Seal of Magna Charta.

FREE GOVERNMENT

IN

ENGLAND AND AMERICA:

CONTAINING

THE GREAT CHARTER,
THE PETITION OF RIGHT,
THE BILL OF RIGHTS,
THE FEDERAL CONSTITUTION.

BY

S. M. JOHNSON.

NEW YORK:
Carleton, Publisher, 413 Broadway.
MD CCC LXIV.

It is said never to be diplomatic, seldom courteous or civil, and not always safe, to call things by their right names. If an exception is anywhere to be found to this suggestion of policy, it should surely exempt the discussion of the wide-spread and destructive opinions which seem now to govern the American people.

The spectacle of an admirable system of laws shamelessly overridden, or wantonly administered, is surely an occasion for plain speech.

This work is submitted in the hope that an examination of its contents may lead to a better understanding of the principles and structure of the States and the Union, and to a higher appreciation of the duties and obligations of the people in the maintenance of a free system of laws.

I have discussed at some length the leading doctrines of Free Government as they have been developed by the Anglo-American race, and have given a sketch of their progress through the struggles of the Great Charter, the Petition of Right, the Bill of Rights, up to the adoption of the Federal Constitution.

These great events teach us the important lesson that Experience is the only safe guide in the creation and maintenance of free institutions. These institutions embrace not alone the mere theory of Free Government, but the practical enforcement of its principles in all the affairs of life. Accuracy and completeness of form, in other words, are valueless without perfect fidelity to the law on the part of the people and the public administration. All this is exhibited by our English ancestors in a light so clear as to sink opposing theories to the level of fiction. In the struggle of 1628, no man did more to build up the free system of English laws than that great and honest statesman, Sir Edward Coke. He is found, nevertheless, to admit the right of royal dispensation—the right of the king to dispense, in certain cases, with the laws of the state. That was the light in which a great majority of the people, at the time, viewed their own and the legitimate authority of the crown. Subsequent experience and observation disclosed the necessity of making the law supreme, *in all cases.*

This principle of political progress is just as applicable to us as it was to our progenitors. It is illustrated with peculiar force in the history of the American States which, with rare exceptions, have ever maintained a free system of laws. Descending from this platform of freedom to the practical life of the Union—to the exercise of power more remote from its source—we find even the ancient prerogative of royal dispensation not only revived, but so extended as to set aside both the laws and the Federal Constitution.

I have sought to present a clear view of the great Experiments in Free Government, of England and America. The various subjects discussed have, to some extent, a separate interest, but their general connection is obvious. It is apparent, in going over so much ground, that many of the lights and shadows of political history and many subjects of the greatest practical importance, at the present day, must be passed over without that minute pencilling and investigation which their merits claim. History and biography are so closely united, that he who undertakes to separate them, runs some risk of making his work lifeless and practically valueless. This is especially the case in reviewing the great subject of Free Government, which necessarily embraces the biography of many of the highest and noblest men of history, as it too often involves the sacrifice of their lives and estates. I have not altogether neglected the narration of such personal incidents; though, I confess, I have not dealt as largely in them as I could have wished.

In that portion of the work devoted to English and American political history, I have drawn freely upon cotemporaneous writers, and have used their reflections, with some necessary modifications of the text, with and without special credit, as would best carry out my design.

NEW YORK, *October*, 1864.

CONTENTS.

PART I.

CHAPTER I.

FREE GOVERNMENT—ITS CHARACTER AND OFFICE.

CHAPTER II.

THE STATE AND FEDERAL GOVERNMENTS.

CHAPTER III.

THE JUDICIARY.

CHAPTER IV.

THE HABEAS CORPUS ACT.

CHAPTER V.

MARTIAL LAW.

PART II.

CHAPTER I.

THE ANGLO-SAXON SYSTEM OF LOCAL SOVEREIGNTIES.

CHAPTER II.

THE FEUDAL SYSTEM OF CONSOLIDATED MILITARY POWER.

CHAPTER III.

ENGLAND UNDER THE YOKE.

CHAPTER IV.

THE GIVING OF MAGNA CHARTA.

CHAPTER V.

THE RISE OF PARLIAMENTARY REPRESENTATION.

CHAPTER VI.

TRIAL BY JURY.—THE HIGH COURT OF STAR-CHAMBER.—SLAVERY IN ENGLAND.

CHAPTER VII.

THE STUARTS.—JAMES I.

CHAPTER VIII.

THE STUARTS, CONTINUED.—CHARLES I.—FIRST THREE PARLIAMENTS TO THE PETITION OF RIGHT.

CHAPTER IX.

CHARLES I.—FROM THE PETITION OF RIGHT TO THE GRAND REMONSTRANCE.

CHAPTER X.

CHARLES I.—THE REIGN OF PURITANISM—FROM THE GRAND REMONSTRANCE TO THE END OF CONSTITUTIONAL LEGISLATION UNDER CHARLES.

CHAPTER XI.

CHARLES II.—THE RESTORATION.—ABOLITION OF THE FEUDAL TENURES.—HABEAS CORPUS ACT.

CHAPTER XV.

INDEPENDENCE.

CHAPTER XVI.

CONFEDERATION.

CHAPTER XVII.

ADOPTION OF THE CONSTITUTION.

ADDENDA TO PART SECOND.

LOCKE ON GOVERNMENT.

BURKE ON THE AMERICAN WAR.

PART FIRST.

CHAPTER I.

FREE GOVERNMENT—ITS CHARACTER AND OFFICE.

IT IS A STATE OF LAWS—THE BRITISH SYSTEM—ITS RIGID ENFORCEMENT—THE UNION AN ELECTIVE SYSTEM—ITS ELECTIVE PRESERVATION—ITS POPULAR FAILURE—ORGANIC LAWS—THEIR OFFICE—CERTAIN RIGHTS OF PERSON NEVER ENTER INTO GOVERNMENT—TOO MUCH POWER A SOURCE OF WEAKNESS.

IT would seem to be an easy task to arrange a just system of relations between government and people; certainly so on the basis that the former is an agency created by and for the sole benefit, advantage, and protection of the latter. In theory, this is the purpose and end of every description of polity, the public good being the grand objective point to be reached.

The application of this principle, in the creation and maintenance of government, in different countries, has produced widely different forms of administration. This is neither paradoxical nor illogical, any more than it is illogical in the physician who varies his remedies to suit the constitution and overcome the peculiar malady of his patient. Precisely so it is in the institution of government. What is suited to one people, is evidently unsuited to another.

In discussing the principles of free government, it would be unfair to test their practical benefits, by reference to the history of those nations where free speech and a free press have been the mere dreams of enthusiasts. With rare exceptions, the laws of any named people will be found to express just what is best adapted to their necessities, and indicate the true state of popular intelligence of the country;—in other words, what may be the very best government for one nation, may be the worst for another. This is simply the adaptation of means to ends.

It has been very much the habit of public writers, on both sides of the water, to draw conclusions concerning matters of government, from the operation of certain systems of administration, which have been found to work admirably in specified countries, without taking any account of the peculiar political habits of the people, their intelligence, or the character of their religious opinions. Hence it is that the French, always the most prosperous and successful under absolute government, are convinced that imperialism is better than republicanism—that the will of one man is better than the laws of many.

The English, on the other side, are equally certain that their free system of laws is the perfection of wisdom.

They are, in our judgment, both in the right.

The British government expresses a far higher intelligence on the part of the people, more complete and defined notions of personal rights and liberty, more dignity and nationality, than that of the French. It has elicited, in its establishment, more mind, and involved vastly heavier personal sacrifices. *It is a state of laws* —a state in which individualism no longer exists as a governing power—*in which the law is supreme.*

If we take any account of the ambitions of men, we must admit that the creation of such a system is a most wonderful achievement. It may be doubted, indeed, if any other people have encountered so many difficulties in the creation of government as the English. We know of no other where classes are so distinctly marked—the high, the middling, and the low; as there is no other, where, under the laws, classes are so absolutely obliterated, where laws, not individuals, have such supreme control.

It will be admitted that a state of laws, so established as to secure public tranquillity, and maintain the rights of person, against the encroachments of influence and individual power, and of the state itself, is the best civil polity. This is precisely what we understand to be the British government. It has had a slow, but sure and healthy growth. Unlike the government of the Union, which consists of a simple compact of independent States, covering a few specified interests, created, as it were, by a body of representatives, commenced and ended in a day, that of England has been the patient work of many centuries, its progress evolving principles of freedom, which had to be won by battle and by argument. It is a singular feature of British history, that the people have never taken a step backwards. Often checked in their onward course, slow to secure obvious rights of person and property, obstructed or crippled by the hand of power and ambition, they have, through every trial, vindicated their grand purpose *to establish a free system of laws, and make them supreme, at all times and in every exigency, over individuals.* This is the distinguishing feature of all free government.

It is common to maintain that this species of polity, being in its nature more stately and inflexible than absolute government, is ill adapted to meet and overcome great trials and difficulties. It is urged that while it is admirable in peace, economical in administration, and effective in rule, in the ordinary affairs of life, it is cumbrous, heavy, slow, and expensive, in periods of peril or civil commotion. This argument goes to the main question—to the very power of any people to maintain free government on any terms; for a state is clearly worthless, and something worse, if it has not the capacity, energy, and patriotism necessary to sustain its own life in hours of peril. If what is called a government of laws, is incapable of doing this, without invoking the discretionary powers of individuals—without, in other words, substituting the will of the latter for the inflexible rule of the former, it follows that it is a radical and mischievous error.

It is far better, under every description of government, to rely upon the enforcement of laws, than to trust the wisdom of persons, however honest, in times of civil commotion. It is hardly possible, at such periods, to find individuals to rule, who do not enter upon their work as partisans; and it is more than has been found safe, in this country, to trust this class of persons in time of peace, much less should they be trusted with administrative discretion, in war.

Those who maintain the necessity of this rule under any circumstances, are no friends of constitutional government. It is a sort of appeal from free institutions to absolutism—from the government of the many to that of the few; a resolution to abandon the organism of the state in favor of a few persons in authority.

It is no answer to this statement to say, that individual government proposes to lay aside only a limited portion of the written law. It is not the extent of the change, but its character, its nature, to which we object. The authority to alter constitutional covenants is lodged in the States, which must act in strict obedience to the organic law. Statute laws, State and federal, come within the legislative authority. It is now proposed to ordain a third estate, giving or conceding power to persons in charge of affairs, under the constitutions and laws, to alter, modify, or annul the one for the time being, and disregard the other. This, we take it, is authority, in point of fact, to ordain a new government.

It will not be maintained that we have adhered, in strict fidelity, even in the ordinary administration of the Government, to the Federal Constitution. In more than one instance, we have, as a people, sanctioned the complete surrender of fundamental rules, and given the full force of law and the indorsement of majorities to measures which were utterly incompatible with the peaceful maintenance of the National Government.

The Missouri Compromise is one of these—a law which ordained and established disunion—which distinctly recognized the separate existence of a political North and a political South; a law which created, as far as it could do so, two governments, permitting certain things to be done in one, which it prohibited in the other, thus ordaining positive inequality between citizens of the same common country. We allude to this matter, not to discuss it, but to show the tendency of our people, in time of peace, to disregard or overlook the Constitution of the United States as the supreme law of the States over the interests delegated to the Union. Whether that compact was absolutely perfect or not, it is certain that the least departure from its provisions was not only unjustifiable, but fatal to the whole scheme of government, of which it was the only law. If, in other words, it was not supreme to the extent of preventing even compromises, by any other than State action, which violated its covenants, it was no law at all. If it had no power to vindicate itself against the action of majorities or even absolute unanimity, on the part of the people, except in its own prescribed way, then it follows, that, instead of a constitutional government, we had a purely democratic majority government. The real law of the Union was not the Constitution, but the will of greater over lesser numbers. The recognition of the right to give force to laws, made in contravention of the fundamental law of the Union, concedes at once the right of the people, without reference to the States, to alter, modify, or annul the latter, at pleasure. Of course, in such case, the government is a democracy, under which minorities have no rights, and majorities are supreme.

Our career as a nation, though short, is full of evidence that however perfect may have been our theory of self-government, we have, after all, understood little of its practical philosophy. We have had a broad and a rich field; but our husbandry has been sadly defective, our labor misapplied, and our productions meagre and unsatisfactory.

Our failure, for such it is, may be accounted for, by a simple reference to one or two leading features of the national mind. Self-reliance is a great virtue when kept within reasonable bounds. It quickens invention, stimulates industry, widens the channels of enterprise, and gives energy and force to those who possess it. But like every other good quality it is liable to run into excess—to become swollen into such inordinate vanity as to reject the lessons of experience and all the counsels of history. It is folly to seek to conceal this turn of an excellent characteristic of the American people. The great evils of its existence and dominion, at the present moment, are too obvious, damaging, and pervading, to admit of either extenuation or justification. It is the dominion of self-conceit over wisdom and patriotism.

It is no answer to point to the industrial successes of the people, during the period of what we call our national existence; for these very triumphs of labor indicate far more the source of the evils referred to, than prove our capacity to maintain the government under which they were achieved. It is better at once to admit that we are indebted to exemption from trials—that our great success has resulted from the absence of political disturbances, rather than from ability, by strict adherence to fundamental principles of justice and freedom, to manage and control them, when they arise. Until recently we had been called upon only to overcome trifling disturbances. No great, disintegrating elements had before presented themselves. We had an elective system, embracing exclusive elective remedies. This was the corner stone and foundation of the political edifice. It embraced no other principle, touching the matter of its creation, existence, or maintenance. It was indestructible, too, so long as this principle should have sovereign control in its administration. The exclusion of the ballot, in the adjustment of differences, under such a system, was the abandonment of the Constitution—the practical abdication of government by the people, and the installation of another kind of government, by irresponsible men.

In point of fact, we have signally failed, on the first great trial, to maintain free government. What is now of greatest interest, is to ascertain, if possible, the cause of this failure, which must be the source of our greatest weakness.

A review of the past and present position of the States and Union, it seems to us, discloses this striking defect :

Ignorance, on the part of the people, of the real office and what is necessary to maintain a free system of laws; or non-appreciation of the necessity, *at all times*, of maintaining the supremacy of the laws over individuals.

It would be difficult to find testimony more complete, in support of this suggestion, than that which the present National Administration has presented, within the short period of its rule. Starting with the open declaration that the public exigencies demanded the removal of all legal restraints, its measures, from that time to the present, have, in no material respect, been made to conform to the Federal Constitution. It is due to candor to say, however, that both Congress and the people have distinctly approved, and, as far as their action could do so, justified, the annulment of the organic law and the substitution of the will of the chief magistrate, as the governing power of the country. In other words, if the President violated the Constitution and the rights of persons and property, his criminality is no greater than that of the people, who either indorsed, or gave a qualified assent to, all his acts of usurpation. The offence, in this way, was compound. There was no other process so sure to ruin the President, on the one hand, and the institutions of government, on the other. No man could withstand such temptations, and no system of laws such a terrible shock.

We deem it unnecessary to point to the public records of the country, to show that we have not drawn our conclusions from an imaginary condition of public affairs. The announcement, by the President, of the imperial power of war, under his exclusive control; his suspension of the writ of habeas corpus; his abrogation of many provisions of the Constitution, trial by jury, free speech, the press; his wilful confiscation of estates; his new law of treason; his emancipation; his assumed jurisdiction over all the people, even to their expulsion from the country by military force, are surely enough to justify what we have said.

Granting that the highest motives of patriotism governed him, it makes nothing in his favor, as a political trustee, under defined powers; for there was nothing but the Union to save, and there could be no legal agency employed in the work other than those ordained by the States.

The States had ordained a limited, but perfect government of laws, to be maintained by them, within the sphere of its authority. It was fearfully menaced, not by mere casual disobedience, but by organic, internal convulsion.

Its authority was openly set aside by large and influential States, four of which were original parties to the Union. Our duty was a plain one—to vindicate the laws within the scope of the authority of the Constitution, and by its appointed agencies.

There could be no other vindication; for the instant we transcended this limit, no matter with what motive, we became assailants, not defenders of the Union. If the latter provided one remedy for a certain political disease, and we failed to employ it, and substituted another, it follows that we would not trust the law nor wait till we could modify it in obedience to prescribed forms. We preferred to rely upon the discretionary power of public agents.

This is a plain proposition. The Union, based entirely upon living governments, existing purely under written laws, was incapable of admitting into it the least discretion, as it was impossible to maintain it on any other than an elective basis. Force was as foreign to its maintenance as to its ordination. It is believed by many, that it never could have been permanently ruptured without force, and by more, that it can never be restored with force. Force is personal discretion, the law of individuals, in direct antagonism to the written law. The British Constitution, as it is called, though its powers and prohibitions are sufficiently defined by various royal charters and parliamentary declarations, is what may be termed a system of political common law—a sort of prescriptive government—the result of a most protracted effort on the part of the people to secure their rights as freemen. There is no pretence of equality, as that word is now understood, in it. The people are not born equal, unless we mean that they have an equal right to breathe the air, to speak their sentiments, and enjoy the blessings of liberty. The foundations of the British Government were all laid in absolutism, from which has been raised its superstructure of laws. From one man it has grown up to be every freeman of the kingdom. From allegiance to that one man, it is now allegiance to laws. So it is in the United States. Yet the two systems widely differ in structure and administration. It took many centuries, involving vast sacrifices of persons and property, to achieve the present Constitution of England, while that of the United States was the work of a few days—the work of States, as free as the Empire of England. We have been parties to both systems. When we separated from our great ancestors, we dissolved all the political relations subsisting between us, but retained everything else. Their experience was ours. Their knowledge was ours. Their martyrs to liberty, all their lessons of adversity in struggling for a free system of laws, their hostility to military power, their language, their literature, their ancient love of freedom and independence, were ours. The States combined to effect their separation. When this was achieved they stood before the world as thirteen nationalities. They subsequently ordained the Union, not by sinking their nationalities, but by creating a government of States—a government of independent authority over individuals within the scope of the powers delegated to it by the States, but in nothing else. This is seen in the act of confederation, and in the fact that it is a government of States. It contains not one dynastic element, not one grant of discretionary authority to its representatives. This was the principle and the policy of its creation, for the obvious reason that its constituent parties maintained, respectively, perfect civil institutions. The latter embrace quite all the concerns of life. The relations of husband and wife, parent and child, guardian and ward, the collection of debts, the settlement of estates of deceased persons, the tenures of real property, the punishment of crime, the maintenance of the poor, education, charitable institutions, the authorization of corporate bodies, local municipal police, and a hundred other matters of familiar life, come within the scope of the State governments.

It is illogical to claim that these living governments, which created the Union, which confer upon it all the machinery of administration and all means for its maintenance and support, are in any sense subject to the discretionary power of individuals. Such a conclusion might, possibly, be admissible under a concrete system, but it is clearly inadmissible under that of the Union. Its agents are all elected, directly or indirectly, by the people of the States, in obedience to their respective laws. There is not one approach to it, except through the States. They make its president, its legislature, and, indirectly, its judiciary. They give up their citizens to constitute its army and navy. Without them, it is nothing. It is the law, and the only law, of their being. They are its constituents, not as a people, but as so many independent nationalities.

It requires but a moment's reflection to see that, under such a system, the laws must, at all times, be supreme over individuals. It is unquestionably better that it should be so in every government, but absolutely necessary under this, for the obvious reason, as we have stated, that the Union is the law of the States and not of the people.

Exactly the opposite of this theory of the Union has been its administration during the last three years. Its law has been treated as a cumbrous, heavy weight, and its strict maintenance punished as treason to the Government. Patriotism has been made to consist in upholding the action of persons in direct opposition to it. Those who would show the least regard for its obligations and the greatest contempt for its solemn injunctions, have been most honored and trusted.

We have passed through years of great political trial. The institutions of the country have been put to a severe test indeed. It was not enough that we should meet and overcome the military force which assailed and sought to overthrow them. We had a character as a free people, as well as a government of laws, to uphold. We could not sustain the latter and give up the former. Our enemies are those who violate our laws, who set aside the Constitution, no matter on what pretext. Our institutions were put upon trial. Their practical utility must undergo the terrible test of a widespread civil war. The question was, whether the laws should prevail over the illegal and treasonable action of individuals. We must determine not only who are the open, but also the concealed enemies of the Union. He is quite as much an enemy who transcends the authority of the Union, professing to sustain it, as the rebel who openly defies its authority. We have no right to make war for anything else than the enforcement of the laws, as we have no right to punish rebels for anything else than their violation. If we do not ourselves know what our institutions are, or, what amounts to the same thing, permit public agents to modify them at will, then it is clear that we cannot determine what is loyalty on the one hand or treason on the other.

We are confident that our political bankruptcy is due, not to the defects of our institutions, but to the dominion of great popular errors, which have made it impossible, for the moment, to say. whether, the Administration at Washington or Richmond have done us most harm. Pride, ambition, and ignorance have ever warred against free government. What we have said of these passions in England is quite applicable to us. The English people have repeatedly done just what we are doing—and they have done again just what we shall yet do—they have vindicated the supremacy of their free system of laws over all personal discretion.

In this view, our comprehensive and damaging mistakes and omissions, during the present war, may be charged to non-appreciation of what was required of us rather than to defects of our system, or inability or indisposition to maintain it in all its legal force and integrity.

Good practical government may unquestionably exist, embracing freedom of speech and of the press and the largest measure of personal liberty, without a Constitution, Magna Charta, Bill of Rights, or any such law as the Habeas Corpus Act. So it is possible to maintain order, for a limited time, without the aid of civil institutions of any kind.

The general tendency of all self-governed communities is sufficient, under ordinary circumstances, to assure not only public tranquillity, but to enforce the rights of persons and property. Governments are ordained not alone to secure these ends, but so constructed as to be able to meet and overcome great trials and difficulties. To assure this, with greater certainty, organic laws are enacted. These laws govern the corporate body, just as statute laws govern the magistrate and the people. They are said to be supreme laws, not because they are irrepealable or indestructible, but because they are supreme over all the agencies of government, whose powers they define, whose duties they enjoin, and whose jurisdiction they determine. They are supreme over the executive, the legislature, and the judiciary. They constitute an official chart which should be ever present in their deliberations and ever control their action.

It is their office not only to direet what may be done, by the law-making, the executive, and judicial power, but, through the last-named department, declare what shall not be done—to command and to interdict action.

In addition to these obvious intendments of the organic law, it is one of its chief offices, in a free government, to define what interests and things *shall be exempt* from the operations of the polity —what, in the language of the Federal Constitution, "shall be reserved to the States respectively or to the people."

For instance, free government, being ordained exclusively in the interest of the people and for their protection in person and property, can never rightfully gain jurisdiction over either, except for the punishment of crime. The sacrifice of either, on any other ground, is sufficient to show that its ends have been perverted, and that, instead of a government of laws, it is a system of robbery, arson, murder, and personal aggrandizement.

Government is rightfully limited to the accomplishment of

certain ends, all of which must accord with the public good and advantage. These are its only legitimate mission. It is certainly not necessary, in the maintenance of such a system, to take the property or interfere with the liberty of persons of the commonwealth. It is the right of every well-conducted citizen to say and publish what he wills, being always responsible to injured persons for the abuse of this right. He is never responsible to the Government, for any such abuse, because the policy of the state demands the utmost liberty of speech and the press. This is not only essential to the integrity of its administration, but it is that which has always been admitted to be the very soul of our institutions. These institutions signify general discussion, criticism, and condemnation. They are the product of free inquiry and speech. To admit the right to suppress either, would be exactly equivalent to the suppression of the Government. The silly pretence set up that it is necessary to keep them within reasonable bounds by political agents, is an impeachment of the laws for the protection of persons, because persons alone have a right to complain. The Government itself cannot be injured, except on the hypothesis that the agent for the time being is the state.

But we go farther than all this. The right of free speech and a free press is absolute, with or without constitutional guarantees. It is exempt from the operation of the polity—*beyond its jurisdiction.* No people in ordaining civil institutions are authorized to trench upon this right. It is original and inalienable. The cause of good government, of morality, religion, and human progress, forbids that it shall ever, under any possible circumstances, be surrendered by the people. It is their birthright, their weapon of defence against aggression and wrong. Without it they are subjects, not freemen. They have no right to yield up this natural gift of a beneficent God, because it is inalienable, and for a better reason, because no people have a right to go from light into political darkness.

The Federal Constitution, we repeat, was framed on this theory. It expressly declares that the powers not delegated to the Union are "reserved to the States respectively or to the people." The latter portion of this clause bears no other signification than the reservation of certain rights, ordinarily embraced in political governments, "to the people." These include exemption from arrest, except for crime, to be determined by judicial authority; all rights of property; perfect religious freedom; free speech and a free press. The States of the original confederation, without a single exception, recognized these rights as beyond their legal jurisdiction. The safeguards thrown around them in the Amendments to the Constitution, evince alike distrust of Federal agents and a determination to protect them.

It will be found, we apprehend, under every description of polity, that the recognition of this principle would not only impart stability to the state, but be the source of its greatest social, industrial, and intellectual progress.

It is said of the common law, that it is the perfection of reason. If so, it is because its authors have treated all subjects of investigation in absolute freedom. In this spirit it is time to investigate not only what are the legitimate ends and mission of government, but what interests should be reserved from its operations. These reservations or limitations, we imagine, will be seen to be far more important matters and more effective guarantees of stability, strength, and efficiency, than its positive grants. It is nothing more than the simple recognition of the well-established principle, that power is a source of weakness as well as strength. When unlimited, it is apt to degenerate into licentiousness, and thus make an enemy of one, on account of its moral failings, and of another, by reason of its illegal oppressions. It is seen, in practical life, which is the only test of usefulness, to be just as necessary to withhold as to confer authority upon government. We refer, of course, to a free system.

Now, while the Federal Constitution is an open record, defining every power that may be exercised; expressly reserving certain rights of person and property; prescribing, in numerous cases, the mode of prosecution for offences, and measuring the extent of punishment, as for treason; declaring what magistrates and others shall do to gain jurisdiction of alleged offences, is it not true, from whatever motive, that quite all these provisions of the law have been either disregarded or annulled, for the time being, by the Administration? Let us see:

Trial by jury has been habitually denied.

Persons have been arrested and imprisoned by military authority, in utter disregard of the Constitution.

Private property has been taken for public use, by military orders.

Freedom of speech and the press has been suppressed by like orders.

Property has been confiscated by legislative and executive authority, in utter violation of the Constitution.

Persons have been seized, tried by military commission, and transported beyond the jurisdiction of the States, by express order of the President.

The privilege of the writ of habeas corpus has been suspended, in the loyal States, and all the machinery of martial law put in operation throughout the whole Union.

The United States have been transformed by these measures into a purely military government, and the civil authority everywhere subjected to the arbitrary orders of the commander-in-chief of the army and navy and the militia, in actual service.

This array of treason to the Union and to every principle of free government, embraces only the most prominent offences committed against the constitutional authority of the United States by the people's representatives. They are, too, not only avowed and continued by the ministers, but were explicitly indorsed and justified by the Republican National Convention at Baltimore. They stand, then, as their settled maxims of government. It is claimed that these proceedings have been instituted *in aid* of the Constitution. Lord Brougham, speaking of the proposed suspension of the Habeas Corpus Act, in 1817, says:

"It is said by those who now call for the suspension of the Habeas Corpus Act, that in times of danger the Constitution requires support. I beg leave to protest against this doctrine. The Constitution of England is not made merely for fair weather, and if it cannot defy and outlive the storm, it is not worth preserving. If this measure is unfortunately passed, I hope never again to be compelled to listen to the pharisaical cant of how much happier and more free the subjects of this country are than the nations by whom they are surrounded; for what does the suspension of the Habeas Corpus Act prove, but that the Constitution of England is of no use, and the liberty of England of no value?"

We allude to this subject, not to discuss the character of the existing Administration, but to show how necessary it is that a free system of laws should be restricted in the exercise of powers, in order that it may command the confidence of the people, without which it cannot and ought not to be successful. This confidence is an outbirth of freedom, and a vital element of all social, political, and industrial progress. But it can never be attained, in this country or in England, except on condition of the entire protection of person and property. A failure to do this, from whatever cause, is a compound offence here; an offence against the States, against the citizen, and against the legitimate government of the Constitution.

It is due to candor to say, that the people of the United States, though sincerely attached to a free system of laws, entertain very questionable ideas, upon a single point, at least, in reference to what should constitute such a system. They admit the right to ordain a constitution, conferring unlimited authority upon the legislature to enact and enforce such laws as their constitution may permit or command. This we hold to be a radical and damaging error.

There is no right, surely, in the people, in framing government, to do more than is absolutely necessary to be done, in order to put into operation a perfect system of laws. For instance, trial by jury, by its long and beneficent agency, has become an essential feature of free government—a sort of vested right, which persons charged with offence may invoke, and which there is no power in the state to withhold. Freedom of speech and the press, the rights of the habeas corpus, and the subordination of the military to the civil authority, and many other interests of the same nature, are necessary elements of this species of government. They are rights which the citizen cannot be called upon to surrender, for the simple reason, that jurisdiction by the state over them would add nothing to its strength or efficiency, but take much from both.

Military authority, in the United States, is purely ministerial in its nature. It may enforce laws in certain cases, ordained by competent authority; but it can never, under any circumstances, exercise legal jurisdiction over either persons or property, outside of the military service. There is no authority, in Congress or the President, to confer such jurisdiction. The existence of war adds nothing to its legitimate powers in this respect. Whenever and wherever it has done so, it has committed a flagrant violation of the Constitution, and a more flagrant and damaging assault upon the character of the American people.

We hold the latter to have been, in this way, its most serious and injurious offence.

To the American people had been committed, more than any other, the great trust of maintaining a free system of laws. We had promised more and accomplished more in the short period of our national existence, than any other people. It was here that labor received its highest reward, that genius and invention achieved their greatest triumphs, that education was most widely disseminated; and it was here that freedom, peace, and prosperity had made their cherished home.

We had done more as a People than as a Government.

It is thus seen that the domination of the military power is something more than a mere political offence. Our estates are not all made up of civil institutions. When we gave up those institutions we surrendered the greatest name as a People, the highest dignity and the noblest mission ever organized by freemen. It was a sacrifice so complete that, from being the first people in all the world, in character and works, we became the last in practical freedom and political wisdom. This fall is due exclusively to the fact that we have tamely surrendered the dominion of laws to a wanton military rule.

We had a mission to fulfil as well as a state to maintain. Separated from the great governments by an impassable barrier, which protected us through all the stages of our early career, we had grown to colossal proportions, with ample power to vindicate, by arms and by labor, the free system of laws which we had adopted for our government. We had advanced so far that our example became an eloquent and powerful assailant of absolutism everywhere, while it conveyed to every people unquestionable proof of the capacity of man for self-government.

Without a thought of active intervention with the local politics of others, we had declared, in the name of the people, that hostile European colonization on this continent would in no case be permitted. This was no more than a legitimate expression of our political system. There was nothing of menace or presumption in it. As a measure, it was timely and regular. Europe had combined at Vienna, to declare to the world that her people should in no case recognize free institutions. England had joined in this decree of exclusion. If Europe could rightly interdict free government on the other side of the water, we certainly could interdict absolutism on this. There was as much moral and legal weight in our ideas as theirs. They addressed us, it is true, through their governments, while we addressed them as a people. We listened to them because we knew they had power to enforce their decree; they listened to us because they knew we had power to enforce ours.

So long as we remained true to the principle which gave us that power we were potential and unconquerable; when we abandoned that principle and practically adopted that which governed the Congress of Vienna, we became weak and contemptible. This abandonment stands to us as a subjugation by a foreign power. It is not armies alone, commanded by Frenchmen or Germans, which constitute foreign invasion. Whatever is not indigenous to our institutions, whatever partakes of absolutism, is utterly foreign to us in a political sense. We care not where a ruler comes from, if his will, instead of our law, is to govern. Abraham Lincoln is a foreigner to us, when he rules in opposition to the Constitution of the United States.

NOTES.

The Constitution and its Dangers.—Lord Brougham, in the House of Commons, June 23d, 1817, says:

"It is now reckoned childish or romantic to profess any veneration for the Constitution of the country, or respect for popular rights. My honorable friend

(Sir S. Romilly) has been taunted with romance for defending its general principles; but I will say, that, if it is a romance, it is a romance which has given us all the advantages which those who know not their origin cannot overlook. It has made us the admiration and envy of our neighbors; and by frequent derelictions of it, like the present, we shall soon cease to be the only free and happy country in Europe, or in the world. If the house thinks to do its duty to the country by agreeing to every unconstitutional measure at the bare suggestion of the minister—if you think you will be doing your duty to your constituents by refusing to investigate their complaints, and by rushing headlong, without inquiry, into every measure which is recommended against them—if the new doctrine of confidençe in ministers, whoever they may be, obtains, I should then say that it is a matter of little consequence in which form the constitution exists—the substance is gone. It is plainly avowed that it is fit only for fair weather—to be got rid of as soon as a storm arises—and that the rights of the people of England are not to be held even during their good behavior, but at the good will and pleasure of the ministers of the crown."—BROUGHAM'S *Opinions*, p. 96.

"I know that the general answer to all that has been hitherto alleged on this subject is that martial law had been proclaimed at Demerara. But, sir, I do not profess to understand, as a lawyer, martial law of such a description; it is entirely unknown to the law of England. I do not mean to say in bad times of our history, but in that more recent period which is called constitutional. It is very true that formerly the crown sometimes issued proclamations, by virtue of which, civil officers were tried before military tribunals. The most remarkable instance of that description, and the nearest precedent to the case under our consideration, is the well-known proclamation of the august, pious, and humane Philip and Mary, stigmatizing as rebellion, and as an act that should subject the offender to be tried by a court martial, the having heretical, that is to say, Protestant, books in one's possession, and not giving them up without previously reading them.

"Similar proclamations, although not so extravagant in their character, were issued by Elizabeth, by James I., and (of a less violent nature) by Charles I., until at length the evil became so unbearable that there arose from it the celebrated Petition of Right, one of the best legacies left to this country by that illustrious lawyer Lord Coke, to whom every man who loves the constitution owes a debt of gratitude, which unceasing veneration for his memory can never pay.

"The Petition declares that all such proceedings shall henceforth be put down; it declares that 'no man shall be forejudged of life or limb against the form of the Great Charter,' that 'no man ought to be adjudged to death but by the laws established in this realm, either by the custom of the realm, or by acts of Parliament;' and that 'the commissions for proceeding by martial law should be revoked and annulled, lest, by color of them, any of his majesty's subjects be destroyed, or put to death contrary to the laws and franchise of the land.' Since that time no such thing as martial law has been recognized in this country; and courts founded on proclamations of martial law have been wholly unknown. And here I beg to observe that the particular grievances at which the Petition of Right was levelled were only the trials, under martial law, of military persons, or of individuals accompanying or in some measure connected with military persons. On the abolition of martial law, what was substituted? In these days a standing army in times of peace is considered a solecism in the constitution.

"Accordingly, the whole course of our legislation proceeded on the principle that no such establishment was recognized.

"Afterwards came the annual Mutiny Acts, and courts martial, which were held only under those acts. These courts were restricted to the trial of soldiers for military offences, and the extent of their powers was pointed out and limited by law."—*Ibid.*, 220–222.

Trial by Jury.—"The jury are sometimes right when the judge is wrong. Judges themselves sometimes admit that they took, what they afterwards found out to be, a wrong view of the case, while the jury took a right one; and how can it be otherwise than a frequent case? One may be very excellent for deciding a point of law; nothing can be better than one for superintending a jury, from his long experience and long practice; but twelve men are much better for deciding in cases where there is conflicting evidence, and where that evidence is to be brought before them in an uncertain shape, because there are a great variety of points in the case; one man takes one view, and another another, each taking it, as it were, by a different handle, until, by reflection and argument, they come to a unanimous decision. Nothing can be better, I am convinced, than the decision of these twelve men, instructed as they are by the counsel and the judge."—*Ibid.*, vol. ii. p. 80.

Right of the Subject to Demand Protection from the Crown.—"Protection, your lordships are aware, protection affording security of person and property, is the first law of the state. The legislature has no right to claim obedience to its laws, the crown no right to demand allegiance from its subjects, if the legislature and the crown do not afford, in return for both, protection for person and property. Without protection, the legislature would abdicate its functions if it demanded obedience; without protection, the crown would be an usurper of its right to enforce allegiance."—*Ibid.*, p. 94.

Effects of Oaths in Weakening the Moral Principle.—"Increasing unnecessarily the number of oaths to be taken operates injuriously in a twofold manner—it not only diminishes the sanctity of an oath, and begets an indifference to what ought to be a high, moral, and religious ordination; but it hath another tendency, to check the law in its course in punishing crime. Everything that diminishes the sanctity of an oath begets a carelessness about swearing, and generates a habit of perjury and prevarication, which those who have to administer the law know to be the most difficult thing to deal with."—Brougham, vol ii. p. 109.

CHAPTER II.

THE STATE AND FEDERAL GOVERNMENTS.

THEIR UNITY—THE STATE EXCLUSIVE JUDGE OF PROHIBITED POWERS—THE UNION NOT A CIVIL POLITY—NOT A DEMOCRACY—PERSONS AND MAJORITIES—HOW REGARDED—THE SLAVERY QUESTION—ITS ALLEGED INCOMPATIBILITY WITH FREE INSTITUTIONS—THE LAW OF ITS EXISTENCE AND ITS EXTIRPATION.

Now, let us consider that the States of the Union, in respect to all ordinary matters of government, are just what they have ever been since the first organization of civil institutions in this country. For example, the State of New York is just what she was a century ago, an independent State, having an executive, legislative, and judicial department. Scarcely an acre of its territory, or a noticeable fraction of its political rights, or an iota of its liberty, as a free State, has ever been surrendered. The control of its foreign relations, the coining of money, postal matters and a few other specific interests, of a general nature, were transferred, not to an independent power, but to a power of its own creation and government.

In making this transfer, it is hardly possible that New York intended in any sense, to make herself a subject State, not even in reference to those things over which she declared the authority of the United States supreme. The supremacy here accorded is strictly legal in its nature, partaking far more of exclusive jurisdiction over the subjects than of dominion.

The general and the State law, so far as the people of the State are concerned, are identical—they are both, to all practical intents and purposes, the laws of the State. The Government of the State draws to it and makes part of it, all laws of the Union, made in obedience to the Federal Constitution.

This expresses the true unity of the system. It does not admit the existence of two governments. It is all one system. By so treating it, it is possible to maintain the rights and dignities of the States on the one hand, and the integrity of the confederation on the other.

It is nothing to the American people how persons abroad shall see them. Whether the General Government is regarded as the embodiment of power and the aggregation of legal authority or not, is of no consequence. We are viewing the structure of our institutions, not a picture exhibiting their lights and shadows from a distant standpoint. They are extremely complicated, and, as we have found, most difficult of enforcement. The latter is due to the practical recognition, by the States, of two distinct, and in many respects, antagonistic polities.

It may seem anomalous, and extra-speculative, to maintain, in the face of what has been written, said, and done by the people, that, instead of two systems, we have, in reality, but one. Nevertheless, if we regard the true structure of the States, and the objects they sought to accomplish in ordaining the Union, it seems impossible to come to any other conclusion. As we have departed from this vital doctrine of union, by recognizing the independent power and authority of the General Government, making it not only supreme over delegated interests, but building it up as a colossal foreign state, in many respects, so have the signs of discord and civil commotion multiplied upon us.

It is folly, and something worse, to suppose that two schemes of independent government can be maintained. We must have unity in fact as well as name. It is not in the power of human wisdom and integrity to maintain independent government in the States, and the independent government of the Union, unless it be on the basis that the latter is purely the government of the States, having no separate mission whatever.

Accountability, except as to those matters which have been delegated to the Union, must ever be *to the States*. They remain in the confederation as its only sustaining power. They fill, from their citizens, all its offices, executive, legislative, and judicial. It is their duty to see that its laws are faithfully executed, because it is their government for specific national purposes—what Mr. Hamilton called their political, in contradistinction to their civil or

State Governments. It is their duty to see that its powers shall be executed just as they were delegated; because that was their agreement. Just as they were delegated! It is as much a violation of the compact to exercise the least Federal authority not delegated, as to refuse to carry into effect the delegated powers. To refuse to send Senators and Members of Congress to the Federal capital, to neglect to appoint a Federal judiciary, would be a violation of the Constitution, but no more so, than for the Senators and Members of Congress and judiciary to assume to exercise unwarranted authority. Concerning all delegated powers, the judiciary is made the exclusive judge. That is the agreement. But in respect to the prohibited powers, the States have retained the right of exclusive judgment. From the character of the compact, the parties to it, and the ends sought to be accomplished, we hold this law of construction to be equally necessary and reasonable. It is necessary, because the parties to the compact remain in the Union, as sovereign, independent States. These attributes make it clear that they ought to retain the exclusive right to judge of all matters affecting their systems of local government, which they did not expressly delegate. This right cannot be relinquished without placing it in the power of the Union to sweep away all State institutions and laws. Self-preservation demands that they shall retain it. It is the vital element of local freedom and independence.

The best reasons of State policy also demand it. It is just as necessary that the Union should be kept within the strict letter and spirit of its organic law as that the States should preserve their freedom and independence. We need not be told that the extinguishment of either of these elements of State government would result only in their transfer to the Union, and not in their destruction. That, we know, is the theory of many persons intrusted with the discharge of Federal duties. But it is not the theory of the Union. It is dominion, which such men want, not a free system of laws—it is individual, discretionary government, and not the ancient free institutions of this country, without which, in all their integrity, it will be found impossible, for many years, to rescue the people from anarchy and bloodshed.

This rule of construction will be found, too, on examination, to be entirely consistent with the provisions of the Constitution.

It is hardly necessary to say that that compact delegates certain powers to the United States; declares that none other shall be exercised; and that the powers not delegated nor prohibited to the States, shall be retained by them respectively or the people. After enumerating all the delegated powers, and prescribing, in many cases, in what manner, where and how, they shall be executed, a schedule of prohibitions is added. It is declared, for instance, that "the freedom of speech and of the press shall not be abridged."[1]

This is the declaration of the States to the General Government, a declaration which constitutes no part of that government, conferring no power upon it, intended, not only to limit its authority over persons and property, in respect to free speech and a free press, but to affirm the exclusive jurisdiction over both by the States. It is manifest, then, that the Federal judiciary and all Federal officers, of whatever character, are utterly prohibited from the least control over these rights of the people: first, because they are natural, or what the Constitution denominates *reserved rights;* and secondly, because the governments of the States never delegated to the Union the least control over them.

A reference to the delegated powers will render this conclusion still more satisfactory.

The Federal system embraces exclusive authority over the revenues, postal accommodation, the coinage of money, weights and measures, and a few other interests of a general nature. These are Federal matters, not because they differ essentially from others reserved to the people, but because their management was turned over to the Union. They are the subjects of its jurisdiction. It would be folly to question the authority of the United States over any of the delegated powers; but a much greater folly to concede the least authority over subjects not delegated, and worse still over matters specifically reserved or prohibited.

These reservations and prohibitions mean nothing, if they do not assert the exclusive jurisdiction of the State over all the subject matters embraced in them. The States must take care of their citizens, when their liberty and rights are taken away. The policy of the law demands, in all cases, that it shall never be placed in the hands of individuals to maintain their rights, however plain. Resort must be had to the tribunals of justice. It is the State's business to execute justice. It is, then, where a citizen has been deprived of either liberty or property, by persons without authority, or by Federal officials, without authority, far more an offence against the State than the injured person. The latter is powerless, while the former is an independent member of the confederation, and as such is bound by all the dignities and obligations of nationality to vindicate the rights of its citizens, especially against every Federal aggression. We say especially against Federal aggression, because aggression from that quarter is first to be resisted, as a double means of preserving the Union on the one hand, and the independent authority of the States on the other.

The real character of the Union, as a limited state, must not be overlooked. It was no part of the design of the States, in creating it, to establish a civil polity. Their civil institutions were already complete; and they were based on the clearest written guarantees of freedom, and sustained by a public sentiment which had never recognized, in government, any other principle. Just relieved of an oppressive war, and threatened by the antagonistic polities of Europe, they saw the necessity of coöperation in respect to certain matters of government. It was believed by quite all the leading statesmen of the day, that one foreign intercourse, commerce, and navigation, one currency, one postal accommodation, and a few other matters of a general nature, would add strength to the parts and greatly advance their material interests. The Union was ordained on precisely this basis.

It took the form of an independent government, and was clothed with the powers of such a government touching the interests to which we have referred, *but in nothing else.* To a political system, embracing original authority over the people, with powers of legislation, a judiciary, and an executive, it bears little resemblance. It has but few of the attributes of such a polity. There was no occasion to put in force any such scheme. All that was required of that kind of government, already existed in perfection, as is abundantly shown in the fact that the States which ordained the Union, without a single exception, maintain the exact forms of administration to-day that they then did. This fact is positive proof of two things:

First, that the Union was not intended to be a free civil polity, in any just sense, but a compact of States of a political nature, for certain economical purposes; second, that the States intended to retain their right to continue to exercise sovereign authority over all those interests which they had not delegated to the Union.

It makes nothing against this theory, that, in ordaining the Union, they minutely defined its powers, and, in so many cases, forbade the exercise of others. There was, unquestionably, sufficient power conveyed to render this precaution necessary. The men of the Revolution were no believers that the wisdom and integrity of mankind were sufficient guarantees to assure the freedom of the people, in the absence of positive restraints and prohibitions. They knew that power was inclined to strengthen itself by exercise. They had authorized the creation of an army and navy, for purposes of defence and security; and they accompanied this authorization by every conceivable guarantee, that neither should ever be wielded except against the enemies of the people.

A free system of laws, and all the details of practical government, they had enjoyed from the very origin of society in America. They were indebted, in point of fact, to their isolation, and to the perils of frontier life, for this. So that, in ordaining the Union, it was their settled purpose, not to create a new system, but to *extend* the old one, on such terms, limitations, and restrictions, as would preserve the freedom and independence of the people. They proceeded upon the theory that the surrender of free speech, a free press, and the least measure of personal rights and property, was in no contingency necessary to the maintenance of good government; that, on the other hand, such surrender, by removing an effective restraint, would be justly construed as a license for the commission of the gravest crimes on the part of the public administration. It would change, at once, the very character of the whole scheme, make the agent the principal, the States subject parties, and the Union an imperial power. That such a polity is not what was designed to be created, that it is utterly incompatible with a free system of government, and that it would be impossible to maintain it in this country, we hold to be equally clear. And if this is true of the whole, it is true of every part of it. We are entitled to absolute freedom, in respect to all the interests referred to, or we are entitled to none. The people are supreme, under the forms of their own established government, or the government is supreme over them. There is no middle ground to be occupied in this matter.

There is, we are aware, a wide distinction between a free people and a free system of laws. We are discussing the latter on the bases of the existing institutions of the States and of the Union, neither embracing, by any fair construction, the least jurisdiction or legal control over the liberties or property of the citizen. All that was sought to be accomplished was the establishment of rules regulating and governing the ordinary relations of the people, so that each individual member of the body politic might be protected in person and property. We have passed from a mere democracy to a government of laws. We have surrendered the control of majorities to the domination of an agreement, by which all matters of state are to be determined. This agreement was not entered into for the purpose of protecting majorities, for they can take care of themselves, but for the purpose of protecting minorities, even down to the least worthy citizen of the commonwealth.

The former, in the absence of legal restraint, are absolute, or, rather, their action is itself law. It is so simply because, in such case, majorities can be held to no account—they are the state. There are neither moral nor logical elements in such a system of government. Personal liberty and popular tyranny, absolute freedom and the most degrading bondage, unrestrained dominion and hopeless subjection, are rudely blended into one scheme of administration.

A government of laws, whether free or otherwise, is impossible on any other basis than the protection of minorities. That of the States and the Union exhibits this principle perhaps more perfectly than any other known to history. We speak, of course, of the theory and philosophy of the polity, and not of its practical workings; for in the latter we find far more acts tending to its subversion than its maintenance. Judged by what we have done since the adoption of the Federal Constitution, it would seem that, instead of a government of States, bound together for certain specified general purposes, we have a government of majorities; instead of a free system of laws, carefully guarding the rights of minorities, and limiting the power of majorities, we have a government of majorities. Their actual control of the administration, at least, is incontestable. Their right to govern is also widely asserted. This right can be contested only by showing that the Union was adopted on another basis—that the voice of a majority is entitled to no more weight than that of the smallest minority, in support of any measure which violates the Constitution of the United States, or the rights of the people of the States which have been reserved. The controlling power is in the compact of union. Majorities can legally govern only within the scope of that compact.

It must not be assumed that we regard majorities as always in the wrong, or disposed to act in opposition to the public welfare. Far from it, especially in a country like this, where the people have the amplest means of acquiring information of public affairs. It is, perhaps, the misfortune of an elective republic, that when the majority-rule once gets control of the government, in opposition to its organic law, it is capable of *tainting* the whole scheme. And justly so, because it shows not only a determination not to abide by the agreement, but a spirit of shameless persecution of those who insist upon its fulfilment. It may be that the majority is quite in the right, judged by any other standard than that of the compact. It would be great folly to maintain the perfection of any system of government. But if errors exist in the system, it is far better to effect its modification in a legal way, than to overthrow it by the despotic will of majorities.

A complete illustration of these reflections is found in the career of the States and the Union touching the slavery question.

It must be admitted that a majority of the people of the States are hostile to slavery; but it is equally true, that under the Constitution of the United States, the Government of the Union could, in no manner and in no place, except in the District of Columbia, gain jurisdiction of slavery. There is not one provision of the compact of Union which, directly or by implication, confers such jurisdiction.

Nevertheless, it is a historical fact, that the slavery question has occupied a large portion of the time of Congress for the last fifty years. Nor has it been a mere idle debate in that body, upon the moral attributes and character of this relation. Congress, by the sole agency of majorities, by the instructing power of majorities, by the mad will, command and imperious dictation of majorities, has not only assumed jurisdiction of the subject, but legislated upon it, abolished it where it existed, prohibited its introduction where it did not exist; and finally, in the ordinary course of usurpation, assumed to exercise unlimited control of it in every part of the Union.

No well-informed and well-disposed man will maintain that this action of Congress is authorized by the States or the compact of Union. And no student of government will venture to say, that such action was consistent with the maintenance of a free system of laws. It was neither. Laws must, under our scheme, be supreme over individuals and majorities, or they are nothing. Whatever might be the result of a radical violation of the laws under other governments, their complete maintenance in this country, since the adoption of the Federal Constitution, is absolutely necessary. The more so here, because the structure of our institutions is of a compound nature, embracing many separate and distinct nationalities in one General Government, created by compact, by and between those nationalities. It is not, then, purely a scheme of laws, but a compact of States also, leaving no discretionary authority to alter or suspend either, and making the life of both to depend entirely upon their rigid and complete enforcement, in every essential particular.

Whether the existence of slavery was compatible or not with the establishment of such a system, is another and utterly foreign question. It is to be observed that in ordaining the Union, slavery was an institution already legalized, extending to quite all the States of the original confederation. It is manifest, then, that those who maintain the incompatibility of slavery with free institutions, are bound to go farther, and show that the States of 1789 were incapable, by reason of the existence of slavery, of ordaining such institutions. This argument, we apprehend, followed to its legitimate end, accomplishes more than the enemies of slavery, at the present time, desire. It was one of their weapons, used in demolishing the bulwarks of the Constitution, but now that they have removed the obstacles in the way of federal jurisdiction and are wielding the powers of the Union to override the States and slavery together, it is no longer necessary to impeach the legal authority of the old Union, on the ground of its incompatibility with slavery. This authority was the legitimate subject of overthrow by majorities, until those majorities got control of it. It was illegal and void so long as it refused to recognize the mission of anti-slavery. It is legal, binding and sacred, in the exclusive execution of such mission.

We bring up this subject, not with a view of the least examination of the abstract question of slavery. Right or wrong, it is a purely domestic interest, which those who maintain must defend. It was so regarded by all the States when they ordained the Union. It was so left by the compact of Union. Whatever has been done since, by the President or Congress, to change its *status*, we hold to be evidence of the ignorance of the people of what was required to maintain a free system of laws. In this work the laws have been subordinated to the dominion of individuals.

Whatever may be the public judgment on the subject of slavery, we are bound, at least, to acknowledge its existence in this country. This simple fact brings before us more than four millions of people of an inferior race. To release them from bondage and make them coequal inhabitants with a dominant superior race, would be a fearful experiment indeed. We have no right to disturb the present order of things, except on the basis of the improvement of the condition of the blacks. The naked assertion of their right to freedom goes for nothing, unless by freedom we mean to assure their improvement. Freedom to a people disqualified to maintain their rights, is of no possible advantage. The recent establishment of republican government, in France, did not actually enfranchise that people. Invention is valueless to those who know nothing of its uses or the process of its operation. The daily experience of the whole world attests the truth of these suggestions. Our own recent history exemplifies it. It is as applicable to nations as to individuals. Its force was never more apparent than in the treatment of the slavery question. Granting the ability of the negro race to maintain free government, if separated from the whites, it will hardly be contended that they will be able to cope with the latter, as coequal inhabitants. The races are certainly antagonistic. The one or the other will have dominion; which, we apprehend, it is not difficult to determine. It is, in this view, simply impossible to benefit the negroes by abolishing slavery. If there is no other mode by which they can be improved in condition, their welfare demands that they shall, for the present, at least, be let alone. What the future holds in promise for them, it is not for us to determine. There is not a day's observation, or a single lesson of experience, which does not teach us that there is a fitting time for all things. Perhaps this admonition is more impressively conveyed to the American people in the history of slavery, in this country, than anywhere else. The process and progress of its expulsion here and there, its removal from one State and its introduction into another, show clearly that there is a law which not only governs its existence, but which will, in the work of time, effect its overthrow.

Great caution, we know, is required in dealing with all such questions. They are too apt to be viewed as mere abstract matters. In this way we come to the ready conclusion, that slavery ought, at once, to be abolished; simply because to hold man in bondage, is wrong and sinful. This reasoning is conclusive with all men who view the subject in the abstract. But in point of fact slavery exists in this country, as it must in every other, as a social institution. It is involuntary labor rendered by an obviously inferior race, to a superior race. Its violent overthrow, in the very nature of things, must produce general disorder, anarchy, and bloodshed. If the blacks could be removed from the country and assisted to maintain civil government, *the knowledge they have acquired solely through the agency of bondage*, might be sufficient to enable them to better their present condition. As a competing race of freemen, with the white inhabitants of this country, they are certain to fail. We have the most complete and overwhelming testimony upon this point, in the career of the free Indian tribes. They were not only free, but organized into nations. We met three millions of them, and never once made an effort to subject them to our laws. They were our competitors for empire and dominion, in the field of mind and labor. They now number about three hundred and fifty thousand persons. This result, surely, has not been brought about by undue oppression on our part. On the contrary, we have sought, by every means which genuine benevolence and humanity could suggest, to elevate them in the scale of moral and Christian life. We have instructed them in the use of machinery, and taught them lessons in agriculture. But all to no purpose. There was one lesson they never could understand—*how to take care of themselves.* Right on the opposite page of our history is written an account of another inferior race, who have been held in slavery to the whites. They have increased from a few hundred thousand to four and a half millions. They were once held by all the American States. As population crowded on production, their labor became unprofitable here and there, *and this* was sure, in a little time, to abolish the relation. This, we apprehend, is the only legitimate process of its extinction. We doubt, indeed, if it is the moral right of any State of the Union to abolish slavery by any other means. The blacks are entitled to protection, and they can secure it only by remaining as they are, subject to the law referred to.

There are two radical passions which may be counted as the peculiar and ever-active enemies of free government—partisanism and fanaticism. The former is inherent in the system, or rather, the necessary production of elective institutions. It is a pervading and damaging evil.

Civil liberty presupposes intense political action through all the organs of the body politic. Without necessarily involving the equality of the whole people, it opens the way to every citizen, by which it is made possible to secure, not only equal consideration in the State, but command its highest offices and honors. The very statement of this feature of free institutions is quite enough to show that intellectual progress under it is greater than under absolute or despotic rule. There is more expansive power in every view, more energy, more mind, more thought, more invention, and, we apprehend, far more material production. It would be an exception to all rules, if there should not be found something to counterbalance these great benefits and advantages of civil liberty. It is not often that blessings are dispensed without something to remind us that they are to be enjoyed only on certain conditions. The wisdom of a free system of laws, when wisely administered, none will question. But the very advantages it assures are often the cause of its failure. This is especially the case in the almost necessary, certainly most probable, growth of partisanism. It springs immediately out of the scramble for office and place which is sure to result from the number and character of claimants. These persons may enter the field full of patriotism and purpose to promote the general good. In a little time they consult public prejudices, and shape their course more by what will promote their own interest than that of the state. It is easy to see, in this way, how the people may be led to give their allegiance to party, and actually to forget or overlook the obligations of their laws.

These suggestions find the completest verification in the progress of slavery and anti-slavery in the United States. Very much of the hostility, so far as the great body of the people is concerned, to slavery, has a purely partisan origin. It has been promoted as a means of acquiring office and government. It has grown, in numerous instances, to be stronger than patriotism, stronger than the Constitution. The natural product of this hostility to slavery, one which could hardly fail to follow its connection with elective institutions, is fanaticism. This species of lunacy is far less reasonable and more difficult to govern than the other. It is a sort of hurricane which sweeps everything before it. All its powers are concentrated upon one object. Everything else is lost in the pursuit of its one cherished end. It may be temperance to-day, native Americanism to-morrow, slavery next, Catholicism next, masonry next, and so on to the end of its mission. History is a falsehood, experience a deception and a snare, Christianity a cunning fraud, when they cross the path of these monster enemies of free institutions.

They have issued an edict against slavery. They are armed for its overthrow. They are now fighting battles for its extirpation. What they have done and what they have sacrificed, no man can tell.

NOTE.

1. *Liberty of the Press.*—Jeremy Bentham, in his letter, written in 1820, to the Spanish people on the subject of the freedom of the press, says: "Spaniards! The Madrid intelligence of the prosecution of a newspaper editor for comments on the Madrid system of police, and of the proposed law against political meetings, has just reached me. I am astounded! What? is it come to this? So soon come to this? The men being men, of their disposition to do this, and more, there could not be any room for doubt. But that this disposition should so soon ripen into act, this (I must confess) is more than I anticipated, that the impatience of contradiction, not to say the thirst for arbitrary power, should so soon have ventured thus far; these in my view are of themselves highly alarming symptoms. By the prosecution, if successful, I see the liberty of the press destroyed; by the proposed law, if established, I see the almost only remaining check to arbitrary power destroyed. Taken together, they form a connected system—these two measures. By the authors of this system you have of course been told, that it is indispensably necessary—necessary to *order*, to GOOD *order*, to tranquillity—and perhaps honorable gentlemen may have ventured so far into the region of *particulars* and *intelligibles* as to say, to *good government*, and some other good things. Spaniards! It is neither necessary, nor conducive to, nor other than exclusive of, any of those good things. What says experience? In the Anglo-American United States (alas! alas! when Bentham wrote he wrote truth, but were he living now he could scarcely refer, with any good effect, to this country to support his views), of the two parts of this system, neither the one nor the other will you see. No prosecution can there take place for anything written against the Government, or any of its functionaries as such. No restriction whatever is there on public meetings held for any such purpose as that of sitting in judgment on the Constitution—on any measures of the Government—or on any part of the conduct of any of its functionaries. There is no more restriction upon men's speaking together in public than upon their eating together in private.

"Against the allowance of the liberty of the press, considered with a view to its effect on the goodness of the government, no arguments that have been or may be adduced will bear the test of examination.

"I. First comes *dangerous*. Dangerous it always and everywhere is; for it may lead to insurrection, and thus to civil war; and such is its continual tendency.

"*Answer:* In all liberty there is more or less of danger; and so there is in all power. The question is—in which there is most danger—in power limited by this check, or in power without this check to limit it. In those political communities in which this check is in its greatest vigor, the condition of the members, in all ranks and classes taken together, is, by universal acknowledgment, the happiest. These are the United States, and the kingdom of Great Britain and Ireland. In the republic this liberty is allowed by law, and exists in perfection: in the kingdom it is proscribed by law, but continues to have place, in considerable degree, in spite of law.

"II. Next comes *needlessness.* To the prevention of misgovernment, the other remedies that government itself affords, are adequate. The rulers in chief, whoever they are, have nothing so much at heart as the happiness of all over whom they rule.

"*Answer:* The rulers in chief, whoever they are, if they are men, have their own happiness more at heart than that of all over whom they rule put together: the very existence of man will in every situation be found to depend upon this general and habitual self-preference.

"As to *wisdom,* it can never be so near to perfection without as with these all-comprehensive means of information, which nothing but the liberty here in question can give. The characteristic, then, of *an undespotic* government—in a word, of every government that has any tenable claim to the appellation of a *good government*—is the allowing and giving facility to a free communication of thought by vehicles of all sorts; by signs of all sorts; signs to the ear, signs to the eye, by spoken language, by written, including printed language, by the liberty of the tongue, by the liberty of the writing *desk,* by the liberty of the *post office,* by the liberty of the *press.*"

CHAPTER III.

THE JUDICIARY.

ITS OFFICE IN A GOVERNMEMT OF LAWS—ITS HIGH TRUSTS AND DUTIES—SUSPECTED AND CONVICTED PERSONS—HOW REGARDED—HABEAS CORPUS—EXTRA-CONSTITUTIONAL MEASURES—DEVICE FOR VIOLATING LAWS—BOLD USURPATIONS—THE UNION A BROTHERHOOD—ACCOUNTABILITY OF FEDERAL OFFICIALS TO THE JUDICIARY—THE EQUILIBRIUM OF THE SYSTEM.

THE judicial department of a free system of laws, is by far the most important of all the branches of the public service. With no legislative power or partisan influence, its sphere is confined to the execution of the weighty trusts devolved upon it, by the state on the one side, and the people on the other. It is purely an umpire, with power to enforce existing laws. It contemplates all public institutions as a party, and recognizes its duty to protect them. The people are also a party, and entitled, in like manner, to protection. The judicial power of the state, in this general sense, is called upon to exercise, what may be termed, political functions. The relations between the people and their Government are purely reciprocal. Obedience to laws is no more a duty of the former, than their honest enforcement by the latter. Their violation, by either, is a crime.

These reflections indicate the general office of the judiciary. It is the exclusive judge of what is due to the state and what is due to the citizen.

The constitution of the Federal Judiciary limits its power to nine specific trusts :

1. " To all cases in law and equity arising under this Constitution, the laws of the United States, and the treaties made or which shall be made under their authority.

2. " To all cases affecting ambassadors, other public ministers, and consuls.

3. "To all cases of admiralty and maritime jurisdiction.

4. "To controversies to which the United States shall be a party.

5. "To controversies between two or more States.

6. "Between a State and the citizens of another State.

7. "Between citizens of different States.

8. "Between citizens of the same State, claiming lands under grants of different States.

9. "Between a State and the citizens thereof and foreign states, citizens, or subjects."

The first of these specific delegations of power, is far more general and comprehensive than the others, extending to all cases in law and equity arising under the compact of Union. If this language bears any signification, beyond a mere limitation of jurisdiction to the federal system, it makes the judges of the Supreme Court of the United States a tribunal, with exclusive power to determine, not only the rights of litigant parties in suit, but the constitutionality of all federal laws which shall be brought before it for enforcement. In this respect, the "judicial power," as it is denominated, is intrusted with the very highest of political functions. It is as much its duty to interdict the enforcement of illegal acts as to execute those which are legal.

It has been found, in the practical life of every description of administration, that the judicial authority has maintained, through every trial, a far higher tone; more incorruptible integrity; more capacity and disposition to allay excitement, reconcile differences, and adjust disputes personal and general, than any other branch of the public service. Less ostentatious than the legislature, unobtrusive and almost unnoticed in its deliberations; earnest, profound and impartial in its decisions, it commands public confidence, and exacts a willing obedience to its awards. It is preëminently the tribunal of the people; an umpire, with power, not only to determine all controversies between persons, but an international commission to adjust questions of difference between the States and the Union and the citizen and the Union. [1]

In the enforcement of all local laws, embracing the internal administration of justice through the whole range of civil institutions, the collection of debts, the punishment of crime, the maintenance of order, the judiciary is the mainspring of the political machine. It is, to all intents and purposes, the animating principle of the state.

Under general regulations, covering the ordinary intercourse of life, it exercises absolute power. The character of its administration is indicated by the fact, that its decisions constitute a body of laws, of higher merit and wider influence than those ordained by the legislature. It is impossible indeed to conceal this feature of the government of the States and the Union. That there is something in the structure of these great departments of administration, or in the nature of the duties assigned to each, which enables the judiciary to command higher qualifications and intellect, we do not question.

In this connection it is a noteworthy fact that of all the complaints made by parties and sections against the general Administration, involving, in many cases, alleged violations of the Constitution, and in others, of fundamental principles of political economy, not one has been laid at the door of the judiciary. Usurpation of authority has been charged upon the Executive and the legislature, and, at times, a general tendency to disregard constitutional obligations and duties manifested; but we know of no instance, beyond the lowest partisan circles, where the judicial authority of the States or the nation has been held responsible for the least offence of the kind.

It must not be admitted, in explanation of this, that its office is comparatively of little account. On the contrary, in a government of laws, it is by far the highest, most important and responsible of all the institutions of state. Its range is broader; its duties more weighty and elaborate; its government more complete and universal; its trusts more sacred; and, we may add, its decisions more satisfactory, than any other department. It is the state, to all practical intents and purposes. When the privilege of the writ of habeas corpus was partially suspended in England, Mr. Burke denounced and declared it a dissolution of government. In this denunciation we see the true theory of the English Constitution. It is a free system of laws, and such a system is impossible on any other basis than the maintenance of a free, impartial, and unrestricted judiciary. This freedom, too, must be absolute. It must be, as Goethe says, " a courageous magistracy," for that is the greatest blessing a free people can have. The rights of the Habeas Corpus Act, under it, are inalienable and indestructible. Their suspension, by whomsoever ordered, undermined and destroyed the whole scheme of government. It was not a mere political offence, but a fatal blow at the system, which alone was the object of preservation and the source of authority. There was no extravagance in the speech of Mr. Burke, as will be seen by an examination of the duties of the judiciary.

It is the province of the legislature to enact laws for the punishment of crime; but crime exists alone by the decision of the courts. The entire innocence of parties charged with offence, is presumed until they are convicted by the tribunals of justice. Hence the classification of offenders, as *suspected* and *convicted persons*. This distinction is clearly recognized in the laws of the States, and in the Constitution and laws of the Union. While no limitation is put upon the judges, in dealing with convicts, simply because they are outlaws, they are charged with the greatest circumspection, and bound to the severest restraints, touching the treatment of persons *suspected of crime.*

The reason of this is too obvious to justify comment. It is the most vital feature of a government of laws. There must be certain written evidence of guilt submitted to a peace officer before suspicion can legally attach to the offender. He cannot be held as a suspected person on any other condition. If he has violated the law, let the proof of the facts be laid before the judges of the law. It is just as reasonable to expect the judiciary to be proficient in the military service as to suppose that soldiers are qualified to discharge the duties of the legal profession.

The Federal Constitution provides, what was supposed, at the time, to be the amplest precautionary restrictions, upon any and all persons having the right of arrest and imprisonment, against the abuse of such right and its corresponding injury. It declares, for instance, that " no warrant shall issue, but upon probable cause, supported by oath or affirmation; " and " no person shall be held in answer for a capital or other infamous crime, unless on a presentment or indictment of a grand jury;" and "no person shall be deprived of life, liberty, or property, without due process of law;" and "excessive bail shall not be required."

These provisions apply exclusively to *persons suspected of crime*, and, in no case, to persons convicted of crime. There is nothing in them but the exercise of a wise and humane precaution against the abuse of power, by magistrates or others in authority.

The direct office of the writ of habeas corpus is to recover the freedom of a citizen wrongfully taken away.

This law was enacted *in aid* of the provisions of the Constitution quoted, and exclusively for the benefit of suspected persons. It recognizes the possibility of illegal imprisonment, in spite of the protective features of the organic law, to which we have referred, and provides for a rehearing of the case.

There is nothing new in all these ordinances and regulations. They are a part, and a necessary part, of the machinery of all free governments. They are the very features of such a system which distinguish it from absolutism. They take away, not only all right to exercise individual will and judgment, but every semblance of authority to do so. They make the law supreme, by prescribing certain forms of proceeding; and then, conceding the possibility of its evasion, they provide the means of recovering the freedom of a citizen thus illegally deprived of his liberty.

All these safeguards against oppression are of no possible account without an appropriate agency in the government to enforce them. A right, without a corresponding remedy, in the event of its violation, is a mere word of promise to the ear. The Federal Constitution is not only a chart, pointing out political shoals and treacherous currents, but a complete system of political navigation. It is a state, fixing with almost mathematical precision, the rights of persons and property, and on this basis giving power to enact and enforce laws. It was intended that these rights should be maintained precisely as they are placed in the compact. For this distinct and avowed purpose, among others, the judiciary was organized. Its constitution and powers are explicit. It is made a coördinate department of the government, its jurisdiction extending over all federal grants of which it is the only judge. With no authority to enact laws, it is its duty to determine the legality and constitutionality of those enacted by Congress.[2]

If we have fairly stated the office of the judiciary, it is hardly necessary to add that its suppression is fatal to the Union. It leaves a quivering, lifeless body to testify that the heart has been torn from it by the ruthless hand of ambition.

It is certainly a wonderful turn of the wheel of fortune, which imposes upon the American people an occasion for the discussion and maintenance of rights of persons and property, which are not only inherent in every freeman, but which are acknowledged in every line of their Constitution and laws. Nothing but the most astounding events of the day could have provoked this extraordinary condition of things. We cannot believe, as thousands of the best informed unquestionably do, that a disposition anywhere prevails to overthrow our free system of laws. That we have committed great mistakes in managing public affairs; that we have shamefully violated almost every principle of constitutional government; that we have conceded too much power to the Executive, where power is never legally exercised; that we have, in short, trusted most to that which, in the nature of things, should be trusted least, cannot be questioned. The plea on which these things have been done, too, is scarcely less criminal and treasonable, than the acts and omissions of which we complain. A large portion of the people proclaimed that the civil commotions of the state made it necessary practically to abandon the government of the Constitution in favor of the existing Administration. This monstrous heresy has borne its legitimate fruit. We have a despotism without a dynasty.

With no partiality for dynastic government, and no belief in the possibility of its maintenance, in the present temper of the American people, it is certainly much to be preferred to the reckless system now in force at Washington.

The President of the United States, by a strict construction of the Constitution, is endowed with no creative powers whatever. He is called the Executive, and required to fill certain offices, by the advice and consent of the Senate. As the political head of the nation, it is his duty to conduct all foreign relations and generally to see to it that the laws shall be faithfully executed. He is not intrusted with the power, by virtue of his own action, to execute a single law of Congress governing the ordinary affairs of the people.

It is the province of Congress to create all local executive offices necessary to carry into effect the laws of the Union. The President may appoint incumbents, by the consent of the Senate. He is a sort of commander to give orders to engineers, whose duty it is to execute the laws. In the event of failure, his power is exhausted by removing the delinquent, who is then turned over to the judiciary, where justice is administered and the rights and dignities of the state vindicated. There is not an element of constitutional government in the executive department. Compare this theory of the Union with its present administration, and let us see what we have done.

Without the dignity which commands respect, the stability which assures order, or the magnanimity which often springs from the exercise of supreme power, we have a weak, vacillating political hybrid, so vulgar and offensive as to be no longer endurable even to its own parasites. It is the revel of the midnight robber in the house of the peaceful but despoiled citizen. It is that prodigal use of power, which in itself establishes its abuse.

The governments of the States and the Union are not a mere arbitrary arrangement of covenants and obligations. They were founded on great moral rights and principles, every one of which would be binding, without a single section of law authorizing their enforcement.

It would, for instance, be wrong and sinful to take life, liberty, or property without resorting, in every case, to recognized legal tribunals; so of trials and punishments, without an impartial jury; so of arrests of persons, without written proof of guilt; so of forfeitures of property for treason or other felony. It would be wrong and sinful, in the event of arrest, to deny the right of a rehearing.

Any departure from these settled principles, aside from the guilt involved in the deliberate violation of the Federal Constitution, is a great moral crime. The rights assailed are inherent and indestructible, except by violence. The President, in no event, can have jurisdiction over them. They are matters which, in their very nature, come within the exclusive government of the judiciary. The latter is far more an executive department, so far as the enforcement of laws is concerned, than that of the President; because it is charged with the special duty of enforcing laws, and endowed with absolute power to determine their binding force and constitutionality. For illustration, the Constitution declares that "treason shall consist only in levying war against them (see Sec. 5), or in adhering to their enemies, giving them aid and comfort;" and that "no attainder of treason shall work corruption of blood or forfeiture, except during the life of the person attainted." Convictions for treason and forfeiture of property on any other ground than this are void. It is the exclusive office of the judiciary to declare them so, and to hold to legal account those who act in violation of this fundamental law of the Union.

But it is urged, we repeat, that pressing exigencies of public affairs demand the exercise of unrestricted power by the chief of the state; and justify a disregard of acknowledged principles and obligations of law. This is the philosophy of despotism.

Wherever it prevails, we apprehend, however, it will be found that extra-constitutional measures have not only preceded such exigencies, but caused them—that civil commotions have been fomented for the sole purpose of justifying such measures. Upon this point we need refer only to the conduct of the Federal Government, during the existing war, in all the border Slave States; to the policy adopted to degrade those States into the merest dependencies upon the public administration; to the suppression of the judiciary in all the States, which might otherwise have vindicated the laws of the Union; to the exercise of legislative powers by every local military commander; and finally, to the practical exercise of supreme and absolute power, over the people, by the President of the United States.

These examples of usurpation not only prove the wickedness of the pretence that extra-constitutional measures were demanded to meet unlooked-for and overwhelming difficulties; but they show conclusively, in the sequence of events, that such difficulties were created for the very purpose of justifying the assumption of absolute power. They indicate the process by which the free system of laws, under which the American people have lived and prospered for more than two centuries, has been swept away, almost unnoticed, within the few months of our criminal civil war.

It must be confessed, in reviewing this degrading picture of public affairs, that there has been no midnight intrigue and deception in the work. This is the President's view of his powers: "As commander-in-chief of the army and navy *in time of war*, I have the *right* to take any measure which may best subdue the enemy."

It is equally candid and explicit. If trial by jury, though an explicit constitutional right, should interfere with the efficiency of the army, he may suspend it. If the judicial arm of the States and of the Union, in his judgment, should render the military less effective, he may set it aside. If the seizure of private property for public uses without compensation, the arrest and imprisonment of citizens without any process of law, the suppression of the press, of religious freedom, free speech, and the confiscation of estates[3, 4] by military commissions, provost marshals and their county deputies, should, in his judgment, be regarded as appropriate war measures, he would have the right to enforce them.

Then comes, from the same exhaustless fountain of despotic power, the right of transportation on the part of the President by order of military commissions—the right to seize a citizen, try him by court martial, sentence him to imprisonment or death, and to commute his punishment by an arbitrary edict, commanding that he be sent beyond the jurisdiction of the United States. It will not do to pass this flagrant outrage upon the people and the Federal Constitution by a reference to one or two prominent cases. It is the regular and every-day practice of the Administration in quite all the border States; and the power is exercised by local commanders and provost marshals, without any supervisory control by the war department. Blackstone, speaking of this gross violation of the plainest rights of the people and of the highest dignities of the state, in the same act, says:

" A natural and regular consequence of personal liberty is, that every Englishman may claim a right to abide in his own country so long as he pleases; and not to be driven from it, unless by the sentence of the law. The king, indeed, by his royal prerogative, may issue out his writ *ne exeat regum*, and prohibit any of his subjects from going into foreign parts without license. This may be necessary for the public service and safeguard of the commonwealth. But no power on earth, except the authority of Parliament [which is the same as that of the States and the people in this country], can send any subject of England *out* of the land *against his will*—no, not even a criminal. For exile and transportation are punishments unknown to the common law; and wherever the latter is now inflicted, it is either by the choice of the criminal himself to escape a capital punishment, or else by the express direction of some modern act of Parliament. To this purpose the great charter declares that no freeman shall be banished unless by the judgment of his peers or by the law of the land. And by the Habeas Corpus Act (that second Magna Charta and stable bulwark of liberties) it is enacted that no subject of this realm, who is an inhabitant of England, Wales, or Berwick, shall be sent prisoner into Scotland, Ireland, Jersey, Guernsey, or places beyond the sea (where they cannot have the full benefit and protection of the common law), but that all such imprisonments shall be illegal, and that the person *who shall dare to commit another contrary to the law, shall be disabled from bearing any office, shall incur the penalty of a premunire, and be incapable of receiving the king's pardon;* and the party suffering shall also have his private action against the person committing, and all his aiders, advisers, and abettors, and shall recover treble costs, besides his damages, which no jury shall assess at less than five hundred pounds."[5, 6]

So far is this exemption of the subject from exile carried, in England, that the Government has no power to force one of its people to discharge diplomatic or other duties abroad, except persons in the naval and military service, because such a power might be construed into a right of actual transportation.

It must be conceded, if the President has a right to take any measure he may deem proper, in time of war, in order to subdue the enemy, it extends to transportation as well as absolute domestic rule.

That other Governments, including England, with two or three Continental exceptions, have abolished martial law, is no argument against its legal existence here. We must go to our own records to prove it to be one of the institutions of our society. If we cannot find its authorization there, it is clearly a usurpation. The President says he is authorized to enforce its powers in time of war. Its origin is, then, war. It had been abolished in England long before the Revolution. It had of course been abolished in this country at the same time. It made no part of the institutions of the States when they adopted the Constitution. Even military law, except strictly *in the military service*, and confined exclusively to the preservation of discipline, was entirely unknown in both countries. This principle is illustrated in a case which originated at Fort Niagara, in the State of New York. A soldier committed an offence within the jurisdiction of the fort, and while strictly in the military service. He was indicted by the civil authorities. It was claimed that it was an offence cognizable only by military tribunals. The court held that Fort Niagara, though a post occupied by the troops of the United States, had never been conveyed to the latter so as to exclude the jurisdiction of the State—that the United States could acquire jurisdiction within the limits of a State only by positive cession. It was argued in the case, that Fort Niagara was held by the British authorities at the close of the war, and surrendered to the United States; and that the State, therefore, never had acquired jurisdiction of its grounds. Against this plausible reasoning the court opposed the great doctrine of State sovereignty and independence.

We allude to this event to show how the authority of the United States was regarded at the time, rather than to illustrate the powers and duties of the Union or the States "in cases of rebellion." If the former can gain jurisdiction within the territorial limits of the latter only by cession, it determines, clearly enough, at least, the identity of the States as a governing power. Chief-Justice Taney says: "Unquestionably a State may use its military power to put down an armed insurrection too strong to be controlled by the civil authority." So, unquestionably, a State, finding its civil and military authority insufficient to put down armed insurrection or rebellion, may call *to its aid* the military arm of the

Union. Such a call is its cession of jurisdiction to the latter within the limits of the State. The preservation of the civil authority of the State and the political authority of the Union is the end to be attained.

How, then, is it, that the President may, under such circumstances, take any measure which he may think will best put down rebellion? Is he clothed with power not only to put down rebellion, but to suspend the civil institutions of the State, which he was called upon to sustain and uphold? Does rebellion in one or more States, at the option of the Administration, transform the Union into an army and navy? Certainly so, if he may declare martial law and exercise its powers; for martial law, as he has enforced it, is a complete supersedeas of all civil authority. But he is not content with martial law. Hume, speaking of this species of government, says:

"The Star Chamber and High Commission and court martial, though arbitrary jurisdictions, yet had some pretence of trial, at least of a sentence; but there was a grievous punishment very familiarly inflicted in that age (Elizabeth), without any other than the warrant of a SECRETARY OF STATE or of the privy council, and that was imprisonment in any jail, and during any time, that the ministers should think proper. *In suspicious times all the jails were full of prisoners of state*, and these unhappy victims of public jealousy were sometimes thrown into dungeons and loaded with irons, and treated in the most cruel manner, without being able to obtain any remedy from law. This practice was an indirect way of inflicting torture."

This step, beyond the jurisdiction and forms of martial law, has been taken, by the existing Administration, even so accurately as to make the historian's description of the practice of the English queen's government an exact account of the present Government of the United States. This little picture would be incomplete without another extract from the same learned author, touching the offices of one or two other institutions of Elizabeth's administration. He says:

"One of the most ancient and most established instruments of power was the Star Chamber, which possessed an unlimited and discretionary authority of fining, imprisoning, and inflicting corporal punishment, and whose jurisdiction extended to all sorts of offences, contempts, and disorders, that lay not within the reach of the common law.

"There needed but this one court in any government, to put an end to all regular, legal, and exact plans of liberty. For who durst set himself in opposition to the crown and ministry, or aspire to the character of being a patron of freedom, while exposed to so arbitrary a jurisdiction? I much question whether any of the absolute monarchies in Europe contain, at present, so illegal and despotic a tribunal. . . . But martial law went beyond even these two courts, in a prompt and arbitrary and violent method of decision. Whenever there was any insurrection or public disorder, the crown employed martial law, and *it was during that time* exercised not only over the soldiers, but over a whole people. Any one might be punished as a rebel or as an aider and abettor of rebellion, whom the provost martial or the lieutenant of a county or their deputies pleased to suspect."

It must be remembered that these things occurred in England before martial law had been abolished, through the Petition of Right, which declares that "no man shall be prejudged of life or limb against the forms of the Great Charter," "that no man ought to be adjudged to death, but by the laws established by this realm, either by the custom of the realm, or by act of Parliament, and that the commissions for proceeding by MARTIAL LAW should be revoked and annulled, lest by color of them any of his majesty's subjects be destroyed or put to death contrary to the laws and franchise of the land;" and long before the feeble colonies of this country had become objects of serious political interest. So that so far as the American people are concerned, they are indebted to Mr. Lincoln's Cabinet for their first practical lessons in this species of arbitrary government. Military law, as it is understood and enforced in England, would answer none of the ends sought to be accomplished; because that would leave the judiciary perfectly free to exercise absolute control over every pretended offence, committed outside of the military service. There is no possible way open to the latter, under the British system, by which, in any contingency, the military can acquire jurisdiction over civil offences. It is this feature of the system, which more than anything else, marks the transition from feudal or arbitrary rule to the present government of laws. The Star Chamber, High Commission, and court martial are fair expressions of the old law of England—the old covenant which has been superseded by the Christian politics of the present day.

But it is maintained, with some plausibility, that it may not always best subserve the interest of the state, faithfully to execute its laws; that this species of political heresy may be extended to the enforcement of arbitrary orders, even in direct opposition or contravention of its organic laws. Without admitting the propriety or justice of this terrible doctrine, its enforcement surely should be limited, if it is ever recognized, in such manner *as never, in the slightest degree, to impair the integrity of the political system.* Those who claim it as necessary, in order to preserve the life of the state, assert of course, that its institutions are defective—that they are deficient, at the very time when they ought to be sufficient. In the case of the United States, in the present rebellion, the Administration have assumed not only extra-constitutional powers, but have set aside every constitutional guarantee of the liberty of the people. If they were authorized by overwhelming circumstances to take measures of an arbitrary nature, they must be limited to the first meeting of Congress, and, then, in no case, so as to impair the rights of a single citizen of the republic. The Government could be preserved only by protecting the rights of every man in the country. That was its only great office. Their preservation was the only end in view. We cared not to conquer an enemy, but to make a friend. If we lose free government, it is a poor consolation to reflect that we have won a battle. We can triumph only by convincing the world that we are capable of maintaining a free system of laws; and this we can never do except by subordinating the military, in war and in peace, to the civil power. It is the civil power that makes war against the South. It is the civil power which is struggling for existence and maintenance. It employs the army, and must ever command the army. This command, too, must be absolute. It is the law of the state, and there is no other law.

Battles lost, in the present fearful struggle, have not been our greatest misfortunes. When we surrendered an independent judiciary, and admitted the governing power of circumstances over the most venerable and freest system of laws in existence, we did more to degrade the people of the United States before the world, than could have been done by the loss of a thousand battles. We undertook to trade off the fame and success of a great nation for the transient and criminal honors of martial glory. We preferred the Norman law of conquest and its feudal government, to the Saxon law of liberty, equality, and justice. We would have the dominion of the sword, with all its blood and waste. It was our right. The majority of the people said so. Majority is power. We had the power. Minorities must come to us for terms of reconciliation and peace. There is no magnanimity in politics—certainly none in war! It is a trial of strength, not an issue of fact. We are not debaters, but fighters. We have no civil institutions to save, but an enemy to punish!

We have referred to the conduct of the present Administration, we repeat again, with no intention of discussing its measures, but solely for the purpose of illustrating the principles of free government. There is not a question but that the State and Federal systems were as perfect as it is possible for human intellect and patriotism to make. If we have failed to maintain them, it is our fault, not theirs. In the judgment of many, the Union of the States was in great danger of failure through its elective corruptions. Public demoralization was almost universal. The confidence of the people in the integrity of their agents was greatly impaired. These evils, we believe, have led to the present unfortunate war between the States of the North and the South. It is a war against free government, if not the Union, by both belligerents. War between the States is disunion. It is much to be doubted if the separation could have been effected by any other process; as it is certain that reconciliation is impossible through its agency. There must be reconciliation, or there can be no union. Successful war, even to subjugation, is separation with a terrible vengeance. It will not only destroy the principle of union, but the power of maintaining free government in the victorious States.

What we want, in any event, is free government. With that, we cannot fail. It is that we have had. It gave us greater prosperity, more happiness and less misery, than any other people ever had enjoyed. It was, too, the freest system; assured a nearer approach to equality, a more general distribution of labor and capital; it had more inherent elements of strength, political and geographical, more positive power for good, and a higher and nobler mission, than any other. It recognized what we call the institution of slavery—an apparent incongruity, we admit, of which we shall speak in another place; but it was so constituted, that no citizen or State or party could have an anti-slavery mission, for the simple reason, that no citizen or State or party could right fully alter or modify one single law of another State, or one single provision of the compact of Union. It was understood that a violation of this principle would cause a sort of leak in the vessel of state, capable of wasting all that was valuable within. This is no new idea, on the subject of legal government; but it is peculiarly applicable to our compound system, because the Union is a government, not of persons, but of States.

It is this feature of the system which makes it necessary to recognize two legal parties—the people of the States, on the one hand, and federal representatives or agents, on the other—both being amenable to the law. It would indeed be a strange anomaly in a free government, if the people should be held to account, and not the agent or representative. The scheme was based on the idea that both might offend, and that both should be held responsible to the law. It is too common for the former to regard themselves as bound to submit to the dictation of the latter—to confound power with right—to admit, in all cases, the duty of obedience to whatever is exacted, on the part of political representatives. This is not only a great practical error, but one which, if carried out, can hardly fail to overthrow the best popular government which it is in the power of wisdom and patriotism to establish.

It destroys, at once, the equilibrium of the system, by taking away its representative character, and removing from it the principle of accountability, without which it is not easy to see how a government of laws is to be maintained.

Every citizen is clothed with legal authority to make resistance to such laws or ordinances as he may deem to be unconstitutional and therefore void. The judicial department was created expressly to enable him to appeal from the law-making and the executive power. It is the only check he is able to put upon Congress and the President, when his rights are invaded or his liberty taken away by unauthorized legislation or executive acts. The judiciary, in such cases, is not only the state, but the only possible means of avoiding either tame submission to arbitrary laws, on the one hand, or open resistance, on the other.

On this subject, more than any other, we have the most interesting and timely events of British history to aid us. The struggle for the free system of English laws, which commenced under the Saxons, and which can hardly be said to have ended till after the close of the Napoleonic wars, discloses, at every stage of its progress, an inflexible purpose to maintain, at every cost and sacrifice, the complete independence of the judiciary. This has evidently been regarded, from the beginning, as the corner stone and foundation of the political edifice. It has been, indeed, a struggle between the crown and the courts—a struggle for dominion on the one side, and for the right of impartial and independent judgment on the other.

In the days of feudal government, it will be remembered, to the date of Magna Charta, the divine right of the king to reign, and passive obedience, were almost universally recognized. The executive government had all the advantages of prescription and established political habits. Those who have studied the practical events of history, will understand the magnitude and strength of those powers of state. The assailants of the crown came to their work with ideas alone. It was ideas that made war upon the whole scheme of royal prerogatives. It was a war of reason, of philosophy, of rational liberty, against effete, decrepit forms, against blind, stupid convictions, and Asiatic habits and customs. It was this war which gave England the purest and ablest literature, the highest judiciary, and the greatest statesmen, philosophers and historians. It made it apparent to all the world, that no mere despotism, however protected by bayonets, can maintain itself against the forces of reason and the searching power of truth.

It is a singular feature of American and English history, that while the people of this country, since the establishment of the Government of the Union, have manifested a tendency at least to increase the powers of their chief magistrate, and to sustain and justify the exercise of almost every act of doubtful constitutional authority; the people of England have struggled through centuries to strip their king of quite all authority, to increase the powers of their legislature, and to make their judiciary an independent tribunal having jurisdiction over both.

This anomaly is the more remarkable, because the people of the States, especially during the last thirty years, have continued to withdraw authority from their governors; insomuch, that in many cases, they have left little more than a name to distinguish the office.

But there is a lesson of profound interest to the American people and to the friends of free government everywhere in these events of history. They disclose the workings of two governments, both based upon principles of popular liberty, both successful, beyond all precedent, in whatever marks the prosperity of the people, in education, industry, enterprise, the distribution of labor, the accumulation of wealth, both starting substantially upon the same mission, but suddenly, as if controlled by some supernatural power, thrown as widely from parallel lines of administration as those which mark the governments of the Asiatic and European races. The point of separation is exactly where we abandoned the judiciary.

The exercise of unconstitutional powers by the executive and legislative departments was a mere political offence, so long as the judiciary remained in freedom; because the right and the agencies of punishment still existed. So long there was the means to hold official delinquents to account. Their enforcement might, indeed, have been difficult, and in many cases impossible. The law was violated, but not set aside. The machinery of government was perfect, though the engineer had neglected his duties.

Impeachment, it must be remembered, is not the only process of punishment for official delinquents. That process is one prescribed in certain cases in order to establish the right of their removal from place. Violations of the rights of persons carry with them direct responsibility to injured parties. These parties may resort to the tribunals of justice. When the latter are stricken down, their remedy is gone, and, with it, all accountability and legal responsibility of official trespassers upon the rights of the people. The overthrow of the judiciary is always the first step of those who aspire to supreme control.

NOTES.

1. The responsibility of all federal agents to injured parties is affirmed in the following decision of the Supreme Court: "These orders given by the Executive under the construction of the act of Congress made by the department to which its execution was assigned, enjoin the seizure of American vessels sailing from a French port. Is the officer who obeys them liable for damages sustained by this misconstruction of the act, or will his orders excuse him? If his instructions afford him no protection, then the laws are legally awarded against him; if they excuse an act not otherwise excusable, it would then be necessary to inquire whether this is a case in which the probable cause which existed to induce a suspicion that the vessel was American would excuse the captor from damages when the vessel appeared, in fact, to be neutral.

"I confess, the first bias of my mind was very strong in favor of the opinion that though the instructions of the Executive could not give a right, they might yet excuse from damages. I was much inclined to think that a distinction ought to be taken between acts of civil and those of military officers; and between proceedings within the body of the country and those on the high seas. That implicit obedience which military men usually pay to the orders of their superiors, which, indeed, is indispensably necessary to every military system, appeared to me strongly to imply the principle that those orders, if not to perform a prohibited act, ought to justify the person whose general duty it is to obey them, and who is placed by the laws of his country in a situation which in general requires that he should obey them. I was strongly inclined to think that where, in consequence of orders from the legitimate authority, a vessel is seized with pure intention, the claim of the injured party for damages would be against the Government from which the orders proceeded, and would be a proper subject for negotiation. But I have been convinced that I was mistaken, and I have receded from this first opinion. I acquiesce in that of my brethren, which is, that the instruction cannot change the nature of the transaction, or legalize an act which, without those instructions, would have been a plain trespass."

2. Chief-Justice Marshall defines with wonderful accuracy the character of the government and the great offices of the judiciary in the following lucid exposition:

"This, then, is a plain case for a mandamus, either to deliver the commission, or a copy of it from the record; and it only remains to be inquired,

"Whether it can issue from this court. The act to establish the judicial courts of the United States authorizes the Supreme Court 'to issue writs of mandamus, in cases warranted by the principles and usages of law, to any courts appointed, or persons holding office, under the authority of the United States.'

"The Secretary of State, being a person holding an office under the authority of the United States, is precisely within the letter of the description, and if this court is not authorized to issue a writ of mandamus to such an officer, it must be because the law is unconstitutional, and therefore absolutely incapable of conferring the authority and assigning the duties which its words purport to confer and assign.

"The Constitution vests the whole judicial power of the United States in one Supreme Court, and such inferior courts as Congress shall, from time to time, ordain and establish. This power is expressly extended to all cases arising under the laws of the United States; and, consequently, in some form, may be exercised over the present case; because the right claimed is given by a law of the United States.

"In the distribution of this power it is declared that 'the Supreme Court shall have original jurisdiction in all cases affecting ambassadors, other public ministers and consuls, and those in which a State shall be a party. In all other cases the Supreme Court shall have appellate jurisdiction.'

"It has been insisted, at the bar, that, as the original grant of jurisdiction to the supreme and inferior courts is general, and the clause assigning original jurisdiction to the Supreme Court contains no negative or restrictive words; the power remains to the legislature to assign original jurisdiction to that court in other cases than those specified in the article which has been recited; provided those cases belong to the judicial power of the United States.

"If it had been intended to leave it in the discretion of the legislature to apportion the judicial power between the supreme and inferior courts according to the will of that body, it would certainly have been useless to have defined the judicial power, and the tribunals in which it should be vested. The subsequent part of the section is mere surplusage, is entirely without meaning, if such is to be the construction. If Congress remains at liberty to give this court appellate jurisdiction, where the Constitution has declared their jurisdiction shall be original; and original jurisdiction where the Constitution has declared it shall be appellate; the distribution of jurisdiction, made in the Constitution, is form without substance.

"Affirmative words are often, in their operation, negative of other objects than those affirmed; and in this case a negative or exclusive sense must be given to them, or they have no operation at all.

"It cannot be presumed that any clause in the Constitution is intended to be without effect; and, therefore, such a construction is inadmissible, unless the words require it.

"If the solicitude of the convention, respecting our peace with foreign powers, induced a provision that the Supreme Court should take original jurisdiction in cases which might be supposed to affect them; yet the clause would have proceeded no farther than to provide for such cases, if no farther restriction on the powers of Congress had been intended. That they should have appellate jurisdiction in all other cases, with such exceptions as Congress might make, is no restriction, unless the words be deemed exclusive of original jurisdiction.

"When an instrument organizing fundamentally a judicial system, divides it into one supreme and so many inferior courts as the legislature may ordain and establish; then enumerates its powers, and proceeds so far to distribute them as to define the jurisdiction of the Supreme Court by declaring the cases in which it shall take original jurisdiction, and that in others it shall take appellate jurisdiction; the plain import of the words seems to be, that in one class of cases its jurisdiction is original, and not appellate; in the other it is appellate, and not original. If any other construction would render the clause inoperative, that is an additional reason for rejecting such other construction, and for adhering to their obvious meaning.

"To enable this court then to issue a mandamus, it must be shown to be an exercise of appellate jurisdiction, or to be necessary to enable them to exercise appellate jurisdiction.

"It has been stated, at the bar, that the appellate jurisdiction may be exercised in a variety of forms, and that if it be the will of the legislature that a mandamus should be used for that purpose, that will must be obeyed. This is true, yet the jurisdiction must be appellate, not original.

"It is the essential criterion of appellate jurisdiction that it revives and corrects the proceedings in a cause already instituted, and does not create that cause. Although, therefore, a mandamus may be directed to courts, yet to issue such a writ to an officer for the delivery of a paper is in effect the same as to sustain an original action for that paper, and, therefore, seems not to belong to appellate, but to original jurisdiction. Neither is it necessary in such a case as this to enable the court to exercise its appellate jurisdiction.

"The authority, therefore, given to the Supreme Court, by the act establishing the judicial courts of the United States, to issue writs of mandamus to public officers, appears not to be warranted by the Constitution; and it becomes necessary to inquire whether a jurisdiction so conferred can be exercised.

"The question whether an act, repugnant to the Constitution, can become the law of the land, is a question deeply interesting to the United States; but, happily, not of an intricacy proportioned to its interest. It seems only necessary to recognize certain principles, supposed to have been long and well established, to decide it.

"That the people have an original right to establish for their future government such principles as, in their opinion, shall most conduce to their own happiness, is the basis on which the whole American fabric has been erected. The exercise of this original right is a very great exertion; nor can it, nor ought it to be frequently repeated. The principles, therefore, so established, are deemed fundamental. And as the authority from which they proceeded is supreme, and can seldom act, they are designed to be permanent.

"The original and supreme will organizes the Government, and assigns to different departments their respective powers. It may be either stopped here, or establish certain limits not to be transcended by those departments.

"The Government of the United States is of the latter description. The powers of the legislature are defined and limited; and that those limits may not be mistaken or forgotten, the Constitution is written. To what purpose are powers limited, and to what purpose is that limitation committed to writing, if these limits may at any time be passed by those intended to be restrained? The distinction between a government with limited and unlimited powers is abolished if those limits do not confine the persons on whom they are imposed, and if acts prohibited and acts allowed are of equal obligation. It is a proposition too plain to be contested, that the Constitution controls any legislative act repugnant to it; or, the legislature may alter the Constitution by an ordinary act.

"Between these alternatives there is no middle ground. The Constitution is either a superior, paramount law, unchangeable by ordinary means, or it is on a level with ordinary legislative acts, and, like other acts, is alterable when the legislature shall please to alter it.

"If the former part of the alternative be true, then a legislative act contrary to the Constitution is not law; if the latter part be true, then written constitutions are absurd attempts, on the part of the people, to limit a power in its own nature illimitable.

"Certainly all those who have framed written constitutions contemplate them as forming the fundamental and paramount law of the nation, and consequently the theory of every such government must be, that an act of the legislature repugnant to the Constitution is void.

"This theory is essentially attached to a written constitution, and is consequently to be considered, by this court, as one of the fundamental principles of our society. It is not therefore to be lost sight of in the further consideration of this subject.

"If an act of the legislature repugnant to the Constitution is void, does it, notwithstanding its invalidity, bind the courts, and oblige them to give it effect? Or, in other words, though it be not law, does it constitute a rule as operative as if it was a law? This would be to overthrow in fact what was established in theory, and would seem, at first view, an absurdity too gross to be insisted on. It shall, however, receive a more attentive consideration.

"It is emphatically the province and duty of the judicial department to say what the law is. Those who apply the rule to particular cases, must of necessity expound and interpret that rule. If two laws conflict with each other, the courts must decide on the operation of each.

"So if a law be in opposition to the Constitution, if both the law and the Constitution apply to a particular case, so that the court must either decide that case conformably to the law, disregarding the Constitution, or conformably to the Constitution, disregarding the law, the court must determine which of these conflicting rules governs the case. This is of the very essence of judicial duty.

"If then the courts are to regard the Constitution,—and the Constitution is superior to any ordinary act of the legislature,—the Constitution, and not such ordinary act, must govern the case to which they both apply. Those then who controvert the principle that the Constitution is to be considered in court as a paramount law, are reduced to the necessity of maintaining that courts must close their eyes on the Constitution, and see only the law.

"This doctrine would subvert the very foundation of all written constitutions. It would declare that an act which, according to the principles and theory of our government, is entirely void, is yet, in practice, completely obligatory. It would declare that if the legislature shall do what is expressly forbidden, such act, notwithstanding the express prohibition, is in reality effectual. It would be giving to the legislature a practical and real omnipotence, with the same breath which professes to restrict their powers within narrow limits. It is prescribing limits, and declaring that those limits may be passed at pleasure.

"That it thus reduces to nothing what we have deemed the greatest improvement on political institutions—a written constitution—would of itself be sufficient, in America, where written constitutions have been viewed with so much reverence, for rejecting the construction. But the peculiar expressions of the Constitution of the United States furnish additional arguments in favor of its rejection.

"The judicial power of the United States is extended to all cases arising under the Constitution.

"Could it be the intention of those who gave this power to say that, in using it, the Constitution should not be looked into? That a case arising under the Constitution should be decided without examining the instrument under which it arises?

"This is too extravagant to be maintained. In some cases then the Constitution must be looked into by the judges. And if they can open it at all, what part of it are they forbidden to read or to obey?

"There are many other parts of the Constitution which serve to illustrate this subject.

"It is declared that 'no tax or duty shall be laid on articles exported from

4

any State.' Suppose a duty on the export of cotton, of tobacco, or of flour, and a suit instituted to recover it; ought judgment to be rendered in such a case? ought the judges to close their eyes on the Constitution and only see the law?

"The Constitution declares that 'no bill of attainder or *ex post facto* law shall be passed.'

"If, however, such a bill should be passed, and a person should be prosecuted under it, must the court condemn to death those victims whom the Constitution endeavors to preserve?

"'No person,' says the Constitution, 'shall be convicted of treason unless on the testimony of two witnesses to the same overt act, or on confession in open court.'

"Here the language of the Constitution is addressed especially to the courts. It prescribes, directly for them, a rule of evidence not to be departed from. If the legislature should change that rule, and declare *one* witness, or a confession *out* of court sufficient for conviction, must the constitutional principle yield to the legislative act?

"From these, and many other selections which might be made, it is apparent that the framers of the Constitution contemplated that instrument as a rule for the government of *courts* as well as the legislature.

"Why otherwise does it direct the judges to take an oath to support it? This oath certainly applies, in an especial manner, to their conduct in their official character. How immoral to impose it on them if they were to be used as the instruments, and the knowing instruments, for violating what they swear to support!

"The oath of office too, imposed by the legislature, is completely demonstrative of the legislative opinion on this subject. It is in these words: "I do solemnly swear that I will administer justice without respect to persons, and will do equal right to the poor and to the rich; and that I will faithfully and impartially discharge all the duties incumbent on me as ———, according to the best of my abilities and understanding, agreeably to *the Constitution* and laws of the United States.'

"Why does a judge swear to discharge his duties agreeably to the Constitution of the United States, if that Constitution forms no rule for his government—if it is closed upon him, and cannot be inspected by him?

"If such be the real state of things, it is worse than solemn mockery. To prescribe, or to take this oath, becomes equally a crime.

"It is also not entirely unworthy of observation, that in declaring what shall be the *supreme* law of the land, the *Constitution* itself is first mentioned; and not the laws of the United States generally, but those only which shall be made in *pursuance* of the Constitution, have that rank.

"Thus the particular phraseology of the Constitution of the United States confirms and strengthens the principle supposed to be essential to all written constitutions—that a law repugnant to the Constitution is void, and that *courts*, as well as other departments, are bound by that instrument."

3. Speaking of the *attack upon security* in France under the monarchy, Bentham says, under the head of *General Confiscations:* "I refer to this head those vexations exercised upon a sect, upon a party, upon a class of men, under the vague pretence of some political offence, in such manner that the imposition of the confiscation is pretended to be employed as a punishment, when in truth the crime is only a pretence for the imposition of the confiscation. History presents many examples of such robberies. The Jews have often been the object of them; they were too rich not to be always culpable. The financiers, the farmers of the revenue, for the same reason, were subjected to what were called *burning chambers.* When the succession to the throne was unsettled, everybody, at the death of the sovereign, might become culpable, and the spoils of the vanquished formed a treasury of reward in the hands of the successor. In a republic torn by factions, one half of the nation became rebels in the eyes of the other half. When the system of confiscations was admitted, the parties, as was the case at Rome, alternately devoured each other.

"The crimes of the powerful, and especially the crimes of the popular party in democracies, have always found apologists. 'The greater part of these large fortunes,' it has been said, 'have been founded in injustice, and that was only restored to the public which had been stolen from the public.' To reason in this manner is to open an unlimited career to tyranny; it is to allow it to presume the crime, instead of proving it. Ought so grave a punishment as confiscation to be inflicted by wholesale, without examination, without detail, without proof? A procedure which would be deemed atrocious if it were employed against a single person; does it become lawful when employed against an entire class of citizens? Can the evil which is done be disregarded because there is a multitude of sufferers whose cries are confounded together in their common shipwreck?"

4. Commenting upon the fallacies in the Declaration of Rights by the French National Assembly in 1791, Jeremy Bentham remarks on its declaration that "*All men are born and remain free, and equal in respect of rights:*"

"*All men are born free? All men remain free?* No, not a single man; not a single man that ever was, or is, or will be. All men, on the contrary, are born in subjection, and the most absolute subjection—the subjection of a helpless child to the parents on whom he depends every moment for his existence. In this subjection every man is born—in this subjection he continues for years—for a great number of years—and the existence of the individual and of the species depends upon his so doing.

"What is the state of things to which the supposed existence of these supposed rights is meant to bear reference?—a state of things prior to the existence of government, or a state of things subsequent to the existence of government? If to a state prior to the existence of government, what would the existence of such rights as these be to the purpose, even if it were true, in any country where there is such a thing as government? If to a state of things subsequent to the formation of government—if in a country where there is a government, in what single instance—in the instance of what single government is it true? Setting aside the case of parent and child, let any man name that single government under which any such equality is recognized.

"*All men born free?* Absurd and miserable nonsense! When the great complaint—a complaint made perhaps by the very same people at the same time, is—that so many men are born slaves. Oh! but when we acknowledge them to be born slaves, we refer to the laws in being, which laws being void, as being contrary to those laws of nature which are the efficient causes of those rights of man that we are declaring, the men in question are free in one sense, though slaves in another—slaves and free at the same time—free in respect of the laws of nature—slaves in respect of the pretended human laws, which, though called laws, are no laws at all, as being contrary to the laws of nature. For such is the difference—the great and perpetual difference betwixt the good subject, the rational censor of the laws, and the anarchist—between the moderate man and the man of violence. The rational censor, acknowledging the existence of the law he disapproves, proposes the repeal of it; the anarchist, setting up his will and fancy for a law before which all mankind are called upon to bow down at the first word—the anarchist, trampling on all truth and decency, denies the validity of the law in question—denies the existence of it in the character of law, and calls upon all mankind to rise up in a mass and resist the execution of it.

"*All men are born equal in rights.* The rights of the heir of the most indigent equal to the rights of the heir of the most wealthy? In what case is this true?

"*All men* (i. e., all human creatures of both sexes) *remain equal in rights.* The apprentice then is equal in rights to his master; he has as much liberty with relation to the master as the master has with relation to him; he has as much right to command and to punish him; he is as much owner and master of the master's house as the master himself. The case is the same as between ward and guardian. So again as between wife and husband. The madman has as good a right to confine anybody else as anybody else has to confine him. The idiot has as much right to govern everybody as anybody can have to govern him. The physician and the nurse, when called in by the next friend of a sick man seized with a delirium, have no more right to prevent his throwing himself out of the window, than he has to throw them out of it. All this is plainly and incontestably included in this article of the Declaration of Rights; in the very words of it, and in the meaning—if it have any meaning. Was this the meaning of the authors of it?—or did they mean to admit this explanation as to some of the instances, and to explain the article away as to the rest? Not being idiots, nor lunatics, nor under a delirium, they would explain it away with regard to the madman, and the man under the delirium. Considering that a child may become an orphan as soon as it has seen the light, and that in that case, if not subject to government, it must perish, they would explain it away, I think, and contradict themselves, in the case of the guardian and ward. In the case of master and apprentice I would not take upon me to decide; it may have been their meaning to proscribe that relation altogether—at least this may have been the case, as soon as the repugnancy between that institution and this oracle was pointed out; for the professed object and destination of it is to be the standard of truth and falsehood, of right or wrong, in everything that relates to government. But to this standard, and to this article of it, the subjection of the apprentice to the master is flatly and diametrically repugnant. If it do not proscribe and exclude this inequality, it proscribes none; if it do not do this mischief, it does nothing.

"So again, in the case of husband and wife. Amongst the other abuses which the oracle was meant to put an end to, may, for aught I can pretend to say, have been the institution of marriage. For what is the subjection of a small and limited number of years in comparison of the subjection of a whole life? Yet without subjection and inequality no such institution can by any possibility take place; for of two contradictory wills, both cannot take effect at the same time.

"The same doubts apply to the case of master and hired servant. Better a man should starve than hire himself; better half the species starve than hire itself out to service. For, where is the compatibility between liberty and servitude? How can liberty and servitude subsist in the same person? What good citizen is there that would hesitate to die for liberty?—and, as to those who are not good citizens, what matters it whether they live or starve? Besides that, every man who lives under this constitution being equal in rights, equal in all sorts of rights, is equal in respect to rights of property. No man, therefore, can be in any danger of starving—no man can have so much as that motive, weak and inadequate as it is, for hiring himself out to service."

5. "For the destruction of everything by which the constitution of this country has ever been distinguished to its advantage, no additional measures need be employed; let but the principles already avowed continue to be avowed—let but the course of action dictated by those principles be persevered in—the consummation is effected. As for the Habeas Corpus Act, better that the statute book were rid of it. Standing or lying as it does, up one day, down another, it serves but to swell the list of sham securities with which, to keep up the delusion, the pages of our law books are defiled. *When no man has need of it, then it is that it stands; comes a time when it might be of use, and then it is suspended.*"—BENTHAM.

6. The letter of Napoleon to M. Fouché, his Minister:

"M. FOUCHÉ: I read in *The Journal de l'Empire* of the 9th instant that at the end of a comedy, by Colin d'Harleville, this note occurs:

"'Seen and permitted the printing and sale, pursuant to the decision of his Excellency, the Minister of General Police Senator. Dated 9th of this month. By order of his Excellency, P. LAGARDE,

'Chief of the Division of the Liberty of the Press.'

"I am astonished at these new forms, which the law only could authorize.

If it were proper to establish a censorship, it could not be established without my permission. When my will is that the censorship shall not exist, I have a right to be surprised at seeing in my empire forms which may be good at Vienna and Berlin. If these be the result of an old usage, send me a report on it. I have a long time calculated the means of reëstablishing the social edifice, and now I am obliged to watch over the maintenance of public liberty. I do not mean that the French should become serfs. In France, all that is not prohibited is permitted; and nothing can be prohibited except by the laws and the tribunals, or by measures of high police, where public morals and public order are concerned. I repeat, I will not have a censorship; because every bookseller answers for the work he puts into circulation; because I have no wish to be responsible for the nonsense that may be printed; and because I will not allow a mere clerk to tyrannize over mind and mutilate genius. NAPOLEON."

CHAPTER IV.

THE HABEAS CORPUS ACT.

ITS LEGAL OFFICE—NECESSARY TO FREE GOVERNMENT—HOW SUSPENDED—THE RIGHT OF THE PRESIDENT AND CONGRESS DENIED—ORIGINATED WITH US—SUBORDINATION OF THE MILITARY POWER—CONSTITUTION SUSPENDED BY OVERTHROW OF JUDICIARY—MILITARY GOVERNMENT A USURPATION—HABITS AND TRADITIONS A PART OF OUR SYSTEM—DEMORALIZING EFFECTS OF MILITARY RULE UPON THE CIVIL POWER.

THE Act of Habeas Corpus simply provides that all persons deprived of their liberty, shall have the right to demand a review of the proceedings of magistrates or others leading thereto. This right is utterly valueless to guilty parties, and was given solely in the interest of accused or suspected persons, in order that the innocent may be protected against the tyranny or usurpation of those in authority. The Constitution of the United States makes it a part of our political system, not by express provision, but by the restriction it imposes upon the authorities, in reference to its suspension. It existed in all the States of the original confederation, and, as was evidently supposed, transmitted to the government of the United States, as a settled element in a free system of laws.

It is one of those provisions which can be removed only by showing that freedom is an evil, and absolutism a benefit. It is incapable of doing the least damage to a free state, of preventing the execution of the least rightful authority, of shielding offenders, or in any way defeating the ends of justice.

It constitutes a sort of reserve force against those intrusted with the right of arrest, with power to keep them within the scope of the laws, and with no other authority whatever. It is purely protective in all its features; to the state, because it is the compass of its administration; to the citizen, because, while it never shields an offender, it never permits innocent parties to be confounded with the guilty.

Among the many perplexing anomalies which have arisen in the course of our political career, the disclosure of hostility to the free exercise of the rights of the Habeas Corpus Act, is the most difficult of solution. With no party or citizen who dares to oppose it, we find it suspended, not, according to the Constitution, by the supervening power of the army, in cases and places of rebellion, but by the proclamation of the President of the United States, over the entire Union.

The right to suspend the writ is given in these words (1st Art., 9th sec., Con. U. S.):

"The privilege of the writ of habeas corpus shall not be suspended, unless when in cases of rebellion or invasion the public safety may require it."

It will be observed that the authority of suspension is here declared, while nothing is said of the manner or by whom it may be done. In the absence of all reflections upon the nature of the government, and of the State systems, existing at the time of the adoption of the Constitution, the inference would be fair, that the President of the United States might legally take jurisdiction of the case and suspend the writ. But it is clearly seen that no such power was ever intended to be lodged in his hands, simply because, by another provision of the Constitution, he is made commander-in-chief of the army. It is not possible that the head of the army was clothed with affirmative power to subordinate the least civil authority to his command.

In this case, too, we have the origin of the writ, as it were, in our own family. It grew out of a controversy involving the alleged right of the Crown of England to imprison, at will, its subjects. This right the people not only denied, but affirmed that they would be held alone in answer to the laws. In order to effect this great end of free government, they enacted that all freemen should have the right to be heard before the courts, whenever their liberties had been taken away without due warrant of law. This was no more than a simple declaration that they would be governed by laws, and not by the arbitrary will of an executive magistrate.

All this, we repeat, is a part of the record of our own political household. It was the work, in a legal sense, of our own people. It is our own history. Its honor, and its example, are ours. We cannot go behind it, without an open abandonment of free government.

It is clear, then, that the President was clothed with no authority to suspend the writ; and such, we apprehend, is the almost unanimous opinion of the country.

The right of the legislative department to do in this case what principle, policy, and history concur in denying to the executive, is another and far more important question. It is more important, simply because that department has assumed to exercise the power of suspension. It has ordained a precedent, and although it may not be received as good law that congressional legislation is proof of constitutional right, yet it is undeniably true that there are many persons—far too many—who are satisfied with this kind of reasoning.

We well understand, that a denial of the right of Congress or the President, to suspend the privilege of the writ imposes upon the person who urges it, the duty of showing by what authority and action it may be suspended.

It is impossible to overlook, in discussing the subject, not only the character of the Union, but of the States which created it. Nowhere else in the world was there a system of laws more absolutely free, or a people more resolute or vigilant in their maintenance. What was prominent over every other matter of government, was their resolution to maintain, at all times and in all exigencies, the complete subordination of the military to the civil authority. This was not a mere theory or fancy of the day, but a great law of public opinion, of universal acceptation and government.

It is hardly possible that such a people, not only jealous of military rule, but expressing fears of the domineering civil power of the Union, should so construct the latter as directly or indirectly to be able to violate this fundamental idea of freedom. If Congress may suspend the writ or authorize its suspension, though it places before the President one impediment to the exercise of irresponsible power, it does not close the door against it, as was the evident purpose of the States in creating the Union. It makes it little better, that Congress instead of the President has authority to break down the barrier between the civil and the military power. That barrier was universally regarded as necessary to the preservation of the former and the control of the latter. The governments of the States and the Union are purely civil institutions. In no event was it intended that they should be anything else. Military authority, as an element of government, was never contemplated. The army was recognized as sheriffs, marshals, and other ministerial officers were recognized, to perform ministerial duties, not legislative or judicial. There was no original authority placed in its hands. Its duty was to obey, not make laws. It possessed neither peace nor war powers, of a civil or political nature.

How are we then justified in the conclusion that either Congress or the President is authorized to suspend the writ? Such suspension, if legal, inaugurates the military head of the nation, and of necessity makes it supreme over all civil institutions; for it is the right of every people to have government.

If military rule was not contemplated by the States, if its subordination to the civil authority was universally demanded, is it not morally impossible that the framers of the Constitution should have conferred upon Congress the least authority to emasculate the judiciary?

What need was there for inserting in that compact its stringent prohibitions against the arbitrary exercise of authority over persons and property, if, by a sweeping power, they intended to permit their practical suspension by Congress on precisely the occasions when power is most likely to be abused?

Were civil institutions of such doubtful utility and efficiency, that they could be trusted only in peace?

From what events in our own or the history of England, was it determined that military government may be inaugurated over the whole country "in cases of rebellion or invasion" in any particular part of it?

Was rebellion, in one State, regarded as sufficient to deprive the people of all the others of their civil institutions?

It is obvious to the least-informed person that no authority is conferred upon Congress to suspend the writ. Yet it may be suspended, and in such manner and place as to effect the end desired, the invigoration of the civil authorities, without inflicting a fatal wound upon the body politic. The Constitution, we repeat, is silent touching the manner and the authority to suspend the writ. Granting the right, we are restricted in its enforcement, at least to the limits of its previous exercise by the governments of the States. In other words, the *status* of the military had been fixed, by an irrepealable law of public sentiment in this country and England, and we have no right, on the authority of the vague grant in question, to interfere with that *status*. We have no right to infer, simply because the right of suspension is conceded, that it may be carried out so as to confer authority upon the military to assume superior control over the laws of the United States, and the States. If those laws, in a particular place or locality, are menaced or overthrown, by rebellion or invasion, the best thing the civil authorities can do, is to invoke the *aid* of the military; for it is then that the public safety is endangered, and it is then, and then only, that the latter is warranted to supervene, and assume control, to the end that the civil administration may go on with its peaceful work. Meanwhile, in every other part of the Union the example of absolute civil government, within the scope of the laws, is held up to the rebels or insurgents of the disaffected district or section. By this simple theory of the case, the great end sought to be attained, the maintenance of the Union, is achieved, without the least infringement of the system. We can better afford to lose the General Government, than the general character of the people as the peculiar guardians of liberty. It will be much easier to reconstruct the former than to recover the latter when lost.

Rebellion consists of combinations to resist or overthrow the laws of the state. When it becomes so formidable as to endanger the public safety—which means, we repeat, the inability of the civil power to enforce the laws within the circle of the disaffection it is the right of the military to suspend the writ. There would seem to be no right to further invade the ordinary functions of the judiciary, because that department is coequal with the legislative and the executive, and there is no semblance of authority to interfere with its duties beyond that of the suspension of this particular warrant. General Jackson at New Orleans disregarded the command of the judiciary, " in time of war ; " and was subsequently fined for contempt. He paid the amount cheerfully, and with it, that deference to the supremacy of the civil power, which he never failed to assert over the military. The fine was subsequently refunded to him, by direction of Congress, which was a testimonial to his integrity, without any confession of his right to disregard the orders of the court. He might well have maintained, had that been the question, that by virtue of the grant now under discussion, his suspension of the writ was so far legal as to exempt him from liability to injured persons on account of the act. But even then, his exemption could only be established by showing that the public safety demanded it.

The language of the Constitution partakes far more of the character of a guarantee of the rights of the Habeas Corpus Act, than of a delegation of power to suspend it. It reads: "The privilege of the *writ* shall *not* be suspended," except in certain cases of "rebellion or invasion." The means of judging when the public safety may require it, is necessarily confined to the authorities of the locality. This was peculiarly so when the Constitution was adopted. It exhibits, we imagine, the intention of its framers. Had it been their purpose to confer the right upon Congress, they would surely have said so. If it was their purpose to provide for local contingencies, they would most naturally have entrusted the right with persons of the place, who could best determine when the public safety is endangered and therefore the suspension required.

Nothing is better established than that the governments of the States and the Union are purely civil governments. Military authority is not only no part of their polities, but is excluded from their administration, by positive law and long and well settled national habits and traditions. This is confirmed by the whole analogy of the governments of the States and the Constitution of the United States. As Hume says of England. " A free monarchy, in which every individual is a slave, is a glaring contradiction." There is, we maintain, in these habits and traditions, a moral power scarcely less cogent and binding than the obligations of the Constitution and laws. They constitute the very basis of government. It was the violation, on the part of England, of these traditional rights, far more than the actual sacrifice of material interests, that led to the war of the Revolution. In the great act which declared our separation, we proclaimed to the world that the king had "affected to render the military independent of and superior to the civil power;" that he had deprived us of "the benefits of trial by jury;" that he had created new offences; that he had quartered soldiers upon the people.

We allude to these records of history to show the force of certain ideas or convictions, which, we maintain, constitute a part of our free system of laws.

The authority claimed and exercised by Congress to suspend the functions of the judiciary, or to authorize the President to do so, is not only inconsistent then with the political governments of the States and the Union, but in plain opposition to the national habits and traditions of the people. Nothing short of absolute necessity, involving, through its agency, the preservation of the Union, could have justified the lodgment of such a power with the army; and we are bound to show, before we acknowledge its existlance there, not only the great peril of the state, but that its exercise is necessary to its preservation. There is a total absence of words conveying authority to any particular person or department. This leaves the clause to be construed by the application of general principles, having in view, at all times, the character of the States and the Union, and the habits and traditions of the people. Nor must it be forgotten, that general rebellion, embracing all the States, is quite impossible. There will always be what we call loyal States; for without loyal States there can be no pretence either for rebellion or Union. The proposition to cripple the civil administration of the faithful, in order to conquer and subdue the unfaithful, is too monstrous for consideration. If punishment is to be inflicted, let it fall upon the transgressor. It is enough for the loyal people that they employ themselves and their means to put down the disloyal. They are limited in this work to the enforcement of the laws. They are willing to sacrifice their blood and treasure to this end, but not their civil institutions, their freedom, and their manhood.

It is certainly more in consonance with our system to admit the right of Congress to enact the suspension, than to lodge it in the hands of the Executive. At least there is one objection less to its exercise by the legislature than by the President. But it is unnecessary and suicidal to confer it upon either. That it has been received and enforced by Congress, as a legislative grant, in the most arbitrary and unjustifiable manner, is the very best proof that it should not have been placed in the hands of that body. The precedent goes for nothing, beyond the solemn warning it conveys to the people of the danger, disorder, and demoralization, which must ever follow the surrender of the civil to the military power. It is another impressive illustration of the principle we have advanced, that too much power, in a free government, is a source of weakness, rather than strength. It is undeniably true, in the present instance, that the Union sentiment of the people has become fearfully weakened by this and kindred measures, which have gone far to prove that free governments are made for sunshine and not for the storm. Of course, such things indicate, if they have any political significance at all, that the federal system was radically defective, that it needed *aid*, not of military force, not of patriotism and determination on the part of the people to sustain it, but of measures, which it failed to authorize, or worse yet, which it positively prohibited. In this category we place the unwarranted suspension of the writ of habeas corpus, the suppression of trial by jury, of free speech and the press, and finally, the general inauguration of martial law, all over the Union.

If the right of suspension was conferred upon Congress or the President, the language used being general, in respect to the extent of its exercise, over all the territories of the Union, the power is equally so. There is not a word of limitation, of this nature, in it. "In cases of rebellion or invasion, when the public safety requires it," the suspension is authorized. This clearly contemplates *cases* of rebellion in certain localities, and the inference is fair, that it was intended to confine the act of suspension to the places or States where it might exist. It was very much the habit of the times when the Constitution was adopted, to take a practical view of things. To authorize the suspension of the writ in New York, because the people of Virginia had entered into rebellion against the authority of the former State through that of the Union, would be little less than absurd. It would certainly raise a reasonable presumption that New York was a party to the rebellion, and so on through all the States.

This view is completely sustained by the proceedings of the Constitutional Convention, touching this particular grant.

The proposition to confer the power, in general and unqualified terms, upon Congress, was embraced in Mr. Pinckney's plan of a constitution, presented on the 20th of August, 1787. This particular subject came up, for consideration, on the 28th of the same month, when Gouverneur Morris submitted a substitute for the proposition of Mr. Pinckney, in these words:

" The Privilege of the Writ of Habeas Corpus shall not be suspended, unless *where* in cases of rebellion or invasion the public safety may require it."

There was no difference of opinion in the convention on the first part of this substitute, viz.: " The privilege of the writ of habeas corpus shall not be suspended," it was therefore adopted *nem. con.* The vote on the remaining portion of the substitute, to wit: " unless *where* in cases of rebellion or invasion, the public safety may require it," stood, seven States for it, and three against it. So the Morris substitute, entire, was adopted.

This is the simple history of the adoption, by the convention, of the clause in question, and afterward, so far as we can find, no reference is made to the subject. There was very decided opposition made to giving power in any contingency to suspend the writ. It was declared unnecessary, unsafe, and especially in the general and unlimited form proposed by Mr. Pinckney. It was distinctly and positively said, in behalf of the proposition to authorize the suspension on some terms, that its general suspension would be an impossibility, for it would signify that all the States might be in rebellion at the same time, or that the civil establishment might be overthrown in all the States at the same time. Hence, in order to satisfy the opponents of the power, Mr. Gouverneur Morris framed his substitute in a negative form, authorizing the suspension only "WHERE, in cases of rebellion or invasion, the public safety may require it." How, and when, this significant word, WHERE, was lost, and "when" put in its place, we cannot discover from the record. *The Madison Papers* make no mention of the subject matter again after the 28th of August, up to the reference of all the adopted provisions to the committee on order and finish, from which the Constitution came back for signature. There was no consideration, by the convention, of this particular matter again. Whether the word "where," in Mr. Morris' substitute, was so written that the copyist made it "when," or whether the committee on form, without much reflection, substituted the latter for the former, we leave to the curious to determine.

Meanwhile the original design of the convention of the States is made too clear to be disputed. Mr. Pinckney's general legislative power of suspension was rejected; three States opposed any restriction; while seven States were willing to confer the power of suspension, *where* there should be rebellion or invasion. This simple history of the origin of the grant, indicates the spirit and purpose of the body which framed the Constitution.

There is no light in which the subject can be seen, which gives the least color of authority to suspend the privilege of the writ, beyond the district, State, or section, which may be invaded or in rebellion. The design certainly was to uphold the Union and enforce its laws. To this end the employment of the military was authorized. It is absurd to claim that the authority of the latter in such "cases" is not limited to those in rebellion or the public enemy, Not so, however, if the right to suspend the writ has been lodged with Congress or the President, because they are two chief departments of the Federal Government, and the power being general in its language, they may command it over all the United States, at least so far as to interdict the Federal Judiciary.

The Union was ordained by sovereign States, acting separately and remaining in the confederation with all their original powers of government, excepting those which they delegated. The delegated powers are almost exclusively of a political nature, such as foreign intercourse, commerce, and navigation, the regulation of the value, of foreign coin, and so on through the whole range of the delegated interests. The Federal Judiciary was so constituted as to take cognizance of these things, and at the same time, to act in obedience to the civil institutions of the States—"to adopt and follow the decisions of the State courts," in the language of Chief-Justice Taney, "in all questions which concern merely the constitution and laws of the State." When we reflect that titles to real estate and other kindred matters are almost exclusively determined by State laws, and that the jurisdiction of the courts of the latter is absolute over quite all the relations of the people, the reason of this obedience will be seen.

In view of these things, how is it possible, in the absence of direct and positive authority, to that end, to sustain the conclusion, that the writ may be suspended over all the Union, including the Federal and State Judiciary, by the mere enactment of Congress, or the more summary process of Executive proclamation?

The least that can be said of such a proceeding, if the power is conceded, is, that Congress is clothed with authority, in fact, to change or overthrow the whole scheme of government. It is folly to contend that an elective republic can be maintained on any other basis than an untrammelled, independent judiciary.

It is most unlikely that a people, unreasonably jealous of the aggregate civil powers of the Federal Union, would clothe any department thereof with the right and the means of overthrowing the civil institutions of the States and transforming their Union into a military despotism. All this is possible by the exercise of such a power. The first step in the progress of the transformation, is the removal of a tribunal which has exclusive power to judge of the constitutionality of the acts of both Congress and the President.

But it is answered, it is the suspension only of a single function of the courts, and that, in all other respects, they are as free to act, within the scope of the law, as before.

If this special pleading has any force, it proves too much. If the courts are free to execute the laws, there can be no justification for the suspension of the writ. If the civil government is ample, the intervention of the military is surely wanton. The writ of habeas corpus can do no injury to a free people, or a free state when its laws are not obstructed by civil disabilities. It was ordained *in aid of the people*, and expressly to prevent the violation of their rights of person, by the arbitrary acts of those in authority. No honest man ever sought the suspension of this great remedy, when the courts were free to exercise their judicial functions.

It is not, then, the mere suspension of the writ which is demanded; it is the practical overthrow of the judicial power of the state. So we find it. The President made it partial at first; and followed the act almost immediately by the declaration of martial law. Finding the two measures to work admirably in the interest of consolidation, they were again followed by another proclamation, suspending the writ in all the States and Territories of the Union. But it was not alone, we repeat, the writ of habeas corpus that was suspended; all the powers of the judiciary, State and Federal, were either interdicted or placed under the actual government of military commanders. These events are too recent and well authenticated to be doubted or denied. We live to-day under the surveillance of marshals and provost marshals; and are everywhere told, that the President was authorized, by virtue of power conferred upon him by Congress, drawn from an express constitutional grant, to do and direct these things!

Having shown, as we think, that neither Congress nor the President has any legal right to suspend the writ, and that its suspension is only authorized, in any event, over certain localities where the overthrow of the civil authorities has been effected by "rebellion or invasion," and then only by the supervening power of the army, we now propose to discuss the legal *limits* of suspension, by whomsoever declared.

The subject comes before the country in the form of a paragraph taken from the Constitution of the United States. In another part of that instrument a judicial department is authorized. In order that we may be perfectly accurate, we repeat entire the second section of the third article, which covers all the grants of power made to the Federal Judiciary:

"The judicial Power shall extend to all cases, in law and equity, arising under this Constitution, the laws of the United States, and treaties made, or which shall be made, under their authority;—to all cases affecting ambassadors, other public ministers, and consuls;—to all cases of admiralty and maritime jurisdiction;—to controversies to which the United States shall be a party;—to controversies between two or more States;—between a State and citizens of another State;—between citizens of different States;—between citizens of the same State, claiming lands under grants of different States, and between a State or the citizens thereof, and foreign states, citizens, or subjects."

The jurisdiction of the United States is here expressly limited to specific relations, the first of which is by far the most important, embracing "all cases arising under the Constitution, the laws of the United States, and treaties made or which shall be made under their authority." It is obvious that this clause covers all the expressly delegated powers, and such as may be necessary to carry them into effect, and nothing else. For illustration, all postal and revenue matters, currency, the regulation of commerce, and all other powers delegated to the Union, come within the jurisdiction of the federal courts. So of all controversies "between a State and citizens of another State," "between citizens of different States," and so on through the special cases laid down.

On the other hand, the federal courts have no jurisdiction (with the single exception embraced in the section quoted), covering all the ordinary relations and interests of life. They are as clearly beyond their control in respect to everything of the kind, as of the courts of England or France. The Union is to them, touching such matters, a foreign government; because the States not only retain original and exclusive jurisdiction over them, but maintain a complete system of laws, with ample executive and judicial powers for their enforcement. These laws, as we have shown, embrace quite all the interests of society. They are manifestly the rule, while the powers delegated to the Union constitute the obvious exception.

It seems incredible, with the chart of the latter before us, and the operation of all the machinery of the States by our own hands, under the direction of engineers of our own appointment, that we should be capable of running into controversy upon the subject, or commit or permit the least error, in a case so clear.

It will be remembered, that in ordaining the Federal Judiciary, it was made to cover all the delegated powers. It is the judicial machinery of a complete government. Its powers are coextensive with the powers of that government. They are limited; because those of the United States are limited. Whatever the President may rightfully do, the judiciary may act upon. So of Congress. The opposite of this is equally true. Whatever the judiciary has no constitutional jurisdiction over, in respect to persons and property, the President and Congress are excluded from; because the authority of the three coördinate departments of the government was delegated to them by the States, and the whole was organized into and constituted *one system of laws*, on the express condition, that "the powers not delegated to the United States by the Constitution, nor prohibited by it to the States, are reserved to the States respectively or to the people." This certainly fixes the unity of the three departments. With different duties and obligations, their boundaries are identical, the scope of their authority the same.

How, then, is it within the constitutional power of any federal agency to suspend the privilege of the writ of habeas corpus, *beyond the jurisdiction of the Federal Judiciary?* The habeas corpus act existed in all the States, when the Union was adopted; is it competent for Congress to travel out of the federal beat and command its suspension by the State Courts, in respect to matters which the State not only never delegated to the United States, but expressly reserved to themselves or their people?

It makes nothing in favor of this pretension, that the suspension is intrusted to Congress, because that body, like the judiciary, is limited to the delegated powers. It will not be urged, surely, that the restrictive words of the grant, viz., "The privilege of the writ shall *not* be suspended" except in certain cases, confers authority to suspend it over things not embraced in the Federal Union. The organic law reads, "The Congress shall have power" to do certain enumerated things (the right of suspension not one of them), and it is otherwise provided, as we have seen, that nothing else shall be done.

The legal inference to be drawn from this statement, is clearly against the right of that body to suspend the writ, on any terms, and absolutely conclusive against the power of suspension, *beyond* the legal jurisdiction of the Federal Judiciary, or what is the same thing, beyond the limits of the federal syscem.

The latter would be rightly classed as a measure proposing an amendment to the Constitution, for it involves, in its enforcement, not only a modification of fundamental principles, but can hardly fail to change the very character of the government.

The union of the civil and the military powers, limited exclusively to the federal system, under the control of the President or Congress, would be bad enough; but its extension so as to absorb State institutions, the concretion of all the parts of our complicated political machinery into one compact whole, is a proposition so monstrous, disloyal, and treasonable, that to name ought to be enough to defeat it. The existence of civil commotions should stimulate every true friend of civil liberty to struggle with all energy to preserve the integrity and uphold the authority of the Constitution and laws of the country. Instead of affording a just ground for relaxing our fidelity to the great principles of free government, they impose upon every honest man a necessity for increased vigilance in their strict maintenance.

There are dangers enough to be apprehended from the workings of the civil administration, without needlessly adding to them those inherent in military rule. We have witnessed the revolutionary power of majorities; the tendency of one department to encroach upon the legal functions of another; the enactment and enforcement of laws having no other foundation than the alleged necessities of the day; the suppression of free speech, of the press, and the overthrow of personal rights—the exercise, indeed, of almost absolute government, by the civil authorities. Superadd to these political errors the despotic enforcement of martial law, and our fall will be complete. The recognition, to the least degree, of the latter, or even of military rule, is fatal to the integrity of the former. It is that loss of virtue which justifies licentiousness and makes regeneration and atonement impossible. Governments can no more escape the effects of this species of license than individuals; while the difficulties of reformation are obviously greater.

It may be stated as a never-failing principle, that the mainteance of a free system of laws is impossible, by any other than an exclusive civil administration. There can be no compromise between the two estates; for the simple reason that their powers are unequal. Military government is absolute in its very nature. It has no deliberative features. It is a single person; a law in itself, with all the powers necessary to its enforcement.

But it is urged, that a government of laws, in the sense here described, is also practically impossible; that every state must enter into the great family of nations, and adopt for its government international rules and regulations; and that, in order to preserve the rights and dignities of a state, it is compelled to maintain an army and navy. The absence of these agencies, it is said, would certainly invite aggression and produce evils superior to any to be apprehended from the exercise of military power.

If these considerations have any force at all, they go to the extent of proving that military law, in the present condition of the world, is a sort of necessity—that we cannot maintain government without its distinct recognition as a political element of the state. This results, not from the condition of public sentiment here, but from the fact that we are, as a nation, drawn into association with others, who are not as honest as they might be. It follows, of course, that the American people, by the force of circumstances, cannot be permitted to maintain a government of their choice.

It is true, that as a nation, we must take our place in the family of nations, and subscribe to the code of general laws adopted for the government of all; that we must have an army and navy; that we must be prepared to meet aggression and repel invasion. All this is suggested by wise precaution. But it does not follow, that it may not be done under the exclusive direction of the civil power. Such was the design of the Union. No other principle of government has ever been recognized in this country. It is this principle which has distinguished ours from the Continental systems. Its grand agency is the judiciary. The range of its duties are coextensive with the jurisdiction of the state.

There is, undoubtedly, great virtue in the popular enthusiasm of the day, in behalf of the Government of the Union. Its preservation, in all its integrity, is an object dear to every citizen. We want it all, just as it was ordained. We want it as a means to an end. Its restoration, simply because it was our government, under which we had been most prosperous and happy, is not enough. We want it, bcause it was a free government—an exclusive civil government—with vast powers for doing good, when honestly administered. We want it, because it was a standard political system, with vastly more capacity to benefit mankind than to assure peculiar advantages to our people.

We have placed ourselves under some obligations to all the world. It has been our interest to invite emigration hither, because we possessed a great continent, a large portion of which was unproductive. Our labor was disproportioned to our territories.

We called our country an asylum for the oppressed. We proclaimed everywhere, that our civil institutions were as free as the air. We opened wide the doors to citizenship; and millions entered, and millions more, yet unborn, we supposed, would come to join us in the great mission of free government. That mission became sacred, far beyond the range of present life. It was for the future. It can succeed only on the basis of the strict maintenance, *at all times*, of the supremacy of the civil over the military power.

One of the most striking and fatal popular errors of the day, is that which justifies the exercise of extra-constitutional powers, on the alleged ground of necessity. This is a pervading and damaging political heresy. It is an impeachment of the whole scheme of government, a declaration of its incapacity to answer the simplest purposes of its creation. A nation of laws, so deficient in foresight as to render their abrogation a necessity, on the first trial of their strength and efficiency, is certainly not worth preserving. If the Union could be maintained only by the overthrow of civil liberty, we do not perceive the wisdom of the sacrifices we have made in its behalf. These sacrifices go for nothing, if not offered up on the shrine of free government. To admit the right of our political agents, in a period of trial, to substitute their laws for ours, their discretion, no matter with what motive, for the deliberate judgment of the States and the people, would be a confession not only that our institutions had entirely failed, but that we had *authorized* those agents to institute government for us. There is no way by which this conclusion can be avoided. And yet there are great numbers of the people who justify the almost absolute exercise of discretionary power on the part of the President and others under him—power not confined to military operations, but of a legislative and judicial character. Taxes have been levied and collected. Property has been confiscated. Persons have been arrested, tried, and convicted, or held in prison, at the mere will of provost marshals and military commissions. These things too are of daily occurrence. They show how completely the civil administration has been subordinated to the military, in every part of the Union.

It would be extraordinary virtue, if the civil power, in such a condition of things, should retain its wonted purity and integrity—if it should escape the evil influence of that general demoralization, which never fails to follow such exhibitions of public disorder and anarchy. The wonder is, with such fearful examples before us, in connection with the great disasters of the war, the derangement of business, the exhaustion of national credit,[2] and the almost universal loss of confidence in the general administration, that we are able to exhibit so much tenacity of purpose and real devotion to the free system of laws we have so recklessly abandoned.

NOTES.

1. "SUCH attention was paid to this charter by our generous ancestors, that they got the confirmation of it reiterated thirty several times, and even secured it by a rule which seems in the execution impracticable. They have established it as a maxim, *that no statute, which should be enacted in contradiction to any article of that charter, can have force or validity.* But with regard to that important article which secures personal liberty, so far from attempting, at any time, any legal infringment of it, they have corroborated it by six statutes, and put it out of all doubt and controversy. If in practice it has often been violated, abuses can never come in place of rules; nor can any rights or legal powers be derived from injury and injustice. But the subject's title to personal liberty not only is founded on ancient, and, therefore, the more sacred laws: it is confirmed by the whole ANALOGY of the government and constitution. A free monarchy, in which

every individual is a slave, is a glaring contradiction; and it is requisite, when the laws assign privileges to the different orders of the state, that it likewise secure the independence of all the members. If any difference could be made in this particular, it were better to abandon even life or property to the arbitrary will of the prince, nor would such immediate danger ensue from that concession, to the laws and to the privileges of the people. To bereave of his life a man not condemned by any legal trial, is so egregious an exercise of tyranny, that it must at once shock the natural humanity of princes, and convey an alarm through the whole commonwealth. To confiscate a man's fortune, besides its being a most atrocious act of violence, exposes the monarch so much to the imputation of avarice and rapacity, that it will seldom be attempted in any civilized government.

"But confinement, though a less striking, is no less severe a punishment; nor is there any spirit so erect and independent as not to be broken by the long continuance of the silent and inglorious sufferings of a jail. The power of imprisonment, therefore, being the most natural and potent engine of arbitrary government, it is absolutely necessary to remove it from a government which is free and legal."—HUME'S *History of England.*

"Ashby, the king's sergeant, having asserted, in a pleading before the peers, that the king must sometimes govern by acts of state as well as by law; this position gave such offence that he was immediately committed to prison, and was not released but upon his recantation and submission."—*Ibid*, vol. vi. p. 250.

2. "What is meant by the 'constitutional currency,' about which so much is said? What species or forms of currency does the Constitution allow, and what does it forbid? It is plain enough that this depends on what we understand by *currency.* Currency, in a large, and perhaps in a just sense, includes not only gold and silver and bank notes, but bills of exchange also. It may include all that adjusts exchanges and settles balances in the operations of trade and business. But if we understand by currency the *legal money* of the country, and that which constitutes a lawful tender for debts, and is the statute measure, then undoubtedly, nothing is included but gold and silver. Most unquestionably there is no legal tender, and there can be no legal tender, in this country, under the authority of this Government or any other, but gold and silver, either the coinage of our own mints, or foreign coins, at rates regulated by Congress. This is a constitutional principle, perfectly plain, and of the very highest importance. The States are expressly prohibited from making anything but gold and silver a tender in payment of debts; and although no such express prohibition is applied to Congress, yet, as Congress has no power granted to it, in this respect, but to coin money and to regulate the value of foreign coins, it clearly has no power to substitute paper, or anything else, for coin, as a tender in payment of debts and in discharge of contracts. Congress has exercised this power fully in both its branches. It has coined money, and still coins it; it has regulated the value of foreign

coins, and still regulates their value. The legal tender, therefore, the constitutional standard of value, is established, and cannot be overthrown. To overthrow it would shake the whole system. . . . . . The constitutional *tender* is a thing to be preserved, and it ought to be preserved sacredly, under all circumstances."—WEBSTER.

CHAPTER V.

MARTIAL LAW.

THE GUARDIANS OF CIVIL LIBERTY SHOULD UNDERSTAND WHAT IS MARTIAL LAW—ITS ORIGIN AND ORIGINAL POWERS IN ENGLAND—THE EXTENSION OF THE CIVIL ESTABLISHMENT—MARTIAL LAW CONFINED AFTER THE GREAT CHARTER EXCLUSIVELY TO THE MILITARY SERVICE—ITS COMPLETE SUBORDINATION TO THE CIVIL POWER BY THE PETITION OF RIGHT—THE ENGLISH SYSTEM OURS—MARTIAL LAW IN THE UNITED STATES—REVOLUTIONS—CROMWELL—HIS MILITARY GOVERNMENT THROUGH TWELVE MAJOR-GENERALS—WHERE LAWS FAIL IT IS A DESPOTISM—EXPOSITION OF MARTIAL LAW BY THE SUPREME COURT OF THE UNITED STATES—ITS EXPOSITION IN ENGLAND BY LORD LOUGHBOROUGH.

A PEOPLE who have undertaken to maintain free government, and have held themselves up before the world, in no very modest speech, as the peculiar guardians of civil liberty, ought to understand exactly what is martial law, military law, and civil authority. If we look back upon the career of the Anglo-Saxon race, these three widely different phases of government become as distinct as the reign of the hostile families who have been raised at times to the throne of England. They mark, indeed, three distinct stages of progress, from the Norman Conquest to the time of the execution of the Great Charter, as the first; to the enactment of the Petition of Right, as the second; to the Bill of Rights and the final triumph of the people in the firm establishment of the Habeas Corpus Act, as the third.

It is a curious and instructive fact that the progress of English liberty is exactly indicated by the progress of the civil over the military power. Starting under the Norman conquerors with an absolute and licentious military government, the utter overthrow of Saxon liberty, and the complete confiscation of estates, parcelled out to the followers of the chief, and again to sub-dependants, we pass on to the great conflict between the barons and the king, resulting in the conquest of Magna Charta, the reduction of the military and the extension of the civil power, and again, to that greater achievement of civil liberty, the Petition of Right, when, in point of fact, the military power ceased to be an element of the Constitution of England. All this, we repeat, is simply a history of martial law, as it was understood and enforced from the Norman Conquest, up to about the time of the wresting of the Great Charter from King John; of military law, its successor in government, as it was enforced before the Petition of Right and the Habeas Corpus enactment, to the final and complete triumph of the civil establishment.

Martial law, as rudely exercised by the conquerors, was absolute military government, not limited in its jurisdiction to military persons, but extended to every citizen or subject, even to the right of compelling service to those intrusted with command. It would seem, from an examination of the structure of society at that period and what was actually done, that it was the policy of the conquerors of our honest Saxon ancestors, to confer supreme power upon the military, as the easiest and shortest process of overthrowing, not only their civil institutions, but the entire eradication of their social and political habits and convictions. There were none but martial honors to be won, and no submission, short of slavery, could be received.

In the progress of events this early phase of martial law became modified, so as to confine its authority to military persons in all circumstances. Even their debts and obligations were subject to inquiry by military commissions. Every species of offence committed by any person in the army must be tried, not by a civil judicature, but by the judicature of the regiment or corps to which he might belong. It was yet made to extend to a great variety of cases not relating to the discipline of the army. Plots against the sovereign, intelligence furnished to the enemy, and numerous other kindred matters, were all considered as cases within the cognizance of military authority.

This was its phase for many centuries in England, and although shorn, as was intended, by the Great Charter, through the extension of the civil establishment, of much of its offensive and damaging power, its exercise, far beyond what was necessary to preserve discipline and order in the military service, was continued till the time of Sir Edward Coke, when it received its final blow, from which it has never entirely recovered.

It is a remarkable fact—at least very remarkable to the American people—that martial law, as enforced in England, after the treaty of Runnymede, was a weak, harmless power, when compared with the exercise of military authority in this country during the last three years. It was absolute over all persons in the army, and assumed that certain persons, not in the service, but acting against the service, were thereby brought within the jurisdiction and government of martial law. There was no pretence of power to determine crimes against the state, such as treason or other felony. The right to sit in judgment upon the citizen, for any offence, opinion, or speech he might commit or utter, touching the character or conduct of the general administration, was never claimed.

Those who have carefully studied the history of governments, where there have been two acknowledged forces in the state, the civil and the military, need not be told that the latter is constitutionally inclined to extend its powers, during war or civil commotions. This has been especially the case in England even, where there has ever been more distrust of military authority, and a more profound sense of the necessity of keeping it within the strict limits of the law, than in any other country. But with all the robust political health of Englishmen, and their long-established devotion to civil liberty, their career is full of instances, in which the military power has broken over the boundaries of legal authority, and trampled down, for the day, the civil institutions of the kingdom.

It is thus seen how war may be as dangerous to a free state, on account of its inherent tendencies to weaken or overthrow the civil establishment, as hostile invasion by a powerful public enemy. In the long struggle of the British people for free institutions—a struggle, which, all the circumstances of the case considered, evinces more earnest, patient, and profound knowledge of mankind, than is elsewhere to be found in the history of the human family—there is not to be seen one event in time of peace, since the establishment of the existing constitution, which has seriously threatened the legal authority of Parliament. It has been when the army was employed by the direction and for the civil establishment, that it has extended its powers beyond the authority conferred upon it by the latter. But in every such event there has been, on the part of the people, a prompt, earnest, and resolute rebuke administered to the offending power, and a reassertion of the supreme authority of the civil establishment.

"The army being established," says an eminent English judge, "by the authority of the legislature, it is an indispensable requisite of that establishment, that there should be order and discipline kept up in it, and that the persons who compose the army, for all offences *in their military capacity*, should be subject to trial by their officers. That has induced the absolute necessity of a mutiny act accompanying the army." "It is one of the objects of that act to provide for the army, but there is a much greater cause for the existence of a mutiny act, and that is the preservation of the peace and safety of the kingdom; for there is nothing so dangerous to the civil establishment of a state, as a licentious and undisciplined army." "The object of the mutiny act, therefore, is to create a court invested with authority to try those who are a part of the army, in all their different descriptions of officers and soldiers; and the object of the trial is limited to breaches of military duty. Even by that extensive power granted by the legislature to his majesty, to make articles of war, those articles are to be for the better government of his forces, *and can extend no farther.*"

These extracts exhibit the structure of the civil establishment in England, and show clearly that the military is held in complete subordination to it. The mutiny act confers jurisdiction to the army over offences committed by persons *in a military capacity.* Without such a delegation of power, we take it, the army would have no authority, of any kind, to punish persons in its own service. Its power is limited by the act exclusively to such persons —is conferred by the state to that extent only. And then over all is constituted a court, having superior jurisdiction of all those who are a part of the army, in all their different descriptions of officers and soldiers.

The important right to ordain articles of war, existing in the

Crown of England, and delegated by the States to Congress here, can in no event be exercised, in either country, so as to confer jurisdiction upon the army, beyond what is necessary to preserve and maintain discipline. The law here is precisely what it is in England, with this exception: that there is no power in Congress, as there unquestionably is in Parliament, to extend the authority of the army beyond the limits set upon it by the existing British system. That system, in this respect, is ours. All our notions of civil liberty, and what is necessary to maintain it, we inherited from England. We started in our career of independent government on this distinct basis: that as long as the civil establishment can be maintained, it must be absolute over the military. We went farther than this, and maintained that the latter should always be held as an agent of the former, subject to its orders at all times, and that every person in the army, who assumes to exercise original authority, is an offender against the laws, liable to punishment through the courts, and personally liable to every citizen who may be injured thereby. This doctrine has been repeatedly affirmed in England. Extreme punishments have been enforced against military commanders, in cases where there was some difficulty in ascertaining whether the original offence was strictly military in its nature.

The most celebrated, perhaps, of this class of criminal trials, was that of Governor Wall, who, by commission of a court martial, caused a soldier to be flogged, so that he died. Twenty years after the commission of the offence, Wall was tried by the civil authorities, convicted, and executed. The case turned upon a single point, whether the alleged offence of the soldier was strictly military in its nature. This having been determined in the negative, the original trial by court martial could not screen the unfortunate commander, because by that decision the military authority was left wholly without any jurisdiction of the soldier's offence.

Lord Coke says: "If a lieutenant or any other that hath commission of martial law *in time of peace*, hang or otherwise execute any man, by color of martial law, this is murder." What is here meant by the words "in time of peace," is explained by judicial decisions to be "when the courts are open"—when, in other words, the civil establishment is in full operation. The Count de Lancaster, having been taken *in open insurrection*, was, by judgment of martial law, put to death; and this, though it was conceded that Lancaster was taken in an armed effort to overthrow the laws, was adjudged murder. The reason assigned by the great English lawyers in the case of the Count de Lancaster, was that the courts were in full operation, with exclusive jurisdiction of the offence, and that the courts martial could in no case exercise authority over persons outside of the military service. The question of the actual guilt of the offender did not come before the court. Nor was it a question of jurisdiction between two courts of civil judicature. It was the exercise of illegal authority, by a tribunal which the common judgment of the nation regarded with distrust and aversion, and which the common experience of mankind had found necessary to keep within the strict limits of its constitutional powers. A more extreme illustration of this idea cannot be conceived than that of the execution of Governor Wall, twenty years after the offence had been committed.

The Federal Government has delegated power to Congress to ordain articles of war for the government of the land and naval forces of the United States. The purpose of this grant is too obvious to justify comment. Its language indicates the scope of the authority delegated. It is necessary, everybody admits, to institute separate and positive rules for the government of every military establishment. Hence, even in an elective republic like that of the Union, where the sovereign power, by common consent, remains in the people, whose General Government provides for the periodical return to them of all authority, it was found necessary to ordain for the army and navy distinct and positive regulations, of an arbitrary nature, to the end that discipline and efficiency might be preserved therein. Nobody will question the fact, that these regulations are in conflict, most essentially, with the great principles which underlie a free system of laws. There is no freedom, properly speaking, in military government. Nor can there be any. The best that can be done, is to so construct the political system of the state, that its civil establishment shall authorize and empower the military to do certain things within its own service—

limited exclusively to persons legally enrolled therein—which, by its constitution and the philosophy of the system, can be done nowhere else. But even this authority must be strictly confined to the preservation of discipline; for on no other basis can it be justified, either by logical or analogical reasoning. Every officer, from the commander-in-chief to the lowest subaltern, is accountable to the civil establishment for the manner and extent of its exercise. The military is a creature of the law, and never a judge of the law. Its tribunals are limited by the Constitution of the United States, and by the practice of our own and the British Government, to the narrow sphere of its own service, and in that service, to the simple preservation of discipline.

Another consideration of the subject, it appears to us, is entitled to great weight in connection with the federal system. The authority of the Union is limited to certain specific grants, the States having retained to themselves all the powers of government not expressly delegated. The Supreme Court of the United States, in the case of Luther *vs.* Bordan, growing out of what is known as the Dorr Rebellion, stated expressly that they would follow the decisions of the State courts in all questions which concern merely the constitution and laws of the State.

It will be remembered that the legislature of Rhode Island declared martial law within the limits of the State; and that its officers, under the authority thus given them, not only assumed exclusive military jurisdiction over persons within the service, but enforced absolute rule over all the people. The case was an extreme one, indeed; for martial law, as enforced, had not been thus enlarged, since the presentation and enactment of the Petition of Right, in England. It was carried out without any pretence of aid to the civil authorities, without any apparent recognition of the existence of a civil establishment at all, but by all the forms of arrest without warrant, oath, or affirmation, by breaking into houses, where no alleged offenders were found, and acting exclusively under military orders of the State.

Chief-Justice Taney, without giving any opinion upon the legality of the proceedings, in rendering the decision of the court, declares that the United States have no power to go behind the action of the constituted authorities of a sovereign member of the Union. The case did not, in other words, come within the legal jurisdiction of the United States. It was for the State of Rhode Island alone to determine whether she would recognize an exclusive military government over her people, or not.

We allude to this phase of our compound system, to show that there are more powers than one to be consulted, in cases involving the unwarranted exercise of military authority in this country. That of the United States is limited to the federal army, within the scope of the laws, and to the single end of preserving discipline therein. On this subject we give entire, at the close of this chapter, the minority report of the judges, by Mr. Justice Woodbury, in the case of Luther *vs.* Bordan, because it is a full exposition of martial law, and its legal accuracy is not questioned by the majority decision, the latter resting the case exclusively on the ground that they had no right to go beyond the action of the authorities of a sovereign State. This report will be found very full in argument and authority, and will well repay, in these times, a careful reading. In further illustration of the subject, we give entire the exposition of Lord Loughborough, of what in England is regarded as the relation of martial law to the civil establishment of the kingdom.

Having traced out the origin of martial law (or military law, or the war power, as the arbitrary enforcement of military government has been indifferently denominated), its decline, under the gradual enlargement of the civil establishment, to its final overthrow, at the close of the sixteenth and commencement of the seventeenth centuries, we have now only to refer to the ordinary practice of the existing Administration to put the reader in possession of all that is necessary to enable him to form an enlightened judgment upon the current events of the day touching the maintenance of our free system of laws. It is quite unnecessary to reiterate what we have already stated upon this point. The exercise of martial law, to the utmost limit of its enforcement in England, up to the year 1688; its actual control over all persons at will, both in and out of the military service; its extension to the every-day exile or transportation of persons beyond the limits of the authority of the

United States; its levy and collection of taxes; its arbitrary imposition of fines; its arrest and imprisonment of citizens without any warrant of law; its suppression of free speech, the press, religious freedom, and trial by jury; its confiscation of estates; its summary execution or murder of persons; and, finally, the open justification of all these acts, by high officers of state, are simple historical facts. It matters little, to a suffering people, by whose direction or order, or in what name, or by what pretended authority, these things have been done. They stand as historical events, justified by those who have caused them, and the power that commanded them is still supreme over public affairs. We will not undertake to argue the question whether they are legal or illegal. To any man of common understanding, they must be received as conclusive evidence of great depravity or great ignorance.

It is too late in the progress of free government to argue the question whether the governor of a State is authorized, by the existence of war or rebellion, to become a despot. We must submit tamely to the surrender of all that makes a nation of freemen, or we must vindicate our rights, enforce our laws, and cherish our ancient habits, customs, and traditions. We cannot command the respect of the world and permit such despotic institutions as martial law to govern our people. If we prefer a despotism to civil liberty, let us have it in its usual forms, and with its usual responsibilities. We cannot well suffer the agonies of a struggle for absolute rule. It would be far better, at once, to accept the new order, and aid to clothe it with the dignities and formalities of dynastic government.

There are excuses to be urged in behalf of those who choose to submit to the arbitrary orders of a great military commander. Mankind are often disposed to yield a sort of homage to those whose career marks their superiority over their fellow men. The history of the world is full of instances of this nature, and we all dwell upon them with peculiar interest, and often feel our sympathies turning to those whose brilliant deeds have raised them to dynastic honors, even at the expense of the liberties of the people.

We are not permitted to avail ourselves, however, of this species of justification for abandoning that noble structure of free government, under which we have lived and prospered from the very first day of our occupation of this continent. All our great men, without a single exception, have evinced the most earnest and profound love of our institutions. We remember no instance, in the whole history of the country up to the year 1861, in which a great public man has not shown his entire devotion to our free system of laws, and made their strict maintenance the first and last duty of every good citizen. Precisely when we had most need of fidelity and patriotism we have found both most wanting, among representatives and people. The Union, menaced by widespread and thoroughly organized rebellion against its authority, not by detached masses of the people, but by great and powerful constituent States, acting on the theory of the right of secession, we have undertaken to enforce its powers over all its original territories, not by the command and direction of the civil establishment, but solely by the command and power of the military. It is impossible to overlook the great fact that the employment of civil officers has ceased to be a perceptible feature in the general administration of the Union. Those duties which, with rare exceptions, under the British system, have not, for more than five hundred years, been intrusted to the military, are now habitually discharged by that arm of the public service. We venture to say that there is not one single general officer engaged in active service who, judged by English or federal law, has not made himself liable to infamous punishment through the courts of civil judicature; nor is there the least question but those courts have legal jurisdiction of every such offence. But the actual power is all in the hands of the military; at precisely the time, too, it must be borne in mind, when the people are called upon to submit to the heaviest sacrifices to uphold the authority and enforce the laws of the Union! Just when we require the greatest integrity as an example to offenders, and as a means of uniting and strengthening the friends of the Government, precisely then we are made to feel that other than patriotic considerations control the councils and direct the policy of the nation. It is surely not martial law and military government, extended over the "loyal" people of this country, which will best put down the "disloyal," and restore the supremacy of the laws. We cannot comprehend the wisdom of the policy which commands that if one State turns against the Union the authorities of the latter should disfranchise all the others, as the best means of restoring order and good neighborhood; that if one section renounces its obligations, the others should be deprived of the power of fulfilling theirs.

If the seceding States of the South were guilty of a great wrong in resisting the authority of the confederation, how is it possible to make the proof of it available to us otherwise than by a faithful and honest effort, on our part, to restore that authority? If we consent that the laws shall be set aside, from whatever motive or on whatever pretext, are we less guilty of disobedience to their authority and commandment than the people of the seceding States? There is surely nothing else to maintain than our free government. Mr. Webster says: "Whatever government is not a government of laws is a despotism, let it be called what it may." This is a plain proposition. If it is not the law that governs, what is it but a man? Hence we find the same great statesman to lay down this principle in connection with the maintenance of a free system of laws:

"Nothing can be more repugnant, nothing more hostile, nothing more directly destructive, than excessive, unlimited, and unconstitutional confidence in men; nothing worse than the doctrine that official agents may interpret the public will in their own way, in defiance of the Constitution and laws; or that they may set up *anything* for the declaration of that will except the Constitution and the laws themselves; or that any public officer, high or low, should undertake to constitute himself, or to call himself, *the representative of the people*, except so far as the Constitution and laws create and denominate him such representative."

This language is equally plain and conclusive. The subject under discussion was the exercise of executive powers by the President of the United States. Those powers are all expressly defined. To go beyond their authority is "repugnant, hostile, and destructive to the Constitution and laws of the state;" for when "official agents" go beyond that authority, then surely we have not a government of laws, but a despotism, "let it be called what it may." The inquiry is returned to us, can we be ranked as vindicators of the Constitution and laws of the Union, so long as we permit our official agents to set up anything else as the governing power over the people?

Do we come to the work with clean hands to enforce the laws, or seek the restoration of friendly intercourse and political brotherhood between the North and the South, when throughout all the loyal States we find the civil establishment to have been superseded or driven out by the military?

Can we be considered Union men, battling for the preservation of the Constitution and the enforcement of the laws, until we have stricken down that dominant military power which now governs all the "loyal" States?

If we are contending for anything, it is for the civil establishment. It is a great misfortune for a free state ever to be compelled to call into being a military force of any considerable numbers, and a great crime to permit its employment in any other way than in aid of and obedience to the orders of civil tribunals.

A free state can never have any sufficient occasion for the enforcement of martial law, for when that species of arbitrary and irresponsible government is really necessary, the evidence will be conclusive that it has ceased, to all practical intents and purposes, to be a free state. A despotism is made by the exercise of original and supreme power by the chief of a state. It consists in the simple fact that such power *may* be exercised. It would be not less a despotism in the event of the assumption of supreme power, in particular cases, whether the chief should enforce the former laws of the community or not. Cromwell governed through established English tribunals and laws long after his assumption of dictatorial powers. Hume says, on this subject, that "all the chief offices in the courts of judicature were filled with men of integrity; amidst the violence of faction the decrees of the judges were upright and impartial; and to every man *but himself, where necessity required the contrary*, the law was the great rule of conduct and behavior."

Nobody will question the completeness of the revolution which conferred upon the Lord Protector dictatorial and despotic powers. The process of its exercise is admirably described by the same learned historian:

"The Protector instituted twelve major-generals, and divided the whole kingdom of England into so many military jurisdictions. These men, assisted by commissioners, had power to subject whom they pleased to decimation, to levy all the taxes [see recent proceedings of General Hugh Ewing in Kentucky, and like proceedings in Missouri and other States] imposed by the Protector and his council, and to imprison any person who should be exposed to their jealousy or suspicion; nor was there any appeal from them but to the Protector himself and his council. Under color of these powers, which were sufficiently exorbitant, the major-generals exercised authority still more arbitrary, and acted as *if absolute masters of the property and person of every subject.* All reasonable men now concluded that the very mask of liberty was thrown aside, and that the nation was forever subjected to military and despotic government, exercised not in the legal manner of European nations, but according to the maxims of Eastern tyranny. Not only the supreme magistrate owed his authority to illegal force and usurpation, he had parcelled out the people into so many subdivisions of slavery, and had delegated to his inferior ministers the same unlimited authority which he himself had so violently assumed."

Perhaps no chief of a state ever made more sanctimonious professions of friendship for the people, or more repeated promises to preserve and maintain the civil establishment, than Cromwell. If he exercised absolute powers, it was necessary, he claimed, in order to put down "disloyal" persons. Without the time or disposition to enter at large into the enormous wrongs of the Protector's government, one great fact is apparent, that he was not only the chief of a Puritan faction, but his administration of the state was so conducted as to practically exclude from the body politic every subject who did not enter fully into his policy. All such persons were regarded and treated as "disloyal" to the government. It is not difficult to see from this basis how readily and conclusively the right was established to forage on all those who did not either really or nominally sustain his "God-ordained Protectorate." He had made ample provision for carrying out his work of oppression and confiscation, by parcelling out the people into military sections, and setting over each a major-general.

The employment of the civil establishment, even through the

most pliant of agents, was too cumbrous, heavy, and uncertain to answer his purpose. There is always too much light in courts of judicature to render their employment in works of oppression either safe or effective. "An army," on the other hand, says Hume, "is so forcible, at the same time so coarse a weapon, that any hand which wields it may, without much dexterity, perform any operation and attain any ascendant in human affairs."

It is hardly necessary to add, that neither persons nor property have ever been respected under the government of military law.

Mr. Webster says: "We have no experience that teaches us that any other rights are safe where property is not safe. Confiscations and plunder are generally, in revolutionary commotions, not far before banishment, imprisonment, and death. It would be monstrous to give even the name of government to any association in which the rights of property should not be completely secured. . . . . . The English Revolution of 1688 was a revolution in favor of property, as well as of rights. It was brought about by the men of property, for their security; and our own immortal Revolution was undertaken not to shake or plunder property, but to protect it."

The civil establishment, under every government, represents and enforces the legal rights of the whole people, while the military establishment, under every known system, has been found practically to represent a faction. It is the very law of faction. It bears complete resemblance, in all its features and in all its actions, to a faction. Impatient of control, unruly, dictatorial, and uncompromising, it commands where expostulation would be better, and punishes where restraint alone is needed. We cannot do better in illustration of this idea than again to summon Mr. Webster:

"Liberty is the creature of law, essentially different from that authorized licentiousness that trespasses on right. It is a legal and a refined idea, the offspring of high civilization, which the savage never understood and never can understand. Liberty exists in proportion to wholesome restraint; the more restraint on others, to keep off from us, the more liberty we have. . . . . The working of our complex system, full of checks and restraints on legislative, executive, and judicial power, is favorable to liberty and justice. Those checks and restraints are so many safeguards thrown around individual rights and interests. That man is free who is protected from injury."

This power of protection exists solely in the law. Beyond the law it is all despotism. Revolutions involving the mere overthrow of one dynasty and the substitution of another, which takes up the old system of laws and enforces them, are of little comparative consequence. Beyond the derangement of business, for the day, and the displacement of one set of officers for another, their influence is scarcely felt. We may, without any extravagance, denominate our periodical elections as so many constitutional revolutions. They are important only as they involve greater or less fidelity to the law, in those who come in and those who go out of office. It is certainly a weak point in the system, that in the nature of things, the highest order of statesmanship is hardly eligible to the highest dignities of the state. The very term, "popular elections," indicates the necessity of giving one ear, if not both, to policy. He who can get the most votes is a better man in the judgment of partisans than he who is most learned, honest, truthful, and experienced in the conduct of public affairs. Policy is far more potent than the law. So we have found it. When it demanded the suspension of the civil establishment and the enforcement of martial law, we promptly gave up the one and sanctioned the other. Nothing was more common in the earlier stages of the present rebellion than for public writers to enter solemn protests against the enforcement of martial law, in the State of New York, for instance, while they justified its exercise in the border States, whose rights rest upon precisely the same foundations as those of the people of New York. It was policy that dictated those protests. It was not principle, because, had they been governed by its rules, they would never have justified so gross and clear a violation of them.

The minority report by Mr. Justice Woodbury, of the Supreme Court of the United States, in the case of Luther against Bordan embraces a very full and accurate review of the power of martial law:

"This is no new distinction in judicial practice any more than in judicial adjudications. The pure mind of Sir Matthew Hale, after much hesitation, at last consented to preside on the bench in administering the laws between private parties under a government established and recognized by other governments, and in full possession *de facto* of the records and power of the kingdom, but without feeling satisfied on inquiring, as a judicial question, into its legal rights. Cromwell had 'gotten possession of the government,' and expressed a willingness 'to rule according to the laws of the land'—by 'red gowns rather than red coats,' as he is reported to have quaintly remarked. And this Hale thought justified him in acting as a judge. (Hale's Hist. of the Com. Law, p. 14, Preface.) For a like reason, though the power of Cromwell was soon after overturned, and Charles the Second restored, the judicial decisions under the former remained unmolested on this account, and the judiciary went on as before, still looking only to the *de facto* government for the time being. Grotius virtually holds the like doctrine. (B. I., ch. 4, sec. 20, and B. II., ch. 13, sec. 11.) Such was the case, likewise, over most of this country, after the Declaration of Independence, till the acknowledgment of it by England in 1783. (3 Story's Com. on Const., §§ 214, 215.) And such is believed to have been the course in France under all her dynasties and *régimes*, during the last half century.

"These conclusions are strengthened by the circumstance, that the Supreme Court of Rhode Island, organized since, under the second new constitution, has adopted this principle. In numerous instances, this court has considered itself bound to follow the decision of the State tribunals on their own constitutions and laws. (See cases in Smith *v.* Babcock, 2 Woodb. & Min.; 5 Howard, 139; Elmendorf *v.* Taylor, 10 Wheat. 159; Bank of U. States *v.* Daniel et al., 12 Peters, 32.) This, of course, relates to their validity when not overruling any defence set up under the authority of the United States. None such was set up in the trial of Dorr, and yet, after full hearing, the Supreme Court of Rhode Island decided that the old charter and its legislature were the political powers which they were bound to respect, and the only ones legally in force at the time of this transaction; and accordingly convicted and punished the governor chosen under the new constitution for treason, as being technically committed, however pure may have been his political designs or private character. (Report of Dorr's Trial, 1844, pp. 130, 131.) The reasons for this uniform compliance by us with State decisions made before ours on their own laws and constitutions, and not appealed from, are given by Chief-Justice Marshall with much clearness. It is only necessary to refer to his language in Elmendorf *v.* Taylor, 10 Wheat. 159. Starting, then, as we are forced to here, with several political questions arising on this record, and those settled by political tribunals in the State and General Government, and whose decisions on them we possess no constitutional authority to revise, all which, apparently, is left for us to decide is the other point—whether the statute establishing martial law over the whole State, and under which the acts done by the defendants are sought to be justified, can be deemed constitutional.

"To decide a point like the last is clearly within judicial cognizance, it being a matter of private personal authority and right, set up by the defendants under constitutions and laws, and not of political power, to act in relation to the making of the former.

"Firstly, then, in order to judge properly whether this act of Assembly was constitutional, let us see what was the kind and character of the law the Assembly intended in this instance to establish, and under which the respondents profess to have acted.

"The Assembly says: 'The State of Rhode Island and Providence Plantations is hereby placed under martial law, and the same is hereby declared to be in full force until otherwise ordered by the General Assembly, or suspended by proclamation of his excellency the Governor of the State.' Now, the words 'martial law,' as here used, cannot be construed in any other than their legal sense, long known and recognized in legal precedents as well as political history. (See it in 1 Hallam's Const. Hist., ch. 5, p. 258; 1 MacArthur on Courts Martial, 33.) The legislature evidently meant to be understood in that sense by using words of such well-settled construction, without any limit or qualification, and covering the whole State with its influence, under a supposed exingency and justification for such an unusual course. I do not understand this to be directly combated in the opinion just delivered by the Chief-Justice. That they could mean no other than the ancient martial law, often used before the Petition of Right, and sometimes since, is further manifest from the fact, that they not only declared 'martial' law to exist over the State, but put their militia into the field to help, by means of them and such a law, to suppress the action of those denominated 'insurgents,' and this without any subordination to the civil power, or any efforts in conjunction and in coöperation with it. The defendants do not aver the existence of any civil precept which they were aiding civil officers to execute, but set up merely military orders under martial law. Notwithstanding this, however, some attempts have been made at another construction of this act, somewhat less offensive, by considering it a mere equivalent to the suspension of the habeas corpus, and another still to regard it as referring only to the military code used in the armies of the United States and England. But when the legislature enacted such a system 'as martial law,' what right have we to say that they intended to establish something else and something entirely different? A suspension, for instance, of the writ of habeas corpus—a thing not only unnamed by them, but wholly unlike and far short in every view of what they both said and did? Because they not only said, *eo nomine*, that they established 'martial law,' but they put in operation its principles; principles not relating merely to imprisonment, like the suspension of the habeas corpus, but forms of arrest without warrant, breaking into houses where no offenders were found, and acting exclusively under military orders rather than civil precepts.

"Had the legislature meant merely to suspend the writ of habeas corpus, they, of course, would have said that, and nothing more. A brief examination will show, also, that they did not thus intend to put in force merely some modern military code, such as the Articles of War made by Congress, or those under the Mutiny Act in England. They do not mention either, and what is conclusive on this, neither would cover or protect them, in applying the provisions of those laws to a person situated like the plaintiff. For nothing is better settled than that military law applies only to military persons; but 'martial law' is made here to apply to all. (Hough on Courts Martial, 384, note; 27 State Trials, 625, in Theobald Wolfe Tone's case.)

"The present laws for the government of the military in England, also, do not exist in the vague and general form of martial law; but are explicitly restricted to the military, and are allowed as to them only to prevent desertion and mutiny, and to preserve good discipline. (1 Bl. Com. 412; 1 MacArthur on Courts Martial, p. 20.) So, in this country, legislation as to the military is usually confined to the General Government, where the great powers of war and peace reside. And hence, under those powers, Congress, by the act of 1806 (2 Stat. at Large, 359), has created the Articles of War, 'by which the armies of the United States shall be governed,' and the militia when in actual service, and only they. To show this is not the law by which *other* than those armies shall be governed, it has been found necessary, in order to include merely the drivers or artificers 'in the service,' and the militia after *mustered* into it, to have special statutory sections, (See articles 96 and 97.) Till mustered together, even the militia are not subject to martial law. (5 Wheat. 20; 3 Stor. Com. Const. § 120.) And whenever an attempt is made to embrace others in its operation, not belonging to the military or militia, nor having ever agreed to the rules of the service, well may they say, we have not entered into such bonds—*in hæc vinculæ, non veni.* (2 Hen. Bl. 99; 1 Bl. Com. 408, 414; 1 D. & E. 493, 550, 784; 27 State Trials, 625.) Well may they exclaim, as in Magna Charta, that 'no freeman shall be taken or imprisoned but by the lawful judgment of his equals, or by the law of the land.' There is no pretence that this plaintiff, the person attempted to be arrestod by the violence exercised here, was a soldier or militiaman then mustered into the service of the United States, or of Rhode Island, or subject by its laws to be so employed, or on that account sought to be seized. He could not, therefore, in this view of the case, be arrested under this limited and different kind of military law, nor houses be broken into for that purpose and by that authority.

"So it is a settled principle even in England, that, 'under the

British Constitution, the military law does in no respect either supersede or interfere with the civil law of the realm,' and that 'the former is in general subordinate to the latter' (Tytler on Military Law, 365); while 'martial law' overrides them all. The Articles of War, likewise, are not only authorized by permanent rather than temporary legislation, but they are prepared by or under it with punishments and rules before promulgated, and known and assented to by those few who are subject to them, as operating under established legal principles and the customary military law of modern times. (1 East, 306, 313; Pain *v.* Willard, 12 Wheat. 539, and also 19; 1 MacArthur, Courts Martial, 13 and 215.) They are also definite in the extent of authority under them as to subject-matter as well as persons, as they regulate and restrain within more safe limits the jurisdiction to be used, and recognize and respect the civil rights of those not subject to it, and even of those who are in all other matters than what are military and placed under military cognizance. (2 Stephen on Laws of Eng. 602; 9 Bac. Abr., *Soldier*, F; Tytler on Military Law, 119.) And as a further proof how rigidly the civil power requires the military to confine even the modified code martial to the military, and to what are strictly military matters, it cannot, without liability to a private suit in the judicial tribunals, be exercised on a soldier himself for a cause not military, or over which the officer had no right to order him; as, for example, to attend school instruction, or pay an assessment towards it out of his wages. (4 Taunt. 67; 4 Maule & Selw. 400; 2 Hen. Bl. 103, 537; 3 Cranch, 337; 7 Johns. 96.)

"The prosecution of Governor Wall in England, for causing, when he was in military command, a soldier to be seized and flogged so that he died, for an imputed offence not clearly military and by a pretended court martial without a full trial, and executing Wall for the offence after a lapse of twenty years, illustrate how jealously the exercise of any martial power is watched in England, though in the army itself and on its own members. (See Annual Register for 1802, p. 569; 28 State Trials, p. 52, Howell's ed.)

"How different in its essence and forms, as well as subjects, from the Articles of War was the "martial law" established here over the whole people of Rhode Island, may be seen by adverting to its character for a moment, as described in judicial as well as political history. It exposed the whole population, not only to be seized without warrant or oath, and their houses broken open and rifled, and this where the municipal law and its officers and courts remained undisturbed and able to punish all offences, but to send prisoners, thus summarily arrested in a civil strife, to all the harsh pains and penalties of court martial or extraordinary commissions, and for all kinds of supposed offences. By it, every citizen, instead of reposing under the shield of known and fixed laws as to his liberty, property, and life, exists with a rope round his neck, subject to be hung up by a military despot at the next lamp-post under the sentence of some drumhead court martial. (See Simmons's Pract. of Courts Martial, 40.) See such a trial in Hough on Courts Martial, 383, where the victim on the spot was 'blown away by a gun,' neither 'time, place, or persons considered.' As an illustration how the passage of such a law may be abused, Queen Mary put it in force in 1558, by proclamation merely, and declared, 'that whosoever had in his possession any heretical, treasonable, or seditious *books*, and did not presently burn them, without reading them or showing them to any other person, should be esteemed a *rebel*, and without further delay be executed by the *martial law*.' (Tytler on Military Law, p. 50, ch. 1, sec. 1.)

"For convincing reasons like these, in every country which makes any claim to political or civil liberty, 'martial law,' as here attempted and as once practised in England against her own people, has been expressly forbidden for near two centuries, as well as by the principles of every other free constitutional government. (1 Hallam's Const. Hist. 420.) And it would be not a little extraordinary if the spirit of our institutions, both State and national, was not much stronger than in England against the unlimited exercise of martial law over a whole people, whether attempted by any chief magistrate or even by a legislature.

"It is true, and fortunate it is that it is true, the consequent actual evil in this instance from this declaration of martial law was smaller than might have been naturally anticipated. But we must be thankful for this, not to the harmless character of the law itself, but rather to an inability to arrest many, or from the small opposition in arms, and its short continuance, or from the deep jealousy and rooted dislike generally in this country to any approach to the reign of a mere military despotism. Unfortunately, the legislature had heard of this measure in history, and even at our Revolution, as used by some of the British generals against those considered rebels; and, in the confusion and hurry of the crisis, seem to have rushed into it suddenly, and, I fear, without a due regard to private rights, or their own constitutional powers, or the supervisory authority of the General Government over wars and rebellions.

"Having ascertained the kind and character of the martial law established by this Act of Assembly in Rhode Island, we ask next, how, under the general principles of American jurisprudence in modern times, such a law can properly exist, or be judicially upheld? A brief retrospect of the gradual, but decisive repudiation of it in England will exhibit many of the reasons why such a law cannot be rightfully tolerated anywhere in this country.

"One object of parliamentary inquiry, as early as 1620, was to check the abuse of martial law by the king which had prevailed before. (Tytler on Military Law, 502.) The Petition of Right, in the first year of Charles the First, reprobated all such arbitrary proceedings in the just terms and in the terse language of that great patriot as well as judge, Sir Edward Coke, and prayed they might be stopped and never repeated. To this the king wisely replied, '*Soit droit fait comme est desire*—Let right be done as desired.' (Petition of Right, in Statutes at Large, 1 Charles I.) Putting it in force by the king alone was not only restrained by the Petition of Right early in the seventeenth century, but virtually denied as lawful by the Declaration of Rights in 1688. (Tytler on Military Law, 307.) Hallam, therefore, in his Constitutional History, p. 420, declares its use by 'the commissions to try military offenders by martial law a procedure necessary within certain limits to the discipline of an army, but unwarranted by the constitution of this country.' Indeed, a distinguished English judge has since said, that 'martial law,' as of old, now 'does not exist in England at all,' 'was contrary to the constitution, and has been for a century totally exploded.' (Grant *v.* Gould, 2 Hen.

Bl. 69; 1 Hale's P. C. 346; Hale's Com. Law, ch. 2, p. 36; 1 MacArthur, 55.) This is broad enough, and is correct as to the community generally in both war and peace. No question can exist as to the correctness of this doctrine in time of peace. The Mutiny Act itself, for the government of the army, in 36 Geo. III., ch. 24, sec. 1, begins by reciting, 'Whereas, no man can be forejudged of life and limb, or subjected in time of peace to any punishment within the realm by martial law.' (Simmons's Pract. of Courts Martial, 38.)

"Lord Coke says, in 3 Inst. 52: 'If a lieutenant, or any other that hath commission of martial authority in time of peace, hang or otherwise execute any man by color of martial law, this is murder.' 'Thom. Count de Lancaster, being taken *in open insurrection*, was by judgment of martial law put to death,' and this, though during an insurrection, was adjudged to be murder, because done in time of peace, and while the courts of law were open. (1 Hallam's Const. Hist. 260.) The very first Mutiny Act, therefore, under William the Third, was cautious to exonerate all subjects except the military from any punishment by martial law. (Tytler on Military Law, 19, note.) In this manner it has become gradually established in England, that in peace the occurrence of civil strife does not justify individuals or the military or the king in using martial law over the people.

"It appears, also, that nobody has dared to exercise it, in war or peace, on the community at large, in England, for the last century and a half, unless specially enacted by Parliament, in some great exigency and under various restrictions, and then under the theory, not that it is consistent with bills of rights and constitutions, but that Parliament is omnipotent, and for sufficient cause may override and trample on them all, temporarily.

"After the civil authorities have become prostrated in particular places, and the din of arms has reached the most advanced stages of intestine commotions, a Parliament which alone furnishes the means of war—a Parliament unlimited in its powers—has, *in extremis*, on two or three occasions, ventured on martial law beyond the military; but it has usually confined it to the particular places thus situated, limited it to the continuance of such resistance, and embraced in its scope only those actually in arms. Thus the 'Insurrection Act' of November, 1796, for Ireland, passed by the Parliament of England, extended only to let magistrates put people 'out of the king's peace,' and subject to military arrest, under certain circumstances. Even then, though authorized by Parliament, like the General Government here, and not a State, it is through the means of the civil magistrate, and a clause of indemnity goes with it against prosecutions in the 'king's ordinary courts of law.' (Annual Register, p. 173, for A. D. 1798; 1 MacArthur, Courts Martial, 34.) See also the cases of the invasions by the Pretender in 1715 and 1745, and of the Irish rebellion in 1798. (Tytler on Military Law, 48, 49, 369, 370, App. No. 6, p. 402, the act passed by the Irish Parl.; Simmons's Practice of Courts Martial, App. 633.)"

In the case of Grant *vs.* Sir Charles Gould, 1792, Lord Loughborough rendered the following opinion touching the *status* of martial law in England:

"The suggestion begins, by stating the laws and statutes of the realm, respecting the protection of personal liberty. It goes on to state, that no person ought to be tried by a court martial, for any offence not cognizable by martial law, and so on. In the preliminary observations upon the case, my brother Marshall went at length into the history of those abuses of martial law which prevailed in ancient times. This leads me to an observation, that martial law, such as it is described by Hale, and such also as it is marked by Mr. Justice Blackstone, does not exist in England at all. Where martial law is established and prevails in any country, it is of a totally different nature from that which is inaccurately called martial law, merely because the decision is by a court martial, but which bears no affinity to that which was formerly attempted to be exercised in this kingdom; which was contrary to the constitution, and which has been for a century totally exploded. Where martial law prevails, the authority under which it is exercised claims a jurisdiction over all military persons, in all circumstances. Even their debts are subject to inquiry by a military authority; every species of offence, committed by any person who appertains to the army, is tried, not by a civil judicature, but by the judicature of the regiment or corps to which he belongs. It extends also to a great variety of cases not relating to the discipline of the army, in those states which subsist by military power. Plots against the sovereign, intelligence to the enemy, and the like, are all considered as cases within the cognizance of military authority.

"In the reign of King William there was a conspiracy against his person in Holland, and the persons guilty of that conspiracy were tried by a council of officers. There was also a conspiracy against him in England, but the conspirators were tried by the common law. And within a very recent period, the incendiaries who attempted to set fire to the docks at Portsmouth were tried by the common law. In this country, all the delinquencies of soldiers are not triable, as in most countries in Europe, by martial law; but where they are ordinary offences against the civil peace, they are tried by the common law courts. Therefore it is totally inaccurate to state martial law as having any place whatever within the realm of Great Britain. But there is, by the providence and wisdom of the legislature, an army established in this country, of which it is necessary to keep up the establishment. The army being established by the authority of the legislature, it is an indispensable requisite of that establishment, that there should be order and discipline kept up in it, and that the persons who compose the army, for all offences in their military capacity, should be subject to a trial by their officers. That has induced the absolute necessity of a mutiny act, accompanying the army. It has happened, indeed, at different periods of the government, that there has been a strong opposition to the establishment of the army. But the army being established and voted, that led to the establishment of a mutiny act. A remarkable circumstance happened in the reign of George the First, when there was a division of parties on the vote of the army. The vote passed, and the army was established, but from some political incidents which had happened, the party who opposed the establishment of the army would have thrown out the mutiny bill. Sir Robert Walpole was at the head of that opposition, and when some of their most sanguine friends proposed it to them, they said, as there was an army established, and even if the army was to be disbanded, there must be a mutiny act, for the safety of the country. It is one object of that act to provide for the army; but there is a much greater cause for the existence of a mutiny act, and that is the preservation of the peace and safety of the kingdom; for there is nothing so dangerous to the civil establishment of a state as a licentious and undisciplined army; and every country which has a standing army in it is guarded and protected by a mutiny act. An undisciplined soldiery are apt to be too many for the civil power; but under the command of officers, those officers are answerable to the civil power that they are kept in good order and discipline. All history and all experience, particularly the experience of the present moment, give the strongest testimony to this. The object of the mutiny act, therefore, is to create a court invested with authority to try those who are a part of the army, in all their different descriptions of officers and soldiers; and the object of the trial is limited to breaches of military duty. Even by that extensive power granted by the legislature to his majesty, to make articles of war, those articles are to be for the better government of his forces, and can extend no farther than they are thought necessary to the regularity and due discipline of the army. Breaches of military duty are in many instances strictly defined; they are so in all cases where capital punishment is to be inflicted; and in other instances where the degree of offence may vary, it may be necessary to give a discretion with regard to the punishment, and in some cases it is impossible more strictly to mark the crime than to call it a neglect of discipline.

"This court being established in this country by positive law, the proceedings of it, and the relation in which it will stand to the courts of Westminster Hall, must depend upon the same rules with all other courts which are instituted and have particular powers given them, and whose acts, therefore, may become the subject of application to the courts of Westminster Hall for a prohibition. Naval courts martial, military courts martial, courts of admiralty, courts of prize, are all liable to the controlling authority which the courts of Westminster Hall have from time to time exercised, for the purpose of preventing them from exceeding the jurisdiction given to them; the general ground of prohibition being an excess of jurisdiction, when they assume a power to act in matters not within their cognizance."

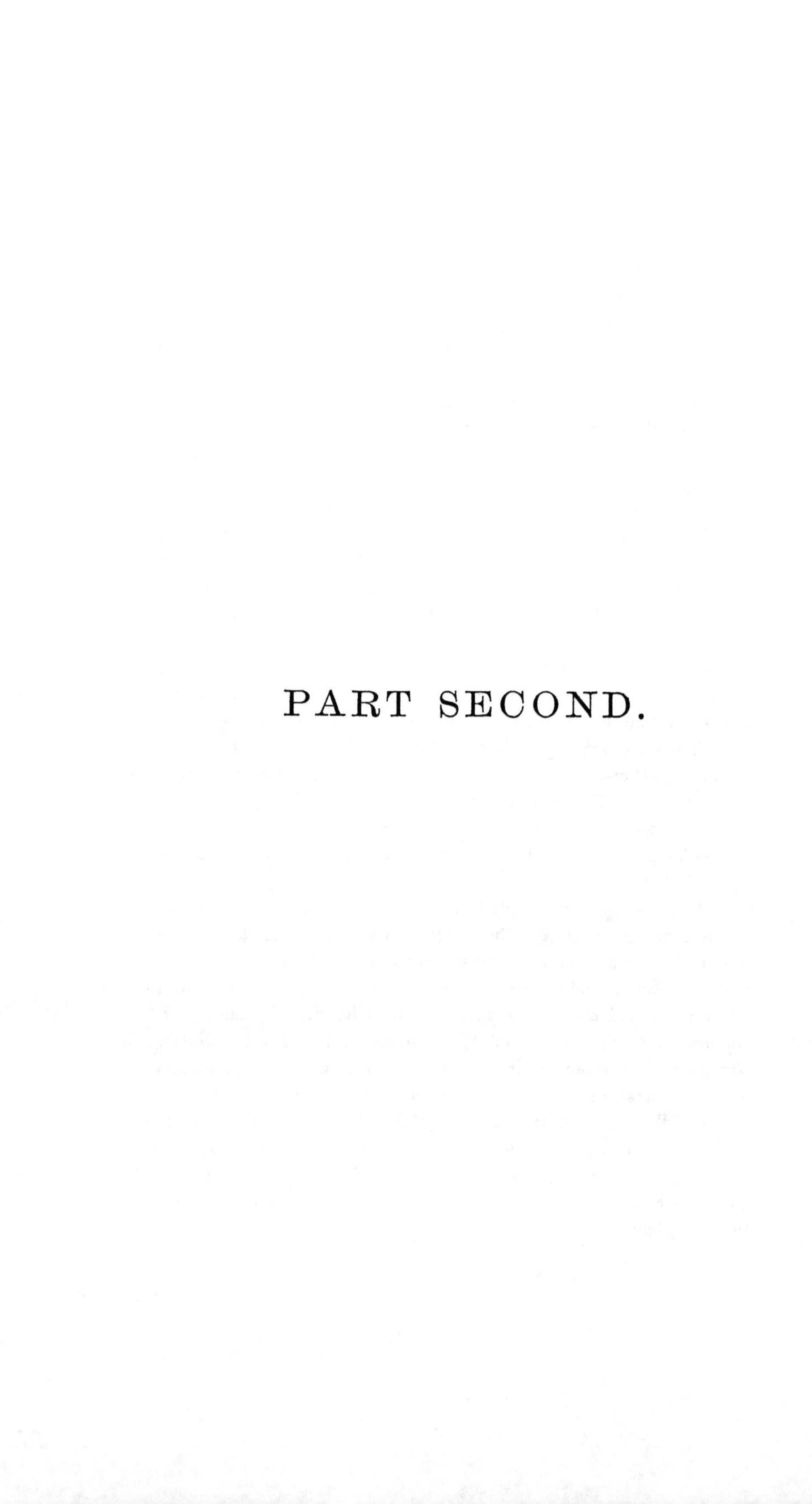

PART SECOND.

CHAPTER I.

THE ANGLO-SAXON SYSTEM OF LOCAL SOVEREIGNTIES.

OBJECT OF THE PRESENT WORK—FREEDOM AMONG THE ANGLO-SAXONS—EORLS AND CEORLS—ORIGIN OF THE DISTINCTION—LOCAL CHARACTER OF THE SAXON SYSTEM—THE TYTHING AND FRANK-PLEDGE—THE HUNDRED—THE BURGH—THE SHIRE—ILLUSTRATION OF COUNTY COURT PROCEEDINGS—ORIGIN OF LEGAL CUSTOMS IN THE FOLK-COURTS—CONSTITUTION AND POWERS OF THE WITTENA-GEMOTE—CONSTITUTION OF THE SAXON EMPIRE—DECADENCE OF THE SAXON SYSTEM.

THE liberties of England—and of these United States—as they exist to-day, were not created by the generosity of princes, nor devised by legislative wisdom. They were the unquestioned birthright of our Anglo-Saxon forefathers a thousand years ago, and only wrested after centuries of contest from the royal power which had unlawfully suppressed them. Freedom is the natural condition of mankind: but when, in the formation of political organizations, the freedom of the people is surrendered to the ruling power, it cannot be regained but by a long, persistent, and determined struggle, waged through revolution after revolution, till at length the people wins back only that which it ought never to have lost. In such a sequence of events, nothing can be certainly predicted but the bloody penalty of infidelity to freedom. It is never certain that the ancient liberty will be recovered. Of the modern nations sprung from the German tribes which took possession of the Roman territories at the great upbreaking of the Empire, and established in their new homes the free customs and immunities which were their immemorial inheritance, not one, save England, has been able to this day to cast off utterly the yoke of bondage set upon their necks by mediæval feudalism; and even England had to struggle for six centuries before she was secure in the enjoyment of the rights which no man dared to question in the days of Saxon Edward the Confessor.

We believe the time has come when these United States must choose deliberately and finally between the principles of Saxon freedom and of feudal servitude. If they shall choose the former, unborn generations will rise up to call them blessed: if the latter, no one can foretell the heritage of blood and strife they will bequeath to their posterity.

Our purpose is to show the animating spirit of the Saxon system; the antagonistic principle of feudalism which superseded it; the dire necessities which forced the Norman barons to repudiate their feudal obligations and fall back on ancient statutes of the Saxon kingdom, battling with the Saxon commons for their ancient Saxon rights; and the successive steps by which the long-lost liberties of England were won back from the strong grasp of kingly usurpation.

As the subject of the present chapter is the Anglo-Saxon system, it is important to observe that every Saxon man was free; and free not merely in the sense of being his own master, but because he was "a living unit in the state." He held lands in his own right. He was entitled to attend the courts, and join in their deliberations. He could bear arms, and had the legal power to use them in maintaining his just rights, even to the extent of making violent reprisals for the injuries inflicted on him by his enemies. Indeed, so far was this right of the freeman carried, that the Saxon, like the ancient Hebrew, was permitted voluntarily to abdicate his freedom and become the vassal of another under whose control he chose to place himself.

It is true the freedom of the Saxons did not necessarily include the notion of equality. Far otherwise. They were divided into two great classes, eorls and ceorls, or gentlemen and commons; a distinction which the learned Lingard says was merely personal, conveying neither property nor power. The eorls were said to be ethel-born, that is, of noble birth; which, probably, among a people who acknowledged no merit superior, or even equal, to that of martial prowess, was applied only to those whose fathers had never exercised the occupations of husbandry or the mechanic arts. "Yet the eorl possessed important advantages. In fact, he was also designated as twelf-haend-man, while to the ceorl was given the appellation of twi-haend-man, which would place their comparative worth in the estimation of the Saxon law in the ratio of twelve to two, or six to one;" and in certain judicial and other proceedings an actual advantage attached to the eorls in this ratio. The ceorl, however, was by no means a degraded person. He might raise himself by industry or enterprise to be an eorl. A merchant who went thrice across the sea in his own craft became an eorl. Or, if a ceorl acquired five hides of land—about six hundred acres—having thereupon a church and mansion for his family, he too, became an eorl. Thus the distinction appears to have been chiefly honorary, though in certain matters evident advantages attached to the superior rank.

The sense of personal freedom and responsibility was strangely mingled in the Saxon mind with reverence for rank, which to the Saxon represented martial glory. Moreover, the notion of the family relation was extended to the tribe, of which the chief, whose office was elective, was the head and representative. Tacitus informs us that in his time the German chieftains were surrounded by bands of adherents or companions, who voluntarily attached themselves to their respective leaders. They were the chieftain's ornament and pride in peace; in war, the chief source of his power. The only tie which bound them to his person was that of honor and affection. He considered it his duty to reward their services; but his rewards were not regarded in the light of pay. The notion of obligatory or purchased service was repudiated by the chief no less than by his free companions. In such estimation was this institution held, that every freeman was, for a long time, required to be connected with some chieftain, who was called his hlaford, *i. e.* lord, although his choice was wholly unrestrained as to the particular chieftain under whom he placed himself. The freeman did not become a vassal, and still less a slave, to his superior. Their connection was a simple social contract, freely entered into both by lord and man, and might be terminated at the choice of either. While it lasted, they were bound to mutual defence against all wrongs and enemies whatever. The lord was the man's legal surety and the champion of his man's right, and to fail in this regard was held to be dishonor. On the other hand, the man was present and took part in the lord's courts and councils, and attended him in war. Desertion of the standard of his lord in open fight was treason; but he was at liberty at any other time to leave his lord and choose another.

Evidently this relationship of lord and freeman must have exercised a potent influence in the development of Anglo-Saxon institutions. The settlements of the Germanic tribes in Britain were effected at successive times, in different localities, and under different leaders, who established on the soil of Britain many tribes which, though of kindred blood and speech, were not identical. Eight independent kingdoms therefore soon appeared, in all of which the public polity was of the same free type, although their mutual independence necessarily prevented uniformity. Of the various steps whereby these different kingdoms were at length united under one crown, it is not our purpose now to speak at length. Suffice it, for the present, to observe that the union of the crowns did not at all imply a union of the kingdoms. These, as we shall see, remained distinct, and unless when voluntary coalitions were effected, they retained their own laws, with their independent witena-gemotes or parliaments.

In sketching such a simple system as the Anglo-Saxon, the most ready way of giving a complete view is to begin with the Individual. This we have already done, and shown sufficiently that every Saxon man was in the best and highest sense a freeman. Slaves, among the Anglo-Saxons, were their subjugated enemies. We are now to show the various institutions and divisions of the people which made up the sum of the Anglo-Saxon government; and we shall find throughout the whole, that its one animating principle was that of LOCAL SOVEREIGNTY. Consolidated power was totally unknown among them. From the least matters to the greatest, every right of jurisdiction vested in the local power alone, to the exclusion of all others whatsoever. In a word, the local powers were sovereign and independent in all local matters.[1]

The first and elemental division of the Anglo-Saxon people was the Tything, with its officer and representative, the tything-man. It was founded on no territorial basis, but was simply the embodiment of every ten households or families of such freemen as were not in the "mund," or under the protection of a superior lord. It was a police division, in which each man of the ten became responsible in some degree for all the rest, under a kind of suretyship, called Frank-Pledge. If one of them committed a crime, it was the duty of the rest to produce him in justice, that the wrong-doer might make reparation by his own property, or by personal punishment. In case of his escape, the tything was allowed to purge itself of all participation in the crime and the escape; but, failing such an exculpation, if the malefactor's property proved insufficient for the payment of the penalty, the tything was compelled to make it good. The influence of such a local system of responsibility in rude times can be easily conceived. It was the interest of every man that each should keep the peace; and in this simplest distribution of the Anglo-Saxons, we perceive at once the presence of that principle of local unity and local supervision which becomes but clearer as we carry our investigations farther.

Next in order to the tything was the Hundred, which was represented by its officer, the hundred-man. Concerning its organization, antiquarians have had much dispute—some holding it to be a territorial division of the country into tracts, containing each one hundred hides of land; while others with much plausibility maintain that hundreds, like the tythings, were numerically organized, containing each one hundred families. The truth is, both opinions are most probably correct. In the southern kingdoms of the Octarchy, the hundred could not have been organized on the same principle as in the northern. Sussex, for example, was divided into sixty-five hundreds, and Dorset into forty-three; while Yorkshire had but twenty-six, and Lancashire not more than six. So wide a difference as this must have arisen from a difference of plan in the construction of the hundreds; and as Alison observes, "the divisions of the north, properly called wapentakes, were planted upon a different system [from the hundreds of the south], and obtained the denomination of hundreds incorrectly, after the union of all England under a single sovereign." However this may be, the union of the Anglo-Saxon crowns produced no change in the local law, either in the northern or the southern kingdoms; and the wapentakes of the north, like the hundreds of the south, continued in the full enjoyment of their local customs. Every hundred held a hundred court once in each month, in which it took cognizance of causes both civil and criminal. The freemen of the hundred were at once the witnesses, the judges, and the jury in these courts. The hundred-man, with an ecclesiastic, aided them with his advice on points of law or right, but the decision rested absolutely with the freemen of the hundred. So closely did our Saxon fathers guard the sovereignty of their local institutions, that it is questionable whether an appeal was suffered to be made from the decision of the hundred court, unless where litigants were residents of different hundreds. Yet it seems but reasonable to suppose that such appeals were sometimes made to the superior county courts.

The Burgh was a hundred, or, perhaps often, a union of hundreds, surrounded by a moat, wall, or stockade. Its business was transacted in its burgh courts, which had jurisdiction over causes arising within their limits.

But the most important distribution of the country was into shires, or counties, which were strictly territorial divisions, and included within definite boundaries the freemen who composed the tythings and hundreds, lords with the men belonging to their "munds," burghs with their burghers, and religious houses with their tenants and dependants. In the shire courts, whose presiding officer was called an Ealdor-man, the most important judicial business of the county was transacted at half-yearly sessions. Of their importance, Hallam observes as follows: "It has been justly remarked by Hume, that among a people who lived in so simple a manner as the Anglo-Saxons, the judicial power is always of more importance than the legislative. The liberties of the Anglo-Saxon thanes (freemen) were chiefly secured—next to their swords and free spirits—by the inestimable right of deciding civil and criminal suits in their own county courts: an institution which, having survived the Conquest, contributed in no small degree to fix the liberties of England upon a broad and popular basis."[2] The procedure of the county court was summary and simple. It was composed of all the freemen of the county who assembled at the regular time, or on a special summons if the court were held at any other time. The ealdorman, in later times, assisted by a bishop or other ecclesiastic, presided, and, no doubt, instructed these unlearned judges, but he had no power to force or overrule their verdict. The freemen of the shire decided the whole controversy. They judged the fact and applied the law. The only duty of the ealdorman was to execute their judgments. The following account from an old chronicle of the proceedings in an Anglo-Saxon shire gemote or county court, will illustrate the summary and informal judgments of the times: "To this gemote came Edwin and spake against his mother concerning some lands. The bishop asked who would answer for her. Thurcil the White said he would answer for her if he knew the complaint, but that he was ignorant of it. Then three thanes of the gemote were showed where she lived, and rode to her and asked what dispute she had about the land for which her son was impleading her. She said that she had no land that belonged to him, and was angry with her son. So she called Lleofleda her kinswoman, the wife of Thurcil the White, and before the thanes spake thus: Here sits Lleofleda my kinswoman. I give thee both my lands, my gold, and my clothes, and all that I have after my life. Then said she to the thanes, Do thane-like, and tell well to the gemote before all good men what I have said, and tell them to whom I have given my lands and my goods, but to my son nothing; and pray them to be witnesses of this. And they did so, and rode to the gemote, and told all the good men there what she had said to them. Then stood up Thurcil the White in that gemote, and prayed all the thanes to give to his wife all the lands which her relation had given her. And they did so, and Thurcil the White rode to St. Ethelbert's church by all the folk's leave and witness, and left it to be set down in our Christ's book." The decision of the shire gemote or county court was irreversible, unless by the great council of the kingdom. Appeal from it was not permitted even to the king. Persons, such as slaves, who were not *law worthy*—that is, capable of bringing suits at law—or who could not obtain a hearing in their county court, might lay their cause before the king; but even Edgar, the most powerful of the Saxon monarchs, found it necessary to proclaim by the following ordinance that he would hear none but the causes that legitimately might be brought before the throne: "Now this is the secular ordinance which I will that it be held. This then is just what I will; that every man be worthy of folk-right, as well poor as rich; and that righteous dooms be judged to him; and let there be that remission in the *bot* as may be becoming before God and tolerable before the world. And let no man apply to the king in any suit unless he at home may not be law worthy or cannot obtain law. If the law itself be too heavy, let him seek a mitigation of it from the king; and for any *bot*-worthy crime let no man forfeit more than his *wer*." *Bot*, in the glossary, signifies *amends*, *atonement*, *compensation*, and *emancipation*. A man's *wer* is the estimated value of his life—every man's life, among the Saxons, being estimated at a certain money value, according to his rank.

Such was the judicial system of our Anglo-Saxon forefathers, and the character of local sovereignty which attached to the assemblies of the people in their various organizations. Evidently courts like these must often have been forced, from ignorance of law, to *make* the law in a particular case: and it is also to be kept in mind that they were courts of voluntary jurisdiction. "All transactions by which property might be acquired or lost, the purchase and sale of land, and the payment of money, were effected in the assemblies of the hundred. Here charters and deeds were produced and read, or, if they had been lost, they were established and confirmed." The shire court possessed the same jurisdiction as that of the hundred, and (perhaps) an appellate power in addition. The precedents of each court would be remembered afterward on like occasions, and hence local *customs* would grow up at variance with established *customs* in the neighboring shires. Many such customs survive the Conquest, and continue to the present day, an irrefutable proof of local sovereignty among the Saxon people.[3]

The general legislation of the Anglo-Saxon kingdom after the union of the crowns was done by the Witena-gemote, or council of the wise. It was composed of the archbishops, bishops, abbots, subject kings, earls, and thanes; and, as Prof. Lappenberg declares, "there is no reason extant for doubting that every thane had the right of appearing and voting in the witena-gemote, not only of his shire, but of the kingdom." The powers of this imperial council, according to Kemble, were as follows:

1. They had a right to consider every public act which could be authorized or done by the king.

2. They deliberated upon new laws which were to be added to the existing folk-right, and which were then promulgated by the joint authority of the king and the gemote.

3. They made alliances and treaties of peace.

4. On them devolved the duty of electing the king.

5. They had the right to depose a king whose government was not for the benefit of the people.

6. They, conjointly with the king, appointed prelates to vacant sees.

7. They regulated ecclesiastical affairs.

8. They levied taxes for the public service.

9. They provided for defence, by raising forces for land and sea.

10. They had the power of recommending and assenting to grants of land.

11. They were empowered to pronounce the lands of criminals and intestates forfeit to the crown.

12. They were in certain cases a supreme court of judicature both in criminal and civil matters.

Yet, with all these weighty powers, the witena-gemote was limited in its authority, says Sir Francis Palgrave, "by the privileges of the different states composing the Anglo-Saxon empire; and which dominions, as I have often remarked, had never amalgamated into one kingdom. Kent, for instance, under the victorious Athelstane, had lost all the appearance of an independent state. But when he had made a law, by the assent of the Witan of Wessex, which, according to Lappenberg, was the great council of the united Saxon states), he could not impose it upon the men of Kent without their concurrence. He transmitted the enactment to them, and they then accepted the proposition by an address which they returned to their sovereign. I can quote the very words of such a document:

"'Beloved lord, thy bishops of Kent, and all Kentshire aldermen, thanes, and churls, return thanks to thee for the directions which thou hast given us concerning the conservancy of the peace, for great is the benefit which results to all of us, both poor and rich, thereby.'

"They then state the several articles or chapters of the statute, being ten in number, seriatim, and signify the manner in which they have received and modified the same. Grateful for the legislation thus bestowed upon them, the Kentishmen speak with thankfulness and humility; yet the form of the proceeding implies that their assent, so asked, might have been refused. In proportion as the sovereign gained in prerogative, the powers of the witena-gemote of Wessex, the predominant kingdom, would gradually gain strength also. The minor states annexed to Wessex would tacitly submit to be bound by its legislation, and, from the reign of Edgar, the lesser authorities seem in most cases to have been merged in the three leading states or territories of Wessex, Mercia, and Danelaghe. Mercia clearly maintained its independence; Northumbria equally so. East Anglia seems to have been sometimes considered as annexed to Mercia, sometimes as constituting a separate state, and sometimes as classing with Danish Northumbria. The laws which Edgar enacted at the request or with the assent of the Witan of Wessex were to be implicitly observed by his own immediate subjects. As to the others, they were to be adopted according to the model enacted by the assembly. The laws were transmitted to the earls by writ: it is most probable that they were usually received without hesitation, yet there was no absolute coercive power in the crown of Wessex; and it was not until the reign of Canute that the Mercians received King Edgar's laws."

Thus we have traced the political organization of the Saxon empire, and from the hundred to the witena-gemote, we have discovered everywhere the principle of local self-control, while in the constitution of the united Saxon states, state sovereignty is manifestly seen to be the basis of their union. Though under one king, elected from the royal family by the joint suffrages of the freemen of all the kingdom, yet the witena-gemotes of the respective kingdoms had an absolute power of rejecting the decrees of the great national witena-gemote of Wessex, and no power of coercing states was claimed for the crown.

But even before the conquest by the Norman, it is evident from the quotation given above from Palgrave, that the genuine spirit of the Saxon system had already fallen into decay. Of the original eight kingdoms, only three retained the vigorous vitality of independence. One still maintained a sickly struggle, which could hardly be deemed successful, and the remaining four had either voluntarily united with the more powerful states, or at best presented but a *caput mortuum* of their original defiant independence. It is also to be observed that the *centralizing* influences of the stationary monarchy were sapping the foundations of the Saxon institutions. As the royal prerogative gained in power, the king's original dominion of Wessex gained a preponderating influence, to the disparagement of her coequal sister states. The king was known as the king of Wessex, and the witena-gemote of the united Saxon states came to be called the Witan of Wessex. Hence, though their local liberties were still untouched by king or witan, the great body of the Saxons had become accustomed to forget the primitive idea of the sovereign independence of their several states, and to the conception of a royal central power, of which the states were merely subjects and dependants. In other words, the Saxon principle of local sovereignty had been insidiously undermined, and the imperial principle of absolute and centralized authority was gradually but surely gaining ground. The notion of imperial centralism once entertained, it mattered little who should be the tyrant. Two claimants, one a Norman, one a Saxon, had a contest for the crown, and when the sun set on the bloody field of Hastings, casting his last rays on the victorious banners of the Norman conqueror, the crumbling fabric of the Anglo-Saxon system fell before his feet. The men who had already sacrificed their independence to a Saxon, made no long defence against the Norman. One fierce, bloody battle, and the sun of Anglo-Saxon freedom set, to be succeeded by the Egyptian darkness of the feudal system. Thus a strife of centuries was laid up for the English people; and instead of working out their own free system through continuous and glorious spontaneous developments, by the assistance of enlightened Christianity and increased knowledge, they were forced to rise by slow steps, from a state of bondage, through a din of never-ceasing battle, to their ancient heritage of freedom.

NOTES.

1. PROBABLY the best illustration of the local character of the *subordinate* Anglo-Saxon institutions is to be found in the United States.

I have thus given a very general outline of the more important Anglo-Saxon institutions. To notice the minuter variations, special provisions, and occasional changes, would lead me into too wide a discussion, and would not aid the purposes of so elementary a work as this: enough has been said, however, to indicate those of our own legal ideas and forms which have a Saxon origin.

Prominent among these is that most important, and to us sacred principle of local self-government. This element lay at the foundation of the whole Saxon polity. It has been preserved in the English shires and ancient municipal corporations or boroughs, with their immemorial privileges. In many of the American States it is guarded with even more jealousy than in the mother country. The New England and New York divisions of towns, each with its own officers and stated convocations of citizens, and of counties, each with a local representative assembly legislating for much that concerns the welfare of the district, and a court possessing a jurisdiction co-extensive with the territorial limits, embody with much simplicity and purity the essential idea of the Saxon commonwealth."—POMEROY'S *Municipal Law*, p. 240, 241.

2. Few persons have an adequate conception of the degree to which the principle of local self-government is carried in England at the present day. The following extract, therefore, will be useful:

"The principle of local self-government which exists in England has doubtless exercised very great influence in the production of the freedom enjoyed under the Constitution. It is not intended to make an attempt to trace that influence through the gradual advance of the institutions, but only to suggest some facts without which the full extent of the liberty and power possessed by the people cannot be fully appreciated. The nature of the Anglo-Saxon courts and motes was favorable to self-exertion and self-reliance on the part of the people; but at a later period the chartered boroughs stand out conspicuously as institutions imbued with the spirit of freedom, and at the same time furnished with power to advance and defend it. These fought out their own independence from their feudal lords, and became the seats of self-government, on principles opposed to arbitrary or centralized power. The burgesses, with the mayor or portreeve and aldermen as their executive officers, elected by them, regulated the affairs of their boroughs, in trade and police, independently of any direct supervision on the part of the crown or its officers, and without any appeal on the part of the inhabitants except through the courts of law, when cases arose of an illegal character. The tendency of these institutions was republican or democratic, rather than monarchical; and the election of members to the House of Commons being vested in the boroughs, they returned to Parliament, for the most part, those patriots by whom the battle of the Constitution was fought. Charles II. made an attempt to get the boroughs, returning members to Parliament, under the influence of the crown, by an attack upon their ancient charters, and by forcing or persuading the burgesses to accept new charters; but he did not disturb their municipal authority. That has now been regulated and brought under one system by the act to provide for the regulation of the municipal corporations in England and Wales. It vests in the inhabitant householders rated to the relief of the poor, the election of burgesses, from whom the mayor and alderman are elected. The mayor becomes a justice of the peace, and returning officer of the borough at elections of members of Parliament; and the mayor, aldermen, and burgesses are the council of the borough, in whom, or a majority in case of division, all authority is vested. They are empowered to make rates on the inhabitants for watching, lighting, and paving the borough, to appoint constables, to make by-laws, and, in general, to regulate the municipal affairs of the borough; and all without the control or supervision (except in the disposal of their property) of any other central authority than the courts of law and equity.

"The affairs of the counties are, in like manner, intrusted to the management of their principal inhabitants. The magistrates appointed by the crown, through the medium of the lord-lieutenant, and consisting of the principal landowners of the county, regulate the county affairs by a system of self-government. Assembled in their court of quarter sessions, they have jurisdiction to try small felonies, and to decide appeals from the several parishes of the county, in regard to rates and assessments for the relief of and the settlement of the poor. They regulate, in sessions or at county boards, the construction and repair of bridges, public roads, shire halls, prisons, and lunatic asylums; and they superintend the apprehension, conveyance, and prosecution of criminals, the expenses of witnesses, and of the county police. For these, in quarter sessions, they make county rates on the freeholders. These important duties are discharged by persons resident within the counties, and who are necessarily the most considerable contributors to the rates; and over whose acts there is no other central control than the courts of law and equity, when cases arise in which the legality of their acts is questioned.

"The several parishes of the kingdom exercise self-government in parochial affairs, by the election, from the inhabitants, of churchwardens and overseers, who administer the laws for the relief of the poor, and of boards of parishioners, who discharge the various duties of the acts for the repair of the highways and the sewers, and for the preservation of health. The magnitude of the funds raised and distributed for the relief of the poor, throughout the kingdom, and the effect of their distribution on the public prosperity, made it necessary to adopt a uniform system of management and relief; and therefore the functions of the parochial boards for relief of the poor are exercised under the superintendence of a supreme poor-law board, appointed by the crown, but responsible to Parliament. Its president is usually in the cabinet, and a member of the House of Commons. There is also a supreme board of health, but with these exceptions, the administration of the local affairs of each division and subdivision of the kingdom is vested in its inhabitants, with an authority controlled only by the law and the courts of justice.—ROWLAND'S *Manual of the English Constitution*, p. 570–572."

3. The following, from Blackstone, will serve to show the influence of the Saxon courts in establishing the present local *customs* of England:

"The second branch of the unwritten laws of England are particular customs, or laws which affect only the inhabitants of particular districts.

"These particular customs, or some of them, are without doubt the remains of that multitude of local customs before mentioned, out of which the common law, as it now stands, was collected at first by king Alfred, and afterward by King Edgar and Edward the Confessor; each district mutually sacrificing some of its own special usages, in order that the whole kingdom might enjoy the benefit of one uniform and universal system of laws. But, for reasons that have been now long forgotten, particular counties, cities, towns, manors, and lordships, were very early indulged with the privilege of abiding by their own customs, in contradistinction to the rest of the nation at large: which privilege is confirmed to them by several acts of Parliament.

"Such is the custom of gavelkind in Kent and some other parts of the kingdom (though perhaps it was also general till the Norman conquest), which ordains, among other things, that not the eldest son only of the father shall succeed to his inheritance, but all the sons alike; and that, though the ancestor be attainted and hanged, yet the heir shall succeed to his estate, without any escheat to the lord. Such is the custom that prevails in divers ancient boroughs, and therefore called borough-english, that the youngest son shall inherit the estate in preference to all his elder brothers. Such is the custom in other boroughs that a widow shall be entitled, for her dower, to all her husband's lands; whereas at the common law she shall be endowed of one third part only. Such also are the special and particular customs of manors, of which every one has more or less, and which bind all the copyhold and customary tenants that hold of the said manors.—Such likewise is the custom of holding divers inferior courts, with power of trying causes, in cities and trading towns, the right of holding which, when no royal grant can be shown, depends entirely upon immemorial and established usage. Such, lastly, are many particular customs within the city of London, with regard to trade, apprentices, widows, orphans, and a variety of other matters.

"All these are contrary to the general law of the land, and are good only by special usage; though the customs of London are also confirmed by act of Parliament."—BLACKSTONE'S *Commentaries*, i. 74, 75.

CHAPTER II.

THE FEUDAL SYSTEM OF CONSOLIDATED MILITARY POWER.

ORIGIN OF THE FEUDAL SYSTEM—NATURE OF THE FEUDAL TENURE OF LAND IN CONSIDERATION OF MILITARY SERVICE—SOCAGE—HOMAGE—ALLEGIANCE—AMOUNT OF SERVICE—SCUTAGE—RELIEFS—HERIOTS—FINES ON ALIENATION—ESCHEATS—AIDS—WARDSHIP—MARRIAGE—CONVERSION OF ALLODIAL LANDS INTO FEUDAL TENURES—SERFDOM—ESTABLISHMENT OF FEUDALISM IN ENGLAND.

THE Saxon and the feudal systems were exact antipodes. The former, as we have already shown, was one of independent local sovereignties in the hands of freemen. The latter was a rising series of consolidated military powers, reaching its climax in a central monarchy which tolerated not one freeman.

The feudal system sprang up upon the continent of Europe, among the German tribes of Normans, Franks, Burgundians, Visigoths, and Lombards, who swept down upon the falling Roman Empire, and divided its vast territories among themselves. It is not our purpose to give its history. It doubtless had its moving cause in the custom of the German warriors, which we have mentioned in the previous chapter, of joining themselves to military chiefs, whom for their martial glory they regarded with an almost superstitious reverence. In their invasions of the south, these chiefs in like manner united under various leaders, who on their conquest of the several provinces, became their kings. Here it was not long ere the civilization of the vanquished gained upon the victors, who without much difficulty adopted the religion and laws of the Empire. Under the teachings of the Christian priesthood—always forward in supporting kingly and imperial prerogative—the sovereigns and their subjects learned to look upon the royal office in a yet more lofty point of view. The ceremonies of the church in the anointing and investiture of these barbarian princes made a strong impression on the warm imaginations of the newly converted Northmen. Henceforth the king became to them God's representative in civil matters, as the priest was in the matters of the faith, and, next to God and holy church, they gave implicit submission to the anointed king, who was supposed to hold his office by divine appointment. Meanwhile, jurists learned in the law were not behind the priesthood in supporting and increasing the pretensions of the kings. They taught that these barbarian sovereigns were the successors of the Cæsars, and that all the high prerogatives of the imperial crown were now legitimately vested in them. Moreover, they had gained their title by conquest, and had consequently every right claimed by the emperors in subjugated territories. Hence the *lands* they had subdued were the king's individual property. This was a mighty cornerstone of the feudal system; and upon this, with the other notion, that the king's right was a right divine, that is, a right of God, the whole tremendous fabric may be said to have been based. But though he was the absolute proprietor of all the lands within his territories, it was impossible on any system for a single man personally to enjoy so wide a domain. The lands of the kingdom were therefore distributed among the warriors who had followed him. Not that they thereby were invested with the *ownership* of these lands. The ownership (*dominium directum*) rested with the king. But they received the actual possession and profitable use of them (*dominium utile*). Thus the king was able to reward his faithful retainers, by making to them grants of land under the name of benefices.

Under these beneficial grants we find the first historic traces of the feudal system. The benefice was not an absolute gift vesting the recipient with the ultimate ownership; that still remained in the king, and the grant was liable to be revoked at any disloyal or hostile act of the beneficiary. In return for this gift to him from the monarch, the subject was bound to give the king, when called upon, his military service and aid, from time to time, as they should be required. Thus the favored subject entered into the possession of the land, and enjoyed all of its benefits as though he were the absolute owner: still, as he was not the absolute owner, he was said, in the subsequent language of the feudal law, to *hold* the land of his sovereign; and the method or relation by which he thus held was denominated a *tenure*, or holding. (Pom. p. 255).

Sometimes the grant was for the life of the grantor; but more generally for that of the grantee. At what time custom or agreement made the enjoyment of the property hereditary in the family of the grantee, we have no means of accurately ascertaining in any country. As late as the end of the sixth century, the lands which had been parcelled out returned in most European states to the prince, and were only continued to the family as an act of favor, and by a new gift; although undoubtedly instances of hereditary tenure occurred even at this early date.

Now a benefice (*beneficium*), or grant of land by a chief to his followers upon condition of military service, was called a fief, feud, fee, or feo (from *feo*, wages, and *od*, land), and it constituted the grantee a feudatory, or vassal of the chief or superior to whom he owed service in consideration of the land. The use of the land was his wages, which he earned for doing service to his master, the owner or grantor of the land. This, we repeat, is the cornerstone of the feudal system. It is the root from which all its peculiarities spring.

Attempts have been made to deduce the feudal relations from other sources. It has been said that traces of it are to be found in the customs of the Germans and Saxons; and the relation of chief and follower was no doubt the moving cause which led those hardy people to adopt the system so universally. But it is to be remembered that the companions of the chief cannot be likened to vassals, to whom, indeed, they bear a very faint resemblance; and that, in their primitive abode, payment of any kind, and certainly in land, was altogether wanting. Some have imagined that the feudal relation is to be traced in the Roman connection of patrons and clients—a practice, among men of consequence and power, of taking under their protection inferior persons, who rendered in return such services as were within their means, often paying money, and not unfrequently bequeathing property, to their patron. But no real resemblance exists between the two cases; for here, again, in the Roman custom there is no holding of land in consideration of allegiance and service. The only case which resembles feudal service in the early history of Europe is to be found in the reign of Alexander Severus at the beginning of the third century, who settled some barbarous tribes along the Danube, making to them grants of land on the express condition of their serving him in wars against the neighboring tribes.

This was a simple feudal tenure, arising out of circumstances identical with those out of which the feudal relation grew and became general two centuries later; and on reflection it seems probably the most natural form in which the custom of free companionship prevailing in the unsettled German tribes could coalesce with the imperial power appropriated by their chiefs, on their establishment as settled rulers of the conquered Romans and provincials.

When a chief, then, established himself and parcelled out the lands seized, the leading companions of the expedition shared some of the lands taken, on condition of allegiance and military service. When the feuds became hereditary and the favor of succeeding princes had increased the grants, the comites or counts possessing large tracts exercised great influence in the state. For the acquisition of feuds, when the tenures became hereditary, and perhaps even sooner, was attended with another operation. As the practice of renting land was unknown, whoever had more land given him than he could cultivate, whether a count or any inferior person, was obliged to make a similar grant to other persons, in return for which they were to do him service. Thus every one who had a considerable estate given him, retained part for himself, and parcelled out the rest among inferiors, who rendered him the same service as he rendered to the chief or prince—following him in war when he followed the prince, assisting him in peace, and attending his courts. The practice of making these inferior grants of land was called sub-infeudation, and originally there was no limit to it. The smaller proprietors had of course fewer inferior vassals, or subfeudatories; but, like the counts and other important vassals of the crown, they had the same courts and administration of justice over their vassals as the king himself over his tenants *in capite*, or tenants in chief. From this distribution of land among the crown's vassals, and by them among their dependants, arose the great power of the feudal lords or barons; for the allegiance of their feudatories to them was in theory as rigorous as their own to the sovereign; and in practice it was much more effectual. The count or baron passed his whole time at home, surrounded by his followers, who also were the suitors or members of his courts where justice was administered, while the more distinguished among them were his companions in the chase and at his feasts. Occasionally the great lord might go to the sovereign's court, and in his wars he accompanied his armies; but the constant occupation of his life was such as to maintain his power over his own vassals.[1]

It happened, however, that in every country overrun by the barbarians, a considerable portion of the land remained the property of the former inhabitants, and some part of it was granted out in absolute possession, without any direct obligation of service. This land was called *allodial*, and its holders *allodists*, or *allodial proprietors*; but its amount in every country underwent constant diminution. This was principally owing to the disordered state of society, and the insecurity arising from thence and from foreign invasion, During many centuries there was continual commotion; petty private wars were waged between the feudal lords; there was no generally acknowledged law and no respect for private property; and the allodial proprietors having incurred no obligation of service, and therefore having no title to protection from the sovereign and no laws from which to seek redress, were exposed to the perpetual rapacity of counts and other nobles. "The owners of the castles and fastnesses would sweep down upon these proprietors, ravage their possessions, and carry them off, to be ransomed at any exorbitant charges. The military tie of lord and vassal was the only barrier to these attacks, for while it imposed a duty of warlike service upon the vassal, it also afforded the protection of the lord." Hence many allodial proprietors surrendered their lands into the hands of some more powerful proprietor, to receive them back as feuds, with the condition of allegiance and service imposed upon them, but also with the duty of protection cast upon the lord. Even those lords themselves, owners of larger allotments, were frequently reduced by similar apprehensions to become vassals of the crown in respect of lands formerly held by them as allodial; and to such an extent was this practice of infeudation carried, that in the tenth and eleventh centuries it appears that almost all the allodial possessions of France had been converted into feudal tenures held by vassals of superior lords on the condition of military service.

When the feudal relation had become established, it extended itself to various kinds of property, not in their nature the subject of such a conditional holding. Thus rents, tolls, pensions, tithes, and offices were made the subjects of feudal grant, and given on condition of military service. Even perquisites of the priests for saying mass were sometimes seized by the barons, and held by them of the church, on the condition of giving their service in protecting it; and such spoils were shared by sub-infeudation among their followers. But some lands, and generally property in towns, were in England held for fixed payments, or for services not military; and this was called *socage*, or *free* and *certain* service.

Having now traced the establishment of the feudal relation of lord and vassal, we are next to examine the rights and duties which it constituted, and the important effects which it produced upon the structure of the government and the condition of society.

The first duty of the vassal to the lord was allegiance. He did homage by uncovering his head and ungirding his sword, and kneeling before the lord, in whose hands he placed his own. In this attitude he solemnly promised to become *his man*—*homme* (whence the word *homage*); and to serve him faithfully with life and limb in return for the land held of him. This ceremony generally was ended by his kissing the lord's cheek, and the lord kissing his mouth; and a remnant of this is retained in England at the coronation of the king, the peers all kneeling before the king uncovered, and then kissing his cheek. The bishops still do homage to him for their temporal possessions, which return to the crown on the see being vacant, and are granted again to the successor. The homage, chiefly confined to military tenure, was performed to the lord in person. The oath of fidelity, or *fealty*, which belonged to all tenures, followed; but the lord might receive it by proxy.[2] The *investiture* of the vassal in the land was that for which he owed allegiance, and the lord either gave actual possession on the spot, or delivered it over by symbols, as turf for a field, a stone for a house, and so forth.

Allegiance comprehended the duty of attempting nothing against the lord, disclosing all information that might affect him, and not divulging his counsel when trusted by him. The vassal was also bound to side with him in war, and be a hostage for him if captured. But military service, to which was added *suit service*, or attendance on the lord's court, was the most important duty, and in most cases, perhaps at first in all, was the foundation of the tenure.

Allegiance was at all times due, and continued always the same. Military service was originally coextensive with allegiance, and was due whenever the lord was attacked. Whether, if he waged offensive war, the same absolute right existed to the vassal's service, may be questioned. Cæsar tells us that the ancient Germans volunteered to accompany their chief on an expedition which he announced at a general assembly, and that, having once promised, it was infamy not to perform. Probably, then, the barbarians, when they settled and granted out lands in feudal tenure, held assemblies where the expedition was resolved upon, and the lord had a right to service while it lasted. But by degrees this came to be regulated and limited, and the vassals became bound to serve only a given number of days, each according to the extent of his possession. Thus, for a knight's fee (or land of the value of twenty pounds a year), forty days were due; which in France was extended to sixty days. But in the course of time the extent of service came to be specified in the deed or charter by which the land was granted. Men of sixty, women, priests, and public functionaries, were allowed to find substitutes. Sometimes the service was limited to the lord's territory; sometimes it was general and unrestricted. The non-performance incurred a forfeiture of the land to the lord, because it was a breach of the condition upon which the grant had been made. But afterward the practice grew up of commuting the service for a fine, which was called *escuage*, or *scutage*, and proved a source of revenue to the chief.

But besides the service of war, other rights were possessed by the lord, some of them connected with the land, and arising from its having been originally his own altogether, and never wholly given to the vassal; others acquired by usurpation upon the vassal

As the land was at one time granted for life, when the lord gave it at a vassal's death to his heir, he exacted something in consideration of the favor. This was called a *relief* (from *re*, back, and *levare*, to raise), as if the land had fallen into the lord's hands, and was to be relieved out of them by payment of the fine; or had fallen down, as it were, and was to be raised up again. The amount to be paid was probably at first quite arbitrary—as much as the lord chose to ask, and the vassal could afford to pay. Afterward it became fixed by custom, and even by law. The charter of Henry I., of England, enacted that reliefs in future should be reasonable, and Magna Charta fixed them at what was supposed to be one fourth of the yearly real value. In some countries, relief was also due on the death of the lord; and at the present day, we find the remains of this, as well as the ordinary relief, in many manors in the North of England, where copyholders pay a fine, on the death both of the lord and of the tenant. It is most probable that this kind of relief, on the lord's death, originated in the remoter period, when the feud was granted wholly at pleasure, or at least, only during the grantor's life; and when he died, the heir, not being bound to continue the grant during the vassal's life, required a consideration for remembering his ancestor's grant. *Heriots*, still known in some English manors, are probably another remnant of the temporary nature of the feud out of which reliefs arose. They are due on the tenant's decease, and consist of his best chattel. A valuable racehorse was some years ago claimed in Surrey as a heriot. The same custom prevailed in Italy and France as early as the eleventh century; in England, at least two centuries before. The custom with regard to reliefs differed in different countries. Thus, in most parts of France, they were not due at all on direct, but only on collateral succession. This, however, may have been a limitation of late introduction, when the right of inheritance was established. Originally, they were probably due on all descents alike.

The right to alienate the feud was of comparatively late introduction; for the fealty and service of the vassal were properly personal, and could not be transferred. Indeed, the original relation of lord and tenant was so strict, that neither party could dissolve it at pleasure. The lord's consent was necessary to a change of tenant; the tenant's to a change of lord; expressed by a form called his *attornment*, which continued to be required in England until the eighteenth century. At a much earlier period, however, the lord had become accustomed, in all feudal states, to permit alienation by the tenant, upon payment of a sum of money, and the person to whom the transfer was made became the lord's vassal, and did homage upon admission as tenant.

When feuds became hereditary, they descended either according to the order of succession pointed out in the grant, or according to some general law of succession prevailing in the state at large, or confined to the particular district. It was not till late in the history of most nations that the right to dispose of property by will was introduced, and it may be asserted that while the feudal system remained in full force, no such power was enjoyed generally in any part of Europe. When it was given anywhere, it at first extended only to a part of the land, the rest being still required to go in a particular line pointed out by the original terms of the grant, or the general law of the state, or the local law of the district. But while the feudal system remained entire, the death of the vassal without heirs, or without such heirs as were designated in the grant, caused the fief to return, fall, or *escheat*, as it was called, to the lord. The word signifies a casualty, or falling in consequence of an accident. But want of heirs was not the only cause of forfeiture. If the vassal committed any act inconsistent with his fealty, the fief returned to the lord; and refinements were introduced, by which many things were held to be constructive rebellion, or contempt of the lord's authority. Thus, encroaching on his share of the land, whether on the waste not parcelled out, or on the lord's private property, as well that of which he had the beneficial ownership as that of which he had the feudal dominion, was termed *purpresture* or *pourprision*, and forfeited the feud to the lord; though in England this term has for ages been confined to encroachments upon the crown's rights. Thus, too, disclaiming the lord's right and the tenure under him was a cause of forfeiture. And in general alienating without license, and even making certain alterations upon the form and disposition of the land, were causes of forfeiture.

But besides these rights and perquisites which arose out of the relation between the lord of the soil and him who had only the enjoyment, and that limited, of its fruits, there were others which grew out of the vassal's allegiance and dependence upon the superior.

Of these, *aids* were the chief. They were sums, like a tax or contribution, levied upon all the vassals, to defray expenses of the lord on certain extraordinary occasions—such as a pilgrimage to the Holy Land; the costs of his own relief to an over lord; the making his eldest son a knight; the portioning his eldest daughter; and his ransom, if taken in battle.

These three last are alone permitted by Magna Charta; and by the laws of France and other Continental monarchies, *ward* or *wardship* and *marriage* were not so universally established as the aids of which we have just been speaking. But in England they existed, and to an oppressive extent, as they also did in Germany and in Normandy. On the ground of training the infant vassal to arms after his father's death, and because he lost his service during his minority, the lord took possession of his estate until he became of age; and an abuse of a vexatious kind soon crept in—the lord bestowing the guardianship and possession of the land upon strangers, from favor or for money. This was called, in English law, *guardianship in chivalry*, and was only abolished first during the Commonwealth, and then by a perpetual act at the Restoration, after having been the source of extreme oppression down to that late period.

Marriage (*maritagium*) was the right to marry a ward, and receive a price for the match. The custom was still more rigorous in Jerusalem, where the Crusaders introduced the feudal system; for there, maiden or widow, in order that there might never be wanting a male vassal to perform service, was compelled to take one of three husbands presented to her by the lord, unless she was sixty years old, and resolved to die single. In some parts of Germany and France, and in Scotland till the eleventh century, it is certain that a custom more outrageous still prevailed, the lord having a right to enjoy the person of the vassal's bride. This, in France, was called *droit du seigneur*, and in Scotland the fine paid for it was termed *woman's mark;* but it is doubtful whether it existed in respect of the vassals who held by military service, or was only incident to other tenures of a baser kind. Of these it is now necessary to speak.

We have hitherto confined our attention to those persons who, being soldiers, companions in arms of the chief, freemen and warriors, shared the fruits of the conquests made, and obtained land either freely and unconditionally, or on the condition of certain allegiance and service—the holders of the former or allodial land gradually becoming holders by feudal tenure. There existed, however, in all the provinces overrun by the northern nations, a twofold division of the inhabitants, some being freemen and some being slaves. In all parts of the Roman Empire the legal right and the practice was established of holding persons in absolute slavery; and that the barbarians found the people in this state is plain, among other things, from the laws of the Burgundians, which mention their having, on their settlement in France, seized two thirds of the land, and one third of the slaves or serfs.

But the northern nations had also slavery as a part of their own customs, although their domestic slaves were in an easy condition, and did not much differ in their circumstances from the other poorer classes of the community. Captives made in war; persons who sold themselves, or who were sold by their parents from poverty; convicts condemned to pay fines, and made slaves on default; gamesters who staked their personal liberty upon the issue of play, to which the Germans were passionately addicted—all these classes increased the number of slaves among those rude nations. Upon conquering any district, they sometimes reduced all the people to slavery, except such as could ransom themselves. Subsequently, revolt or other acts of violence extended the numbers of the slaves. Another reason operated in the same direction. The violence of the early feudal times, and the consequent dangers in which poor men were placed, made it highly desirable to obtain protection from the more powerful members of the community. Personal protections were obtained from these lords, called *commendations*, resembling the *patronage* of the Romans, or the relation in which the upper classes stood toward their *clients*. For this protection, payments in money were made, called *salvamenta*, or *salvages*, and many who could pay nothing, became serfs or slaves to such as would not be content with mere allegiance or with occasional service. Allodial proprietors used at first to obtain *commendations*, as they had no law to protect them, until by degrees the tenure of their land became feudal, as we have already seen. Men who had no land were deprived of this resource, and very often became serfs. Many, too, in those superstitious ages, parted with their liberty to monasteries and churches in return for their prayers and masses, together with some small share of their temporal possessions. It thus happened that, as all the land became feudal, and the maxim of the law arose, "*Nulle terre sans seigneur*"—"*No land without a lord*"—so almost every one was either a vassal in respect of his land, or a serf in respect of his person, and the common people came to be almost universally in a state of slavery.

But land in those countries constituted the whole, or nearly the whole, wealth of the community. It was in some sort, too, the currency in which services of every kind were paid. A proprietor desiring to retain the services of any one, gave him a rent issuing out of his land; and this constituted him a vassal; for it was by a refinement of the feudal law reckoned (not *feudum*, but) *quasi feudum*—a kind of fief, or an improper fief—a fee or feud of land. In order to obtain inferior services, or to support serfs, they were settled on small portions of land in the neighborhood of the lord's residence, and these allotments were entirely held at will by the serfs, whom the lord could at any time dispossess. Thus, to obtain land, needy freemen became serfs—another source of domestic slavery. But this kind of contract had very important consequences; for as the servitude of these voluntary slaves only could last as long as they held the land, they and their children came no longer to be regarded as tenants at will, and liable to be dispossessed; and so the slaves, who had no rights at all, but were merely settled on their owner's land as the best way of supporting them and securing their services, came gradually to be considered like the others, and were allowed first to retain their allotments for life, afterward to transmit them to their children, and finally to their collateral heirs. No uniform rule, however, was established as to these rights or permissions. Different lords gave different rights and different courses of succession; different rights of alienation by conveyance or by will were established in different districts or lordships, and different sums were paid to the lord as fines upon descent or alienation. One thing, however, was common originally to the whole—some service was exacted by the lord, and this service was of an inferior or base kind; never the military service by which free land was held by the freemen, vassals of the lord. These were the freeholders of each manor or lordship, owed suit service to the freeholders' court, and were bound to follow the lord in war. But the serfs, even when established in their rights of property, only attended customary courts of an inferior kind, and served the lord in a humbler way.

Thus, throughout the whole of what was once the Empire of the West, the feudal system was effectually established; and thus, from the degraded serf, who eked a miserable sustenance from the allotment made him by the holder of a knight's fee, who, perhaps, was vassal to a baron holding from some count, who was retainer to a duke, who was *tenant in capite*, or the immediate vassal of the king himself, until we reach the royal head of this vast system of servitude, we find not one freeman. True, the terms of the relationship were made to seem sufficiently inviting. *Nominally* "the feudal relation of lord and vassal was one of mutual support and assistance. Heavy burdens were laid upon the one, but they demanded corresponding duties and obligations from the other. If the vassal was bound to furnish an uncertain amount of personal military attendance to his superior, in his wars, public or private, and in later times to contribute much money, the lord was in turn obliged to warrant and secure his dependant in the quiet possession of his land, and to defend him against all enemies." No language, however, can conceal the fact that the whole system was one of petty despotisms, rising to an irresponsible and central military head; that it was emphatically a system of brute force; that it gave no defence from lawlessness but by submission to a lawless tyranny; that it reduced the poor man to a state of slavery, and that the best it could make any man was the bound vassal of a higher lord than he.

Such was the substitute for the free Saxon institutions, brought to England by the Norman conqueror, and we repeat what we asserted in the first page of the present chapter—that it was *a rising series of consolidated military powers, reaching its climax in a central monarchy which tolerated not one true freeman.* But fortunately for the liberties of England, William made himself too powerful. The royal power in France had been reduced almost into contempt by the immense power of the immediate feudatories of the crown. The counts and dukes—though nominally vassals of the king—holding enormous territories, and, by the practice of sub-infeudation, having multitudes of military followers, had become in reality all but independent sovereigns. William himself, as duke of Normandy, had been too powerful to pay much respect to his French suzerain; but in distributing the lands of his defeated Saxon subjects among the Norman knights whose swords had won his crown, he saw to it that none should be so powerful as to dare, in any case, contest the royal will. He thus made tyranny over the barons possible whenever he or his successors should desire to play the tyrant. The result could not be doubtful. Tyranny, when possible, is always certain. He had made the individual barons too weak individually to make an issue with the king. When, therefore, royal tyranny became intolerable, the resistance to it necessarily assumed the best form of resistance to a tyranny—that of a united and determined coalition. Better still, it made the Saxon commons an important element in the baronial contests with the crown; and hence the charters, wrung from kings in England by the hands of nobles, have invariably been charters of the people's rights much more than of baronial privileges. Thus, through generation after generation, the united lords and commons, making common cause for rights and liberties dear to them both, have gradually won back to the people from the royal power what, but for the insatiable rapacity and keen sagacity of William, they might never have united to achieve. How the first great step of this mighty march was made we shall proceed to tell hereafter.[3]

NOTES.

1. *Guizot on the Social Working of the Feudal System.*—" Let us investigate this society in itself, and see what part it has played in the history of civilization. First of all, let us take feudalism in its most simple, primitive, and fundamental element: let us consider a single possessor of a fief in his domain, and let us see what will become of all those who form the little society around him.

" He establishes himself upon an isolated and elevated spot, which he takes care to render safe and strong: there he constructs what he will call his castle. With whom does he establish himself? With his wife and children; perhaps some freemen who have not become proprietors, attach themselves to his person, and continue to live with him at his table. These are the inhabitants of the interior of the castle. Around and at its foot, a little population of colonists and serfs gather together, who cultivate the domains of the possessor of the fief. In the centre of this lower population, religion plants a church; it brings hither a priest. In the early period of the feudal system, this priest was commonly at the same time the chaplain of the castle and the pastor of the village: by and by these two characters separated; the village had its own pastor, who lived there beside his church. This, then was the elementary feudal society, the feudal molecule, so to speak. It is this element that we have first of all to examine. We will demand of it the double question which should be asked of all our facts: What has resulted from it in favor of the development, 1, of man himself—2, of society?

" We are perfectly justified in addressing this double question to the little society which I have just described, and in placing faith in its replies; for it was the type and faithful image of the entire feudal society. The lord, the people on his domains, and the priest: such is feudalism upon the great as well as the small scale, when we have taken from it royalty and the towns, which are distinct and foreign elements.

" The first fact that strikes us in contemplating this little society, is the prodigious importance which the possessor of the fief must have had, both in his own eyes, and in the eyes of those who surrounded him. The sentiment of personality, of individual liberty, predominated in the barbaric life. But here it was wholly different: it was no longer only the liberty of the man, of the warrior; it was the importance of the proprietor, of the head of the family, of the master, that came to be considered. From this consideration an impression of immense superiority must have resulted; a superiority quite peculiar, and very different from everything that we meet with in the career of other civilizations. I will give the proof of this. I take in the ancient world some great aristocratical position, a Roman patrician for instance. Like the feudal lord, the

Roman patrician was head of a family, master, superior. He was, moreover, the religious magistrate, the pontiff in the interior of his family. Now his importance as a religious magistrate came to him from without; it was not a purely personal and individual importance; he received it from on high; he was the delegate of the Divinity; the interpreter of the religious creed. The Roman patrician was, besides, the member of a corporation which lived united on the same spot, a member of the senate; this again was an importance which came to him from without, from his corporation, a received, a borrowed importance. The greatness of the ancient aristocrats, associated as it was with a religious and political character, belonged to the situation, to the corporation in general, rather than to the individual. That of the possessor of the fief was purely individual; it was not derived from any one; all his rights, all his power came to him from himself. He was not a religious magistrate; he took no part in a senate; it was in his person that all his importance resided; all that he was, he was of himself, and in his own name. What a mighty influence must such a situation have exerted on its occupant! What individual haughtiness, what prodigious pride—let us say the word—what insolence must have arisen in his soul! Above himself there was no superior of whom he was the representative or interpreter: there was no equal near him; no powerful and general law which weighed upon him; no external rule which influenced his will; he knew no curb but the limits of his strength and the presence of danger. Such was the necessary moral result of this situation upon the character of man.

"I now proceed to a second consequence, mighty also, and too little noticed, namely, the particular turn taken by the feudal family spirit.

"Let us cast a glance over the various family systems. Take, first of all, the patriarchal system of which the Bible and oriental records offer the model. The family was very numerous, it was a tribe. The chief, the patriarch, lived therein in common with his children, his near relations, the various generations which united themselves around him, all his kindred, all his servants; and not only did he live with them all, but he had the same interests, the same occupations, and he led the same life. Was not this the condition of Abraham, of the Patriarchs, and of the chiefs of the Arab tribes who still reproduce the image of the patriarchal life?

"Another family system presents itself, namely, the *clan*, a petty society, whose type we must seek for in Scotland or Ireland. Through this system, probably, a large portion of the European family has passed. This is no longer the patriarchal family. There is here a great difference between the situation of the chief and that of the rest of the population. They did not lead the same life. The greater portion tilled and served, the chief was idle and warlike. But they had a common origin: they all bore the same name, and their relations of kindred, ancient traditions, the same recollections, the same affections, established a moral tie, a sort of equality between all the members of the clan.

"These are the two principal types of the family society presented by history. But have we here the feudal family? Obviously not. It seems at first that the feudal family bears some relation to the clan; but the difference is much greater than the resemblance. The population which surrounded the possessor of the fief were totally unconnected with him; they did not bear his name: between them and him there was no kindred, no bond, moral or historical. Neither did it resemble the patriarchal family. The possessor of the fief led not the same life, nor did he engage in the same occupations with those who surrounded him; he was an idler and a warrior, while the others were laborers. The feudal family was not numerous; it was not a tribe; it reduced itself to the family, properly so called, namely, to the wife and children; it lived separated from the rest of the population, shut up in the castle. The colonist and serfs made no part of it: the origin of the members of this society was different, the inequality of their situation immense. Five or six individuals in a situation at once superior to and estranged from the rest of the society—that was the feudal family. It was of course invested with a peculiar character. It was narrow, concentrated, and constantly called upon to defend itself against, to distrust, and at least to isolate itself from, even its retainers."

*   *   *   *   *   *   *   *   *

"No doubt, after a certain time, some moral relations, some habits of affection, became contracted between the colonists and the possessor of the fief. But this happened in spite of their relative position, and not by reason of its influence. Considered in itself, the position was radically wrong. There was nothing morally in common between the possessor of the fief and the colonists; they constituted part of his domain; they were his property; and under this name property were included all the rights which, in the present day, are called the rights of public sovereignty, as well as the rights of private property, the right of imposing laws, of taxing, and of punishing, as well as that of disposing of and selling. As far as it is possible that such should be the case where men are in presence of men, between the lord and the cultivators of his lands there existed no rights, no guarantees, no society.

"Hence I conceive the truly prodigious and invincible hatred with which the people at all times have regarded the feudal system, its recollections, its very name. It is not a case without example for men to have submitted to oppressive despotisms, and to have become accustomed to them; nay, to have willingly accepted them. Theocratic and monarchical despotisms have more than once obtained the consent, almost the affections, of the population subjected to them. But feudal despotism has always been repulsive and odious; it has oppressed the destinies, but never reigned over the souls of men. The reason is that in theocracy and monarchy, power is exercised in virtue of certain words which are common to the master and to the subject; it is the representative, the minister of another power superior to all human power; it speaks and acts in the name of the Divinity, or of a general idea, and not in the name of man himself, of man alone. Feudal despotism was altogether different; it was the power of the individual over the individual; the dominion of the personal and capricious will of a man. This is, perhaps, the only tyranny of which, to his eternal honor, man will never willingly accept. Whenever, in his master, he beholds a mere man, from the moment that the will which oppresses him appears a merely human and individual will like his own, he becomes indignant, and supports the yoke wrathfully. Such was the true and distinguishing character of feudal power; and such was also the origin of the antipathy which it has ever inspired.—*History of Civilization.*

2. *Act of Homage and Fealty.*—It may be worth while here to give the ceremonies performed in conferring feudal tenures:

"The manner of entering into the homage of another is this: that is to say, the feudal seigneur must be requested, with bare head, by the man who wishes to do faith and homage, to be received into his faith; and if the seigneur will, he sits down, and the vassal unbuckles his girdle, if he have one, lays down his sword and staff, kneels on one knee, and says these words: 'I become your man from this day forth, of life and limb, and will hold faith to you for the lands I claim to hold of you.' And when the freeholder shall do fealty to his lord, he shall put his right hand upon a book, and shall say these words: 'This hear, my lord, that I will be faithful and loyal to you, and will keep faith to you for the lands which I claim to hold of you, and will loyally fulfil unto you the customs and services that I shall owe you on the conditions belonging thereto, so help me God and the saints.' And then he shall kiss the book; but he shall not kneel when he does fealty, nor make so humble a reverence as is before prescribed for homage. And there is a great difference between doing fealty and doing homage; for homage can only be done to the seigneur himself, whereas the seneschal of the seigneur's court or his bailiff may receive fealty in his name."

3. *Oppressions of the Feudal System in England.* "In England, women and even men, simply as tenants in chief, and not as wards, fined to the crown for leave to marry whom they would, or not to be compelled to marry any other. Towns not only fined for original grants of franchises, but for repeated confirmations. The Jews paid exorbitant sums for every common right of mankind, for protection, for justice. In return they were sustained against their Christian debtors in demands of usury, which superstition and tyranny rendered enormous. Men fined for the king's good will; or that he would remit his anger; or to have his mediation with their adversaries. Many fines seem, as it were, imposed in sport, if we look to the cause, though their extent and the solemnity with which they were recorded, prove the humor to have been differently relished by the two parties. Thus the bishop of Winchester paid a tun of good wine for not reminding the king (John) to give a girdle to the countess of Albemarle; and Robert de Vaux five best palfreys, that he might hold his peace about Henry Pinel's wife. Another paid four marks for leave to eat (*pro licentiâ comedendi*). But of all the abuses which deformed the Anglo-Norman government, none was so pernicious as the sale of judicial redress. The king,

we are often told, is the fountain of justice; but in those ages it was one which gold alone could unseal. Men fined to have right done them; to sue in a certain court; to implead a certain person; to have a restitution of land which they had recovered at law. From the sale of that justice which every citizen has a right to demand, it was an easy transition to withhold or deny it. Fines were received for the king's help against the adverse suitor; that is, for the perversion of justice, or for delay. Sometimes they were paid by opposite parties, and, of course, for opposite ends. These were called counter fines; but the money was sometimes, or as Lord Lyttleton thinks, invariably, returned to the unsuccessful suitor."—HALLAM'S *Middle Ages*, vol. ii. p. 316.

Abuses of Prerogative—Purveyance.—"The real prerogatives that might formerly be exerted, were sometimes of so injurious a nature, that we can hardly separate them from their abuse: a striking instance is that of purveyance, which will at once illustrate the definition above given of a prerogative, the limits within which it was to be exercised, and its tendency to transgress them. This was a right of purchasing whatever was necessary for the king's household, at a fair price, in preference to every competitor, and without the consent of the owner. By the same prerogative, carriages and horses were impressed for the king's journeys, and lodgings provided for his attendants. This was defended on a pretext of necessity, or at least of great convenience to the sovereign, and was both of high antiquity and universal practice throughout Europe. But the royal purveyors had the utmost temptation, and doubtless no small store of precedents, to stretch this power beyond its legal boundary, and not only to fix their own price too low, but to seize what they wanted without any payment at all, or with tallies, which were carried in vain to an empty exchequer. This gave rise to a number of petitions from the commons, upon which statutes were often framed; but the evil was almost incurable in its nature, and never ceased till that prerogative was itself abolished. Purveyance, as I have already said, may serve to distinguish the defects from the abuses of our Constitution. It was a reproach to the law that men should be compelled to send their goods without their consent; it was a reproach to the administration that they were deprived of them without payment.

"The right of purchasing men's goods for the use of the king was extended by a sort of analogy to their labor. Thus Edward III. announces to all sheriffs that William of Walsingham had a commission to collect 'as many painters as might suffice for our works in St. Stephen's chapel, Westminster, to be at our wages as long as shall be necessary,' and to arrest and keep in prison all who should refuse or be refractory; and enjoins them to lend their assistance. Windsor Castle owes its massive magnificence to laborers impressed from every part of the kingdom. There is even a commission from Edward IV. to take as many workmen in gold as were wanting, and to employ them at the king's cost upon the trappings of himself and his household."—HALLAM'S *Middle Ages*, vol. iii. p. 148.

CHAPTER III.

ENGLAND UNDER THE YOKE.

NECESSITIES OF DESPOTISM—SUPPRESSION OF THE ANGLO-SAXON SYSTEM AND LANGUAGE—CONFISCATION—THE NEW FOREST AND FOREST LAWS—TYRANNY OF THE KING OVER THE NOBLES—EXACT DEFINITION OF CONQUEST—REMNANTS AND TRADITIONS OF THE SAXON SYSTEM—CHARTERS—RUFUS—HENRY I.—STEPHEN—MATILDA—HENRY II.—RICHARD II.—FIRST IMPEACHMENT BY PARLIAMENT.

DESPOTIC power can only be sustained by acts of despotism. In the idea of subjection to the will of a mere mortal, there is something so revolting to our nature that the bare conception rouses an involuntary spirit of resistance. Despotism is war with human nature; and the first necessity of despots is defence against the instincts of mankind. The necessities of their position force them to crush out the spirit of resistance to their usurpation. It is not enough to crush resistance. They must crush the spirit which inspires resistance, or they cannot be secure. It is a combat *a l'outrance.* The law of self-defence demands relentless war upon their foe, and that foe is the nature God has breathed into the nostrils of mankind. Hence it is that tyrants, naturally amiable and humane, have not unfrequently become the scourges of their race. Compelled at first to use brute force against their open enemies, and then to wage a ceaseless warfare with their hidden foe, in the heart of every man worthy of the name of freeman, habit has at last brought them to be willingly what tyrants must be actually —enemies of man. Self-preservation, calling for continual intimidation, leads to an inveterate habit of trampling on all human rights and obligations, till the tyrant learns that his true enemy is human nature. Then his task is clear. The arm of power and the allurements of temptation are his only instruments; and he becomes the corrupter and destroyer of his race.

The English people felt the full force of these horrible necessities during the first five Norman reigns. Under the iron hand of William, almost every vestige of the Anglo-Saxon system disappeared. The great mass of the freemen were disfranchised and made serfs. The ealdormen and eorls were attainted and exiled, and their lands delivered to the Norman followers of the king. The Anglo-Saxon priests and prelates were degraded from their offices, and Norman creatures of the king appointed in their stead. The Saxon language was proscribed, and the procedures of the courts required to be in Norman French. The native people, ground down by exactions and exasperated by the insults heaped upon them by their foreign masters, were lashed into occasional revolt; and thus furnished to the king pretexts for further confiscations, and excuses for more violent oppressions. From the Domesday Book we learn that of seven hundred tenants *in capite*, or immediate vassals of the crown, not one was a Saxon; and though of the 60,215 knights' fees in England, it is probable that some—perhaps many—were still held by Saxons, we must recollect that they were now no longer freeholders, but were compelled to surrender their own lands into the hands of Norman barons, and to receive them back as vassals, burdened with the usual imposts of the feudal tenure. As the landless Saxon freemen were degraded into serfs, so were the free proprietors of lands degraded into feudal vassals.

Thus the people felt the full weight of the conqueror's heel. But the necessities of arbitrary power demand intimidation of its subjects, and the conqueror proceeded to strike terror to the people's hearts by acts of ruthless cruelty which, if not prompted by this cause, could only be described as acts of fiendish wantonness. Under the thin pretence that he was apprehensive of a Danish invasion, he caused the whole region from the Tyne to the Humber to be laid waste. Thousands of the people died of want beside the ruins of their wasted homes; and for nine years, thoughout the desolated district there was not one village—scarcely one house—left for human occupation. Fear of an invasion, flimsy as the reason was, was yet some reason for this wholesale cruelty; but no excuse was even attempted for a similar destruction, both of life and property, caused in the making of the king's "New Forest." Thousands of persons died of hunger, that the king's deer might be fed. Thousands of homes were given to the torch, that in their ruins the wild boar might make his lair. Thousands of acres were withdrawn from cultivation for the use and benefit of man, to furnish pastures for the royal game. And if the starving Saxon churl presumed to kill a boar or deer, his punishment was the loss of his eyes. This trampling on the common instincts of humanity was not mere wantonness. It was part of the policy of the conqueror, and was intended to inspire his subjects with a terror of his power. To overawe his Norman as well as his Saxon vassals, he kept up a standing army of mercenary soldiers from the Continent, and their support he furnished by the manifold exactions which the feudal system gave the opportunity of making. The comparative smallness of the fiefs enabled him to put down that pernicious system of marauding by the barons which prevailed upon the Continent. This he did, not as an act of justice, but as a means of making his power felt and respected. In his realm of England he endured no robber but himself. Rightly, indeed, does Hallam say that "England had passed under the yoke;" yet England bore no other yoke than that which any free people must endure which yields its freedom to the hand of foreign or domestic usurpation. The necessities of tyranny are everywhere the same. It has the same position to maintain; the same war with the inborn instincts of mankind to wage; the same means of corruption and intimidation to apply; and the same heartless recklessness in working out its aims.[1]

It was not long before the Normans, under William and his immediate successors, found out that the royal despotism was not a despotism merely to the Saxons. With that they might have been content; but they were not long in discovering that they themselves were as much objects of oppression to their sovereign as the subjugated Saxons. The effect of this was to make common cause between them and the Saxons as against the crown: and it is singular to notice that the causes which eventually led to the deliverance both from kingly tyranny were the few remnants of the ancient Saxon institutions that had been permitted to remain. William did not affect to have conquered *England*, but to have conquered the *crown* of England; the term conquest not being in feudal language understood in its modern sense, but signifying simply *acquisition* in any way other than by inheritance; and as William claimed to have acquired the crown, not by inheritance, but by a real or pretended grant from Edward the Confessor, and was thus the original *acquirer* of it to his family, he was called the conqueror, *i. e.*, the acquirer of the crown of England. He did not consequently pretend to have subjugated England by the sword, but by the sword to have won his rightful crown from Harold. At his coronation he took the same oaths as the Saxon kings had taken theretofore, and swore in the same formula to support and defend the laws of the realm. It is true that William, like more modern rulers, held official oaths but lightly, and completely overturned the Anglo-Saxon constitutions. Yet in some respects the former institutions still remained. The shire and burgh courts—now called courts of assize—and the hundred courts—now called the quarter sessions—continued to be held. In these the ancient laws and customs of the kingdom were preserved; in many matters they retained that local sovereignty which was their great characteristic before the Conquest; and in all of them tradition still spoke of a time when laws and statutes were not emanations from the arbitrary will of a despotic king, but were enacted by a free and independent council of the kingdom, to whose laws the prince and people were alike amenable. Thus the idea of constitutional government was preserved. When groaning under the oppressions of the kings, the Norman barons, no less than the Saxons, clamored for the laws of Edward the Confessor; and as the necessities of the crown afforded opportunity, they called for and obtained successive charters recognizing the ancient Saxon laws. Such charters were, however, always looked upon as acts of royal grace. No parliament or council ventured to assume the functions of the Saxon witena-gemote; nor, till the time of Richard I. did Parliament assert any authority beyond that of a council of advice. In their subjection to the throne, their only hope lay in the partial recollection of the ancient liberties of England, which was kept alive by a few feeble remnants of the Anglo-Saxon polity.

For a hundred and fifty years after the Conquest, the history of

England, so far as it relates to constitutional developments, may be summed up in a few sentences.

William Rufus, the immediate successor of the Conqueror, followed in the footsteps of his father, and extended his oppressions to the church. He seized upon the temporalities of vacant bishoprics and abbeys, and delayed appointments to them, that he might continue to enjoy their revenues. In many instances he sold or gave away the church lands to his favorites. When he purchased the duchy of Normandy from his brother Robert for 10,000 marks, this sum was raised by general extortions both from church and laity, so rigorous that convents were compelled to melt their plate in order to supply the amounts required of them.[2]

Henry I., having usurped the crown in defiance of the right of his brother Robert, duke of Normandy, endeavored to secure himself in his possession by concessions to his subjects. He immediately gave a charter which professed to do away with the abuses of his predecessor's reign; and as an earnest of his purpose he degraded and imprisoned Ralph Flambard, bishop of Durham, who had been the agent of his brother's tyranny.[3] He also reconciled the Saxons to his government by marrying Matilda, daughter of Malcolm III. of Scotland, and niece to Edgar Atheling. Thus both the Normans and the Saxons looked to better days under the rule of Henry; but though by no means so unscrupulous a prince as Rufus, he had hardly given his charter before he broke it by seizing on the temporalities of the see of Durham, which he held for five years; and when he went on his invasion of Normandy, he raised the means for his expedition by exactions not less ruinous than those of Rufus.

Stephen, a usurper like his predecessor, sought, like him, to win the barons to his cause by a pretended abolition of abuses. He gave a solemn charter in which he promised that church benefices falling vacant should immediately be filled, and that the crown should no more seize their temporalities; that the royal forests should be diminished; that certain obnoxious taxes levied for fictitious purposes should be abolished, and that the wholesome laws of Edward the Confessor should be restored. To win the favor of the barons, he allowed them privileges hitherto unknown. The baronial strongholds became dens of highway robbers. New castles, built at first for safety, were in turn applied to purposes of violence; and England in the reign of Stephen was one scene of turbulence and bloodshed. Charters and laws in such a reign were of but little value. When Stephen thought his crown safe on his head, he spurned the solemn obligations he had sworn before the altar to fulfil; and the historian tells us that not laws nor charters, but his "power, was the sole measure of his conduct." Such a monarch could not be otherwise than hateful to his subjects of all classes; and the anarchy which overspread the realm must have impressed them with the absolute necessity of fixed laws founded, not in the caprice or the necessities of vicious princes, but on the eternal principles of right. Hence, when MATILDA, the true heir to the succession came with her son Henry to assert her right, she found the people of all classes ready to support her claims, and Stephen was before long beaten and made prisoner. But England had by this time learned that her prosperity depended, not upon the person of their king, but on the equitable administration of just laws. When the queen was in the pride of her triumph, it was firmly but respectfully demanded by the people that she should promise to govern them by the laws of Edward. Their prayer was haughtily refused; and the result was the desertion of her standard by the people, her defeat by Stephen's partisans, and, ere long, the restoration of a king who, faithless as he was, at least was willing to confess his obligation to obey the fundamental constitutions of the kingdom over which he ruled.

HENRY II. was a monarch of another stamp. Firm and determined, he applied himself to the correction of the multiform abuses which had grown up in the previous reign. His first act was to dismiss the mercenaries who had been collected by his predecessor at a ruinous expense to overawe the barons. Then he demolished the baronial castles which had been productive of such monstrous evils; but required that every man throughout the country should be armed and practised in the use of weapons suited to his rank in life; thus aiming to establish peace within the country and security against invasions from without. Still more to repress the violence of the barons, he commissioned four justiciaries, whose duty was to travel through the country, holding courts in the king's name; and being armed with full power to decide the causes brought before them, they were able to curb the barons in their very strongholds.

Henry's disposition was unquestionably to do right; yet one important act of this reign shows how loose were all ideas both of parliaments and legislation. A law was made that if a feudal lord contracted debts, his vassal's goods should not be seized to satisfy the creditor; but that, until the debt were paid, the creditor should be entitled to receive the rents paid by the vassal to his lord. This equitable law was not enacted by an English parliament, but was made at Verneuil, in a council of prelates and barons of Normandy, Poictou, Anjou, Maine, Touraine, and Brittany; yet it was readily accepted as a valid law in England—so completely had the royal power at this time overshadowed, and indeed extinguished the remembrance of the national legislature.

In the next reign, favorable circumstances tended to the reëstablishment of the authority of Parliament. During the protracted absence of King Richard in the Crusades, William Longchamp, who had been left joint regent and judiciary with the bishop of Durham, wielded his power with so high a hand, that Parliament, on its own responsibility, removed him from his office. There is reason to believe that Richard was not displeased with this act of his barons, but, at all events, the act stood; and for the first time since the days of Saxon witena-gemotes, another voice than that of the sovereign was heard in the administration of the national affairs. The first blow had been struck at the unlimited autocracy established by the Norman conqueror in England. The first step toward the building up of a free government with a well-balanced constitution had been taken. Centuries of conflict still had to be passed through ere the work could be accomplished; but in this act of the barons the great work had been begun. The Parliament of England was by this act reëstablished; and before that generation passed away, the abject baseness and the treacherous tyranny of John inspired the will, afforded the occasion, and called forth the power to set the liberties of England on a permanent foundation.[4]

NOTES.

1. *Character of the Reign of the Conqueror.*—" The commencement of his (William the Conqueror's) administration was tolerably equitable. Though many confiscations took place in order to gratify the Norman army, yet the mass of the property was left in the hands of its former possessors. Offices of high trust were bestowed upon Englishmen, even upon those whose family renown might have raised the most aspiring thoughts. But partly through the insolence and injustice of William's Norman vassals, partly through the suspiciousness natural to a man conscious of having overturned the national government, his yoke soon became more heavy. The English were oppressed; they rebelled, were subdued, and oppressed again. All their risings were without concert and desperate; they wanted men fit to head them, and fortresses to sustain their revolt. After a very few years they sank in despair, and yielded for a century to the indignities of a comparatively small body of strangers without a single tumult. So possible is it for a nation to be kept in permanent servitude, even without losing its reputation for individual courage, or its desire of freedom."—HALLAM'S *Middle Ages*, vol. ii. p. 301.

" England passed under the yoke; she endured the annoyance of foreign conquerors; her children, even though their loss in revenue may have been exaggerated, and still it was enormous, became a lower race, not called to the councils of their sovereign, not sharing his trust or his bounty. They were in a far different condition from the provincial Romans after the conquest of Gaul, even if, which is hardly possible to determine, their actual deprivation of lands should have been less extensive; for, not only they did not for several reigns occupy the honorable stations which sometimes fell to the lot of the Roman subject of Clovis or Alaric, but they had a great deal more freedom and importance to lose. Nor had they a protecting church to mitigate barbarous superiority. Their bishops were degraded and in exile; the footstep of the invader was at their altars; their monasteries were plundered and the native monks insulted. Rome herself looked with little favor on a church which had preserved some measure of independence. Strange contrast to the triumphant episcopate of the Merovingian kings!"—*Ibid.* vol ii. p. 308.

" The tyranny of William displayed less of passion or insolence than of that indifference about human suffering which distinguishes a cold and far-sighted statesman. Impressed by the frequent risings of the English at the commencement of his reign, and by the recollection, as one historian observes, that the mild government of Canute had only ended in the expulsion of the Danish line, he formed the scheme of riveting such fetters upon the conquered nation that all resistance should become impracticable. Those who had obtained honorable offices were successively deprived of them; even the bishops and abbots of

English birth were deposed—a stretch of power very singular in that age. Morcar, one of the most illustrious English, suffered perpetual imprisonment. Waltheoff, a man of equally conspicuous birth, lost his head upon a scaffold by a very harsh if not iniquitous sentence. It was so rare in those times to inflict judicially any capital punishment upon persons of such ranks that his death seems to have produced more indignation and despair in England than any single circumstance. The name of Englishman was turned into a reproach. None of that race for a hundred years were raised to any dignity in the state or church. Their language and the characters in which it was written were rejected as barbarous; in all schools, if we trust an authority often quoted, children were taught French, and the laws were administered in no other tongue. It is well known that this use of French in all legal proceedings lasted till the reign of Edward III."—*Ibid.* vol. ii. p. 302, 303.

The condition of England under the Conqueror may be readily conceived from the account given with apparent impartiality by the Saxon chronicler:

"If any one wish to know what manner of man he was, or what worship he had, or of how many lands he were the lord, we will describe him as we have known him; for we looked on him, and some while lived in his herd. King William was a very wise man and very rich, more worshipful and strong than any his foregangers. He was mild to good men who loved God; and stark beyond all bounds to those who withsaid his will. Yet truly, in his time, men had mickle suffering, and yet very many hardships. Castles he caused to be wrought and poor men to be oppressed. He was so very stark. He took from his subjects many marks of gold, and many hundred pounds of silver; and that he took, some by right, and some by mickle might, for very light need. He had fallen into avarice, and greediness he loved withal. He let his lands to fine as dear as he could; then came some other and bade more than the first had given, and the king let it to him who bade more; then came a third and bade yet more; and the king let it into the hands of the man who bade the most. Nor did he reck how sinfully his reeves got money of poor men, or how many unlawful things they did. For the more men talked of right law, the more they did against the law. He also set many deer-friths; and he made laws therewith that whosoever should slay hart or hind, him man should blind. As he forbade the slaying of harts, so also did he of boars; so much he loved the high deer, as if he had been their father. He also decreed about hares that they should go free. His rich men moaned, and the poor men murmured; but he was so hard that he recked not the hatred of them all. For it was need they should follow the king's will withal, if they wished to live, or to have lands, or goods, or his favour. Alas, that any man should be so moody, and should so puff up himself, and think himself above all other men! May Almighty God have mercy on his soul and grant him forgiveness of his sins."—*Saxon Chronicle.*

Assuredly the Norman king had good need of the devout prayer of his Saxon subject.

2. *Rufus.*—Rufus was as reckless in the use of arbitrary power, and as fond of a rude joke, as some more modern rulers. Witness the following:

"For a while, the new monarch, William Rufus, made himself popular by pledging himself to rule with justice, and to relieve the native English from several irksome restraints; and by giving away or spending freely the accumulated wealth which came into his possession. But his temper was too violent to let him observe his promises. And when Lanfranc remonstrated with him, the king was not ashamed to reply in words which amounted to a confession that he neither had kept nor intended to keep them. 'Who,' said he, 'can perform all he promises?'

"Instead of removing restraints, he probably added to those imposed by his father that severe one by which all families were compelled to extinguish their lights and fires at the sound of the evening bell, which was thence called curfew, that is, cover fire. As to the *liberality* of Rufus, it was but the extravagance of a thoroughly selfish man. The money he wasted had cost him no labor, and he therefore chose to set no bounds to his profusion; caring nothing for the burdens which he thereby forced an unprincipled minister to impose upon his subjects. It is related of him, that his chamberlain having bought him a new pair of hose, William asked what they cost. 'Three shillings,' was the reply; and this was at that time the price of a quarter of wheat. 'Away with them,' said he; 'a king should wear nothing so cheap; bring me a pair ten times as dear.' The shrewd attendant brought him an inferior pair, but said he had with difficulty prevailed with the tradesman to part with them at the price named by the king. On which William replied: 'You have now served me well; those I will have.'

"Such silly pride and wilful prodigality, when extended to all the occasions of expense to which a sovereign is necessarily subject, must as certainly consume the revenues of a kingdom as they would on a smaller scale destroy any private fortune. And a king, like any other spendthrift, will be too surely driven by his folly from pride to meanness. Though too haughty to wear clothes of ordinary goodness, William could lower himself to cheat a Jew. One of that unhappy race complained to him with tears, that his son had been converted; and besought the king to command the youth to deny Christ, and return to the faith of his fathers. William gave no answer, but at the same time showed no horror at the request; so that the Jew was encouraged to offer his sovereign sixty marks as a bribe for compliance. On this he sent for the young man, told him what his father required, and bade him acknowledge himself a Jew again. The youth expressed his hope that the king could not be in earnest. 'Son of a dunghill,' exclaimed William, 'do you think I would joke with you? Obey me instantly, or, by the cross of Lucca, you shall lose your eyes.' Though thus threatened by a tyrant, who was known to fear neither God nor man, and whose passionate tone and fierce look seemed to declare that his threats would be executed the next moment, the young man calmly replied that he must suffer whatever the king should choose to inflict; but that he had hoped a Christian sovereign would have protected such as embraced the Christian faith. Finding him thus firm, William neither punished the convert, nor continued his threats, but, turning to the father, demanded the promised sum. The Jew objected that his son was as much a Christian as ever. 'I did what I could,' said William; 'and do you think I will work without my reward? As I have been unsuccessful, give me half.' The Jew was obliged to comply, and the king took his thirty marks."—WALTER'S *Hist. of England*, vol. i. p. 288–290.

3. *Charter of Henry I.*—"Besides taking the usual coronation oath to maintain the laws and execute justice, Henry I. passed a charter which was calculated to remedy many of the grievous oppressions which had been complained of during the reigns of his father and brother. He therefore promised that, at the death of any bishop or abbot, he never would seize the revenues of the see or abbey during the vacancy, but would leave the whole to be reaped by the successor; and that he would never let to farm any ecclesiastical benefice, nor dispose of it for money. After this concession to the church, whose favor was of so great importance, he proceeded to enumerate the civil grievances which he purposed to redress. He promised that upon the death of any earl, baron, or military tenant, his heir should be admitted to the possession of his estate, on paying a just and lawful relief, without being exposed to such violent exactions as had been usual during the late reigns; he remitted the wardship of minors, and allowed guardians to be appointed, who should be answerable for the trust; he promised not to dispose of any heiress in marriage, but by the advice of all the barons; and if any baron intended to give his daughter, sister, niece, or kinswoman in marriage, it should only be necessary for him to consult the king, who promised to take no money for his consent, nor even to refuse permission, unless the person to whom it was purposed to marry her should happen to be his enemy. He granted his barons and military tenants the power of bequeathing by will their money or personal estates; and if they neglected to make a will, he promised that their heirs should succeed to them; he renounced the right of imposing moneyage, and of levying taxes at pleasure on the farms which the barons retained in their own hands; he made some general professions of moderating fines; he offered a pardon for all offences; and he remitted all debts due to the crown; he required that the vassals of the barons should enjoy the same privileges which he granted to his own barons; and he promised a general confirmation and observance of the laws of King Edward. This is the substance of the chief articles contained in that famous charter."—HUME, i. 313.

4. *Saxon Serfdom.*—The most perfect picture of the condition of England under the Norman princes I have yet found is in the "Ivanhoe" of Sir Walter Scott. In language, costume, and all minor details, it is marked by the usual accuracy of that great and learned writer:

"The human figures which completed this landscape were in number two, partaking, in their dress and appearance, of that wild and rustic character which belonged to the woodlands of the West Riding of Yorkshire at that early period. The eldest of these men had a stern, savage, and wild aspect. His garment was of the simplest form imaginable, being a close jacket with sleeves, composed of the tanned skin of some animal, on which the hair had been originally left, but which had been worn off in so many places, that it would have been difficult to distinguish from the patches that remained, to what creature the fur had belonged. This primeval vestment reached from the throat to the knees, and served at once all the usual purposes of body clothing; there was no wider opening at the collar than was necessary to admit the passage of the head, from which it may be inferred that it was put on by slipping it over the head and shoulders, in the manner of a modern shirt or ancient hauberk. Sandals, bound with thongs made of boar's hide, protected the feet, and a roll of thin leather was twined artificially around the legs, and ascending above the calf, left the knees bare, like those of a Scottish Highlander. To make the jacket sit yet more close to the body, it was gathered at the middle by a broad leathern belt, secured by a brass buckle; to one side of which was attached a sort of scrip, and to the other a ram's horn, accoutred with a mouthpiece, for the purpose of blowing. In the same belt was stuck one of those long, broad, sharp-pointed, and two-edged knives, with a buck's-horn handle, which were fabricated in the neighborhood, and bore even at this early period the name of a Sheffield whittle. The man had no covering upon his head, which was only defended by his own thick hair, matted and twisted together, and scorched by the influence of the sun into a rusty dark-red color, forming a contrast with the overgrown beard upon his cheeks, which was rather of a yellow or amber hue. One part of his dress only remains, but it is too remarkable to be suppressed: it was a brass ring resembling a dog's collar, but without any opening, and soldered fast round his neck, so loose as to form no impediment to his breathing, yet so tight as to be incapable of being removed, excepting by the use of the file. On this singular gorget was engraved, in Saxon characters, an inscription of the following purport: "Gurth, the son of Beowulph, is the born thrall of Cedric of Rotherwood." Beside the swineherd, for such was Gurth's occupation, was seated, upon one of the fallen Druidical monuments, a person about ten years younger in appearance, and whose dress, though resembling his companion's in form, was of better materials, and of a more fantastic appearance. His jacket had been stained of a bright purple hue, upon which there had been some attempt to paint grotesque ornaments in different colors. To the jacket he added a short cloak, which scarcely reached halfway down his thigh; it was of crimson cloth, though a good deal soiled, lined with bright yellow; and as he could transfer it from one shoulder to the other, or at his pleasure draw it all around him, its width, contrasted with its want of longitude, formed a fantastic piece of drapery. He had thin silver bracelets upon his arms, and on his neck a collar of the same metal, bearing the inscription: "Wamba the son of Witless, is the thrall of Cedric of Rotherwood." This person had the same sort of sandals with his companion, but instead of the roll of leather thong, his legs were cased in a sort of gaiters, of which one was red and the other yellow. He was provided also with a cap, having around it more than one bell, about the size of those attached to hawks, which jingled as he turned his head to one side or other; and as he seldom remained a minute in the same posture, the sound might be considered as incessant. Around the edge of this cap was a stiff bandeau of leather, cut at the top into open work, resembling a coronet, while a prolonged bag arose from within it, and fell down on one shoulder, like an old fashioned nightcap, or a jelly bag, or the head gear of a modern hussar. It was to this part of the cap that the bells were attached; which circumstance as well as the shape of his head-dress, and his own half-crazed half-cunning expression of countenance, sufficiently pointed him out as belonging to the race of domestic clowns or jesters, maintained in the houses of the wealthy, to keep away the tedium of those lingering hours which they were obliged to spend within doors. He bore, like his companion, a scrip, attached to his belt, but had neither horn nor knife, being probably considered as belonging to a class whom it is considered dangerous to intrust with edge tools. In place of these he was equipped with a sort of sword of lath, resembling that with which Harlequin operates his wonders upon the modern stage.

" The outward appearance of these two men formed scarce a stronger contrast than their look and demeanor. That of the serf or bondsman was sad and sullen; his aspect was bent on the ground with an appearance of deep dejection, which might be almost construed into apathy, had not the fire which occasionally sparkled in his red eye, manifested that there slumbered, under the appearance of sullen despondency, a sense of oppression and a disposition to resistance. The looks of Wamba, on the other hand, indicated, as usual with his class, a sort of vacant curiosity, and fidgety impatience of any posture of repose, together with the utmost self-satisfaction respecting his own situation, and the appearance which he made. The dialogue which they maintained between them was carried on in Anglo-Saxon, which, as we said before, was universally spoken by the inferior classes, excepting the Norman soldiers and the immediate personal dependants of the great feudal nobles. But to give their conversation in the original would convey but little information to the modern reader, for whose benefit we beg to offer the following translation.

" 'The curse of St. Withold upon these infernal porkers!' said the swineherd, after blowing his horn obstreperously, to collect together the scattered herd of swine, which, answering his call with notes equally melodious, made, however, no haste to remove themselves from the luxurious banquet of beech mast and acorns on which they had fattened, or to forsake the marshy banks of the rivulet, where several of them, half plunged in mud, lay stretched at their ease, altogether regardless of the voice of their keeper. 'The curse of St. Withold upon them and upon me!' said Gurth; 'if the two-legged wolf snap not up some of them ere nightfall, I am no true man. Here, Fangs! Fangs!' he ejaculated at the top of his voice to a ragged, wolfish-looking dog, a sort of lurcher, half mastiff, half greyhound, which went limping about as if with the purpose of seconding his master in collecting the refractory grunters; but which, in fact, from misapprehension of the swineherd's signals, ignorance of his own duty, or malice prepense, only drove them hither and thither, and increased the evil which he seemed designed to remedy. 'A devil draw the teeth of him,' said Gurth, 'and the mother of mischief confound the ranger of the forest that cuts the foreclaws off our dogs, and makes them unfit for their trade! Wamba, up and help me, an thou beest a man; take a turn round the back o' the hill, to gain the wind on them; and when thou'st got the weather gage, thou mayst drive them before thee as gently as so many innocent lambs.'

"'Truly,' said Wamba, without stirring from the spot, 'I have consulted my legs upon this matter, and they are altogether of opinion, that to carry my gay garments through these sloughs would be an act of unfriendship to my sovereign person and royal wardrobe; wherefore Gurth I advise thee to call off Fangs, and leave the herd to their destiny, which, whether they meet with bands of travelling soldiers, or of outlaws, or of wandering pilgrims, can be little else than to be converted into Normans before morning, to thy no small ease and comfort.

"'The swine turned Normans, to my comfort!' quoth Gurth, 'expound that to me, Wamba, for my brain is too dull and my mind too vexed to read riddles.'

"'Why, how call you these grunting brutes running about on their four legs?' demanded Wamba.

"'Swine, fool, swine,' said the herd, 'every fool knows that.'

"'And swine is good Saxon,' said the jester; 'but how call you the sow when she is flayed, and drawn, and quartered, and hung up by the heels like a traitor?'

"'Pork,' answered the swineherd.

"'I am very glad every fool knows that too,' said Wamba; 'and pork I think is good Norman-French; and so when the brute lives and is in the charge of a Saxon slave, she goes by her Saxon name; but becomes a Norman, and is called pork, when she is carried to the castle hall to feast among the nobles; what dost thou think of this, friend Gurth, ha?'

"'It is but too true doctrine, friend Wamba, however it got into thy fool's pate.'

"'Nay, I can tell you more,' said Wamba in the same tone; 'there is old Alderman Ox continues to hold his Saxon epithet while he is under the charge of serfs and bondsmen such as thou, but becomes Beef, a fiery French gallant, when he arrives before the worshipful jaws that are destined to consume him. Mynheer Calf, too, becomes Monsieur de Veau in the like manner; he is Saxon when he requires tendance, and takes a Norman name when he becomes matter of enjoyment.'

"'By St. Dunstan,' said Gurth, 'thou speakest but sad truths; little else is left to us but the air we breathe, and that appears to have been reserved with much hesitation, solely for the purpose of enabling us to endure the tasks they lay upon our shoulders. The finest and the fattest is for their board; the loveliest is for their couch; the best and bravest supply their foreign masters with soldiers, and whiten distant lands with their bones, leaving few here who have either will or the power to protect the unfortunate Saxon.

* * * * * * * * *

"'Gurth,' said the jester, 'I know thou thinkest me a fool, or thou wouldst not be so rash in putting thy head into my mouth. One word to Reginald Front de Bœuf, or Philip de Malvoisin, that thou hast spoken treason against the Norman, and thou art but a castaway swineherd; thou wouldst waver on one of these trees as a terror to all evil speakers against dignities.'

"'Dog, thou wouldst not betray me,' said Gurth, 'after having led me on to speak so much at disadvantage?'

"'Betray thee!' answered the jester; 'no, that were the trick of a wise man; a fool cannot half so well help himself,' &c., &c.—*Ivanhoe.*

CHAPTER IV.

THE GIVING OF MAGNA CHARTA.

STATE OF THE KINGDOM AT THE ACCESSION OF JOHN—EARLY ACTS OF HIS REIGN —MURDER OF PRINCE ARTHUR—REFUSAL OF THE BARONS TO FOLLOW JOHN INTO FRANCE—HIS SEIZURE OF THE TEMPORALITIES OF CANTERBURY—APPOINTMENT OF LANGTON TO THE ARCHBISHOPRIC—ENGLAND UNDER INTERDICT—THE KINGDOM GIVEN BY THE POPE TO PHILIP OF FRANCE—THE INTERDICT REMOVED—JOHN'S OATH BEFORE RECEIVING ABSOLUTION—DISCOVERY OF THE CHARTER OF HENRY I. BY LANGTON—THE BARONS SWEAR TO MAINTAIN IT, AND DEMAND THAT JOHN SHALL RATIFY IT—THEY RAISE AN ARMY—LONDON DECLARES FOR THE BARONS—THE MEETING AT RUNNYMEDE —THE CHARTER GRANTED—ITS CHARACTER AND PROVISIONS—RECOGNITION OF THE RIGHT OF REBELLION—HUME AND HALLAM ON THE CHARTER.

AT the accession of King John the power of Parliament as a legislative body was distinctly recognized, but it is doubtful whether any clear idea of the vast importance of the privilege of parliamentary legislation had been formed. During the various disturbances which had ensued upon the seizure of the crown by princes who had no legitimate title to it, the barons had been taught their power in the disposition of a vacant throne. Their power to check a crowned king they had not yet learned. Again, the insecurity of these usurping princes had from time to time induced them to give charters promising to rule their people by the good laws of the Saxon kings. But of the purport of these laws the people were profoundly ignorant. Contrasted with the violence of Norman rule, the days of equitable Saxon government were remembered in the popular traditions as the golden age, and these charters of the kings were gratifying to a general desire, however vague, for fixed and fundamental laws. But they were never clearly understood. The Norman barons knew, as yet, no government but that of feudalism; the

Saxon people had been crushed till they had lost the recollection of their ancient liberties; and neither had yet learned their power to force a sovereign to respect his subjects' rights. Hence the successive charters were neglected equally by prince and people, and soon passed into oblivion. In the reign of John, only one copy of the charter given by Henry I. was to be found in the whole kingdom, though a copy had been sent to every shire and diocese throughout the land! It needed such a reign as that of John to rouse the people to activity. Had he possessed the strong will, the sagacious forecast, and the iron nerve of the Conqueror, the history of England might have been like that of France; but his unequalled course of murder, meanness, falsehood, perjury, licentiousness, extortion, and oppression roused both lords and commons to a sense of the necessity of a fixed constitution which should bind both prince and people; his pusillanimous weakness was a tower of strength to the great confederacy which was formed to vindicate their liberties; and the sound wisdom and discretion of the patriot archbishop, Stephen Langton, guided them in their endeavors, till the fundamental law of England, which has never to this day been changed but by the development of its inestimable principles, was laid down in the instrument called MAGNA CHARTA.

The early acts of John's reign were but little likely to inspire the people with respect for royalty. He was not the true heir to the throne; for though his elder brother Geoffrey was dead, Arthur the son of Geoffrey still lived, and was, in right, the king of England. Not content, however, with supplanting Arthur, John, having defeated his adherents and gained possession of his person, murdered him in prison. This foul assassination of a child whose early qualities gave promise of a noble manhood, inspired the barons with resentment and disgust. Philip of France, availing himself of the occasion furnished by the crime of John and the alienation of his subjects, marched upon, and took possession of the Norman duchy; and when John summoned the English barons to accompany his standard in an expedition for the recovery of his lost province, they indignantly refused to follow him. Thenceforward he applied himself to the oppression of his English subjects. The limits of our space forbid us to relate the story of his tyranny.

Unlimited licentiousness, rapacity, and prodigality, and a succession of arbitrary fines, imprisonments, and taxes, are the chief points of the tale. At length his insolent extortion brought him into conflict with the only power which could effectually cope with him, —the church. The see of Canterbury falling vacant, he seized upon its lands and revenues, expelled the monks of Christ Church, who, according to their ancient custom, were about to elect a prelate to the vacant see, and of his own power named a new archbishop. Innocent III., the reigning Pope, was little likely to submit to this invasion of the church's rights. He instantly annulled the appointment of the king, required him to give up the church lands, with the revenues he had appropriated, and appointed Stephen Langton to the archiepiscopal throne. John's reply to the Pope's requisitions was another seizure of church lands; and Innocent laid England under interdict. For nearly seven years England groaned beneath that fearful sentence. Public worship was suspended, and the people lived and died without the offices of their religion, and, so far as priestly ministrations were concerned, without God in the world. Had John possessed the affections of his people, he might have defied the Pope, declared the independence of the English Church, and so anticipated, partially at least, the events of a much later period. But his arbitrary conduct had arrayed all classes of his subjects in hostility against him. Laity and clergy, lords and commons hated and despised him ; and when Innocent, proceeding to extremities, declared his people released from their allegiance, and appointed Philip II., king of France, to the throne of England, so few of the barons seemed disposed to stand by him, that, as we learn from Matthew Paris, the historian of his reign, he actually sent for succor to Murmelius, the Moslem king of Spain and Africa, offering, in return for his assistance, to apostatize to Islamism, and hold his kingdom as a vassal of the Moorish king. But Philip gave him short space to make such alliances ; and John submitted to the Pope on terms which showed how utterly he was humiliated. He submitted to the censures of the church, resigned his crown to the Pope's legate, and received it back again as the Pope's gift, to be held as the Pope's vassal. On these conditions Innocent consented to require the French king to abstain from his invasion of the realm of England. The interdict was raised, and John was solemnly absolved at Winchester by the primate Langton, in June, 1214. But before the primate gave him absolution, he required the king to swear "that he would diligently defend the ordinances of Holy Church, and that his hand should be against all her enemies; *that the good laws of his ancestors, and especially those of King Edward the Confessor, whose restoration had been promised by the charter of Henry I., should be recalled, and evil ones destroyed; and that his subjects should receive justice, according to the upright decrees of his courts.*" John also swore "that all corporations and private persons whom the interdict had damaged should receive a full restitution of all which had been taken away, before the time of the approaching Easter, if his sentence of excommunication were first removed. He swore, moreover, fidelity and obedience to Pope Innocent and his catholic successors, and that he would give them that superiority which was already contained in writing."

John held his oaths but lightly, and months passed away without redress of grievances, without the abolition of oppressive laws and customs, and without that restoration of the ancient constitutions which had been promised by the charter of King Henry, and confirmed by John's oath.

It is probable that John was not aware of the importance of that charter. Certainly the barons were in utter ignorance of its provisions. But the patriotic Langton was as learned as he was heroic and discreet. Calling the barons to him, he informed them that he had a copy of the charter of King Henry, read it to them article by article, and, as he did so, showed them its immense importance, and the ease with which it might be applied to their existing circumstances.[2] Overjoyed at this discovery, and filled with hope, the barons joined in a confederacy, with the primate at their head, to force John to make good the oaths which he had taken; and the hands of the confederates were strengthened on the very threshold of their enterprise by an outbreak of the king's unbridled lechery.[3] Assembling at the abbey of St. Edmund, in Edmundsbury, on the 20th of November (St. Edmund's day), they swore before the high altar to stand by each other, and make war upon the king till he should by a solemn charter ratify their liberties, with provisions under which they might themselves be able to compel him to respect them. On Epiphany they came to him with such a military force as challenged his respect,and solemnly demanded that he would make good his oaths. John asked till Easter to consider their demands, in hopes that through the papal influence he might be able to dissolve the confederacy. The time was granted, but John's hopes were disappointed. In the week succeeding Easter the confederates assembled at the town of Stamford with two thousand knights and their retainers. Thence they marched to Brackly on the 27th of April. John held the town of Oxford, fifteen miles from Brackly, and despatched the archbishop with the earl of Pembroke to the camp of the confederates. When they returned, they brought an abstract of the articles demanded by the barons, which was subsequently made the basis of the charter, and announced their purpose to make war upon the king till he should grant what they desired. "And why," said the excited monarch with a scornful sneer, "And why demand they not my kingdom likewise? By God's teeth, I will never grant them liberties that will make myself a slave." It was not long before he found it necessary to break this oath like the rest. London declared for the confederates, and it is said that London even then could muster 80,000 men-at-arms. The barons took possession of the capital on the 22d of May, and issued writs of summons to all the nobles who had not yet joined them. The effect was magical; and in a few days John was left at Oldham with but seven attendants, some even of whom, though they had not deserted him, were cordially in sympathy with the confederates. The king had no choice left but to comply with the demands of his revolted barons; and, after a few unimportant preliminaries, met them on the plain of Runnymede, beside the Thames, where they encamped apart, like enemies, from June 15th till June 19th, when the negotiations were completed. The articles embodied in the first demand of the confederates were, with some verbal alterations, made into a royal grant; and MAGNA CHARTA, the GREAT CHARTER of the Liberties of England, signed and sealed by the king's hand, was solemnly declared, with grave formalities, to be, what it has ever since remained—the fundamental law of England. This time at least the people understood the meaning of the royal charter. The tyrannies of John had fortunately been so flagrant, so distinct, so universal among all classes of his subjects, that a bare recital of his acts, coupled with a prohibition of the like in time to come, was a complete protection to the people for the future. In the charter we find not one abstraction, theory, or maxim of government, but a distinct and sharp enumeration of things which the king shall and which he shall not do, that shows clearly both the wrongs he had committed and the rights he had denied.[4] It is for this reason, doubtless that the charter has proved to be so good and fruitful. For having ever afterward been regarded as the root and ground of the whole English Constitution, the judges have from time to time applied to it for precedent as cases of a novel character arose; and in its multifarious clauses they have seldom failed to find one which contained a principle applicable to the cause in hand. To this directness, therefore, of the charter we must trace much of the equity and reason of the common law. A charter, however good, expressing abstract theories and maxims of laws or government, must inevitably have led to inextricable confusions: some judges straining the law to the utmost, and others restraining it to the least it could mean. But given as it was in direct application to existing facts, it became a chapter of judicial precedents from which there could be no escape, and being gradually developed in the course of ages only as new circumstances called for some new application of the principles of equity on which it was established, centuries have vindicated its claim to be known as the Great Charter of the Liberties of England.

As it is our purpose to give a translation of this venerable monument of freedom, with such copious notes as will make it perfectly intelligible to the ordinary reader, we shall not here enter largely into the provisions of the charter, but content ourselves with an enumeration of its chief heads. It granted, then, the freedom of the English church forever; it mitigated the chief burdens of the feudal system, by decreasing the king's power over his immediate tenants, or tenants *in capite*, and by extending these provisions to sub-feudatories; it did away, particularly, with the abuses of the feudal right of wardship and marriage, which had so oppressed the helpless; it defined and limited the aids which might be lawfully assessed by lords upon their vassals, and provided that *in case of any further taxation, a parliament must be summoned to grant and assess it;* it protected trade and commerce by a guarantee of safety to foreign merchants, and a recognition of the ancient rights, liberties, and free customs of all boroughs, towns, and cities; it provided for more regular administration of the laws by promising that the king's courts should henceforth be held at a fixed place, instead of following the royal person, thus at the same time removing judges from unwholesome influences; it declared *that justice should neither be denied, sold, nor delayed to any man;* that "NO FREEMAN SHOULD BE TAKEN, OR IMPRISONED, OR DISPOSSESSED, OR OUTLAWED, OR BANISHED, OR IN ANY WAY DESTROYED, BUT BY THE LAWFUL JUDGMENT OF HIS PEERS OR BY THE LAW OF THE LAND;" and that a *writ* of *inquisition*, equivalent in its effect to a *writ* of HABEAS CORPUS, SHOULD BE INSTANTLY AND GRATUITOUSLY GRANTED TO ACCUSED PERSONS WHO DESIRED A SPEEDY TRIAL; it provided that unlawful fines which had been levied by the king and his immediate predecessors should be remitted or repaid, that the new forests should be disforested, that is, restored to cultivation, and that the king's foreign mercenaries should be banished. It concluded with a general amnesty to all who had taken part against the king in the discord between him and his barons, and with a SOLEMN RECOGNITION OF THE RIGHT OF REBELLION if the king should violate the charter. Five and twenty barons were appointed to compel him to fidelity. In case he injured any man, complaint was to be made to any four out of the twenty-five, who were to make a solemn application for redress, and if redress were not given them, the five and twenty barons were to make war on the king, to harass and distress him in every way possible, by taking his castles, lands, and possessions, saving harmless only the persons of the royal family, till the wrong should be redressed *according to their verdict*, after which they were to return to their allegiance as before. In security of these things John delivered to the barons the custody of London, and to Langton the Tower of London, to be held till his concessions should have been fulfilled. Never was humiliation more complete; never was victory more perfect; but the victory was that of freedom over despotism, and the humiliation was that of a tyrant before freemen whose rights he had contemned, whose firesides he had sought to violate, and over whom he had attempted to usurp unlimited and irresponsible authority.[5]

Thus, by a great rebellion of the barons, England's worst and weakest monarch was compelled to grant a charter which declared rebellion lawful, and provided means for lawfully conducting it. No great step in the onward march of constitutional government has ever yet been made but by such righteous rebels as the barons of King John; and while it is a truth that an unjustifiable rebellion is a heinous crime, it is no less true that without rebellion constitutional freedom never could have been achieved in any country. Magna Charta, the Petition of Right, the Bill of Rights, the Constitution of these States, were all successively the offspring of rebellion; and if these States now abandon their free system to the hand of arbitrary power, the only hope for their posterity will be that they may follow the example of rebellion set them by our English and colonial ancestors.

The provisions of the charter of King John involve, as Hume says, "all the chief outlines of a legal government, and provide for the equal distribution of justice and the free enjoyment of property; the great objects for which the *people have a perpetual and inalienable right to rebel;* and which no time, nor precedent, nor statute, nor positive institution ought to deter them from keeping ever uppermost in their thoughts." Neither Hume nor the heroes of Runnymede appear to have been very firm believers in the doctrine of "unconditional loyalty." That article in the provisions of a constitutional government it was reserved for an American Republican to invent, in the year of grace—we had almost said *disgrace*—1863.

We cannot better end the present chapter than with the following quotation from Hallam:

"In the reign of John, all the rapacious exactions usual to these Norman kings were not only redoubled, but mingled with other outrages of tyranny still more intolerable. These too were to be endured at the hands of a prince utterly contemptible for his folly and cowardice. One is surprised at the forbearance displayed by the barons, till they took up arms at length in that confederacy which ended in establishing the great charter of liberties. As this was the first effort toward a legal government, so is it beyond comparison the most important event in our history, except that Revolution, without which its benefits would have been rapidly annihilated. The Constitution of England has indeed no single date from which its duration is to be reckoned. The institutions of positive law, the far more important changes which time has wrought in the order of society, during six hundred years subsequent to the great charter, have undoubtedly lessened its direct application to our present circumstances. But it is still the keystone of English liberty. All that has since been obtained is little more than a confirmation or commentary; and if every subsequent law were to be swept away, there would still remain the bold features that distinguish a free from a despotic monarchy. It has been lately the fashion to depreciate the value of the Magna Charta, as if it had sprung from the private ambition of a few selfish barons, and redressed only some feudal abuses. It is indeed of little importance by what motives those who obtained it were guided. The real characters of men most distinguished in the transactions of that time are not easily determined at present. Yet if we bring these ungrateful suspicions to the test, they prove destitute of all reasonable foundation. An equal distribution of civil rights to all classes of freemen forms the peculiar beauty of the charter. In this just solicitude for the people, and in the moderation which infringed upon no essential prerogative of the monarchy, we may perceive a liberality and patriotism very unlike the selfishness which is sometimes rashly imputed to those ancient barons. And so far as we are guided by historical testimony, two great men, the pillars of our church and state, may be considered as entitled beyond the rest to the glory of this monument: Stephen Langton, archbishop of Canterbury, and William, earl of Pembroke. To their temperate zeal for a legal government, England was indebted during that critical period for the two greatest blessings that patriotic statesmen could confer: the establishment of civil liberty upon an immovable basis, and the preservation of national independence under the ancient line of sovereigns, which rasher men were about to exchange for the dominion of France.

"But the essential clauses of Magna Charta are those which protect the personal liberty and property of all freemen, by giving security from arbitrary imprisonment and arbitrary spoliation. 'No freeman' (says the 29th chapter of Henry III.'s charter, which, as the existing law, I quote in preference to that of John, the variations not being very material) 'shall be taken or imprisoned, or be disseized of his freehold, or liberties, or free customs, or be outlawed or exiled, or any otherwise destroyed; nor will we pass upon him, nor send upon him, but by lawful judgment of his peers, or by the law of the land. We will sell to no man, we will not deny or delay to any man justice or right.' It is obvious that these words, interpreted by any honest court of law, convey an ample security for the two main rights of civil society. *From the era therefore of King John's charter, it must have been a clear principle of our Constitution, that no man can be detained in prison without trial.* Whether courts of justice framed the writ of habeas corpus in conformity to the spirit of this clause, or found it already in their register, it became from that era the right of every subject to demand it. *That writ*, rendered more actively remedial by the statute of Charles II., but founded upon the broad basis of Magna Charta, *is the principal bulwark of English liberty; and if ever temporary circumstances, or the doubtful plea of political necessity, shall lead men to look on its denial with apathy, the most distinguishing characteristic of our Constitution will be effaced.*"—HALLAM'S *Middle Ages*, vol. ii. p. 322 et seq.

NOTES.

1. *The Former Charters.*—"A charter of Henry I., the authenticity of which is undisputed, though it contains nothing specially expressed but a remission of unreasonable reliefs, wardships, and other feudal burdens, proceeds to declare that he gives his subjects the laws of Edward the Confessor, with the emendations made by his father with consent of his barons. The charter of Stephen not only confirms that of his predecessor, but adds, in fuller terms than Henry had used, an express concession of the laws and customs of Edward. Henry II.

is silent about these, although he repeats the confirmation of his grandfather's charter. The people, however, had begun to look back to a more ancient standard of law. The Norman conquest, and all that ensued upon it, had endeared the memory of their Saxon government. Its disorders were forgotten, or rather were less odious to a rude nation than the coercive justice by which they were afterward restrained. Hence it became the favorite cry to demand the laws of Edward the Confessor; and the Normans themselves, as they grew dissatisfied with the royal administration, fell into these English sentiments. But what these laws were, or, more properly perhaps, these customs subsisting in the Confessor's age, was not very distinctly understood."—HALLAM'S *Middle Ages*, vol. ii., p. 320.

2. *Langton's Discovery of the Charter of Henry I. to the Barons.*—"The barons, finding that John was only temporizing with them, convened a general assembly of the peers and ecclesiastics at St. Paul's, when Langton, the archbishop, stood up and addressed the convocation in these terms: 'Ye have heard, when at Winchester, before the king was absolved, I compelled him to swear that the existing evil statutes should be destroyed, and that more salutary laws, namely, those of King Edward the Confessor, should be observed by the whole kingdom. In support of these things are ye now convened; and I here disclose to you a newly discovered charter of King Henry I. of England, the which if ye are willing to support, your long-lost liberties may be restored in all their original purity of character.' The prelate then proceeded to read the charter with a loud voice, which so animated the minds of all present, that with the greatest sincerity and joy they swore, in the archbishop's presence, that at a proper season their deeds should avouch what they had then declared, and that even to death itself they would defend those liberties. Langton, on the other hand, promised his most faithful assistance in the execution of their arduous undertaking, and at the same time assured them that the covenant then made would reflect honor on their names through successive generations. This, then, was the conclusion of the first meeting for securing the king's consent to the Magna Charta; from the decisions of which none of that assembly for a moment withdrew their support until the object which they had so long sought was obtained, and the liberties which preceding kings refused to grant were entirely and wholly theirs."—THOMPSON'S *Magna Charta*, p. 12, 13.

3. *Case of De Vesci.*—"Henry Knighton, a canon-regular of Leicester abbey, who lived in the time of Richard II., relates an improbable circumstance (to others the affair appears extremely probable) particularly connected with this baron—De Vesci—wherein he affirms that the incontinence of John was the real cause of the general insurrection of the peerage against him, charging him with vitiating their wives, and then deriding them. He adds, too, that Eustace de Vesci, having married a very beautiful woman—Margaret, daughter of William, king of Scotland—whom he kept far distant from the court, John became

enamored of her, and carefully considered how he might possess her. Sitting one day at table with the baron, King John, observing a ring he wore, took it from him, and said that he had a similar stone, which he would have set in gold of the same pattern; and having thus procured it, he immediately sent it in De Vesci's name to his wife, charging her by that token instantly to come to him, if she ever expected to see him alive. Believing this message, she speedily departed to the court, but on her arrival there, she met her husband, who happened to be riding out; and an explanation having taken place, a disguised courtesan was sent to the king as her substitute. Upon John's discovery of this deceit, he was so enraged that De Vesci fled into the north, destroying some of the king's houses in his passage; whilst many of the nobles who had experienced the same treatment, going with him, they seized upon the king's castles, and at length were joined by the citizens of London. As this baron was so inveterate an enemy to King John, it is not surprising to find him a principal leader in the insurrection that followed."—Thompson's *Magna Charta*, p. 291.

4. *Simplicity of the Charter.*—It is observable that the language of the great charter is simple, brief, general without being abstract, and expressed in terms of authority, not of argument; yet commonly so reasonable as to carry with it the intrinsic evidence of its own fitness. It was understood by the simplest of the unlettered age for whom it was intended. It was remembered by them; and though they did not perceive the extensive consequences which might be derived from it, their feelings were, however, unconsciously exalted by its generality and grandeur.

It was a peculiar advantage that the consequences of its principles were, if we may so speak, only discovered gradually and slowly. It gave out on each occasion only as much of the spirit of liberty and reformation as the circumstances of succeeding generations required, and as their character would safely bear. For almost five centuries it was appealed to as the decisive authority on behalf of the people, though commonly so far only as the necessities of each case demanded. Its effect in these contests was not altogether unlike the grand process by which nature employs snows and frosts to cover her delicate germs, and to hinder them from rising above the earth till the atmosphere has acquired the mild and equal temperature which insures them against blights. On the English nation, undoubtedly, the charter has contributed to bestow the union of establishment with improvement. To all mankind it set the first example of the progress of a great nation for centuries, in blending their tumultuary democracy and haughty nobility with a fluctuating and vaguely limited monarchy, so as at length to form, from these discordant materials, the only form of free government which experience had shown to be reconcilable with widely extended dominions. Whoever, in any future age, or unborn nation, may admire the felicity of the expedient which converted the power of taxation into the shield of liberty, by which discretionary and secret imprisonment was rendered impracticable, and portions of the people were trained to exercise a larger share of judicial power than was ever allotted to them in any other civilized state, in such a manner as to secure instead of endangering public tranquillity;—whoever exults at the spectacle of enlightened and independent assemblies, who, under the eye of a well-informed nation, discuss and determine the laws and policy likely to make communities great and happy;—whoever is capable of comprehending all the effects of such institutions, with all their possible improvements upon the mind and genius of a people, is surely bound to speak with reverential gratitude of the authors of the great charter. To have produced it, to have preserved it, to have matured it, constitute the immortal claim of England on the esteem of mankind. Her Bacons and Shakspeares, her Miltons and Newtons, with all the truth which they have revealed, and all the generous virtue which they have inspired, are of inferior value, when compared with the subjection of men and their rulers to the principles of justice; if, indeed, it be not more true that these mighty spirits could not have been formed, except under equal laws, nor roused to full activity without the influence of that spirit which the great charter breathed over their forefathers.—MACKINTOSH'S *England*, i. 219–222.

5. *Effect of the giving of the Charter on King John.*—A celebrated English historian speaks in the following terms concerning the manner in which the late grant of Magna Charta preyed upon the health and the disposition of John: 'Great reioising," says Holinshed, "was made for this conclusion of peace betwixt the king and his barons, the people iudging that God had touched the king's heart, and mollified it, whereby happie daies were come for the realm of England, as though it had beene delivered out of the bondage of Ægypt; but were much deceived, for the king having condescended to make such grant of liberties, farre contrarie to his mind, was right sorrowful in his heart, cursed his mother that bare him, the houre that he was borne, and the paps that gave him sucke, wishing that he had received death by violence of sword or knife, in steed of naturall norishment: he whetted his teeth, he did bite now on one staffe, and now on an other, as he walked, and oft brake the same in pieces when he had done, and with such disordered behauior and furious gestures he uttered his greefe in such sort that the noblemen verie well perceiued the inclination of his inward affection concerning these things, before the breaking up of the councell, and therefore sore lamented the state of the realme, gessing what would become of his impatiencie and displeasant taking of the matter."

If this melancholy description was a real picture of John's mind after the conclusion of Magna Charta, he was indeed reduced to a miserable state; and this in a twofold sense, for he was not only bent under the weight of his present evils, but his peers, perceiving how much his extorted concession oppressed his thoughts, and fearful of his swerving from it, were prepared to resort to the same violent methods for its preservation as those which they had already made use of to gain it. The future actions of John's life were then smouldering in his breast, like the sleeping, yet unsubdued fires of a volcano: his intentions were however already suspected by many of his peers, and while the king was secretly providing for the success of his plans, they were not less anxious for the security of theirs. Hence arose a mutual mistrust, which the sealed deed of Magna Charta could by no means dissipate; but it was regarded, by one party at least, as only a temporizing expedient, to put an end to the civil feuds which were spread over all the kingdom. In the midst of the schemes which John had commenced to render void that engagement, which he could never remember but with agony, he died suddenly at Newark, on the 19th of October, 1215, by poison, as it is related by some writers, or through the infirmities induced by a broken heart and constitution, as it is asserted by others. There are but few, however, at the present time, who give any degree of credence to the former relation; yet whoever attentively considers the utter hatred which was entertained for John by almost all his subjects, and more especially by the ecclesiastics, will perceive but little reason why this account should be supposed wholly traditional. The celebrated Rapin, and his annotator Morant, have thought it a sufficient argument against its truth to remark that it was improbable for "a man to poison himself to be revenged of another;" but as the mistaken friar believed he was acting in the most patriotic and virtuous manner, in rescuing England from a tyrannic power, so he gave himself without scruple as a martyr to the cause, confidently expecting as a reward, an immediate and eternal beatitude. The same authors also observe that this circumstance is neither mentioned by any contemporary historians, nor even by any one who lived within sixty years of that time. This argument will go, however, but a short distance to prove the falsity of the relation. Matthew Paris, and from him the principal account of John's reign is derived, was too great an enemy of that king to allow of any vices in the opposing party; particularly in that class of society by a member of which this act is said to have been committed. During the space of sixty years it was in every one's memory, and after that period it is more than probable, that, had there not existed some foundation for such a report, it could never have descended to later times through the medium of written history."—THOMPSON'S *Magna Charta*, p. 32 et seq.

6. *Personal Liberty as Secured by the Charter.*—"The thirty-ninth article of this charter is that important clause which forbids arbitrary imprisonment and punishment without lawful trial: 'Let no freeman be imprisoned or outlawed, or in any manner injured, nor proceeded against by us, otherwise than by the legal judgment of his peers, or by the law of the land.' In this clause are clearly contained the writ of habeas corpus and the trial by jury—the most effectual securities against oppression which the wisdom of man has hitherto been able to devise. It is surely more praiseworthy in these haughty nobles to have covered all freemen with the same buckler as themselves than not to have included serfs in the same protection: 'We shall sell, delay, or deny justice to none.' No man can carry farther the principle that justice is the grand debt of every Government to the people, which cannot be paid without rendering law cheap, prompt, and equal.

Nor is the twentieth section unworthy of the like commendation: 'A freeman shall be amerced in proportion to his offence, saving his contenement, and a merchant saving his merchandise.' And surely the barons must be acquitted of an exclusive spirit who subjoin 'and the villain saving his wagonage.' It seems to be apparent from Glanville that villainage was a generic term for servitude in the reign of Henry II., so that the villain of the Great Charter must have been at least a species of serf. The provision which directs that the supreme civil court shall be stationary, instead of following the king's person, is a proof of that regard to the regularity, accessibility, independence, and dignity of public justice, of which the general predominance peculiarly characterizes that venerable monument of English liberty. The liberty of coming to England and going from it, secured to foreign merchants of countries with whom this kingdom is at peace (unless there be a previous prohibition, which Lord Coke interprets to mean by act of Parliament), even if we should ascribe it to the solicitude of the barons for the constant supply of their castles with foreign luxuries, becomes on that very account entitled to regard, inasmuch as the language must be held to be deliberately chosen to promote and insure the purpose of the law."—Mackintosh.

Magna Charta.

John, by the grace of God, king of England, lord of Ireland, duke of Normandy and Aquitaine, and count of Anjou; to his archbishops, bishops, abbots, earls, barons, justiciaries, foresters, sheriffs, governors, officers, and to all his bailiffs and liegemen, greeting:

Know ye, that in presence of GOD, and for the health of our soul and the soul of our ancestors and heirs, and to the honor of God and to the exaltation of His Holy Church, and for the amendment of our kingdom; by advice of our venerable fathers, Stephen, archbishop of Canterbury, primate of all England, and cardinal of the Holy Roman Church; Henry, archbishop of Dublin; William of London, Peter of Winchester, Jocelyn of Bath and Glastonbury, Hugh of Lincoln, Walter of Worcester, William of Coventry, and Benedict of Rochester, bishops; Master Pandulph, our lord the Pope's subdeacon and servant; Brother Aymeric, master of the Temple in England; and the noblemen William Marescall, earl of Pembroke, William earl of Salisbury, William earl of Warren, William earl of Arundel, Alan de Galloway, constable of Scotland, Warin Fitzgerald, Peter Fitzherbert, Hubert de Burgh, seneschal of Poictou, Hugh de Neville, Matthew Fitzherbert, Thomas Basset, Alan Basset, Philip de Albiney, Robert de Roppelaye, John Marescall, John Fitzhugh, and others our liegemen; we have granted to GOD, and by this our present charter confirmed, for us and our heirs forever:

1. That the English church shall be free and enjoy her whole

liberties inviolate. And that we will have them so to be observed, appears from this that of our mere good will we granted, and by our charter confirmed, the freedom of elections which was reckoned most necessary for the English church, and obtained the confirmation thereof from our lord the Pope Innocent the Third, before the discord which has arisen between us and our barons; which charter we will ourselves observe, and will that it be observed in good faith by our heirs forever. We have also for us and our heirs forever granted to all the freemen of our kingdom, all the underwritten liberties to have and to hold to them and their heirs from us and our heirs.

2. If any of our earls or barons, or others holding lands of us *in capite* by military service shall die, and when he dies his heir shall be of full age and owe a relief, the heir shall have his inheritance by the ancient relief; the heir or heirs of an earl for a whole earl's barony, by one hundred pounds; of a baron for a whole barony, by one hundred pounds (marks); of a knight for a whole knights fee, by one hundred shillings at most; and he who owes a less relief shall pay less according to the ancient custom of his fee.

3. But if the heir shall be under age, and shall be in ward, when he comes of age he shall have his inheritance without relief or fine.

4. The warden of the heir under age shall take only reasonable issues, customs, and services; and that without destruction or waste of men or things. And if we shall commit the guardianship of these lands to the sheriff or any other who is answerable to us for their revenues, and he shall make destruction or waste on the ward lands, he shall make satisfaction; and the lands shall be intrusted to two lawful and discreet men of that fee, who shall be answerable to us. Or, if we shall give or sell the wardship of lands to any one, and he shall make destruction or waste, he shall lose his wardship, and the lands shall be intrusted to two discreet men of that fee, who shall be answerable to us as aforesaid.

5. The warden, for as long as he shall hold the land, shall, from the revenues thereof, maintain the houses, parks, warrens, ponds mills, and other things thereto pertaining; and he shall restore to the heir when he comes of age his whole land stocked with ploughs

and carriages according as the time of wainage shall require, and the revenue of the estate will reasonably allow.

6. Heirs shall be married without disparagement of their rank, yet in such wise, that before the marriage is contracted the blood relations of the heir shall be acquainted with it.

7. A widow, after the death of her husband, shall forthwith and without difficulty have her marriage and her inheritance; nor shall she give anything for her dower, marriage, or her inheritance which she and her husband may have held on the day of his decease; and she may remain in the house of her husband forty days after his death, within which term her dower shall be assigned.

8. No widow shall be distrained to marry herself while she shall desire to live without a husband; but she shall give security not to marry without the king's assent, if she holds of him; or without the consent of the lord of whom she holds, if she holds of another.

9. Neither we nor our bailiffs shall seize any land or rent for any debt, so long as the chattels of the debtor are sufficient for the payment of the debt. Nor shall the sureties of the debtor be distrained, so long as the principal debtor is sufficient for the payment of the debt. And if the principal debtor fail in the payment of the debt, not having wherewithal to discharge it, then shall the sureties be answerable for the debt. And, if they will, they shall have the lands and rents of the debtor until they shall be satisfied for the debt they have paid for him; unless the principal debtor shall show himself acquitted thereof against the said sureties.

10. If any one shall have borrowed any thing from the Jews, more or less, and shall die before that debt be paid, the debt shall pay no interest so long as the heir shall be under age, of whomsoever he may hold; and if that debt shall fall into our hands, we will take nothing but the chattel named in the bond.

11. And if any one shall die indebted to the Jews, his wife shall have her dower and shall pay nothing of that debt; and if children of the deceased shall remain, under age, necessaries shall be provided for them according to the tenement which belonged to the deceased; and out of the residue the debt shall be paid, saving the

rights of lords (from whom the lands are held). In like manner let it be done with debts due to others than Jews.

12. No scutage nor aid shall be imposed in our kingdom excepting for the ransom of our person, to make our eldest son a knight, and once to marry our eldest daughter; and for these none but a reasonable aid shall be demanded. So, likewise, let it be concerning the aid of the city of London.

13. And the city of London shall have all its ancient liberties and free customs, as well by land as by water. Furthermore, we will and grant that all other cities, burghs, towns, and ports, have all their liberties and free customs.

14. And for the holding of the common council of the kingdom to assess aids other than in the three aforesaid cases, and for the assessing of scutages, we will cause the archbishops, bishops, abbots, earls, and greater barons to be summoned individually by our letters; moreover, we will cause all others in general who hold of us *in capite* to be summoned by our sheriffs and bailiffs on a certain day, to wit: forty days at least (before the meeting), and to a certain place; and in all letters of summons, we will declare the cause of the summons. And the summons being thus made, the business shall proceed on the day appointed, according to the advice of those who shall be present, although all that shall be summoned may not come.

15. We will not, for the future, give leave to any one to take an aid from his own free tenants, unless to redeem his own body, to make his eldest son a knight, and once to marry his eldest daughter; and for these none but a reasonable aid shall be paid.

16. No man shall be distrained to do more service for a knight's fee or other free tenement, than what is justly due therefrom.

17. Common pleas shall not follow our court, but shall be holden in some certain place.

18. Trials upon the writs of *novel disseisin*, *mort d'ancestre*, and *darrein presentment*, shall be taken only in their proper counties, and after this manner: We, or, if we shall be out of the realm, our chief justiciary, will send through every county, four times in

the year, two justiciaries, who, with four knights of the county, elected by the county, shall hold the aforesaid assizes in the county, on the county day, and at the county place.

19. And if the aforesaid assizes cannot be held on the county day, let as many of the knights and freeholders, who have been present at the county court, remain behind, as shall be sufficient to conduct the trials, according as the business shall be, more or less.

20. A freeman shall not be amerced for a slight offence, but in proportion to the degree of the offence; and for a great offence he shall be amerced according to its magnitude, saving to him his contenement; likewise, a merchant shall be amerced, saving to him his merchandise; and a villain in the same way, saving his wainage if he falls under our mercy; and none of the aforesaid amerciaments shall be assessed, but by the oath of honest men of the neighborhood.

21. Earls and barons shall not be amerced but by their peers and according to the degree of their offence.

22. No clerk shall be amerced for his lay tenement but in the manner of the others aforesaid, and not according to the quantity of his ecclesiastical benefice.

23. Neither town nor man shall be distrained to build bridges over rivers, save those who anciently and rightfully are bound to do it.

24. No sheriff, constable, coroners, or other our bailiffs shall hold pleas of our crown.

25. All counties, hundreds, trethings, and wapentakes shall stand at their old rents without increase, except in our demense manors.

26. If any one, holding of us a lay fee, dies, and the sheriff or our bailiff shall show our letters patent of summons concerning a debt due to us from the deceased, it shall be lawful for the sheriff or our bailiff to attach and register the chattels of the deceased found upon his lay fee, to the amount of that debt, by the view of lawful men, so that nothing be removed until our whole debt be paid: and the rest shall be paid to the executors to fulfil the will

of the deceased; and if there be nothing due from the deceased to us, the chattels shall remain to the deceased, saving to his wife and children their reasonable shares.

27. If a freeman shall die intestate, his chattels shall be distributed by the hands of his nearest relations and friends, by view of the church, saving to every one the debts which the deceased owed.

28. No constable or other our bailiff shall take the corn or other goods of any man unless he instantly pay money for it, or obtain a respite of payment by the free will of the seller.

29. No constable (of a castle) shall distrain any knight to give money for castle guard, if he be willing to do guard in his own person, or by another able man, if he himself, for reasonable cause, cannot perform it. And if we shall have led or sent him to the army, he shall be excused from castle guard according to the time he shall be in the army by our order.

30. No sheriff nor bailiff of ours, nor any other person, shall take the horses or carts of any freeman, for carriage, without the free consent of the said freeman.

31. Neither we nor our bailiffs, will take another man's timber for our castles or other uses, unless by the consent of the owner of the timber.

32. We will not retain the lands of those who have been convicted of felony, but for one year and a day, and then they shall be delivered to the lord of the fee.

33. All wears shall, for the future, be wholly removed from the Thames and Medway, and throughout all England except on the seacoast.

34. The writ which is called *præcipe* shall not for the future be granted to any one of any tenement whereby a freeman may lose his court.

35. Throughout our whole kingdom there shall be one measure of wine; and one measure of ale; and one measure of corn; namely, the quarter of London; and one width of dyed cloths, and russets,

and halberjects, namely, two ells within the lists. And it shall be with weights as with measures.

36. From henceforth nothing shall be given or taken for the writ of *inquest* of life or limb; but it shall be given without charge and not denied.

37. If any man hold of us by fee-farm, socage, or burgage, and hold land of another by military service, we shall not have the wardship of the heir or of the land which belongs to another man's fee on account of the aforesaid fee-farm, socage, or burgage; nor shall we have the wardship of the free-farm, socage, or burgage, unless the fee-farm owe military service. We shall not have the wardship of any man's heir, or of the land he holds of another on account of any petty serjeantry he holds of us by the service of giving us daggers, arrows, or the like.

38. No bailiff shall henceforth put any man to his law upon his own single accusation without credible witnesses produced for that purpose.

39. No freeman shall be taken, or imprisoned, or dispossessed, or outlawed, or banished, or in any way destroyed; nor will we pass upon him, nor commit him, but by the lawful judgment of his peers, or by the law of the land.

40. To no man will we sell, to none will we delay, to none will we deny right or justice.

41. All merchants shall have safety and security in coming into England and departing out of England, and in tarrying and travelling through England, as well by land as by water, to buy and sell without any evil tolls, according to the ancient and just customs; except in time of war, when they shall be of any nation at war with us. And if any such be found in our land at the beginning of a war, they shall be apprehended without injury of their bodies or their goods, until it shall be known to us or our chief justiciary how the merchants of our country are treated who are found in the country at war with us. And if ours be safe there, the others shall be safe in our land.

42. Henceforth it shall be lawful to any person to go out of our

kingdom and to return safely and securely, by land or by water, saving his allegiance to us, unless for some short space in time of war, for the common good of the kingdom; except prisoners and outlaws by the law of the land, people of a country at war with us, and merchants who shall be treated as aforesaid.

43. If any man hold of any escheat, as of the honor of Wallingford, Nottingham, Boulogne, Lancaster, or any other escheats which are in our hand and are baronies, and shall die, his heir shall not give any other relief, nor do any other service to us, than he would to the baron if the barony were in a baron's hand; and we will hold it in the same way in which the baron held it.

44. Men who dwell without the forest shall not hereafter come before our justiciaries of the forest on a common summons, unless they are parties to a plea or sureties for any who have been apprehended for something concerning the forest.

45. We will not make justiciaries, sheriffs, or bailiffs except of such as know the law of the land, and are disposed duly to observe it.

46. All barons who have founded abbeys which they hold by charter of the kings of England, or by ancient tenure, shall have the custody thereof when they fall vacant, as they ought to have.

47. All forests which have been made in our time shall be immediately disforested; and it shall be so done with the embankments which have been erected as obstructions to the rivers in our reign.

48. All evil customs of forests and warrens, foresters and warreners, sheriffs and their officers, embankments and their keepers, shall forthwith be inquired into in every county by twelve sworn knights of the same county, who must be elected by the good men of the county; and within forty days after the holding of the inquisition they shall, by the said knights, be utterly abolished so as never to be restored; provided that we be first notified thereof, or if we be not in England, our chief justiciary.

49. We will forthwith restore all hostages and charters which

have been delivered to us by the English in security of peace and faithful service.

50. We will remove from their bailiwicks the kinsmen of Gerard de Athyes, so that henceforth they shall have no bailiwick in England; Engelard of Cygony; Andrew, Peter, and Gyone de Chancell; Gyone de Cygony; Geoffrey de Martin and his brothers; Philip Mark and his brothers, and Geoffrey his brother, and all their retinue.

51. And immediately after the conclusion of peace we will remove from the kingdom all foreign knights, crossbowmen, and mercenary soldiers who have come with horses and arms to the injury of the kingdom.

52. If any man hath been by us deprived or dispossessed, without the lawful judgment of his peers, of lands, castles, liberties, or rights, we will forthwith make restitution; and if any dispute arise on this head, then the matter shall be settled by the judgment of five and twenty barons hereinafter mentioned for the preservation of the peace. Concerning all those things of which any man hath been deprived or dispossessed, without the legal judgment of his peers, by King Henry our father, or King Richard our brother, which we hold in our own hand or others hold under our warrant, we shall have respite until the common term of the Crusaders; except those concerning which a plea has been moved, or an inquisition made by our direction, before our taking the cross; but so soon as we shall return from our expedition, or if by chance we should not go upon our expedition, we will forthwith do therein full justice.

53. We shall have like respite, and upon the like conditions, in doing justice by disforesting the forests which Henry our father or Richard our brother afforested, and the same concerning the wardship of lands belonging to another man's fee, of which we have hitherto had wardship on account of some fee held by the tenant from us by military service; and concerning abbeys founded in a fee which is not ours, and in which the lord hath claimed a right; and when we shall have returned, or if we should not go upon our expedition, we shall forthwith do full justice to complainants in these matters.

54. No man shall be taken or imprisoned on the appeal of a woman for the death of any other than her husband.

55. All fines that have been made unjustly and contrary to the law of the land, and all amerciaments imposed unjustly, contrary to the law of the land, shall be wholly remitted; or order shall therein be taken by the five and twenty barons hereinafter mentioned for the security of the peace, or by the verdict of the greater part of them, together with the aforesaid Stephen, archbishop of Canterbury, if he can be present, and such others as he may think fit to bring with him; but if he cannot be present, the business shall nevertheless proceed without him; yet so, that if any one or more of the aforesaid five and twenty barons have a like plea, they shall be removed from that particular trial, and others elected and sworn for that trial only by the residue of the five and twenty shall be substituted in their room.

56. If we have deprived or dispossessed any Welshmen of their lands, or liberties, or other things, without a legal verdict of their peers, restitution shall forthwith be made; and if any dispute shall arise upon this head, then let it be determined in the Marches by the judgment of their peers; for tenements of England, according to the law of England; for tenements of Wales, according to the law of Wales; and for tenements of the Marches, according to the law of the Marches. The Welsh shall do the same to us and to our subjects.

57. Also, concerning those things of which any Welshman hath been deprived or dispossessed without the lawful judgment of his peers, by King Henry our father, or King Richard our brother, and which we hold in our hand or others hold under our warrant, we shall have respite until the common term of the Crusaders, except for those concerning which a plea hath been moved, or an inquisition made by our command before taking the cross. But as soon as we return upon our expedition, or if by chance we should not go upon our expedition, we shall immediately do full justice therein, according to the laws of Wales and of the parts aforesaid.

58. We will forthwith release the son of Llewellyn, and all the

charters and hostages of Wales which were delivered to us for security of the peace.

59. We will do to Alexander, King of Scotland, concerning the restoration of his sisters and hostages, and concerning his liberties, and concerning his rights, according to the form in which we do to our other barons of England, unless it ought otherwise to be according to the charters which we have from William, his father, the late King of Scots; and this shall be by the judgment of his peers in our court.

60. All the aforesaid customs and liberties which we, for our part, have granted to be holden in our kingdom by our people, let all within the kingdom, as well clergy as laity, observe toward their vassals.

61. But forasmuch as we have granted all these things aforesaid to GOD, both for the amendment of our kingdom and for the better settling of the discord which has sprung up between us and our barons; and forasmuch as we desire that these things should remain in perfect and complete stability forever; therefore we do make and grant them the security underwritten, to wit: that the barons may elect twenty-five barons of the kingdom, whom they please, who shall, with their whole power, observe, keep, and cause to be observed, the liberties which we have granted and confirmed to them by this our charter: that is to say, if we or our justiciary, or our bailiffs, or any of our officers, shall have injured any one in anything, or shall have transgressed any article of peace or security, and the injury shall be shown to four of the aforesaid five and twenty barons, the four barons shall come to us, or to our justiciary if we shall be out of the kingdom, and making known to us the wrong committed, shall petition us to cause it to be redressed without delay. And if we, or our justiciary if we be not in the kingdom, do not redress the wrong within the term of forty days, to be reckoned from the time when we were notified thereof, or when our justiciary was notified, if we were not within the kingdom, the aforesaid four barons shall lay the cause before the residue of the five and twenty barons; and they, the five and twenty barons, with the community of the whole land, shall harass

and distress us in whatever ways they shall be able, by the capture of our castles, lands, and possessions, and by any other means they can, until the injury have been redressed according to their judgment: saving harmless our own person and the persons of our queen and children: and when the wrong hath been redressed, they shall behave to us as they have done before. And whoever of our land shall please, may swear that he will obey the commands of the aforesaid five and twenty barons in accomplishing all these aforesaid things, and that, together with them, he will harass us according to his power. And we do publicly and freely grant, to every man who chooses, leave to take this oath, nor will we ever forbid any man to take it. But all men of our land, who, of themselves and of their own choice, shall be unwilling to swear to the five and twenty barons to distress and harass us, together with them, we will compel by our command to swear as is aforesaid. And if any of the five and twenty barons shall die, or leave the country, or in any other way be hindered from the execution of the things aforesaid, then the rest of the aforesaid five and twenty barons shall, at their pleasure, choose another in his stead, who shall be sworn in the same manner as the rest. Now, in all the things which are intrusted to be executed by these five and twenty barons, if it happen that the five and twenty shall be present, and shall disagree concerning any matter; or if some of them, having been summoned, be unwilling or unable to attend, that which the greater part of those who may be present shall determine or decree, shall be held as firm and valid as if all the twenty-five had been agreed therein; and the aforesaid five and twenty men shall swear that they will faithfully observe all the aforesaid things, and to the utmost of their power cause them to be observed. And neither by ourself nor through another will we obtain anything from any man, through which any of these grants and liberties may be revoked or lessened. And if any such thing shall have been obtained, it shall be null and void; and we will never use it, through ourself or through another.

62. And to all men we have fully remitted and pardoned all the ill wills, resentments, and rancors, which have arisen between

us and our subjects, lay and clerical, from the commencement of our disagreement. Moreover, we have fully remitted, and so far as in us lies, have fully pardoned to all the clergy and laity, all transgressions, committed by occasion of the same disagreement, from the Easter of the sixteenth year of our reign to the conclusion of the peace. And further, we have caused testimonial letters patent to be made for them concerning this security and the aforesaid grants from the lord Stephen, archbishop of Canterbury, the lord Henry, archbishop of Dublin, and from Master Pandulph.

63. Wherefore we do will and firmly do command that the Church of England be free; and that all men in our kingdom have and hold all the aforesaid liberties, and rights, and grants, well and in peace, freely and quietly, fully and wholly, as aforesaid, to them and their heirs, from us and our heirs forever. It is also sworn, as well on our part as on that of the barons, that all the things aforesaid shall be observed in good faith and without evil intention. Witnessed by the above and many others. Given by our own hand, in the mead called Runnymede, between Windsor and Staines, this fifteenth day of June, in the seventeenth year of our reign.

Covenant of Security.

Tʜɪs is the covenant made between our lord John, king of England, on the one part, and Robert Fitzwalter, elected marshal of GOD and of the Holy Church in England, and Richard earl of Clare, Geoffrey earl of Essex and Gloucester, Roger Bigod earl of Norfolk and Suffolk, Saher earl of Winchester, Robert earl of Oxford, Henry earl of Hereford, and the barons underwritten: that is to say, William Marshall the younger, Eustace de Vescy, William de Mowbray, John Fitz Robert, Robert de Mont-Begon, William de Lauvalay, and other earls and barons and freemen of the whole kingdom, on the other part: namely, That they, the earls and barons, and others before written, shall hold the custody of the city of London in bail from our lord the king; saving that they shall clearly render all the debts and revenues within the same to our lord the king, until the term of the Assumption of the Blessed Virgin Mary, in the seventeenth year of his reign.

And the lord of Canterbury shall hold, in like manner of bail, from our lord the king, the custody of the tower of London, to the aforesaid term: saving to the city of London its liberties and free customs, and taking his oath, in the keeping of the said tower, that our lord the king shall, in the meanwhile, not place a guard, or other forces, in the aforesaid city, nor in the tower of London.

And that, also, within the aforesaid term, the oaths to the twenty-five barons be tendered throughout all England, as it is tendered in the charter granted concerning the liberties and security of the kingdom, or to the attorneys of the twenty-five barons, as it is contained in the letters granted concerning the election of twelve knights for abolishing evil customs of the forests, and others. And moreover, within the said term, all the other demands which the earls, barons, and other freemen do ask of our lord the king, which he himself has declared to be granted to them, or which by the twenty-five barons, or by the greater part of them, shall be judged proper to be granted, are to be given according to the tenor of the said charter. And if these things shall be done, or if our lord the king, on his part, shall agree to do them within the term limited, then the city and tower of London shall, at the same term, be delivered up to our lord the king; saving always to the aforesaid city its liberties and free customs, as it is before written. And if these things shall not be done, and if our lord the king shall not agree to do them within the period aforesaid, the barons shall hold the aforesaid city, and the lord archbishop the tower of London, until the aforesaid deed shall be completed. And in the meanwhile, all of both parts shall recover the castles, lands, and towns which have been taken in the beginning of the war that has arisen between our lord the king and the barons.

NOTES ON THE GREAT CHARTER.

Introduction.—The four causes for granting Magna Charta are the prominent parts of the opening: the honor of God, the benefit of the king's soul—as a pious action—the exaltation of the church, and the amendment of the kingdom. The last expression to be observed is, that the words *spontaneously and of our own free will*, were added in the subsequent charter of Henry III. because King John endeavored to avoid the execution of his grant, asserting that it had been extorted from him by force.

Ch. I.—The expression to *grant unto God*, with which this section commences, was an ancient legal phrase, employed when anything was bestowed for the use and maintainance of the church; since the thing so given was supposed to be granted to God, as it was for his service. King John was the first sovereign who used the plural pronoun We in his grants, as all the preceding monarchs wrote in the first person singular.

Ch. II.—This section of the Great Charter refers to an ancient law connected with feudal tenures, by which it was supposed that the lord of the estate was the real proprietor of all: though the tenant, while he was able to do service for the land, held it in possession and enjoyed its products. The grants issued by the superior lord lasted for life only; and, upon the decease of a tenant, if his heir were not of an age sufficient to discharge all the services belonging to that fee, or estate, it still remained in the possession of the chief lord until he should be able to do so; for, it must be observed, that these services were, for the most part, doing duty in the field.

The most ancient relief is called a heriot, from the Saxon *here-geat*, which literally signifies armor and weapons. "A tribute," says Somner, in his 'Dictionarium Saxonico-Latino-Anglicum,' "of old given to the Lord of a manor, for his better preparation towards warre. We now call it a Heriot, and understand by it, the best horse, ox, cow, or such like chattell, which the Tenant hath at the houre of his death, due to the Lord by custome." It was probably from this circumstance, then, that the original reliefs were ordained to be paid in armor: and by the laws of King William the First, the relief of an Earl was eight horses saddled and bridled, four helmets, four coats of mail, four shields, four spears. four swords, four chasors, or hunting horses, and one palfrey bridled and saddled. A baron was to give half as much with the palfrey. A vavasor, the next degree to a peer, was to present his lord with his best horse, his helmet, coat of mail, shield, spear, and sword, or instead of these one hundred shillings. A countryman's relief was his best beast, and he who farmed his lands gave a year's rent. Thus there was originally a scale of settled sums for the lands of the different degrees, from the highest downward; but previous to John's reign, especially in those of King William Rufus and Henry II. reliefs became arbitrary, and often, under the title of a reasonable relief, considerable oppressions were imposed. The sums mentioned in the text would be about twenty times their value in modern currency; ten times in allowing for the difference of coin, and ten more in the quantity and worth of the article to be procured. The ancient relief, however, to which the present chapter of Magna Charta alludes, was the giving up the fourth part of the value of an earldom, a barony, or a knight's fee for one year.

Ch. III.—The intent of this chapter is to preserve the old statute of the common law regarding military service, by which it is provided that the lord of an estate cannot both have guardianship of the heir and his land, and also a relief when he shall come of age to do knight's or warlike service for it. For this cause, then, if a person held lands of the king in chief, and different lands under some other lord, both by military duty; the king by his prerogative had the wardship of all, and, upon the heir's coming of age, a relief was paid to the other by way of recompense.

Ch. IV.—The intent of this and the following chapter of the great charter, was to prevent the sovereign from placing rich estates of heirs under age in the custody of mercenary men, who might exact heavier rents and services than the land had ever before been rated at; or who could destroy or neglect any of the property so committed to them.

Guardians of estates held by military service were, as Lyttleton observes, of two kinds: a guardian in *right*, which was when the superior lord upon the decease of his tenant became, in virtue of his title, the possessor of the heir and his lands; and a guardian in *fact*, which is where the superior lord, after having made his claim, grants the wardship to another, who comes into possession by the force of that grant. This latter species of guardian is that mentioned in the text.

Issues, or as the original word may be better translated, outgoings, signify the rents and profits issuing from the lands or tenements of the ward, which are to be taken by the guardian in a reasonable manner, according to what is allowed by law. *Customs* are privileges due or appendant to the lands of the ward, such as advowsons or presentations to ecclesiastical livings, commons, waifs and strays, tenant fines, &c. *Services* were those duties accruing to the lord from his copyhold tenants, which were of the nature of feudal services, being annual and accidental, as well as comprising homage and fealty. The reasonableness of these various provisions was to be decided by the king's justices.

With regard to the saving clause in this chapter, concerning the destruction and waste of the men or goods, it will be proper to explain it, as it concerns the legal signification of those terms. *Waste* is committed in neglecting to repair houses, in damage done to gardens, and in the cutting down of timber trees. *Destruction* of goods is cutting down of young timber plants, and any other kind of trees set for the defence of the house. Exile, or destruction of men, is when by any oppression they are reduced to poverty, and forced to quit their dwellings upon the estate. It should be observed that the fair profits of the land were claimed by the lord of an heir under age, that out of them he might provide some person to supply his defect of service until he should be able to act for himself. (*Wright.*)

CH. V.—The laws enforced by this chapter of Magna Charta are similar to the agreement of repair which exists between a landlord and tenant for years, as may be seen by a reference to Sir Edward Coke's *Commentary upon Littleton*, Book I., chap. vii., sec. 67.

CH. VI.—The tenure of military service was connected with the right of a superior lord to bestow his tenants in marriage; or at least his consent was required before any union could take place with one of his followers, and the reason for this was certainly a fair one; because, according to the principles of feudal tenures, it was proper to prevent any person who enjoyed a part of the land from bringing into the joint possession of it either an enemy of the superior lord, or one of a family at enmity with him. If therefore a military tenant married without his lord's consent, his fee was forfeited.

A female heir might be given in marriage by her father at the age of twelve, but fourteen was called her age of discretion, or time when she might consent or disagree to marriage under a feudal lord; but if her ancestor died before she had reached the age of fourteen or was married, then she was to remain in ward until the age of sixteen, in which two years it was supposed that her lord might tender to her a suitable marriage. This if he neglected to do, at the end of the two years she could enter on possession of her estate. If, on the contrary, she were married under the age of fourteen, in the life of her progenitor, and was also under that age at his death, then the lord was to have wardship of her until she attained to it, when her husband and she were immediately to enter on possession of her lands. The age of discretion for a male heir was fourteen, at which time he might consent or disagree to any marriage his lord had formerly provided for him; and the old law was such that if he did then disagree to such marriage, although his lands remained in wardship until he should come to the full age of twenty-one, yet he was free from ward as to his body, and his lord had no right to marry him a second time.

One who gave his daughter in marriage without the consent of his lord, forfeited his inheritance.

During the time, however, that these laws existed, the present chapter of Magna Charta was intended as an ancient institute of the common law, and was doubtless inserted as a provision against mercenary or interested guardians involving their wards in any improper connection, by way of securing the estates for themselves. There were many kinds of disparagements; but for any of these four principal ones, the heir, if married before the age of fourteen, when he arrived at that age might disagree to the match, and it should then be dissolved by law: firstly, the marriage might be refused, if the party provided were an idiot or lunatic; secondly, if they were of an inferior degree, one of attainted blood, or illegitimate; thirdly, if they were imperfect in person, or deformed; and fourthly, if the bride were a widow, because that was considered as bigamy, and precluded benefit of clergy. The latter, however, was provided against in 1541, the first year of Edward VI., cap xii. § 16, by an act entitled "An Act for the repeal of certain statutes concerning treasons, felonies, &c.," in which it was declared that benefit of clergy should be allowed to any persons, notwithstanding their marriage with widows.

Chs. VII., VIII.—Before the Norman conquest, a widow had no power to marry again until one year should have expired after the death of her husband.

The word *maritagium*, as it occurs in the original text, is a technical expression signifying liberty to marry again, whereby the year of mourning was set aside, so far as the law was concerned. The whole of this and the succeeding chapter relates to the general right of widows, as they regarded the feudal system; for as females at that period possessed no personal fortune to entitle them to a jointure, so the immediate provision of dower for their maintenance was of the greatest importance. The widow, however, might remain in her late husband's dwelling (if it were not a castle) for forty days, which time was called her quarantine, and which began on the day of his death, and continued to thirty-nine days after; if during that time she married, her widowhood was then past, and she forfeited her dower.

With respect to the quantity of the dower, when granted, it was generally the third part of the deceased's possessions, and thence called *dos legitima*, or lawful dower.

Ch. IX.—This is the first act of grace contained in the great charter; for by the common law, the king had execution of the body, lands, and goods of the debtor, and he might also, by his prerogative, distrain for his rent in any other lands which his tenant possessed, although they were not of his own fee. A similar process was likewise used by many of the barons, and this was afterward carried to such an extent that they levied their distresses in the common streets and highways.

Ch. X.—By the laws of King Edward the Confessor, and the testimony of Glenville and others, it was anciently not lawful for Christians to take any sort of usury, so that interest for money was paid to the Jews alone, and to them only while the ancestor was living, or after his successor came to full age.

Ch. XI.—The expression in the text, *saving the rights of the lords*, is a provision that all their lawful customs and services are not barred by this protection of a tenant's property; and it infers that if they be neglected or denied, the lord of the fee might distrain for wardship, relief, or marriage.

Ch. XII.—This chapter is to be found in its fullest extent in the great charter of King John only; and its subject is the levying of scutage, a tax anciently paid by such as held lands by knight's service, toward furnishing the royal army, at the rate of one, two, or three marks for every knight's fee. It was originally derived of the Saxon words *scyld* and *penig*, the shield-penny; whence it was translated into the Norman French *escuage*, and the law Latin expression of *scutagium*, or service of the shield: this, says Lord Coke, "was in respect of the *scutum*, or shield, which ought to be borne both by lord and tenant in such wars."

The kings of England, therefore, anciently taking advantage of, or probably complying with this custom of their tenants, and sometimes on occasion of war, assessed without summons a moderate sum upon every knight's fee, as an escuage, wherewith they might provide foreign stipendiaries to supply their defect of service. But as this species of escuage was really a previous commutation between a tenant and his lord, and not incurred as a fine, it was not long acceded to; and in the reign of King John it was not only insisted upon as an undoubted right of the king's tenants, but the barons procured the insertion of the present chapter of Magna Charta, that it should be imposed only by the common council of the kingdom.

The amount of escuage assessed upon any estate was, of course, according to the extent of it; this being estimated sometimes by the number of knight's fees it contained, and at others by the value of the land.

This chapter in King John's charter also provides for another privilege claimed by the superior lords under the feudal system, namely the assessing of aids for defraying some of their own private charges. Strictly speaking, however, aids were not at first a direct feudal obligation, but were originally sums of money obtained from the tenants, out of a regard to the person and claims of the lord. In their most ancient state, too, both the amount and nature of aids were as uncertain as the occasions which arose to demand them and the property of the tenant could furnish; but in the course of years they became established renders of duty, of which the three events mentioned in the text gave, in Normandy, the most general opportunities for claiming. These soon became fixed and established, to the exclusion of certain other unreasonable demands made by the inferior lords of fees, which passed also under the title of aids; as an assessment upon the tenants, to enable a lord to discharge his debts; and one termed aide de relief, to furnish the sum required by the law of reliefs already treated of. In the reign of King Henry II. also, it was doubted whether the lords might not require aids toward the perfecting of their military preparations; but all these illegal aids were abolished by the present chapter of King John's great charter. At the same time, three certain aids were permitted to be taken, as well by the king as by his barons: see chap. xv., to which also this note will be a sufficient commentary. They were ordained, however, to be taken in a lawful manner, and were, firstly, *for redeeming the king's or a lord's body*, that is to say, whenever he became a prisoner of war; secondly, *for making his eldest son a knight*; and thirdly, *for once marry-*

ing his eldest daughter. For the first of these causes the aid was less frequent and more uncertain than any of the others; but at the same time it was of the highest consequence that he should be ransomed at any rate, so often as he might be made a prisoner of war. Sir William Blackstone, in his *Commentaries*, Book II., chap. 5, page 63, observes that as this species of aid was a natural consequence of feudal attachment and fidelity, the omission of it, whenever it was in the tenant's power, was, by the rigor of the feudal law, the absolute forfeiture of his estate. The second species of aid was for *making the lord's eldest son a knight*, "a matter," says the same authority, "that was formerly attended with great ceremony, pomp, and expense." The intent of this was to bring up the heir of the lordship to arms and chivalry, for the better defence of the nation, and the assessment could not be made until the young chief had attained the age of fifteen, or at least was capable of bearing arms; but anciently, Sir Edward Coke observes, the lords would pretend that their eldest sons were hopeful and forward, as in their abilities and stature, and they would thence demand an aid larger than was due from their tenants, and also before the proper time. The same grievance was likewise imposed, with respect to the third kind of aid mentioned in the text, that of *once marrying the lord's eldest daughter;* "by giving her," says Blackstone, "a suitable portion, for daughters' portions in those days were extremely slender, few lords being able to save much out of their income for this purpose; nor could they acquire money by other means, being wholly conversant in matters of arms; nor, by the law of their tenure, could they charge their lands with this or any other encumbrances."

CH. XIII.—The present chapter of Magna Charta specifies two kinds of franchises, namely, *its ancient liberties* and *its free customs;* the first of which signify a royal privilege or branch of the king's prerogative, held by grant or prescription, and existing in the hands of his subjects, by which he or they enjoy privileges not common to ordinary persons. Free customs are liberties enjoyed by custom or usage, which, in its legal sense, signifies a law not written, but established by long use and the consent of ancestry.

CH. XIV.—The first members of the English council, down to the time of King Henry III., were those persons only who held of the king in chief, and who are ordained to be summoned by the present chapter of Magna Charta; and they are designated in the more ancient histories and works on law by several names importing superior rank, as barons of the kingdom, the greater barons, &c., and the assembly which they formed is called the Great Council or King's Court, the word Parliament not coming into use until the latter part of the reign of King Henry III. Baron Maseres supposes in his paper that this council met at the least thrice in the year, at the feasts of Christmas, Easter and Whitsuntide, which meetings being in the ordinary course, required no issue of summons, though there were occasionally others called for a special purpose, when the king issued his command for the council to come together. The occupations, however, were the same in each, as debates concerning war and peace, the granting of aids to the king, the regulation of the laws, and the trial of great causes between the barons. The king however, at this period, had not the power of omitting to call a baron to the Great Council, nor of summoning any person who was not a tenant in chief.

The tenants in chief, according to Domesday, amounted to about seven hundred persons; but their baronies being very unequal in extent, and being in the course of years repeatedly divided and subdivided, especially by partitions with female heirs, they were diminished in quantity, while the number of tenants in chief was considerably increased. There are instances, says Baron Maseres, of persons holding the hundredth, and even the three hundredth part of a barony; yet all these had a title to a seat in Parliament, and hence arose the distinction between the greater and lesser barons. A difference between these is noted in the present chapter of Magna Charta; for the king was therein bound to summon the former to Parliament *individually* by his letters, but the latter were to be summoned in general by his sheriffs or bailiffs.

CH. XVI.—This statute was intended to relieve such as had no remedy by the common law; and it was a restoration of the ancient law of England. It is usually stated that the writ, entitled from its commencing words, "Ne injuste vexes," was originally grounded upon this act. Sir William Blackstone, however, adopts the general belief following the "New Natura Brevium" of Fitzherbert; and explains that the writ is available where a tenant, who has held of a lord by certain services, has inadvertently given his lord possession of more and of greater.

The Court of Common Pleas, which this chapter made permanent in its situation, is one of the king's courts now constantly held in Westminster Hall; but in ancient time it was movable at the king's will, according to the place of the royal residence: whereupon, says Lord Coke, "many discontinuances ensued, and great trouble of jurors, charges of parties, and delay of justice; for these causes this statute was made." Sir William Blackstone states that, in the Saxon Constitution, there was only one superior court of justice in the kingdom, namely the General Council, of which some account has been already given. After the Norman invasion, the ecclesiastical jurisdiction was separated from the civil; and King William soon after effected another separation, of the judicial and parliamentary power vested in the remaining members. On this account he established a constant court in his own residence, entitled "Aula Regis," or the King's Hall, which was composed of the great officers of state. Of these, the Lord Marshal generally presided in matters relating to honor and arms, and the military and national laws; the Lord Chancellor kept the royal seal, and had cognizance of all letters, writs and grants, to which it was affixed; the Lord Treasurer was the chief authority in affairs of the revenue; and certain persons who had carefully studied the laws, called the king's justices, all of whom were assisted by the greater barons of the realm, formed a court to be consulted in cases of appeal or difficulty. Over this assembly presided an officer of great rank and power, who was denominated the Chief Justiciary of all England. He was esteemed the second person in the kingdom, of which, by virtue of his office, he was guardian in the king's absence; and it was he who principally determined the vast variety of causes that were brought before this court. As such an establishment was bound to follow the king's household to whatsoever place it might remove, the trial of common causes became so difficult to the people, that its permanence formed one of the petitions of the barons in the preliminary articles of the great charter; and it was in consequence settled in Westminster Hall, the place where the ancient kings of England were accustomed to reside, in which it has in general ever since continued. At the same time were appointed justices of the common pleas, having a chief whose jurisdiction was to hear and determine all pleas of land and injuries between subject and subject.

Trials for *novel disseisin*, for which this statute first provides, were inquisitions for the recovery of lands or tenements of which any party had been disseized or dispossessed; and the term *novel*, or new, was applied, because the justices who travelled went their circuits only from seven years to seven years; and no assize was allowed before them which had commenced previously to the last circuit, as such was called an ancient assize; while that which was concerning a later dispossession, was termed an "assize of novel disseisin." A trial of "*mort d'ancestre*" was an inquiry after the death of any ancestor or relative who was possessed of lands, &c., as estates which subsequently to their decease were abated —broken down or destroyed—by a stranger; but the writ for this trial must be brought within fifty years, or the right may be lost by the neglect. The term ancestor is here considered to stop at the father in the ascending line, and the writ assumes a new name for the more ancient relations. It should be observed that both this writ and the former are now nearly obsolete, being almost superseded by the action of ejectment, excepting in some very peculiar cases. A trial or assize of *darrien presentment* takes place when a person, or his ancestors under whom he claims, have presented a clerk to a benefice, and upon the next vacancy a stranger presents, disturbing him who is the real patron. In such a case, the true patron shall have a writ of last presentation directed to the sheriff, to summon an assize or jury, to inquire who was the last patron that presented to the vacant church; and according as the cause is decided, a writ is issued to the bishop to institute that clerk in favor of whose patron it is determined. Assizes of this nature were formerly conclusive, but they are now wholly disused, in consequence of a statute of the 7th of Anne, 1708, cap. xviii., by which a person has a right to recover if his title be good, notwithstanding the writ of last presentation. Previously to the making of this charter, all the above writs were required to be brought before the king or his justiciary, wherever they might happen to be; but the present chapter tended considerably to relieve the jurors and parties in the plea, both in time and in expense, since by it justice was ordained to be administered to them in their own counties, without their following the king's court, or that of the common pleas, to a distant place.

CH. XXI., XXII.—The term "amerciament" is derived of the French *a merci*, and signifies the pecuniary mulct laid upon an individual who has offended, and therefore lies *at the mercy* of the king. Amerciaments, properly so called, are penalties assessed by the peers or equals of the offending party; and they are considered as more merciful than fines, because, if they are too heavy, a release may be sued by an ancient writ founded upon Magna Charta.

The next species of amerciament mentioned in the text, is that to be assessed on a merchant, and this was to be done, *saving his merchandise*, upon the same principle as before; "for trade and traffic," says Lord Coke, "are the livelihood of the merchant and the life of the commonwealth."

Of villains in England under the feudal system, there were two kinds: the first were called villains in gross, and were such as belonged to the person of a lord and his heirs; and the second were those who belonged to a manor, and appertained to the lord thereof only while he held it. These were termed villains regardant. But though the condition of a pure villain was such, that his lord was entitled to impose upon him those aids and taillages already treated of, and even to dispossess him of all his property, yet the great charter has, with great humanity, a clause in its favor which states that he shall *be amerced with safety to his wainage.* This word is derived from the Saxon *wagna*, which signifies a cart or wagon; and the most liberal meaning of the passage is, that tillage and husbandry shall not be hindered by levying a distress or amerciament.

CH. XXIII.—The original intent of this statute was to avoid the repetition of those fictitious exactions which, during the reigns of Richard I. and John, were made in the king's name for making of bridges, banks, fortrésses, and bulwarks, contrary to law.

CH. XXIV.—Pleas of the crown, which it is the object of this chapter to preserve, are those suits which the king commences against all crimes and misdemeanors; "because," says Sir William Blackstone, "in him centres the majesty of the whole community, and he is supposed by the law to be the person injured by every infraction of the public rights belonging to that community, and is therefore in all cases the proper prosecutor for every public offence." The persons, then, by whom these pleas could not be held, comprise all classes of the royal officers, although four degrees only are mentioned in the text. Sheriffs were the chief officers under the king in every county, deriving their title from the two Saxon words *shire* and *reve*, the bailiff or steward of the division. They are called, however, in the Latin text of the great charter, *vicecomes*, which signifies, in place of the earl of the county, who anciently governed it under the king. The next officer mentioned in this chapter of Magna Charta, is called *constabularius*, or *constable*, which is sometimes derived from the Saxon; but other authorities have conceived it, more truly, to come from the Latin *comes stabuli*, a superintendent of the imperial stables, or master of the horse. This title, however, began, in the course of time, to signify a commander, in which sense it was introduced into England. In the present instance, the word is put for the constable, or keeper of a castle, frequently called a castellan, of whose dignity mention will be made in a future note. They were possessed of such considerable power within their own precincts, that previously to the present act they held trials of crimes, properly the cognizance of the crown, as the sheriffs did within their respective bailiwicks, and sealed with their own effigies on horseback.

As prisons were considered to be an important part of all ancient castles, these officers are sometimes called constables of fees, which signifies those who were paid for keeping of prisons. In this part of their duty they appear often to have been guilty of great cruelty.

The title of *coroner* implies that he was an officer of the crown, to whom, in certain cases, pleas of the crown, in which the king is more immediately concerned, are properly belonging; and in this sense the lord chief justice of the king's bench is the principal coroner of the kingdom. Previously to the statute of Magna Charta a coroner might not only receive accusations against offenders, but might try them.

Ch. XXV.—From the time of the Norman invasion downward, the cities and towns of England were vested either in the crown, the clergy, or the barons; that is to say, persons of one of these classes were the immediate lords of towns, &c. Those which appertained to the king were of several kinds; for he possessed some by the original inheritance of his crown, which were termed *ancient demesne;* and others became his by way of escheat, want of heirs, attainder, or forfeiture.

From the reign of William I. also, the king was accustomed to let out the several counties of the realm at a farm or rent, concerted between the crown and the holder, or else they were committed to custody, the nature of which is shown in the note on Chapter IV.

When a county was let out at a greater farm than it had been formerly rated at, the advance money was usually termed *crementum*, the increase, &c.

The word *county*, in Latin *comitatus*, is derived from *comes*, the earl, a principal governor of it, to whom the sheriff was anciently a deputy; the term *hundred* is supposed to have been introduced by King Alfred, and to signify a division of country containing ten towns, each of which consisted of ten families of freeholders; a *trething*, or *trithing*, amounted to a third part of a county; and a *wapentake*, which is equivalent to a hundred, was so called because the governor of the district, when he first entered on his office, appeared in the field on horseback holding a lance, which all the chief men of the hundred touched with a similar weapon, thereby evincing their unanimity. (*Blackstone*, *Jacob.*)

Ch. XXVI., XXVII.—The ancient common law respecting wills was, in general, peculiarly compulsory; for in the time of Henry II. a person's goods were to be divided into three parts, of which one went to his wife, another to his heirs, and a third he was at liberty to dispose of. If he were childless, his widow claimed half; and if he were a widower with children, they also claimed an equal portion; and these were termed their reasonable shares, as the expression is used in the text of Magna Charta.

It was also an ancient custom for the clergy to claim a gift on the decease of any of their parishioners, called a mortuary, which was intended as a species of amends to the ecclesiastics for personal tythes, or other duties, which the deceased had forgotten or omitted to pay. The mortuary consisted of the second best chattel remaining, after the lord had taken out his heriot.

Such were the chief points required in the ancient English testaments; and if a person died without making any disposition of that part of his property which he might bequeath, the king, as the general trustee of the kingdom, and father of the country, was empowered to seize upon it. In process of time this branch of the prerogative was given to the church, which was done because spiritual men were supposed to have a better knowledge of what would conduce to the benefit of the soul of the deceased.

As these ecclesiastics, however, were not accountable to any one for the faithful discharge of their trust, they too frequently abused it; and it appears that, so late as about 1250, the clergy took the whole residue of the deceased's estate after the widow's and children's two thirds had been deducted, without even paying his lawful debts; for which reason, in 1284, it was enacted that the ordinary should be bound to pay the debts of the intestate so far as the goods would extend.

The intention of the *inventory* mentioned in this chapter, was not less to prevent the executor from concealing any part of the property of the deceased, than to secure the payment of the king's debts.

The following chapter (XXVII.) relates to such persons only as die intestate: who, according to Matthew Paris, were anciently considered as eternally condemned, because by the canon they were obliged to leave a tenth of their property to pious uses for the redemption of their souls; which he who did not, regarded not his own salvation. There was also no distinction made between one who died without a will, and a suicide; for the goods of the former were forfeited to the chief-lord, and of the latter to the king. As, however, sudden deaths might frequently cause intestates, the bishops, in the course of time, received power to make such a distribution from the goods of the deceased as he himself was bound to do, under the term of *Eleemosyna rationabilia.*

Chs. XXVIII., XXIX., XXX., XXXI.—The four chapters which are next to be considered have one principal aim, the regulation of purveyance, and the duties to be taken for the maintenance of castles. They were intended to remedy the heavy oppressions inflicted by the governors of castles upon the surrounding tenants, and even on the military, as well in peace as in war. Some notice of the evil practice of these castellans has already been given; but previously to entering upon a particular illustration of the text in this place, it will be proper to give some notice of the nature of purveyance in general. The term itself is derived of the French *pourvoir*—to provide—and its legal acceptation was a providing for the king's household by his officers, who exercised his prerogative of buying provisions, &c., at a certain rate, to the preference of all others, and even without the owner's consent. It embraced also the power of impressing the horses and carriages of the subject to execute the king's business on the public roads, in the conveyance of timber, baggage, &c., however inconvenient to the proprietor, upon paying him a settled price.

Lord Coke, in commenting on the first of these chapters, says, that the constable of a castle had no right to make purveyance at all; though the fortress were to be kept for the defence of the realm, as it might be taken for the houses of the king and queen only. "Constables," says the author of the Mirror, "should defend the rights of all persons around them; for there is no difference between taking ill care of them, and robbery—the which is this seizing of their horses, provisions, merchandise, carriages, lodging, or any kind of their goods."

Castle-guard was an essential part of knight's service, but it did not extend to the fortress of any other than the peculiar lord, nor even to that if it were alienated; and the part to be watched, as a door, tower, bridge, or sconce, was to be specified in the tenure. The duty of watching, however, might be discharged either by the tenant or his deputy; but though there was not any certain term ordained by law for the performance or duration of it, the tenant was to receive, says Littleton, *Lib.* II., ch. iv., sect. 3, a reasonable notice, when his lord hears that the enemies will come, or come into England; and Lord Coke adds, that he was not bound to attend until such notice was given. If any damage happened to the fortress from careless keeping, the lord was entitled to distrain for it, and recover satisfaction from his tenant.

The wood is protected on the ground, that being part of the subject's inheritance, it could therefore no more be taken than the inheritance itself.

Ch. XXXII.—The prerogative mentioned in this division of Magna Charta, that the sovereign should hold the lands of a felon for a year and a day, exists also in the French and Danish laws. The ancient custom was that in detestation of the crime committed, the felon's property, if it were held of a subject, was to be destroyed—as the houses to be thrown down, the gardens extirpated, the woods eradicated, and the meadow-land ploughed up—this was termed waste, and of right belonged to the king as part of the felon's forfeiture; but for the common benefit the lords of estates were afterward contented to resign such lands to be retained by the king for a year and a day, in consequence of which, waste was omitted in this chapter of Magna Charta, and no waste was to be made after they returned to the lord of the fee. The word *felony* in this chapter signifies that kind which is punished by death, though nearly all felonies carry with them forfeiture of estates, and thus Sir William Blackstone supposed the word to have been derived of the Teutonic terms *fel*, an estate, and *lon*, the price or value—that is to say, the consideration for which the land has been resigned.

Ch. XXXIII.—The intent of this brief fragment of the old common law was to prevent any persons from appropriating to themselves a fishery of any part of the river Thames which was common property.

Wears are large dams made across rivers for the taking of fish, or the conveyance of water to a mill; and the peculiar kind mentioned in the text, called Kydells, were dams having a loop or narrow cut in them, and furnished with wheels and engines for catching of fish. They are now called kettles, or kettle nets, and are still in use on the sea coasts of Kent and Cornwall.

Ch. XXXIV.—The writ mentioned in the text is of that class properly termed writs of right, its ancient name of *Præcipe in Capite*, being derived from the first words of the instrument.

The chief intent of the present chapter appears to be to prevent any false transfer of property under color of this writ, from one lord to another, by which the former lost both his fee and his tenant's services. The writ of right should be first brought into the court baron of the lord of whom the lands are held, but if he do not hold any, or have waived his right, then it might be brought into the king's. As in this instance also it was sometimes falsely pretended that a lord had waived his right, the present chapter of Magna Charta restrains any improper use of the writ Præcipe, by which a lord might be dispossessed of his right of court of jurisdiction over his tenants.

Ch. XXXV.—Two peculiar kinds of cloth are mentioned in this division of Magna Charta: halberjects, or haubergets, and russets. The first was a kind of very coarse and thick mixed English cloth, of various colors, sometimes used for the habits of monks; and its name was probably derived from the German words *al*, all, or *haltz*, or *hals*, the neck, and *bergen*, to cover. Russets were also a monastic dress, made of an inferior cloth, sometimes spun by rustics, and dyed by them of a dull reddish hue, with bark. John de Neville, in the year 1386, ordered by his will that his coffin should be attended by twenty-three paupers in russet cloaks, bearing torches, and carried by as many more in cloth of russet wool, bearing a red cross. The name of this material is doubtless derived of the Latin *russus*, a kind of red.

Ch. XXXVI.—The intent of this short but important chapter, was to prevent the long imprisonment of a person charged with a crime, without examining his guilt or innocence. "For the intent of imprisoning such," says Lord Coke, "is only for their security, that they may be duly tried." There is a striking similarity between this division of the great charter, and the act of habeas corpus, of which it may, in some measure, be considered as the ancient prototype; for the purpose of each was to bring an accused person to trial without an extended confinement. The writ of inquisition or inquiry mentioned in the text, was denominated *Odio et Aciâ* of hatred and malice, and was anciently called *Breve de bone et Malo*—the writ concerning good and evil, from those words appearing in it; and it was assigned by the common law to any imprisoned person, to prevent his remaining in prison until the arrival of the justices in Eyre, when he should be tried. "The former was available," says Lord Coke, "for the most odious cause, even for the death of a man, which, without the king's writ, could not be bailed; but in that instance a writ of inquisition was issued to the sheriff of the county, that he should assume the holding of a court of pleas of the crown, and, in full county, by the oath of true and lawful men, inquire whether the accused person were guilty of hatred and malice; unless he had been previously indicted or called before the justices in Eyre, because then his accusation became matter of record, against which this writ could not stand, being grounded on a surmise. The latter writ mentioned above, was issued when any person was committed to prison for the death of a man, and was addressed to the justices of jail delivery. It set forth that "if N, taken and detained in prison for the death of M, be willing to place himself upon his country for good and evil, and for this occasion, and for no other, is detained in the same, and not by any special mandate of ours, then let N be delivered from the prison aforesaid, according to the laws and customs of England." Without this writ the justices of jail-delivery would not, anciently, proceed to trial. This statute was altered and amended by three others, passed in the reign of Edward I.; and in 1354, the 28th of Edward III., chapter ix., the writ *de Odio et Aciâ* was taken away, because the sheriffs of counties made inquests for the indicting of the people, and then took fines and ransoms for their delivery, without ever bringing them before the king's justices. Lord Coke, however, observes that it was enacted in 1237 that all statutes contrary to Magna Charta should be void, on which account the writs still remained. "And therefore," adds he, "the king's justices in general have not suffered the prisoner to remain long in prison, but have speedily brought him to trial at their next coming." This practice is also commanded and described in the statute of Gloucester, 6th Edward I.

Ch. XXXVII.—There are five different species of tenures mentioned in this division of the great charter, one of which—military tenure—has already been sufficiently described. Concerning the remaining four, it will be proper to give some explanation, previously to considering the intent of the statute itself.

Fee farm is when the lord of an estate, on creation of a tenancy, reserves to himself either the rent for which it was before let, or was reasonably worth, or at least a fourth part of the value, without any extraordinary services.

The term *socage* is derived by some from the old French word *soc*, a ploughshare, and signifies a portion of lands held by tenure of certain inferior offices in husbandry, or any conventional services that were not military. It was anciently the most popular English tenure, and was of so wide an extent, that Littleton states that all the tenures which were not held by knights' service, were held by socage.

Tenure by *burgage* bears a very close resemblance to socage, and it is defined to be where the king or any other person is lord of an ancient borough, in which tenements are held by a rent certain; whence it has been called a species of *town socage*, as common socage is generally rural.

Petit or *petty serjeantry* consisted, according to Littleton, in holding lands of the king by the service of giving him some small weapon of war, as a bow, a sword, a lance, an arrow, &c., as it is stated in the text of Magna Charta; and hence, as it was the payment of a certain rent, it has also been considered as a species of socage.

The intent of the present chapter of the great charter, was to prevent the king from claiming, by virtue of the tenure of petty serjeantry, which could be held of him only, the profit attached to the wardship of the heir, and his lands. The famous statute of the 12th of Charles II., rendered this portion of the *great charter* obsolete, by taking away wardship and most of the feudal tenures; although the honorary services belonging to grand serjeantry were not wholly abolished by it.—*Coke—Blackstone—Statutes at Large.*

Ch. XXXVIII.—The expression used in the 38th chapter, *to be put to his law*, is equivalent to putting a person upon his oath, which is the medium furnished him by the law, of proving himself innocent of any charge. The trials which were anciently used by the Saxons were by wager of law, by ordeal, and by jury; of which the first and third properly belong to the present chapters, the trial by ordeal being referable to the 54th division of the great charter.

The *wager of law* received its name from the similarity it bore to that proof which is called the *wager of battle;* for as in the latter instance the defendant gave a pledge or gage to try the cause by combat, so in the former he put in sureties, or *vadios*, that at a certain day he would take the benefit which the law had provided him.

The expression wager is derived either from the old French *gager*, to pledge, or from the German *waegen*, to attempt anything dangerous. Before, however, the wager of law could be demanded of the defendant, the accuser was obliged, beyond his own declaration, to produce his *secta*, suit, followers, or witnesses, whose testimony was to be consistent, and by whom a probable case was to be made out.

When the charge was complete, and the defendant had given security to make his law, he came into court with eleven of his neighbors, and, standing at the end of the bar, was asked by the secondary whether he would wage his law, and admonished by the judges of the danger of a false oath. If he persisted, an oath similar to the following form was administered to him: "Hear this, ye justices! That I do not owe to ——— the sum of ——, nor any penny thereof, in manner and form as the said ——— hath declared against me, so help me God!" The defendant's eleven neighbors or compurgators then avowed, upon their oaths, that they believed in their consciences that he had spoken the truth; thus, whilst he was sworn to faithfulness, they were sworn to declare as faithful a belief. Previously to these oaths being administered, the plaintiff was thrice called into court; if he did not appear, he was nonsuited, though he might bring a new action; but if he appeared, and the defendant, &c., made the oaths, his claim was barred forever, the wager of law being equal to a verdict against him. This species of trial was never permitted but in cases where the defendant bore a fair and irreproachable character; and it is supposed to have had its original in the Mosaical law mentioned in Exodus xxii. v. 10, 11. It is also to be traced in the legal codes of most of the northern nations; and its intent was, that an innocent man of good credit might find a remedy when he was overborne by a multitude of false witnesses.

Ch. XXXIX.—Sir Edward Coke, in commenting upon this chapter, shows that the evils from which the law of the land are to protect any person, are recited in the order in which they most affect him; as, firstly, loss of liberty—"no free man shall be taken or imprisoned;" because the freedom of a man's person is more precious to him than all the succeeding particulars; and the word "taken," which occurs in this clause, signifies being restrained of liberty by petition or suggestion to the king or his council.

Secondly, the chapter declares, that none "shall be disseized of his free tenement, his liberties, or his free customs," meaning that neither the king nor others shall seize upon any of his possessions, and that a man shall not be put from his livelihood without answer. Against this law, it seems, even a royal patent could not stand. The word *liberties* has several significations; as the laws of the realm, privileges bestowed by the king, and the natural freedom possessed by the subjects of England, for which cause monopolies in general are against the enactments of the great charter.

The present chapter ordains, thirdly, that none shall be outlawed, exiled, or in any way destroyed. By *outlawry* is signified the ejecting of a person by three public proclamations from the benefit of the law, which, from the time of Alfred until long after the reign of William I., could be done for felony only, for which the penalty was death; and therefore an outlaw, being considered as a wolf, might be slain by any man.

The expression being *exiled* is equivalent with transportation, and it signifies to be banished or forced to abjure the realm against one's consent.

The chapter next declares that none shall be, "in any manner, *destroyed* contrary to the law of the land;" which Sir Edward Coke interprets to signify being "forejudged of life or limb, disinherited, or put to torture or death." He also observes that the words "in any manner" are added to the expression "destroyed," and to no other in the sentence, because they prohibit any means being used by which this destruction may be brought about; thus, if any individual be accused or indicted of felony, his goods or lands can neither be seized into the king's hands, nor granted, nor even promised to another, before his attainder.

In the original Latin of this charter, the above engagement is followed by the words "*nec super eum ibimus, nec super eum mittemus;*" of which the literal translation is, "nor will we pass upon him, nor commit him," &c.; but, as the margin of the statutes at large observes, these words do by no means express the sense of the original; and Sir Edward Coke states that they signify that none shall be condemned at the king's suit, either before the king in his bench, where the pleas are supposed to be held in his presence, or before any judge or commission whatever.

The word *peer* was probably originally derived of the Latin *par*, an equal, but was afterward used to signify the vassals or tenants of the same lord, who were equals in rank, and were obliged to attend him in his courts. They were also called *peers of fees*, either because they held their fees or estates under him, or because they sat in his courts to judge with him of disputes arising upon fees; and if there were too many in one lordship, the lord selected twelve of his tenants, who received the title of peers by way of distinction, whence it is said that juries have been derived.

To be judged according to "the law of the land," is the last privilege secured by the present chapter; which expression Sir Edward Coke interprets to signify the law of England, in its most extensive sense, binding both the sovereign and the subject; for which cause it is not written in the name of either. It likewise signifies that none of the foregoing penalties were to be imposed, but after due process of the common law.

CH. XL.—The intent of this chapter, which in the third great charter of King Henry III., vide page 140, was added to the preceding, was to abolish those fines which were anciently paid to delay or expedite law proceedings and to procure favor. Madox, who in his history of the exchequer, chap. xii., gives numerous instances of these fines, states that the counties of Norfolk used to pay an annual composition at the exchequer, that it might "be fairly dealt with."

By the expression, "to none will we *sell*," were abolished those excessively high fines paid for procuring of right or judgment. The words, "to none will we *deny*," referred to the stopping of suits or proceedings, and the denial of writs; and the engagement, "to none will we *delay* right or justice," provided against those delays which were caused by the counter-fines of defendants, who would sometimes outbid the plaintiff, or by the will of the prince.

The concluding words of this chapter are all which require to be noticed, namely, "*right and justice.*" The former, according to Lord Coke, signifies the law, because it guides as a right line, discovers that which is wrong, is the best birthright of the subject, and is supposed to allude to the Writ of Right, which must be given without fine. The passage then ordains that neither right, nor law, which forms the means of procuring justice, nor justice itself, which is the end of the law, shall be bought, sold, or denied. Such are the contents of these important chapters, which admit of the most extensive commentary and analysis; for it is aptly though quaintly observed by Lord Coke, in concluding his minute illustrations of these passages: "As the gold-finer will not, out of the dust of shreds of gold, let pass the least crum, in respect of the excellency of the metall, so ought not the learned reader to passe any syllable of the law, in respect of the excellency of the matter."

CHS. XLI., XLII. The protection from "evil tolls" is a security from paying so large a custom or imposition upon any goods, that the fair profit is lost therein, and the trade thereby prevented.

Lord Coke, in his Commentary on Pleas of the Crown contained in his *Third Institute*, chapter 84, shows that there were certain orders of men under a continual prohibition of quitting the realm without the king's previous license; though by the common law, every one had liberty to go where he would, provided he was under no injunction to remain at home. Some of the persons who were not to depart without the king's license were peers, because they were the councillors of the crown; knights, because they were to defend the kingdom from invasion; all ecclesiastics, because they were confined by a special law, on account of their attachment to the See of Rome; and all archers and artificers, lest they should instruct foreigners how to rival the manufactures of England.

By the writ called "*ne exeat regno*," the sovereign has still the power of confining his subjects within the kingdom, under severe penalties, because every man ought of right to defend the king and his realm; and to this reason Magna Charta has a reference, when it states that in time of war persons may be restrained from going abroad "for some short space for the good of the kingdom."

Ch. XLIII. The signification of the title *Honor*, is a more noble sort of lordship, on which other inferior estates depend, by the performance of certain services to the superior chief, who is called the Lord Paramount; and his seigniory is frequently termed an honor, not a manor, especially if it ever have belonged to the king or to an ancient feudal baron. To constitute an honor, however, it was essential that it should have been originally created by the king, and that it should be holden of the king; for, though the king might grant it to a subject, yet if it were assigned to another, it could not be holden of a subject.

The word escheat, which also occurs in this chapter, is derived of the old French word, *escheoir*, to return or happen: and it signifies the return of an estate to a lord, either on failure of issue from the tenant, or upon account of such tenant's felony. The nature of reliefs paid to the chief lord at the entry of a new heir, has already been particularly described; and it was usual for honors to be let out to the sheriffs to farm, in the manner already stated.

Chs. XLIV., XLVII., XLVIII., LIII.—"When a conqueror," says Mr. Lewis, "settled the economy of a country which he had previously vanquished, it behoved him, in order to secure his new acquisition, to keep the natives of the country (who were not his military tenants) in as humble a condition as possible; and more especially to restrain them from the use of arms; and as nothing could do this so effectually as the prohibition of hunting and shooting, it became a matter of policy to reserve this right to himself, or to those of his capital feudatories (the greater barons), on whom he thought proper to bestow it." On this account these laws were both instituted and executed with much cruelty; but in Canute's charter, granted at Winchester, in the year 1016, many of the offences committed, both on the vert and venison, were to be redeemed by fines; and this restriction extended only to the royal forests. The succeeding century produced a terrible alteration in these statutes; beasts of venery were then considered to belong solely to the king, and the right of taking them to be vested only in him; and while the Norman government carried these regulations to their greatest extent, a wide range of country was appropriated for the chase by the command of William the First, which was then denominated the New Forest. Within these limits, and under the color of forest law, the most horrid tyrannies and oppressions were exercised; the penalties attached to the destroying a beast within the bounds of a forest, were made almost as severe as taking away the life of a human being. These principles, if we credit the assertion of Matthew Paris, seem to have influenced the mind of John more than that of any other monarch, for his interdict touching the chase, extended to the winged as well as to the four-footed creation. It is not surprising that from such laws as these the people of England should contend as earnestly for liberation, as from the other oppressions of the feudal system; and John would have been as reluctant to confirm the charter of forests, as he was to ratify the charter of liberties; but the former instrument was granted in the ninth year of his successor, King Henry the Third.

CH. XLV.—Dr. Brady supposes that the office of chief justiciary was originally derived from Normandy, where he believes him to have been the same as the grand seneschal; in England he had extensive power over all the inferior officers of the law, took cognizance of all crimes, and was often general, viceroy, and guardian of the kingdom. The annals of Waverley (which are contemporary with Magna Charta), besides the oppression and incontinence of the king himself, ascribe the anger of the barons to the ill use which Peter, Bishop of Winchester, who in 1213 was constituted chief justiciary, made of his newly acquired power, during the absence of King John in France. And this appears the more probable, because the nobility were from the first extremely disgusted at his promotion, taking it very ill that a foreigner should be preferred above them all; and because in the great charter we find the power of the chief justiciary considerably curbed in many instances, and a strong innuendo given, that the officers of justice had been deficient in the knowledge, or at least in the observance, of the laws of the land.—THOMPSON'S *Magna Charta.*

CH. XLIX.—These hostages were first taken about the year 1208, during the time of the interdict, when King John, fearing that the Pope might absolve all his subjects from their allegiance, demanded pledges of all the barons, &c., whom he suspected, to be delivered to him as securities for their future fidelity. "Many of them," says Dr. Brady, "gave their sons, their nephews, or their nearest relations to the messengers whom he sent for them. In July, 1211, when he marched into Wales and subdued it, he received twenty-eight hostages from the nobles of that nation, who were executed on account of a revolt in the year following.

CH. LI.—The 51st chapter of John's charter provides for the dismission of certain alien soldiers, distinguished by the names of foreign knights, crossbowmen, and stipendiaries, who had been probably hired by the king to assist him against his barons. Even under the feudal system, paid or stipendiary troops, both national and foreign, were engaged by the monarchs, with the sums given by such as commuted for their services; and their duties were castle guards, foreign garrisons, or the protecting of the marches, or borders of the kingdom, adjoining Wales and Scotland. Their pay was sometimes out of the privy purse, or else they were suffered to live at free quarters; and being actually a party of wandering brigands from all nations, ready to embrace any side for hire, they gave rise to that cause of complaint alleged against them in the text, that they came with horses and arms to the molestation of the kingdom.

As the crossbow, or *hand arbalist*, is said to have been introduced into France by the first crusaders, and to have been used early in the reign of Louis le Gros, which began in 1108, it may probably account for the balistarii, or crossbowmen, being foreigners.

Ch. LII.—This chapter provides for the restoration of any possessions which had been unjustly seized on during his dispute with the barons; though at the same time it has a retrospective effect, by referring to such as were seized in the reigns of Henry II. and Richard I., then remaining in the king's hands. This demand, however, appears to have been already, in some degree, complied with; for, about February or March, 1214, John assumed the cross as a protection, and the present clause refers to some estates concerning which pleas had before been moved, and inquisitions previously taken. The text observes that all others were to be respited for the usual term of the crusaders, by which was signified the space of three years, allowed to all who took the cross, during which time their debts bore no interest, even from the day on which they joined the crusade; nor could a crossed debtor be cited before any court, until his return from beyond the seas. On account of these privileges, and from their suspicions that King John had assumed the cross only to secure himself and his possessions, the barons probably inserted that peculiar clause in the text, providing that if he did not go upon the crusade, he would immediately grant them their petitions.

Ch. LIV.—The particular species of action indicated in this chapter, is called an appeal to death, which is of two kinds, murder properly so named, and manslaughter; these being the only crimes for which an appeal can be brought for a relation, all others referring to the parties themselves. The appeal of death, however, cannot be brought for every relation, but only by a widow for the death of her husband, and by the heir male for that of his mother or ancestor, which heirship was extended, by an ordinance of King Henry I., to the four nearest degrees of blood. The writ of appeal is a natural consequence annexed to the widowhood of a woman, and is allowed her on account of the loss of her husband; if, therefore, she marry before or during her appeal, it is entirely lost; and if after judgment, she cannot demand execution.

The principal value of appeals of murder can hardly be estimated at the present day; though anciently there were reasons for thus prosecuting offences rather than by indictment. Blackstone and Barrington suppose that they had their origin in those times when a pecuniary satisfaction was paid for the expiation of great crimes; and princes were accustomed to pardon even murder, considering it as homicide, for a certain sum, entitled a *weregild*, to be paid to the nearest relation.

An acquittal, in the case of an appeal, protected the party from being afterward indicted for the same offence; and it was provided by the statute of Westminster, ch. xii., that in such a case the appellor or prosecutor should suffer a year's imprisonment, pay a fine to the king, and make restitution to the defendant for his imprisonment and infamy; which provision was of considerable effect in discouraging the common use of appeals. If, on the contrary, the appellee were found guilty, he suffered the same judgment as if he had been convicted by indictment; the king having no power to pardon him, any more than he had to permit the payment of the weregild.

CHS. LVI., LVII.—The text of King John's great charter declares, that all these disputes shall be decided by a threefold law, peculiar to that place to which they might refer: as the law of England for English tenements; that of Wales for Welsh possessions; and that of the Marches, for those estates situate on the borders of the two countries. The term marches is derived either from the German word *marck*, a mark, limit, or boundary, or from the old French *marque*, *signum;* and it signifies the line of distinction between two territories, considered as enemies' countries, which was anciently the case betwixt England, Wales, and Scotland. The Welsh marches are situate on the western and northern sides of Shropshire. They were governed by certain of the nobility called lords marchers, or marquesses of the marches of Wales, who possessed a kind of palatine authority in their respective territories, administered justice to the inhabitants in their own courts, and were gifted with several privileges and immunities, particularly under certain circumstances, with an exemption from the royal writ.

The law of Wales, which is also mentioned in this part of the great charter, refers to that code which was left to the ancient inhabitants, with such parts of the country as were not taken from them. It consisted of the statutes drawn up by Howel Dha, king of South Wales, in 940, and his council at "the White House on the River Taf," which were formed of the ancient laws and customs of the country, then fallen into decay, amended and increased.

CH. LVIII.—The 58th and 59th chapters of this charter relate to two events in the life of King John, and his connection with the princes of Wales and Scotland. In 1211, the lords of the Welsh marches made several heavy complaints to John against Llewellyn, the great prince of North Wales, concerning his ravages and incursions into England, and the king, assembling an army, marched through the whole country, whence, however, he soon returned, with considerable loss. In 1212 he entered Wales, and, as many of the Welsh nobility were of his party, Prince Llewellyn, who had married Joan, the king's natural daughter, sent her to him to make terms of peace, which were afterward confirmed between the prince and the king. Hostages were then given, and Llewellyn promised the king toward his charges, 20,000 head of cattle and 40 horses. The patent roll of the 16th of John, 1215, membrane 9, records a warrant for the delivery of certain Welsh hostages, probably some of those mentioned in the text.

CH. LIX.—John's agreement with Alexander II., king of Scots, which occupies the 59th chapter, refers to the capture of his father William I., in 1173, at Alnwick in Northumberland, when he covenanted to restore all that he had taken from England, to do homage for his crown, and give as security the castles of

Roxburgh, Berwick, Sterling, and Edinburgh. On November 22d, 1200, the same king did homage to John at Lincoln, and then demanded of him the restoration of the counties of Northumberland, Cumberland, and Westmoreland, with all their appurtenances, as his ancient right and inheritance; but as they came to no agreement, William returned discontented into Scotland. But though this claim remained unanswered until the king's death in December, 1214, he had entered into such a friendly compact with John, as to send his son Alexander over to England, where he was knighted in 1212. In the civil wars of the barons, they invited Alexander to join them, after the conclusion of Magna Charta; and in 1216, he entered England, where Norham Castle was surrendered to him upon terms. As he marched farther into the country, he took homage of Northumberland, and the barons of Yorkshire fled to him for protection from John's advancing army, before which, however, he was at length forced to retreat into his own kingdom. He afterward married Joanna, King John's eldest daughter by his third queen, Isabella of Angoulême, at York, on June 25th, 1221.

Ch. LX.—The insertion of this clause of the great charter, by which all the engagements and limitations between the king and his barons, &c., are made binding on them toward their own dependents, has been sometimes attributed to John himself. "For," says Dr. Henry, in his History of Great Britain, after mentioning this probability, "though the great barons were very desirous to prevent the tyrannical exercise of the feudal authority toward themselves, many of them were much inclined to exercise it in that manner toward their vassals, and continued to do so after this charter was granted." "This," he continues, "both encouraged our kings to violate all its limitations, and furnished them with a ready answer to all the complaints of their barons." Lord Coke, however, views this clause in a very different aspect, since he says of it: "This is the chief felicity of a kingdom, when good laws are reciprocally, of prince and people, as is here undertaken—duly observed." Dr. Lingard, in his History of England, Vol. II., ch. xiv., page 257, seems to believe that as the great body of freemen was composed of the subvassals of the immediate tenants of the crown, the clause was inserted for them, because they had assisted in procuring the charter itself. By Samuel Henshall, it is asserted that John himself caused this passage to be included in the articles of the great charter; and it is to be observed to be the only clause which affects the whole body of the people.

Ch. LXII.—After the extended and violent hostilities, between the king and his peers, the great charter properly contains one section, as an act of oblivion and reconciliation; which it may be observed, has so much of a retrospective view, as to commence at the preceding Easter, April 29th, 1215. The peace was actually concluded on Friday, June 19th, and it was announced to the king's party by the following letter, which is entered on the patent rolls, and which in referring to the fines and tenseriæ,—a military tax or contribution—may be thought to have some allusion to the taking away of unlawful amerciaments, provided by chapter lv. of King John's charter.

"The king to Stephen Harengod, &c. Know ye, that a firm peace was, by the grace of God, made between us and our barons, on the Friday next after the feast of the Holy Trinity, at Runnemede near to Staines, and that there we took homage of the same. Wherefore, we steadfastly command and instruct you, as ye have respect unto us, and our honour, and the peace of our kingdom, that you shall no further disturb, nor do any evil to our barons, nor to others, for the future; nor permit any occasion to be taken from the former discord between us and them. We also command you, that of the fines and tenseriæ taken by us on account of that discord, if any remain to be paid after the aforesaid Friday, nothing shall be taken. And the bodies of the prisoners, and hostages, and such as are detained on account of those wars, or fines, or tenseriæ, aforesaid, shall be liberated without delay. All the aforesaid shall be done as ye have respect to our person. And in testimony of this matter we send to you: Witness myself, at Runnemede, the 18th day of June, in the Seventeenth year of our reign."

CHAPTER V.

THE RISE OF PARLIAMENTARY REPRESENTATION.

SUFFICIENCY OF MAGNA CHARTA—NECESSITY OF FURTHER GUARANTEES—POWER OF PARLIAMENT IN THE REIGN OF JOHN—ABSENCE OF THE REPRESENTATIVE PRINCIPLE—HENRY'S RATIFICATION OF THE CHARTER OF KING JOHN—BLENDING OF THE NORMAN AND SAXON RACES—HENRY'S MORTGAGE OF THE KINGDOM TO THE POPE—THE GOVERNMENT INTRUSTED TO TWENTY-FOUR BARONS—THE CIVIL WAR—DE MONTFORT'S PARLIAMENT—OVERTHROW OF DE MONTFORT—FIRST CONSTITUTIONAL HOUSE OF COMMONS—ACCESSION OF EDWARD I.—HIS CONFIRMATION OF THE CHARTERS—STATUTE DE TALLAGIO NON CONCEDENDO—FINAL SETTLEMENT OF PARLIAMENTARY REPRESENTATION.

THE Charter of King John, had its provisions been faithfully executed, would unquestionably have been found sufficient to ensure the safety of the subject and the quiet of the kingdom. As yet the refinements of a high civilization were unknown, and a complicated system of government could only have resulted in confusion. To secure mankind in the possession of life, liberty, and property, are the sole objects of all government; and that form is the best for every people, which in its peculiar circumstances is the best adapted to attain this end. Ideal systems for the government of mankind are the dream of the philosopher, but the Republic of Plato and the Arcadia of Sydney only serve to show what man's condition might be if man were not what man is. Magna Charta was sufficient for its time, so far as any mere agreement could suffice; but it is not in human nature to surrender power without a desperate struggle, and the successors of King John were always ready to evade the plainest promises of an instrument which they alleged was only binding on the monarch who had granted it. We are not, then, to imagine that the usurpations and oppressions of the crown ceased with the giving of the charter. Far from it.[1] It was in consequence of royal wrongs that the necessity of further guarantees of rights came to be manifest to every class in the community, and that the people were from time to time compelled to wrest from their sovereigns some part of the functions of government, until the crown became the weakest of the three estates. The great advantage acquired through the charter to the cause of freedom was this, that the people's ordinary rights were clearly stated and distinctly guaranteed, and that the right of revolution and rebellion was acknowledged to exist when other rights were outraged by the crown. The hope to be derived from these acknowledgments and recognitions lay in this, that a free parliament existed, jealous of its liberties and watchful of the sovereign, ready, as occasion offered, to restrain his power and to provide securities against the overweening claims of his prerogative. With such an institution, it could hardly be a matter of doubt that checks would be from time to time set on royal power, and that new agencies of government would be created which must in the end destroy the autocratic claims of English sovereigns, and in their stead erect a commonwealth of freemen. Some, perhaps, of the brave barons who took part in the long contest, of which Runnymede was but the first great battle ground, saw in the objects they attained a glimmering of something greater for posterity than they had yet imagined for themselves; but these were at the best but vague hopes. To overthrow consolidated and prescriptive power is no slight task; and it was only long-continued and repeated wrongs which educated them to know and guard their rights. Through the long term of years which intervened between the death of John and the accession of the Stuarts, there is little to be seen but a succession of vain contests, in wild civil wars, with now and then a step made or a step lost in the development of constitutional government. Freedom blooms more slowly than the century plant of South America; and once destroyed, it cannot be restored to life and vigor but by copious waterings of blood. The moral of our illustration needs no exposition.

We have said that in the Parliament of England, and the recognition of its rights of legislation and taxation, lay the chief hope of the people. Yet the Parliament as it existed in the reign of John was but the shadow of a representative assembly. It is true that Magna Charta promises that the greater barons shall be summoned to Parliament by special writ, while all other tenants in chief are to be summoned in gross, and that this distinction of the barons into greater and lesser, obscure as it is, *may* be the first hint of a representation of the commons. But yet none were admitted to the parliamentary assembly but tenants in chief of the crown, whether their tenures were great or small. All subfeudatories were excluded. Parliament was, therefore, less a national assembly than the feudal council of the immediate vassals of the king. We are now briefly to trace its gradual development into the present Parliament of England.

The long and weak reign of Henry III., from 1216 to 1272, with all its indiscretions, was eminently favorable to the progress of free institutions. Had the reign of such a prince as Edward I. succeeded that of John, the charter might have been suppressed; but Henry's long minority, his folly, and his weakness gave the barons every opportunity to strengthen and confirm the privileges they had won from John. Moreover, the continued civil war which soon arose between the barons and the king, revealed the fact that either side, in order to success, must gain the affections of the commons. Hence the commons were invited to take part in Parliament by chosen representatives, and in the following reign the principle of popular representation came to be a fundamental principle of the English constitution.

At the accession of this prince in 1216, the Earl of Pembroke, the great advocate of the popular cause, was by the Parliament, appointed governor of the kingdom, and through his influence the charter of King John was revised and confirmed. In 1223, Henry was declared of age, and being utterly incapable of governing the kingdom, the supreme power was entirely exercised by his justiciary, Hubert de Burgh. In 1225, when war with France broke out, De Burgh was forced to apply to Parliament for an extraordinary aid; and one-fifteenth of all movables was granted by the barons, on condition that the king should now, in his majority, ratify and confirm the charters. This was done.[2] But the war terminating in disaster, Parliament refused to grant another aid, and popular indignation hurled the justiciary from power. During the discontents which followed the disaster of the English forces, Henry added greatly to the disaffection of the people by marrying a French princess, Eleanor of Provence, and by introduction into the chief places of the court and kingdom of her foreign relatives. Enraged at being governed by a band of foreign favorites, the barons more than once took arms against the king, who just as often swore to dismiss the obnoxious persons, and as often broke his oaths. The spirit of dissatisfaction reached its culminating point with the defeat of Henry in the French war he had undertaken contrary to the advice of Parliament, which forthwith peremptorily refused further supplies. The loss of the king's French possessions proved of immense advantage to England. The king could no longer threaten one part of his dominions with a foreign force to be brought from the rest: the barons, separated from their continental associations, now regarded themselves as English peers rather than as Norman nobles; and the distinction of the Normans from the English began gradually to disappear. "The two races," says Macauley, "so long hostile, soon found that they had common interests and common enemies; both were alike grieved by the tyranny of a bad king—both were alike indignant at the favor shown by the court to the natives of Poitou and Aquitaine. The grandsons of those who had fought under William, and the great-grandsons of those who had fought under Harold, began to draw near to each other in friendship;" and, as the great charter had been the first pledge of their reconciliation, so the formation of a representative government was the consummation of their identity.

After his serious repulse, Henry endeavored to conduct his government without advice or aid from Parliament, but his necessities compelled him in 1253 to meet the barons, who solemnly but firmly asked for a redress of grievances. The clergy seconded the barons. When they assembled in Westminster Hall, the bishops and abbots in their robes went in a solemn procession to the king with lighted tapers in their hands, and the archbishops then pronounced the fearful sentence of excommunication against whoever should have violated the great charter. Terror-stricken, the weak-minded king exclaimed, "So help me God, I will keep the charters inviolate, as I am a man, as I am a Christian, as I am a knight, as I am a king!" It was in vain. The king's devotion was as temporary as it doubtless was sincere; and his imprudence now led him to an act which might have brought about the ruin of his family, but fortunately had the happier result of furnishing the occasion for establishing the representative assembly of the English Commons. At the instigation of Pope Innocent III., Henry undertook the conquest of Sicily for his son Edmund, and the pope supplied him with the sum of 14,000 marks on a mortgage of his kingdom. Mortgages to popes in those days were no empty form; for the successors of St. Peter were good stewards of the patrimony of the apostolic fisherman. When Sicily was conquered, the then reigning pope, Alexander IV., demanded the immediate completion of their contract under threat of excommunication of the king, and interdict of the whole kingdom. Driven to despair, he called upon his Parliament to aid him in the payment of his debt. They were astonished at the impudence of the demand that they should pay so vast a debt, which they had never authorized him to contract; and they insisted that a committee should be appointed by the Parliament to administer the affairs of the kingdom, which their sovereign obviously was unfit to govern. The king consented, and the Parliament appointed twenty-four persons to conduct the government; and it was furthermore resolved, that four knights should be elected in each county to represent the grievances of their constituents in the next Parliament. But the barons were determined on more sweeping reforms. They had learned by long experience how little confidence could be reposed in kingly faith or prudence, and they determined once for all to cleanse the kingdom from the corruption which had grown upon it. For the sake of greater efficiency, Simon de Montfort, the ruling spirit among the barons, caused twelve instead of twenty-four to be appointed to the task of reformation, who forthwith dismissed the whole of the king's officers and advisers. The king himself became a cipher in the state; and in a monarchy, as Mr. Hallam justly says, a king divested of prerogatives by his people, soon appears even to themselves an injured party The decision and promptness of De Montfort and the twelve barons doubtless carried with it an air of usurpation which strengthened the hands of the the royalists; and Prince Edward flew to arms to vindicate the lost prestige of royalty. He was speedily defeated, the king prince were taken prisoners, and de Montfort, who had no desire to found a tyranny, determined to summon a parliament which should give a constitutional sanction to the acts he was determined to accomplish. The royalists of course were chiefly in the ranks of the nobility; while the citizens of London, and the commons generally, were enthusiastic for the cause of Leicester. It was obviously the policy of Leicester to call the citizens and commons to his aid. Writs were therefore issued, ordering the Sheriff to elect and return two knights for each county, and two burgesses and citizens for each borough and city respectively; and thus the principle of representation was established in the English Government, and the foundation of the present House of Commons laid.[3]

The conduct of the commons in this Parliament was a striking proof that the people of a country are always more ready to endure the government to which they are accustomed, while it is in any degree tolerable, than to fly into the uncertainties of revolution. Much as they had suffered at the hands of Henry, and deeply as they sympathized with Leicester, they had no desire to overturn the throne or change the constitution of their country. On the contrary, while they were firm in their demand for the redress of grievances, and stipulated that the chief authority should rest with Leicester, yet they no less steadily demanded the restoration of the king and the enlargement of the prince. Their wishes were accomplished; and the first result was that Prince Edward, making his escape, gathered an army, overthrew Simon, the son of Leicester, in the battle of Kenilworth, and turning to meet Leicester, who was hastening to the succor of his son, surrounded and destroyed his army, giving no quarter to any rank. Leicester himself was slain, but long lived in the affections of his countrymen, especially of the commons, as the champion of liberty and equal rights. He was for generations known among them as Sir Simon the Righteous; and though he died excommunicate, the popular credulity believed that notable miracles were wrought at his tomb.

For once the king now acted with prudence. Conscious of his weakness, notwithstanding the late triumph, he appears to have shown no disposition to trample on the charters or to reassert those ancient claims of prerogative which would have plunged the kingdom once more into revolt. Measures of retribution against the late rebels were left to Parliament; but the rigorous acts of this assembly, consisting as it now did of those barons only who had been the steady partisans of Henry, produced such disturbances that Henry wisely overruled them. Nor did his moderation end here. His most powerful partisan, the Earl of Gloucester, taking umbrage at some measures of the court, rose in rebellion and seized the tower of London. The disturbance was, by a mild course, soon brought to an end; the earl was freely pardoned, and the kingdom was restored to quiet. But the king was sensible that he must now concilitate the commons also to his cause, if he would hold his kingdom in tranquillity; for with them remained the balance of power in any discord between him and the barons. He accordingly determined by the advice of his council to convene a Parliament on the plan of Leicester, in which counties, cities, and boroughs[4] should be duly represented: and this body, from which many good laws—called the Statutes of Malbridge—emanated, having been assembled by the free will of the king and barons, with a distinct concession of a right of parliamentary representation to the Commons, is justly regarded as the first body of constitutional English legislators, in which the House of Commons was a constituent part.

During the rest of Henry's reign he lived in peace; and having in a period of bloodshed and rebellion, reaped the bitter fruits of violence and usurpation, he at length enjoyed in quiet, honor, and security, the blessings which could only have been won for him and his distracted kingdom by a course of prudence, moderation, and conciliation. But the fiery Edward who succeeded him was made of sterner stuff than the weak Henry; and in other circumstances this great sovereign might have swept away the limitations of the royal power which had been made during the last two reigns. But his own energy embarrassed him. His victorious wars in England and Scotland speedily impoverished his treasury; and when affairs upon the Continent demanded an immediate expedition into France,

Edward, who had never yet confirmed the charters of the previous reigns, resorted to measures of the most violent nature to provide the necessary funds. Without the consent of Parliament he levied tallages on all personal property, both of barons and commons, made an arbitrary tax on wool, and demanded of merchants loans equal to the full value of their cargoes. A strong spirit of resistance was aroused. Henry Bohun, Earl of Hereford, and Roger Bigod, Earl of Norfolk, resisted the exactions of the king and so intimidated the officers of the crown as to compel them to desist. They even refused to allow troops to be mustered for the expedition into France, alleging that the levy was unlawful, they not being bound to render military service otherwise than in attendance on the royal person, and declaring that they would not go unless the king himself went. Indignant at this unexpected opposition to his will, Edward is said to have exclaimed to Hereford, "By the eternal God, sir earl, you either go or hang!" "By the same oath, sir king," said the undaunted noble, "I will neither go nor hang!" With this defiancė the two earls departed to their castles and many of the barons followed their example. Edward's affairs admitted no delay; and having endeavored to win over the populace of London, and to conciliate the clergy to his cause, he departed into Flanders. Thereupon the clergy sided with the country, and ere long the warlike Edward was by force of circumstances driven to subscribe a confirmation of the charters of the previous reigns; and moreover to assent to the important Statute *de tallagio non concedendo*, which provided that no tallage or aid should be levied without the consent of the lords and commons assembled in Parliament; that in future no seizure of wool, hides or other merchandise should be made to the crown, and that no tolls or customs should be levied contrary to the charters. The better to secure the observance of these important provisions, it was enacted that copies of the charters should be sent to the sheriff, and justices in Eyre; that they should be publicly read in the cathedrals and sheriff courts, accompanied by a solemn sentence of excommunication against all who should presume to violate their sanctity; and that knights should be indifferently chosen in every shire to inquire into every abuse and infringement of these statutes, and to grant redress where it was not otherwise provided by law. From this time forth we may consider that the right of parliamentary representation was so firmly established in the English constitution, that no tax could be assessed on any portion of the people, lords or commons, laity or clergy, without the express assent of the class or order to be taxed; and it was fortunate that this admission was conceded by so powerful and great a prince as Edward. Hitherto concessions from the crown had been extorted from unwise and weak kings; so that even in the people's own minds there was still a doubt whether those solemn acts were permanently and unalterably established. But when they were ratified by Edward, who, by his contemporaries no less than by posterity was admitted to be one of the most wise, sagacious, powerful, and determined monarchs of his age, no doubt remained that they would stand forever.[6]

"From this period" says Lord Brougham, "we may truly say, that the constitution of Parliament, as now established, took its origin; and however that body may have occasionally had to struggle for its privileges, how often soever it may have submitted unworthily to oppression, how little soever it may have shown a determination to resist cruelty and injustice, and even the disposition to become the accomplice in such acts, we must allow that, generally speaking, it has ever since the end of the thirteenth century, formed a substantive and effective part of the constitution, and that the monarchy then assumed the mixed form which it now wears. "The English nation," continues the same noble author, "ought piously to hold in veneration the memory of those gallant and virtuous men who thus laid the foundation of a constitution to which they are so justly attached. The conduct of the barons in John's reign is indeed above all praise, because it was marked by as much moderation and wisdom as firmness of purpose and contempt of personal danger." "But to withstand the measures of Edward, a prince unequalled by any who had reigned in England, since the Conqueror, for prudence, valor and success, required a far more intrepid patriotism;" it is therefore to the sacred names of Henry Bohun, Earl of Hereford and Essex, and Roger Bigod, Earl of Norfolk, that we must award the meed of praise as the greatest patriots England has produced: and it is to the reign of Edward that we must refer the firm and final settlement of the great principles of constitutional liberty in England.[6]

It is easier to lose than to win back. From the conquest by the Normans to the confirmation of the charters by king Edward I., and the enactment of the statute *de tallagio*, two hundred and thirty years of wrong, oppression, usurpation, rebellion, civil discord, and intestine war were suffered; and nearly four hundred years of contest and vicissitude had yet to pass, before the rights so long acknowledged and so clearly understood, were to be quietly enjoyed :—a lesson which the freemen of all nations should not fail to bear in mind when they are tempted, on whatever grounds, to sacrifice their liberties to a supposed necessity.

NOTES.

1. *Tone of English Government from Magna Charta to Henry VI.*—Although the restraining hand of Parliament was continually growing more effectual, and the notions of legal right acquiring more precision from the time of Magna Charta to the wars under Henry VI., we must justly say that the general tone of administration was not a little arbitrary. The whole fabric of English liberty rose step by step, through much toil and many sacrifices; each generation adding some new security to the work, and trusting that posterity would perfect the labor, as well as enjoy the reward. A time, perhaps, was even then foreseen, in the visions of generous hope, by the brave knights of Parliament, and by the sober sages of justice, when the proudest ministers of the crown should recoil from those barriers which were then daily pushed aside with impunity.

There is a material distinction to be taken between the exercise of the king's undeniable prerogative, however repugnant to our improved principles of freedom, and the abuse or extension of it to oppressive purposes. For we cannot fairly consider as part of our ancient constitution, what the Parliament was perpetually remonstrating against, and the statute book is full of enactments to repress. Doubtless the continual acquiescence of a nation in arbitrary government, may alternately destroy all privileges of positive institution, and leave them to recover, by such means as opportunity shall offer, the natural and imprescriptible rights for which human societies were established. And this may, perhaps, be the case at present with many European kingdoms. But it would be necessary to shut our eyes with deliberate prejudice against the whole tenor of the most unquestionable authorities, against the petitions of the commons, the acts of the legislature, the testimony of historians and lawyers, before we could assert that England acquiesced in those abuses and oppressions, which, it must be confessed, she was unable fully to prevent.—HALLAM'S *Middle Ages*, vol. iii. p. 146.

2. *Hume, on Charter of Henry III.*—"Thus these famous charters were brought very nearly to the shape in which they have ever since stood; and they were, during many generations, the darling of the English nation, and esteemed the most sacred rampart to national liberty and independence. As they secured the rights of all orders of men, they were anxiously defended by all, and became the basis, in a manner, of the English monarchy, and a kind of original contract, which both limited the authority of the king, and ensured the conditional allegiance of his subjects. Though often violated, they were still claimed and recalled by the nobility and people; and as no precedents were supposed valid that infringed them, they rather acquired than lost authority from the frequent attempts made against them in several ages by regal and arbitrary power."

3. *Leicester's Parliament.*—The commencement of the year 1265 is rendered forever memorable by a measure destined to have the most important influence on the development of the British constitution; and which, as it has been elegantly expressed, has "afforded proof from experience that liberty, order, power and wealth are capable of being blended together in a degree of harmony which the wisest men had not before believed to be possible." Hitherto the great councils of the nation had consisted only of the prelates, barons, and tenants in chief of the crown; but Leicester, in the summons for a parliament at this time, directed the "sheriffs to elect and return two knights for each county, two citizens for each city, and two burgesses for each borough in the county; thus establishing the principle of representation, and giving the people of the towns, who had hitherto been taxed at will, a share in the legislature of the realm. By a fortunate chance also, they were allowed to sit along with the knights of the shire and not in a separate chamber; a circumstance which greatly contributed to give them dignity and importance. That Leicester could have foreseen the full effects of what he was doing is not to be supposed. The measure was one which, in the natural course of things, must inevitably have occurred within a few years; deputies for the towns had sitten for the last century in the Cortes of Spain; towns were everywhere rising into importance, and becoming of too great weight in the balance of states to be any longer subject to the arbitrary power of princes and nobles. Leicester may, doubtless, have seen much of this, but his probable motive was merely to the parliament members who he knew would be wholly devoted to himself, and the ready agents of his will."—KEIGHTLEY'S *History of England*, vol. i. p. 221.

4. *Admission of Borough Representatives to Parliament.—Separation of the two Houses.*—There is no great difficulty in answering the question why the

deputies of boroughs were finally and permanently ingrafted upon Parliament by Edward I. The government was becoming constantly more attentive to the wealth that commerce brought into the kingdom, and the towns were becoming more flourishing and more independent. But, chiefly, there was a much stronger spirit of general liberty, and a greater discontent at violent acts of prerogative, from the era of Magna Charta; after which authentic recognition of free principles, many acts which had seemed before but the regular exercise of authority, were looked upon as infringements of the subject's right. Among these the custom of setting tallages at discretion would naturally appear the most intolerable; and men were unwilling to remember that the burgesses who paid them were indebted for the rest of their possessions to the bounty of the crown. In Edward I.'s reign, even before the great act of confirmation of the charters had rendered arbitrary impositions absolutely unconstitutional, they might perhaps excite louder murmurs than a discreet administration would risk. Though the necessities of the king, therefore, and his imperious temper, often led him to this course, it was a more prudent counsel to try the willingness of his people, before he forced their reluctance, and the success of his innovation rendered it worthy repetition. Whether it were from the complacency of the commons at being thus admitted among the peers of the realm, or from a persuasion that the king would take their money if they refused it, or from inability to withstand the plausible reasons of his ministers, or from the private influence to which the leaders of every popular assembly have been accessible, much more was granted in subsidies, after the representation of the towns commenced, than had ever been extorted in tallages.

It has been a very prevailing opinion, that Parliament was not divided into two houses at the first admission of the commons. If by this is only meant that the commons did not occupy a separate chamber till some time in the reign of Edward III., the proposition, true or false, will be of little importance. They may have sat at the bottom of Westminster Hall, while the lords occupied the upper end. But that they were ever intermingled in voting, appears inconsistent with likelihood and authority. The usual object of calling a parliament was to impose taxes; and these, for many years after the introduction of the commons, were laid in different proportions upon the three estates of the realm. Thus, in the 23 E. I., the earls, barons, and knights gave the king an eleventh, the clergy a tenth, while he obtained a seventh from the citizens and burgesses; in the twenty-fourth of the same king, the two former of these orders gave a twelfth, the last an eighth; in the thirty-third year, a thirtieth was the grant of the barons and knights and of the clergy, a twentieth of the cities and towns; in the first of Edward II., the counties paid a twentieth, the towns a fifteenth; in the sixth of Edward III., the rates were a fifteenth and a tenth. These distinct grants imply distinct grantors; for it is not to be imagined that the commons intermeddled in those affecting the lords, or the lords in those of the commons. In fact, however, there is abundant proof of their separate existence long before the seventeenth of Edward III., which is the epoch assigned by

Carte, or even the sixth of that king, which has been chosen by some other writers. Thus the commons sat at Acton Burnell in the eleventh of Edward I., while the upper house was at Shrewsbury. In the eighth of Edward II., "the commons of England complain to the king and his council, &c." These must surely have been the commons assembled in Parliament, for who else could thus have entitled themselves? In the nineteenth of the same king we find several petitions, evidently proceeding from the body of the commons in Parliament, and complaining of public grievances. The roll of 1 E. III., though mutilated, is conclusive to show that separate petitions were then presented by the commons, according to the regular usage of subsequent times. And, indeed, the preamble of 1 E. III., stat. 2, is apparently capable of no other inference.

5. *Final Settlement of the English Parliament.*—In the Parliament held at Gloucester in 1407 (9 Henry IV.), we find the constitution of Parliament finally settling into its present form. The king had assembled the lords, spiritual and temporal, into his presence, and a debate took place between them about the state of the kingdom, and its defence; and on the necessity that the king should have an aid and subsidy. The king demanded of the lords what aid would be sufficient and requisite; who answered that, considering the necessity of the king on the one side, and the poverty of his people on the other, no less aids could be sufficient than those which they then specify. The king then sent to the commons, to cause a certain number of their body to come before the king and the lords; and the commons sent twelve of their companions, to whom the answer given by the lords was communicated. It was the pleasure of the king that the commons should report to their fellows, to the end that they might take the shortest course to comply with the intention of the lords. But the report having been made to the commons, they were greatly disturbed at it, saying and asserting it to be much to the prejudice and derogation of their liberties. The king became alarmed by the intelligence of the displeasure of the commons, and it is stated on the roll that "the king, after he had heard this, not willing that anything should be done at present, or in time to come, that might any wise turn against the liberty of the estate for which they are come to Parliament, nor against the liberty of the lords, wills, and grants, and declares, by the advice and consent of the lords, that it shall be lawful *for the lords to commune among themselves* in this present Parliament, and in every other in time to come, *in absence of the king*, of the state of the realm, and of the remedy necessary for the same. And that, in like manner, it should be *lawful for the commons*, on their part, *to commune together* of the state and remedy aforesaid. Provided always, that the lords, on their part, and the commons, should not make any report to the king of any grant, *by the commons granted and the lords assented to*, nor of the communications of the said grants, before the *lords and commons should be of one assent* and accord in such matters, and then in manner and form as had been accustomed: that is, *by the mouth of the speaker of the commons*. The king willing, moreover, by assent of the lords, that the communication made in

that Parliament, as before stated, should not be drawn into example in time to come, nor turn to the prejudice or derogation of the liberty of the estate for which the commons were then come, neither in that parliament nor in any other in time to come; but he willed that himself, and all the estates, should be as free as they were before."

But notwithstanding these solemn arrangements, the rights of the commons were not observed, and the commons, in the Parliament held in 1414 (2 Henry V.), made a protestation against statutes passed without their assent. In a petition addressed to the king, they assert it to be their liberty and freedom that there should be no statute nor law made, unless they gave thereto their assent; "considering that the commons of your land, which is, and ever hath been, a member of your Parliament, are as well assenters as petitioners; that from this time forward, on complaint of the commons of any mischief, asking remedy by the mouth of their speaker, or by written petition, there be no law made thereupon, and engrossed as statute and laws, neither by additions nor diminutions, nor by any manner of terms which should change the sentence, and the intent asked by the speaker's mouth, or the petitions given in writing; considering our sovereign lord, that it is nowise the intent of your commons, that if they ask you, by speaking or by writing, two things or three, or as many as they list, but that it ever stand in the freedom of your high regalie to grant which of them that you list, and to deny the remainder." To this the king's answer was as follows:—"The king, of his grace especial, granteth that from henceforth nothing be enacted to the petitions of his commons that be contrary of their asking, whereby they should *be bound without their assent;*—saving always to our liege lord his royal prerogative, to grant and deny what he lists of their petitions and askings aforesaid." *—Rowland's *English Constitution*, p. 104 et seq.

6. *Rowland on the Origin of Parliamentary Representation.*—It will not be found unprofitable to peruse the following *resumé* of the subject from Rowland's English Constitution, though it does not exactly present the same view as the text.

By the feudal system, as has been explained, large estates were granted to the Norman barons, on condition of military service and suit in the king's court; and these barons, with the prelates—the latter in right of their baronies—formed the great council of the king. The councils were summoned by the king at his pleasure and by his writ—the common mode of communicating his commands to all ranks of persons and public bodies. The councils, after the Conquest, were often called parliaments—a name which was applied to assemblies of various kinds; to the Aula Regis, and to the convention from which the great charter issued, which was called *Parliamentum Runnymedæ.*

In progress of time, as the original baronies escheated and returned to the crown, it became the policy of the king to divide them into smaller baronies, and

* Rot. Parl. Henry V. p. 22. This is the first instance on the rolls of the use of the English language.

thus to provide adherents against the power of the greater barons. But the new grants were made to the new grantees as tenants *in capite*, and they thus became of the same order as the greater barons; but not being possessed of the same wealth and power, they came to be distinguished as the lesser or smaller barons. They were equally entitled with the great barons to be summoned to, and to sit in, the great council. But although they possessed that right, and regarded it as a privilege and distinction attached to their order, attendance at the council was a burden, and they were satisfied to be exempt from it, or with only an occasional attendance.

The great numbers of the military tenants of the crown, whether called lesser barons or knights (for both were tenants *in capite* of the king, and any distinction between them soon merged in their common knighthood), would have made it difficult for the king to summon them individially and personally by his writ or letter, like the great barons. Magna Charta solved the difficulty by providing that "for holding the general council of the kingdom to assess aids, and for the assessing of scutages, we shall cause to be summoned the archbishops, bishops, abbots, earls, and great barons (majores barones) of the realm, singly by our letters; and furthermore, we will cause to be summoned in general by our sheriffs and bailiffs all others who hold of us *in capite*." This separation of the baronage into two classes—those summoned by writs, directed to each individually, and those summoned by sheriffs, under the direction of writs addressed to them—laid the foundation of the distinction which afterward arose between the ranks of nobility and gentry.

The next step toward the representation of the inferior class, arose from the necessity of consulting the convenience as well of the king and council, as of the knights themselves. The knights were a numerous class in each county. All persons holding land under the crown as tenants-in-chief, of the yearly value of twenty pounds, were compellable to receive knighthood. The attendance of so large a body, even if it were practicable, would have rendered deliberation impossible. Attendance by representatives must, therefore, when it was desired to act upon the provision of Magna Charta, have suggested itself as the natural mode of giving effect to the general but impracticable right; and thus representation of the counties arose. An election of representative knights took place at the county court, before the sheriff; the choosers (as the electors are called in the ancient statutes) being the knights themselves; but whether with or without the freeholders, is a question much controverted. At the present day the counties are supposed to be represented by actual knights. The writ directs the sheriff to return two knights; and each member, when his election is declared, is girt with a sword, to supply the fiction of knighthood.

But Magna Charta—out of which the representation of the counties by knights, as members of the feudal union, may be considered to have almost directly sprung—gave not the remotest ground for foreseeing, as a coming event, the attendance in the great council, of representatives of cities and boroughs; it provided, as we have seen, that the city of London and all other cities and boroughs, should have their ancient liberties and free customs; but these places, at the time of Magna Charta, were too completely excluded from the feudal union, to be allowed any share whatever in the national government. London was, indeed, a city of considerable importance; but the other cities and boroughs, with the exception of a few to whom charters of immunity had been granted, belonged to the king or the great barons, who treated them as property, exacting from them toll or tallage. But as trade and commerce extended, the cities and boroughs increased in population; and as their citizens and burgesses then also increased in power and importance, they were able to procure or to force from their lords, charters of liberties, which were numerously granted in the reign of John; so that, in the reign of Henry III., they had begun to acquire self-government, and oftentimes the ownership of land in the vicinity of the city or borough; and, what was more important, the abolition of the arbitrary power of tallage, by the substitution of a fee farm rent, or rent certain. The charters by which these changes were produced, were often wrung from the lords of the boroughs; and they have been well called treaties of peace between the burgesses and their lords.

It is remarkable that the first summoning of representatives of counties and boroughs to a great council, did not proceed from the sovereign, but from a faction which, in the reign of Henry III., obtained, for a time, the command of the kingdom. Henry had displeased his subjects by his devotion to and his enrichment of foreigners. He paid no regard to the great charter, or to the laws which it promulgated, although he was forced frequently to recognize and confirm it. The pusillanimity of his character was unequal to the control of the turbulent barons; many of the most powerful of whom lived in continual opposition to his administration and government. At length Simon de Montfort, Earl of Leicester, conspired with other barons to get the king into their power. They forced him to call a great council or parliament at Oxford, which assembled there on the 11th of June, 1258; it consisted of the prelates and barons only; they came to the assembly armed, and attended by their military vassals, and the king found himself a prisoner in their hands. Through their coercion, certain laws were passed, called "The Provisions of Oxford," which, until they were revoked by the restored authority of the king, took all power from him, and put the government under the control of twenty-four selected barons. Civil war was the result: a battle was fought between the king and the barons, at Lewes, on the 14th of May, 1264, in which the king's army was routed, and the king surrendered himself prisoner to the barons; his son, Prince Edward, being detained a hostage in Dover Castle.

Through this success, Leicester acquired the exercise of the sovereign power; and to strengthen his power, by increasing his popularity, he summoned, in the name of the captive king, a great council or parliament, to meet in London on 20th of January, 1265, in the forty-ninth year of Henry's reign. The record of this parliament exists: it shows that twenty-three lay lords, and one hundred and twenty-two ecclesiastics, including abbots, priors, and deans, attended the assembly. Leicester also ordered the attendance of two knights from each shire, and two citizens and burgesses from each city and borough. That is the origin of the representation of the people. The writs for summoning this parliament are the earliest writs of summons now extant on record. Some historians have contended that earlier instances of representation may be inferred from the facts and documents of history; but the best authorities and the highest research have made it manifest that the assembly convened by Simon de Montfort is the first instance of popular representation in parliament.—ROWLAND'S *Manual of the English Constitution*, p. 71–75.

CHAPTER VI.

TRIAL BY JURY.—THE HIGH COURT OF STAR-CHAMBER.—SLAVERY IN ENGLAND.

OBSERVATIONS ON THE PERIOD FROM EDWARD I. TO THE STUARTS—ESSENTIAL FEATURE OF THE JURY TRIAL—THE ROMAN JURY TRIAL—PECULIARITY OF THE ENGLISH JURY TRIAL—ITS ORIGIN IN THE SAXON COURTS—COMPURGATORS—RECOGNITORS—TRIAL BY PEERS IN MAGNA CHARTA—WITNESSES CALLED IN AID OF JURORS UNDER EDWARD III.—MODERN CONSTITUTION OF THE JURY SETTLED UNDER HENRY IV.—SUBSEQUENT CHANGES—BLACKSTONE ON THE JURY TRIAL—COURT OF STAR-CHAMBER—ITS ORIGIN—HOW SETTLED UNDER HENRY VII.—ITS JURISDICTION UNDER HENRY VIII.—HISTORICAL DISCUSSION—MODE OF PROCEDURE—ITS ABUSES AND EFFECTS—CIVIL JURISDICTION OF THE STAR-CHAMBER—ITS ENORMITIES DESCRIBED BY CLARENDON—OBSERVATIONS—SAXON SLAVERY IN ENGLAND—GENERAL REMARKS ON SLAVERY—ACCOUNT FROM HALLAM OF ITS GRADUAL DISAPPEARANCE IN ENGLAND—CONCLUSION.

THE constitutional history of England, from the reign of Edward I. to that of James I., hardly falls within the scope of the present volume. Our object is to trace the gradual recognition of rights, and the still more gradual development of constitutional contrivances for their protection. The period just indicated was preëminently barren in such matters. The rights of English subjects may be fairly taken to have been completely recognized by the statute *de tallagio;* and, from the epoch of the settlement of Parliament on its present basis, no change of importance took place in the English constitution. Such changes as occurred were merely local peculiarities, embodying no principle, and developing no general truth. They are therefore not within the scope of a work which aims at utility to the American citizen, rather than the enlightenment of the laborious student in English jurisprudence.

Yet the period which intervened between the two reigns above mentioned, is by no means the least interesting to the student. Throughout the whole of it we see the doubtful struggle of free institutions for existence. We behold a Parliament at one time so strong and so conscious of its strength, as to depose the sovereign of the country from his kingly office, and change the succession to the crown;[1] and at another, we behold the same great council stooping from its high prerogative, to become the servile register of kingly proclamations, legalizing, in advance, the acts of royal tyranny:[2] and it is startling to observe that at the very time when knowledge was increasing, and a right conception of the true foundation of all government was becoming most clear, the nearest approach to despotism was made by English monarchs. Of the line of princes who have governed England, from the Conqueror down, none have been more completely arbitrary in their sway than the Tudors. Yet it is precisely in their reigns that the most rapid strides were made in knowledge, and that the clearest expositions of the rights of subjects were produced. No one since the time of Hooker, has excelled that writer in the clearness of his views on government; yet his writings were produced under the arbitrary reign of Elizabeth.[3]

But neither do we propose to enlarge on these apparently paradoxical phenomena. There is, however, one great institution which attained nearly its present form during this period, and which, from its immense importance, we conceive it necessary to trace through the various phases of its history. We mean TRIAL BY JURY. And there are two other English institutions to be named hereafter, from which we believe important lessons may be learned; and for a sketch of which we think the present is the proper place. But first of Juries.

I. The essential feature of the Jury Trial is that it provides two judges, one of whom decides the *law* in the particular case to be determined, while to the other is reserved the duty of pronouncing on the *facts*, and rendering a final judgment thereupon according to the law as it has been previously expounded. This, we say, is the *essential* feature of the Jury Trial, separated from the adjuncts which have been connected with it in the common law of England and the United States; and this separation of the trial of the law from the trial of the facts, conducing as it obviously does to equity in judicial procedures, is by no means novel in the history of jurisprudence.

Among the Romans, the trial of a cause was first held before the Prætor. To him the prosecutor stated his case without any evidence of its truth: the defendant in like manner made his answer; and the Prætor then stated the law in the case. With the truth or falsehood of the statements made by prosecutor and defendant, the Prætor had no concern whatever. He simply cited the law to show what would be the legal decision of the cause *if* the facts were as had been alleged on either hand. This was called the trial *in jure*, or trial of the *law*. On its conclusion the cause was committed to a court of jurors (*judices*), for decision by a trial *in judicio*, or final judgment of the *facts;* which ended the proceedings. How the Roman judices were selected is not altogether certain. It appears, however, that they were a body of official persons from whom details were made for the trial of particular cases. Nor is the number of the jurors known. But it is probable that it was varied according to the importance of the cause to be decided. This mode of trial was the ordinary mode among the Romans. Extraordinary trials were occasionally held—perhaps at the pleasure of the parties to the suit—in which the whole matter was left to the Prætor, who then pronounced the law, decided on the facts, and rendered judgment. Under the emperors, as might have been anticipated, the principle of consolidation, which was so triumphant in the executive and legislative powers, was soon extended to the judicial. The office of the judices fell into disuse; the extraordinary trial by the Prætor, became the ordinary course of justice; and the Roman jury trial—for so it may with perfect truth be called —was utterly abolished. Despotism has little love for juries.

The peculiar feature of the English jury trial, is the choice of jurors from the whole body of freemen, dwelling within the jurisdiction of the court which tries the cause; and this, which is in fact the greatest safeguard of the citizen against the arbitrary despotism of executive authority, is the legitimate outgrowth of the Saxon system. We have already described (chap. I.) the folk-courts of the Saxons in their hundreds and counties, in which the assembled freemen of the district decided both the law and facts of the causes brought before them, and the ealdorman, though he no doubt instructed and advised them, had no power to force or alter their decision. These courts were unquestionably common to all the Germanic tribes who founded kingdoms in the middle and southern parts of Europe at the fall of the empire. The Arimanns among the Franks, the Rachinbourgs among the Lombards, and the *boni homines* among all the tribes, had originally, no doubt, the same institutions, and the same privileges as the freemen of the Anglo-Saxons of England. And if it be asked why the jury trial should have grown up step by step in England to its present form, while no such institution has arisen on the Continent, the answer is an obvious one. For on the Continent, the German conquerors fell very shortly into the legal system of the Roman colonists they had subdued, and hence the code and practice of the imperial courts came to be very generally substituted for the rude methods of administering justice they had hitherto pursued. In England, on the contrary, the Roman laws could have no influence upon the Saxons. England had been totally deserted by the Romans, and the aboriginal inhabitants were so completely subjugated by the invaders that the greater part took refuge in the fastnesses of Wales, where they maintained a savage independence till the reign of Edward I., and those who still remained among the invaders were reduced to abject slavery. Before the Saxon tribes in England every vestige of the Roman government and jurisprudence disappeared; and in respect to juries and all other matters the folk courts were left to follow out their course of natural development. It may be well to state, in this connection, that the development of jury trial in England was but hindered by the Norman conquest. For though the feudal courts held by the lords among their vassals must have had a much more extensive jurisdiction than the like courts of the Saxon earls among the ceorls belonging to their mound, yet the folk courts were not by any means abolished. On this subject we have spoken in a former chapter. We shall now proceed to trace the steps by which the tumultuous jury of the Saxon folk courts gradually formed itself into the modern English and American jury.

Among the Germanic tribes the ordinary way of settling questions was originally by means of *conjurators* or *compurgators*, a method concerning which there has been and still is much controversy. According to some writers, and among them a no less authority than Mr. Sharon Turner, the compurgators—whose number varied with the importance of the case—were essentially a committee of the folk court empowered regularly to try the cause, to hear the testimony brought by the parties, and to render a judicial verdict. If this view of the case be true, these compurgators lacked but one particular of being identical with our own jurors; and indeed the parties who sustain it, further hold that at the period of the conquest, jury trial was already as completely perfected among the Saxons as it is among ourselves. Of this, to say the least, there must be very grave doubts; and the evidence adduced in proof of it is not sufficient to sustain the theory. But neither, on the other hand, is there sufficient evidence adduced by their opponents in the opposite extreme. These men affirm that compurgators, so far from being jurors, were not even witnesses of facts, but persons who, without the slightest knowledge of the facts, might be brought forward either by the plaintiff or the defendant to swear to their belief of the probability or improbability of the complaint or charge made. And it is further maintained that the decision of the cause was given to the party who produced the greater number of compurgators, or whose compurgators were of higher rank than those of his opponent. It is difficult to believe that any system so absurd could have prevailed in any country; and although it would appear that some such system did for a time prevail among the Frankish tribes, analogy is not enough to prove that it was ever settled as an institution among the Saxons. Truth lies probably between the two extremes of these opinions. It is likely that the oaths of compurgators, intimately acquainted with the parties to the cause, had great weight with the voters in the folk courts, especially as it was always probable that they would have a knowledge of the cause at issue, and that witnesses for either party would be sought by him *among his compurgators.* But it is not likely that the testimony of witnesses was disregarded or excluded,

Be this as it may, the functions of the compurgators were speedily determined, and ere long we find them under the new appellation of *recognitors*. These were persons chosen from the neighborhood of the matter to be tried—generally twelve or some multiple of twelve—whose office it was to decide the cause from their own knowledge, and from the information they were able personally to give each other. As they were themselves chosen on account of their acquaintance with the litigants and the matters in litigation, they heard no witnesses, and received no allegations, but in cases of doubt they were required to state the ground on which they rendered their decision or verdict (*vere dictum*), which was always given on oath. When these recognitors were first employed is doubtful. Some would fix the date long before the conquest, others not till afterward. In this case likewise the truth probably lies between. There is no date at which this step toward jury trial was universally made. It was adopted doubtless by some shire and hundred motes long before the conquest, but it probably did not become a universal institution before a later date; and it is not before the period of the Norman reigns that we have documentary proof that it had been accomplished—a circumstance at which we cannot be surprised when we consider the destruction of the Saxon monuments and records which was made by the Conqueror.

From the date of Magna Charta we have little difficulty in tracing the remaining steps of jury trial. When it had been decreed that no freeman should be taken or imprisoned, or dispossessed, or banished, or in any way destroyed, but by the lawful judgment of his peers, it could not but be that a people jealous of its rights, and daily growing in enlightenment and civilization, should improve upon the rude contrivances of an epoch less advanced in knowledge, and as yet untrained by wrongs to guard their rights.

It was an obvious defect in the system of recognitors, that they were not permitted to call witnesses to their assistance; and in the reign of Henry III., we find that witnesses on either side were joined with the recognitors, in one body, for the trial of the cause. This constitution of the jury must undoubtedly have been often perverted to injustice in a manner that would naturally suggest its own remedy.

Accordingly, in the reign of Edward III., A. D. 1350, witnesses were called in aid of the recognitors, to whom they gave their testimony. They were not, however, joined with them, and took no part in their decision. Here, therefore, we may join with the historian of the court of Chancery, Mr. Spencer, in saying that the jury was complete in its developments, and that it now remained only that proper regulations for its action should be framed, and due restrictions brought to bear on it for the prevention of abuses, in order to present it in that perfect form which is the pride of England and America.

And now that the recognitors were permitted to call witnesses in evidence, little was necessary to be added to the constitution of the jury trial, but that it should be protected against irregular and improper testimony, and that its proceedings should be so directed as to insure the gravity becoming in a court of justice. Therefore, in the reign of Henry IV., a most important change was made, which put the jury under the direction of the judges in open court. The witnesses were now required to give their evidence in presence of the judges, who controlled the whole proceedings of the court and jury, and rejected all such evidence as was improper to be given. Since that time witnesses have not been questioned merely by jurors, but submitted to examination by the judge, the jury, and the counsel in the cause; so that their evidence is fairly tested in a searching cross-examination, and the court has every opportunity of judging from their manner and appearance how much credit is to be reposed in what they say.[4] The jury trial was thus brought into its present state. The separation of the trial of the law from the trial of the facts was now complete, and while the assistance of a competent judge was afforded to the jurors to instruct them in the law and aid them in receiving testimony, the decision of the cause was not left to a single person, who might be the corrupt appointee of an unscrupulous and arbitrary Government, but to a jury of freemen, whose interest it must be to sustain rights which were their own.

One change only remained to be made. Hitherto the jurors or recognitors had been selected from the neighborhood in which the crime had been committed, or the property in litigation lay—a provision, which, when the recognitors rendered their verdict from personal knowledge, was essential; but which, now that more reliance was reposed in the extraneous depositions of witnesses, was likelier to cause prejudice, and a perversion of the judgment of the juror, that would lead him to give little heed to the importance of evidence produced in court, when it might happen to conflict with prepossessions of his own. To remedy this evil—for an evil it was felt to be—" numerous partial changes were made from time to time, until, by statutes in the reigns of Anne and of George II., the rule requiring the jurors to be summoned from the vicinage was abolished, and the selection was directed to be made from the county at large. And by a decison of the court of King's Bench, it was declared that if a jury gave a verdict upon their own private knowledge, it was an error, and that they ought to have informed the court, so that they might have been sworn as witnesses. This brought trial by jury to its present perfected condition. As anciently a most careful scrutiny was made to select such men only as were familiar with the parties and the facts, the endeavor is now equally strenuous to obtain such alone as are absolutely unacquainted with the parties and circumstances of the case, and shall stand unbiassed by any preconceived opinions and prejudices." (POMEROY'S *Municipal Law*, p. 76.)

Thus, then, from this rapid and imperfect sketch, the reader will perceive that jury trial, like all other guarantees of human freedom, has proceeded from a slight germ through ages of progress, every step of which is marked in blood, rebellion, revolution, to that perfect consummation which it is our right now to enjoy. This venerable institution, which from the first Saxon settlement in England, to the reign of George the Second, must be counted to have passed through nearly thirteen centuries of growth—this venerable institution, cherished by our Revolutionary fathers, who declared that in these States the sacred English right of trial by jury should never be denied—this venerable institution is not merely threatened in this free (?) Republic, it is trampled under foot. And yet the people hesitate! The writer of these pages is no party politician, but thus much a student may say even to the statesman: It is easier to pull down than to build up! The oak that grows for ages perishes before the woodman in an hour, and liberty, which grows more slowly, perishes as quickly if the violence of arbitrary power is suffered, unrebuked, to rise against it. To the American citizen there is at present a sad warning in the termination of the first of the following glowing paragraphs from Blackstone:

"The trial by jury ever has been, and I trust ever will be, looked upon as the glory of the English law. And if it has so great an advantage over others in regulating civil property, how much must that advantage be heightened when it is applied to criminal cases! It is the most transcendent privilege which any subject can enjoy or wish for, that he cannot be affected either in his property, his liberty, or his person, but by the unanimous consent of twelve of his neighbors and equals. A constitution that I may venture to affirm has, under Providence, secured the just liberties of this nation for a long succession of ages. And, therefore, a celebrated French writer, who concludes that because Rome, Sparta, and Carthage have lost their liberties, therefore those of England in time must perish, should have recollected that *Rome, Sparta, and Carthage, at the time when their liberties were lost, were strangers to the* TRIAL BY JURY.

"Great as this eulogium may seem, it is no more than this admirable constitution, when traced to its principles, will be found in sober reason to deserve. The impartial administration of justice, which secures both our persons and our properties, is the great end of civil society, but if that be entirely intrusted to the magistracy (a select body of men, and those generally selected by the prince, or such as enjoy the highest offices of the state), their decisions, in spite of their own natural integrity, will have frequently an involuntary bias toward those of their own rank and dignity; it is not to be expected from human nature that *the few* should be always attentive to the interests and good of *the many.* On the other hand, if the power of judicature were placed at random in the hands of the multitude, their decisions would be wild and capricious, and a new rule of action would be every day established in our courts. It is wisely therefore ordered that the principles and axioms of law, which are general propositions, flowing from abstracted reason, and not accommodated to times or to men, should be deposited in the breasts of the judges, to be occasionally applied to such facts as come properly ascertained before them. For here partiality can have little scope; the law is well known and is the same for all ranks and degrees; it follows as a regular conclusion from the premises of fact preëstablished. But in settling and adjusting a question of fact when intrusted to any single magistrate, partiality and injustice have an ample field to range in; either by boldly asserting that to be proved which is not so, or by more artfully suppressing some circumstances, stretching and warping others, and distinguishing away the remainder. Here, therefore, a competent number of sensible and upright jurymen, chosen by lot from among those of the middle rank, will be found the best investigators of truth, and the surest guardians of public justice. For the most powerful individual in the state will be cautious of committing any flagrant invasion of another's right, when he knows that the fact of his oppression must be examined and decided by twelve indifferent men, not appointed till the hour of trial; and that when once the fact is ascertained, the law must of course redress it. This, therefore, preserves in the hands of the people that share which they ought to have in the adminstration of public justice, and prevents the encroachments of the more powerful and wealthy citizen. Every new tribunal, erected for the decision of facts, without the intervention of a jury (whether composed of justices of the peace, commissioners of the revenue, judges of a court of conscience, or any other standing magistrates), is a step toward establishing aristocracy, the most oppressive of absolute governments. The feudal system, which, for the sake of military subordination, pursued an aristocratical plan in all its arrangements of property, had been intolerable in times of peace, had it not been wisely counterpoised by that privilege, so universally diffused through every part of it, the trial by the feudal peers. *And in every country on the Continent, as the trial by the peers has been gradually disused, so the nobles have increased in power, till the state has been torn to pieces by rival factions, and oligarchy, in effect, has been established, though under the shadow of regal government, unless where the miserable commons have taken shelter under absolute monarchy, as the lighter evil of the two.* And particularly, it is a circumstance well worthy an Englishman's observation, that in Sweden the trial by jury, that bulwark of Northern liberty, which continued in its full vigor so lately as the middle of the last century, is now fallen into disuse; and that there, *though the regal power is in no country so closely limited, yet the liberties of the commons are extinguished, and the government is degenerated into a mere aristocracy.* IT IS THEREFORE, UPON THE WHOLE, A DUTY WHICH EVERY MAN OWES TO HIS COUNTRY, HIS FRIENDS, HIS POSTERITY, AND HIMSELF, TO MAINTAIN TO THE UTMOST OF HIS POWER THIS VALUABLE CONSTITUTION IN ALL ITS RIGHTS: TO RESTORE IT TO ITS ANCIENT DIGNITY, IF AT ALL IMPAIRED by the different value of property, or otherwise deviated from its first institution; TO AMEND IT WHEREVER IT IS DEFECTIVE; AND ABOVE ALL, TO GUARD WITH THE MOST ZEALOUS CIRCUMSPECTION AGAINST THE INTRODUCTION OF NEW AND ARBITRARY METHODS OF TRIAL, WHICH, UNDER A VARIETY OF PLAUSIBLE PRETENCES, MAY IN TIME IMPERCEPTIBLY UNDERMINE THIS BEST PRESERVATIVE OF ENGLISH LIBERTY." (BLACKSTONE, vol. iii. p. 378–381.)

II. Despotism, as we have said, has little partiality for juries; and when royalty in Engand failed to crush out the free spirit of the people, and to sweep away the safeguard of the ordinary jury trial, it availed itself of the tyrant's ever ready and generally plausible plea—necessity—to erect a court which should be wholly in the royal interests, and utterly subservient to the crown. This court was the High Court of Star Chamber—an institution which from the reign of Charles I. has had no parallel in England or America, until, in 1861, a Secretary of State of these United States assumed to concentrate its powers in his own person—powers so monstrous, so iniquitous, so utterly repugnant to the plainest principles of justice, that their exercise conduced in no small degree to bring about that revolution which brought Charles I. to the block; whose exercise in France produced the scathing whirlwind of another and more bloody revolution; which here in these United States—OUR SECRETARIES WOULD DO WELL TO LAY ASIDE.

The Star Chamber is said to have been in early times one of the apartments of the king's palace at Westminster allotted for the despatch of public business. The Painted Chamber, the White

Chamber, and the Chambre Markolph were occupied by the triers and receivers of petitions, and the king's council held its sittings in the Camera Stellata, or Chambre des Estoylles, which was so called probably from some remarkable feature in its architecture or embellishment.

"The lords sitting in the Star Chamber" is used as a well-known phrase in records of the time of Edward III., and the name, becoming permanently attached to the jurisdiction, continued long after the local situation of the court was changed. The judicature of the court of Star Chamber appears to have originated in the exercise of a criminal and civil jurisdiction by the king's council, or by that section of it which Lord Hale calls the *Consilium Ordinarium*, in order to distinguish it from the *Privy Council*, who were the deliberative advisers of the crown. (HALE'S *Jurisdiction* of the *Lords' House*, ch. v.; PALGRAVE'S *Essay on the Original Authority of the King's Council.*) The exercise of jurisdiction by the king's council was considered as an encroachment upon the common law, and being the subject of frequent complaint by the Commons, was greatly abridged by several acts of Parliament in the reign of Edward III. It was discouraged also by the common law judges, although they were usually members of the council; and from the joint operation of these, and some other causes, the power of the *Concilium Regis* as a court of justice had materially declined previously to the reign of Henry VII, although, as Lord Hale observes, there remain "some straggling footsteps of their proceedings" till near that time.

The statute of the 3d Henry VII. c. i. empowered the chancellor, treasurer, and keeper of the privy seal, or any two of them, calling to them a bishop and temporal lord of the council and the two chief justices, or two other justices in their absence (to whom the president of the council was subsequently added), upon bill or information exhibited to the lord chancellor or any other, against any person for maintenance, giving of liveries, and retainers by indentures or promises, or other embraceries, untrue demeanings of sheriffs in making panels and other untrue returns, for taking of money by juries, or for great riots or other unlawful assemblies, to call the offenders before them and examine them, and punish them according to their demerits. The object and effect of this enactment are extremely doubtful. It appears to have been the opinion of the courts of law at the time the statute was passed that it established a new jurisdiction entirely distinct from the ordinary jurisdiction of the council; for, five years afterward, it was resolved by all the judges, according to the plain words of the law, that the only judges of the court under the statute were the lord chancellor, the treasurer, and the keeper of the privy seal, the bishop and temporal lord being merely "called to them" as assistants or assessors, and not as constituent members of the court. This view of the effect of the statute is confirmed by the fact that, more than forty years afterward the president of the council was expressly added to the judges of the court; "a decisive proof," as Mr. Hallam observes, that it then existed as a tribunal perfectly distinct from the council itself.

However this may have been, there is no doubt that previously to the time of Coke, this court, whether distinct, or only a modification of the ancient jurisdiction, had again so completely merged in the general jurisdiction of the lords of the council, as to justify his statement that the opinion expressed in the judicial resolution was "contrary to continual experience." Sir Thomas Smith, who wrote his "Treatise on the Commonwealth of England," in the year 1565, makes no mention of a limited court, though he treats particularly of the court of Star Chamber, and says that the judges were the lord chancellor, the lord treasurer, all the king's council, and all peers of the realm; and he ascribes the merit of having renewed the vigor of the court to Cardinal Wolsey. At the beginning of the reign of Elizabeth, therefore, the court of Star Chamber was unquestionably in full operation, in the form in which it was known in the succeeding reigns; and at this period, before it had degenerated into a mere engine of state, it at least appeared to be by no means destitute of utility. It was professedly the only court in the land in which great and powerful offenders had no means of setting at defiance the administration of justice, or of corrupting its course. And during the reign of Elizabeth, when the jurisdiction of the Star Chamber had reached its maturity, it seems, *except in political cases*, to have been administered with wisdom and discretion. In trials having any political tendency, it is needless to observe that this court never was, nor indeed, could be equitable in its jurisdiction.

The proceedings in the court of Star Chamber were by information, or bill and answer; interrogatories in writing were also exhibited to the defendant and witnesses, which were answered on oath. The attorney-general had the power of exhibiting ex-officio informations; as had also the king's almoner to recover deodands and goods of a felo-de-se, which were supposed to go in support of the king's alms. In cases of confession by accused persons, the information and proceedings were oral; and hence arose one of the most oppressive abuses of the court in political persecutions. The proceeding by written information and interrogatories was tedious and troublesome, often involving much nicety in pleading, and always requiring a degree of precision in setting forth the accusation, which was embarrassing in a state prosecution. It was with a view to these difficulties that Lord Bacon, on one occasion, discouraged the king from adopting this mode of proceeding, saying that "the Star Chamber, without confession, was long seas." In political charges, therefore, the attorney-general derived a great advantage over the accused by proceeding *ore tenus*. The consequence was, that no pains were spared to procure *confessions*, and pressure of every kind, including torture, was unscrupulously applied. According to the laws of the court, no person could be orally charged, unless he acknowledged his confession at the bar, "freely and voluntarily, without constraint." But this check upon confessions improperly obtained, seems to have been much neglected in practice during the later periods of the history of this court. "Therein," says Hudson, writing in the reign of James I., "there is sometimes dangerous excess; for, whereas the delinquent confesseth the offence, *sub modo*, the same is strained against him to his great disadvantage. Sometimes many circumstances are pressed and urged to aggravate the matters which are not confessed by the delinquent, which surely ought not to be urged, but what he did freely confess, and in the same manner. And happy were it if these might be restrained within their limits, for that this course of proceeding is an exuberancy of prerogative, and, therefore, great reason to keep it within the circumference of its own orb." Upon admissions of immaterial circumstances, thus aggravated and distorted into confessions of guilt, the Earl of Northumberland was prosecuted *ore tenus* in the Star Chamber, for being privy to the gunpowder plot, and was sentenced to pay a fine of £30,000, and to be imprisoned for life, " but by what rule," says Hudson, " that sentence was, I know not, for it was *ore tenus*, and yet not upon confession." And it frequently happened during the last century of the existence of the Star Chamber, that enormous fines, imprisonments for life, or during the king's pleasure, banishment, mutilation, and every variation of punishment short of death, were inflicted by a court composed of members of the king's council, upon a mere oral proceeding, without hearing the accused, without a written charge or record of any kind, and without appeal.

The civil jurisdiction of the Star Chamber comprehended mercantile controversies between English and foreign merchants, testamentary causes, and differences between the heads and commonalty of corporations, both lay and spiritual. The court also disposed of the claims of the king's almoner to deodands, as above referred to, and also such claims as were made by subjects to deodands and the goods of convicted felons, by virtue of charters from the crown. The criminal jurisdiction of the court was very extensive. If the king chose to remit the capital punishment, *the court had jurisdiction to punish as crimes even treason, murder, and felony.* Under the comprehensive name of contempts of the king's authority, all offences against the state were included, forgery, perjury, riots, maintenance, embracery, fraud, libels, conspiracy, and false accusation : misconduct by judges, justices of the peace, sheriffs, jurors, and other persons connected with the administration of justice, were all punishable in the Star Chamber.

A court of criminal judicature, composed of the immediate agents of prerogative, possessing a jurisdiction very extensive, and at the same time imperfectly defined, and authorized to inflict any amount of punishment short of death, must, even when best administered, have always been viewed with apprehension and distrust; and accordingly in the earlier periods of its history we find constant remonstrances by the commons against its encroachments. As civilization, knowledge, and power increased among the people, the jurisdiction of the lords of the council became more odious and intolerable. Unfortunately, too, the court of Star Chamber, which at one time appears to have been serviceable in the manner described by Sir Thomas Smith, "as bridling such stout noblemen or gentlemen which would offer wrong by force to any manner of men, and could not be content to demand or defend the right by order of law, degenerated in the reigns of James I. and Charles I. into a mere engine of state, and was employed as one of the main instruments for the assertion of prerogative, pretension, and the enforcement of illegal taxation. "They extended their jurisdiction," says Clarendon, "from riots, perjury, and the most notorious misdemeanors *to the asserting of all proclamations and orders of state; to the vindicating of illegal commissions and grants of monopolies; holding for honorable that which pleased, and for just that which profited; and becoming both a court of law o determine civil rights, and a court of revenue to enrich the treasury; the council table by proclamation enjoining to the people that which was not enjoined by the laws, and prohibiting that which was not prohibited; and the Star Chamber, which consisted of the same persons in different rooms, censuring the breach and disobedience to these proclamations by very great fines, imprisonments, and corporal severities; so that any disrespect to any acts of state, or to the persons of statesmen, were in no time more penal, and the foundations of right never more in danger to be destroyed.*"

Let the patriotic American of this day carefully read this description by Lord Clarendon of the usurped prerogatives of the Star Chamber court of England, weighing calmly each expression as he comes thereto: let him then think of the condition of his country at the present moment, and the more than kingly prerogatives usurped by our court of star chamber, the President and cabinet, in presidential "proclamations and orders of state," which have "enjoined upon the people that which is not enjoined by the laws, and prohibited that which by the laws is not prohibited;" in illegal "commissions" issued to so-called military governors of sovereign States and a multitude of unnecessary officers whose functions have no legal sanction or authority—in grants of cotton "monopolies" so freely issued from the Treasury Department to the partisans of the Administration—in the holding for "loyal" of that which pleases a mere faction of the people, and for "just" of a dishonest legal-tender paper currency, which is the *reverse* of profitable"—in the erection of the President or any member of his cabinet into a sufficient "court of law to determine civil rights," and thereupon to trample on them—in the empowering of major-generals and others to assume that they may hold courts both of law and "revenue," in which they confiscate estates and money which *do not* "enrich the treasury"—and in the punishment of disobedience to these proclamations and other usurpations "by very great fines" unlawfully assessed, by arbitrary "imprisonments" in forts and arsenals of the United States, and "by corporal severities" at the Dry Tortugas and elsewhere—let him, we say, thus read, thus meditate, and then declare to his own conscience whether he believes "that any disrespect to acts of state" has ever been "more penal" than it has been in these States for three years past, and whether "the foundations of right" were ever "in more danger to be destroyed" than they are now, to-day. These questions must ere long be *effectually* answered, or we and our posterity must reap a bitter harvest from the seeds of tyranny we madly suffer a corrupt Administration to sow over every one of our most ancient and most cherished rights and institutions.

For the present we must leave the High Court of Star Chamber. We shall have more to say of it when we come to the unhappy reign of Charles I.

III. During this period (from Edward I. to James I.) English history supplies us with a pregnant illustration of the wisdom of our English ancestors and our own stupendous folly. The institution of slavery, in attempting to destroy which, we have perhaps destroyed a nation, is no novelty in history. It is the creature of peculiar circumstances always, and always disappears with the peculiar circumstances which have brought it into being. Slavery among the Jews, in Greece, in Rome, in the Germanic kingdoms into which the Empire was divided, and in England, thus rose and thus passed away; and the same system in America, had it been left to run its natural course, would, in the providence of God, have found its own solution in the influence of natural causes. During the period of English history with which we are at present concerned, the problem of Saxon slavery was solved; and we have thought that Hallam's outline of the steps by which this end was reached might not improperly be introduced here to show how slavery was done away in England, not by legislation or coercion, and still less by arbitrary royal proclamation, but by a simple change in the original circumstances of the masters and their slaves; in order to show further that in any country the same institution may be naturally expected to arrive at a like end when it has ceased to be of service in the commonwealth. We have preferred to give the version of Hallam verbatim, lest it might be thought that we had in any way distorted or concealed facts, from a desire to give them a peculiar coloring; and therefore, before giving his account, we venture to present the following points to the attention of the reader to be borne in mind during his perusal of it:

1. The Saxon churl was as absolute a slave to the Norman as the Southern negro to his master.

2. The right of the Norman master to the labor of his villain was a prescriptive and unquestioned right, in no respect differing from that of the American slaveholder.

3. The abolition of Saxon slavery was not effected by legislation, coercion, or proclamation, but was gradual, natural, and for the most part voluntary on the master's part.

4. Had coercive emancipation been attempted by any power in the state to the prejudice of the prescriptive rights of masters, it cannot be doubted that the Normans would have offered as determined a resistance to it as they did to every other invasion of their rights. Nor can it well be doubted that an attempt at forced emancipation, by arousing opposition to it in the Norman masters, would have indefinitely delayed the emancipation of the churls.

5. If it be said that Southern slavery is governed by the strict rules of the Roman slave code, and not by the rules of English common law, our answer is: That under Roman law, slavery disappeared as effectually as under English law; that slavery in any country must have some peculiar characteristics which do not exist in any other country; that history shows that, soon or late,

the growth of population or some other cause leads to a gradual and natural emancipation, independently of law; and therefore that a knowledge of the progress of emancipation in the peculiar case of England is peculiarly valuable in any other case where plans and systems of emancipation are considered. Judging from all past experience—and not least from the experience of England—we believe that the best plan is to have no plan, and that the only certain system is that which is naturally evolved by circumstances in each several case. Interference only retards the progress of emancipation. With these remarks we now proceed with Hallam.

In a former passage I have remarked of the Anglo-Saxon churls, that neither their situation nor that of their descendants for the earlier reigns after the conquest appears to have been mere servitude. But from the time of Henry II., as we learn from Glanvil, the villain so called was *absolutely dependent upon his lord's will, compelled to unlimited services, and destitute of property, not only in the land he held for his maintenance, but in his own acquisitions.* If a villain purchased or inherited land, the lord might seize it; if he accumulated stock, its possession was equally precarious. Against his lord he had no right of action, because his indemnity in damages, if he could have recovered any, might have been immediately taken away. If he fled from his lord's service, or from the land which he held, a writ issued *de nativitate probanda*, and the master recovered his fugitive by law. His children were born to the same state of servitude; and contrary to the rule of the civil law, where one parent was free and the other in villainage, the offspring followed the father's condition.

This class was distinguished into villains regardant, who had been attached from time immemorial to a certain manor, and villains in gross, where such territorial prescription had never existed, or had been broken. In the condition of these, whatever has been said by some writers, I can find no manner of difference; the distinction was merely technical, and affected only the mode of pleading. The term, in gross, is appropriated in our legal language to property held absolutely and without reference to any other. Thus it is applied to rights of advowson or of common, when possessed simply, and not as incident to any particular lands. And there can be no doubt that it was used in the same sense for the possession of a villain. But there was a class of persons, sometimes inaccurately confounded with villains, whom it is more important to separate; villainage had a double sense, as it related to persons or to lands. As all men were free or villains, so all lands were held by a free or villain tenure. As a villain might be enfeoffed of freeholds, though they lay at the mercy of his lord, so a freeman might hold tenements in villainage. In this case his personal liberty subsisted along with the burdens of territorial servitude. He was bound to arbitrary service at the will of the lord, and he might, by the same will, be at any moment dispossessed, for such was the condition of his tenure. But his chattels were secure from seizure, his person from injury, and he might leave the land whenever he pleased.

From so disadvantageous a condition as this of villainage, it may cause some surprise that the peasantry of England should have ever emerged. The law incapacitating a villain from acquiring property, placed, one would imagine, an insurmountable barrier in the way of his enfranchisement. It followed from thence, and is positively said by Glanvil, that *a villain could not buy his freedom, because the price he tendered would already belong to his lord;* and even in the case of free tenants in villainage, it is not easy to comprehend how their uncertain and unbounded services could ever pass into slight pecuniary commutations, much less how they could come to maintain themselves in their lands, and mock the lord with a nominal tenure according to the custom of the manor.

This, like many others relating to the progress of society, is a very obscure inquiry. We can trace the pedigree of princes, fill up the catalogue of towns besieged and provinces desolated, describe even the whole pageantry of coronations and festivals, but we cannot recover the genuine history of mankind. It has passed away with slight and partial notice by contemporary writers, and our most patient industry can hardly at present put together enough of the fragments to suggest a tolerably clear representation of ancient manners and social life. I cannot profess to undertake what would require a command of books as well as leisure beyond my reach;

but the following observations may tend a little to illustrate our immediate subject, the gradual extinction of villainage.

If we take what may be considered as the simplest case, that of a manor divided into demesne lands of the lord's occupation, and those in the tenure of his villains, performing all the services of agriculture for him, it is obvious that his interest was to maintain just so many of these as his estate required for its cultivation. Land, the cheapest of articles, was the price of their labor; and though the law did not compel him to pay this or any other price, yet necessity, repairing in some degree the law's injustice, made those pretty secure of food and dwelling, who were to give the strength of their arms for his advantage. But in course of time, as alienations of small parcels of manors to free tenants came to prevail, the proprietors of land were placed in a new situation relatively to its cultivators. The tenements in villainage, whether by law or usage, were never separated from the lordship, while its demain was reduced to a smaller extent, through subinfeudations, sales, or demises for valuable rent. The purchasers under these alienations had occasion for laborers; and these would be free servants in respect of such employers, though in villainage to their original lord. As he demanded less of their labor, through the diminution of his domain, they had more to spare for other masters; and, retaining the character of villains and the lands they held by that tenure, became hired laborers in husbandry for the greater part of the year. It is true that all their earnings were at the lord's disposal, and that he might have made a profit of their labor, when he ceased to require it for his own land. But this, which the rapacity of more commercial times would have instantly suggested, might escape a feudal superior, who, wealthy beyond his wants, and guarded by the haughtiness of ancestry against the desire of such pitiful gains, was better pleased to win the affection of his dependants, than to improve his fortune at their expense.

The services of villainage were gradually rendered less onerous and uncertain. Those of husbandry indeed are naturally uniform, and might be anticipated with no small exactness. Lords of generous tempers granted indulgences which were either intended to be or readily became perpetual. And thus, in the time of Edward I., we find the tenants in some manors bound only to stated services as recorded in the lord's book. Some of these perhaps might be villains by blood; but free tenants in villainage were much more likely to retain this precision in their services; and from claiming a customary right to be entered in the court-roll upon the same terms as their predecessors, prevailed at length to get copies of it for their security. Proofs of this remarkable transformation from tenants in villainage to copyholders are found in the reign of Henry III. I do not know however that they were protected at so early an epoch in the possession of their estates. But it is said in the year book of the 42d of Edward III. to be "admitted for clear law, that if the customary tenant or copyholder does not perform his services, the lord may seize his land as forfeited." It seems implied herein that so long as the copyholder did continue to perform the regular stipulations of his tenure, the lord was not at liberty to divest him of his estate; and this is said to be confirmed by a passage in Britton, which has escaped my search; though Littleton intimates that copyholders could have no remedy against their lords. However, in the reign of Edward IV. this was put out of doubt by the judges, who permitted the copyholder to bring his action of trespass against the lord for dispossession.

While some of the more fortunate villains crept up into property as well as freedom under the copyholders, the greater part enfranchised themselves in a different manner. The law which treated them so harshly, did not take away the means of escape; nor was this a matter of difficulty in such a country as England. To this, indeed, the unequal progression of agriculture and population in different counties would have naturally contributed. Men emigrated, as they always must, in search of cheapness or employment, according to the tide of human necessities. But the villain who had no additional motive to urge his steps away from his native place, might well hope to be forgotten or undiscovered when he breathed a freer air, and engaged his voluntary labor to a distant master. The lord had indeed an action against him; but there was so little communication between remote parts of the country, that it might be deemed his fault or singular ill fortune if he were compelled to defend himself. Even in that case the law inclined to favor him; and so many obstacles were thrown in the way of these suits to reclaim fugitive villains, that they could not have operated materially to retard their general enfranchisement. In one case, indeed, that of unmolested residence for a year and a day within a walled city or borough, the villain became free, and the lord was absolutely barred of his remedy. This provision is contained even in the laws of William the Conqueror, as contained in Hoveden, and, if it be not an interpolation, may be supposed to have had a view to strengthen the population of those places which were designed for garrisons. This law, whether of William or not, is unequivocally mentioned by Glanvil. Nor was it a mere letter. According to a record in the sixth of Edward II., Sir John Clavering sued eighteen villains of his manor of Cossey, for withdrawing themselves therefrom with their chattels; whereupon a writ was directed to them; but six of the number claimed to be freemen, alleging the Conqueror's charter, and offering to prove that they had lived in Norwich, paying scot and lot, about thirty years; which claim was admitted.

By such means a large proportion of the peasantry before the middle of the fourteenth century had become hired laborers instead of villains. We first hear of them on a grand scale, in an ordinance made by Edward III., in the twenty-third year of his reign. This was just after the dreadful pestilence of 1348, and it recites that, the number of workmen and servants having been greatly reduced by that calamity, the remainder demanded excessive wages from their employers. Such an enhancement in the price of labor, though founded exactly on the same principles as regulate the value of any other commodity, is too frequently treated as a sort of crime by lawgivers, who seem to grudge the poor that transient melioration of their lot, which the progress of population, or other analogous circumstances, will, without any interference, very rapidly take away. This ordinance therefore exacts that every man in England, of whatever condition, bond or free, of able body, and within sixty years of age, not living of his own nor by any trade, shall be obliged, when required, to serve any master who is willing to hire him at such wages as were usually paid three years since, or for some time preceding; provided that the lords of villains or tenants in villainage shall have the preference of their labor, so that they retain no more than shall be necessary for them. More than these old wages is strictly forbidden to be offered, as well as demanded. No one is permitted, under color of charity, to give alms to a beggar. And to make some compensation to the inferior classes for these severities a clause is inserted, as wise, just and practicable as the rest, for the sale of provisions at reasonable prices.

This ordinance met with so little regard that a statute was made in Parliament two years after, fixing the wages of all artificers and husbandmen, with regard to the nature and season of their labor. From this time it became a frequent complaint of the commons that the statute of laborers was not kept. The king had in this case probably no other reason for leaving their grievances unredressed than his inability to change the order of Providence. A silent alteration had been wrought in the condition and character of the lower classes during the reign of Edward III. This was the effect of increased knowledge and refinement, which had been making a considerable progress for full half a century, though they did not readily permeate the cold region of poverty and ignorance. It was natural that the country people, or uplandish folk, as they were called, should repine at the exclusion from that enjoyment of competence, and security for the fruits of their labor, which the inhabitants of towns so fully possessed. The fourteenth century was in many parts of Europe the age when a sense of political servitude was most keenly felt. Thus the insurrection of the Jacquerie in France, about the year 1358, had the same character, and resulted in a great measure from the same causes as that of the English peasants in 1382. And we may account in a similar manner for the democratical tone of the French and Flemish cities, and for the prevalence of a spirit of liberty in Germany and Switzerland.

I do not know whether we should attribute part of this revolutionary concussion to the preaching of Wickliffe's disciples, or look upon both one and the other as phenomena belonging to that particular epoch in the progress of society. New principles, both as to civil rule and religion, broke suddenly upon the uneducated mind, to render it bold, presumptuous and turbulent. But at least

I make little doubt, that the dislike of ecclesiastical power, which spread so rapidly among the people at this season, connected itself with a spirit of insubordination and an intolerance of political subjection. Both were nourished by the same teachers, the lower secular clergy; and however distinct we may think a religious reformation from a civil anarchy, there was a good deal common in the language by which the populace were inflamed to either one or the other. Even the scriptural moralities which were then exhibited, and which became the foundation of our theatre, afforded fuel to the spirit of sedition. The common original, and common destination of mankind, with every other lesson of equality which religion supplies to humble or to console, were displayed with coarse and glaring features in these representations. The familiarity of such ideas has deadened their effects upon our minds; but when a rude peasant, surprisingly destitute of religious instruction during that corrupt age of the church, was led at once to these impressive truths, we cannot be astonished at the intoxication of mind they produced.

Though I believe that, compared at least with the aristocracy of other countries, the English lords were guilty of very little cruelty or injustice, yet there were circumstances belonging to that period which might tempt them to deal more hardly than before with their peasantry. The fourteenth century was an age of greater magnificence than those which had preceded, in dress, in ceremonies, in buildings; foreign luxuries were known enough to excite an eager demand among the higher ranks, and yet so scarce as to yield inordinate prices; while the land-owners were on the other hand, impoverished by heavy and unceasing taxation. Hence it is probable that avarice, as commonly happens, had given birth to oppression; and if the gentry, as I am inclined to believe, had become more attentive to agricultural improvements, it is reasonable to conjecture that those whose tenure obliged them to unlimited services of husbandry were more harassed than under their wealthy and indolent masters in preceding times.

The storm that almost swept away all bulwarks of civilized and regular society seems to have been long in collecting itself. Perhaps a more sagacious legislature might have contrived to disperse it; but the commons only presented complaints of the refractoriness with which villains and tenants in villainage rendered their due services; and the exigencies of government led to the fatal poll tax of a groat, which was the proximate cause of the insurrection. By the demands of these rioters we perceive that territorial servitude was far from extinct; but it should not be hastily concluded that they were all personal villains, for a large proportion were Kentish men, to whom that condition could not have applied; it being a good bar to a writ *de nativitate probanda*, that the party's father was born in the county of Kent.

After this tremendous rebellion, it might be expected that the legislature would use little indulgence toward the lower commons. Such unhappy tumults are doubly mischievous, not more from the immediate calamities that attend them, than from *the fear and hatred of the people which they generate in the elevated classes.* The general charter of manumission extorted from the king by the rioters of Blackheath, was annulled by proclamation to the sheriffs, and this revocation approved by the lords and commons in Parliament; who added, as was very true, that "such enfranchisement could not be made without their consent; which they would never give to save themselves from perishing altogether in one day." Riots were turned into treason by a law of the same Parliament. By a very harsh statute in the 12th of Richard II., no servant or laborer could depart, even at the expiration of his service, from the hundred in which he lived, without permission under the king's seal; nor might any who had been bred to husbandry till twelve years old, exercise any other calling. A few years afterward, the commons petitioned that villains might not put their children to school, in order to advance them by the Church, "and this for the honor of all the freemen of the kingdom." In the same Parliament they complain that villains fly to cities and boroughs, whence their masters cannot recover them; and if they attempt it, are hindered by the people; and prayed that the lords might seize their villains in such places, without regard to the franchises thereof. But on both these petitions the king put in a negative.

From henceforward we see little notice taken of villainage in parliamentary records, and there seems to have been a rapid tendency to its entire abolition. But the fifteenth century is barren of materials; and we can only infer that, as the same causes which in Edward III.'s time had converted a large portion of the peasantry into free laborers still continued to operate, they must silently have extinguished the whole system of personal and territorial servitude. The latter, indeed, was essentially changed by the establishment of the law of copyhold.

I cannot presume to conjecture in what degree voluntary manumission is to be reckoned among the means that contributed to the abolition of villainage. Charters of enfranchisement were very common upon the Continent. They may perhaps have been less so in England. Indeed, the statute *de donis* must have operated very injuriously to prevent the enfranchisement of villains regardant, who were entailed along with the land. Instances however occur from time to time; and we cannot expect to discover many. One appears as early as the fifteenth year of Henry III., who grants to all persons, born or to be born within his village of Contishall, that they shall be free from all villainage in body and blood, paying an aid of twenty shillings to knight the king's eldest son, and six shillings a year as a quit rent; so in the 12th of Edward III., certain of the king's villains are enfranchised on payment of a fine. In strictness of law, a fine from the villain for the sake of enfranchisement was nugatory, since all he could possess was already at his lord's disposal. But custom and equity might easily introduce different maxims; and it was plainly for the lord's interest to encourage his tenants in the acquisition of money to redeem themselves, rather than to quench the exertions of their industry by availing himself of an extreme right. Deeds of enfranchisement occur in the reigns of Mary and Elizabeth; and perhaps a commission of the latter princess in 1574, directing the enfranchisement of her bondmen and bondwomen on certain manors upon payment of a fine, is the last unequivocal testimony to the existence of villainage; though it is highly probable that it existed in remote parts of the country some time longer.—HALLAM'S *Middle Ages*, vol. III., pp. 171–182.

At this epoch, to continue nearly in the language of the

author just quoted, we must pause before proceeding with these inquiries into the English constitution; a sketch very imperfect and unsatisfactory, but which may at least answer the purpose of fixing the reader's attention on the principal objects, and of leading him to consult the purest fountains of constitutional knowledge. From the accession of the house of Tudor, a new period is to be dated in our history; far more prosperous in the diffusion of opulence, and the preservation of general order, than the preceding, but less distinguished by the spirit of freedom and jealousy of tyrannical power. This period, therefore, we shall not attempt to illustrate, but pass on to the more tumultuous, but more fruitful epoch of the Stuarts. We have already seen, through the twilight of our Anglo-Saxon records, a form of civil policy established by our ancestors, marked, like the kindred governments of the Continent, with aboriginal Teutonic features; barbarous, indeed, and insufficient for the great ends of society, but capable and worthy of improvement, because actuated by a sound and vital spirit, the love of freedom and of justice. From these principles arose that venerable institution, which none but a free and simple people could have conceived, trial by peers; an institution common in some degree to other nations, but which, more widely extended, more strictly retained, and better modified among ourselves, has become perhaps the first, certainly among the first, of our securities against arbitrary government. We have seen a foreign conqueror and his descendants trample almost alike upon the prostrate nation, and upon those who had been companions of their victory, introduce the servitudes of feudal law with more than their usual rigor, and establish a large revenue by continual precedents upon a system of universal and prescriptive extortion. But the Norman and English races, each unfit to endure oppression, forgetting their animosities in a common intererst, enforce by arms the concession of a great charter of liberties. Privileges wrested from one faithless monarch, are preserved with continual vigilance against the machinations of another; the rights of the people become more precise, and their spirit more magnanimous, during the long reign of Henry III. With greater ambition and greater abilities than his father, Edward I. attempts in vain to govern in an arbitrary

12*

manner, and has the mortification of seeing his prerogative fettered by still more important limitations. The great council of the nation is opened to the representatives of the commons. They proceed by slow and cautious steps to remonstrate against public grievances, to check the abuses of administration, and sometimes to chastise public delinquency in the officers of the crown. A number of remedial provisions are added to the statutes; every Englishman learns to remember that he is the citizen of a free state, and to claim the common law as his birthright, even though the violence of power should interrupt its enjoyment. It were a strange misrepresentation of history to assert that the constitution had attained anything like a perfect state in the fifteenth century; but we know not whether there are any essential privileges of our countrymen, any fundamental securities against arbitrary power, so far as they depend upon positive institutions, which may not be traced to the time when the house of Plantagenet filled the English throne.

NOTES.

1. *Deposition of Richard II. by Parliament.*—The Parliament closed this reign, Richard II.'s, and exercised the supreme power of government by the removal of Richard II. from the throne and the election of Henry, Duke of Lancaster, to succeed him as king. The rolls of Parliament describe the proceedings at great length: the king's renunciation of the throne, for causes of inability and insufficiency by himself confessed; his absolution of the people from all allegiance; and his recommendation of the duke of Lancaster as his successor. The parliament pronounced sentence of deposition against him and Henry claimed the vacant throne. The lords spiritual and temporal, and commons, as the three estates of the realm, accepted Henry as king, he disclaiming all right by conquest. The justices and other officers of state were sworn into their offices, and proclamation was made for his coronation. Procurators announced to Richard their acceptance of his resignation, and his deposition; and renounced and gave back to him the homage and fealty formerly made to him.

2. *Proclamations of the Sovereign declared by Act of Parliament to have the force of Laws.*—The Parliament having thus resigned all their ecclesiastical liberties, proceeded to an entire surrender of their civil; and without scruple or deliberation they made by one act a total subversion of the English constitution.

They gave to the king's proclamations the same force as to a statute enacted by Parliament; and to render the matter worse, if possible, they framed this law as if it were only declaratory, and were intended to explain the natural extent of the regal authority. The preamble contains, that the king had formerly set forth several proclamations, which froward persons had wilfully contemned, not considering what a king by his royal power may do; that this license might encourage offenders not only to disobey the laws of Almighty God, but also to dishonor the king's most royal majesty, *who may full ill bear it;* that sudden emergencies often occur, which require speedy remedies, and cannot await the slow assembling and deliberations of Parliament; and that, though the king was empowered, by his authority, derived from God, to consult the public good on these occasions, yet the opposition of refractory subjects might push him to extremity and violence. For these reasons, the Parliament, that they might remove all occasion of doubt, ascertained by a statute this prerogative of the crown, and enabled his majesty, with the advice of his council, to set forth proclamations, enjoining obedience under whatever pains and penalties he should think proper; and these proclamations were to have the force of perpetual laws.

What shows either a stupid or a wilful blindness of Parliament is, that they pretended, even after this statute, to maintain some limitations in the government; and they enacted that no proclamation should deprive any person of his lawful possessions, liberties, inheritances, privileges, franchises; nor yet infringe any common law or laudable custom of the realm. They considered not that no penalty could be inflicted on the disobedience of proclamations, without invading some liberty or property of the subject; and that the power of enacting new laws, joined to the dispensing power, then exercised by the crown, amounted to a full legislative authority.—HUME, iv. 207, anno 1539.

The Parliament also facilitated the execution of the former law, by which the king's proclamations were made equal to statutes. They appointed that any nine counsellors should form a legal court for punishing all disobedience to proclamations. The total abolition of juries in criminal causes, as well as of al Parliaments, secured, if the king had so pleased, the necessary consequence of this enormous law. He might issue a proclamation for the execution of any penal statute, and afterward try the criminals, not for a breach of the statute, but for disobedience to his proclamation. It is remarkable, that the lord Mountjoy entered a protest against this law; and it is equally remarkable, that that protest is the only one entered against any public bill during this whole reign.—HUME, iv. 250, anno 1543.

This law, the destruction of all laws, by which the king's proclamation was made of equal force with a statute, was repealed under Edward VI. During the reign of Elizabeth, however, the rights conferred by it upon the sovereign were exercised with such extravagance as to be even ridiculous. Hume says:

In reality, the crown possessed the full legislative power, by means of proclamations, which might effect any matter, even of the greatest importance, and which the Star Chamber took care to see more rigorously executed than the laws themselves. The motives of these proclamations were sometimes very frivolous and even ridiculous. Queen Elizabeth had taken offence at the smell of woad; and she issued an edict prohibiting any one from cultivating that useful plant. She was also pleased to take offence at the long swords and high ruffs then in fashion. She sent about her officers, to break every man's sword, and clip every man's ruff, which was beyond a certain length.—HUME, v. 458.

3. The following paragraphs will suffice as an illustration of the style and views of Hooker. Showing the evils of anarchy, and the necessity of *consent* to the validity of government, he says:

"To take away all such mutual grievances, injuries, and wrongs, there was no way but only growing into composition and agreement amongst themselves, by ordaining some kind of government public, and by yielding themselves subject thereunto: that unto whom they granted authority to rule and govern, by them the peace, tranquillity, and happy estate of the rest might be procured. Men always knew that when force and injury was offered they might be defenders of themselves; they knew that howsoever men may seek their own commodity, yet if this were done with injury unto others, it was not to be suffered, but by all men and by all good means to be withstood; finally they knew that no man might in reason take upon him to determine his own right, and according to his own determination proceed in maintenance thereof, inasmuch as every man is towards himself and them whom he greatly affecteth partial; and therefore that strifes and troubles would be endless, except they gave their common consent all to be ordered by some whom they should agree upon: without which consent there were no reason that one man should take upon him to be lord or judge over another; because, although there be according to the opinion of some very great and judicious men a kind of natural right in the noble, wise, and virtuous, to govern them which are of servile disposition; nevertheless for manifestation of this their right, and men's more peaceable contentment on both sides, the assent of those who are to be governed seemeth necessary.

"The lawful power of making laws to command whole politic societies of men belongeth so properly unto the same entire societies, that for any prince or potentate of what kind soever upon earth to exercise the same of himself, and not either by express commission immediately and personally received from God, or else by authority derived at the first from their consent upon whose persons they impose laws, it is no better than mere tyranny.

"Laws they are not, therefore, which public approbation hath not made so. But approbation not only they give who personally declare their assent by voice, sign, or act, but also when others do it in their names, by right originally at the least derived from them. As in parliaments, councils, and the like assemblies, although we be not personally ourselves present, notwithstanding, our assent is by reason of others, agents there in our behalf. And what we do by others, no reason but that it should stand as our deed, no less effectually to bind us than if ourselves had done it in person."—*Eccl. Pol.*, Bk. I., ch. x. sec. 2, 3, 4, 8.

Of limited or constitutional government, usurpation, and the right of revolution, Hooker speaks thus:

"Even in these very actions which are proper unto dominion, there must be some certain rule, whereunto kings in all their proceedings ought to be strictly tied.

"The cause of deriving supreme power from a whole entire multitude unto some special part thereof, is partly the necessity of expedition in public affairs; partly the inconveniency of confusion and troubles, where a multitude of equals dealeth; and partly the dissipation which must needs ensue in companies, where every man wholly seeketh his own particular. Men by that which is proper are severed, united they are by that which is common. Wherefore, besides that which moveth each man in particular to seek his private, there must of necessity in all public societies be also a general mover, directing unto the common good, and framing every man's particular to it. The end whereunto all government was instituted, was *bonum publicum*, the universal or common good."—*Eccl. Pol.*, Bk. VIII., ch. ii. sec. 16, 18.

"First unto me it seemeth almost out of doubt and controversy, that every independent multitude, before any certain form of regiment established, hath, under God's supreme authority, full dominion over itself, even as a man not tied with the bond of subjection as yet unto any other, hath over himself the like power. God creating mankind did endue it naturally with full power to guide itself, in what kind of societies soever it should choose to live. A man which is born lord of himself may be made another's servant; and that power which naturally whole societies have, may be derived into many, few, or one, under whom the rest shall then live in subjection."—HOOKER, Bk. VIII., ch. ii. sec. 5.

"I cannot choose but commend highly their wisdom, by whom the foundations of this commonwealth have been laid; wherein though no manner of person or cause be unsubject to the king's power, yet so is the power of the king over all and in all limited, that unto all his proceedings the law itself is a rule. The axioms of our regal government are these: 'Lex facit regem;' the king's grant of any favour made contrary to the law is void; 'Rex nihil potest nisi quod jure potest.' Our kings therefore, when they take possession of the room they are called unto, have it pointed out before their eyes, even by the very solemnities and rites of their inauguration, to what affairs by the said law their supreme authority reacheth."—*Eccl. Pol.*, Bk. VIII., ch. ii. sec. 13.

"Subjection therefore we owe, and that by the law of God; we are in conscience bound to yield it even unto every of them that hold the seats of authority and power in relation unto us. Howbeit, not all kind of subjection unto every such kind of power. Concerning scribes and pharisees, our Saviour's precept was, 'Whatsoever they shall tell you, do it;' was it His meaning that if they should at any time enjoin the people to levy an army, or to sell their lands and goods for the furtherance of so great an enterprise; and in a word, that simply whatsoever it were which they did command, they ought without any exception forthwith to be obeyed? No; but 'whatsoever they shall tell you,' must be understood *in pertinentibus ad cathedram*, it must be construed with limitation, and restrained unto things of that kind which did belong to their place and power. For they had not power general, absolutely given them to command them.

"The reason why we are bound in conscience to be subject unto all such power, is because all "powers are of God." They are of God either instituting or permitting them. Power then is of divine institution when either God himself doth deliver, or men, by light of nature, find out the kind thereof. So that the power of parents over children, and of husbands over their wives, the power of all sorts of superiors, *made by consent of commonwealths within themselves, or grown from agreement amongst nations*, such power is of God's own institution in respect of the kind thereof.

"As for them that exercise power altogether against order, although the kind of power which they have may be of God, yet is their exercise thereof against God, and therefore not of God, otherwise than by permission, as all injustice is.

"Usurpers of power, whereby we do not mean them that by violence have aspired unto places of high authority, but them that use more authority than they did ever receive in form and manner before mentioned (for so they may do, whose titles unto the rooms of authority which they possess no man can deny to be just and lawful: even as contrariwise some men's proceedings in government have been very orderly who, notwithstanding, did not attain to be made governors without great violence and disorder); such usurpers, therefore, as in the exercise of their power do more than they have been authorized to do, cannot in conscience bind any man unto obedience."—*Eccl. Pol.*, Bk. VIII., Appendix No. I.

In the first months of Elizabeth's reign, Aylmer, afterward Bishop of London, published an answer to a book by John Knox, against female monarchy, or, as he termed it, "Blast of the Trumpet against the Monstrous Regiment of Women;" which, though written in the time of Mary, and directed against her, was of course not acceptable to her sister. The answerer relies, among other arguments, on the nature of the English Constitution, which by diminishing the power of the crown, renders it less unfit to be worn by a woman. His clear conception of the nature of a government of laws is well worthy of notice: "Well," he says, "a woman may not reign in England! Better in England than anywhere, as it shall appear to him, that without affection, will consider the kind of regiment. While I compare ours with others, as it is in itself, and not maimed by usurpation, I can find none either so good or so indifferent. The regiment of England is not a mere monarchy, as some, for lack of consideration, think, nor a mere oligarchy, nor democracy, but a rule mixed of all these, wherein each one of these have, or should have, like authority. The image whereof, and not the image, but the thing indeed, is to be seen in the parliament house, wherein you shall find these three estates: the king or queen, which representeth the monarchy; the noblemen, which be the aristocracy; and the burgesses and knights, the democracy. If the Parliament use their privileges, the king can ordain nothing without them; if he do, it is his fault in usurping it, and their fault in permitting it. Wherefore, in my judgment, those that in King Henry VIII.'s days would not grant him that his proclamations should have the force of a statute, were good fathers of the country, and worthy of commendation in defending their liberty. But to what purpose is all this? To declare that it is not in England so dangerous a matter to have a woman ruler as men take it to be. For first, it is not she that ruleth, but the laws, the executors whereof be her judges appointed by her, her justices, and such other officers. Secondly, she maketh no statutes or laws, but the honorable court of Parliament; she breaketh none, but it must be she and they together, or else not. If, on the other part, the regiment were such as all hanged on the king's or queen's will, and not upon the laws written; if she might decree and make laws alone without her senate; if she judged offences according to her wisdom, and not by limitation of statutes and laws, if she might dispose alone of war and peace; if, to be short, she were a mere monarch, and not a mixed ruler, you might, peradventure, make me to fear the matter the more, and the less to defend the cause."—HALLAM'S *Constitutional History of England*, vol. i. pp. 280, 281.

4. *Blackstone on the open Examination of Witnesses.*—"This open examination of witnesses *viva voce*, in the presence of all mankind, is much more conducive to the clearing up of truth, than the private and secret examination, taken down in writing before an officer, or his clerk, or in the ecclesiastical courts, and all others that have borrowed their practice from the civil law, where a witness may frequently depose that, in private, which he may be ashamed to testify in a public and solemn tribunal. There an artful or careless scribe may make a witness speak what he never meant, by dressing up his depositions in his own forms and language; but he is here at liberty to correct and explain his meaning, if misunderstood, which he can never do after a written deposition is taken down. Besides, the occasional questions of the judge, the jury, and the counsel, propounded to the witnesses on a sudden, will sift out the truth much better than a formal set of interrogatories, previously penned and settled; and the confronting of adverse witnesses is also another opportunity of obtaining a clear discovery, which can never be had upon any other method of trial. Nor is the presence of the judge during the examination a matter of small importance; for, besides the respect and awe with which his presence will naturally inspire the witness, he is able, by use and experience, to keep the evidence from wandering from the point in issue. In short, by this method of examination, and this only, the persons who are to decide upon the evidence have an opportunity of observing the quality, age, education, understanding, behavior, and inclinations of the witness; in which points all persons must appear alike, when their depositions are reduced to writing, and read to the judge, in the absence of those who made them; and yet, as much may be frequently collected from the manner in which the evidence is delivered, as from the matter of it. These are a few of the advantages attending this, the English way of giving testimony *ore tenus*."—BLACKSTONE, vol. iii. p. 373, 374.

CHAPTER VII.

THE STUARTS. JAMES I.

CHARACTER OF THE STUART PERIOD—ACCESSION OF JAMES—HIS SPEECH ON OPENING HIS PARLIAMENT—DEFINITION OF TYRANNY—THE DOCTRINE OF DIVINE RIGHT—SEVERITIES AGAINST ROMAN CATHOLICS—PARLIAMENT OF 1609—ACT FOR COMPELLING OATHS OF ALLEGIANCE—THE COMMONS MAINTAIN THEIR RIGHT OF DECIDING ELECTION RETURNS—PARLIAMENTARY PRIVILEGE—THEIR "APOLOGY" TO THE KING—THEY EXPEL A MEMBER AT HIS DICTATION—HIGH PREROGATIVE SPEECH OF JAMES TO THE PARLIAMENT IN 1610—ILLEGAL EXACTION OF TONNAGE AND POUNDAGE—REMONSTRANCE OF THE COMMONS—CASE OF DR. COWELL—CONSIDERATION OF GRIEVANCES—ATTEMPT AT UNION BETWEEN ENGLAND AND SCOTLAND, AND AT THE ABOLITION OF FEUDAL TENURES—EXPEDIENTS OF JAMES FOR RAISING MONEY—THE UNDERTAKERS' PARLIAMENT—PARLIAMENT OF 1620–1—JAMES'S SPEECH—DISPUTE OF THE COMMONS WITH THE KING ON ADJOURNMENT—PARLIAMENT REASSEMBLED—THE PROPOSED SPANISH MATCH—PETITION OF THE COMMONS—ANGRY LETTER OF JAMES TO THE SPEAKER—SECOND PETITION AND REMONSTRANCE OF THE COMMONS—JAMES'S ANSWER—PROTESTATION OF THE COMMONS—IT IS TORN OUT FROM THE RECORD BY THE KING—PUNISHMENT OF MEMBERS—PARLIAMENT OF 1623—MONOPOLIES, TOGETHER WITH THE SUSPENDING AND DISPENSING POWERS OF THE KING ABOLISHED—CONCLUDING OBSERVATIONS.

WE come now to a period in the constitutional history of England when all that had been gained for liberty was once more to be brought into dispute, and the long controversy between prerogative and freedom was to receive its ultimate decision. Under the Stuart kings the absolutism that existed in the constitution girded on its strength, did battle for existence, fell before the chartered rights of a brave people resolute to guard them, and was blotted out forevermore. The story of this period has none of the romance which is connected with the giving of the first great charter. Here we see no lordly barons with their retinues of belted knights and sturdy yeomen marching in the pomp and circumstance of war to win a bloodless triumph from a recreant king. Here we have no true English prelate like the archbishop Langton standing for a nation's right against a tyrant's usurpation. In this strife we have on one side royalty with all its prestige; on the other a plain English House of Commons; and between, we see the church arrayed upon the side of royalty against the people; while the peers sustain the commons at the same time that they strive to reconcile a quarrel which portends so terrible an end. On the surface nothing tells at first of the volcanic fire that threatens the existence of the constitution of the kingdom or the sovereign's throne. The war—for war it is—seems to be but a paper fusillade. The king sends messages to Parliament; adjourns, prorogues, dissolves the Parliament; proclaims the nullity of laws passed by the Parliament; gives orders for the levying of taxes, and imprisons freemen without trial, in defiance of the Parliament; *all on paper.* Parliament, on the other hand, sends back what is apparently a shower of paper balls and nothing more. It passes resolutions, signs addresses, and remonstrances, and humble parliamentary petitions, and asserts its rights—*on paper.* But anon the papers glow with passion and men's hearts burn, and the torch of civil war lights up the land; and by and by, as oftenest happens in the course of revolutions, people, weary of the strife, give up all they have fought for to the hands of a worse tyrant than they had before—enduring under a man they call (in mockery is it?) *Lord Protector of a Commonwealth* (!) more grinding and degrading despotism than they suffered in the worst days of their beheaded king. Yet were the Greeks wise who said, All things are born of battle. For by the paper fusillade, no less than the civil strife, and the hatred roused against the puritan *Lord Destroyer of the Kingdom*, the atmosphere of English mind was cleared. And liberty, at length, defined and guarded by sufficient safeguards, grew, as she only can grow, by the aliment of strife and war. He who has no imagination would do well to pass over the outwardly dull details of parliamentary contention we are now about to lay before him. But he who has eyes to see the national life that burns and glows, or sometimes only faintly smoulders, under their paper protocols and manifestoes, may learn much therefrom not altogether useless in this epoch of the history of the United States. We are now about to give the parliamentary history of England under the Stuart kings, in order to bring clearly out the necessities which called for the second and third Great Charters of the liberties of England, commonly called the Petition of Right and the Bill of Rights. The same necessities may arise again; many citizens of these States think they have occurred already in the past three years. Nor are there wanting those who hold that Charles I. never did, in all his reign, commit more flagrant outrages upon the English constitution and the rights of Englishmen, than have been openly and boldly committed on the fourth Great Charter—the incomparable Constitution of the United States, and on free-born Americans by a so-called republican (!) administration. Whether these accusations be true or not, we leave our readers to determine. We shall tell the simple tale, neither extenuating nor maliciously exaggerating anything whatever.

James the Sixth of Scotland and First of England, the successor of Elizabeth, ascended the throne on the 24th of March, 1603. He was received with great and hearty welcome by the people, who had become tired of their long submission to Elizabeth; and it is probable that the ardent patriots who had sprung up in the nation toward the end of her reign looked forward to the occupation of the throne by a foreigner, for an opportunity to establish the principles of liberty, for which they had contended under her repressive system. Yet in the outset of James's reign the most extreme flattery—which we have no mind to repeat—was addressed to the monarch; though we must observe that it was always flattery of his person, never flattery of his official prerogative. Such as it was, it proved acceptable to James; and nothing could have been more promising or more fallacious than the concord which at first prevailed between the first king of the House of Stuart and the kingdom he had come to govern. The assembling of Parliament was delayed on account of the plague which prevailed during the year of James's accession, and did not meet before the 19th of March, 1604. It was opened with a long speech from the king, in which he so plainly defined the rights and duties of a constitutional sovereign, that his words are quoted by Locke in support of his definition of *tyranny*, which the philosopher describes as "*the exercise of power beyond right.*" James said, "I will ever prefer the weal of the public and of the whole commonwealth, in making of good laws and constitutions, to any particular and private ends of mine; thinking ever the wealth and weal of the commonwealth to be my greatest weal and worldly felicity—a point wherein a lawful king doth directly differ from a tyrant. For I do acknowledge that the special and greatest point of difference that is between a rightful king and a usurping tyrant, is this:—that whereas the proud and ambitious tyrant doth think his kingdom and people are only ordained for satisfaction of his desires and unreasonable appetites, the righteous and just king doth by the contrary acknowledge himself to be ordained for the procuring of the wealth and property of the people." It is curious to find such constitutional principles laid down at the commencement of the career of the Stuart kings—a dynasty to which we owe the monstrous doctrine of DIVINE RIGHT. This doctrine, which we do not hesitate to stamp as monstrous, was thoroughly believed by James and his immediate successor, Charles I., and being in fact the platform of their principles, must be clearly understood if we would have an intelligent conception of the motives which actuated the Stuarts in their long struggle with their subjects. It was current in the reign of James, who went so far as to employ his pen to enforce it; but we may collect a more concise account of it, and of the arguments by which it was maintained, from a later and more celebrated work, called the "Patriarch," written by Sir Robert Filmer in the reign of Charles I., and published after the restoration of Charles II. "All government (it is asserted) is absolute monarchy. No man is born free; and therefore could never have the liberty to choose either governor or form of government. The father of a family governs by no law but his own. Kings, in the right of parents, succeed to the exercise of supreme jurisdiction. They are above all laws. They have a divine right to absolute power; and are not answerable to human authority." The consequence of these propositions was assumed to be "that all laws, privileges, and grants of princes have no force but during their lives, if they be not ratified by the express consent or the sufferance or the prince following; and that a perfect kingdom is that where the king rules all things according to his own will." This doctrine was preached by the Church and acted upon by the Stuart kings.

This Parliament was chiefly occupied with passing and restoring penal laws against the Roman Catholics. Its most important acts will be described hereafter. The second session of Parliament commenced on the 5th of November, 1605, the day after the discovery of the Gunpowder Plot; and the act which was immediately passed for establishing an annual public thanksgiving for the deliverance of the king, was used as an occasion for more of that fulsome and even blasphemous adulation which had been addressed to him at the beginning of his reign. This Parliament was chiefly noted for severities against the Roman Catholics.

The Parliament held in 1609 continued the same course of severity against the papists (*i. e.*, to enforce the established religion upon them). It passed an act that no person should be naturalized, or restored in blood (in other words, relieved from the penalties of attainder), unless he received the sacrament before the bill was exhibited, and took the oath of allegiance and supremacy before it was read a second time.

An act of the same session, 1609, shows the willing concurrence of Parliament in severe laws. It was "for administering the oath of allegiance, and reformation of married women recusants." "To show how greatly your loyal subjects approve the oath, they prostrate themselves at your majesty's feet, that the oath may be administered to all your subjects." It required the oath to be taken by all persons, ecclesiastical and temporal, of both sexes, above the age of eighteen years. Numerous clauses describe the officials before whom the several orders and ranks in the state—the church, the law, the army and navy, members of the universities and of Parliament, doctors of physic, aldermen, and freemen—should take the oath, which was to be taken by all within six months. Any of the privy council, or a bishop, might require any baron or baroness above the age of eighteen—and two justices of the peace might require any other person above the same age—to take the oath.

If refused, the person tendering the oath was to commit the

offender to the common jail, there to remain without bail, until the next assizes, or quarter sessions; where if the oath were again refused, the person refusing incurred the penalties of *præmunire;* except married women, who were to be *imprisoned without bail*, until they would take the oath. Persons refusing the oath were disabled to hold any public place of judicature, to bear any office, or to practise the common law, or civil law, or physic, or surgery, or the art of an apothecary, or any liberal science for gain, until they should receive the oath.

But ere long a change became apparent in the actions of the Commons. James—" the wisest fool in Christendom "—was little likely to sustain the reverence inspired by his position. He was a striking contrast to his predecessor; and the House of Commons, relieved from the dread with which Elizabeth had inspired them, soon gave James to understand that he must not expect submission to his absolute will where their privileges were concerned. These they brought forward, and enforced with an energy and spirit, in striking contrast with the humble language of their statutes. In the first Parliament they entered into a contest, in which the king took personal part, as to their right to decide upon election returns. The king having assumed a right to limit the selection of the people in regard to the persons whom they might return as members of the House of Commons, and in the Court of Chancery to set aside elections not made in accordance with his proclamation, the house made so determined a resistance to this manifest invasion of its privilege, that James was glad to end the matter by a compromise which left the house substantially victorious; and from this time forward no attempt ever was made to dispute their jurisdiction over the returns of their members.

In the same Parliament they established (not without a struggle) their privilege to deliver out of custody members arrested in execution for debt, and to punish those who made or procured such arrest; which privilege was put into an indisputable position by an act of the same Parliament.

Besides these successes, the House of Commons of James's first Parliament laid a strong foundation for the future efforts by a bold and explicit statement of their constitutional rights and liberties, which they caused to be drawn up by a committee of the house, in order to be delivered to the king. It is entitled "A Form of Apology and Satisfaction to be delivered to his Majesty;" and must ever be considered as an important constitutional document. It is addressed to the king, and it commences by expressing a desire to remove from the mind of the king (whom they style "a king of such understanding and wisdom as is rare to find in any prince in the world") misinformation touching the estate of the House of the Commons, as to the privileges of the commons, and their several proceedings during this Parliament. They reduce these misinformations to three principal heads. "1st, Touching the cause of the joyful receiving of your majesty into the kingdom;—2dly, Touching the rights and liberties of your subjects of England, and the privileges of this house;—3dly, Touching the several actions and speeches passed in the house."

They "declare, as to the first, that they received him not with fear, but with joy and cheerfulness, and with a general hope that, under his reign, peace, justice, and all virtue, should renew again and flourish. Touching the privileges (the second) the misinformation delivered was—1st, That we hold not privileges of right, but of grace only, renewed every Parliament, by way of donation, upon petition, and so to be limited; 2dly, That we are no court of record, nor yet a court that can command view of records, but that our proceedings here are only to acts and memorials, and that the attendance with the records is courtesy, not duty; 3dly, and lastly, That the examination of the return of writs for knights and burgesses is without our compass, and due to the chancery.

"They, in the name of the whole commons of England, and for themselves and their posterity, protest against these assertions, and desire that their protestation may be recorded to all posterity. And contrariwise, against these misinformations they most truly avouch:

"1st. That our privileges are our rights and due inheritance, no less than our lands and goods.

"2dly. That they cannot be withheld from us, denied, or impaired, but with apparent wrong to the whole state of the realm.

"3dly. That our making of request, in the entrance of Parliament, to enjoy our privilege, is an act only of manners, and doth weaken our right no more than our suing to the king for our lands by petition, which form, though new and more decent than the old by præcipe, yet the subject's right is no less now than of old.

"4thly. We avouch also, that our house is a court of record, and so ever esteemed.

"5thly. That there is not the highest standing court in the land that ought to enter into competency, either for dignity or authority, with this high Court of Parliament; which, with your Majesty's royal assent, gives laws to other courts, but from other courts, receives neither laws nor orders.

"6thly and lastly. We avouch that the House of Commons is the sole proper judge of return of all such writs, and of the election of all such members as belong to it—without which the freedom of election were not entire; and that the chancery, though a standing court under your majesty, be to send out these writs and receive the returns, and to preserve them, yet the same is done only for the use of Parliament; over which neither the chancery, nor any other court ever had, or ought to have, any manner of jurisdiction."

The strain of such high principles, in a body which had addressed so much fulsome flattery to James, in the first acts of the Parliament, may be conceived; and in the session of 1606 the Commons receded so far as to expel a member at the king's dictation. The circumstances were as follows: Sir Christopher Pigott, having introduced into a speech some by-matters of invectives against the Scotch and the Scottish nation, the house was so amazed at the speech that they took no notice of it at the time, nor until three days afterward, when they received a message from the king saying, "how much he did mislike and tax the neglect of the house, in that the speech had not been interrupted in the instant, and the party committed before it became public, and came to his highness's ear."

The house sent the sergeant-at-arms for the offender: but after all, they said, they knew not what way to censure him for it; for freedom of speech in their house was a darling privilege. But it was resolved to expel him; and on his knees he received from the speaker the judgment of the house, committing him to the Tower during the pleasure of the house, and dismissing him from his place as knight of the shire.

Nevertheless the growing boldness of the Commons required from the king a counter assertion of his authority and principles of government, and, in a speech with which he opened the sessions of Parliament of 1610, he declared these in the highest strain of divine right. The contest, now commenced between prerogative and Parliament, was, in this reign, carried on by speeches, or state papers—the protocols, as it were, which preceded the declaration of actual war—and it is in these we must look for the pretensions and demands of the contending parties. From the long and pedantic speeches of James, a few extracts will show his view of his royal prerogative and position. "The state of monarchy is the supremest thing upon earth; for kings are not only God's lieutenants, and sit upon God's throne, but, even by God himself, they are called gods. Kings have like power with God: they make and unmake their subjects; they have power of raising and casting down; of life and death; are judges over all their subjects, and in all causes, and yet accountable to God alone." He admits that "a king is bound to protect his people, and to govern them according to his laws; and therefore a king governing in a settled kingdom, leaves to be a king, and degenerates into a tyrant, as soon as he leaves off to rule according to his laws; . . . and they that persuade them to the contrary are vipers and pests, both against them and the commonwealth; yet their punishment is with God, and no Christian man ought to allow any rebellion of people against the prince." He concludes with this climax of divine right: "That as to dispute what God may do is blasphemy, so is it sedition in subjects to dispute what a king might do in the height of his power; but just kings will ever be willing to declare what they will do, if they will not incur the curse of God. I will not be content that my power be disputed upon; but I shall ever be willing to make the reason appear of all my doings, and rule my actions according to my laws."

These high pretensions did not intimidate the Commons, who, in this session, called in question a proceeding of the king's in relation to the custom of tonnage and poundage. An act of his first Parliament granted to James the subsidy of tonnage and poundage for his life; but afterwards, by his own sole authority, he increased the duty on currants from two shillings and sixpence to five shillings per hundred weight. This being an imposition without the consent of Parliament, Bates, a Turkey merchant, refused payment, and he was prosecuted by the crown. The Court of Exchequer, subservient to the crown, had justified the imposition on the principle of the divine right of kings, and their superiority to all laws which they had not concurred in enacting. In the session of 1610, the Commons, although forbidden by the king, remonstrated against the imposition, and excused themselves from compliance with his command not to enter upon the matter, by declaring that they claimed it "as an ancient, general, and undoubted right of Parliament to debate freely all matters which do properly concern the subject, which freedom of debate being once foreclosed, the essence of the liberty of Parliament is withal dissolved." And as to the imposition and judgment in the exchequer, after premising "that the policy and constitution of the kingdom appropriates unto the kings, with the assent of Parliament, as well the sovereign power of making laws, as that of taxing, or imposing upon the subjects' goods or merchandises, as may not, without their consents, be altered or changed;" they say that "finding that your majesty, without advice or consent of Parliament, hath lately, in time of peace, set both greater impositions, and far more in number, than any your noble ancestors did ever in time of war—have, with all humility, presumed to present this most just and necessary petition to your majesty, that all impositions set without the assent of Parliament, may be quite abolished and taken away; and that your majesty, in imitation likewise of your noble progenitors, will be pleased that a law be made during this session of Parliament, to declare that all impositions set, or to be set upon your people, their goods and merchandises, save only by common consent in Parliament, are and shall be void." The Commons followed up their protest with a bill abolishing impositions; but it was thrown out of the upper house.

The king's high notions of prerogative found a supporter in Dr. Cowell, a clergyman, who published a book called "The Interpreter," dedicated to Archbishop Bancroft. It was rumored that the king had spoken favorably of the book, and the indignation of the Commons was roused. It must be admitted that the royal prerogative was asserted in an extravagant form. The author's principles were these: 1st. That the king was *solutus a legibus* and not bound by his coronation oath. 2d. That it was not *ex necessitate* that the king should call a Parliament to make laws, but he might do it by his absolute power; for *voluntas regis* was *lex populi.* 3d. That it was a favor to admit the consent of his subjects in giving of subsidies. The Commons sent a message to the Lords that they had noticed Cowell's book; which, as they conceived contained matters of scandal and offence towards the high Court of Parliament, and was otherwise of dangerous consequence and example. Conferences were held between the Lords and Commons, and the king called the author before him, and heard his defence of his doctrines. He afterwards transmitted his judgment to the Lords to be communicated to the Commons; but it never was communicated, and the matter dropped, the Commons probably thinking that their remonstrance was sufficient.

The Commons in the same Parliament, when asked for a subsidy, gave priority to their grievances in ecclesiastical and temporal concerns. They complained of the high commission court, and of its proceeding to fine and imprisonment, powers beyond its jurisdiction. They disputed the king's power *to make or alter laws by proclamations:* they said that there was nothing more precious than to be governed by the *certain rule of law*, and not by any *uncertain or arbitrary form of government. . . .*" They asserted "the indubitable right of the people of this kingdom not to be made subject to any punishment that should extend to their lives, lands, bodies, or goods, other than such as were ordained by the common laws of this land, or the statutes made by their common consents in Parliament; and they pointed out that proclamations had of late years been more frequent, extending not only to the liberty and property of men, but altering the old laws and making new—even when the latter had been rejected in the same session of Parliament, and imposing penalties and punishments, so that a general fear was conceived and spread amongst the people, that proclamations could by degrees grow up and increase to the strength and nature of laws."

Two great measures—which, however, were not carried out in this reign—occupied much of the attention of this Parliament. The first was the union of England and Scotland as one nation under the same Parliament and government, which the king was extremely anxious to bring about; expressing his desire that as there was *unus rex*, so there might be *unus grex*, and *una lex*, one king, one country, one law. In this, however, he was not cordially met by Parliament. The other measure was the abolition of the feudal revenues of the crown, which the Commons desired, and for which they were willing that the king should receive an adequate compensation. This affair acquired the name of the *great contract* between the king and people. James sent a message to the Lords, offering to accept a commutation of £200,000 yearly. The Commons, after contending for £180,000, at length came up to the price demanded; but while the Lords were striving to carry through the contract on the part of the king, the Commons suddenly changed their minds, from a feeling, it is supposed, that they could have no security for the performance of the arrangement, from the laxity of the prevailing doctrines of divine right. The king was displeased, and dissolved the Parliament, with no good humor on either side.

The failure of the great contract, and the dissolution of Parliament without the grant of a supply, left James in great embarrassment. He was not involved in war, but the supply of his court and favorites required large sums of money. Its effect upon the people is described as beneficial. "Freedom from war made riches flow; no taxes anyways burdensome—the grant of subsidies during this king's reign being but a poor pittance compared with those of Elizabeth. How he kept up his estate and expense of court is a secret." Various devices were adopted to raise money for the royal treasury. A new order of dignity—that of *baronets*—was invented, for patents to which a fee of £1,000 was paid. The current value of the gold coin was raised; and a lottery, the first drawn in England, was instituted.

These resources proving insufficient, and the king's necessity being great, he was induced again to try the effect of a Parliament. He was strongly urged to do so by Sir Francis Bacon, who, seconded by others of the king's ministers and courtiers, undertook to assemble such a House of Commons, and so to manage it when assembled, as that it should be subservient to the king's wishes. These therefore got the name of *undertakers*.

The Parliament met on the 5th of April, 1614, but the scheme was eminently unsuccessful. The Commons passed a unanimous vote against the king's right of imposing taxes without the consent of Parliament; and they desired a conference with the Lords touching the point of impositions. The Lords desired the opinions of the judges on the subject, in order to regulate their answer to the Commons: but the judges, headed by Sir Edward (Lord) Coke, declined to give an opinion, on the ground that the question might come before them judicially; and the Lords, unable to settle a satisfactory answer, sent a message to the Commons declining the conference. The Commons thereupon declared that they considered a great wrong had been done to them, which they had so taken to heart that they had determined to forbear all parliamentary matter, until they might receive a different answer from the Lords. This threat was directed against a bill of supply, which the king's secretary had introduced into the lower house. The Lords, to whom the king had sent a commission to dissolve, gave the Commons time to reconsider their resolution; but on the 7th of June, there being no change, the Parliament was dissolved. Not a single bill was passed in this Parliament.

Six years elapsed before another Parliament was called; and during that time the king and his ministers supported the court and state from the ordinary resources, or by such loans and benevolences as they could procure. This period is described as the "halcyon days in England, no taxes being now paid, trade open to all parts of the world, a profound peace reigning everywhere;" but in 1620, this quietude was disturbed by a war which broke out in Germany, by which Frederic, Count Palatine of the Rhine, who had married the king's daughter, the princess of England, was dispossessed of all his hereditary dominions. James's pacific temper was roused to revenge his son in law, and to recover his territories: and the inclination of the people being in favor of the support of the Protestant interest in Germany, he ventured to call a Parliament.

It met on the 30th of January, 1620–'1, and was opened by a rather lugubrious speech from the king, in which he humbled himself in a manner inconsistent with high prerogative principles. He said to them, "I have often piped to you, but you have not danced; I have often mourned, but you have not lamented." He asks, "Why are you called?" and replies, "To advise the king in his urgent affairs; to give him your best advice in such errands as he shall ask of you, or you shall think fit to ask his advice in." To the House of Commons he said, "You are the authors of sustenance to the king, to supply his necessities, and this is the proper use of Parliaments." "The main errand, to speak the truth, which I have called you for, is for a supply of my urgent necessities." He reminds them of the eighteen years of peace they had enjoyed, "and yet, with these eighteen years, I have had less supplies than many kings before. The last queen had what came, by computation, to £135,000 a year at least. I had never above four subsidies and six fifteenths." He told them that "bis dat qui cito dat;" that in his first Parliament he was led by the old counsellors he found, which the old queen had left; and in the last Parliament there came up a strange kind of beasts called *undertakers*, a name which in his nature he abhorred, and which had caused a dissolution.

Mr. Secretary Calvert put the house in mind of what the Parliament was principally called for; and it was agreed that the occasion was more pressing than any since the recovery of the Holy Land. But the Commons were in no hurry to supply the king's necessities, and Sir Edward Coke moved for a committee of the whole for grievances; sarcastically saying, that "the remedying of them would encourage the house and enable them to increase the supply." The committee was appointed, and the supply was deferred; but the Commons, who were favorable to the recovery of the Palatinate, and had assented to a resolution encouraging the king to attempt it, passed a subsidy bill, and received the thanks of the king for their cheerfulness in passing it.

Parliament had sat several months, and many bills had been introduced, but none had been brought to a conclusion, when the House of Commons incurred the displeasure of James. On the 28th of May the lord treasurer announced that the king intended to adjourn the Parliament, and to *adjourn* rather than *prorogue:* and the judges, on being consulted, announced their opinion that the effect of an adjournment by royal commission was to reserve all bills not passed, in the same state, until their next meeting. The Commons urged the Lords to join them in a petition to prevent the adjournment, and in a conference expressed "their grief and passion that they could not perform what they had promised for the good of the commonwealth." But the king was not to be moved from his determination. He attended the House of Lords to adjourn the Parliament, affirmed that if the Commons had behaved with humility, he would have granted them ten days longer, but that now he would not yield to their requests. Yet, if the Lords thought ten days more would be of advantage, he would grant it to them. The Lords thereupon had a conference with the Commons, but the latter indignantly refused to ask for further adjournment.

On the reassembling of Parliament, on the 20th of November following, a session commenced, in which the struggle between the king and Commons reached its climax. After a speech by the lord keeper Williams, the lord treasurer urged the king's wants; declared that the two subsidies which had been granted by the Parliament had been spent about the Palatinate; promised that future supplies should be wholly employed for the recovery of the Palatinate; and ended by expressing a wish "that the Commons would so handle this business as to make his majesty in love with parliaments."

The Commons were in no haste to grant supplies, but went upon the old topic of grievances. The principal of these was the danger to the established religion which they apprehended from the intended match between Prince Charles and the Infanta of Spain, then publicly talked about. They drew up a petition, to be presented to the king, in which they pointed out the evils which, they believed, would fall on the nation from the Spanish match. The king, having received a copy of the petition before the Commons had time to present it in form, was so displeased, that he sent a letter to the speaker, forbidding it to be sent to him. He said, in his letter, that he had heard by reports, that some fiery and popular spirits of the House of Commons had argued and debated publicly, of matters far above their reach and capacity, tending to his high dishonor, and breach of prerogative royal. He commanded that " none should presume to meddle with anything concerning his government or deep matters of state ; " adding that " we think ourself very free and able to punish any man's misdemeanor in Parliament, as well during the sitting, as after, upon any occasion of any man's insolent behavior that shall be ministered unto us."

The Commons despatched messengers to bring back the members whom they had sent to deliver the remonstrance, and they drew up a second petition or remonstrance, which they sent along with the former by twelve of their members. The latter opens with the expression by the Commons, of loyal and submissive feelings toward the king, and proceeds to justify their having taken into consideration (being invited to do so by the king) both the war abroad and the security of our peace at home. They did not, they said, assume to encroach or intrude upon the sacred bounds of the royal authority, " to whom, and to whom only, it belonged to resolve of peace or war, and of the marriage of the prince his son. But as his humble subjects, representing the whole commons of the kingdom, they resolved, out of their cares and fears, to demonstrate these things to his majesty; and that without expectation of any answer than what at his good pleasure and in his own time should be held fit." They besought him to receive their former declaration, and added, " But whereas your majesty, by the general words of your letter, seems to restrain us from intermeddling with matters of government, in particulars which have their motion in courts of justice—the generality of which words might involve those things which are the proper subjects of parliamentary occasions and discourse—and whereas your majesty doth seem to abridge us of the ancient liberty of Parliament, for freedom of speech, jurisdiction, and just censure of the house, and other proceedings there— . . . . the same being our ancient and undoubted right, received from our ancestors, without which we cannot freely debate, nor clearly discourse of things in question before us, nor truly inform your majesty, ... —we are, therefore, now again enforced, in all humbleness, to pray your majesty to allow the same."

The king sent the Commons a written answer on the 11th of December, 1621, drawn up in his usual scholastic style, and often treating the positions of the Commons sarcastically and contemptuously. Referring to their request to him not to trust reports against them, he said, "We wish you to remember that we are an old and experienced king, needing no such lessons; being in our conscience, freest of any king alive, from hearing or trusting idle reports; which many in your house could bear witness, if ye would give as good ear to them as you do to some tribunitial orators among you. . . . In your petition you usurp upon our prerogative royal, and meddle with things far above your reach; and then, in a conclusion, you protest the contrary; as if a robber would take a man's purse, and then protest he meant not to rob him. For first you presume to give us your advice concerning the match of our dearest son with some Protestant (we cannot say *princess*, for we know of none of these fit for him), and dissuade him from his match with Spain, urging us to a war with that king; and yet, in the conclusion, forsooth, ye protest ye intend not to press upon our most undoubted and royal prerogative."

Adverting to their excuse of not determining anything concerning the match, but only to tell their opinion, and lay it at his feet, he desired to know "how ye could have presumed to determine on that point, without committing high treason." And as to the receiving of their former petition, he justly rejected that suit; "for what have you left unattempted in the highest points of sovereignty in that petition of yours, except the striking of coin? For it contains the violation of leagues, the particular way how to govern a war, and the marriage of our dearest son. These are unfit things to be handled by Parliament, except your king should require it of you. For who could have wisdom to judge of things of this nature, but such as are daily acquainted with the particulars of treaties, and of the variable and fixed connection of affairs of state, together with the knowledge of the secret ways, ends, and intentions of princes in their several negotiations? Otherwise, a small mistake of matters of this nature may produce more effects than can be imagined. And, therefore, *ne sutor ultra crepidam.* And besides, the intermeddling of Parliament with peace or war, and the marriage of our dearest son, would be such a diminution to us and our crown in foreign countries, as would make any prince neglect to treat with us, except they might be assured by the assent of Parliament. We cannot omit to show you how strange we think it, that you think we meant to restrain you of your ancient privileges in Parliament. Although we cannot allow of the style calling it *your ancient and undoubted right of inheritance*, but could rather have wished that ye had said that your privileges were derived from the grace and permission of our ancestors (for most of them grew from precedents, which shows rather a toleration than an inheritance), yet we are pleased to give our royal assurance that, so long as you contain yourselves within the limits of your duty, we will be as careful to maintain your lawful liberties and privileges as ever any of our predecessors were; nay, as to preserve our own royal prerogative."

The Commons met the king's answer (which even the lord keeper considered so harsh that he wished it to be mitigated) by giving over all business; and foreseeing that the king, despairing of supply, would dissolve the Parliament, they resolved to place on record a declaration of their privileges. They, therefore, drew up a bold and comprehensive protestation, in vindication of their privileges, which was recorded in the journals of the house on the 18th of December. On the same day the prince, by virtue of a commission from the king, adjourned the Parliament to the 8th of February following. This great constitutional protestation is as follows:

"The Commons now assembled in Parliament, being justly occasioned thereunto concerning sundry liberties, franchises, privileges, and jurisdictions of Parliament, do make this protestation following: That the liberties, franchises, privileges, and jurisdictions of Parliament, are the ancient and undoubted birthright and inheritance of the subjects of England, and that the arduous and urgent affairs concerning the king, state, and the defence of the realm and of the Church of England, and the maintenance and making of laws, and redress of mischiefs and grievances which daily happen within the realm, are proper subjects and matter of counsel and debate in Parliament; and that, in the handling and proceeding of those businesses, every member of the house of Parliament hath, and of right ought to have, freedom of speech, to propound, treat, reason, and bring to conclusion the same; and that the commons in Parliament have like liberty and freedom to treat of those matters, in such order as in their judgment shall seem fittest; and that every member of the said house have like freedom from all impeachment, imprisonment, and molestation (other than by the censure of the house itself), for or concerning any speaking, reasoning, or declaring any matter or matters, touching the Parliament or Parliament business; and that if any of the said members be complained of, and questioned, for anything done or said in Parliament, the same is to be showed to the king, by the advice and assent of all the commons assembled in Parliament, before the king give credence to any private information."

The king sent for the journals, and he "rent out the protestation with his own hand;" and afterwards published a declaration, declaring it invalid, annulled, void, and of no effect. In a subsequent proclamation he reviewed the proceedings of the Parliament, and attributed its failure to "some ill-tempered spirits, who by their cunning diversions had imposed on him the necessity of discontinuing it." But he stated his intention to govern his people in the same manner as his predecessors; and in due time to call another Parliament. The "ill-tempered spirits" to whom the king referred, were soon made known, by the steps taken to punish them. Some were committed to the Tower; some were imprisoned or confined; some, by a sort of honorable banishment, were sent to Ireland as commissioners, under a royal commission, to inquire into sundry matters for his majesty's service; and a few *were raised to the peerage.*

A new Parliament met on the 19th of February, 1623. The first period of its sitting was occupied chiefly with the treaties with Spain touching the proposed match of the Prince with the Infanta, which was speedily broken off. They, moreover, sanctioned the king's entering into a war for the recovery of the Palatinate, for which they granted the largest aid ever given by Parliament—three entire subsidies and three fifteenths—stipulating only for a commission to see that the money was appropriated according to the purpose of Parliament.

But the great subjects which occupied the attention of this Parliament, were the grants of monopolies, and the power of dispensing with penal laws and forfeitures exercised by the crown. In the time of Elizabeth, Parliament had remonstrated against the injury done by monopolies to trade and manufactures; but in this reign they were still continued to a great extent. The crown now also assumed as its prerogative a power, called the *dispensing power*, to dispense with the action of laws; and by this prerogative it exempted favored individuals from the operation of penal laws, and from the forfeitures which a breach of them demanded. By another nearly similar prerogative, called the *suspending power*, it made royal grants to favored individuals, contrary to the terms of existing statutes, by inserting in the grants or letters patent a *non obstante* clause—*i. e.*, *notwithstanding* the particular statute which the grants contravened. It also made to its friends and courtiers grants of fines and penalties, which had accrued, or were expected to accrue to the crown, from persons convicted, or expected to be convicted under penal statutes; and of the profits to be derived from escheats.

No prerogatives could be more unjust or more injurious than these; and they were effectually ended by an act of this Parliament. Its title is, "An Act concerning Monopolies, and Dispensations with Penal Laws and the Forfeitures thereof." In its preamble it refers, as the foundation of its enactments, "to a royal judgment which King James did, in 1610, publish in print to the whole realm, and to all posterity, that all grants of monopolies, and of the benefit of penal laws, or of power to dispense with the law, or to compound for the forfeiture, were contrary to the laws;—which royal declaration was truly consonant and agreeable to the ancient and fundamental laws of the realm."

It, therefore, declared that all monopolies, commissions, grants, licenses, charters, and letters patent for the *sole* buying, selling, making, working, or using anything within the realm, or of any other monopolies; or of power, liberty, or faculty to dispense with any others; or to give license or toleration to do, use, or exercise anything against the tenor or purport of any law or statute; or to give or make warrant for any such dispensation, license, or toleration to be had and made; or to agree or compound with any others for any penalty or forfeitures limited by any statute; or of any grant or promise of the benefit, profit, or commodity of any forfeiture, penalty, or sum of money that was or should be due by any statute, before judgment thereupon had; and all proclamations, inhibitions, restraints, warrants of assistance, and all matters and things whatsoever, any way tending to the strengthening, furthering, or countenancing of the same or any of them—were altogether contrary to the laws of the realm, and so were, and should be, utterly void, and in no wise be put in use or executed.

This declaration of the law is enforced by provisions for making monopolies impracticable; and one provision saves from the operation of the act, and declares that it "shall not extend to letters patent and grants of privilege for the term of fourteen years and under, thereafter to be made, of the sole working or making of any manner of *new* manufactures within this realm, to the true and first inventor or inventors of such manufactures, which others, at the time of making such letters patent and grants, shall not use." It is under this exception from the act, that the British crown has exercised, and now exercises, the right of granting letters patent for new inventions.

With this great act of Parliament we leave the reign of James. The pretensions of prerogative were now clearly understood, and had been manfully resisted. The seeds of civil discord had been sown; and in the following reign of the unfortunate and misguided Charles, a harvest of contention was to be gathered, to be followed, at a later and a better time, by liberty and peace. In their disputes with James, no lover of the people will admit that Parliament made one false or imprudent step. They were in all their acts calm, and, though firm, conciliatory and respectful. In religion, it is true, they were not yet advanced to our opinions in regard to toleration. But as yet, at least, they had not fallen into the hands of Puritanism. In the next reign we shall perceive how they preserved the same course of consistent and conservative determination to preserve their rights, and how they had already won the amplest guarantees of every right they had asserted, when the pestilent viper of Puritanism, whose clamorous love for freedom is but a devilish, hypocritical mask, assumed to hide its lust of domination, carried on its agitations, till it overthrew the constitution of the kingdom and set up the *gentle* rule of Cromwell.

CHAPTER VIII.

THE STUARTS CONTINUED.—CHARLES I.—FIRST THREE PARLIAMENTS TO THE PETITION OF RIGHT.

INTRODUCTORY OBSERVATIONS—FIRST PARLIAMENT—CHARLES'S SPEECH—TONNAGE AND POUNDAGE GRANTED FOR ONE YEAR BY THE COMMONS—ILLEGAL COLLECTIONS OF THEM BY CHARLES—HATRED AGAINST BUCKINGHAM—DISSOLUTION OF PARLIAMENT—EXACTIONS AND FORCED LOANS—SECOND PARLIAMENT—HAUGHTINESS OF CHARLES—PREPARATION OF THE COMMONS TO IMPEACH BUCKINGHAM—COMMONS PASS SUPPLY BILLS TO BE GRANTED WHEN GRIEVANCES HAVE BEEN HEARD—UNCONDITIONAL SUPPLY DEMANDED—COMMONS' REMONSTRANCES—IMPEACHMENT OF BUCKINGHAM—IMPRISONMENT OF DIGGS AND ELLIOT—ABRUPT DISSOLUTION OF PARLIAMENT—RENEWED EXACTIONS AND IMPRISONMENTS—EXPEDITION TO ROCHELLE—THIRD PARLIAMENT—UNCONCILIATORY SPEECH OF CHARLES—COMPLAINT OF GRIEVANCES—SIR PETER HAYMAN—RESOLUTIONS OF THE COMMONS—ADDRESS TO THE KING—THE PETITION OF RIGHT FIRST AGITATED—CHARLES ENDEAVORS TO PREVENT DISCUSSION, OFFERING HIS ROYAL PROMISE TO MAINTAIN THE CHARTERS—PERMISSION FOR A BILL GIVEN—SPEECHES OF ELLIOT AND COKE—CONFERENCE WITH THE LORDS—THEIR PROPOSITION—OUTLINE OF THE PETITION—CHARLES'S AMBIGUOUS ASSENT—CLERICAL POLITICS—DR. MAINWARING—CHARLES FORBIDS CENSURE OF MINISTERS—EXCITEMENT IN THE HOUSE—EXPLANATORY MESSAGE FROM THE KING—REGULAR AND FINAL PASSAGE OF THE PETITION OF RIGHT—JOY OF THE PEOPLE.

CHARLES I. ascended the throne on the 27th of March, 1625. His reign is, perhaps, the most exciting in the constitutional history of England: in it the great contest between prerogative and freedom was brought to decision by the *ultima ratio* of war, followed by the execution of the king. These events long divided the nation into two parties; one of which deprecated the war as a great rebellion, and the execution of the king as sacrilegious parricide: while the other justified the war, as a national and just resistance of arbitrary and illegal power; and the king's execution as the lawful punishment of a tyrant.

It is not necessary to our purpose to follow the course of that memorable history through the civil war; but the contest between Charles and his parliaments, prior to the civil war, abounds with events and circumstances that must not be overlooked. The commons then asserted and maintained principles of constitutional freedom with indefatigable perseverance and boldness; and transmitted them to posterity as privileges of Parliament, or in general statutes. Of the latter, the most important is that known as the PETITION OF RIGHT; a landmark of the Constitution, inferior only in importance to Magna Charta and the Confirmatio Chartarum of Edward I. It was the constitutional result of the first three parliaments of Charles; but unlike its great predecessors which were the work of the barons, this proceeded from the commons.

The characteristic feature of Charles's reign, in the relation between him and his first three parliaments, was, on his part, a constant endeavor to obtain supplies without diminishing the absoluteness of his prerogative; on their part, to make the supplies the condition of concessions in favor of civil liberty. He was but twenty-five years of age when he ascended the throne; and, as might have been expected from his education under his father James, he was imbued with the highest notion of his royal power and prerogative. But he had to encounter in Parliament the same band of patriots that had so boldly struggled with his father—the most able and determined men in the nation. Against them, Charles, firm in "the divinity that doth hedge a king," pitted his friend and favorite the Duke of Buckingham, as his chief minister, a nobleman who had been popular in the latter Parliament of James, but of "whose exorbitant power and abusive carriage" the Parliament of Charles had conceived the greatest apprehension and dislike.

Charles, moreover, placed himself in a disadvantageous condition for a contest with Parliament, by adopting the war with Spain, which his father had threatened, but which was not yet commenced, for the recovery of the Palatinate; and from which his accession gave him an excuse for withdrawing. By entering into war he increased his necessities to an extent so great that they could not be supplied by the ordinary means of the crown, which had been so reduced as to be barely sufficient for peaceful times; on the other hand, the people gaining a positive advantage by the withholding of subsidies, their representatives in Parliament could coolly and deliberately pursue their policy of requiring redress of grievances as the condition of supply.

CHARLES'S FIRST PARLIAMENT.

Charles was anxious to assemble Parliament immediately after his accession, in order to obtain supplies for the war; but a plague was raging, and his marriage with the Princess Henrietta Maria of France occupied his attention. Two days after his marriage, on the 18th of June, 1625, Parliament assembled. He opened it in a good-humored speech, in which, referring to the votes of the parliaments of James, he held the present Parliament responsible for the war; and he reminded them that he was employed by Parliament to advise his father to break off treaties with Spain for peace, and his own match with a Spanish princess.

He was followed by the lord keeper Williams, who explained that the king's main reason for calling the Parliament was to remind them of their engagements for the recovery of the Palatinate and to let them understand that the supplies granted in the last Parliament of James were spent (whereof the account was ready), together with as much more of the king's own revenue. He added that the king desired them to bestow this first meeting on his, or rather on their actions; and the next should be theirs, to be applied to domestic purposes, as soon and as long as they pleased.

The Commons tried to procrastinate. The plague was raging; and they complained that they were distracted from business, by the tolling of the bell every minute whilst they were speaking. They petitioned the king for a recess "this sickly season." He answered that as soon as he should hear that they were ready with their bills, he would put an end to the session. Next day the Commons passed a bill, granting two entire subsidies. They also passed a bill granting tonnage and poundage for one year, instead of for life, and thus opened an unceasing dispute between the king and the Parliament. The Lords, on the ground that former grants to the king's predecessors had been for life, refused their consent to the bill, and Charles caused the duties to be collected without any parliamentary authority.

The Parliament adjourned on the 11th of July, on account of the plague; it reassembled in August at Oxford, in the great hall of Christ Church. The king again addressed them, and reminded them of their obligations to provide for the war. His secretaries informed the House of Commons that the two subsidies they had granted were either spent or anticipated, and they moved for a further supply of two subsidies and two fifteenths. The Commons debated this motion at great length, without coming to any decision; their antipathy to the Duke of Buckingham influencing them against the king. The debate resulted in no supply, and after various matters had been agitated, Charles, believing there was no present intention to grant a supply, resolved to show his displeasure by dissolving Parliament.

By its dissolution the ordinary constitutional means of providing money to defray the charge of the fleets and armies were cut off. Recourse was therefore had to the old expedient of compulsory gifts and loans. Letters were addressed in the king's name to the lord lieutenants of counties, directing them to collect as many persons' names as might be of ability to furnish the king with money; but they were cautioned not to deal with noblemen, nor with the clergy, who were to be left to their metropolitans. The privy seal followed the return, and left the involuntary contributor little room for escape.

SECOND PARLIAMENT.

Although these loans were industriously pressed, they were not sufficiently productive to meet the king's urgent necessities, and he resolved to call another Parliament, which assembled on the 6th of February, 1625–'6, still in the first year of his reign. From the first, it was hostile to him. Charles in no way attempted to conciliate the Commons. His view of his relation to the House of Commons was that he was an absolute prince; and that if the Commons, who assembled by his permission, did not perform their duty of raising supplies with the least inconvenience to the people, he was empowered by his prerogative to tax them without consent of Parliament. The Commons had practically admitted this theory in the reigns of the Tudors; but the spirit and freedom of the Plantagenet period were now revived; and, led by men of commanding intellect and great determination of purpose, the Commons presented an unwavering opposition to every illegal or enlarged exercise of the royal prerogative. Sir Thomas Coventry, the new lord keeper, opened the Parliament in a high prerogative speech. The Commons, on the other hand, widened the difference between the king and themselves by impeaching the Duke of Buckingham; and whilst they were preparing materials for the charges, the king sent a letter to the speaker, urging for a full and perfect answer of what they would give for his supply, according to his expectation and their promises. The Commons, full of their intended impeachment of the Duke of Buckingham, answered "that because they could not doubt that the king would be pleased graciously to accept the faithful and necessary information and advice of his Parliament (which could have no end but the king's honor and safety of his realm) in discovering the causes, and proposing the remedies, of those great evils which had occasioned his wants and his people's griefs; they therefore in full confidence and full assurance of redress therein, did with one consent propose that they really intend to supply and assist the king, in such a way, and in so ample a manner, as might make him safe at home, and feared abroad."

Charles received their observations as directed against Buckingham, and he sent a haughty reply to the speaker. After thanking the Commons for their answer, he observed that he must let them know that he would not allow any of his servants to be questioned among them, much less such as were of eminent place and near unto him. He concluded by saying, "I wish you would hasten my supply, or else it will be worse for yourselves; for, if any ill happen, I think I shall be the last that shall feel it;"—a threat which shows that Charles had not calculated the difficulty of his position in a contest with the Parliament, or that he confidently reckoned on obtaining sufficient money by force of his prerogative.

The Commons resolved that three subsidies and three fifteenths should be granted to the king, payable at three different times; *the bill to be brought in when they had presented their grievances and received the king's answer to them.* That resolution, which was an indefinite procrastination of the supply, gave the king great offence; and on the following day he sent a message to both houses, requiring their attendance at Whitehall on the next day. He addressed them in a speech in which he complimented and thanked the Lords for their care of the kingdom, and expressed his sorrow to the Commons that he might not justly give the same thanks to them; but he must show them their errors and, as he might call it, their unparliamentary proceedings. The lord keeper, as on the former occasion, enforced the king's speech, requiring, as their final answer, what further supply they would add to that they had already agreed on; and that to be *without condition either directly or indirectly*, for the supply of the king's great and important affairs.

The king's rebukes and his lord keeper's demands called forth a remonstrance from the Commons to the king, which was presented to him on the 5th of April by a select committee. They justified their proceedings against Buckingham by one of those declarations of rights which had now become usual on important occasions; by which, as they could not resist, they recorded on their journals their protest against the prerogatives assumed by the king. They declared "that it had been the usual, constant, and undoubted right and usage of Parliament to question and complain of all persons, of what degree soever, found grievous to the commonwealth, in abusing the power and trust committed to them by their sovereign. And as to the supply, that though it had been the long custom of parliaments to handle the matter of supply with the last of their businesses; yet, at that time, out of extraordinary respect to his person and care of his affairs, they had taken the same into speedy consideration, and had agreed to a resolution for a present supply, as was well known to the king."

Having thus asserted their constitutional rights, the Commons proceeded to the consideration of the supply. It was pointed out, on the part of the king, that the subsidies had decreased in productiveness, and therefore that one subsidy and one fifteenth more ought to be given, payable after the three agreed to had been collected. A bill for a grant of tonnage and poundage was also in the course of preparation by the house; but concurrently with it, the house ordered to be drawn up a remonstrance to the king against his taking those duties without grant of Parliament. The addition of a fourth subsidy was agreed to, and when the account of the whole grant was signified to the king, he said "that he accepted it in very good part, but desired such speed might be used in it that it might do him good."

It would not promote the object we have in view, to enter into the details of the impeachment of Buckingham which now took place. The charges against him were founded on the abuse of his influence with the king, and thus obtaining a plurality of appointments—trafficking in offices—and the abuse of his power as lord high admiral; and they conclude with a charge of having given a posset and a plaister to the late King James in his last illness, referring to suspicions of poison, which were publicly talked of at the death of James. These were not treated otherwise than as personal charges. No constitutional question of ministerial responsibility was involved. But there arose a question of privilege of constitutional importance, which requires our notice. The Commons presented their charges against the duke to the Lords, and appointed eight of their most distinguished members to support the charges before a committee of the upper house. Two of them, Sir Dudley Diggs and Sir John Elliot, gave offence to the king in their speeches before the Lords, and he committed them to the tower.

The Commons resented the imprisonment of their two members, and resolved to suspend all business till they should be righted in their privileges. The Lords came forward to the relief of this difficulty with the assurance of a large number of the peers that there had been a misapprehension as to the words used by Sir Dudley at the conference; and the king being satisfied that Sir Dudley had not spoken the words imputed to him, he was released from the tower. On the next day he took his seat in the house, and made a protestation " that the words charged on him were so far from being his words, that they never came into his thoughts."

But the case of Sir John Elliot was not so easily disposed of. In addition to the freedom of his remarks on Buckingham, he had used in speaking of him contemptuous expressions. It was particularly complained that he had spoken of him as "*that man.*" The chancellor of the exchequer informed the house that "although the king disliked the whole manner of his delivery of that which he had commandment from the house to speak, yet the king charged Sir John Elliot with things *extra-judicial* to that authority." It was desired that the word extra-judicial should be explained. Mr. Chancellor said it was the king's own word, and therefore he could not do it. On the 20th of May a motion was made, with apparent irony, that Sir John Elliot should *come and take his seat*, having been charged with high crimes, *extra-judicial to that house.* The ministers allowed of his coming, and the vice-chamberlain having repeated the charges, Sir John justified what he had said, as authorized by his instructions from the house. The house resolved that Sir John Elliot had not exceeded the commission given him in the late conference with the Lords; and a like resolution was carried in the case of Sir Dudley Diggs—both without one negative.

The subsidies, which the House of Commons had agreed to, were a very liberal supply, and, as we have seen, were approved by Charles, " provided he had them with speed, so that they might do him good." But several weeks elapsed without any progress towards completing the grant. Charles, impatient of delay, and, it would seem, having taken the resolution to punish it by a dissolution of Parliament, showed his displeasure in a letter to the speaker, which he desired to be read publicly to the house. He pointed out that unless the supply were presently concluded, it would be of little use; and if by their denial or delay, anything of ill consequence should fall out, either at home or abroad, he called God and man to witness that he had done his best to prevent it, by calling his people together to advise with him; by opening the weight of his occasion to them; and by requiring their timely help and assistance in those actions wherein he stood engaged by their own counsel. The Commons prepared a declaration by way of answer to the king's letter. It was agreed to on the 14th of June, and ordered to be presented to the king by the speaker, attended by the whole house. But in the mean time the king had determined to dissolve the Parliament; and on the 15th of June the Commons were summoned to the House of Lords, to hear the royal commission for the dissolution read. The peers petitioned the king, and offered him their loyal and faithful advice to continue the Parliament, by which the dangers at home and abroad might be prevented, and his majesty made happy in the duty and love of his people. The king, angry and impetuous, answered, "No, not a minute," and the Parliament was dissolved.

This abrupt and ill-considered measure forced the king upon the old illegal projects for supplying his necessities. An order in council commanded all the tonnage and poundage duties to be levied and paid. A commission was issued to arrange with Jesuits, popish priests, and recusants, to dispense with the laws and penalties affecting them, in consideration of money to be paid to the king. The nobility were applied to; and a loan of £100,000 was demanded from the city of London. All the sea-port towns were ordered to fit out ships for the guarding of their own coasts—the city of London being ordered to set out twenty of the best that lay in the Thames.

Many persons refused payment of the imposed loan, and were committed to prison. Amongst these we find the eminent names of Sir Thomas Wentworth and John Hampden, who were, by an order in council, *removed to prisons distant from their own counties.* Other five gentlemen, so imprisoned, obtained writs of habeas corpus; but they were remanded to prison by the judges, as being imprisoned by the command of the king. Sir Peter Hayman, refusing payment, was called before the council, who sent him on service to the Palatinate. But the opposition of these eminent men, on constitutional grounds, did not prevent the compliance of great numbers of the people, and a large sum was raised. It was employed in fitting out an expedition for the relief of the Protestants of Rochelle. The conduct of the affair was entrusted to Buckingham, who abandoned the Protestants to the tender mercy of the French king, and made a descent on the Isle of Rhé.

The expedition was wholly unsuccessful, and the people, finding themselves at war with both France and Spain, became alarmed at their defenceless state. A general desire was expressed that Parliament should assemble. The king held a great council at Whitehall, to which Sir Robert Cotton was called to give his advice. He advised that a Parliament should be called, at which the king should endeavor, by a gracious yielding to their just petitions, to win the people's hearts, which would give him their purses; and that Buckingham, to remove the people's personal dislike toward him, should appear as a prominent adviser for calling the Parliament. "But could it be imagined," says Lord Clarendon, "that those men would meet again, in a free convention of Parliament, without a sharp and severe expostulation and inquisition into their own right, and the power that had imposed upon that right?"

THIRD PARLIAMENT.

A new Parliament met on the 17th of March, 1627–'8, in the third year of Charles's reign. It had been deemed advisable to release the persons imprisoned for refusing the loan; and seventy-eight, *of whom some were chosen into the new Parliament*, were released. Charles opened it in a threatening and unconciliatory speech. "There is none here," he said, "but knows that common danger is the cause of this Parliament, and that supply, at this time, is the chief end of it. . . . . I will use but few persuasions; for if these be not sufficient, then no eloquence of men or angels will prevail. If you (as God forbid) should not do your duties, in contributing what the state at this time needs, I must, in the discharge of my conscience, use those other means which God hath put into my hands, to save that which the follies of some particular men may otherwise hazard to lose. Take not this as a threatening, but an admonition; for I scorn to threaten any but my equals."

The Commons, as in the preceding Parliament, all took the sacrament, and at their desire the king appointed a general fast. The late proceedings furnished them with numerous grievances; and complaints were made against the Government for billeting of soldiers upon the people, raising money by loans, and, above all, for the imprisonments for refusal of the loan;—and especially for the violation of the principle of the writ of habeas corpus in the case of the five gentlemen whom the judges recommitted to prison because it was returned that they were committed by command of the king. A motion was made for a committee of grievances; and the utmost concession which the king's secretary could obtain, in the way of attention to his demand of ships and men for the king's use, was, that the same committee should take the king's propositions into consideration. The house went into committee, with instructions to take into consideration the liberty of the subject in his person and in his goods, and also the king's supply. The grievances were reduced in the debate that followed to six heads: 1. Attendance at the council board; 2. Imprisonment; 3. Confinement; 4. Designation to foreign employment; 5. Martial law; 6. Undue proceedings in matters of judicature.

Sir Peter Hayman described to the house the manner in which he was dealt with by the council, and sent to the Palatinate. "I was called before the lords of the council; for what, I knew not; but I heard it was for not lending on a privy seal. I told them, if they will take my estate, let them; I would give it up; lend I would not. They laid to my charge my unwillingness to serve the king. I said I had my life and my estate to serve my country and my religion. They told me that if I did not pay, I should be put upon an employment of service. I was willing. After ten weeks waiting, they told me I was to go with a lord into the Palatinate, and that I should have employment there, and means befitting. I told them I was a subject, and desired means. Some put on very eagerly, some dealt nobly. They said I must go on my own purse. I told them, *nemo militat suis expensis.* Some told me I *must* go. I began to think, what *must* I. None were ever sent out in that way. Lawyers told me I could not be sent. Having this assurance, I demanded means, and was resolved not to stir but upon those terms, and in silence and duty I denied. Upon this, having given me a command to go, after twelve days they told me they would not send me as a soldier, but to attend on an ambassador. I knew that stone would hit me, therefore I settled my troubled estate and addressed myself to that service."

The debate was continued on the other heads. *Confinement* was distinguished from *imprisonment*, as being the restraint of a subject to his own house or elsewhere. But (it was said) either was an interference with that liberty which is the right of the subject, and of which none can be deprived but by the law of the land. The remedy for regaining the liberty of the person when illegally restrained is the writ of habeas corpus; which was shown in the debates to be coeval with the statutes passed for the liberty of the subject by Edward III., cases having been cited of the use of the writ in that reign; so that the laws which gave liberty of the person were accompanied by a remedy for regaining it when restrained. Mr. Selden, at a conference with the lords, explained the mode of procedure; that the writ of habeas corpus is the highest remedy for him that is imprisoned by the special command of the king, or the lords of the privy council, without showing the cause of commitment; and if any man be imprisoned, by that or any other authority, this writ is to be granted to him, and ought not to be denied. It is directed to the keeper of the prison, in whose custody the prisoner is, commanding him that after a certain day, he bring in the prisoner, with the cause of his detention, and sometimes with the cause of his caption; and he, with the return, filed to the writ, brings the prisoner to the bar at the time appointed; and the court judges of the sufficiency or insufficiency of the return. If they find him bailable, he is committed to the marshal, the proper officer of the court, and then afterward delivered to bail. But if it appear to the court that the prisoner ought not to be bailed, nor discharged from the prison whence he is brought, then he is remanded and sent back again to the prison from whence he came, there to continue, till by due course of law he be delivered.

The debate terminated in the following resolutions, unanimously agreed to in a committee of the whole house on the 3d of April:

1. That *no freeman ought to be committed, or detained in prison, or otherwise restrained* by command of the king, or the privy council, or any other; unless some cause of the commitment, detainer, or restraint be expressed, for which, *by law, he ought* to be committed, detained, or restrained.

2. *That the writ of habeas corpus cannot be denied, but ought to be*

granted to every man that is committed or detained in prison, or otherwise restrained by command of the king, OR THE PRIVY COUNCIL, OR ANY OTHER; *he praying the same.*

3. That if a freeman be committed or detained in prison, or otherwise restrained by command of the king, privy council, or any other, no cause of such commitment being expressed, and the same be returned upon an habeas corpus, granted for the said party,—then that he ought to be delivered or bailed.

4. That the ancient and undoubted right of every freeman is, that he hath a full and absolute property in his goods and estate; and that no tax, tallage, loan, benevolence, or other like charge, ought to be commanded or levied by the king or his ministers, without common assent of Parliament.

On the subjects of these resolutions, the Lords, at the request of the Commons, appointed a conference, at which the managers of the Commons were instructed to endeavor to induce the Lords to join in a petition to the king for a confirmation of these resolutions. But before the conference was concluded, the Commons, after receiving another message from the king to hasten the supply, came to a unanimous vote that five subsidies should be given to the king. This gave Charles great joy. Mr. Secretary Cook reported to the house the king's acceptance of the subsidies, and the great satisfaction which the vote had given him. But another message, a few days afterward, urging the completion of the vote by an act without delay—in which he cautioned the Commons *not to bend themselves against the extension of his royal power*, but to meddle only with pressures and abuses of power—gave the Commons offence, and they appointed a committee of ten members to consult on their grievances, and to give their substance under several heads, as instructions for their speaker to deliver them to the king in a speech. In these instructions, besides other matters, it was asserted—That it is the ancient right of Parliament to dispose of matters there debated in their own method;—that it is their ancient custom to consider grievances before matters of supply;—that yet, nevertheless, in this Parliament, to express our affection to his majesty, contrary to our ordinary proceedings, we have proceeded to supply as far as we could in committee; and, so far from delaying, that, postponing the common and pressing grievances of the nation, we have given precedency to the supply; joining with it only the fundamental and vital liberties of the kingdom that give subsistence to the subject.

The speaker presented at the same time a petition from the House of Commons concerning the billeting of soldiers, denouncing the practice as against the absolute property which every freeman, by the fundamental laws of the realm, had in his goods and estate. The petition pointed out in long detail the mischiefs and exactions arising from the king's subjects being compelled to receive and lodge soldiers in their houses, and to contribute toward the maintenance of them; the service of Almighty God was greatly hindered, the people in many places not daring to repair to church, lest in the mean time the soldiers should rifle their houses; the government of the country contemned, *the officers of justice being resisted and endangered;* the rents of the gentry diminished, as the farmers, to secure themselves and families from the soldiers' insolence, retired themselves to places of more secure habitation; husbandmen corrupted; tradesmen and artificers discouraged; markets unfrequented; and robberies, rapes, rapines, murders, and barbarous cruelties generally complained of—of which few have been so much as questioned, and fewer punished.

These grievances, under the general title of "The Liberty of the Subject," occupied the attention of the House of Commons, and, through their influence, the attention also of the House of Lords, almost exclusively of all other business, for two months, when the debates terminated in the celebrated Statute or "PETITION OF RIGHT."

The king tried to avert the further consideration of this matter by the Commons, by offering his royal word to observe the liberties of the subject as declared by the ancient statutes. He went on the 28th of April to the House of Lords; and sending for the Commons, the lord keeper, by order of the king, addressed them, and referred to the expense of time that had been occasioned by the debate in both houses—in which as they professed that they would not diminish or blemish the king's prerogative, so he presumed that "they would all confess it a point of extraordinary grace and justice in him to suffer it to rest so long in dispute without interruption. But as the debate took more time than the affairs of Christendom could permit, his majesty had thought of an expedient to shorten the business, by commanding him to let them know that he holds Magna Charta and the other statutes all in force, and that he will govern according to them; and that you shall find as much security in his royal word and promise as in the strength of any law you can make."

The House of Commons, not moved by the king's expedient, appointed a committee of lawyers to draw a bill, containing the substance of Magna Charta and the other statutes concerning the liberty of the subject. Another message from the king was delivered by Mr. Secretary Cook, that, "to show clearly that it would not be the king's fault if this be not a happy Parliament, he had commanded him to desire the house clearly to let him know whether they would rest on his royal word, which he did assure them should be really and royally performed." But on his own account as a privy counsellor, the secretary told the house that he must commit, on the king's order, and neither express the cause to the jailer nor to the judges, nor to any counsellor in England, except the king himself. Yet (he said) "this power was not unlimited, and was rather a charge and danger; for if by this power he should commit the poorest porter upon what should appear not a just cause, he should suffer a burden heavier than the law could inflict, for he should lose his credit with his majesty and also his place."

Before the house had come to any conclusion on that message, the secretary delivered, on the 2d of May, another message from the king, "that time would not admit of more debate or delay, and that the session of Parliament must continue no longer than Tuesday come sevennight at the furthest; in which time his majesty, for his part, would be ready to perform what he had promised; and if the house were not as ready to do what was fit for themselves, it should be their own faults." It was intimated that, upon assurance of their good despatch and correspondence, it was his majesty's intention to have another session of Parliament at Michaelmas next, for the perfecting of such things as could not then be done. The Commons, by their speaker, answered the several messages, expressing full trust and confidence in the royal word and promise; yet, as there had been public violation of the laws and the subjects' liberties, by some of the king's ministers, they conceived that no less than a public remedy would raise the dejected hearts of his subjects to a cheerful supply of his majesty, or make them receive content in the proceedings of the house. The king answered by the lord keeper that, to show the sincerity of his majesty's intention, he is content that a bill be drawn for a confirmătion of Magna Charta, and the other six statutes insisted upon for the subjects' liberties, but so as to be without additions, paraphrases, or explanations.

But notwithstanding the permission given for a bill, Mr. Secretary Cook, on the next day, again pressed the house to rely on the king's word as an assurance that bound the king further than the law could. He urged that the debate should take place in the house, and not in a committee of the whole house, but Sir John Elliot replied, "that the proceeding in a committee is more honorable and advantageous both to the king and the house; for that way tends most to truth, as it is a more open way, where every man may add his reasons, and make answer upon the hearing of other men's reasons and arguments." The debate accordingly proceeded in committee; "and the key was brought up, and none were to go out without leave first asked. Sir Edward Coke persuaded the house to proceed by bill. "Was it ever known," said he, "that general words were a sufficient satisfaction to particular grievances? The king's answer is very gracious; but WHAT IS THE LAW OF THE REALM? that is the question. I put no diffidence in his majesty; but the king must speak by record, and in particular, and not in general. Let us put up a PETITION OF RIGHT; not that I distrust the king, but that I cannot take his trust but in a parliamentary way.

The Commons having finished the PETITION, desired a conference with the Lords, which was held on the 8th of May, but their proceedings were suspended by a letter from the king, sealed with the royal signet, and delivered by the Duke of Buckingham. Referring to the leave he had given for debate on the highest points of royal prerogative—which none of his predecessors would have permitted—he found it still insisted upon, notwithstanding his several messages, that neither he nor his privy council have power to commit any man without cause shown; whereas it often happened that, should the cause be shown, the service itself would thereby be destroyed and defeated. He informed the Lords that without the overthrow of his sovereignty, he could not suffer that power to be impeached: but he declared that neither he nor his privy council should or would commit or command to prison, or otherwise restrain the person of any man for not lending money to him, nor for any other cause which in his conscience did not concern the public good of himself and his people; that he would not be drawn to pretend any cause, wherein his judgment and conscience were not satisfied; and that in all cases, upon the humble petition of the party, or address of the judges to him, he would readily and really express the true cause of their commitment or restraint, so soon as, with convenience and safety, the same was fit to be disclosed and expressed. This he thought fit to signify, to shorten any long debate upon this question.

The king's letter impressed the House of Lords with a desire to render the petition acceptable to him. They prepared a saving clause of the king's sovereign power—"*to leave entire the sovereign power of the king*"—which in a conference the Commons rejected. The king also interposed messages to the Lords, urging a speedy decision; but at length, on the 26th of May, the Lords, after several conferences with the Commons, agreed to the petition as prepared by them, with a few verbal alterations. They contented themselves with a declaration, by their own house alone, to the king, that their intention was not to lessen or impeach anything which by the oath of supremacy they had sworn to assist and defend. The petition was delivered on the 28th of May, by the lord keeper, to the king, in the presence of both houses, and it was requested that his majesty would please to give his assent to it in full Parliament.

The substance of this great constitutional statute is as follows: It is the petition of the lords spiritual and temporal and commons, in Parliament assembled, and is addressed to the king. It begins by—

1. Reciting the ancient laws against taxation without consent of Parliament;—it declares that, *notwithstanding such laws*, commissions have issued, by which the people have been assembled and

required to lend money to your majesty; and many upon their refusal, *have had an oath administered to them, not warrantable by the laws and statutes, and have been constrained to become bound to make appearance, and to give attendance before your privy council, and in other places; and others have been imprisoned, confined, and sundry other ways molested and disquieted.* Divers other charges have been laid and levied on the people, in several counties, by lord lieutenants, deputy lieutenants, commissioners for musters, justices of peace, and others, by command or direction from your majesty, or your privy council, against the laws and customs of the realm.

2. *Reciting the ancient laws for securing the liberty of the subject, the petition declares that against the tenor of such laws, divers of your subjects have of late been imprisoned without any cause showed; and when for their deliverance they were brought before your justices, by writs of* HABEAS CORPUS, *there to undergo and receive as* THE COURT *should order—and their keepers commanded to certify the causes of their detainer—no cause was certified, but that they were detained by* YOUR MAJESTY'S SPECIAL COMMAND, *signified by the* LORDS OF YOUR PRIVY COUNCIL; *and yet were returned back to several prisons,* WITHOUT BEING CHARGED WITH ANYTHING TO WHICH THEY MIGHT MAKE ANSWER ACCORDING TO THE LAW.

3. Great companies of soldiers and mariners (it declares) have of late been dispersed into several counties; and the inhabitants, against their wills, have been compelled to receive them into their houses, and there to suffer them to sojourn, *against the laws and customs of the realm*, and to the great grievance and vexation of the people.

4. Reciting Magna Charta and the ancient statutes, that no man should be tried, or be adjudged to death, but by the law of the realm, it declares that of late, commissions under your majesty's great seal have issued forth, by which certain persons have been assigned and appointed commissioners, *with power and authority to proceed, within the land, according to the justice of* MARTIAL LAW, against such soldiers or mariners, or other dissolute persons joining with them, as should commit murder, robbery, felony, mutiny, or other outrage or misdemeanor whatever; and by such summary cause and order as is agreeable to martial law, and is

used in armies in time of war, to proceed to the trial and condemnation of such offenders, and to cause them to be executed and put to death, according to the martial law. *By pretext whereof some of your majesty's subjects have been put to death, when, if they deserved death, they ought* BY THE STATUTES OF THE LAND, AND BY NO OTHER, *to have been adjudged and executed;* and other grievous offenders have escaped the punishment due to them by the laws of the realm, by reason that your officers and ministers of justice have unjustly refused or forborne to proceed against such offenders, according to the laws of the realm, upon pretence that the offenders were punishable only by martial law, and by authority of the commissions; *which commissions,* AND ALL OTHERS OF A LIKE NATURE, *are directly contrary to the laws and statutes of your realm.*

1. The petitioners prayed that no man hereafter be compelled to make or yield any gift, loan, benevolence, tax, or such like charge, without common consent by act of Parliament; and that none be called to make answer, or take such oath, or to give attendance, or be confined or otherwise molested or disquieted concerning the same, or refusal thereof.

2. *That no freeman, in any such manner as is before mentioned, be imprisoned or detained.*

3. That your majesty would be pleased to remove the soldiers and mariners, and that your people may not be so burdened in time to come.

4. *That the commissions for proceeding by* MARTIAL LAW *may be revoked and annulled; and that hereafter no commissions of like nature may issue forth to any person or persons whatsoever to be executed as aforesaid, lest by color of them any of your majesty's subjects be destroyed, or put to death,* CONTRARY TO THE LAWS AND FRANCHISE OF THE LAND.

All which they most humbly pray of your most excellent majesty AS THEIR RIGHTS AND LIBERTIES ACCORDING TO THE LAWS AND STATUTES OF THIS REALM: and that your majesty would also vouchsafe to declare that the awards, doings, and proceedings to the prejudice of your people in any of the premises, shall not be drawn hereafter into consequence or example; and that your majesty would be also graciously pleased, for the further comfort and safety of your people, to declare your royal will and pleasure—that in the things aforesaid, *all your officers and ministers shall serve you according to the laws and statutes of this realm*, as they tender the honor of your majesty and the prosperity of this kingdom.

The king attended in the House of Lords on the 2d of June, to give his royal assent to the petition, in the presence of the Lords and Commons. It was read over by the clerk; but instead of adopting the ancient form of the royal assent—"Soit droit fait comme est desire"—the king made the following answer:

"The king willeth that right be done according to the laws and customs of the realm; and that the statutes be put in due execution, that his subjects may have no cause to complain of any wrong or oppressions, contrary to their just rights and liberties; to the preservation whereof he holds himself, in conscience, as well obliged, as of his own prerogative."

On the return of the Commons to their house the king's answer was read, and dissatisfaction was expressed at the departure from the legal form. But the consideration of it was postponed, for another matter had arisen, more absorbing than even that of the liberty of the subject.

The Church sympathized with the king in his struggle for prerogative, and the pulpit had been used to intimidate the people by the terrors of Divine punishment from resisting the royal demands. Among these clerical politicians, one Dr. Mainwaring had become conspicuous for his enforcement of unconditional loyalty. He had preached two sermons before the king, and a third in his parish church, and these he afterward published in a book entitled 'Religion and Allegiance.' He maintained that the king's royal command imposing taxes and loans without consent of Parliament was so binding on the conscience of a subject of the kingdom that he could not refuse payment without peril of damnation! And he moreover enforced it as a principle that the authority of Parliament was not necessary for the raising of aids and subsidies. Such a conversion of the Church into a political arena is always fraught with danger to a commonwealth. Nothing is so beneficial to society as the faithful preaching of the gospel of Jesus Christ;

and nothing is so great a curse as the perversion of the pulpit to the purposes of politics; but in England, where the Church and State are united, the use by the king of so potent an instrument as the established Church for the dissemination of his principles of absolutism was manifestly not to be endured.

The Commons, therefore, prepared charges against Mainwaring, which they presented to the House of Lords, and called upon that house to make inquiry, and bring him to justice. The king tried to avert the Commons' proceedings by repeated messages to Lords and Commons, promising a faithful adherence to the Petition of Right, notwithstanding the irregularity of form in the assent, but finally intimating his intention to close the session on the 11th of the month; "and because that could not be, if the house entertain more business of length, he required of them not to enter or proceed with any new business which might spend greater time, or which might lay any scandal or aspersion on the state, government, or ministers thereof."

This message produced a debate and a scene in the House of Commons that should not be lost sight of in our constitutional history. A restriction upon their liberties so important as one prohibiting them from censuring the king's ministers, could not be passed over in such a Parliament. A debate was opened, in which Sir John Elliot was the second speaker. He commented on that part of the message, "that they were not to enter on any business which might lay some aspersions on the government." "It is said also," he proceeded, "as if we cast some aspersions on his majesty's ministers. I am confident no minister, howsoever dear, can"— Here the speaker started up from the chair, and supposing that Sir John Elliot intended to censure the Duke of Buckingham, he said, "There is a command laid upon me to interrupt any that should go about to lay an aspersion upon the ministers of state." A deep silence followed;—the speaker desired leave to go forth for half an hour; and the house ordered that he might go forth, if he pleased.

The house, in his absence, resolved itself into committee. The first member who spoke was in consternation; he said, "That for the speaker to desire to leave the house in such a manner was never heard of before, and he feared would be ominous." The next said there were two ways of proceeding: to go to the Lords, or to the king. He thought, " the latter our proper cause, as it doth concern our liberties; and let us not fear to make a remonstrance of our rights." Sir Edward Coke, after quoting several ancient instances of the interference of Parliament with kings' ministers, said, " I think the Duke of Buckingham is the cause of all our miseries, and till the king be informed thereof, we shall never go out with honor, or sit with honor here. As for going to the Lords, that is not *via regia;* our liberties are now impeached; we are deeply concerned. It is not *via regia,* for the Lords are not participants in our liberties. It is not the king, but the duke that saith, 'We require you not to meddle with state government, or the ministers thereof.'" Several members attributed these evils to the prevalence and permission allowed to popery, and " because those that use the king's power seek an utter subversion of our religion." Another said, " It is not the Duke of Buckingham alone that is the cause of the evils, but there are other great persons worthy of blame;" to which it was replied, " Take away the one, and the rest will vanish." Many found excuse for the king, saying, " It is not King Charles counselling himself, but ill counsel followed that is given him by ill counsellors." The house was preparing to put the question, " That the Duke of Buckingham shall be instanced to be the chief and principal cause of all their evils," when the speaker returned with a message from the king, to whom he went when he left the chair—" That his majesty commands for the present, they adjourn the house till to-morrow morning, and all committees cease in the mean time,"—and the speaker adjourned the house accordingly.

The king did not maintain the absolute position which had produced this scene. He sent, on the 6th of June, a message to the Commons, that he had no meaning of barring them of their just right, but only to avoid all scandals on his past counsel and actions; and that his ministers might not be, nor himself, under their names, taxed for their counsel to him. The speaker confessed that, when he left the house with its permission, he went to the king, who confirmed the latter message, stating that, It bars you not of your right in matter; nay, not in manner. The house for the present accepted the explanation as satisfactory.

The Commons had now leisure to consider the king's evasive answer to the Petition of Right. At a conference with the Lords, held on the 7th of June, both houses agreed to address the king, "that he would please to give a clear and satisfactory answer, in full Parliament, to the petition." The message having been communicated to the king, he appointed that day, at four in the afternoon, when he came to the House of Lords; and the speaker, with the Commons being in attendance, the king commanded the clerk of Parliament to cut out his former answer entered in the journal, and he, at the same time, gave him another. After a speech from the lord keeper, requesting a more clear signification of the royal assent, the king made a short speech defending his former assent as sufficient, but concluding with, "Read your petition, and you shall have an answer that I am sure will please you." The petition having been read, the clerk gave the king's assent—"Soit droit fait comme il est désiré." "Let right be done as is desired," and the petition then became, in form and substance, an Act of Parliament.

It is recorded in the Lords' journals that, at the conclusion of the business, the Commons gave a great and joyful applause; and other authorities mention that they returned to their house with unspeakable joy, and resolved so to proceed as to express their thankfulness. The king added to the general satisfaction, by sending a message to the Commons—in anticipation of a request they were about to make—consenting that the petition and his answer should be recorded in the Courts of Westminster, as well as the Houses of Parliament. It is now time to give this great document in full.

The Petition of Right.

THE Petition exhibited to his Majesty by the Lords Spiritual and Temporal, and Commons, in the present Parliament assembled, concerning divers Rights and Liberties of the Subjects, with the King's Majesty's Royal Answer thereunto in full Parliament.

To the King's Most Excellent Majesty.

Humbly show unto our Sovereign Lord the King, the Lords Spiritual and Temporal, and Commons, in Parliament assembled, That whereas it is declared and enacted by a Statute made in the Time of the Reign of King *Edward* the First, commonly called *Statutum de Tallagio non concedendo*, That no Tallage or Aid shall be laid or levied by the King or his Heirs in this Realm, without the good Will and Assent of the Archbishops, Bishops, Earls, Barons, Knights, Burgesses, and other the Freemen of the Commonalty of this Realm; and by Authority of Parliament holden in the five and twentieth Year of the Reign of King *Edward* the Third, it is declared and enacted, That from thenceforth no Person should be compelled to make any Loans to the King against his Will, because such Loans were against Reason and the Franchise of the Land; and by other Laws of this Realm it is provided, That none should be charged by any Charge or Imposition called a Benevolence, nor by such like Charge: by which, the Statutes before mentioned, and other the good Laws and Statutes of this Realm, your Subjects have inherited this Freedom, That they should not be compelled to contribute to any Tax, Tallage, Aid or other like Charge not set by common Consent in Parliament:

II. Yet, nevertheless, of late divers Commissions directed to sundry Commissioners in several Counties, with Instructions, have issued; by means whereof your People have been in divers places assembled, and required to lend certain Sums of Money unto your Majesty, and many of them, upon their Refusal so to do, have had an Oath administered unto them not warrantable by the Laws or Statutes of this Realm, and have been constrained to become bound to make Appearance and give Attendance before your Privy Council and in other Places, and others of them have been therefore imprisoned, confined, and sundry other Ways molested and disquieted; and divers other Charges have been laid and levied upon your People in several Counties by Lord Lieutenants, Deputy Lieutenants, Commissioners for Musters, Justices of Peace, and others, by Command or Direction from your Majesty, or your Privy Council, against the Laws and Free Customs of the Realm.

III. And whereas also by the Statute called *The Great Charter of the Liberties of England*, it is declared and enacted, That no Freeman may be taken or imprisoned, or be disseized of his Freehold or Liberties, or his Free Customs, or be outlawed or exiled, or in any Manner destroyed, but by the lawful judgment of his Peers, or by the Law of the Land.

IV. And in the eight and twentieth Year of the Reign of King *Edward* the Third, it was declared and enacted by Authority of Parliament, That no Man of what Estate or Condition that he be, should be put out of his Land or Tenements, nor taken nor imprisoned, nor disherited, nor put to Death, without being brought to answer by due Process of Law:

V. Nevertheless against the Tenor of the said Statutes, and other the good Laws and Statutes of your Realm to that End provided, divers of your Subjects have of late been imprisoned without any Cause showed; and when for their Deliverance they were brought before your Justices by your Majesty's Writs of *Habeas Corpus*, there to undergo and receive as the Court should order, and their Keepers commanded to certify the Causes of their Detainer, no Cause was certified but that they were detained by your Majesty's special Command, signified by the Lords of your Privy Council, and yet were returned back to several Prisons, without being charged with any Thing to which they might make answer according to the Law.

VI. And whereas of late great Companies of Soldiers and Mariners have been dispersed into divers Counties of the Realm, and the Inhabitants against their Wills have been compelled to receive them into their Houses, and there to suffer them to sojourn, against the Laws and Customs of this Realm, and to the great Grievance and Vexation of the People:

VII. And whereas also by Authority of Parliament, in the five and twentieth Year of the Reign of King *Edward* the Third, it is declared and enacted That no Man should be forejudged of Life or Limb against the Form of the *Great Charter* and the Law of the Land; and by the said *Great Charter* and other the Laws and Statutes of this your Realm, no Man ought to be adjudged to Death but by the Laws established in this your Realm, either by the Customs of the same Realm, or by Acts of Parliament: And whereas no Offender of what kind soever is exempted from the Proceedings to be used, and Punishments to be inflicted by the Laws and Statutes of this your Realm: Nevertheless of late Time divers Commissions under your Majesty's Great Seal have issued forth, by which certain persons have been assigned and appointed Commissioners, with Power and Authority to proceed within the Land, according to the Justice of Martial Law, against such Soldiers or Mariners, or other dissolute Persons joining with them, as should commit any Murder, Robbery, Felony, Mutiny or other Outrage or Misdemeanor whatsoever, and by such summary Course and Order as is agreeable to Martial Law, and as is used in Armies in Time of War, to proceed to the Trial and Condemnation of such Offenders, and them to cause to be executed and put to Death according to the Law Martial:

VIII. By Pretext whereof some of your Majesty's Subjects have been by some of the said Commissioners put to Death, when and where, if by the Laws and Statutes of the Land they had deserved Death, by the same Laws and Statutes also they might and by no other ought to have been judged and executed:

IX. And also sundry grievous Offenders, by color thereof claiming an Exemption, have escaped the Punishments due to them by the Laws and Statutes of this your Realm, by reason that divers of your Officers and Ministers of Justice have unjustly refused or forborn to proceed against such Offenders according to the same Laws and Statutes, upon Pretence that the said Offenders were punishable only by Martial Law, and by Authority of such Commissions as aforesaid; which Commission, and all other of like Nature are wholly and directly contrary to the said Laws and Statutes of this your Realm:

X. They do therefore humbly pray your Most Excellent Majesty, That no Man hereafter be compelled to make or yield any Gift, Loan, Benevolence, Tax or such-like Charge, without common Consent by Act of Parliament; And that none be called to make Answer, or take such Oath, or to give Attendance, or be confined, or otherwise molested or disquieted concerning the same, or for Refusal thereof; And that no Freeman, in any such Manner as is before mentioned, be imprisoned or detained; And that your Majesty would be pleased to remove the said Soldiers and Mariners, and that your People may not be burthened in Time to come; And that the aforesaid Commissions, for proceeding by Martial Law, may be revoked and annulled; And that hereafter no Commissions of like Nature may issue forth to any Person or Persons whatsoever to be executed as aforesaid, lest by Colour of them any of your Majesty's Subjects be destroyed, or put to Death contrary to the Laws and Franchise of the Land.

XI. All of which they most humbly pray of your Most Excellent Majesty as their Rights and Liberties, according to the Laws and Statutes of this Realm; and that your Majesty would also vouchsafe to declare That the Awards, Doings and Proceedings, to the Prejudice of your People in any of the Premises shall not be drawn hereafter into Consequence or Example; And that your Majesty would be also graciously pleased, for the further Comfort and Safety of your People, to declare your Royal Will and Pleasure, That in the Things aforesaid all your Officers and Ministers shall serve you according to the Laws and Statutes of this Realm, as they tender the Honor of your Majesty, and the Prosperity of this Kingdom.

Qua quidem petitione lecta et plenius intellecta, per dictum Dominum Regem taliter est responsum in pleno parliamento, viz., Soit Droit fait comme est desire.

CHAPTER IX.

CHARLES I.—FROM THE PETITION OF RIGHT TO THE GRAND REMONSTRANCE.

FIVE SUBSIDIES GRANTED TO THE KING—PUNISHMENT OF DR. MAINWARING—ILLEGAL COMMISSION OF EXCISE CANCELLED—REMONSTRANCE OF THE COMMONS CONCERNING TONNAGE AND POUNDAGE—PARLIAMENT PROROGUED—CHARLES'S SPEECH—REASSEMBLING OF PARLIAMENT—CONSIDERATION OF GRIEVANCES AND OUTRAGES—THE KING CONSENTS TO TONNAGE AND POUNDAGE AS A PARLIAMENTARY GRANT—FURTHER IRRITATIONS BY THE STAR CHAMBER—CHARLES COMMANDS AN ADJOURNMENT—RESISTANCE OF THE COMMONS—THEIR PROTESTATION—CHARLES'S PROCLAMATION—IMPRISONMENTS—DISSOLUTION—REMARKS OF CLARENDON—DARING PROCLAMATION BY THE KING—PROSECUTIONS OF THE IMPRISONED MEMBERS—DISREGARD OF HABEAS CORPUS BY THE JUDGES—ROYAL EXACTIONS FROM THE PEOPLE—FEUDAL OPPRESSIONS AND FOREST LAWS RESTORED—SHIP MONEY—JOHN HAMPDEN—CHARLES'S DOCTRINE OF MILITARY NECESSITY SUSTAINED BY THE JUDGES IN AN "EXTRA-JUDICIAL OPINION"—THE SHORT PARLIAMENT—GRIEVANCES CONSIDERED—SUPPLIES DEMANDED BY THE KING—ANSWER OF THE COMMONS—DISSOLUTION—THE LONG PARLIAMENT—ITS TEMPER FROM THE FIRST—UNANIMITY OF LORDS AND COMMONS—LATE PROCEEDINGS OF THE KING, AND THE EXTRAJUDICIAL OPINION OF THE JUDGES IN REGARD TO SHIP MONEY DECLARED ILLEGAL—MONOPOLISTS AND PATENTEES EXCLUDED FROM PARLIAMENT—HUMILIATION OF THE KING—TENURE OF JUDGES' APPOINTMENTS TO BE HENCEFORTH FOR LIFE—ACT FOR TRIENNIAL PARLIAMENTS—ACT TO PREVENT SUDDEN ADJOURNMENTS AND DISSOLUTIONS—CHARLES GIVES UP HIS CLAIM TO TONNAGE AND POUNDAGE—ABOLITION OF THE COURT OF STAR CHAMBER AND HIGH COMMISSION COURT—SHIP MONEY, FOREST CLAIMS, AND FEUDAL EXACTIONS ABANDONED—OBSERVATIONS—SATISFACTION OF REASONABLE MEN AMONG THE COMMONS——WELCOME OF THE KING IN LONDON ON HIS RETURN FROM SCOTLAND—PURITANISM.

THE Commons gave proof of the conciliatory effect of the proceedings we have just related by passing a bill granting five subsidies to the king. Sir Edward Coke carried it to the Lords, accompanied by almost the whole house. The Lords took exception to the form of the bill, that the Commons alone were named in the preamble. Several conferences took place, but the Commons evaded any alteration; and from this time settled the custom of making money bills, in form as well as procedure, a grant from the Commons alone.

The king had announced his intention to prorogue the Parliament on an early day, and several important affairs were brought under consideration in the interval, which require our notice.

The impeachment of Dr. Mainwaring was brought to a conclusion by the Lords, who passed sentence upon him—that he should be imprisoned during the pleasure of the house, be fined £1,000 to the king, should make submission at the bar of both houses, be suspended three years from the ministry, and be disabled from ever preaching at court, or holding any ecclesiastical dignity or secular office, and that all the offending books should be called in by proclamation, and burnt. He acknowledged his fault, and made submission on his knees at the bar of the Commons, being led into the house by the warden of the Fleet Prison, to which he was committed.

The Commons now complained of a commission of excise which the king had issued, appointing thirty-three of his counsellors to advise him how to raise money for the war—"the same to be done by impositions or otherwise, as in your wisdoms and best judgments ye shall find to be most convenient in a case of this inevitable necessity, wherein form and circumstance must be dispensed with, rather than the substance be lost or hazarded." After a conference with the Commons, the Lords appointed a special committee to draw up a message to advise the king to cancel the commission. The Commons sent to the lord keeper for the commission, which was sent and read to the house. This business terminated in the lord president of the council acquainting the Lords that the king had caused the commission to be cancelled in his presence. His lordship showed the cancelled commission to the house, and it was sent with a message to the Commons for their inspection.

Tonnage and poundage had not yet been granted to the king, although he appears to have expected that an act, granting the duties for his life, would follow his assent to the PETITION OF RIGHT. The Commons, however, proceeded to prepare a "remonstrance," to explain why the duties had not been granted to him before, and why it was necessary still to postpone the grant. They desired a previous admission from the king that the duties were not leviable by virtue of his prerogative, but of the voluntary grant of Parliament; and they attributed the delay which had occurred to the illegal conduct of King James in raising the duties above the legal rates, and to Charles's collection of the same illegal rates. They declared that the collection of the duties by Charles, without the authority of Parliament, was a fundamental breach of the liberties of the kingdom, and contrary to his answer to the Petition of Right; and they besought him to forbear further receiving them, and not to take it in ill part from those of his subjects who should refuse to make payment without warrant of law.

The king, being informed of these proceedings, and alarmed for his tonnage and poundage, hurried to the House of Lords on the day fixed for the prorogation, several hours earlier than he was expected, and prevented the presentation of the remonstrance by proroguing the Parliament. In his speech he said: "It may seem strange that I come so suddenly to end this session, therefore I will tell you the cause, though I owe the account of my actions to God alone. A while ago the House of Commons gave me a remonstrance—how acceptable every man may judge. Now, I am well informed that a second remonstrance is preparing for me, to take away the profit of my tonnage and poundage, by alleging that I have given away my right thereto by my answer to your petition. This is so prejudicial to me that I am forced to end this session some few hours before I meant, being not willing to receive any more remonstrances, to which I must give a harsh answer. To prevent false constructions of what I have granted in your petition, I declare that I have granted no new, but only confirmed the ancient liberties of my subjects. . . . But as for tonnage and poundage, it is a thing I cannot want, and was never intended by you to ask, nor meant by me, I am sure, to grant."

The speech was ordered by the king to be entered on the Commons' journals. The Bill of Subsidy was presented by the speaker, with the remark "that it was the greatest gift that ever was given in so short a time." The royal assent was given to that and some other bills, and the Parliament was prorogued on the 20th of October.

Before Parliament again assembled one great cause of discord was removed. The Duke of Buckingham was assassinated at Portsmouth by one Felton, an officer, who, previously to the assassination, sewed a paper within his hat, avowing that it was the Parliamentary remonstrance against the duke that had induced him to take him off as an enemy to the country. Buckingham was at the time engaged at Portsmouth in preparing a new expedition for the relief of the Protestants of Rochelle. In consequence of his death the expedition was committed to the conduct of the Earl of Lindsay. But it ended as unfortunately as the former expedition conducted by Buckingham. It was forced to surrender to the Catholic troops of Louis XIII., who entered the town on the 18th of October, and compelled the Protestants to submission.

Parliament was again prorogued from the 20th of October to the 20th of January, on which day it assembled, and the Commons immediately reconstituted committees for privileges, religion, courts of justice, grievances, and trade. A case of extraordinary meanness on the part of the crown was communicated to the House of Commons by Sir John Elliot—that the Petition of Right had been printed by the Government for circulation amongst the people with the first and repudiated answer appended to it, instead of the substituted legal answer. Mr. Selden reminded the house how the Petition of Right had been violated since their last meeting—that the goods of Mr. Rolles, a member of the house, had been seized by the crown for the duties of tonnage, and that the Court of Exchequer had made an order commanding the sheriff not to execute a writ of replevin, issued with the view of trying the legality of the seizure, and restoring the goods in the mean time. He also referred with indignation to the case of Mr. Prynne, who had been deprived of his ears by sentence of the Star Chamber.

The house entered upon the complaint of Mr. Rolles, of the seizure of his goods for tonnage. Before the debate had proceeded far, a message was received from the king that he would speak with both houses on the following day (the 23d of January), in the banqueting house at Whitehall; and on their proceeding thither at the time appointed he made a speech explanatory of his former course in reference to the matter, which made it evident that he was now prepared to relinquish his claim of hereditary right to tonnage and poundage, if he could obtain a parliamentary grant; and this speech was followed by a bill, which Mr. Secretary Cook brought in for a grant of tonnage and poundage, and which he endeavored to induce the house to take into consideration. They gave priority to other business. The king pressed for priority of tonnage and poundage, in successive messages, and would have put the Commons completely in the wrong by fair speeches and propositions, if he had at the same time abstained from enforcing the ungranted duties. But whilst addressing the Commons, his officers were at the same time proceeding against some of the members. The house was irritated by an announcement from Mr. Rolles that "since the last complaint of the breach of the liberties of the house, his house was locked up by one Massey, a pursuivant, and that yesterday he was called forth from the committee in the Exchequer Chamber, and served with a subpœna to appear in the Star Chamber." Although Mr. Rolles announced at the same time that he had since received a letter from Mr. Attorney that it was a mistake, the house would not receive the explanation, but ordered that the messenger who served the subpœna should be summoned to attend the house, and it appointed a committee to see and examine the information in the Star Chamber, and to ascertain by whom the same was put in. The house took very decided measures in opposition to the king's proceedings to recover tonnage and poundage from the merchants; but their success proving at best but doubtful, they adjourned. They met again on the 25th of February, when another scene of interest and excitement was presented. The house proceeded to consider the articles to be insisted and agreed upon at a sub-committee for religion. The debate was interrupted by a message from the king, which the speaker announced, commanding him to *adjourn* the house "until Tuesday come seven night following." It was objected that it was not the office of the speaker to deliver any such command; for the adjournment of the house did properly belong unto themselves; and, after they had settled some things they thought convenient to be spoken of, they would satisfy the king. Sir John Elliot offered a remonstrance which he had prepared, addressed to the king, beseeching him to forbear any further recovery of tonnage and poundage; but the speaker and the clerk refused to read it to the house; and on the former being asked to put the question to the house, whether the remonstrance should be adopted, the speaker said "he was commanded otherwise by the king." "If you will not put the question," said Mr. Selden, "which we command you, we must sit still; and so we shall never be able to do anything. We sit here by command from the king under the great seal; and as for you, you are, by his majesty, sitting in his royal chair before both houses, appointed our speaker. And do you refuse to be a speaker?" The speaker justified his refusal by a command from the king to rise as soon as he had delivered his message. He rose and left the chair, but was drawn into it again by Holles, Valentine, and others. He was held in the chair amidst the scorn and derision of the members, who, foreseeing that a dissolution would follow this outbreak, passed a protestation hastily prepared by Mr. Rolles, containing the following words:

"Whoever shall counsel or advise the taking and levying of the subsidies of tonnage and poundage, not being granted by Parliament, or shall be an actor or instrument therein, shall be likewise reported an innovator on the government, and a capital enemy to this kingdom and commonwealth.

"If any merchant, or other person whatsoever, shall voluntarily yield or pay the said subsidies of tonnage and poundage, not being granted by Parliament, he shall likewise be reputed a betrayer of the liberty of England, and an enemy to the same."

When the protestation had been read and agreed to, the house rose, having protracted their sitting about two hours. In the mean time the king, hearing that their sitting was continued in disregard of his command for adjournment, endeavored to remove them. He first sent a messenger for the sergeant with his mace, that by removing it from the table an end might be put to the sitting. But the sergeant was detained, and the key of the door taken from him and given to a member to keep. The king next sent the usher of the black rod, as for a dissolution; but being informed that neither the usher nor his message would be received, he became enraged, and sent the captain of the pensioners, with his guard, with orders to force open the door. But before that extreme step could be taken, the house had risen and adjourned to the 10th of March.

The king was now roused to violent action: he published a proclamation signifying his intention to dissolve the Parliament on account of the disobedient and seditious carriage of ill-affected persons of the House of Commons; and he entered upon a course of relentless persecution of the unfortunate patriots. Without waiting for the actual dissolution, Sir John Elliot, Selden, Holles, Stodart, Hayman, Coriton, Long, Valentine, and Stroud were summoned before the privy council; and, after having been questioned as to the parts they had respectively taken in preventing the speaker adjourning the house according to the king's command, they were committed to prison. The king's speech, when dissolving the Parliament, manifested his anger and intemperance. He addressed the lords only, although many of the commons were at the bar. "He never came there," he said, "on so unpleasing an occasion, it being for the dissolution of the Parliament. Many may wonder why I did not rather choose to do this by commission, it being a general maxim of kings to lay harsh commands by their ministers, themselves only executing pleasing things. But I thought it necessary to come here this day to declare to you, my lords, and all the world, that it was only the disobedient carriage of the lower house that hath caused this dissolution at this time; and that you, my lords, are far from the causers of it. Nor do I lay the fault equally upon all the lower house; for as I know there are many dutiful and loyal subjects there, so I know that it was only some vipers amongst them that had cast this mist of difference before their eyes."

This was the third Parliament that the king had dissolved in anger within only four years. We may not hesitate to consider these dissolutions impolitic and abrupt, if Clarendon, the historian and apologist of Charles, has so viewed them. "The abrupt and unkind breaking off," says Lord Clarendon, "the two first Parliaments was wholly imputed to the Duke of Buckingham, and of the third, principally, to the Lord Weston, then lord high treasurer of England. No man," he observes, "can show me a source from whence those waters of bitterness, afterwards tasted, more probably flowed than from these unreasonable, unskilful, and precipitate dissolutions, in which, by an unjust survey of the passion, insolence, and ambition of particular persons, the court measured the temper and affection of the country; and by the same standard the people considered the honor, justice, and piety of the court; and so usually parted, at those sad seasons, with no other respect and charity one towards the other than accompanics persons who never meant to meet but in their own defence, in which the king had always the disadvantage to harbor persons about him who, with their utmost industry, false information, and malice, improved the faults and infirmities of the court to the people; and again, as much as in them lay, rendered the people suspected if not odious to the king."

Charles followed up the dissolution of his third Parliament by publishing a declaration of the causes which moved him to dissolve it, and shortly afterwards by proclamation of unparalleled daring, in which he asserted absolute power over the Parliament and people. Referring to rumors spread by ill-disposed persons, he thought it expedient to make known his royal pleasure, that he did not purpose to overcharge his subjects by any new burden, but to satisfy himself with the duties received by his father, which he neither could nor would dispense with. And as to false rumors that he was about again to call a Parliament, he said that although he had showed, by his frequent meeting with his people, his love to the use of Parliament, yet the late abuse having, for the present, driven him out of that course, he should account it presumption for any to prescribe any time to him for Parliaments: the calling, continuing, and dissolving them being always in the king's own power. He should be more inclinable to meet a Parliament again when his people should see more clearly into his intents and actions; when such as had bred this interruption should receive their condign punishment; and those that were misled by them and such ill reports, should come to a better understanding of him and themselves.

Such a proclamation could only have been issued by a king

conscious of power and resolved to use it; and could only have been received with silent acquiescence by a people who acknowledged that power, and their inability to resist it. The imprisoned patriots who had led the House of Commons could no longer stimulate the people nor resist the royal aggressions, whilst their imprisonment operated as a terror to those who were inclined to follow a patriotic cause. The subservience of the judges prevented any hope of stemming the king's will in the courts of law; and the Parliament, the only arena for free discussion, was now denounced as a guilty institution, not to be called together again until it had learnt the lesson of submission.

The proceedings against the members were continued with great oppression. The judges were questioned by the attorney-general, for the purpose of obtaining their private opinions as to the penal liability of the members in the courts of law, for their conduct in the House of Commons. Informations were instituted against some of them in the Star Chamber, and against Sir John Elliot, Denzil Holles, and Benjamin Valentine, in the king's bench. Writs of habeas corpus having been issued to bring up the latter from the prison of the king's bench, they were, by the king's order, and to elude the judgment of the court, transferred to the Tower. They remained there through the long vacation, until November; and being then brought up to the king's bench, the judges having previously conferred with the king, pronounced judgment that they ought to be bailed upon giving security for their good behavior. A decision so contrary to the spirit and purpose of the writ of habeas corpus, and which implied a confession of culpability without trial, could not be submitted to; and the prisoners demanded to be bailed in point of right, and if not of right, they did not demand it. They were remanded to the Tower, and were required to plead to the information. They demurred to the jurisdiction of the court, as being incompetent to try supposed offences done in Parliament, but the demurrer was overruled, and the prisoners persisting in their refusal to plead, sentence was pronounced against them. They were ordered to be imprisoned during the king's pleasure; and not to be delivered until each gave security for his good behavior, and made submission and acknowledgment of his offence. Sir John Elliot, inasmuch as the court thought him the ringleader, was fined £2,000, Mr. Holles, 1,000 marks; and Mr. Valentine, £500. These patriotic men preferred imprisonment to the dishonor of acknowledging their conduct in Parliament to be an offence against the law; and Sir John Elliot died in prison.

It now appeared hopeless to contend against the power of the king; and some, whose ardent patriotism seemed to promise no reward, were gained over to the king's party and accepted office under him. The king further strengthened his position by making peace first with France and afterwards with Spain; and Lord Clarendon informs us that "there quickly followed so excellent a composure throughout the whole kingdom, that the like peace and plenty and universal tranquillity, for ten years, was never enjoyed by any nation." But all the principles of the constitution—the laws relating to taxation, and even the king's own proclamation that he would impose no new burdens—were disregarded. Tonnage and poundage were collected by order of the king's council. New and greater impositions were laid on trade. Obsolete laws were revived and vigorously executed. The ancient prerogative enjoyed by the crown of compelling its tenants *in capite* to take upon them the order of knighthood was revived; and, notwithstanding a restraining statute of Edward II., proclamations were made in every county, summoning all men of full age seized of lands or rents of the annual value of £40 or more, not being knights, to appear personally in the king's presence before a certain day to receive the order and dignity of knighthood. If they made default they were subjected to grievous fines and vexations. Thus, says Lord Clarendon, "the king received a vast sum of money from persons of quality, or of any reasonable condition, throughout the kingdom, by this expedient; which, though it had a foundation in right, in the circumstances of proceeding was very grievous."

Furthermore the oppressions of the ancient forest laws were restored. The ancient boundaries, which had been settled in the reign of Edward III., were by virtue of packed juries extended so as to include adjacent lands, and thus the attempt was made to set up new forests in many parts of the kingdom; and the right thus pretended to belong to the crown was only yielded to the rightful owners in consideration of heavy fines, or great annual rents. This burden," says Lord Clarendon, " lighted most upon persons of quality and honor, who thought themselves above ordinary impressions, and were therefore likely to remember it with more sharpness."

But the most memorable of these unconstitutional and oppressive exactions was that of SHIP MONEY. This was the invention of Noy, who had seceded from the popular party, and become the king's attorney-general. His investigation into old records led to the discovery that in ancient times, when danger of war arose, the seaports and maritime counties had been called upon to furnish ships for the protection of the kingdom; and upon that basis he planned an expedient for raising a large and permanent revenue for the king. The first attempt was made in August, 1634, on the citizens of London; but we shall pass to the time (May, 1635) when the scheme, after the death of Noy, was extended by Lord Keeper Finch to the inland as well as the maritime counties of England and Wales—and especially to that instance which has rendered the name of JOHN HAMPDEN immortal in the annals of the country.

By the plan put in force, writs were issued under the great seal to the sheriffs of all the English and Welsh counties, directing that each county should provide ships of various burden; but which, in the instance of the county of Bucks, in which Hampden resided, was a ship of war of 450 tons, with 180 men, guns, gunpowder, double tackling, victuals, and all other things necessary. It was ordered that she should be brought to Portsmouth on a day named; and from that time, that the county should furnish also victuals and mariner's wages and all other necessaries for twenty-six weeks. But as it was never intended that an actual ship should be provided, the sheriff was further commanded, with the aid of the mayors and bailiffs of the several cities and boroughs within his county, to assess the requisite money on the several boroughs and freeholders of the county; and to return the assessment, with the names of the persons charged, in a schedule to the writ. If payment were not voluntarily made by the party assessed, compulsory process was to be issued to enforce it.

The levy, however obnoxious, had been continued annually for four years, producing a revenue of £200,000 a year, when public opinion set strongly against its legality. An attempt was made to fortify it by the opinions of the judges. They were summoned to the Star Chamber in March, 1636, where a case and question were put into their hands, signed by the king and enclosed in a regal letter. The judges gave their unanimous opinion in affirmation of the question put to them—that, "when the good and safety of the kingdom in general is concerned and the whole kingdom in danger, your majesty may by writ under the great seal of England, command all your subjects, at their charge, to provide and furnish such number of ships, with men, munition, and victuals, and for such time as you shall think fit, for the defence and safeguard of the kingdom from such danger and peril; and that by law you may compel the doing thereof in case of refusal or refractoriness. And we are also of opinion that your majesty is the sole judge both of the danger, and when and how the same is to be prevented and avoided." This opinion became celebrated as an "*extra-judicial opinion;*" and Lord Keeper Finch signified the king's command that it should be entered in all the courts of Westminster, and that the judges should publish it through all their circuits; and he inflicted the keenest rebuke of the baseness and subserviency of the judges, by congratulating them that the king had descended to communicate with them.

The king and his ministers, having secured the judges, could proceed with confidence to put down opposition. Writs of scire facias were issued against the defaulters in the county of Bucks, requiring them to pay the money or to appear in court and show cause against the demand; and the sheriff returned "that he had made it known (*quod sciri fecit*) to John Hampden Esq., who was assessed at 20 shillings, and he hath not paid it."

Hampden justified his refusal of payment, and raised the question of the right of the crown, by a demurrer to the writ of scire facias, which put at issue the law the writ was issued to enforce. The case was argued before the twelve judges in the court of Exchequer Chamber, in April, 1638. The argument occupied twelve days. All the old laws and authorities were cited, which showed that the subject could not be taxed without the consent of Parliament, and finally the confirmation of those laws by the Petition of Right

But a majority of the judges, four dissenting, pronounced judgment in favor of the crown—that the writs were sufficient in law to charge Mr. Hampden with the twenty shillings assessed upon him.

Upwards of eleven years now passed before a Parliament was assembled; a period during which, if we may believe Lord Clarendon, England enjoyed the highest material prosperity; but during which it is also certain that the liberties of the people were defied, and the prerogative of the crown strained to the utmost.

FOURTH (THE SHORT) PARLIAMENT.

At length the king's necessities compelled him to summon a Parliament, when, immediately on their assembling, petitions, representing grievances, were presented from several English counties; and they led to a debate in which the unconstitutional proceedings of the Government, during the long discontinuance of Parliament, were reviewed. This was followed by an inquiry into the circumstances connected with the dissolution of the last Parliament. A resolution was passed that the refusal of the speaker to put the question, by a verbal command from his majesty, was a breach of privilege; and warrants were issued, signed by the speaker, requiring that the records and proceedings of the court of Exchequer, concerning ship money, should be produced by the officers of that court.

These steps indicating the course the Commons were taking, Charles made another effort to call their attention to his supplies Sir Henry Vane delivered a message from the king to the house, that it was his pleasure they should attend him, on the 21st of April, at Whitehall; where the Lords and Commons being assembled in the king's presence, Lord Keeper Finch addressed them.

"Such are his majesty's occasions," he said, "that if the supply be not speedy, it will be of no use; for the army is now marching, and stands at least £100,000 a month. The king doth not expect a great and ample supply for perfecting the work, but only such as without which the charge would be lost and the design frustrated. That done, you may present your grievances to him, and he will hear them with a gracious ear. Concerning ship money, his majesty never had it in his royal heart to make an annual revenue of it, nor to make the least benefit or profit of it, but what he did or intended was for the honor and glory of the nation; and the accounts of such moneys so received have been brought to the council table, and the moneys delivered to the treasurer of the navy. His majesty cannot this year forbear the writs for ship money, because they had gone out before it was possible that Parliament could grant supply; but he expects your concurrence in the levying it for the future. It will comfort every English heart to know that his majesty hath no thoughts of enriching himself by these writs: he doth desire but to live as it behooves a king of England, and as every true English heart desireth."

These fair promises and gracious explanations did not avert the Commons from their course. They admitted the great urgency of the occasion: "Necessity is come upon us like an armed man. Let us not stand too nicely upon circumstances; let us do what may be done with reason and honesty on our part to comply with the king's desires. But let us first give new force to the old laws for maintaining our rights and privileges, and endeavor to restore this nation to its fundamental and vital liberties—the property of our goods, and the freedom of our persons. The kings of this nation have always governed by Parliaments; but now divines would persuade us that a monarch must be absolute, and that he may do all things *ad libitum*. Since they are so ready to let loose the conscience of the king, to enterprise the change of a long-established government, we are the more carefully to provide for our protection against this pulpit law, by declaring and reënforcing the municipal laws of the kingdom. The first thing this house should consider of, should be the restoring to the nation their fundamental and vital liberties, and then to consider of the supply desired."

A Parliament thus begun under Charles I. could not be expected to be very long continued, and it was dissolved by the king's command after an existence of but three weeks. Those who composed it were by no means men of distempered minds, or desirous of revolution. They were fully disposed to supply the king's necessities, but they were no less determined to maintain their own rights and their country's liberty.

Yet the sudden dissolution created great surprise. "There

could not," says Lord Clarendon, "a greater damp have seized upon the spirits of the nation than this dissolution caused, and men had much of the misery in view which shortly after fell out. It could never be hoped that more sober and dispassionate men would ever meet together in that place, or fewer who brought ill purposes with them; nor could any man imagine what offence they had given, which put the king upon that resolution."

FIFTH (THE LONG) PARLIAMENT.

Lord Clarendon informs us that, within an hour after the dissolving of the last Parliament, meeting Mr. St. John, who was seldom known to smile, with a most cheerful aspect, while he himself appeared melancholic, as in truth he was, Mr. St. John asked him what troubled him. He answered that "in such a time of confusion, so wise a Parliament, which alone could have found remedy for it, was so unreasonably dismissed." The other answered that "all was well, and that it must be worse before it could be better;" a prophecy founded on a sound view of the incompetency of the king to contend with his adversaries, and of the increasing difficulty of his affairs. Certainly the king made nothing by the change of the Short Parliament for that which his necessities and the confusions of the kingdom forced him six months afterwards to summon. The latter is known as the Long Parliament, by whose order he was ultimately executed. From the first it was opposed to him. The king had designed that Sir Thomas Gardiner, recorder of London, should be elected speaker of the Commons; and it was not doubted that he could have been chosen to one of the four seats of the city of London. But the citizens exerted themselves so much in opposition to the court, that the recorder was rejected in the city; and through the influence of the citizens, and the prevalence of feelings inimical to the court, he was not elected elsewhere. A large portion of the members of the last Parliament were returned to this, including all the Puritan leaders. "There was observed," says Clarendon, "a marvellous elated countenance in most of the members of Parliament before they met in the house. The same men who six months before were observed to be of very moderate tempers, and to wish that gentle remedies might be applied, without opening the wound too wide and exposing it to the air—and rather to cure what was amiss than too strictly to make inquisition into the causes and original of the malady—talked now in another dialect both of things and persons."

The Lords were animated by the same feelings as the Commons, in whose proceedings they were usually ready to coöperate. They began the work of punishment by summoning Sir William Beecher to the bar of their house, to answer by what warrant or direction he had searched the pockets and houses, and carried away the papers of Lord Brooke and the Earl of Warwick after the last Parliament, and before the expiration of the parliamentary privilege. He justified himself as clerk of the privy council, bound to execute their warrants; and he puzzled the Lords by allowing them to infer that he had acted under the king's direct sanction. But he afterwards confessed that the warrants were signed by the two secretaries of state; and on his humble petition and confession of his error, the Lords released him from imprisonment.

The Commons commenced a long series of impeachments, and having adopted a resolution to accuse Thomas, Lord Wentworth, earl of Strafford, lord lieutenant of Ireland, of high treason, they sent Mr. Pym with a message to the Lords to desire that Lord Strafford might be sequestered from Parliament and committed—a desire which was complied with by the Lords. They did not, however, neglect the king's necessities; for in a few days afterwards, they voted him a supply of £100,000. Ship money was referred to a committee, to inquire into its legality. Upon their report being made to the house, it was resolved, *nullo contradicente*, "that the charge imposed upon the subjects for providing and furnishing of ships, and the assessment and raising of money for that purpose, commonly called ship money; the extra-judicial opinions of the judges, published in the Star Chamber, and enrolled in the courts of Westminster; the writs commonly called ship writs; and the judgment in the exchequer on Mr. Hampden's case—were, severally, against the laws of the realm, the right of property, and the liberty of the subject, contrary to former resolutions of Parliament, and to the Petition of Right." The Lords on a subsequent day passed similar resolutions, declaring the illegality of ship money, and the proceedings connected with it.

The Commons next visited their own house with punishment, by excluding four members, for being monopolists and patentees, from sitting in Parliament.

The king, compelled to submit to all these proceedings, was now thoroughly humbled, and we presently find leaders of the Commons admitted to high offices under the crown; and whatever advantage, present or prospective, was expected from these accessions, it is from this period that we have to note the submission of Charles to the demands of the Parliament, and the rapid descent of his executive power. He acceded to a request of both houses for an alteration in the tenure of the judges' appointments—that for the future the clause *quamdiu se bene gesserint* might be inserted in their patents, instead of *durante bene placito,* that is, during good behavior instead of during the king's pleasure. He next passed the act for triennial parliaments, framed on the principle deprecated in his speech; the title of which is, "An Act for the Preventing Inconveniences happening by the long intermission of Parliament." Although its chief provisions were repealed by Charles II., it is so remarkable an event in the history of the constitution that we must briefly notice its contents. Its foundation is the ancient law that Parliament ought to be holden at least once every year for redress of grievances. It provided that if Parliament were not summoned and assembled before the 3d of September, in every third year, then a Parliament should assemble on the second Monday in November ensuing. The lord chancellor was required to take an oath to issue the writs in due time; and in his default the peers should meet, and any twelve or more should issue the writs. In case of their default, the sheriffs, mayors, and bailiffs should cause elections to be made; and lastly, in their default, the freeholders, citizens, and burgesses should proceed to election. The Parliament should not be dissolved or prorogued within fifty days after the time appointed for their meeting; nor adjourned within fifty days, but by consent of either house respectively.

He subsequently passed another act to prevent inconveniences which may happen by the untimely adjourning, proroguing, or dissolving this present Parliament. It enacted that the Parliament should not be dissolved, nor prorogued or adjourned, unless by an act of Parliament to be passed for the purpose; and that neither the House of Peers nor the House of Commons should be adjourned, unless by themselves, or their own order. This act, in rendering Parliament indissoluble but by their own act, contravened a fundamental principle of the constitution, and whilst it superseded the executive authority of the crown, it also took away the elective rights of the people. The king, however, passed it.

Charles next yielded the contest respecting tonnage and poundage, by passing an act granting him those duties for less than two months, which he had claimed for his life. It declared illegal the right for which he had so long contended, by reciting that the duties had been collected against the laws of the realm, in regard that they had not been granted by Parliament, and that the farmers, customers, and collectors had received condign punishment, and it declared that "it is and had been the ancient right of the subjects of this realm that no subsidy, custom, impost, or other charge whatsoever, might or may be laid or imposed upon any merchandise, exported or imported, by subjects, denizens, or aliens, without common consent in Parliament." Charles must have felt humbled when, by accepting and passing that bill, he gave up his claim, constantly insisted upon since his first Parliament. When passing it, he said, in answer to the speaker, "You cannot but know that I do freely and frankly give over that right which my predecessors have esteemed their own—though I confess disputed, yet so that it was never yielded by any one of them. Therefore you must understand this as a mark of my confidence in you thus to put myself wholly upon the love and affections of my people for my subsistence." Charles was next called upon to give his royal assent to two acts for abolishing the court of Star Chamber and the High Commission Court. He postponed his assent to these bills until, as he said, he had time to consider them; and in consequence some discontent arose, which he alluded to in his speech when be afterwards gave the royal assent: "Methinks it seems strange that any one should think I could pass two bills of such importance as these without taking some fit time to consider them; for it is no less than to alter, in a great measure, those fundamental laws, ecclesiastical and civil, which many of my predecessors have established.

"If you consider (he proceeded) what I have done in this Parliament, discontent will not sit in your hearts. I hope you remember I have granted that the judges hereafter shall hold their places *quamdiu bene se gesserint.* I have bounded the forest, not according to my right, but according to the late customs. I have established the property of the subjects, as witness the free giving up—not the taking away—the ship money. I have established by act of Parliament the property of the subject in tonnage and poundage, which never was done in any of my predecessors' times. I have granted a law for a triennial Parliament; and given way to an act for the securing of moneys advanced for the disbanding of the armies. I have given free course of justice against delinquents. I have put the laws in execution against papists. . . .

"For my part I shall omit nothing that may give you just contentment, and study nothing more than your happiness; and therefore I hope you shall see a very good testimony of it by passing these two bills."

The king had called these laws fundamental. The courts which they abolished had been so long used to oppress the subject, by the Tudors as well as the Stuarts, that their abolition was the greatest blow that had yet been given to irresponsible power. *The constitutional effect of their abolition was the transfer of all accusations and complaints against the subject from the Star Chamber and High Commission Courts to the courts of common law, there to be tried openly by a jury, according to the law of the land.*

The first of these acts is called "An Act for the Regulating of the Privy Council, and for taking away the court commonly called the Star Chamber." It begins with a recital of Magna Charta, and its train of statutes for protecting the liberty of the subject, and refers to the statutes of Henry VII. and of Henry VIII., by the former of which the Star Chamber was established, or at least moulded into a new form; and it declares that the judges had not kept themselves within the limits of the statute of Henry VII.; but had undertaken to punish where no law did warrant, and to make decrees for things having no such authority, and to inflict heavier punishments than by any law was warranted. "And forasmuch (it proceeds) as all matters examinable or determinable in the court of Star Chamber may have their proper remedy and redress, and their due punishment and correction *by the common law of the land, and in the ordinary courts of justice; and the proceedings, censures, and decrees of that court have been found to be an intolerable burden to the subject and the means to introduce an arbitrary power and government;* and forasmuch as the council table hath of late times assumed a power to intermeddle in civil causes between party and party, and to determine of the estates and liberties of the subjects, contrary to the law of the land; it ordained that the court, commonly called the Star Chamber, should be absolutely dissolved, taken away, and determined."

The other act is called "A Repeal of a Branch of Statute, primo Elizabethæ, concerning Commissioners for Causes Ecclesiastical." It recites the act, and the clause contained in it, by which Queen Elizabeth established the High Commission Court, and that the commissioners had to the great and insufferable wrong and oppression of the king's subjects, used to *fine and imprison them;* and, therefore, the branch of the statute on which the court was based was repealed and made void; and persons exercising spiritual or ecclesiastical power by authority derived from the king to inflict fine, imprisonment, or corporal punishment, were deprived of that power.

Charles next conceded the illegality of his proceedings in regard to ship money, the enlargment of forests, and the fines on the refusal of knighthood; and extinguished his claims by giving the royal assent to acts for abolishing them.

The "Act for the declaring unlawful and void the late proceedings touching ship money, and for the vacating of all records and process concerning the same," declared and enacted that the charge imposed upon the subject for the providing and furnishing of ships, commonly called ship money, and the extra-judicial opinions of the justices and barons, and the writs and the judgment against John Hampden, were contrary to the laws and statutes of this realm, the right of property, the liberty of the subject, former resolutions in Parliament, and the Petition of Right.

The "Act for the certainty of forests and of the meets, meers limits, and bounds of the forest," declared that the limits and bounds of the forests should extend no farther than those reputed and taken in the twentieth year of King James; and that all presentments to the contrary should be void.

The " Act for the prevention of vexatious proceedings touching the order of knighthood," declared and enacted that thenceforth no person, of what condition, quality, estate, or degree soever, should be distrained or compelled by any means to take upon him the order or dignity of knighthood; nor suffer or undergo any fine, trouble or molestation, for not having taken on him such order or dignity.

We may here pause to consider the effect of this extensive legislation on the power of the crown. It abolished the principal instruments of tyranny employed by the Tudors, and afterwards by the Stuart monarchs. It declared illegal the expedients to which Charles had resorted to raise money in the absence of Parliament; and it put an end to his long-cherished claim, on the ground of hereditary right, to enjoy tonnage and poundage for his life; giving him in succession grants of that revenue for short periods of weeks or months. The most eminent and powerful of his ministers was attainted and put to death. It was made impossible for him to resist the meeting of Parliament once in three years, and its continuance in session for at least fifty days; while he conferred on the Parliament then existing the prerogative, never before separated from the crown, of continuing or dissolving itself at its will and pleasure. But excepting the latter, which was undoubtedly an unconstitutional interference with the prerogative of the crown, these changes were a just concession to the rights and liberties of the people; and we may also have observed that the speeches in which Charles gave his royal assent to these acts, have none of the defiance and vituperation of his speeches to previous Parliaments, and rather breathe the courteous acquiescence, if they do not also exceed the submission, of a constitutional king.

These concessions were deemed by many a sufficient surrender of the royal power; and Mr. Hyde, Lord Falkland, and others of the popular party, declared in Parliament their disapproval of further demands. After passing the acts, the king went to Scotland, where Scotch affairs required his presence; and on his return the popular feeling had changed so much in his favor, that he made a public entry into London, where "he was received with all imaginary expressions and demonstrations of affection and grandeur." The recorder was warm in his praises and congratulations. He could truly say from the representative body of the city, from whence he had his warrant, that they met his majesty with as much love and affection as ever citizens of London met his royal progenitors; and he added, that these expressions of joy, of love, of loyalty he met with everywhere from the citizens of London. The king answered that he returned with as hearty and kind affections to his people in general, and to the city in particular, as could be desired by his loving subjects; the first he should express by governing them all according to the laws of the kingdom, and in maintaining and protecting the true Protestant religion. In answer to another petition of the city that he would winter at Whitehall, he said that although he had proposed to winter at Hampton Court, he should alter his resolution, and with all convenient speed repair to Whitehall. The king afterwards, in a speech to Parliament, referred to his reception, "not being in doubt," he said, "that his subjects' affections were any way lessened to him in the time of his absence; for he could not but remember, to his great comfort, the joyful reception he had at his entry into London.

Would that we could here end the tale, for England in throwing off the royal yoke was fast becoming subject to an influence not less mischievous—Puritanism. A spirit more arbitrary than monarchy now controlled the Commons, and from the hour of its complete ascendency we read but of confusion, bloodshed, civil war, and by and by the worse than imperial despotism which reached its incarnation in a Cromwell. The affairs of England never had been—never have been in a happier or more hopeful state than at the period we have now reached; and to the restless, meddling fiend of Puritanism in its next act, we must trace the woful tragedy which ended the unhappy reign of the first Charles.

CHAPTER X.

CHARLES I.—THE REIGN OF PURITANISM—FROM THE GRAND REMONSTRANCE TO THE END OF CONSTITUTIONAL LEGISLATION UNDER CHARLES.

THE GRAND REMONSTRANCE CARRIED BY A PURITAN MAJORITY OF ELEVEN—SAYING OF CROMWELL—DIFFERENT OPINIONS CONCERNING THE REMONSTRANCE—ITS FUTILITY—SKETCH OF ITS CONTENTS—OBJECT AND DETERMINATION OF THE PURITANS—THEIR EXASPERATION OF THE KING—ROYAL IMPEACHMENT AND IMPRISONMENT OF LORD KIMBOTTON AND THE FIVE MEMBERS—DECLARATION OF THE COMMONS—RETURN OF THE FIVE MEMBERS—SEPARATION OF KING AND PARLIAMENT—HIS EFFORTS AT A RECONCILIATION—IMPLACABILITY OF THE PURITANS—BISHOPS REMOVED FROM PARLIAMENT—THE "ROOT AND BRANCH BILL"—ABOLITION—MILITIA BILL—THE KING REFUSES HIS ASSENT—MESSAGE TO THE KING FROM PARLIAMENT—HIS ANSWER—GENERAL REVIEW—PURITAN DESPOTISM—CROMWELL.

Shortly before the king's return, the Commons passed through their house a "Declaration of the State of the Kingdom," which, as it has acquired historical celebrity as the "Grand Remonstrance," requires our notice. It was the work of the Puritan members of the house, being objected to and opposed by the others as unparliamentary and inexpedient:—unparliamentary, as being an appeal to the people concerning the government and conduct of the king, and as the work of one only of the constituent bodies of Parliament; inexpedient, as a detail of grievances already redressed. The draft was prepared by a committee, and laid before the house early in November; and after much opposition, a day was fixed for taking it into consideration, clause by clause, by the whole house, the speaker in the chair. The debate commenced at three o'clock in the afternoon, and was continued until three o'clock on the following morning; when, the question being put, whether the declaration as amended should pass, it was carried in the affirmative by a majority of 159 to 148, that is, by a majority of *eleven;* but a motion that it should be printed, terminated in a resolution that it should not be printed without the particular order of the house. The debate produced great passion and vehemence; and the excitement is made evident by a saying of OLIVER CROMWELL, who told Lord Falkland, as they went out of the house after the debate, that "if the Remonstrance had been rejected, he would have sold all he had the next morning, and never have seen England more; and he knew there were several other honest men of the same resolution."

This remonstrance has been considered under different aspects by historians. Forster, the great advocate of Puritanism, would have us think that it "was an appeal to the people, rendered necessary by the falsehood and unfaithfulness of the king to all his engagements, in order to bring about a lasting adjustment of right relations between the Commons and the crown." Mr. Hallam considers that "it was put forward to stem the returning tide of loyalty, which not only threatened to obstruct the further progress of the popular leaders, but, as they would allege, might, by gaining strength, wash away some at least of the bulwarks that had been so recently constructed for the preservation of liberty." We must, however, agree with Hume, who characterizes it "as containing many gross falsehoods, intermingled with some evident truth," and calls it "a plain signal for further attacks on the royal prerogative; and a declaration that the concessions already made, however important, were not to be regarded as satisfactory;" adding that "nothing less was foreseen, whatever ancient names might be preserved, than an abolition almost total" of the constitutional government of England. *The Remonstrance admits that the grievances and oppressions it portrayed had already been removed*—"the difficulties seemed to be insuperable which, by the Divine Providence, *we have overcome.*" It specifies large sums of money that had been raised, "and yet God hath so blessed the endeavors of this Parliament, *that the kingdom is a great gainer by all these charges.*"

"*The ship money is abolished*, which cost this kingdom above £200,000 a year. *The coat and conduct money and other military charges are taken away*, which, in many counties, amounted to little less than the ship money. *The monopolies are all suppressed*, whereof some few did prejudice the subject above a million yearly; the soap, £100,000; the wine, £300,000; the leather must needs exceed both, and salt could be no less than that; besides the inferior monopolies, which if they could be exactly computed, would make up a great sum." It admits that *the king's* POWER OF EVIL *was taken away*. "That which is more beneficial than all this is, *the root of these evils is taken away;* which was the *arbitrary power pretended to be in his majesty*, of taxing his subjects, or charging their estates, without consent of Parliament, which is now declared to be against law, by the judgment of both houses, and also by an act of Parliament."

It reviews the advantages which had resulted from the impeachments and the several new laws. By the former, "the living grievances, the evil counsellors and actors of these mischiefs, *have been so quelled*, that it is likely not only to be an ease to the present time, but a preservation to the future." Among the latter are named the Triennial Act and the Act to prevent the abrupt dissolution of Parliament, which "*secure a full operation of the present remedy and afford a perpetual spring of remedies for the future.*" "The Star Chamber, the High Commission, the courts of president and council in the North, the immoderate power of the council table, *are all taken away;* the canons and the power of canon making *are blasted by the vote of both houses;* the forests are by a good law *reduced to their right bounds;* and other things of main importance for the good of this kingdom are in proposition. The *malignants*"—In this word "malignants" the essential venom of Puritanism already spurts out on its opponents. The Puritans had succeeded in obtaining a majority of ELEVEN in the House of Commons, and already all opposed to them are to be described as malignants! But to continue—"The malignants have endeavored to work on his majesty ill impressions and opinions of our proceedings, as if we had altogether done our own work and not his, and had obtained from him many things very prejudicial to the crown, both in respect of prerogative and profit. To wipe out the first part of this slander, we think good only to say that all we have done is for his majesty, his greatness, honor and support. . . . . As to the second branch of this slander, we acknowledge with much thankfulness that his majesty hath passed more good bills to the advantage of his subjects than have been in many ages."

Having thus fully demonstrated that it is itself a mere *brutum fulmen* of fanaticism, wholly unnecessary in the circumstances of the nation, the Remonstrance next proceeds to declare the reformation in view: "And now what hope have we but in God; when the only means of our subsistence and power of reformation is, under Him, in the Parliament? But what can we, the Commons, do, without the conjunction of the House of Lords? and what conjunction can we expect there, where the bishops and recusant lords are so numerous and prevalent, that they are able to cross and interrupt our best endeavors for reformation, and by that means, give advantage to this malignant party to traduce our proceedings? . . . . We confess our intention is and our endeavors have been, to reduce within bounds that exorbitant power which the prelates have assumed unto themselves, so contrary both to the word of God, and the laws of the land; to which end we have passed the bill for the removing them from their temporal power and employments, that so the better they might with meekness apply themselves to the discharge of their functions; which bill themselves opposed, and were the principal instruments of crossing it." They then declare their own views of discipline and government of the Church; and desire a general synod of divines, the results of whose consultations should be represented to the Parliament, to be there allowed of and confirmed, and receive the stamp of authority. They deny the charge maliciously made, that they intend to destroy and discourage learning, declaring that they "intend to reform and purge the fountains of learning, the two Universities; that the streams flowing from them may be clear and pure, and an honor and comfort to the whole land."

The malignants tell the people, "that our meddling with the power of episcopacy hath caused sectaries and conventicles . . thus with Elijah we are called by this malignant party, the troublers of the state; and still, while we endeavor to reform their abuses, they make us the authors of those mischiefs we study to prevent." The pharisaical hypocrisy of these pretences would be sublime in any but the Puritans. With them it was, and always has been, *customary*.

They finally state the courses for perfecting the work begun, and removing all future impediments, under five heads:

1. To keep Papists in such condition as that they may not be able to do us any hurt; and for avoiding such connivance and favor as heretofore hath been shown to them, that his majesty be pleased to grant a commission to some choice men named in Parliament, who may take notice of their increase, their counsels, and proceedings; and use all due means, by execution of the laws, to prevent any mischievous designs against the peace and safety of the kingdom. 2. That some good course be taken to discover the false conformity of Papists to the Church, whereby they have been admitted to places of trust. 3. That all illegal grievances and exactions be presented and punished at the sessions and assizes; and that judges and justices be sworn to the due execution of the Petition of Right and other laws. 4. That his majesty be humbly petitioned, by both houses, to employ such councillors, ambassadors, and ministers as the Parliament may have cause to confide in, without which we cannot give his majesty such supplies as is desired. 5. That all councillors of state may be sworn to observe the laws which concern the subject in his liberty; not to receive, or give, reward or pension, to or from any foreign prince; that all good courses may be taken to unite the two kingdoms of England and Scotland; to take away all differences among ourselves for matters indifferent concerning religion, and to unite ourselves against the common enemies, and to labor, by all offices of friendship, to unite the foreign churches with us, in the same cause." "If these things," it concludes, "may be observed, we doubt not but God will crown this Parliament with such success as shall be the beginning and founda-

tion of more honor and happiness to his majesty than was ever yet enjoyed by one of his royal predecessors."

Such is the Grand Remonstrance, and it must, by all but Puritans, be confessed that it is difficult to determine from what motive it proceeded, or what object it had in view. Historians have in general considered it as possessing no constitutional value; it is not addressed to any great principle then in danger or in doubt, and a document so lengthy and pretending, ends in a lame and impotent conclusion, when it propounds amongst the remedies for bad government—and those the most prominent—increased vigilance towards Papists, and a more extended union of Protestants against them. Viewing it as a remonstrance of the House of Commons against the tyranny or illegal government of the king, it loses its effect by the confession that the grievances complained of had been fully redressed, and that the king's power of evil was taken away; and it is not to be compared, in that respect, with the bold remonstrances of the Commons to James—or even to those in the early part of this reign, when Charles was in the plenitude of his prerogative—defying the power, and daring the punishments the kings were then able and willing to inflict. If we view it as a measure rendered necessary to insure faithfulness of the king (for which there is no authority in the tenor or terms of the Remonstrance), we object that the king had surrendered by acts of Parliament the prerogatives which he had assumed, and by which he had illegally oppressed his people; and had thus given the highest security known to the constitution, for the abandonment of his assumed prerogatives; and that therefore an appeal to the people in anticipation of his future misconduct, was not only ungracious, but insulting. But the true view of it is that the Remonstrance was intended to aid the design of removing from Parliament the bishops and those lords whom it so strongly denounced as the obstacles to *Puritanism*. The removal of the bishops, in order to obtain the control spiritual as well as temporal of the kingdom, was the great object of the Puritan party; the intention to remove them is confessed in the remonstrance; but it was almost the only point in which they could not get the concurrence of the king and the Lords. It was accomplished, however, within a few months after the Remonstrance; and if we consider the power of ambitious and self-righteous fanaticism when striving for ascendency, and how strongly it governed the actions of the Puritans in Parliament, it will perhaps be felt that this, and this only, in the then subdued condition of the king, fired the energies of these fanatics to the frenzy which the debate produced; and that this is amply adequate to explain the resolution of Cromwell (as the same motives animated the so-called Pilgrim Fathers) to sell all he possessed and leave the country, if the Remonstrance had not been carried.

We now pass to another phase in Charles's eventful life, when, driven by exasperation to relinquish all his compliant submission to the Commons, and losing sight of his pledged regard to their privileges, he entered into a personal contest with them. The attempted seizure of the five members, one of the most ominous passages of English history, is referred to. Since the Grand Remonstrance, several subjects of dispute and irritation (sedulously stirred up and fomented by the Puritans, who were determined that their *majority of eleven* should be made the most of,) had arisen between the king and the Parliament. One arose out of a demand by the Commons, that the king should remove the lieutenant of the Tower from his office, and place another, nominated by the Commons, in his room—a demand which the Peers considered to be an interference with the royal prerogative, and in which, therefore, they refused to concur. Then followed an unpleasant inquiry in the House of Commons, in which the queen was involved. The Commons, too, charged twelve bishops with high treason, for attempting to subvert the laws and being of Parliament. Riots and tumults, stirred up by the Puritan leaders, took place daily in the neighborhood of the houses of Parliament; and the bishops, being particularly obnoxious to the crowd, and not daring to encounter them, they absented themselves from Parliament. Twelve bishops protested in the House of Lords that they had been menaced, affronted, and assaulted, on their way to the house, and put in danger of their lives; and they went the length of protesting, in writing, against all proceedings in the house during what they termed their forced and violent absence. The Lords communicated the bishops' protest to the Commons, who immediately *accused the latter of high treason for interrupting the business of Parliament;* (*!*)

and the Lords were so compliant as to order the bishops to be taken into custody. The king, also, declined to accede to an address from the Commons for a guard; treating their fears for their safety as groundless; assuring them of his protection, and promising condign punishment to any one who should offer them any violence; but in reality hurt and annoyed at their interference with his prerogative.

Events like these, occurring in *one short month*, were calculated to irritate the king's temper and bewilder his judgment; but he would not have fallen into the rash and dangerous project of seizing the five members, if he had consulted the men whom, about this period, he had attracted to his councils. Lord Falkland had become secretary of state in place of Vane; and Sir John Colepepper, knight of the shire of Kent, chancellor of the exchequer; Mr. Hyde, also, had agreed to become a minister, but was without actual office; and to these three the king consented to yield the direction of himself and his affairs. These accessions to the king's ministry were brought about by Lord Digby, who had long served the king as his minister, and whom the king had raised to the House of Lords. It was intended that Lord Digby should have ceased to be the adviser of the king; but between the king and Digby alone the project of the seizure of the five members was agreed and resolved upon, without the least communication with either of the other three.

When the Parliament met after the adjournment for Christmas, the attorney-general attended at the House of Lords, and, standing at the clerk's table, stated that the king had commanded him to accuse, and that he did accuse, Lord Kimbotton, a member of the House of Peers, Mr. Holles, Mr. Pym, Mr. Hampden, Sir Arthur Haselrigge, and Mr. Strode, members of the House of Commons, of high treason. He delivered articles which he had received from the king, charging them with having endeavored to deprive him of his royal power, and to place in the subjects an arbitrary and tyrannical power; by foul aspersions to alienate the affections of the people from the king, and to make him odious to them; to draw the army to disobedience, and to side with them in their treacherous designs; that they had traitorously invited a foreign power to invade the kingdom; that they had traitorously endeavored to subvert the rights and very being of Parliament; that they had, by force and terror, endeavored to compel the Parliament to join them in their traitorous designs, and had actually raised and countenanced tumults against the king and Parliament; and that they had traitorously conspired to levy, and actually had levied, war against the king." The attorney-general demanded a select committee to take the examination of the witnesses to be produced by the king, and that the persons of the accused should be secured. On the same day the king sent the sergeant-at-arms to the House of Commons with a message demanding the five members to be delivered to the sergeant, and being delivered, that he should arrest them of high treason. The Commons immediately ordered Lord Falkland, the chancellor of the exchequer, and two other members, to attend the king, to inform him that the house would take his message into consideration with as much speed as the business would admit, and in the mean time would take care that the gentlemen should be ready to answer any legal charge made against them. The house, also, enjoined the accused members to attend the house daily until further orders. The king, nothing daunted, went on the following day in person to the House of Commons, accompanied by a guard of soldiers, to arrest the accused members. Private information was given of his approach, and the members were removed, the last only quitting the house as the king entered. He passed up to the speaker's chair, which he took, and after looking about the house, and not perceiving Mr. Pym, whose person he knew, he asked the speaker whether any of those persons were in the house, and where they were. The speaker, falling on his knees, replied, "I have neither eyes to see nor tongue to speak in this place, but as the house is pleased to direct me, whose servant I am here, and humbly beg your majesty's pardon that I cannot give any other answer than this to what your majesty is pleased to demand of me." The king, seeing that his attempt had been unsuccessful, addressed the house in a short speech from the speaker's chair, saying that "when he sent the sergeant-at-arms, he expected obedience, and not a message—that though he would be careful of their privileges, they must know that in cases of treason there was no privilege, and that so long as those persons he had accused were in the house, he could not expect that it would be in the right way that he heartily wished it. But since he saw that the birds were flown, he would trouble them no more than to tell them he expected they would send them to him as soon as they returned to the house; otherwise he must take his own course to find them." He retired amidst shouts of "Privilege! Privilege!" and the house, in great excitement, adjourned till the next day.

When the Commons assembled, they passed a declaration that "the king's proceedings were a high breach of the rights and privileges of Parliament, and that they could not, with the safety of their own persons, sit any longer without a full vindication of so high a breach, and a sufficient guard wherein they might confide." They then adjourned to the 11th of January, but they appointed a committee to sit in the mean time at Guildhall, with power to consider and resolve upon all things that might concern the good and safety of the city and kingdom. The House of Lords made a similar adjournment. Mr. Pym vindicated himself before the House of Commons from the king's charges, and the answer of the Puritan leader shows that Charles had founded his charges against the five members wholly on account of their Parliamentary conduct; although small indeed must have been his expectation that the charges could have been sustained in a tribunal which had participated in or sanctioned the acts charged against the accused. But he still continued his efforts, even his personal efforts, to arrest the members. During the short recess of Parliament he went into the city, where the accused members were concealed, and in a speech to the common council assembled at Guildhall, he required their assistance in apprehending the accused. Three days afterwards he issued a proclamation commanding officers and magistrates to apprehend and convey them to the Tower; but on the day before Parliament reassembled, the king quitted London, and retired to his palace at Hampton Court—never again to return to the metropolis of his kingdom until brought there for his trial and execution.

The Parliament met on the 11th of January. The accused members were brought in triumph by water to Westminster, amidst the plaudits of the people, and took their seats in the House of Commons. It was now apparent that all chance of reconciliation was at an end, and both sides prepared for the civil war that was inevitable; although for some time longer the forms of the constitution were complied with, because neither party was prepared nor likely to incur the responsibility of commencing the outbreak. The king and Parliament were now separated, and never afterwards communicated but by messages or petitions, and by royal commission, when it was necessary that acts should be passed. The king was sensible of the great error he had fallen into, and of the mischief he had done to his own cause, by his rash proceeding. He tried to extricate himself from the difficulty, and to conciliate the Parliament by a series of messages, acknowledging that he had interfered with their privileges, and postponing the prosecution of the members; and ultimately he went so far as to abandon any further proceedings against them, and to offer a free pardon. But Puritanism never forgives, and the eleven majority in the Commons would accept no reconciliation, answering every message by requisitions which increased the difficulties of their country.

Charles endeavored to procure the mediation of the Lords. In a message to the house he suggested "that the Parliament should, with all speed, fall into a serious consideration of all those particulars which they should hold necessary, as well for the upholding and maintaining of his just and royal authority, and for the settling of his revenue, as for the present and future establishment of their privileges—the free and quiet enjoyment of their estates and fortunes; the security of the true religion then professed by the Church of England; and the settling of ceremonies in such a manner as to take away all just cause of offence." The Lords acquainted the Commons that they had received a gracious message, which filled their hearts full of comfort and joy; and they prepared an answer to thank the king, and to let him know that they would take his message into such speedy and serious consideration as a proposition of that great importance required. The Puritans refused to second the Peers' views, and coupled their refusal with a demand that "the king would be pleased to put the Tower of London, with all other forts and militia of the whole kingdom, into such hands as the Parliament should confide in." The Lords rejected the proposed addition, and the offer of the king, as well as the demand of the Commons, came to nothing.

The king gave the royal assent to several bills, of which the only one demanding our attention was a bill for taking away the temporal power of the bishops and clergy. It was the third which had been introduced into this Parliament for a similar purpose. The first was "A Bill to restrain Bishops and others in Holy Orders from intermeddling in secular affairs," which was sent up to the Lords on the 1st of May, 1641, and was carried then through all the intermediate stages to the third reading, where it was rejected by a large majority. The second was brought in on the 20th of May, by Sir Edward Dering, and was entitled "A Bill for the utter abolishing and taking away all Archbishops, Bishops, their Chancellors and Commissaries, Deans and Chapters, Archdeacons, Prebendaries, Chanters, Canons, and all other their under officers." This received the name of the "Root and Branch Bill," and is a fair specimen of *Puritan toleration.* Puritanism has but one argument for its opponents and the institutions it desires to overthrow. That argument is—abolition. They are "malignant," and must, therefore, be "utterly abolished." The Root and Branch Bill was debated with great passion for twenty days, but was never brought to a conclusion, having been discontinued on account of the king's departure into Scotland.

The title of the third was "An Act for disabling all persons in Holy Orders to exercise any temporal jurisdiction or authority." It enacted that no archbishop or bishop, or other person in Holy Orders, should at any time after the 15th of February, 1641, have any seat or place, suffrage or voice, or use or execute any power or authority in the Parliaments of this realm; nor should be of the privy council, or justice of the peace, of oyer and terminer, or jail-delivery; or execute any temporal authority by virtue of any commission, but should be wholly incapable and disabled." The Lords passed this bill almost with unanimity, *only three bishops dissenting.* The king took time for consideration, which, being reported to the Commons, they, with the imperious and indecent haste which now characterized their proceedings, resolved that delay was denial, and desired the Lords to join them in reasons for hastening the royal assent. It was given a few days afterwards by commission; and thus the Puritans obtained at last the removal of the bishops from Parliament, for which they had so long and earnestly contended.

It would have been supposed that Charles would have complied with any demand that could be made upon him, if he assented to a measure so sweeping and so repugnant to his feelings as that just described; but he at length took a decided stand against the demand of the Parliament for his assent to an ordinance concerning the militia, by which persons to be nominated by the Commons should be intrusted with authority over the militia of the kingdom. He declined to concur in that ordinance; and in an answer to the Lords, through the lord keeper, he declared "that he could not divest himself of the just power which God and the laws of his kingdom had placed in him for the defence of his people, and to put it into the hands of others for any indefinite time." It was thereupon "resolved that the king's answer was a direct denial of their desires; that those who advised it were enemies to the state; that if the king should persist in it, it would hazard the peace and safety of his kingdom, unless a speedy remedy were applied by the wisdom and authority of both houses of Parliament; that such parts of the kingdom as had put themselves in a position of defence against the common danger, had done nothing but what was justifiable; that it would be a great hazard to the kingdom if the king removed to any remote parts from his Parliament, where they could not have convenient access to him on all occasions; and they desired, also, that the prince might come to St. James's, or to some place near London, where he might continue."

These resolutions were embodied in a message from both houses to the king, in which it was declared "that they were enforced in all humility to protest that if the king should persist in his denial, the dangers and distempers of the kingdom are such as will endure no longer delay; and unless he graciously assured them, by their messengers, that he would speedily apply his royal assent to the satisfaction of their former desires, they should be enforced, for the safety of his majesty and the kingdom, to dispose of the militia in such manner as they had propounded, and they resolved to do it accordingly."

The king returned an answer on the 2d of March, from his

palace of Theobald's. He said: "I am so much amazed at this message, that I know not what to answer. You speak of jealousies and fears. Lay your hands on your hearts and ask yourselves whether I may not likewise be disturbed with fears and jealousies; and if so, I assure you this message hath nothing lessened them. For the militia, I thought so much of it before I sent that answer, and am so much assured that the answer is agreeable to what in justice or reason you can ask, or I in honor grant, that I shall not alter it in any point. For my residence near you, I wish it might be so safe and honorable that I had no cause to absent myself from Whitehall. Ask yourselves whether I have or not. For my son, I shall take that care of him which shall justify me to God as a father, and to my dominions as a king. To conclude: I assure you upon my honor, that I have no thought but of peace and justice to my people, which I shall, by all fair means, seek to preserve and maintain; relying upon the goodness and providence of God for the preservation of myself and my rights."

We must here stop. We have brought the contest between the king and the Parliament to an issue, and we have come to the end of the legislation by which we proposed to limit the extent of our historical inquiries. There is no further statute to record in this reign; all that follows is without regard to the principles or practice of the ancient constitution. The difficult task will not be attempted of estimating the degrees of blame or approval which the parties deserve, in the several stages of the great contest; but upon a general view of it, not many will be found who, testing the incidents by the principles of the constitution, would justify the proceedings of Charles, or condemn those of the Parliament, down to the epoch of the Grand Remonstrance; for few will doubt that if his policy and course of action had not been broken down, despotism would have been established. It is from the time of his departure for Scotland—after having passed the series of acts for extending and confirming the liberties of the people—that it may be unhesitatingly asserted that the Parliament would have served their country best by taking their stand on the laws then established, and on the institutions as modified by those laws, and by directing their great power and influence to keep the king within the bounds of constitutional government, under competent ministers, of whom he about that time made a selection that the Commons might have approved. When we look forward to the Restoration, and notice the laws that were then passed by way of complement to the legislation of this reign, we feel assured that such laws might have been obtained from Charles at the same time as the other laws; and with much less reluctance than those repealed at the Restoration, which he submitted to pass. It is common to reply to such observations by pointing out the perfidiousness of Charles's character, and his secret resolve to overthrow the concessions involuntarily made, if he should recover his power or the vigilance of the Commons should be relaxed; and it must be confessed that his attempt against the five members very much weakened the hope which appears before that attempt to have been entertained, that he would content himself with the constitutional position in which the new laws placed him, and would carry on the government under the guidance of constitutional ministers. But, on the other hand, it must be considered that Charles had received a severe lesson—that he could not hope to avert the vigilance and determination of the Commons—and that the failure of his attack on the five members prepared him for yet greater submission; and it would have required—probably on his part, and certainly on the part of his ministers—the venture of their lives and fortunes, to have attempted again to govern the country, and to raise supplies, on principles put down by law and condemned by all parties. On the whole, therefore, we must observe that all the good in this reign was accomplished before Puritanism had gained an ascendency among the Commons; and that from the day when they discovered, by the vote on the Grand Remonstrance, that they had a petty majority in that house, the downward progress of affairs began. The truth is, Puritanism is always proscriptive—always aiming at despotic domination. In England, in the reign of the unhappy Charles, as in these unhappy States to-day, it must and will rule, *and its rule is ruin!*

The breach between Charles and the Parliament became complete in August, and during nearly eighteen years the country went through the vicissitudes of civil war, of government by the Parliament, by the army, by a council of state, by a council of officers; enjoying the blessings of peace and settled government only when CROMWELL, in the name of Puritanism, obtained and exercised absolute power. During this whole period the constitution was disregarded; and although imitated by Cromwell in the institutions he established, these could not acquire the freedom and independence which distinguished the ancient institutions, and they became merely instruments of Cromwell's will. During the Interregnum, we must not look for any contribution to the history of the constitution; it was suspended throughout the whole period, only recovering its action at the Restoration. To that event, therefore, we must now pass; although we may admit that the events of the intermediate period are of the highest interest, and well deserving of laborious study.

CHAPTER XI.

CHARLES II.—THE RESTORATION.—ABOLITION OF THE FEUDAL TENURES.—HABEAS CORPUS ACT.

ENGLAND UNDER CROMWELL—REACTION FROM PURITANISM AT THE RESTORATION—TENDENCY TO RESTORE ABSOLUTISM—MODERATION OF THE ROYALISTS—THE FEUDAL TENURES—FORMER EFFORTS TO ABOLISH THEM—THEIR FINAL ABOLITION IN THIS REIGN—HABEAS CORPUS—ORIGIN OF THE NAME—PROVISION OF MAGNA CHARTA—HISTORICAL SKETCH—AUTHOR OF THE BILL—ITS REPRODUCTION IN THE UNITED STATES—ITS TWELVE PROVISIONS—ITS IMPORTANCE—ILLUSTRATION FROM THE PARALLEL HISTORY OF FRANCE AND ENGLAND—CONCLUSION.

THE history of England during the period of the Interregnum, displays the agitation of a people deprived of their ancient government, but so enamored of its forms and principles, that when all opposition was subdued, and power was finally concentrated in one ruler, he found it necessary to imitate the ancient system as far and as closely as the new elements would assimilate to the old, Oliver Cromwell, avoiding the title of king from dread of the disapproval of the army, took the title of *Protector*, with analogous powers; and he instituted two houses with similar functions to the houses of Parliament. But not regarding the principle of freedom, which the adoption of the ancient system involved, or being unable to carry on his government in accordance with it, he did not forbear from the exercise of despotic authority; and when he had issued his own ordinances for the levying of taxes, he imitated the worst proceedings of his predecessor, Charles, by the intimidation of parties who resisted payment, by imprisonment of their advocates, and by coercion or removal of the judges.

Seldom if ever has so great a change come over the manners and customs of any nation as took place in England on the accession of Charles II.: instead of that fanatic gloom which, during the reign of the Commonwealth, had repressed every expression of pleasure and induced a rude austerity of manners, a taste for elegance and refinement, too frequently degenerated into luxury and voluptuousness, distinguished the new court and pervaded every class of society. We should, however, form a wrong estimate of the nature of this change did we suppose that the great body of the people had become on a sudden less religious or less moral: it was the reaction which naturally follows a period of undue restraint. "Men," says a contemporary writer, "freed from the bondage under which they had been held, madly rushed into every excess, and indulged in licentiousness in proportion to the severity of the restraint under which they had been held." Even the Puritans themselves had undergone a great and remarkable change since their elevation to power; they were no longer that small and virtuous body which they formerly had been, but a heterogeneous mass, united only by extravagant whims about dress, diversions, and postures, which brought the very name of religion into ridicule with the multitude. Before the civil wars, says Macaulay, even those who most disliked the opinions and manners of the Puritan were forced to admit that his moral conduct was generally, in essentials, blameless; but this praise was now no longer bestowed, and unfortunately was no longer deserved. The general fate of sects is to obtain a high reputation for sanctity while they are oppressed, and to lose it as soon as they become powerful. Soon the world begins to find out that the godly are not better than other men, and argues, with some justice, that, if not better, they must be much worse; and in no long time, all those signs which were formerly regarded as characteristic of a saint, are characteristic of a knave. Such was the tone of public feeling at the time of the Restoration; both Presbyterians and Independents had lost the confidence of the nation; and the character of the restored king tended in no slight degree to favor the spread of latitudinarian opinions. Accustomed to the lax morality of the Continental courts, Charles II., although a thorough gentleman in manners, refined and elegant in tastes, amiable in disposition, and agreeable in conversation, was nevertheless a voluptuary, and addicted beyond measure to sensual indulgence. That such a character in the monarch should have completely impressed itself upon the people, may be fairly charged upon the tyrannous Puritanism—more tyrannous than the most unlimited monarchy—under which the nation had so long groaned.

But, further than to notice that alike in action and reaction, Puritanism is the most vicious pest of a community, we do not care to carry these remarks. Nor does our space permit us to dwell at large on the events of the reign of Charles II. To our purpose it suffices to narrate what are to us the two great acts of this reign—the abolition of the feudal tenures, and the passage of the Act of Habeas Corpus. But for these celebrated acts we could take little pleasure in the story of this period. Throughout the whole of it we witness the recovery of the monarchical element to almost absolute power, through the willing prostration of the people, tired of the changes and insecurity of the Interregnum, eager to place their idol on the highest pinnacle of sovereignty; and owing such liberty as remained to the forbearance of the king's ministers. Hyde, as lord chancellor, was the chief minister. He had resided with Charles abroad, where as titular lord chancellor he had managed Charles's affairs; and now since his return, the king, giving himself up to pleasure, left everything in his chancellor's hands. To his constitutional training are to be ascribed the moderation of the Government, in not taking advantage of the transports that prevailed. He resolved (says Burnet) not to stretch the prerogative to what it was before the wars; and would neither set aside the Petition of Right, nor endeavor to raise the courts of Star Chamber or High Commission again—which could have been easily done if he had set about it; nor did he think fit to move for the repeal of the act for triennial Parliaments, till other matters were well settled. He took care indeed to have all things extorted by the Long Parliament from Charles I. repealed; but in regard to revenues he had no mind to put the king out of the necessity of recourse to Parliament.

"The old civil polity," says Macaulay," was now, by the general consent of both the great parties, reëstablished. It was again exactly what it had been when Charles I., eighteen years before, withdrew from his capital. All those acts of the Long Parliament which had received the royal assent were admitted to be still in force. One fresh concession, a concession in which the Cavaliers were even more deeply interested than the Roundheads, was easily obtained from the restored king. The military tenure of land had been originally created as a means of national defence. But in the course of ages, whatever was useful in the institution had disappeared; and nothing was left but ceremonies and grievances. A landed proprietor who held an estate under the crown by knight service—and it was thus that most of the soil of England was held—had to pay a large fine on coming to his property. He could not alienate one acre without purchasing a license. When he died, if his domains descended to an infant, the sovereign was guardian, and was not only entitled to great part of the rents during the minority, but could require the ward, under heavy penalties, to marry any person of suitable rank. The chief bait which attracted a needy sycophant to the court was the hope of obtaining, as the reward of servility and flattery, a royal letter to an heiress. These abuses had perished with the monarchy. That they should not revive with it was the wish of every landed gentleman in the kingdom. They were therefore solemnly abolished by statute; and no relic of the ancient tenures in chivalry was suffered to remain, except those honorary services which are still, at a coronation, rendered to the person of the sovereign by some lords of manors."

The surrender of these feudal revenues had been the subject of treaty with James I.; but the treaty failed, as we have seen, from the uncertainty felt by the Parliament whether, when they had granted the compensation, the surrender would be binding on the king's successors, on the principles of divine right. Charles I., at the treaty of Newport, consented to surrender the revenues for an annual sum of £100,000. The Long Parliament voted the abolition of them unconditionally, declaring that they had a right to take away the burden, as a recompense to the whole kingdom for having ventured their lives and fortunes in that time of great distraction; and from that period the revenues were not collected, and the court of wards ceased to exercise its functions. The Convention Parliament, as it was called which settled the Restoration, proceeded on the principle of compensation; and resolved, as a consideration of the surrender, to make up the king's entire revenue to £1,200,000 *per annum*, to be derived in part from a perpetual excise of all beer and other liquors; a tax which had been introduced by the Long Parliament for short periods, yet not without being charged with relieving the landowners at the expense of the community. The act which affected the abolition of the feudal tenures, also imposed the duties which were its compensation. It is entitled "An Act for taking away the Court of Wards, and Liveries, and Tenures in Capite and by Knight's Service, and Purveyance, and for settling a Revenue on His Majesty in lieu thereof." It adopted the intermission of that court by the Long Parliament, on the 24th of February, 1645, as the date of the abolition; and it enacted "that the court of wards and liveries, and all wardships, liveries, primer seisins, and ousterlemains, values and forfeitures of marriage, by reason of any tenure of the king's majesty, or *of any other*, by knight service, and all other gifts, grants, charges, or incidents arising for or by reason of wardship, liveries, primer seisins, or ousterlemains, be taken away and discharged from the 24th of February, 1645, and that all fines for alienations, and also *aid pur fil marier*, and *pur fair fitz chevalier*, be taken away and discharged as from the same day."

All tenures of land held of the king or of any other person or persons, bodies politic or corporate, were declared to be turned into free and common *socage*, discharged from the feudal charges and incidents, from the 24th day of February, 1645; and all future grants of lands by the king to be in free and common socage." But it is declared that the act should not take away copyhold tenures, frank-almoign, nor the honorary services of grand-serjeantry.

The act consulted the principles of human nature by transferring the guardianship of children under twenty-one, and not married at the time of their father's death, and the management of their lands and property, to guardians to be appointed by the father, by deed in his lifetime, or by his will.

It was enacted that henceforth "no money or other thing should be paid or levied, in regard of any provision, carriages, or purveyance for the king, his heirs or successors; that no person, under warrant, commission, or authority, under the great seal or otherwise, by color of making provision or purveyance for the king or queen, their children or household, should take any timber, fuel, cattle, corn, grain, malt, hay, straw, victual, cart, carriage, or other thing whatever, of any of the subjects of the king, without the full and free consent of the owner, had and obtained without menace or enforcement; nor summon, warn, take, use, or require any of the king's subjects to furnish or find horses, oxen, or other cattle, ploughs, wains, or other carriages, without such full and free consent; that no preëmption should be allowed or claimed on behalf of the king, queen, or children of the royal family, in market or out of market; but forever after it should be free to all the king's subjects to sell, dispose, or employ their goods to any other persons as they list."

But this statute did not take away that right of the crown called escheat, by which it succeeds to the lands of persons who die without heirs, or whose heritable blood has been attainted by treason or felony, and it still remains a principle of the constitution, that the crown, as *parens patriæ*, is entitled to the property of persons who die leaving no heirs. But in modern days that right is possessed with no advantage to the crown, because its right is surrendered to the public use; and with little advantage to the public, because the Government is always open to petitions for the disposal of the property in favor of persons having equitable or moral claims to it.

Thus ended the oppression of the feudal system in England, which had, for ages, rested like an incubus upon the people. Whatever struggles might yet remain, the spirit of individual freedom was at length established, and we cannot wonder that the same reign which saw the final abolition of this system of obsolete autocracy should have also seen the passage of the Habeas Corpus Act.

Habeas Corpus is an ancient English writ which has been used for a variety of purposes from the remotest antiquity. It is addressed to a sheriff or other officer, and commands him to have the body of the person named at a certain place and time. When all writs were in Latin, the characterizing words of this writ were *ut habeas corpus*, and the name has long survived the use of these words in the writ. One of the purposes for which it was used was to recover freedom which had been wrongfully taken away. Personal liberty was always asserted by the common law from its earliest ages; and it was always assailed by kings who would be tyrants, with an earnestness proportioned to their tyranny. Hence it became necessary to declare in the most solemn manner in Magna Charta, that "no man shall be taken or imprisoned but by the lawful judgment of his peers, or by the law of the land;" and this clause, more than any other, has given to that instrument the name of the palladium of English liberty, a name which is equally deserved by the writ of habeas corpus. For, on the one hand, the great charter did not enact this as a new rule of law, but only declared it to be the law of the land; and on the other, its force and influence gradually faded, in despite of repeated formal confirmations; and this law became actual and operative only by means of the habeas corpus. This writ was issuable from the king's bench, and it was used to protect or restore liberty, by bringing the prisoner before the court, whose duty it was to order his immediate discharge if he were not restrained of his liberty according to law. But it was evaded by courts and sheriffs who were disposed to support royal or ministerial usurpations; and it became so powerless that early in the reign of Charles I. the court of king's bench formally decided that they had no power to release any person imprisoned without any cause assigned, if he were imprisoned by the express command of the king, or by the lords of the privy council. The Petition of Right asserted the illegality of this decision, and declared that "no freeman should be imprisoned or detained without cause shown, to which he may make answer according to law." But the means of enforcing this rule were still imperfect, and personal liberty was still violated; and by 16 Charles I., ch. 10, various provisions were enacted, intended to make the writ of habeas corpus more effectual. But this was not enough. The judges still continued to refuse the writ at their pleasure, or issued it only in term time; and prisoners were sent to distant jails, where sheriffs and jailers refused to obey it; or if the party imprisoned were brought before an examining court, his liberty was still withheld on frivolous pretences. At length, in the thirty-first year of the reign of Charles II. (1679), what is now understood by the Habeas Corpus Act was enacted. It consisted of a variety of provisions, devised with so much skill and so well adapted to give each other mutual support, that it may safely be asserted that personal liberty must be safe so long as this law remains in force. Evasion of it in England is almost impossible; in the United States it was till recently believed to be entirely so; and it can be successful only by a positive and open violation of the law, or by a distinct denial of the writ. We owe this admirable law—which is the protection of the innocent, not the defence of the guilty—to Lord Shaftesbury, who, when he was appointed lord chancellor, had received no legal education whatever, and made no pretence to any knowledge of technical law; nor could his best friends, then or since, claim for him the credit of any especial regard for liberty, or any moral excellence whatever. It happened, however, that his personal purposes at the moment were such as to induce him to make this law as practical and as effectual as possible; and he brought to this object all the resources of his genius and experience, and by their help succeeded in giving to the act an efficiency which the lawyers who had been at work upon it for many generations had never been able to impart.

The English statute has been copied in the United States without essential change; the variations from it being only such as would, in the opinion of various legislatures, make its provisions more stringent, and the security it gives to liberty more certain and available. The provisions of the statutes of habeas corpus, now in force in the different States, may be stated generally thus:

1. The writ commands the sheriff, or other person to whom it is directed, to have the body of the person who is said to be restrained of his liberty forthwith before the justice issuing it, or some other tribunal competent to try the questions the case may present; and to summon the person restraining the alleged prisoner to be there also, and bring with him the cause of the restraint, that all parties may then and there submit themselves to whatever may be lawfully adjudged and ordered in their behalf. The language varies in different statutes which give the form of the writ; but it is always substantially as above.

2. The writ must be granted, *as of right*, by any of the justices of the higher courts, and, in their absence or inaccessibility, by any

of those of a lower court, down to justices of the quorum; the law covering in this respect a wide range, so as to insure to every applicant some one from whom this redress or remedy may come.

3. It must be granted at any time when it is prayed for, whether a court be sitting or not.

4. It must be granted either to the party himself restrained of his liberty, or to any one applying for him; and if his name be unknown, the best description which can readily be given is sufficient.

5. The application must be in writing, and must be verified by the oath of the applicant.

6. The sheriff or other officer to whom it is directed must render prompt obedience and make immediate service, and return the writ forthwith, with a full statement of his doings.

7. It must be returned before the proper magistrate at chambers, if a court to which it is made returnable be not then in session.

8. Upon the return, the alleged prisoner being present, the case is tried; and, unless sufficient cause for his imprisonment is shown, he is ordered to be discharged at once.

9. If not wholly discharged, the court or magistrate may order him to be discharged on giving reasonable bail, if he be held for any bailable offence or cause.

10. In some of the States it is provided that the writ may not issue if the party restrained be imprisoned for crime, or in execution civil or criminal, and by lawful warrant. In others these exceptions are not made, but if facts like these appear on trial the prisoner is remanded.

11. In general, after a party has been discharged on habeas corpus, he cannot again be imprisoned or restrained of his liberty for the same cause.

12. The issuing of the writ by the magistrate applied to, and prompt and full obedience to it by the officer or other person to whom it is directed, are secured by heavy penalties; and also by the fact that any applicant to whom the writ is refused by one magistrate may apply to another, and the number of those to whom he may thus resort is so large that it is hardly possible for them all to be corrupted, or for any reason indisposed to render due obedience to the law.

The vast importance of this law can be appreciated only by those who have experienced or studied the history of despotism. Whether the ruling authority of the nation (be it in the hands of one or many) shall be absolute or subordinated to law, must depend, in the last result, upon its power over the persons of those who are subject to it. Whatever be the law, if there be a sovereign, whether emperor or president, who may disregard it, and put in strict imprisonment those who resist him; if he may substitute his own commands for law, and take away from society and from all power of resort to law those who do not obey him, it is obvious that there can be no disobedience and no resistance which is not rebellion if it be put down, or revolution if it succeed. The histories of France and of England offer the most perfect illustration of this.

Beginning from the feudal ages, those countries stood about upon an equality in respect to the power of the sovereign and the personal rights of the subject. Under some of her monarchs, of the Plantagenet and Tudor families, England seemed to be yielding herself up to a more absolute tyranny than was known to her neighbors. But as the ages went on, it became apparent in France that the subjection of the citizen to the sovereign became with every generation more complete. By insidious rather than open increases, the power of the king, or rather the power of ministers who acted in the name of the king, to imprison at their pleasure whom they would, for political or personal, public or private reasons, became so entirely established that every minister of the crown had, it is said, a large number of blank *lettres de cachet* (or letters under the privy seal of the king), which he could fill with names at his pleasure, and by which the police were authorized and commanded to imprison the party named, and hold him in prison at the pleasure of the minister. The Bastile became a recognized instrument of state; and in its cells lay those who were placed there only at the suspicion or the caprice of some minister, and who remained there only because they were forgotten. Of course this state of things could not last, for no one acquainted with human nature could doubt that such irresponsible and enormous power would be prodigiously abused. Therefore the French revolution came to do the work which must be done, and only revolution could do; and therefore the reign of terror almost necessarily replaced the gilded and graceful despotism which had been its parent. But this could not endure, and perhaps the changes which have since given to that country almost every possible form of government, agree only in proving that in France there is not that training for personal liberty, that inwrought determination to be personally free at all hazards, which can become a part of the life-blood of a nation only after many generations have enjoyed the blessings of freedom, and can alone effectually secure and permanently preserve that liberty which is the fruitful spring of every other good.

If we now turn to England, we have seen that in the Anglo-Saxon times, despotism was rarely attempted and never successful; that the laws and institutions of those days are all founded on the presumption of personal liberty and rights; that this element of character might for a time be suppressed or enfeebled, but that it could never be annihilated; that it rose from time to time into prominence and activity, and, as opportunity could be offered or could be made, gradually asserted itself, first in the fact of a common law, which the courts regarded as binding upon them; then, in the recognition of personal liberty and right as an unquestionable principle of the common law; then by such timely assertions as in Magna Charta, in the Petition of Right, and finally in that Act of Habeas Corpus which we may well hope has settled the question for all time. That the habeas corpus was once sufficiently valued in the United States may be inferred from the fact that the Federal Constitution provides that "the provisions of the act shall not be suspended, unless when in case of rebellion or invasion, the public safety may require it;" and there is a provision to the same effect in some of the State constitutions. Everywhere the statute itself is enacted, and, so far as words can have the effect, made stringent and effectual. The time, however, has now passed when laws and constitutions may be trusted as complete securities and guarantees of rights. It is not certain, it is very doubtful, whether in these States the value of the right of personal liberty is sufficiently apprehended. *Adhuc sub judice lis est.* It is a question that will verily speedily be set at rest.

CHAPTER XII.

JAMES II.—THE REVOLUTION.—BILL OF RIGHTS.—ACT OF SETTLEMENT.

PRELIMINARY OBSERVATIONS—THE EXCLUSION BILL—WHIG AND TORY—LAWS AGAINST ROMANISTS—JAMES, AT HIS ACCESSION, ACKNOWLEDGES THEIR OBLIGATION—SUPPLIES GRANTED BY PARLIAMENT FOR THE TERM OF THE KING'S LIFE—JAMES INSISTS ON SUPPLIES FOR A STANDING ARMY, BUT DECLARES THAT HE HAS BROKEN AND WILL BREAK THE TEST LAWS—ANSWER OF THE COMMONS—ILLEGAL REVIVAL OF THE HIGH COMMISSION COURT—DARING DECLARATION OF INDULGENCE PUBLISHED BY THE KING—EXECUTION OF IT—TRIAL OF THE SEVEN BISHOPS—PRINCE OF ORANGE LANDS—FLIGHT OF JAMES MEETING OF LORDS AND COMMONS AND THE COMMON COUNCIL OF LONDON—CONVENTION AT WESTMINSTER—JOINT RESOLUTION OF LORDS AND COMMONS—SETTLEMENT OF THE CROWN ON WILLIAM AND MARY—SUBSTANCE OF THE BILL OF RIGHTS—ACT OF SETTLEMENT—ITS NECESSITY—SUBSTANCE OF IT—CONCLUSION.

The contest between prerogative and freedom was brought to a conclusion in the reign of James II., who ascended the throne on the 6th of February, 1685. His brief reign, if we estimate it by the events which resulted from it, is perhaps the most important in the history of the constitution. He was a Romanist of the sternest bigotry. He was so confident in his divine right as king, that he seemed blinded to any danger from the open profession of the proscribed religion; and in reliance on that right, and on the passive obedience of the people, he violated almost every fundamental law. The simple narrative of his illegal acts furnished an ample justification of his removal from the throne; and the reaffirmation and parliamentary declaration of the violated laws formed the chief part of the code of rights and liberties deemed necessary for a permanent constitutional government. The Declaration of Rights which followed his abdication was founded, not uoon abstract or theoretical principles of government, but upon what, in legal phrase, may be called James's *overt acts* of treason to the nation.

There had been in the reign of Charles II., so much dislike and even dread of James's succession to the throne—a dread increased by the panic spread by the so-called Popish plot—that a large party in the nation endeavored to exclude him from the succession, on the ground of his being a Papist. The House of Commons passed a bill for that purpose, and for banishing him from the kingdom; from which fate he was only saved by a majority in the House of Lords. The Exclusion Bill long and deeply agitated the nation and the Government; and when James had ascended the throne the people had become divided into two parties, under the then new but now familiar names of Whigs and Tories. Those who were inimical to Popery—as well on religious grounds as from the encouragement it gave to the doctrines of divine right and passive obedience, but who were at the same time favorable to religious toleration among Protestant sects—were called Whigs; while those who, holding those doctrines as of irremovable obligation, and although they supported the exclusive authority of the Protestant established Church, would not concur in depriving even a professed Papist of his right of succession to the throne—were called Tories.

At the accession of James, the laws for the exclusive establishment of the Church of England were clear, and defined by laws not only explicit, but extremely rigorous in their provisions. Charles II. had on several occasions endeavored to produce some alleviation of these, but he was told by Parliament that he had no power of interference, and that no alteration could be made but by an act of Parliament. Those laws, therefore, the king of England was bound to conform to, both in his own person and in his government. James felt the force of these obligations. In his first address to his privy council he said he had been reported to be a man for arbitrary power; but that was not the only story that had been made of him, and he should make it his endeavor to preserve the government in church and state as it was then established. But he made it known after his brother's funeral, that he had died a Roman Catholic; and he himself soon afterwards appeared publicly at mass.

Parliament assembled on the 10th of May, 1685, by virtue of

proclamations issued, as well for the meeting of Parliament as for laying, on James's sole authority, the customs and duties which constituted the revenue of the late king, but which expired at his decease. The House of Commons contained a large majority of adherents of James—the effect of changes made in the last reign in the charters of the corporations of the parliamentary boroughs, for the purpose of bringing them under the influence of the crown. The king opened the session on the 22d of May, and renewed the declaration he had made to the privy council. The House of Commons without delay unanimously voted to him for his life the whole revenue settled on the late king. The same Parliament also granted to James for his life—as a supply for the navy—an imposition on wines and vinegar which had been received by Charles II., and a further sum of £400,000 towards the extraordinary expenses incurred by the rebellion of the Duke of Monmouth. Thus in regard of one of the first constitutional principles, James was rendered independent of Parliament for supplies, unless in case of war. The consequences might have been foretold. The king, thus provided and unrestrained, proceeded to carry out the ardent objects of his life, the restoration of the ascendency of the Roman Catholic religion and the absolute and unshackled power of the monarch. The history of his reign shows that James, in the prosecution of his designs, was restrained by no law—by no compassion for those whom he opposed or oppressed—and by no consideration of his duties as king under a constitutional government. To assist him in these objects he entered into secret arrangements with the king of France, and, notwithstanding the liberality of Parliament, accepted from him large sums of money—that monarch receiving his recompense in the betrayal of the interests of the English nation.

The first open design of James was to obtain the sanction of Parliament for the maintenance of a standing army, and their approval of his having appointed popish officers to serve in the army during Monmouth's rebellion, without having taken the tests against popery. The Parliament met in a new session on the 9th of November, after the supression of the rebellion. James in his speech reflected on the insufficiency of the militia. He hoped "everybody would be convinced it is not sufficient for such occasions; and that there is nothing but a good force of well-disciplined troops, in constant pay, that can defend us from such as either at home or abroad are disposed to disturb us." His concern for the peace and quiet of his subjects, he said, made it necessary to increase the number to the proportion he had done; and to support the charge of keeping such a body of men on foot, he asked for a supply. "Let no man take exception," he added, "that there some officers in the army not qualified, according to the late tests, for their employments. The gentlemen, I must tell you, are most of them well known to me; and having formerly served with me on several occasions, and always approved the loyalty of their principles by their practice, I think them now fit to be employed under me; and I will deal plainly with you, that, after having had the benefit of their service in such a time of need and danger, I will neither expose them to disgrace, nor myself to the want of them, if there should be another rebellion to make them necessary to me."

The proposal for a standing army, and for a violation of the test acts, changed the obsequiousness of the Parliament, and roused an opposition partaking of the spirit of former parliaments. The court party carried a resolution for a supply, but with the addition that a bill be brought in to render the militia more useful, equivalent to a declaration against a standing army; and the Commons afterwards voted an address, in which they represented to the king that "the officers in the army, who had not complied with the tests, could not by law be capable of their employments, and that their incapacities could not be taken away but by act of Parliament." They said they would pass an act to indemnify them from the penalties on this occasion, and they besought the king to give such directions as that no apprehensions or jealousies might remain in the hearts of his subjects. Disapprobation of the king's proceedings spread to the House of Lords, extending even to the bench of bishops; and James, perceiving that resolutions would be passed disapproving of his proceedings, prorogued the Parliament, sacrificing even the vote for the supply, which had not been perfected by an act. Parliament was kept in existence by repeated prorogations for about a year and a half, but without holding a session, and no Parliament assembled again during this reign.

The High Commission Court established by Elizabeth had been abolished by a statute of the Long Paliament, and its abolition had been confirmed by a statute of Charles II., which also declared that no similar court should be constituted. Yet in contempt of those laws a court was erected called the Court of Commissioners for Ecclesiastical Causes, to which, without any other authority than his own, James gave summary and arbitrary jurisdiction over all ecclesiastics, and of which he made his infamous Lord Chancellor, Jeffreys, perpetual president. The Bishop of London, who had offended the king by the part he had taken in Parliament, was the first person summoned before the new court, by which he was suspended from his office.

In exercise of his assumed prerogative to dispense with the statute law, James published a declaration of indulgence, of the most daring character. He declared "that the execution of all, and all manner of penal laws in matters ecclesiastical, should be immediately suspended; and he gave free leave to all his subjects to serve God their own way, either in public or private, provided they took special care that nothing was preached or thought tending to alienate the people from his government." He declared that the oaths of allegiance and supremacy, as also the several tests and declarations of 25 and 30 Charles II., should not for the future be required to be taken by any person who was or should be employed in any place of trust; and that it was his pleasure and intention to grant his royal dispensations under the great seal to all persons so employed, who should not take the said oaths. He gave free pardon to all non-conformists, recusants, and other his loving subjects, for all crimes and things committed against the penal laws.

Under the authority of this declaration (which, however much we may now admire its principles, was clearly *in derogation of law*, and opposed to the feelings of his people) James took Jesuits into his service, and appointed Roman Catholics to the highest offices of the state, and to commands in the army and navy. He went so far as to appoint Roman Catholic priests to ecclesiastical offices in the universities of Oxford and Cambridge; and when his nominees were refused, he deprived the heads of the universities of their dignities. He sent an extraordinary ambassador to the Pope; although intercourse with the Roman pontiff was, *by the laws of England*, high treason. He also gave audience to a nuncio from the Pope. Four Roman bishops were publicly consecrated in the royal chapel, and the popish regular clergy attended his palace in the habits of their order. He appointed a Roman Catholic to be of his privy council, and altered the privy counsellors' oath by expunging the declaration against foreign prelates.

In April, 1688, James renewed his declaration for liberty of conscience, and issued an order in council, requiring the bishops to send copies of it to all their clergy, and to order the clergy to read it on two several Sundays in time of divine service. The archbishop and six bishops petitioned the king to lay before him the reasons that determined them not to obey the order in council. They were admitted to his presence. James threateningly insisted upon being obeyed, and they retired with the words, "The will of God be done." They were immediately committed to the Tower, and an information presented against them for a misdemeanor, on which they were afterwards brought to trial.

The trial of the seven bishops is a memorable instance of the bigotry, injustice, and cruelty of James, and of the corrupt subservience of his judges. But this wicked scheme failed of success. The bishops were triumphiantly acquitted. Universal joy spread throughout the nation. James was informed of the acquittal when he was reviewing at Hounslow the standing army that he unconstitutionally maintained. Whilst partaking of refreshments in the commander's tent, he heard the shouts of the soldiers, and he inquired the cause. "Nothing," was the reply, "but the joy of the soldiers that the bishops are acquitted." "Do you call that nothing?" said the king; "so much the worse for them."

Time was not allowed to James for the fulfilment of the vengeance these words implied. The nation's power of endurance was at an end; the most conscientious believers in the doctrine of the indefeasible right of kings, felt unable to justify the king's conduct, and many of the Tory aristocracy joined the Whigs to remove James from the throne, and to place there, in his room, William, Prince of Orange, and his consort the Lady Mary, daughter of James—both Protestants, and the prince the head of the Protestant interest in

Christendom. An invitation was sent to them by a large number of the peers, both spiritual and temporal, and of the leading men amongst the commons; and William published a declaration, accepting the invitation, with the view, as he stated, "to get a free Parliament assembled, which might secure the national religion and liberty under a just and legal government for the future." James prepared to defend his throne, but when William arrived, supported by an army, James, with his queen and infant son (born at this important juncture), fled to France.

The throne being vacant by the flight of James, the lords spiritual and temporal assembled in their house, to about the number of ninety, and William desired that all persons who had been members of the House of Commons in the reign of Charles II. (for the assembling of James's Parliament might be considered as a recognition of his continued authority), with the lord mayor and aldermen of London, and fifty of the common councilmen, would meet at St. James's, on the 26th of September, 1687.

One hundred and sixty members, with the mayor and corporation, met accordingly, and they adopted an address to the prince, which the Lords had previously voted (and which was subscribed by about ninety peers), humbly desiring him to take upon him the administration of public affairs, and the disposal of the revenue, until the meeting of a convention to be called. They further humbly desired him to cause letters to be written, subscribed by himself, to the lords spiritual and temporal, being Protestants, and to the several counties, universities, cities, boroughs, and Cinque Ports—the letters to the counties to be directed to the coroners or clerks of the peace; of the universities, to the chancellors; and of the cities and boroughs, to the chief magistrates—directing them to choose, within ten days, such a number of persons to represent them, as were of right to be sent to Parliament. They were required to meet at Westminster, on the 22d of January, 1688. The convention met accordingly, and both houses agreed to an address, that the prince should take upon himself the government, which by a message he consented to do. The Commons next proceeded to settle the basis of the future monarchy.

The converse theory to that of the divine right of kings is, that kings reign by virtue of a contract, theoretically assumed to have been made between them and the people at the origin of the government—a theory which implies responsibility on the part of the king, and a remedy in the people if the king violate the assumed contract. The first step of the House of Commons, in which the Whig party was predominant, was to assert that principle in the following resolution:

"That King James II., having endeavored to subvert the constitution of the kingdom, by breaking the original contract between king and people, and having, by the advice of Jesuits and other wicked persons, violated the fundamental laws, and withdrawn himself out of the kingdom, has abdicated the government, and that the throne is thereby vacant."

The resolution was the work of only one day, and it passed without a division of the house. It was carried to the Lords, for their concurrence, on the 28th of January, by Mr. Hampden, the grandson of him of the same name who first shook the prerogative of the Stuart kings.

The Lords took the resolution into consideration in a committee of the whole house, and afterwards communicated to the Commons that they concurred in it, with two amendments. Instead of "abdicated" they would have "deserted" put in, and they would have the words "and that the throne is thereby vacant," left out. Conferences followed, the second being a free conference, in which the resolution was debated, orally, by the managers of the respective houses. The Lords, on the 7th of February, signified to the Commons that they had agreed to the vote without any alterations.

The crown was settled, by both houses, on William and Mary, jointly during their lives, and on the survivor; the administration of the government being committed to William alone during his life. The principles of the future government were embodied in the celebrated Declaration of Rights, which was presented to William and Mary, seated on the throne, at Whitehall, in the presence of both houses of Parliament, by the speaker of the House of Lords, on the 13th of February, 1688. On that day they became, and were proclaimed, king and queen of England, deriving their authority from the joint declaration of the lords and commons, and holding the crown on the principles and subject to the limitations prescribed in the Declaration or Bill of Rights. The substance of this celebrated declaration is as follows:

"Whereas the late King James II., by the assistance of divers evil counsellors, judges, and ministers employed by him, did endeavor to subvert and extirpate the Protestant religion, and the laws and liberties of this kingdom,

"1. By assuming and exercising a power of dispensing with and suspending of laws, and the execution of laws, without the consent of Parliament.

"2. By the committing and prosecuting divers worthy prelates, for humbly petitioning to be excused from concurring to the said assumed power.

"3. By issuing and causing to be executed a commission under the great seal for erecting a court called the Court of Commissioners for Ecclesiastical Causes.

"4. By levying money for and to the use of the crown, by pretence of prerogative, for other time, and in other manner, than the same was granted by Parliament.

"5. By raising and keeping a standing army within this kingdom in time of peace, without consent of Parliament, and quartering soldiers contrary to law.

"6. By causing several good subjects, being Protestants, to be disarmed, at the same time when Papists were both armed and employed, contrary to law.

"7. By violating the freedom of election of members to serve in Parliament.

"8. By prosecutions in the Court of King's Bench, for matters and causes cognizable only in Parliament; and by divers other arbitrary and illegal courses.

"9. And whereas of late years partial, corrupt, and unqualified persons have been returned and served on juries in trials, and particularly divers jurors in trials for high treason, which were not freeholders;

"10. And excessive bail hath been required of persons committed in criminal causes, to elude the benefit of the laws made for the liberty of the subjects;

"11. And excessive fines have been imposed; and illegal and cruel punishments inflicted;

"12. And several grants and promises made of fines and forfeitures, before any conviction or judgment against the persons upon whom the same were to be levied;

"All which are utterly and directly contrary to the known laws and statutes and freedom of this realm."

The declaration then recites the abdication of the throne by James II., the summoning of the convention held on the 22d of January, 1688, and that the lords spiritual and temporal, and Commons, did in the first place (as their ancestors in like case had usually done), for the vindicating and asserting their ancient rights and liberties, declare:

"1. That the pretended power of suspending of laws, or the execution of laws, by royal authority, without consent of Parliament, is illegal.

"2. That the pretended power of dispensing with laws, or the execution of laws, by regal authority, as it hath been assumed and exercised of late, is illegal.

"3. That the commission for erecting the late Court of Commissioners for Ecclesiastical Causes, and all other courts and commissions of like nature, are illegal and pernicious.

"4. That levying money for or to the use of the crown by pretence of prerogative, without grant of Parliament, for longer time, or in any other manner than the same is or shall be granted, is illegal.

"5. That it is the right of the subjects to petition the king, and all commitments and prosecutions for such petitioning are illegal.

"6. That the raising or keeping a standing army within the kingdom in time of peace, unless it be with consent of Parliament, is against law.

"7. That the subjects which are Protestants may have arms for their defence suitable to their conditions, and as allowed by law.

"8. That election of members of Parliament ought to be free.

"9. That the freedom of speech, and debates or proceedings in

Parliament, ought not to be impeached or questioned in any court or place out of Parliament.

"10. That excessive bail ought not to be required, nor excessive fines imposed; nor cruel and unusual punishments inflicted.

"11. That jurors ought to be duly empanelled and returned; and jurors which pass upon men in trials for high treason, ought to be freeholders.

"12. All grants and promises of fines and forfeitures of particular persons before conviction, are illegal and void.

"13. And for redress of all grievances, and for the amending, strengthening, and preserving of the laws, parliaments ought to be held frequently."

The convention on the same day passed an act which declared that the Lords spiritual and temporal, and Commons, convened at Westminster on the 22d of January, 1688, and there sitting on the 13th of February following, were the two houses of Parliament, notwithstanding any defect of form. It repealed the old oaths of allegiance and supremacy required to be taken by members of the houses of Parliament, and substituted a new oath of allegiance to King William and Queen Mary, and acknowledging their supremacy. It also passed an act for establishing a coronation oath. Thus the great event in English history, and change in the constitution and dynasty—THE REVOLUTION—was complete.

Queen Mary died in 1694, and the son of her sister Anne having also died, all hope was lost of the succession to the crown taking place in the course provided by the Bill of Rights. In 1704, therefore, the ACT OF SETTLEMENT was passed, by which the Princess Sophia, electress and duchess-dowager of Hanover—daughter of Elizabeth, late queen of Bohemia, and granddaughter of James I.—was declared to be the next in succession to the throne in the Protestant line; and after the death of William, and of the Princess Anne of Denmark, and in default of issue of Anne and William, the crown was settled on the Princess Sophia, and the heirs of her body, *being Protestants.*

By the course of events the crown passed to her son George I., then elector of Hanover, and the wise foresight of our ancestors in the provisions made, became manifest when the throne actually passed to a king not a native of the kingdom, and being a sovereign of another country. The provisions of the ACT OF SETTLEMENT, which are declared to be "for securing our religion, laws, and liberties," are as follows:

"Whosoever shall hereafter come to the possession of this crown, shall join in communion with the Church of England, as by law established.

"In case the crown and imperial dignity of this realm shall hereafter come to any person not being a native of this kingdom of England, this nation be not obliged to engage in any war for the defence of any dominions or territories which do not belong to the crown of England, without the consent of Parliament.

"No person who shall hereafter come to the possession of this crown shall go out of the dominions of England, Scotland, or Ireland, without consent of Parliament.

"From and after the time that the further limitation by this act shall take effect, all matters and things relating to the well governing of this kingdom, which are properly cognizable in the privy council by the laws and customs of this realm, shall be transacted there, and all resolutions taken thereupon shall be signed by such of the privy council as shall advise and consent to the same.

"After the limitation shall take effect as aforesaid, no person born out of the dominions of England, Scotland, or Ireland, or the dominions thereunto belonging (although he be naturalized or made a denizen), except such as are born of English parents, shall be capable to be of the privy council, or a member of either house of Parliament, or to enjoy any office or place of trust, either civil or military, or to have any grant of lands or tenements or hereditaments from the crown to himself, or to any other or others in trust for him.

"No person who has an office or place of profit under the king, or receives a pension from the crown, shall be capable of serving as a member of the House of Commons.

"After the limitation shall take effect as aforesaid, judges' commissions be made *quamdiu se bene gesserint*, and their salaries ascertained and established; but upon the address of both houses of Parliament, it may be lawful to remove them.

"That no pardon under the great seal of England be pleadable to an impeachment by the Commons in Parliament."

The Declarations of Rights and the Act of Settlement may be considered as the complement of Magna Charta and the Petition of Right, in declaring and fixing the prerogatives of the crown, and the rights of the people in relation to the crown. Since the Act of Settlement there has been no statute expressly directed to curb the royal prerogative; but the executive power of the crown has been diminished by the growth of the power of Parliament—especially of the House of Commons—and the establishment of the system of parliamentary government. That system has silently grown up since the Revolution, and at its root lies the maxim—that all the acts of the crown must be advised and transacted by ministers responsible to Parliament.

The Revolution terminated the contest between prerogative and freedom, and settled the basis of a limited monarchy and constitutional government. From that period the principles laid down in the Bill of Rights have never been disputed, although in the changes of administration, and under the influence of party spirit, they may sometimes have been departed from. They have, however, in our times, obtained a solidity which it is to be hoped is unassailable; and they have been confirmed and added to by, for the most part, a course of wise, enlightened, and impartial legislation, by which the security of the throne has been increased, and the rights and liberties of the people maintained and enlarged.

Bill of Rights.

An Act declaring the Rights and Liberties of the Subject, and settling the Succession of the Crown.

WHEREAS the Lords Spiritual and Temporal, and Commons, assembled at *Westminster*, lawfully fully and freely representing all the Estates of the People of this Realm, did, upon the thirteenth Day of February in the Year of our Lord one thousand six hundred and eighty-eight, present unto their Majesties, then called and known by the Names and Stile of *William* and *Mary*, Prince and Princess of *Orange*, being present in their proper Persons, a certain Declaration in Writing, made by the said Lords and Commons, in the Words following; *viz.*

"Whereas the late King James the Second, by the assistance of divers evil Counsellors, Judges and Ministers employed by him, did endeavor to subvert and extirpate the Protestant Religion, and the Laws and Liberties of this Kingdom.

"1. By assuming and exercising a Power of dispensing with and suspending of Laws, and the Execution of Laws, without Consent of Parliament.

"2. By committing and prosecuting divers worthy Prelates, for humbly petitioning to be excused from concurring to the said assumed Power.

"3. By issuing and causing to be executed a Commission under the Great Seal for erecting a Court called, *The Court of Commissioners for Eclesiastical Causes.*

"4. By levying Money for and to the Use of the Crown, by

Pretence of Prerogative, for other Time, and in other Manner, than the same was granted by Parliament.

"5. By raising and keeping a Standing Army within the Kingdom in Time of Peace, without Consent of Parliament, and quartering Soldiers contrary to Law.

"6. By causing several good Subjects, being Protestants, to be disarmed, at the same Time when Papists were both armed and employed, contrary to Law.

"7. By violating the Freedom of Election of Members to serve in Parliament.

"8. By Prosecutions in the Court of King's Bench, for Matters and Causes cognizable only in Parliament; and by divers other arbitrary and illegal Courses.

"9. And whereas of late Years, partial, corrupt and unqualified Persons, have been returned and served on Juries in Trials, and particularly divers Jurors in Trials for High Treason, which were not Free-holders.

"10. And excessive Bail hath been required of Persons committed in criminal Cases, to elude the Benefit of the Laws made for the Liberty of the Subjects.

"11. And excessive Fines have been imposed; and illegal and cruel Punishments inflicted.

"12. And several Grants and Promises made of Fines and Forfeitures, before any Conviction or Judgment against the Persons, upon whom the same were to be levied.

"All of which are utterly and directly contrary to the known Laws and Statutes, and Freedom of this Realm.

"And whereas the said late King *James* the Second having abdicated the Government, and the Throne being thereby vacant, his Highness the Prince of *Orange* (whom it hath pleased Almighty God to make the glorious Instrument of delivering this Kingdom from Popery and arbitrary Power) did (by the Advice of the Lords Spiritual and Temporal, and divers principal Persons of the Commons) cause Letters to be written to the Lords Spiritual and Temporal, being Protestants; and other Letters to the several Counties, Cities, Universities, Boroughs, and Cinque-ports, for the choosing of such persons to represent them, as were of right to be sent to

Parliament, to meet and sit at *Westminster* upon the two and twentieth Day of *January* in this Year one thousand six hundred eighty and eight, in order to such an Establishment, as that their Religion, Laws, and Liberties might not again be in Danger of being subverted : upon which Letters, Elections having been accordingly made,

"And thereupon the said Lords Spiritual and Temporal, and Commons, pursuant to their respective Letters and Elections, being now assembled in a full and free Representative of this Nation, taking into their most serious Consideration the best Means for attaining the Ends aforesaid; do in the first Place (as their Ancestors in like Case have usually done) for the vindicating and asserting their ancient Rights and Liberties declare :

"1. That the pretended Power of suspending of Laws, or the Execution of Laws, by regal Authority, without Consent of Parliament, is illegal.

"2. That the pretended Power of dispensing with Laws or the Execution of Laws, by regal Authority, as it hath been assumed and exercised of late, is illegal.

"3. That the Commission for erecting the late Court of Commissioners for Eclesiastical Causes, and all other Commissions and Courts of like Nature, are illegal and pernicious.

"4. That levying Money for or to the Use of the Crown, by Pretence of Prerogative, without Grant of Parliament for longer Time, or in other Manner than the same is or shall be granted, is illegal.

"5. That it is the Right of the Subjects to petition the King, and all Commitments and Prosecutions for such Petitioning are illegal.

"6. That the raising or keeping a Standing Army within the Kingdom in Time of Peace, unless it be with Consent of Parliament, is against Law.

"7. That the Subjects which are Protestants, may have arms for their defence suitable to their conditions and as allowed by Law.

"8. That Election of Members of Parliament ought to be free.

"9. That the Freedom of Speech, and Debates or Proceedings

in Parliament, ought not to be impeached or questioned in any Court or Place out of Parliament.

"10. That excessive Bail ought not to be required, nor excessive Fines imposed; nor cruel and unusual Punishments inflicted.

"11. That Jurors ought to be duly impanelled and returned, and Jurors which pass upon Men in Trials for High Treason ought to be Freeholders.

"12. That all Grants and Promises of Fines and Forfeitures of particular Persons before Conviction, are illegal and void.

"13. And that for Redress of all Grievances, and for the amending, strengthening, and preserving of the Laws, Parliaments ought to be held frequently.

"And they do claim, demand, and insist upon all and singular the Premisses, as their undoubted Rights and Liberties; and that no Declarations, Judgments, Doings, or Proceedings, to the Prejudice of the People in any of the said Premisses, ought in any wise to be drawn hereafter into Consequence or Example.

"To which Demand of their Rights they are particularly encouraged by the Declaration of his Highness the Prince of *Orange*, as being the only Means for obtaining a full Redress and Remedy therein.

"Having therefore an entire Confidence, that his said Highness the Prince of *Orange* will perfect the Deliverance so far advanced by him, and will still preserve them from the Violation of their Rights, which they have here asserted, and from all other Attempts upon their Religion, Rights and Liberties,

"II. The said Lords Spiritual and Temporal, and Commons, assembled at *Westminster*, do resolve, That *William* and *Mary*, Prince and Princess of *Orange*, be, and be declared King and Queen of *England*, *France* and *Ireland*, and the Dominions thereunto belonging, to hold the Crown and Royal Dignity of the said Kingdoms and Dominions to them and the said Prince and Princess during their Lives, and the Life of the Survivor of them; and that the sole and full Exercise of the Regal Power be only in, and executed by the said Prince of *Orange*, in the Names of the said Prince and Princess, during their joint Lives; and after their Deceases, the said Crown and Royal Dignity of the said Kingdoms and Dominions to be to the Heirs of the Body of the said Princess, and for Default of such Issue to the Princess *Anne* of *Denmark*, and the Heirs of her Body; and for Default of such Issue to the Heirs of the Body of the said Prince of *Orange*. And the Lords Spiritual and Temporal, and Commons, do pray the said Prince and Princess to accept the same accordingly.

"III. And that the oaths hereafter mentioned be taken by all Persons of whom the Oaths of Allegiance and Supremacy might be required by Law, instead of them; and that the said Oaths of Allegiance and Supremacy be abrogated.

"I, *A. B.*, do sincerely promise and swear, That I will be faithful and bear true Allegiance, to their Majesties King *William* and Queen *Mary*. *So help me God.*

"I, A. B., do swear, That I do from my Heart abhor, detest, and abjure, as impious and heretical, that damnable Doctrine and Position, *That Princes excommunicated or deprived by the Pope, or any Authority of the See of Rome, may be deposed or murdered by their Subjects, or any other whatsoever.* And I do declare that no foreign Prince, Person, Prelate, State or Potentate hath, or ought to have, any Jurisdiction, Power, Superiority, Pre-eminence, or Authority, Ecclesiastical or Spiritual, within this Realm. *So help me God.*"

IV. Upon which their Majesties did accept the Crown and Royal Dignity of the Kingdoms of *England*, *France* and *Ireland*, and the Dominions thereunto belonging, according to the Resolution and Desire of the said Lords and Commons contained in the said Declaration.

V. And thereupon their Majesties were pleased, That the said Lords Spiritual and Temporal, and Commons, being the two Houses of Parliament, should continue to sit and with their Majesties' royal Concurrence make effectual Provision for the Settlement of the Religion, Laws and Liberties of this Kingdom, so that the same for the future might not be in Danger again of being subverted; to which the said Lords Spiritual and Temporal, and Commons, did agree and proceed to act accordingly.

VI. Now, in pursuance of the Premisses, the said Lords Spiritual and Temporal, and Commons, in Parliament assembled, for the ratifying, confirming and establishing the said Declaration, and the Articles, Clauses, Matters, and Things therein contained, by the Force of Law made in due Form by Authority of Parliament, do pray that it may be declared and enacted, That all and singular the Rights and Liberties asserted, and claimed in the said Declarations, are the true, antient, and indubitable Rights and Liberties of the People of this Kingdom, and so shall be esteemed, allowed, adjudged, deemed, and taken to be, and that all and every the Particulars aforesaid shall be firmly and strictly holden and observed, as they are expressed in the said Declaration; and all Officers and Ministers whatsoever shall serve their Majesties and their Successors according to the same in all Times to come.

VII. And the said Lords Spiritual and Temporal, and Commons, seriously considering how it hath pleased Almighty God, in His marvellous Providence, and merciful Goodness to this Nation, to provide and preserve their said Majesties' royal Persons most happily to reign over us upon the throne of their Ancestors, for which they render unto him from the Bottom of their Hearts their humblest Thanks and Praises, do truly, firmly, assuredly, and in the Sincerity of their Hearts think, and do hereby recognize, acknowledge and declare, That King *James* the Second, having abdicated the Government, and their Majesties' having accepted the Crown and royal Dignity as aforesaid, their said Majesties did become, were, are, and of right ought to be, by the Laws of this Realm, our Sovereign Liege Lord and Lady, King and Queen of *England*, *France* and *Ireland*, and the Dominions thereunto belonging, in and to whose princely Persons the royal State, Crown, and Dignity of the said Realms, with all Honours, Stiles, Titles, Regalities, Prerogatives, Powers, Jurisdictions, and Authorities, to the same belonging and appertaining, are most fully, rightfully, and entirely invested and incorporated, united and annexed.

VIII. And for preventing all Questions and Divisions in this Realm, by Reason of any pretended Titles to the Crown, and for preserving a Certainty in the Succession thereof, in and upon which the Unity, Peace, Tranquillity, and Safety of this Nation doth, under God, wholly consist and depend, The said Lords Spiritual and Temporal, and Commons, do beseech their Majesties that it may be enacted, established and declared, That the Crown and regal Government of the said Kingdoms and Dominions with all and singular the premisses thereunto belonging and appertaining, shall be and continue to their said Majesties, and the Survivor, during their Lives, and the Life of the survivor of them : And that the entire, perfect, and full Exercise of the Regal Power and Government be only in, and executed by his Majesty, in the Names of both their Majesties during their joint lives; and after their Deceases the said Crown and Premisses shall be and remain to the Heirs of the Body of her Majesty ; and for Default of such Issue, to her Royal Highness, the Princess *Anne* of *Denmark*, and the Heirs of her Body ; and for Default of such Issue, to the Heirs of the Body of his said Majesty : And thereunto the said Lords Spiritual and Temporal, and Commons, do, in the Name of all the People aforesaid, most humbly and faithfully submit themselves, their Heirs and Posterities for ever; and do faithfully promise, That they will stand to, maintain, and defend their said Majesties, and also the Limitation and Succession of the Crown herein specified and contained, to the utmost of their Powers, with their Lives and Estates, against all Persons whatsoever, that shall attempt any Thing to the contrary.

IX. " And whereas it hath been found by Experience, that it is inconsistent with the Safety and Welfare of this Protestant Kingdom, to be governed by a Popish Prince, or by any King or Queen marrying a Papist ; " the said Lords Spiritual and Temporal, and Commons, do further pray that it may be enacted, That all and every Person and Persons that is, are, or shall be, reconciled to, or shall hold Communion with, the See or Church of *Rome*, or shall profess the Popish Religion, or shall marry a Papist, shall be excluded, and be forever incapable to inherit, possess, or enjoy the Crown and Government of this Realm, and *Ireland*, and the Dominions thereunto belonging, or any part of the same, or to have, use or exercise any regal Power, Authority or Jurisdiction within the same ; and in all and every such Case or Cases the People of these Realms shall be, and are hereby absolved of their Allegiance ; and the said Crown and Government shall from time to time descend to, and be enjoyed by such Person or Persons, being Protestants, as should have inherited and enjoyed the same, in case the said Person or Persons so reconciled, holding Communion, or professing, or marrying as aforesaid, were naturally dead.

X. And that every King and Queen of this Realm, who at any Time hereafter shall come to and succeed in the Imperial Crown of this Kingdom, shall on the first Day of the Meeting of the first Parliament, next after his or her coming to the Crown, sitting in his or her Throne in the House of Peers, in the Presence of the Lords and Commons therein assembled, or at his or her Coronation, before such Person or Persons who shall administer the Coronation Oath to him or her, at the Time of his or her taking the said Oath (which shall first happen) make, subscribe, and audibly repeat the Declaration mentioned in the Statute made in the thirtieth year of the Reign of King *Charles* the Second, intituled, *An Act for the more effectual preserving the King's Person and Government, by disabling Papists from sitting in either House of Parliament.* But if it shall happen, that such King or Queen, upon his or her Succession to the Crown of this Realm, shall be under the Age of twelve Years, then every such King or Queen shall make, subscribe, and audibly repeat the said Declaration at his or her Coronation, or the first Day of the Meeting of the first Parliament as aforesaid, which shall first happen after such King or Queen shall have attained the said Age of twelve Years.

XI. All which their Majesties are contented and pleased shall be declared, enacted and established by authority of this present Parliament, and shall stand, remain, and be the Law of this Realm for ever; and the same are by their said Majesties, by and with the Advice and Consent of the Lords Spiritual and Temporal, and Commons, in Parliament assembled, and by the Authority of the same, declared, enacted and established accordingly.

XII. And be it further declared and enacted by the Authority aforesaid, That from and after this present Session of Parliament, no dispensation by *Non obstante* of or to any Statute, or any Part thereof, shall be allowed, but that the same shall be held void and of no Effect, except a dispensation be allowed of in such Statute, and except in such Cases as shall be specially provided by one or more Bill or Bills to be passed during this present Session of Parliament.

XIII. Provided that no Charter, or Grant, or Pardon, granted before the three-and-twentieth day of *October*, in the Year of our Lord one thousand six hundred and eighty-nine, shall be any ways impeached or invalidated by this Act, but that the same shall be and remain of the same Force and Effect in Law, and no other, than as if this Act had never been made.

Act of Settlement.

[The Act of Settlement (XII. and XIII. William III., Cap. II.) provided that on the decease, without heirs, of William and the Princess Anne of Denmark, the succession to the throne of England should devolve upon the Princess Sophia, Electress and Duchess-Dowager of Hanover, grand-daughter of James I. This act, which it is unnecessary to give entire, is entitled, "An Act for the further Limitation of the Crown, and better securing the Rights and Liberties of the Subject." The following are its constitutional provisions :]

WHEREAS, it is requisite and necessary that some further Provision be made for securing our Religion, Laws and Liberties, from and after the Death of his Majesty and the Princess *Anne* of *Denmark*, and in Default of Issue of the Body of the said Princess, and of his Majesty respectively; Be it enacted by the King's most Excellent Majesty, by and with the Advice and Consent of the Lords Spiritual and Temporal, and Commons, in Parliament assembled, and by the Authority of the same,

"That whosoever shall hereafter come to the Possession of the Crown, shall join in Communion with the Church of *England*, as by Law established.

"That in case the Crown and Imperial Dignity of this Realm shall hereafter come to any person, not being a native of this Kingdom of *England*, this Nation be not obliged to engage in any War for the Defence of any Dominions or Territories which do not belong to the Crown of *England*, without the Consent of Parliament.

"That no Person who shall hereafter come to the Possession of this Crown, shall go out of the Dominion of *England*, Scotland, or *Ireland*, without the Consent of Parliament.

"That from after the Time that the further Limitation by this Act shall take Effect, all Matters and Things relating to the well governing of this Kingdom, which are properly cognizable in the Privy Council by the Laws and Customs of this Realm, shall be transacted there, and all Resolutions taken thereupon shall be signed by such of the Privy Council as shall advise and consent to the same.

"That after said Limitation shall take Effect as aforesaid, no Person born out of the Kingdoms of *England*, *Scotland*, or *Ireland*, or the Dominions thereunto belonging (although he be naturalized or made a Denizen, except such as are born of *English* Parents), shall be capable to be of the Privy Council, or a Member of either House of Parliament, or to enjoy any Office or Place of Trust, either Civil or Military, or to have any Grant of Lands, Tenements, or Hereditaments from the Crown, to himself or to any other or others in Trust for him.

"That no Person who has an Office or Place of Profit under the King, or receives a Pension from the Crown, shall be capable of serving as a Member of the House of Commons.

"That after the said Limitation shall take Effect as aforesaid, Judges' Commissions be made *Quamdiu se bene gesserint*, and their Salaries ascertained and established; but upon the Address of both Houses of Parliament it may be lawful to remove them.

"That no Pardon under the Great Seal of *England* be pleadable to an Impeachment by the Commons in Parliament.

"And whereas the Laws of *England* are the Birth-right of the People thereof, and all the Kings and Queens, who shall ascend the Throne of this Realm, ought to administer the Government of the same according to the said Laws, and all their Officers and Ministers ought to serve them respectively according to the same"—The said Lords Spiritual and Temporal, and Commons, do therefore further humbly pray, That all the Laws and Statutes of this Realm for securing the established Religion, and the Rights and Liberties of the People thereof, and all other Laws and Statutes of the same now in Force, may be ratified and confirmed, and the same are by his Majesty, by and with the Advice and Consent of the Lords Spiritual and Temporal, and Commons, and by Authority of the same, ratified and confirmed accordingly.

CHAPTER XIII.

COLONIAL CONSTITUTIONS.

INTRODUCTORY OBSERVATIONS—CONSTITUTIONAL POSITION OF THE COLONISTS—LAW OF NATIONS ON THE SUBJECT OF COLONIAL SETTLEMENTS: IN COUNTRIES HAVING LAWS AND CONSTITUTIONS; IN COUNTRIES NOT HAVING LAWS AND CONSTITUTIONS—APPLICATION OF IT TO THE COLONIES—THEIR INTERIOR POLITICS—PROVINCIAL ESTABLISHMENTS—PROPRIETARY GOVERNMENTS—CHARTER GOVERNMENTS—MIXED GOVERNMENT—CONSTITUTIONS OF THE COLONIES—VIRGINIA—PLYMOUTH COLONIES—MASSACHUSETTS—NEW HAMPSHIRE—MAINE—CONNECTICUT—RHODE ISLAND—MARYLAND—NEW YORK—NEW JERSEY—PENNSYLVANIA—DELAWARE—NORTH AND SOUTH CAROLINA—GEORGIA.

We have now come to a period at which the justice and enlightenment of England were to be submitted to severe tests. After a contest of four hundred and seventy-three years, extending from the day of Runnymede to the revolution which dethroned the Stuart dynasty, the rights and liberties of every English subject were at length secured by constitutional checks upon the royal power, and by a Parliament in which one house, composed of freely chosen popular representatives, was vested with the power of hindering legislation which might be injurious to the people. The rights of person and of property were now secure in England. It remained to be determined whether Englishmen, in the enjoyment of these rights at home, would stand by and support their fellow subjects in maintaining and defending them in the colonial settlements of North America.

The colonies had been permanently established under various auspices during the troubled reigns of the unhappy Stuarts and the earlier monarchs who succeeded them—apparently an unpropitious period for founding governments. Until the Revolution it was doubtful whether absolute or constitutional authority would prevail in England; and although the monarchy, as regulated by the Bill of Rights and Act of Settlement, was afterwards so limited as to protect the subject from the encroachments of prerogative at home, yet of the constitutional relations of colonial dependencies to the mother country and the crown there still appeared to be no very clear intelligence, as there was certainly no authoritative exposition. Yet the English colonists of North America were clear on one point. They maintained that all the ancient rights and liberties of Englishmen were theirs by birthright; that to them, as much as to the Englishmen at home, belonged the guarantees of Magna Charta, and at a later date, of the Petition and the Bill of Rights; that in removing from their native land to its colonial possessions, they had sacrificed no portion of their ancient rights; and that, as Englishmen, they were entitled still to be protected by the guarantees of liberty which covered them before their emigration.

The law of nations, in the matter of colonial settlements, was altogether in their favor. There are, in general, two cases, which may be briefly stated as follows:

1. If the territory to be colonized is uninhabited, or only occupied by savages or wandering tribes, so that the country is without established laws or government, then the Government of which the colonists are subjects is immediately supreme, and all its laws, both for the regulation and for the protection of its subjects, are at once in force so far as they are applicable to the situation and condition of an infant colony. The artificial refinements and distinctions, says Blackstone, "incident to a great and commercial people, are neither necessary nor convenient for them, and therefore are not in force." What shall be admitted and what rejected, at what times and under what restrictions, must be decided by the joint action of their own provincial judicature, when established, and the sovereign power of which they are the subjects. There must thus be a division of the functions of supreme power; and in this, like every other instance of divided sovereignty, the relations of the provincial to the parent government will often be extremely delicate. But the status of the people is determined from the first. They remain the subjects of the parent Government, and being governed by the same laws, they are bound by the same obligations and invested

with the same rights as before their emigration. The peculiar difficulty of such colonies is this, that laws by which the obligations of the subjects are defined will seem to be immediately in force, while institutions made for the security of rights, being not yet established in the colony, or at best imperfectly established, will be insufficient to protect the colonist in their enjoyment; and in every such case justice will require the spirit of the laws to be regarded rather than the letter. A discretionary application of laws is always dangerous. The tendency of governments is always to encroach upon the franchise of the subject; and the tendency in colonies is always to complete autonomy; so that a conflict is inevitable if the former fail to put a liberal construction on colonial rights, or if the latter fail duly to recognize colonial obligations. When so much is left to human wisdom, virtue, and forbearance, history affords but little reason to expect a happy issue.

2. The second case is when a colony is to be planted in a conquered or ceded country which already has a code of laws, and governmental institutions for their execution. By the law of nations conquest gives to the victorious power an absolute authority over his conquered enemies, to whom, therefore, the conqueror's will becomes the only source of law; but this, "in reason and civil policy, can mean nothing more than that, in order to put an end to hostilities, a compact is either expressly or tacitly made between the conqueror and the conquered, that if they will acknowledge the victor for the master, he will treat them for the future as subjects, and not as enemies." (BLACKSTONE, *Com.* i. 103.) Cession of territory, when no stipulations to the contrary are made, conveys as absolute a sovereignty as conquest. Therefore, in a conquered or ceded country that has already laws of its own, the sovereign has a right to alter or abolish the existing laws; but till he actually does change or abolish them, they remain in full force over the inhabitants; and any of his subjects, colonists, or others who may settle in the conquered or ceded country, fall likewise under their control. In this case, if a colony be planted, there is little likelihood of conflict with the parent Government. The rights and obligations of the colonists being only such as it prescribes, immunities and privileges emanating solely from its gift, and it alone giving protection

against the natives, who may always be supposed to be inclined to win their freedom by rebellion—interest and the instinct of self-preservation equally impel him to sustain the sovereign power. At all events the government is simple. Despotism, and this under any form, is despotism, admits no conflicts of authority or jurisdiction, knows no rights but those it chooses to respect, and recognizes nothing in the subject but his obligation of obedience.

3. The distinction between the two cases is clear. In the former, when a country *having no established laws* is occupied by colonists, they bring with them in full vigor all the laws of their own country, so far as those laws are applicable to colonial circumstances. In the latter, where a country *having legal institutions* falls by conquest, all existing laws remain till they are changed or abrogated by the conqueror; and colonists or settlers in the subjugated country are equally with the natives under the supreme will of the subjugating power. Now, in the country occupied by the American colonies there were no laws for the government of civilized society, because among the Indian aborigines no civilized society existed. From the foundation, therefore, of the colonies, the laws of England were in force in every one of them, and with those laws the rights as well as duties of the subjects of the English crown.

The colonists of North America never lost sight of this. All the anomalies and inconveniences of an ill-regulated colonial system were powerless to alienate them from the English crown. It was their pride that they were Englishmen; their ancient bonds and memories were all in England; but above all things else, their rights and liberties were of English growth, and it was as Englishmen they claimed to hold them. Some cause of dissatisfaction they might have and did have with the Government at home; but in this they suffered only with their fellow subjects from the crown during the troubled period of the Stuarts. It was not till later that their fellow subjects joined the crown in the oppression of the colonies by acts of Parliament, and during the period of trial the Americans could only look with sympathy upon the struggle between royalty and commons' rights, glorying in the triumph of the people, or lamenting the fanaticism which sometimes turned their triumph into cause for grief.

With these preliminary observations we may now proceed to give a sketch of the constitutional history of the thirteen colonies. As to their interior polity, the colonies were properly of three sorts :

1. *Provincial establishments*, in which the governor and council were appointed by the crown. In these the constitutions depended on the respective commissions and instructions issued by the crown to the governors; under the authority of which provincial assemblies, elected by the people, were constituted with the power of making laws and ordinances not repugnant to the laws of England. Such were the governments of VIRGINIA, NEW HAMPSHIRE, NEW YORK, GEORGIA, NEW JERSEY after 1702, and the CAROLINAS after 1728.

2. *Proprietary governments*, granted out to individuals, after the manner of feudatory principalities. In these the proprietary was practically governor of the province, the assembly being chosen by the people. Such were the governments of MARYLAND and PENNSYLVANIA, and at first of NEW JERSEY and the CAROLINAS.

3. *Charter governments*, in which the governor, council, and assembly were chosen by the people. These had the power of local legislation, and such other rights and authorities as were specially given in their charters of incorporation. To this class belonged the governments of the PLYMOUTH COLONY, CONNECTICUT, RHODE ISLAND, and originally of MASSACHUSETTS.

4. In addition to these, a mixed form of government was adopted in MASSACHUSETTS, in which the governor only was appointed by the crown, the council and assembly being both elected by the people.

VIRGINIA.—The first permanent settlement made in America, under the auspices of England, was under a charter to Sir Thomas Gates and his associates, by James I., in 1606, which granted to them the territories in America then commonly called Virginia. The associates were divided into two companies. By degrees, the name of Virginia was confined to the first or south colony. The second assumed the name of the Plymouth Company, and New England was founded under their auspices.

By the tenor of their charter all persons, being English subjects and inhabiting in the colonies, and their children born therein, were declared to have and possess all liberties, franchises, and immunities, within any other of the dominions of the crown, to all intents and purposes, as if they had been abiding and born within the realm of England, or any other dominions of the crown. The patentees were to hold the lands, &c., in the colony, of the king, his heirs and successors, as of the manor of East Greenwich in the county of Kent, in free and common soccage only, and not in *capite;* and were authorized to grant the same to the inhabitants of the colonies in such manner and form, and for such estates, as the council of the colony should direct.

Each colony was to be governed by a local council, appointed and removable at the pleasure of the crown, according to the royal instructions and ordinances from time to time promulgated. These councils were to be under the superior management and direction of another council sitting in England. A power was given to expel all intruders, and to lay a limited duty upon all persons trafficking with the colony; but a prohibition was imposed upon all the colonists against trafficking with foreign countries under the pretence of a trade from the mother country to the colonies.

The settlements in Virginia were earliest in point of date, and were fast advancing under a policy which subdivided the property among the settlers, instead of retaining it in common, and thus give vigor to private enterprise. As the colony increased, the spirit of its members assumed more and more the tone of independence; and they grew restless and impatient for the privileges enjoyed under the government of their native country. To quiet this uneasiness, Sir George Yeardley, then the governor of the colony, in 1619 called a general assembly, composed of representatives from the various plantations in the colony, and permitted them to assume and exercise the high functions of legislation. Thus was formed and established the first representative legislature that ever sat in America. And this example of a domestic parliament, to regulate all the internal concerns of the country, was never lost sight of, but was ever afterwards cherished, throughout America, as the dearest birthright of freemen. So acceptable was it to the people, and so indispensable to the real prosperity of the colony, that the council in England were compelled, in 1621, to issue an ordinance, which gave it a complete and permanent sanction. In imitation of the constitution of the British Parliament, the legislative power was lodged—partly in the governor, who held the place of the sovereign; partly in a council of state named by the company; and partly in an assembly composed of representatives freely chosen by the people. Each branch of the legislature might decide by a majority of voices, and a negative was reserved to the governor. But no law was to be in force, though approved by all three of the branches of the legislature, until it was ratified by a general court of the company, and returned under its seal to the colony. The ordinance further required the general assembly, as also the council of state, "to imitate and follow the policy of the form of government, laws, customs, and manner of trial and other administrations of justice, used in the realm of England, as near as may be."

Charles I. chose to regard and govern his American possessions as conquered territories. He declared the colony to be a part of the empire annexed to the crown, and immediately subordinate to its jurisdiction. During the greater part of his reign, Virginia knew no other law than the will of the sovereign or his delegated agents; and statutes were passed, and taxes imposed, without the slightest effort to convene a colonial assembly. It was not until the murmurs and complaints, which such a course of conduct was calculated to produce, had betrayed the inhabitants into acts of open resistance to the governor, and into a firm demand of redress from the crown against his oppressions, that the king was brought to more considerate measures. He did not at once yield to their discontents; but pressed as he was by severe embarrassments at home, he was content to adopt a policy which would conciliate the colony, and remove some of its just complaints. He accordingly, soon afterwards, appointed Sir William Berkeley governor, with powers and instructions which breathed a far more benign spirit. He was authorized to proclaim that, in all its concerns, civil as well as ecclesiastical, the colony should be governed *according to the laws of England.* He was directed to issue writs for electing representatives of the people, who, with the governor and council, should form a general assembly clothed with supreme legislative authority; and to establish courts of justice, whose proceedings should be guided by the forms of the parent country. *The rights of Englishmen* were thus secured to the colonists.

The laws of Virginia, during its colonial state, do not exhibit as many marked deviations, in the general structure of its institutions and civil polity, from those of the parent country, as those in the northern colonies. The common law was recognized as the general basis of its jurisprudence; and the legislature, with some appearance of boast, stated, soon after the restoration of Charles II., that they had "endeavored, in all things, as near as the capacity and constitution of this country would admit, to adhere to those excellent and often refined laws of England, to which we profess and acknowledge all due obedience and reverence." The prevalence of the common law was also expressly provided for in all the charters successively granted, as well as by the royal declaration when the colony was annexed as a dependency to the crown. Indeed, there is no reason to suppose that the common law was not, in its leading features, very acceptable to the colonists; and in its general policy the colony closely followed in the steps of the mother country. The trial by jury, although a privilege resulting from their general rights, was guarded by special legislation. There was also an early declaration that no taxes could be levied by the governor without the consent of the general assembly; and when raised, they were to be applied according to the appointment of the legislature. The burgesses also, during their attendance upon the assembly, were free from arrest. In respect to domestic trade, a general freedom was guaranteed to all the inhabitants to buy and sell to the greatest advantage, and all engrossing was prohibited. The culture of tobacco seems to have been a constant object of solicitude; and it was encouraged by a long succession of acts sufficiently evincing the public feeling, and the vast importance of it to the prosperity of the colony. We learn from Sir William Berkeley's answers to the lord commissioners, in 1671, that the population of the colony was at that time about 40,000; that the restrictions of the navigation act, cutting off all trade with foreign countries, were very injurious to them, as they were obedient to the laws. And "this (says he) is the cause why no small or great vessels are built here; for we are most obedient to all laws, whilst the New England men break through, and men trade to any place that their interest leads them." This language is sufficiently significant of the restlessness of New England under these restraints upon its commerce. In 1680 a remarkable change was made in the colonial jurisprudence, by taking all judicial power from the assembly, and allowing an appeal from the judgments of the General Court to the king in council.

Plymouth Colonies.—Before their landing, on the 11th of November, 1620, the Plymouth colonists drew up and signed an original compact, in which, after acknowledging themselves subjects of the crown of England, they proceed to declare: "Having undertaken, for the glory of God, and the advancement of the Christian faith, and the honor of our king and country, a voyage to plant the first colony in the northern parts of Virginia, we do, by these presents, solemnly and mutually, in the presence of God and of one another, covenant and combine ourselves together into a civil body politic, for our better ordering and preservation, and furtherance of the ends aforesaid. And by virtue hereof do enact, constitute, and frame, such just and equal laws, ordinances, acts, constitutions, and officers, from time to time, as shall be thought most meet and convenient for the general good of the colony; unto which we promise all due submission and obedience." This compact (signed by forty-one persons) is, in its very essence, a pure democracy; and in pursuance of it, the colonists proceeded soon afterwards to organize the colonial government, under the name of the Colony of New Plymouth, to appoint a governor and other officers, and to enact laws. The governor was chosen annually by the freemen, and had at first one assistant to aid him in the discharge of his trust. Four others were soon afterwards added, and finally the number was increased to seven. The supreme legislative power resided in, and was exercised by, the whole body of the male inhabitants—every freeman, who was a member of the church, being admitted to vote in all public affairs. The number of settlements having increased, and being at a considerable distance from each other, a house of representatives was established in 1639, the members of which, as well as all other officers, were annually chosen. They adopted the common law of England as the general basis of their jurisprudence—varying it, however, from time to time, by municipal regulations better adapted to their situation, or conforming more exactly to their stern notions of the absolute authority and universal obligation of the Mosaic institutions.

The Plymouth colonists acted, at first, altogether under the voluntary compact and association already mentioned. But they daily felt embarrassments from the want of some general authority, derived directly or indirectly from the crown, which should recognize their settlement and confirm their legislation. After several ineffectual attempts made for this purpose, they at length succeeded in obtaining, in January, 1629, a patent from the council established at Plymouth, in England, under the charter of King James, of 1620. This patent, besides a grant of the territory, upon the terms and tenure of the original patent of 1620, included an authority to the patentee (William Bradford) and his associates "to incorporate, by some usual or fit name and title, him or themselves, or the people there inhabiting under him or them, and their successors; from time to time to make orders, ordinances, and constitutions, as well for the better government of their affairs here, and the receiving or admitting any into their society, as also for the better government of his or their people, or his or their people at sea, in going thither or returning from thence; and the same to put or cause to be put in execution, by such officers and ministers as he or they shall authorize and depute; provided, that the said laws and orders be not repugnant to the laws of England, or the frame of government by the said president and council [of Plymouth Company] hereafter to be established."

The charter of 1629 furnished them, however, with the color of delegated sovereignty, of which they did not fail to avail themselves. They assumed under it the exercise of the most plenary executive, legislative, and judicial powers, with but a momentary scruple as to their right to inflict capital punishments. They were not disturbed in the free exercise of these powers until after the restoration of Charles II. Their authority under their charter was then questioned; and several unsuccessful attempts were made to procure a confirmation from the crown. They continued to cling to it, until, in 1684, their charter was overturned. An arbitrary government was then established over them, in common with the other New England colonies, and they were finally incorporated into a province, with Massachusetts, under the charter granted to the latter by William and Mary, in 1691.

After providing for the manner of choosing their governor and legislature, as above stated, their first attention seems to have been directed to the establishment of "free liberties of the free-born people of England." It was therefore declared, almost in the language of Magna Charta, that justice should be impartially administered unto all, not sold or denied; that no person should suffer "in respect to life, limb, liberty, good name, or estate, but by virtue or equity of some express law of the General Court, or the good and equitable laws of our nation suitable for us, in matters which are of a civil nature (as by the court here hath been accustomed), wherein we have no particular law of our own;" and none should suffer without being brought to answer by due course and process of law; that, in criminal and civil cases, there should be a trial by jury at all events upon a final trial on appeal, with the right to challenge for just cause; and, in capital cases, a peremptory right to challenge twenty jurors, as in England; and that no party should be cast or condemned, unless upon the testimony of two sufficient witnesses, or other sufficient evidence, or circumstances, unless otherwise specially provided by law. All processes were directed to be in the king's name. All trials in respect to land were to be in the county where it lay; and all personal actions where one of the parties lived; and lands and goods were liable to attachment to answer the judgment rendered in any action. All lands were to descend according to the free tenure of lands of East Greenwich, in the county of Kent; and all entailed lands according to the law of England.

MASSACHUSETTS.—Application was made for a charter to King Charles, who, accordingly, in March, 1628, granted to the grantees and their associates the most ample powers of government. The charter confirmed to them the territory already granted by the council established at Plymouth, to be holden of the crown, as of the royal manor of East Greenwich, "in free and common soccage, and not in *capite*, nor by knight's service," yielding to the crown one fifth part of all ore of gold and silver, &c. It also created the associates a body politic by the name of "The Governor and Company of the Massachusetts Bay in New England," with the usual powers of corporations. It provided that the government should be administered by a governor, a deputy-governor, and eighteen assistants, from time to time elected out of the freemen of the company, which officers should have the care of the general business and affairs of lands and plantations, and the government of the people there; and it appointed the first governor, deputy-governor, and assistants, by name. It further provided that a court or quorum, for the transaction of business, should consist of the governor or the deputy-governor, and seven or more assistants, which should assemble as often as once a month for that purpose, and also that four great general assemblies of the company should be held in every year. In these great and general assemblies (which were composed of the governor, deputy, assistants, and freemen present), freemen were to be admitted free of the company, officers were to be elected, and laws and ordinances for the good and welfare of the colony made; "so as such laws and ordinances be not contrary or repugnant to the laws and statutes of this our realm of England." At one of those great and general assemblies held in Easter Term, the governor, deputy, and assistants, and other officers, were to be annually chosen by the company present. The company were further authorized to transport any subjects, or strangers willing to become subjects, of the crown, to the colony, and to carry on trade to and from it, without custom or subsidy, for seven years, and were to be free of all taxation of imports or exports to and from the English dominion for the space of twenty-one years, with the exception of a five per cent. duty. The charter further provided that all subjects of the crown, who should become inhabitants, and their children born there, or on the seas going or returning, should enjoy all liberties and immunities of free and natural subjects, as if they, and every of them, were born within the realm of England. Full legislative authority was also given, subject to the restriction of not being contrary to the laws of England.

For three or four years after the removal of the charter, the governor and assistants were chosen, and all the business of the government was transacted, by the freemen assembled at large in a General Court. But the members having increased, an alteration took place, and in 1634, the towns sent representatives to the General Court. They drew up a general declaration, that the General Court alone had power to make and establish laws, and to elect officers; to raise moneys and taxes, and to sell lands; and that, therefore, every town might choose persons, as representatives, not exceeding two, who should have the full power and voices of all the freemen, except in the choice of officers and magistrates, wherein every freeman was to give his own vote. The system thus proposed was immediately established by common consent, although it is nowhere provided for in the charter. And thus was formed the second house of representatives (the first being in Virginia) in any of the colonies. At first, the whole of the magistrates (or assistants) and the representatives sat together, and as one body, in enacting all laws and orders. But at length, in 1644, they separated into two distinct and independent bodies, each of which possessed a negative upon the acts of the other. This course of proceeding continued until the final dissolution of the charter.

The General Court, in their address to Parliament in 1646, in answer to the remonstrance of certain malcontents, used the following language: "For our government itself, it is framed according to our own charter, and the fundamental and common laws of England, and carried on according to the same (taking the words of eternal truth and righteousness along with them, as that rule by which all kingdoms and jurisdictions must render an account of every act and administration in the last day), with as bare an allowance for the disproportion between such an ancient, populous, wealthy kingdom, and so poor an infant, thin colony, as common reason can afford." And they then proceeded to show the truth of their statement by drawing a parallel, setting down in one column the fundamental and common laws and customs of England, beginning with *Magna Charta*, and, in a corresponding column, their own fundamental laws and customs.

After the fall of the first colonial charter, in 1684, Massachusetts remained for some years in a very disturbed state, under the arbitrary power of the crown. At length a new charter was, in 1691, granted to the colony by William and Mary; and it henceforth became known as a province, and continued to act under this last charter until after the Revolution. The charter comprehended within its territorial limits all the old colony of the Massachusetts Bay, the colony of New Plymouth, the province of Maine, the territory called Acadia or Nova Scotia, and all the lands lying between Nova Scotia and Maine; and incorporated the whole into one province by the name of the Province of the Massachusetts Bay in New England, to be holden as of the royal manor of East Greenwich, in the county of Kent. It confirmed all prior grants made of lands to all persons, corporations, colleges, towns, villages, and schools. It reserved to the crown the appointment of the governor, and lieutenant-governor, and secretary of the province, and all the officers of the Court of Admiralty. It provided for the appointment, annually, of twenty-eight counsellors, who were to be chosen by the General Court, and nominated the first board. The governor and counsellors were to hold a council for the ordering and directing of the affairs of the province. The governor was invested with the right of nominating, and, with the advice of the council, of appointing all military officers, and all sheriffs, provosts, marshals, and justices of the peace, and other officers of courts of justice. He had also the power of calling the General Court, and of adjourning, proroguing, and dissolving it. He had also a negative upon all laws passed by the General Court. The General Court was to assemble annually on the last Wednesday of May; and was to consist of the governor and council for the time being, and of such representatives, being freeholders, as should be annually elected by the freeholders of each town who possessed a freehold of forty shillings annual value, or other estate to the value of forty pounds. Each town was entitled to two representatives; but the

General Court was, from time to time, to decide on the number which each town should send. The General Court was invested with full authority to erect courts, to levy taxes, and make all wholesome laws and ordinances, "so as the same be not repugnant or contrary to the laws of England;" and to settle annually all civil officers whose appointment was not otherwise provided for. All laws, however, were to be sent to England for approbation or disallowance; and if disallowed, and so signified under the sign manual and signet, within three years, the same thenceforth to cease and become void; otherwise to continue in force according to the terms of their original enactment. The governor was also made commander-in-chief of the militia, with the usual martial powers; but was not to exercise martial law without the advice of the council. In case of his death, removal, or absence, his authority was to devolve on the lieutenant-governor, or, if his office was vacant, then on the council. With a view also to advance the growth of the province by encouraging new settlements, it was expressly provided that there should be "a liberty of conscience allowed in the worship of God to all Christians, except Papists;" and that all subjects inhabiting in the province, and their children born there, or on the seas going or returning, should have all the liberties and immunities of free and natural subjects, as if they were born within the realm of England. And in all cases an appeal was allowed from the judgments of any courts of the province to the king, in the privy council, in England, where the matter in difference exceeded three hundred pounds sterling. And, finally, there was a reservation of the whole admiralty jurisdiction to the crown; and of a right to all subjects to fish on the coasts.

After the grant of the provincial charter, in 1691, the legislation of the colony took a wider scope, and became more liberal, as well as more exact. At the very first session an act passed, declaring the general rights and liberties of the people, and embracing the principal provisions of Magna Charta on this subject. Among other things, it was declared that no tax could be levied but by the General Court; that the trial by jury should be secured to all the inhabitants; and that all lands shall be free from escheats and forfeitures, except in cases of high treason. A habeas corpus act was also passed at the same session, but it seems to have been disallowed by the crown; and Chalmers asserts that there is no circumstance, in the history of colonial jurisprudence, better established than the fact that the habeas corpus act was not extended to the plantations until the reign of Queen Anne.

New Hampshire.—In November, 1629, Captain John Mason obtained a grant, from the council of Plymouth, of a territory which was afterwards called New Hampshire. The land granted was expressly subjected to the conditions and limitations in the original patent. A further grant was made to Mason by the council of Plymouth about the time of the surrender of their charter (22d April, 1635), covering much of the land in the prior grant, and giving to the whole the name of New Hampshire.

In the exposition of its own charter, Massachusetts contended that its limits included the whole territory of New Hampshire; and, being at that time comparatively strong and active, she succeeded in establishing her jurisdiction over it, and maintained it with unabated vigilance forty years. The controversy was finally brought before the king in council; and in 1679, it was solemnly adjudged against the claim of Massachusetts. And it being admitted that Mason, under his grant, had no right to exercise any powers of government, a commission was, in the same year, issued by the crown for the government of New Hampshire.

New Hampshire continued down to the period of the Revolution to be governed by commission as a royal province, and enjoyed the privilege of enacting her own laws through the instrumentality of a General Assembly, in the manner provided by the first commission.

The laws of New Hampshire, during its provincial state, partook very much the character of those of the neighboring province of Massachusetts.

Maine.—In April, 1639, Sir Ferdinando Gorges obtained from the crown a confirmatory grant of all the land from Piscataqua to Sagadahock and the Kennebeck river, and from the coast into the northern interior one hundred and twenty miles; and it was styled

"The Province of Maine." Of this province he was made lord palatine, with all the powers, jurisdiction, and royalties belonging to the bishop of the county palatine of Durham; and the lands were to be holden as of the manor of East Greenwich. The charter contains a reservation of faith and allegiance to the crown, as having the supreme dominion. It also authorizes the palatine, with the assent of the greater part of the freeholders of the province, to make laws, not repugnant or contrary, but as near as conveniently may be, to the laws of England, for the public good of the province; and to erect courts of judicature for the determination of all civil and criminal causes, with an appeal to the palatine. But all the powers of government so granted were to be subordinate to the "power and *regiment*" of the lords commissioners for foreign plantations for the time being.

A controversy between Massachusetts and the palatine, as to jurisdiction over the province, was brought before the privy council at the same time with that of Mason respecting New Hampshire, and the claim of Massachusetts was adjudged void. Before a final adjudication was had, Massachusetts had the prudence and sagacity, in 1677, to purchase the title of Gorges for a trifling sum; and thus, to the great disappointment of the crown (then in treaty for the same object), succeeded to it, and held it, and governed it as a provincial dependency until the fall of its own charter; and it afterwards, as we have seen, was incorporated with Massachusetts, in the provincial charter of 1691.

Connecticut.—The colony of New Haven was settled by emigrants immediately from England, without any title derived from the immediate patentees. They began their settlement in 1638, purchasing their lands of the natives; and entered into a solemn compact of government. By it no person was admitted to any office, or to have any voice at any election, unless he was a member of one of the churches allowed in the dominion. There was an annual election of the governor, the deputy, magistrates, and other officers, by the freemen. The General Court consisted of the governor, deputy, magistrates, and two deputies from each plantation.

Other courts were provided for; and their laws and proceedings varied in very few circumstances from Massachusetts, except that they had no jury, either in civil or criminal cases.

Soon after the restoration of Charles II., the colony solicited, and in April, 1662, obtained, from that monarch, a charter of government and territory. The charter included within its limits the whole colony of New Haven; and as this was done without the consent of the latter, resistance was made to the incorporation, until 1665, when both were indissolubly united, and have ever since remained under one general government.

In 1685, a *quo warranto* was issued by King James against the colony, for the repeal of the charter. No judgment appears to have been rendered upon it; but the colony offered its submission to the will of the crown; and Sir Edmund Andros, in 1687, went to Hartford, and, in the name of the crown, declared the government dissolved. They did not, however, surrender the charter, but secreted it in an oak, which is still venerated; and immediately after the revolution of 1688, they resumed the exercise of all its powers. The charter continued to be maintained as a fundamental law of the State until the year 1818, when a new constitution of government was framed and adopted by the people. The laws of Connecticut were, in many respects, similar to those of Massachusetts.

Rhode Island.—Roger Williams succeeded in obtaining, from the Earl of Warwick, in 1643, a charter of incorporation of Providence Plantations; and also, in 1644, a charter from the two houses of Parliament (Charles I. being then driven from his capital) for the incorporation of the towns of Providence, Newport, and Portsmouth, for the absolute government of themselves, but according to the laws of England.

Under this charter an assembly was convened in 1647, consisting of the collective freemen of the various plantations. The legislative power was vested in a court of commissioners of six persons, chosen by each of the four towns then in existence. The whole executive power seems to have been vested in a president and four assistants, who were chosen from the freemen, and formed the supreme court for the administration of justice.

They continued to act under this government until the restoration of Charles II. That event seems to have given great satisfaction to these Plantations. They immediately proclaimed the king, and sent an agent to England; and in July, 1663, after some opposition, they succeeded in obtaining a charter from the crown.

That charter incorporated the inhabitants, by the name of "the Governor and Company of the English Colony of Rhode Island and Providence Plantations, in New England, in America," conferring on them the usual powers of corporations.

Rhode Island enjoys the honor of having been, if not the first, at least one of the earliest, of the colonies, and indeed of modern states, in which the liberty of conscience and freedom of worship were boldly proclaimed among its fundamental laws.

In December, 1686, Sir Edmund Andros, agreeably to his orders, dissolved their government, and assumed the administration of the colony. The revolution of 1688 put an end to his power; and the colony immediately afterwards resumed its charter, and, though not without some interruptions, continued to maintain and exercise its powers down to the period of the American Revolution. After the Revolution it continued to act under the same charter as a fundamental law, being the only State in the Union which did not immediately form a new constitution of government.

MARYLAND.—The province of Maryland was included originally in the patent of the Southern or Virginia Company; and, upon the dissolution of that company, it reverted to the crown. King Charles I., on the 20th of June, 1632, granted it by patent to Cecilius Calvert, Lord Baltimore. By the charter, the king erected it into a province, and gave it the name of Maryland, in honor of his queen, Henrietta Maria, the daughter of Henry IV. of France, to be held of the crown of England, he, yearly, forever, rendering two Indian arrows. The first emigration made under the auspices of Lord Baltimore was in 1632, and consisted of about 200 gentlemen of considerable fortune and rank, and their adherents, being chiefly Roman Catholics. "He laid the foundation of this province (says Chalmers) upon the broad basis of security to property and of freedom of religion, granting, in absolute fee, fifty acres of land to every emigrant; establishing Christianity agreeably to the old common law, of which it is a part, without allowing preëminence to any particular sect. The wisdom of his choice soon converted a dreary wilderness into a prosperous colony."

The first legislative assembly of Maryland, held by the freemen at large, was in 1634–1635; but little of their proceedings is known. No acts appear to have been adopted until 1638–1639, when provision was made for a representative House of Assembly, chosen by the freemen; and the laws passed by the Assembly, and approved by the proprietary, or his lieutenant, were to be of full force.

At the same session, an act, which may be considered as in some sort a Magna Charta, was passed, declaring, among other things, that "Holy Church, within this province, shall have all her rights and liberties, and that the inhabitants shall have all their rights and liberties according to the great charter of England." Maryland, like the other colonies, was early alive to the importance of possessing the sole power of internal taxation; and accordingly, in 1650, it was declared that no taxes should be levied without the consent of the General Assembly.

Upon the revolution of 1688, the government of Maryland was seized into the hands of the crown, and was not again restored to the proprietary until 1716. From that period no interruption occurred until the American Revolution.

New York.—Charles II., in March, 1664, granted a patent to his brother, the Duke of York and Albany, by which he conveyed to him the region extending from the western bank of the Connecticut to the eastern shore of the Delaware, together with Long Island, and conferred on him the powers of government, civil and military.

A part of this tract was afterwards conveyed by the duke, by deed of lease and release, in June of the same year, to Lord Berkeley and Sir George Carteret. The territory then claimed by the Dutch as the New Netherlands was divided into the colonies of New York and New Jersey. In September, 1664, the Dutch colony was surprised by a British armament, which arrived on the coast, and was compelled to surrender to its authority.

No general assembly was called for several years; and the people having become clamorous for the privileges enjoyed by other colonists, the governor was, in 1682, authorized to call an assembly, which was empowered to make laws for the general regulation of the State, which, however, were of no force without the ratification of the proprietary. Upon the revolution of 1688, the people of New York immediately took side in favor of the Prince of Orange. From this era they were deemed entitled to all the privileges of British subjects, inhabiting a dependent province of the state.

As soon as the first royal governor arrived, in 1691, an assembly was called, which passed a number of important acts. Among others was an act virtually declaring their right of representation, and their right to enjoy the liberties and privileges of Englishmen by Magna Charta. It enacted that the supreme legislative power should forever reside in a governor and council appointed by the crown, and the people by their representatives (chosen in the manner pointed out in the act) convened in General Assembly; that, in all criminal cases, there should be a trial by a jury; that estates of *femes covert* should be conveyed only by deed upon privy examination; that wills in writing, attested by three or more credible witnesses, should be sufficient to pass lands; that there should be no fines upon alienations, or escheats and forfeitures of lands, except in cases of treason; that no person should hold any office, unless upon his appointment he would take the oaths of supremacy, and the test prescribed by the act of Parliament; that no tax or talliage should be levied but by the consent of the General Assembly.

Perhaps New York was more close in the adoption of the policy and legislation of the parent country, before the Revolution, than any other colony.

New Jersey.—New Jersey, as we have already seen, was part of the territory granted to the Duke of York, and was by him granted, in June, 1664, to Lord Berkeley and Sir George Carteret, with all the rights, royalties, and powers of government which he himself possessed. The proprietors, for the better settlement of the territory, agreed, in February, 1664–1665, upon a constitution or concession of government.

This constitution continued until the province was divided, in 1676, between the proprietors. By that division East New Jersey was assigned to Carteret; and West New Jersey to William Penn and others, who had purchased of Lord Berkeley. Carteret then explained and confirmed the former concessions for the territory thus exclusively belonging to himself. The proprietors also of West Jersey drew up another set of concessions for the settlers within that territory. They contain very ample privileges to the people.

Whether these concessions became the general law of the province seems involved in some obscurity. There were many difficulties and contests for jurisdiction between the governors of the Duke of York and the proprietors of the Jerseys; and these were not settled until after the duke, in 1680, finally surrendered all right to both by letters patent granted to the respective proprietors. In 1681, the governor of the proprietors of West Jersey, with the consent of the General Assembly, made a frame of government, embracing some of the fundamentals in the former concessions. There was to be a governor and council, and a General Assembly of representatives of the people. The General Assembly had the power to make laws, to levy taxes, and to appoint officers. Liberty of conscience was allowed, and no persons rendered incapable of office in respect of their faith and worship. West Jersey continued to be governed in this manner until the surrender of the proprietary government, in 1702.

Carteret died in 1679, and, being sole proprietor of East Jersey, by his will he ordered it to be sold for payment of his debts; and it was accordingly sold to William Penn and eleven others, who were called the Twelve Proprietors. They afterwards took twelve more into the proprietaryship; and to the twenty-four thus formed, the Duke of York, in March, 1682, made his third and last grant of East Jersey. Very serious dissensions soon arose between the two provinces themselves, as well as between them and New York, which threatened the most serious calamities. A *quo warranto* was ordered by the crown, in 1686, to be issued against both provinces.

East Jersey immediately offered to be annexed to West Jersey, and to submit to a governor appointed by the crown. Soon afterwards the crown ordered the Jerseys to be annexed to New England, and the proprietors of East Jersey made a formal surrender of its patent, praying only for a new grant, securing their right of soil. Before this request could be granted, the revolution of 1688 took place, and they passed under the allegiance of a new sovereign.

From this period, both of these provinces were in a state of great confusion and distraction; and remained so until the proprietors of both made a formal surrender of all their powers of government, but not of their lands, to Queen Anne, in April, 1702. The queen immediately reunited both provinces into one province, and by commission appointed a governor over them.

PENNSYLVANIA.—Pennsylvania was originally settled by detachments of planters under various authorities, Dutch, Swedes, and others, which at different times occupied portions of land on South or Delaware river. The ascendency was finally obtained over these settlements by the governors of New York, acting under the charter of 1664, to the Duke of York.

It continued in a feeble state until William Penn, in 1681, obtained a patent from Charles II., by which he became the proprietary of an ample territory called Pennsylvania, of which the charter constituted Penn the true and absolute proprietary. It authorized him, and his heirs and successors, to make all laws for raising money and other purposes, with the assent of the freemen of the country, or their deputies assembled for the purpose. But "the same laws were to be consonant to reason, and not repugnant or contrary, but, as near as conveniently may be, agreeable to law, and statutes and rights, of this our kingdom of England." The laws for the descent and enjoyment of lands, and succession to goods, and of felonies, were to be according to the course in England, until altered by the Assembly. All laws were to be sent to England within five years after the making of them, and, if disapproved of by the crown within six months, to become null and void. It also authorized the proprietary to appoint judges and other officers; to pardon and reprieve criminals; to establish courts of justice, with a right to appeal to the crown from all judgments; to create cities and other corporations; to erect ports, and manors, and courts baron in such manors. Liberty was allowed to subjects to transport themselves and their goods to the province; and to import the products of the province into England; and to export them from thence within one year, the inhabitants observing the acts of navigation, and all other laws in this behalf made. It was further stipulated that the crown should levy no tax, custom, or imposition, upon the inhabitants, of their goods, unless by the consent of the proprietary or Assembly, "or by act of Parliament in England."

A new frame of government was, with the consent of the General Assembly, established in 1683. In 1692, Penn was deprived of the government of Pennsylvania by William and Mary; but it was again restored to him in the succeeding year. A third frame of government was established in 1696. This again was surrendered, and a new, final charter of government was, in October, 1701, with the consent of the General Assembly, established, under which the province continued to be governed down to the period of the American Revolution.

Delaware.—After Penn had become proprietary of Pennsylvania, he purchased of the Duke of York, in 1682, all his right and interest in the territory afterwards called the Three Lower Counties of Delaware, and the three counties took the names of New Castle, Kent, and Sussex. At this time they were inhabited principally by Dutch and Swedes, and seem to have constituted an appendage to the government of New York.

In the same year, with the consent of the people, an act of union with the province of Pennsylvania was passed, and an act of settlement of the frame of government in a General Assembly, composed of deputies from the counties of Delaware and Pennsylvania. By this act the three counties were, under the name of the Territories, annexed to the province, and were to be represented in the General Assembly, governed by the same laws, and to enjoy the same privileges, as the inhabitants of Pennsylvania. Difficulties soon afterwards arose between the deputies of the province and those of the Territories; and, after various subordinate arrangements, a final separation took place between them, with the consent of the proprietary, in 1703. From that period down to the American Revolution, the Territories were governed by a separate legislature of their own, pursuant to the liberty reserved to them by a clause in the original charter or frame of government.

North and South Carolina.—In March, 1662 (April, 1663), Charles II. made a grant, to Lord Clarendon and others, of territory lying on the Atlantic Ocean, and erected it into a province, by the name of Carolina, to be holden as the manor of East Greenwich, in Kent, in free and common soccage, and not in *capite*, or by knight service, subject immediately to the crown, as a dependency, forever.

The grantees were created absolute lords proprietaries, saving the faith, allegiance, and supreme dominion of the crown, and invested with as ample rights and jurisdictions as the Bishop of Durham possessed in his palatine diocese. The charter seems to have been copied from that of Maryland, and resembles it in many of its provisions.

It further required that all laws should "be consonant to reason, and, as near as may be conveniently, agreeable to the laws and customs of this our kingdom of England." And it declared that the inhabitants and their children, born in the province, should be denizens of England, and entitled to all the privileges and immunities of British-born subjects.

In 1665, the proprietaries obtained from Charles II. a second charter, with an enlargement of boundaries.

Several detached settlements were made in Carolina, which were at first placed under distinct temporary governments; one was in Albemarle, another to the south of Cape Fear. Thus various independent and separate colonies were established, each of which had its own Assembly, its own customs, and its own laws—a policy which the proprietaries had afterwards occasion to regret, from its tendency to enfeeble and distract the province.

In the year 1669, the proprietaries, dissatisfied with the systems already established within the province, signed a fundamental constitution for the government thereof, the object of which is declared to be, "that we may establish a government agreeable to the monarchy, of which Carolina is a part, that we may avoid making too numerous a democracy." This constitution was drawn up by the celebrated John Locke.

It provided that the oldest proprietary should be the palatine, and the next oldest should succeed him. Each of the proprietaries was to hold a high office. The rules of precedency were most exactly established. Two orders of hereditary nobility were instituted, with suitable estates, which were to descend with the dignity. The provincial legislature, dignified with the name of *parliament*, was to be biennial, and to consist of the proprietaries or their deputies, of the nobility, and of representatives of the freeholders chosen in districts. They were all to meet in one apartment (like the ancient Scottish Parliament), and enjoy an equal vote. No business, however, was to be proposed until it had been debated in the grand council (which was to consist of the proprietaries and forty-two counsellors), whose duty it was to prepare bills. No act was of force longer than until the next biennial meeting of the Parliament, unless ratified by the palatine and a quorum of the proprietaries. All the laws were to become void at the end of a century, without any formal repeal. The Church of England (which was declared to be the only true and orthodox religion) was alone to be allowed a public maintenance by Parliament; but every congregation might tax its own members for the support of its own minister. Every man of seventeen years of age was to declare himself of some church or religious profession, and to be recorded as such; otherwise he was not to have any benefit of the laws. And no man was to be permitted to be a freeman of Carolina, or have any estate or habitation, who did not acknowledge a God, and that God is to be publicly worshipped. In other respects there was a guaranty of religious freedom. There was to be a public registry of all deeds and conveyances of lands, and of marriages and births. Every freeman was to have "absolute power and authority over his negro slaves, of what opinion or religion soever." No civil or criminal cause was to be tried but by a jury of the peers of the party; but the verdict of a majority was binding. With a view to prevent unnecessary litigation, it was provided that "it shall be a base and vile thing to plead for money or reward;" and that, "since multiplicity of comments, as well as of laws, have great inconveniences, and serve only to obscure and perplex, all manner of comments and expositions on any part of those fundamental constitutions, or on any part of the common or statute law of Carolina, are absolutely prohibited."

After a few years' experience of its ill arrangements, and its mischievous tendency, the proprietaries, upon the application of the people (in 1693), abrogated the constitution, and restored the ancient form of government. Thus perished the labors of Mr. Locke; and thus perished a system, under the administration of which, it has been remarked, the Carolinas had not known one day of real enjoyment, and that introduced evils and disorders which ended only with the dissolution of the proprietary government!

There was, at this period, a space of three hundred miles between the southern and northern settlements of Carolina; and, though the whole province was owned by the same proprietaries, the legislation of the two great settlements had been hitherto conducted by separate and distinct assemblies—sometimes under the same governor, and sometimes under different governors. The legislatures continued to remain distinct down to the period when a final surrender of the proprietary charter was made to the crown, in 1729. The respective territories were designated by the name of North Carolina and South Carolina, and the laws of each obtained a like appellation. Cape Fear seems to have been commonly deemed, in the commissions of the governor, the boundary between the two colonies.

At a little later period (1732), the province was divided; and the divisions were distinguished by the names of North Carolina and South Carolina.

The government conferred on Carolina, when it became a royal province, consisted of a governor and council appointed by the crown, and an Assembly chosen by the people; and these three branches constituted the legislature. The governor convened, prorogued, and dissolved the legislature, and had a negative upon the laws, and exercised the executive authority. He possessed also the powers of the court of chancery, of the admiralty, of supreme ordinary, and of appointing magistrates and militia officers. All laws were subject to the royal approbation or dissent, but were in the mean time in full force.

On examining the statutes of South Carolina, a close adherence to the general policy of the English laws is apparent. As early as the year 1712, a large body of the English statutes were, by express legislation, adopted as part of its own code; and all English statutes respecting allegiance, all the test and supremacy acts, and all acts declaring the rights and liberties of the subjects, or securing the same, were also declared to be in force in the province. All and every part of the common law, not altered by these acts, or inconsistent with the constitutions, customs, and laws of the province, was also adopted as part of its jurisprudence.

In respect to North Carolina, there was an early declaration of the legislature (1715), conformably to the charter, that the common law was, and should be, in force in the colony. All statute laws for maintaining the royal prerogative and succession to the crown; and all such laws made for the establishment of the church, and laws made for the indulgence to Protestant dissenters; and all laws providing for the privileges of the people, and security of trade; and all laws for the limitation of actions, and for preventing vexatious suits, and for preventing immorality and fraud, and confirming inheritances and titles of land, were declared to be in force in the province. The policy thus avowed was not departed from down to the period of the American Revolution.

Georgia.—In the same year in which Carolina was divided (1732), a project was formed for the settlement of a colony upon the unoccupied territory between the rivers Savannah and Alatamaha. The object of the projectors was to strengthen the province of Carolina, to provide a maintenance for the suffering poor of the mother country, and to open an asylum for the persecuted Protestants in Europe; and, in common with all the other colonies, to attempt the conversion and civilization of the natives. Upon application, George II. granted a charter to the company (consisting of Lord Percival and twenty others, among whom was the celebrated

Oglethorpe), and incorporated them by the name of the "Trustees for establishing the Colony of Georgia, in America." The charter conferred the usual powers of corporations in England, and authorized the trustees to hold any territories, &c., in America, for the better settling of a colony.

The charter further granted to the corporation seven undivided parts of all the territories lying in that part of South Carolina which lies from the northern stream of a river, there called the Savannah, all along the seacoast, to the southward, unto the southernmost stream of a certain other great river, called the Alatamaha, and westward from the heads of the said rivers respectively in direct lines to the South Seas, to be held as of the manor of Hampton Court, in Middlesex, in free and common soccage, and not in *capite.* It then erected all the territory into an independent province, by the name of *Georgia.* It authorized the trustees, for the term of twenty-one years, to make laws for the province, "not repugnant to the laws and statutes of England," subject to the approbation or disallowance of the crown, and after such approbation to be valid. The affairs of the corporation were ordinarily to be managed by the common council. It was further declared that all persons born in the province should enjoy all the privileges and immunities of natural-born subjects in Great Britain. Liberty of conscience was allowed to all inhabitants in the worship of God, and a free exercise of religion to all persons except Papists. The corporation were also authorized, for the term of twenty-one years, to erect courts of judicature for all civil and criminal causes, and to appoint a governor, judges, and other magistrates. The registration of all conveyances of the corporation was also provided for. The governor was to take an oath to observe all the acts of Parliament relating to trade and navigation, and to obey all royal instructions pursuant thereto. The governor of South Carolina was to have the chief command of the militia of the province; and goods were to be imported and exported without touching at any port in South Carolina. At the end of the twenty-one years, the crown was to establish such form of government in the province, and such method of making laws therefor, as in its pleasure should be deemed meet; and all officers should be then appointed by the crown.

It continued to languish, until at length the trustees, wearied with their own labors, and the complaints of the people, in June, 1751, surrendered the charter to the crown. Henceforward it was governed as a royal province, enjoying the same liberties and immunities as other royal provinces; and in process of time it began to flourish, and at the period of the American Revolution it had attained considerable importance among the colonies.

In respect to its ante-revolutionary jurisprudence, the same system prevailed as in the Carolinas, from which it sprang. Intestate estates descended according to the course of the English law.

CHAPTER XIV.

THE ANGLO-SAXON SYSTEM IN NORTH AMERICA—DISPUTE WITH ENGLAND—RIGHT OF REVOLUTION.

COMPARISON OF THE COLONIAL WITH THE ANGLO-SAXON SETTLEMENTS—DISTINCTNESS OF THE COLONIES AND ITS CAUSES—DIFFERENT TIMES OF SETTLEMENT—DISTANCE—NAVIGATION LAWS—RELIGIOUS ANIMOSITIES—POLITICAL ANTIPATHIES—NECESSITY OF THE REVOLUTIONARY WAR—THE NEW ENGLAND CONFEDERACY—NATURE OF THE CONTROVERSY OF THE COLONIES WITH ENGLAND—CLAIMS OF THE ENGLISH PARLIAMENT—OPPOSITE VIEW OF THE COLONIES—HOW VINDICATED BY THE PRESENT COLONIAL SYSTEM OF ENGLAND—OBSERVATIONS—FORCE OF CIRCUMSTANCES IN COMPELLING THE ADOPTION OF THE ANGLO-SAXON SYSTEM IN AMERICA—THE RIGHT OF REVOLUTION—FOUNDED IN NATURE—OBJECT OF GOVERNMENTS—THE DOCTRINE OF CONSENT—REVOLUTION ONLY JUSTIFIABLE IN CASE OF TYRANNY OR USURPATION—OBJECTION TO THE RIGHT OF REVOLUTION ON SCRIPTURAL GROUNDS—HOW ANSWERED—CASE OF HEZEKIAH—REVOLUTION IS JUSTIFIABLE POLITICALLY ONLY BY SUCCESS—PRUDENTIALLY BY AN IMPROVED GOVERNMENT—THE AMERICAN REVOLUTION JUSTIFIED RELIGIOUSLY, POLITICALLY, PRUDENTIALLY—A QUESTION.

To the planting of the English colonies in North America we might with all propriety apply even stronger language than was used in our first chapter to describe the Anglo-Saxon settlements in England. Like these the colonies were from the first entirely independent of each other. They were planted at times widely different, at distant places, under different auspices and different leaders, with antagonistic principles of faith and government. Established separately, they remained in all respects distinct and almost without intercourse until the period of the Revolution. Thus, though, like the Saxon tribes, they were of one race and of one speech, yet they were in no sense one people. They were even more distinct than the kingdoms of the Saxon Octarchy. No similarity of natural circumstances availed to unite them. Only common dangers and the sufferance of common wrongs forced them at length to enter into a confederate alliance to maintain their common rights.

Not to reckon the early settlements which failed of success, the first permanent settlement was made in Virginia in 1606. Georgia was not colonized till after 1732. Thus the period of settlements extends over a hundred and twenty-six years at least, and by a different and still fair computation it might be made much more. But at least more than four generations of Virginian colonists had lived, and the fifth generation was already well advanced before the first field had been cultivated or the first house built in the colony of Georgia.

At the present day, with our immense facilities of locomotion, we have but a faint idea of the obstacle to intercourse imposed upon the colonists by distance. From Boston to Savannah was a sea voyage of weeks, along a coast of which there were no charts, and must be made in some small craft but little suited to endure the storms of the Atlantic. Colonists much nearer to each other than the colonists of Georgia and Massachusetts looked upon the distance as immense; and if we observe the difficulties to be overcome in travelling, they were in fact more remote from each other than Europe and America at the present day. Moreover, the Government of England did not favor intercourse between them; and the navigation laws, prohibiting direct trade from the colonies to foreign nations, hindered the development of their marine to an extent which operated almost as a prohibition of trade between themselves.

And apart from interest there was little to create a very strong desire for intercourse. Between the Quaker-burning Puritan of Massachusetts and the Quaker colonist of Pennsylvania, the Roman Catholic of Maryland and the Episcopalian of Virginia or the Carolinas, there were strong religious animosities; and none of them were altogether free from the intolerance of religious rancor. In New England, women who dissented from dissent were whipped naked from Boston to Dedham, and Baptists were *drowned* to death—a rather grim jest on the doctrine of immersion. In Virginia, non-conformists to the Church of England were expelled the colony. And even in Maryland an act was passed in 1649, though it does not appear to have been put in force, which punished Unitarianism with death and confiscation. Religious prejudices so strong and so radically opposite were alone sufficient to prevent friendly communications; and in fact most of the colonies were in this respect as widely separated from each other as Jerusalem and Samaria of old; they had "no dealings" with each other.

Nor were their political antipathies much less decided. The Cavalier of the South and the Roundhead regicide of the New England settlements had no point of agreement, and their mutual bitterness was as intense as that of their respective parties in the mother country. Aside from these direct antagonistic influences, their different colonial constitutions had a tendency to keep them separate. The Plymouth colonies were in the strictest sense democracies. In fact, they were the only radical democracies then in the world. The Carolinas, on the contrary, were, by the constitution framed for them by Locke, established on a basis of aristocratic precedence and power; although the popular principle was made coördinate with the aristocratic. Other colonies, and at a later date the Carolinas also, were brought into near relations to the Government at home by the appointment of their governors and councils by the crown; which, notwithstanding that the assemblies were elected by the people, kept alive a cordial feeling of attachment to the sovereign. In the proprietary governments, particularly that of Maryland, where "Cecilius, Lord Baltimore, sovereign lord and proprietary of the province," exercised in all but name the functions of a constitutional monarch, thus uniting in his single person the office of a king, the status of an English peer, and the enlightenment of a popular leader, a peculiarity of public feeling was produced perhaps more favorable to real progress than any of the others. It was preëminently a government of law. The "sovereign lord" and the free colonist were equally its subjects. Yet the constitution was as far removed from premature democracy as from an effete absolutism. Perhaps of all forms of colonial existence, this, wisely administered, was least objectionable. Conservative and yet progressive, it neither trampled rudely on the institutions of the past, nor rushed with indiscreet haste into the uncertainties of an unripe future. But whichever of these forms of local government may have been best, each was supreme within the colony where it prevailed; each was alike esteemed by those among whom it had been instituted; and where each existed all the others were alike despised.

It was a happy circumstance that there was little intercourse among the colonies in the colonial period, for their intercourse could hardly have been friendly. It was fortunate, also, that this absolute independence of each other as to government was sanctioned by prescription, not less than by law and fact, before their union had been dreamed of; for an unwise union of antagonistic elements could only have produced a strife of factions, civil war, and military despotism, or permanent disruption; and a union of the colonies before the acknowledgment of their entire separate sovereignty would have been an unwise union, offering continual pretexts for sectional aggressions upon local institutions, and compelling sectional resistance to the usurpation of majorities. On the other hand, it was a wise and gracious providence which laid upon the colonies a war of years, to be endured, not in formal union with each other, but as a confederation of independent States; till they should have forgotten ancient discords in the recollection of their common wrongs, their common glory, and their common interests; that is, till they should have been prepared for union under one political organization, which, without destroying or impairing their distinct supremacy as sovereign States, should yet unite them by a common bond in all things in regard to which their interests were identical —a bond which, under God, gave them seventy years of domestic peace, which nothing but judicial blindness could have led the people to assail, and which God's judgment on a thankless people could alone have suffered to be broken.

There was, however, one notable instance of colonial combination and confederation in New England. It was proposed as early as 1637, but difficulties having occurred, the articles of confederation were not adopted till 1643, when "a perpetual league of friendship and amity," styled the United Colonies of New England, was formally entered into, "for purposes of offence and defence, and mutual advice and succor," by the colonies of Massachusetts, Connecticut, New Haven, and Plymouth. Rhode Island asked to be admitted to the league, but was rejected. By the conditions of this union the charges of all wars, offensive and defensive, were to be borne in common, according to an apportionment previously agreed upon. In case of the invasion of any colony, the others were to furnish a certain contingent of armed men for its defence. Commissioners appointed by each colony were to meet and determine all points of war, peace, leagues, aids, charges, &c., and to frame and establish agreements and orders for other general interests. No general government over the confederated colonies was contemplated. Each was still in all respects to govern its own people according to the tenor of its charter. This union, so important during the troubles which then agitated the mother country, was not annulled by Charles II. on his restoration; but though it was styled *perpetual*, it lasted only forty-three years, when it ceased upon the abrogation of colonial charters by King James. It was never afterwards renewed.

In the beginning of the previous chapter, we have shown the constitutional status of the individual colonist. The mutual independence of the colonies has just been illustrated. It remains that we should indicate the status of the colonies in respect of England, which will perhaps be best done if we state at once the opposite constitutional positions assumed by England and the colonies respectively in the controversy which resulted in the Revolution. This was a new question in England, in regard to which there was much confusion of ideas. The general scope, however, of the several arguments was this: On the part of England it was claimed that her American possessions were acquired in part by conquest and in part by cession from the natives; that these possessions were therefore held by *right of conquest*; that colonists and settlers in a conquered country are, in common with the natives of the country, to be governed by such laws as it may please the conqueror to impose, and to enjoy only such rights as he may please to recognize; that the colonies were in no sense parts of England, but separate and subordinate dominions; that they were mere dependencies, not on the crown, but on the realm of England; and hence that the realm, as represented by the Parliament of England, including king, lords, and commons, was entitled by the right of conquest to impose such laws and taxes on them as its sole will should direct.

In answer to this reasoning the colonies maintained that they themselves, whether by conquest or by cession, were the true acquirers of their several territories, which, till settled by them, had belonged to England only by the vague right of discovery; that it was only through them that England had actually become possessed of these dominions; and that it was absurd that they should be subjected to a right of conquest they had themselves acquired. Reverting to the circumstances under which the colonies were planted, they observed that the original colonists were free-born Englishmen; that they had settled in a country which had as yet been neither conquered nor acquired by cession, and in which no laws nor government existed; that therefore by the law of nations they were, from the moment of their landing, governed by the laws of England, as those laws existed at that time and so far as they were applicable to the condition of a colony; and hence that they were from the first fully invested with the rights, as well as obligated by the duties, of natural-born English subjects. They conceded that the colonies were not parts of the realm of England, but separate and distinct dominions, nor did they deny that to a limited extent they were dependent on England. Some of them admitted further that they were dependent, not upon the crown, but on the realm of England. But they declared that this dependence must be so interpreted as not to override the constitutional rights of the colonists as English subjects under the laws of England, as they stood at the time of the plantation of their several colonies. Referring to the Great Charter of King John, the most important of those laws, and the scarcely less important statute *De tallagio non concedendo* of Edward I., they showed that the consent of the subject given through his representatives in Parliament was necessary to the legal levying of taxes. Hence they argued that, according to the letter not less than the spirit of the English Constitution, taxes on the colonists could only be assessed by their consent so given; and since the colonies, being separate dominions from the realm of England, were incapable of being represented in the Parliament of England, the conclusion was inevitable that their own colonial legislatures, in which only they were represented, could alone give constitutional sanction to the imposition of taxes in the colonies. Concerning the claim of Parliament to exercise the rights of paramount sovereignty, they said that the dependence of the colonists, not being such as to vitiate the rights or liberties of their inhabitants, the sovereignty of Parliament, could in reason be no greater in the colonies than the king's sovereignty in England, and hence that, as the sovereign in England could make no laws and impose no taxes but through Parliament, so in the colonies the Parliament of England could have no sovereign right of legislation or taxation, but through the colonial legislatures. Every position thus assumed by the Americans in their controversy with Great Britain, has since that time been completely vindicated by the verdict of the English Parliament itself. The whole colonial system has been constituted on the principles enunciated in America a century ago; and the concessions which would have kept the colonies of North America devoted subjects of the British crown, are now the common axioms of its colonial jurisprudence. A more complete justification there could hardly be of the position of colonial America; but we may well wonder that a legislative body like the Parliament of England, which had battled so determinedly against the usurpations of a monarchy, and by the Bill of Rights and Act of Settlement had so completely limited the crown as to insure the freedom of the subject, should itself have seized so empty a pretext to set up a despotic parliamentary authority over its dependencies. And when we find that one whose mind was so clear, large, and liberal as Blackstone's, could (surely through oversight) accept the empty and self-contradictory reasoning which aimed to prove that the colonial dependencies were to be governed by the right of conquest as subjugated provinces, it would be difficult to give a better exposition of the strange anomaly than is enunciated in the aphorism, that despotism, when possible, is always certain. The saying is as true of parliaments as of princes, and as true of majorities as of parliaments. Wherever power is lodged, there is a certainty that, if not checked by a restraining influence, it will be used to its full limit, if indeed all limitations be not broken down. The cases of King John, the Puritan majority of eleven in the Long Parliament, and the present instance of parliamentary usurpation in the matter of the colonies, will illustrate our meaning. Cases nearer home, however obvious, we cannot here discuss.[1]

We now approach the grand event of the last century, the reëstablishment on a new continent, with all the aids of a mature and still advancing civilization, of the ancient principle which lay at the foundation of the Anglo-Saxon polity. Already we have seen the colonies, established like the Saxon tribes, in perfect independence of each other, growing up in the enjoyment of the rights and liberties, which centuries of bloodshed had at lenght wrung from the Norman monarchs and their various successors. We have seen them educated, by the exercise of local sovereignty as dependencies of a great kingdom, for still more complete self-government. The arrogant assumption of the English Government of a right to govern them as denizens of conquered countries by the arbitrary laws of conquest, left them no choice but to become the slaves of arbitrary power or to exercise the great right of rebellion against tyranny which is so emphatically recognized in Magna Charta. Individually they were too weak to rebel successfully, and hence a confederation became necessary to insure success. Their first confederation showed them the advantages of union, and revealed defects in its extemporary articles; and thus through error and defect they were led to the incomparable form of government provided by the present Constitution, which is a complete revival of the Anglo-Saxon polity. Securing and maintaining the complete right of self-government to every sovereign State, and legislating for them only in matters as to which their interests are identical, the Union, brought into existence by the States under the Constitution, is a full revival of the system of the Anglo-Saxon Empire, differing from it only by the various improvements which the progress of civilization have suggested.

The story of the Revolutionary War lies beyond our province, but before we enter on the constitutional detail reserved to us, we venture to premise a few words on the right of revolution.

The right of revolution is simply a particular application of the general right of self-defence. In the state of nature every individual person has the right to defend by violence his life, liberty, and property, against assaults by whomsoever made. The purpose of political organizations is to substitute the whole power of a community for that of individuals in the protecting of their persons and their properties, by means of laws for the restraint and punishment of wrong-doers within, and military combinations to resist foreign aggressions from without. It is on this ground that the doctrine of consent rests. For in any government it is necessary that a portion of the freedom of the individual should be surrendered that the rest may be preserved. He resigns his right of individual self-defence and submits to the restraints of law in order that he may enjoy more perfect security. But if a government be set over him without his consent, this is itself an invasion of his liberty which the law of nature authorizes him to resist. Hence arbitrary governments, whose subjects have neither expressly nor tacitly consented to their institution, and governments whose title to exist is founded on the so-called right of conquest, are in a perpetual state of war with nature, and their subjects have a perpetual and indefeasible right of rebellion against them. No prescription holds against the laws of nature; and such governments, being governments of force and contrary to nature, hold their power subject to the people's right to reassert the law of nature by resisting, and, if possible, destroying their usurped power.

There are, however, few civilized governments to which the subjects have not yielded an express or tacit consent; and lawful governments can only be lawfully resisted when they are perverted from their lawful purposes. Man is a social being, naturally living in societies; to the existence of society, government is necessary; hence anarchy is repugnant to nature; and therefore the wanton subversion of governments, lawfully instituted by consent of their subjects, being an act which tends to anarchy, is a crime against the law of nature. But when lawful governments, instead of protecting life, liberty, and property, become or threaten to become destructive of these or prejudicial to them, they proclaim war against the law of nature, and their subjects have the right to overthrow them. In this case it is the government that is truly rebellious, and the people who are truly obedient to the law of nature.

To this view there are some who object on Scriptural grounds. "All power is of God;" "the powers that be are ordained of God;"

the magistrate is "the minister of God;" "let every soul be subject to the higher powers." These are the sayings of St. Paul. We have only, however, to carry his injunctions far enough in order to show that they must be received with considerable limitations. If the magistrate is the minister of God who acquires his authority over a kingdom through an armed force of one hundred thousand men, it is difficult to say why a marauding chief who occupies a district at the head of a band of brigands is not equally the minister of God. And if every soul is to be subject to the edicts of the one, it would be hard to find a reason why the same rule should not hold good of the demands of his less mighty but not less righteous imitator. Scripture itself gives warrant for rebellion against arbitrary and unjust power. The exodus of Israel from Egypt was rebellion against a government to which they had consented by their voluntary settlement under it, but from which they were released because it had become oppressive. And in the instance of Hezekiah, so aptly quoted by Locke, we have a case in which the indefeasible right of rebellion against a subjugating power, *even after submission and enforced consent,* is perfectly sustained. Hezekiah and his country had been conquered by Assyria, to the king of which he had submitted. On condition of consenting to the supremacy of Assyria, he had been suffered to retain his throne. But "the Lord was with Hezekiah and he prospered; wherefore he went forth, and he rebelled against the king of Assyria and served him not." (2 Kings xviii. 7.) This is spoken of "the good king Hezekiah," and spoken certainly not in reprehension. The sacred penman represents this godly king's rebellion as the consequence of the divine presence and blessing. Unquestionably lawful magistrates are ministers of God for good to men, but when their lawful powers are prostituted to subserve the devil's purposes, whose ministers do they become? The devil himself is styled in Holy Writ the "prince of this world," and, to judge from what we see around us in this nineteenth century, he is one of the mightiest of the "powers that be;" but here at least resistance to the tyrant is obedience to God. The truth is, the religion of the Holy Scriptures is a religion of common sense, and a religion of righteousness. It does not declare a wrong to be right because it is sustained by force, or because it has the trappings of legitimate authority to cover an unlawful usurpation. Lawful magistrates and lawful governments it is the Christian's duty to obey as ministers of God. Resistance to usurped power—that is, to a robbery of man's most precious heritage—is not contrary either to the letter or the spirit of the Scriptures.

A Christian, then, may lawfully rebel against the government of which he is a subject; but only when it is a lawless government; that is, when its authority is based, not on the law of nature, but of force, or when its power, though lawfully acquired, is not so exercised as to protect the subject in his rights of property and person, which is the object of all government. Against such a government, or one which threatens to become such, but against such only, may a Christian lawfully rebel or aid a revolution.

Politically, however, revolution must be justified by quite a different argument—success. International law takes little cognizance of the original right by which power is acquired. The *fact* of its existence is the only reason for its recognition. Till the revolution is successful by the overthrow of the government whose destruction is attempted, it is in the eye of international law rebellion. Once successful, the authority it sets up becomes legitimate. Politically speaking, the wrongs which may have caused it, or the rights it was intended to secure, are nothing. Revolution is politically justified by nothing but success.

And, prudentially, a revolution must be justified, both by success and by a capacity to organize a better government than that which it subverts. It is not enough that the original government may have been bad or badly administered, for unless it be successful, and unless the new form of administration or the new rules be better than the old, the uncertainties and strife of revolution have been incurred in vain. The French Revolution, though productive in the end of good results, was not, prudentially, a justifiable revolution. Its success was merely temporary, and the government it organized instead of that of the beheaded Louis was in all respects worse than that they cast down. It was wrong prudentially, first, because it failed of permanent success, and second, because, while its power continued, it did not improve the government, but rather made it worse.

The revolution of the colonies was right religiously, politically, and prudentially.

It was right *religiously*, for it was a revolution against a tyranny, that is, against a government which assumed, in the language of King James, to "exercise power beyond right."

It was justified *politically*, by complete and permanent success.

It was justified *prudentially*, by its creation of a government whose constitution is the admiration of the world. If the virtue of the people rise again to an equality with the incomparable wisdom of the Constitution, then the lover of free institutions may cry, *Esto perpetua;* and the prophet may respond, ERIT PERPETUA. If otherwise— ?

NOTE.

1. THE following significant article, which we give verbatim as recently published in a leading daily paper of the city of New York, will serve to show the power of a vigorous and homogeneous MINORITY to turn the machinery of government from its purposes of common benefit to the subservience of petty and peculiar interests:

"THE YANKEE TYRANNY—THE CENTRAL AND WESTERN STATES MERE "HEWERS OF WOOD" TO NEW ENGLAND.

"Previous to the present civil war the agitators of New England were eternally denouncing the alleged ascendency of the seven Cotton States in shaping and controlling the policy of our National Government. 'Everything is shaped to benefit the Cotton States,' was the cry of the New England fanatics. 'The whole Government is in the hands of the South, and every measure of legislation is held subordinate to Southern interests.' That there was a small basis of fact for these assertions is not to be denied, and that basis had this extent, no more: The seven Cotton States demanded that the Constitution of the United States should be upheld, and that no legislation hostile to their property interests in the institution of slavery should be undertaken by Congress. They also further demanded, in one single instance—the Fugitive Slave Law—that Congress should make some legislative provision to enforce one of the rights guaranteed to them by the Constitution against the treasonable and unconstitutional opposition thereto of these same New England fanatics. This was about all the 'peculiar legislation' the South demanded, and, in turn for receiving it, they—a wholly agricultural and producing people—acquiesced without murmur in all the legislation demanded by the complex commercial, agricultural, and manufacturing interests of the remainder of the Union.

"Well, the Union was at last broken up, the South being no longer able to bear peacefully the constant irritation and dangers resulting from the aggressive character of New England's anti-slavery fanaticism. The fourteen Senators from the seven Cotton States not only lost their ascendency in our national affairs, but stepped out of the Union altogether. And now what do we find to be the result? Just this: That the twelve Senators of the six New England States have adopted the *rôle* which they so vehemently denounced in what they were pleased to call the 'Black Gulf Squadron,' and that our whole national policy is to-day subservient to the interests and dictates, the bigotries and narrow, puritanical prejudices, of the twelve Senators who, forming the 'Black Republican Squadron,' are sent from the New England States to Washington. Our present actual masters are more sordid, grasping, and cruel than were the alleged Southern managers of the past. They legislate with a view exclusively to New England interests, and their object would seem to be to throw all the burdens of taxation and revenue upon the other portions of the loyal States, while compelling us all, by high protective and prohibitory importation duties, to purchase New England manufactures, however inferior to those we could obtain much cheaper abroad, at just such prices as may suit the pockets—we will not say consciences, for they appear to have none—of New England's manufacturing aristocracy.

"The main burdens of our internal revenue were thrown by the legislation of last winter upon two articles—whiskey and tobacco—in which the New England States have but the slightest interest, while our custom-house duties were advanced to figures making regular importation all but certainly unprofitable, and of necessity driving the trade, heretofore centred at New York, to be mainly transacted thereafter by active parties of smugglers along the Canadian border. So much is this the case, that the Secretary of the Treasury is now devising means to check this very smuggling, which has reached, even while yet in its infancy, enormous proportions—Secretary Fessenden apparently forgetting Sir Robert Peel's maxim, as the result of English experience, that 'it is utterly impossible to check any smuggling which, if successful, will pay a profit of over thirty per cent. In our case, however, the profits of running certain articles into the United States from Canada will be many hundreds per cent.; nor can this be stopped in any manner, unless we build along the Canadian frontier such a wall as divides the Chinese from the old Tartar empire. Even this would hardly suffice; for, with such a profit as New England greed has left open to the smugglers, it would be a remunerative speculation to start a hundred large balloons in this species of traffic.

"In the last session of the Senate, let it not be forgotten, the chairman of every important committee was a New Englander, the presiding officer was a New Englander, and all the legislation ground out was either to benefit New England interests, or to supply food to New England bigotries and hates. The trade of New York city was to be destroyed by imposing duties which would force foreign merchandise up to Canada, and thence, by smuggling, into the United States; while New England was to avoid the heavy burden of taxation, in great measure, by placing the heaviest excise duties of our internal revenue upon two articles in which her interests are insignificant. Her six States, with an aggregate population of three million one hundred and thirty-five thousand three hundred and one, according to the census of 1860, are represented by twelve Senators, holding the chairmanship of all the most important committees of the Senate of the Union; while New York, with a population of three million eight hundred and eighty-seven thousand five hundred and forty-two, according to the same census, has but two members in the Senate; and these two, upon every occasion in which they attempted to defend the interests of New York and the Central States, were roughly overriden and voted down by the 'Black Republican Squadron' from New England.

"Thus it is that history repeats itself. The Puritans fled to this country under the pretence of a desire to secure religious liberty; but no sooner had they obtained it for themselves than they commenced burning Quakers, nonconformists, witches, and all others whose tenets were not identical with their own, or whose practices they could not understand. They protested against the ascendancy of the 'Black Gulf Squadron' in our national affairs, even provoking a civil war rather than submit to it; but no sooner are they given a chance of power than we find the 'Black Republican Squadron' in full sweep, with the black flag hoisted against the rights, interests, and opinions of every section of the Union. Our whole Government to-day is one of Yankee ideas, and the most miserable sort of Yankee philanthropic notions. The sceptre thrown down by the extreme South as it rushed out of the Union is now wielded more fiercely and remorselessly by the extreme Northeastern section of our people.

"When will the day come, it may be asked, in which the great Central and Western States will assert their natural supremacy, and crush out the extremists, or corner-men of the continent, as we may call them—one faction of these residing in the southeast, and the other in the northeast corner of the Atlantic seaboard? When will the day come that we of the Centre and West shall be 'Americans,' and not 'Yankees,' in the eyes of Europe, and, indeed, of all the world? We are called 'Yankees' now—even by our Southern foes, who know better, geographically—merely because it is seen that we are the helots of a Yankee oligarchy, patiently submitting to Yankee rule, and fighting out a war which had its origin in Yankee intolerance and bigotry. With seven hundred and fifty thousand more population than the six New England States put together, we have but two representatives in the Senate of the United States, while New England has twelve; and not content with foisting on us the greater part of the burdens of the war, while at the same time ruining the trade and marine of our greatest city—the greatest city on the continent—New England has now capped the climax of her oppressions by so arranging it that, while but twelve and a half per cent. of her population has been enrolled for the coming draft, no less than twenty-six per cent. of our population in the first ten districts of New York have been enrolled for the same purpose! Does this really mean that the lives of two and a fraction citizens of New York are but worth the life of one Massachusetts man? Or will the Bay State assert that one of her lanky sons is able to whip two and something over of our New York athletes? The question is a pertinent one: for, as things are now progressing, no one can tell how soon these questions may be brought to a very practical test. The only remedy for these evils is for the Central and Northern States to make a strong alliance, offensive and defensive, during the progress of the Chicago Convention, and to place upon a platform, opposed alike to Southeastern and Northeastern extremists, some conservative soldier or statesman, who shall be the vigorous exponent of a national, anti-corner policy."—New York Herald.

CHAPTER XV.

INDEPENDENCE.

FIRST CONGRESS OF COLONIAL DELEGATES—ASSERTION OF RIGHTS—NON-INTERCOURSE—PETITION TO THE KING—ADVICE TO MASSACHUSETTS—LORD NORTH'S MOTION REJECTED—ADJOURNMENT OF CONGRESS—ITS PROCEEDINGS AFTER REASSEMBLING—DEBATE ON THE PROPOSITION TO DECLARE THE INDEPENDENCE OF THE COLONIES—COMMITTEE APPOINTED TO DRAFT A FORM OF CONFEDERATION—FURTHER STEPS TOWARDS THE ADOPTION OF THE DECLARATION—ITS FINAL SIGNATURE BY THE MEMBERS OF CONVENTION—MATTER OF THE DECLARATION—WHENCE DERIVED—ITS LEGAL AND CONSTITUTIONAL EFFECT—ITS TRUE GRANDEUR.

THE first Congress of delegates "chosen and appointed by the several colonies and provinces in North America to take into consideration the actual condition of the same, and the difficulties subsisting between them and Great Britain," was held in Philadelphia, on the 5th of September, 1774. Delegates attended from New Hampshire, Massachusetts Bay, Rhode Island and Providence Plantations, Connecticut, New York, New Jersey, Pennsylvania, the Delaware Counties, Maryland, Virginia, and South Carolina. On the 14th of September, delegates appeared from North Carolina. It was not till the following year that an informal representative of Georgia was admitted.

On the following day after the adoption of rules of order, Congress appointed a committee "to state the rights of the colonies in general, the several instances in which those rights had been violated or infringed, and the means most proper to be pursued for obtaining a restoration of them." Another committee was appointed "to examine and report the several statutes which affected the trade and manufactures of the colonies."

On the 24th of September, Congress resolved that the delegates would confine themselves to the consideration of such rights as had been infringed by acts of the British Parliament after the year 1763, postponing the further consideration of the general state of American rights to a future day.

On the 14th of October, Congress made a declaration and adopted resolutions relative to the rights and grievances of the colonies. It was unanimously resolved "that the respective colonies are entitled to *the common law of England*, and more especially to *the great and inestimable privilege of being tried by their peers of the vicinage*, according to the course of that law;" "that they were entitled to the benefit of such statutes as existed at the time of their colonization, and which they have, by experience, respectively found to be applicable to their several and local circumstances;" and that their ancestors, at the time of their immigration, were "entitled to all the rights, liberties, and immunities of free and natural-born subjects within the realms of England."

Previously to this date, resolutions of commercial non-intercourse with Great Britain, until the grievances of America should be redressed, had been adopted, and on the 20th of October, a formal agreement for this purpose was entered into by Congress. At different times afterwards letters were sent to the Canadian colonies, inviting their coöperation; and an address to the people of Great Britain was published, setting forth the grievances and justifying the conduct of the people of the colonies; after which and other unimportant matters, Congress adjourned on the 22d of October, to meet again at Philadelphia on the 10th of May, 1775.

On the appointed day Congress reassembled, and on the 13th Lyman Hall was admitted as a delegate from the parish of St. John's, in the colony of Georgia; but not considering himself as the representative of that colony, he declined voting, except on occasions when Congress did not vote by colonies. Non-intercourse with colonies not represented in Congress was resolved upon, including the colony of Georgia, except the parish of St. John's, represented by Mr. Hall.

On the 26th of May, it was determined "that the colonies be put immediately into a state of defence; that a fresh petition to the king, with a view to reconcile differences, be prepared; and that a letter to the people of Canada be reported." This letter, which was approved the day following, and ordered to be signed by the President, solicits the friendship of the Canadians, calls upon them to assert their rights, and exhorts them against hostilities.

On the 9th of June, in consequence of a letter from Massachusetts Bay, which had been previously under consideration, Congress resolved that the governor and lieutenant-governor of that colony were to be considered as absent and their offices vacant; and it was recommended to the Provincial Convention to write letters to the inhabitants of the several places which were entitled to representation in Assembly, requesting them to choose representatives; and that the Assembly, when chosen, should elect councillors; and that such Assembly or Council should exercise the powers of government until a governor of his majesty's appointment would consent to govern the colony according to its charter. This decision of Congress, it will be observed, was exactly in accordance with the limitation of rebellion in Magna Charta, to the continuance of wrong on the king's part. It did not assume the extreme position of the Bill of Rights, that the absence of the sovereign or his representative vacates and abdicates his right of sovereignty.

The most important step was now taken, by the organization of an army under Washington, and Congress at the same time resolved that they would "maintain, assist, and adhere to George Washington, with their lives and fortunes, in the same cause." This step was followed by the emission of bills of credit to the amount of two millions of dollars, for the redemption of which the credit of the twelve confederated colonies was pledged. From this time to the close of the session various acts occupied the attention of Congress. A petition to the king; another address to the British people, invoking sympathy and forbearance; a letter of thanks for sympathy, addressed to the corporation of the city of London; a like address of thanks to the Assembly of Jamaica; a further issue of bills of credit; the appointment of Benjamin Franklin as postmaster-general; and an address to the people of Ireland—all indicate a spirit of conciliation, moderation, and determination worthy of their cause. Two more important circumstances indicate a growing feeling of union among them, and their sense of the increased strength it imparted. On the 20th of July, Congress was informed by a letter from the convention of Georgia that that colony had acceded to the general association, and appointed delegates to attend the Congress. On the 31st, Congress declared a resolution of the British House of Commons, commonly called Lord North's motion, inadmissible as the basis of reconciliation. This resolution proposed, under certain restrictions, to transfer the right of taxing the colonies to the colonial assemblies; and it was rejected, among other reasons, because, in the opinion of Congress it imported only a suspension of the mode, and not a renunciation, of the pretended right to tax the colonies.

On the 1st of August, Congress adjourned to the 5th of September, 1775, and on their reassembling, the delegates from Georgia produced their credentials and took their seats. Its principal acts tending to complete independence of the mother country were as follows: On the 13th of October, Congress ordered two armed vessels to be fitted out. On the 3d of November it was resolved to recommend to the Provincial Council of New Hampshire, which had applied for advice, to call a full and free representation of the people, and to establish such a form of government as would best promote the happiness of the people, &c., during the dispute between Great Britain and the colonies. A similar resolution was entered into in relation to South Carolina. On the 20th of November seizures and captures were authorized under commissions to be granted by Congress, together with the condemnation of British vessels employed against the colonies. On the 2d of December an exchange of prisoners was declared proper. On the 4th of December a proclamation by Lord Dunmore called forth a recommendation to Virginia similar to that formerly made to New Hampshire and South Carolina. On the 6th of December a determination was expressed to retaliate for any undue severities inflicted by the British on persons favoring, aiding, or abetting the cause of the colonies. On the 13th of December a report was sanctioned for fitting out a naval armament of thirteen ships, of which five were to be of thirty-two guns each. On the 17th of February a standing committee of five was appointed for superintending the treasury. On the 27th of February the middle and southern colonies were divided into two military departments. On the 9th of March it was resolved *that no oath by way of test should be exacted of the inhabitants of the colonies by military officers.* On the 23d of March privateering was authorized against the enemies of the United Colonies.

On the 10th of May it was resolved to recommend to the respective assemblies and conventions of the United Colonies, where no government sufficient to the exigencies of their affairs had been established, to adopt such governments as should, in the opinion of the representatives of the people, best conduce to the happiness and safety of their constituents in particular and of America in general. A preamble to this resolution, agreed to on the 15th of May, stated the intention to be totally to suppress the exercise of every kind of authority under the British crown. This resolution was in effect a declaration of independence, only to be consummated by the great measure now to be narrated.

"In Congress, Friday, June 7th, 1776," says Mr. Jefferson, "the delegates from Virginia moved, in obedience to instructions from their constituents, that the Congress should declare that these United Colonies are, and of right ought to be, free and independent States; that they are absolved from all allegiance to the British crown; that all political connection between them and the state of Great Britain is, and ought to be, totally dissolved; and that measures should be immediately taken for procuring the assistance of foreign powers, and a confederation formed to bind the colonies more closely together." The resolutions were debated on Saturday, the 8th, and Monday, the 10th, when able arguments for and against their adoption were presented. Omitting references to considerations of mere expediency, the points of constitutional interest in this discussion, as preserved by Mr. Jefferson, may be compared as follows. It was argued:

Against the resolutions, by Wilson, Robert R. Livingston, E. Rutledge, and others:

That though they were friends to

In favor of the resolutions, by J. Adams, Lee, Wythe, and others:

That no gentleman had argued

the measures themselves, and saw the impossibility that we should ever again be united with Great Britain, yet they were against adopting them at this time:

That the conduct we had formerly observed was wise and proper now, of deferring to take any capital step till the voice of *the people* drove us into it:

That they were our power, and without them our declarations could not be carried into effect:

against the policy or the right of separation from Britain, nor had supposed it possible we should ever renew our connection; that they had only opposed its being now declared:

That the question was not whether, by a declaration of independence, we should *make* ourselves what we are not; but whether we should *declare a fact* which already exists:

That as to the people or Parliament of England, we had always been independent of them, their restraints on our trade deriving efficacy from our acquiescence only, and not from any rights they possessed of imposing them; and that so far our connection had been federal only, and *was now dissolved by the commencement of hostilities:*

That as to the king, we had been bound to him by allegiance, but that this bond *was now dissolved by his consent to the late act of Parliament*, by which he declares us out of his protection, *and by his levying war on us*—a fact which had long ago proved us out of his protection, it being a certain position in law, that allegiance and protection are reciprocal, the one ceasing when the other is withdrawn:

That James II. never declared the people of England out of his protection; yet his actions proved it, and the Parliament *declared* it:

No delegates, then, can be denied, or ever want, a power of *declaring an existent* truth.

That the people of the middle colonies (Maryland, Delaware, Pennsylvania, the Jerseys, and New York) were not yet ripe for bidding adieu to British connection, but that they were fast ripening, and, in a short time, would join in the voice of America.

That the delegates from the Delaware Counties having declared their constituents ready to join, there are only two colonies, Pennsylvania and Maryland, whose delegates are absolutely tied up; and that these had, by their instructions, only reserved a right

That the resolution entered by this house on the 15th of May, for suppressing the exercise of all powers derived from the crown, had shown, by the ferment into which it had thrown these middle colonies, that they had not yet accommodated their minds to a separation from the mother country :

That some of them had expressly forbidden their delegates to consent to such a declaration, and others had given no instructions, and consequently no powers to give such consent:

That if the delegates of any par-

of confirming or rejecting the measure:

That the instructions from Pennsylvania might be accounted for from the time in which they were drawn, near a twelvemonth ago, since which the face of affairs has totally changed:

That within that time it had become apparent that Britain was determined to accept nothing less than a *carte blanche*, and that the king's answer to the lord mayor, aldermen, and common council of London, which had come to hand four days ago, must have satisfied every one of this point:

That the people wait for us to lead the way; that *they* are in favor of the measure, though the instructions given by some of their *representatives* are not:

That the voice of the representatives is not always consonant with the voice of the people, and that this is remarkably the case in these middle colonies.

That the effect of the resolution of the 15th of May had proved this; which, raising the murmurs of some in the colonies of Pennsylvania and Maryland, called forth the opposing voice of the freer part of the people, and proved them to be the majority even in these colonies:

That the backwardness of these two colonies might be ascribed, partly to the influence of proprietary power and connections, and partly to their having not yet been attacked by the enemy:

That these causes were not likely to be soon removed, as there seemed no probability that the enemy would make either of these the seat of this summer's war:

That it would be vain to wait ei-

ticular colony had no power to declare such colony independent, certain they were, the others could not declare it for them; the colonies being as yet perfectly independent of each other:

ther weeks or months for perfect unanimity, since it was impossible that all men should ever become of one sentiment on any question:

That the conduct of some colonies, from the beginning of this contest, had given reason to suspect it was their settled policy to keep in the rear of the confederacy, that their particular prospect might be better, even in the worst event:

That, therefore, it was necessary for those colonies who had thrown themselves forward, and hazarded all from the beginning, to come forward now also, and put all again to their own hazard:

That if such a declaration should now be agreed to, these delegates must retire, and possibly their colonies might secede from the Union:

That the history of the Dutch Revolution, of whom only three states confederated at first, proved that a secession of some colonies would not be so dangerous as some apprehended:

That it was prudent to fix among ourselves the terms on which we would form alliance, before we declared we would form one at all events.

That it would be idle to lose time in settling the terms of alliance, till we had first determined we would enter into alliance.

In the course of this debate it appeared, says Jefferson, "that the colonies of New York, New Jersey, Pennsylvania, Delaware, Maryland, and South Carolina were not yet matured for falling from the parent stem, but that they were fast advancing to that state;" and it was therefore deemed prudent to postpone the final decision to the 1st of July. In the mean time, however, a committee was appointed to draft a declaration to the effect "that the United Colonies are, and of right ought to be, free and independent States; that they are absolved from all allegiance to the British crown; and that all political connection between them and the state of Great Britain is, and ought to be, totally dissolved." The committee consisted of Jefferson, J. Adams, Franklin, Sherman, and R. R. Livingston. Next day, the 11th of June, a resolution was adopted to appoint a committee to prepare and digest a form of confederation to be entered into between the colonies, and another committee to prepare a plan of treaties to be proposed to foreign powers.

On the 25th of June, a declaration of the deputies of Pennsylvania, in their provincial conference assembled, expressing their willingness to concur in a vote declaring the United Colonies free and independent States, was laid before Congress. On the 28th of June, the committee appointed to draft a declaration of independence brought it in, and it was ordered to lie on the table. On Monday the 1st of July, a resolution of the convention of Maryland, passed on the 28th of June, authorizing the deputies of that colony to concur in declaring the United Colonies free and independent States, was laid before Congress and read. On the same day the house "resolved itself into a committee of the whole and resumed the consideration of the original motion made by the delegates of Virginia, which, being again debated through the day, was carried in the affirmative by the votes of New Hampshire, Connecticut, Massachusetts, Rhode Island, New Jersey, Maryland, Virginia, North Carolina, and Georgia. South Carolina and Pennsylvania voted against it. Delaware had but two members present, and they were divided. The delegates from New York declared they were for it themselves, and were assured their constituents were for it; but that their instructions having been drawn near a twelvemonth before, when reconciliation was still the general object, they were enjoined by them to do nothing which should impede that object. They, therefore, thought themselves not justifiable in voting on either side, and asked leave to withdraw from the question; which was given them. The committee rose and reported their resolution to the house. Mr. Edward Rutledge, of South Carolina, then requested the determination might be put off to the next day, as he believed his colleagues, though they disapproved of the resolution, would then join in it for the sake of unanimity. The ultimate question, whether the house would agree to the resolution of the committee, was accordingly postponed to the next day, when it was again moved, and South Carolina concurred in voting for it. In the mean time, a third member had come post from the Delaware Counties, and turned the vote of that colony in favor of the resolution. Members of a different sentiment attended that morning from Pennsylvania also: her vote was changed, so that the whole twelve colonies, who were authorized to vote at all, gave their voices for it; and within a few days (July 9) the convention of New York approved of it, and thus supplied the void occasioned by the withdrawing of her delegates from the vote.

" Congress proceeded, the same day, to consider the Declaration of Independence, which had been reported, and laid on the table the Friday preceding, and on Monday referred to a committee of the whole. The pusillanimous idea that we had friends in England worth keeping terms with still haunted the minds of many. For this reason passages which conveyed censures on the people of England were struck out, lest they should give them offence. The clause, too, reprobating the enslaving the inhabitants of Africa, was struck out in complaisance to South Carolina and Georgia, who had never attempted to restrain the importation of slaves, and who, on the contrary, still wished to continue it. Our Northren brethren also, I believe, felt a little tender under those censures; for though their people had very few slaves themselves, yet they had been pretty considerable carriers of them to others. The debates, having taken up the greater part of the 2d, 3d, and 4th days of July, were, on the evening of the last, closed; the Declaration was reported by the committee, agreed to by the house, and signed by every member present, except Mr. Dickinson." (*Writings of Jefferson*, i. p. 14.) It was thereupon resolved " that copies of this Declaration be sent to the several assembles, conventions, and committees or councils of safety, and to the several commanding officers of the Continental troops, that it may be proclaimed in each of the United States, and at the head of the army."

If we examine the matter of this venerable constitutional document, we discover in it no pretensions to originality or novelty. The doctrine of the natural equality of men; the inalienability of certain human rights; the obligation of governments to secure them; the necessity of the consent of the governed to the validity of governments; and the right of the people to alter or abolish governments which become destructive of their proper ends, are all derived from Locke's treatise on government. The proposition that the king had " abdicated government here by declaring us out of his protection and making war against us," is a simple application of the theory of the feudal law, which presumed that the allegiance of the vassal was always conditional on the protection of the lord. These are the only general propositions of the declaration. The form of its particular accusations of the English sovereign will be readily perceived by those who have attentively observed the clauses of the Petition of Right and of the Bill of Rights, to have been borrowed from those documents. The writer of the Declaration had but an old tale to repeat. The story of the colonies was the old story of usurpation and resistance told in the history of every people which has ever aimed at the achievement of a system of free government. He made no attempt to make it striking by exaggeration or by introducing new features. Setting out with a few general propositions—which he modestly describes as "self-evident truths," but which had never, not even in Locke, been rendered evident but by a labored demonstration, till the wonderful simplicity of their enunciation in the Declaration *made* them axiomatic—he proceeds to tell in language the most simple and direct the tyrannous usurpations of the sovereign, the forbearance of the people, and their final and irrevocable judgment that they were absolved from his allegiance; appealing to the Supreme Judge of the world to attest the righteousness of their cause and the rectitude of their intentions. In the *matter* of the Declaration of Independence there is no new principle for the profound student; but its *manner* is so exquisitely fitted to the subject, so striking in its plain, manly directness, and so touching from the total want of affectation in its style, that it persuades at once the reason and the heart as no display of ostentatious rhetoric or labored argument could possibly persuade. Never was such a tale so well told.

As to its *effect*, the Declaration of Independence was in the strictest sense a *declaration*. It wrought no change in the political status of the States. It simply declared that the usurpations of the sovereign had already brought about a change, by which, from being colonies of England, they had become free and independent States. It did not make them free. Their ancestors, the original colonists, were free-born Englishmen, and had transmitted their rights and liberties undiminished to their children. Magna Charta had ever been the fundamental law in the colonies; and their code was always the equitable code of English common law. The Revolution, therefore, was not undertaken to obtain, but to maintain their freedom :—not because they were not freemen, but because a tyrannous attempt was made to make them slaves. When they became independent they were no more free than they and their fathers had always been. Magna Charta and the English common laws were still theirs, as they are still ours; for, having been the fundamental law in every colony, they still remained supreme when the colonies became States; and never yet having been abrogated, they are still the fundamental law in almost every American State. The Declaration, then, neither made the States free, nor condescended to prove their right to freedom. It simply declared the fact. In like manner, the Declaration did not make them independent. It proclaimed that they were already independent. Their sovereign, by the abuse of a sovereignty lawfully acquired, had given them the right of rebellion and revolution against him; so that they were now justified in rejecting his sovereignty and in achieving their independence by force of arms. But it is not the right to achieve independence that is asserted by the Declaration. It is the fact of actual existing independence. And this assertion was based both on law and on fact. On law, because the king of England had declared them "out of his protection," and as the object of government is protection, his renunciation of the duties was an abdication of the right of sovereignty. On fact, because the royal authority had ceased to exist *de facto* in the colonies, and was sustained only within the lines and posts of his invading army. The Declaration, however, rests its assertion of the independence of the States only on the ground of right under the law of nature and of nations. A government, however legitimate in its authority and righteous in its acts, *might* have been temporarily overthrown by a turbulent people, and the colonial governments might in this way have been independent *de facto* though not *de jure*. The declaration of the independence of the States is therefore wisely made, not on the ground that they had been apparently successful in rebellion against their sovereign, but that their sovereign had forfeited his sovereignty by a repudiation of its obligations, and, by thus leaving them without a sovereign, had forced them, without any act of theirs, into a position of complete independence. The whole legal effect, then, of the Declaration of Independence was to proclaim to the world the fact—and the cause which had produced the fact—that "these United Colonies were and of right ought to be, free and independent States."

The true grandeur of the Declaration is the courage which dared to assume so bold a position, in defiance of so mighty an empire as that of England. That thirteen petty colonies, scattered over half a continent, and with an average population of less than 230,000 inhabitants, should exact the last letter of the bond of civilized society from an empire on whose victorious arms the sun shines through his whole diurnal revolution, was an act whose character could only be discriminated after the event as one of matchless folly or of matchless heroism. Measured by ordinary rules, it was in the last degree rash and imprudent; but the colonists were not guided by those ordinary rules which measure everything by circumstances. They were guided by the rules of heroes, measuring their difficulties by the greatness of their own souls. It is this heroic magnanimity, nowhere expressed but everywhere apparent in the Declaration of Independence, that has made it for all coming time the model and the hope of struggling and oppressed mankind.

IN CONGRESS, *July 4th*, 1776.

THE UNANIMOUS DECLARATION OF THE THIRTEEN UNITED STATES OF AMERICA.

When, in the course of human events, it becomes necessary for one people to dissolve the political bands which have connected them with another, and to assume, among the powers of the earth, the separate and equal station to which the laws of nature and of nature's God entitle them, a decent respect to the opinions of mankind requires that they should declare the causes which impel them to the separation.

We hold these truths to be self-evident, that all men are created equal; that they are endowed by their Creator with certain unalienable rights; that among these, are life, liberty, and the pursuit of happiness. That, to secure these rights, governments are instituted among men, deriving their just powers from the consent of the governed; that, whenever any form of government becomes destructive of these ends, it is the right of the people to alter or to abolish it, and to institute a new government, laying its foundation on such principles, and organizing its powers in such form, as to them shall seem most likely to effect their safety and happiness. Prudence, indeed, will dictate that governments long established, should not be changed for light and transient causes; and, accordingly, all experience hath shown, that mankind are more disposed to suffer, while evils are sufferable, than to right themselves by abolishing the forms to which they are accustomed. But, when a long train of abuses and usurpations, pursuing invariably the same object, evinces a design to reduce them under absolute despotism, it is their right, it is their duty, to throw off such government, and to provide new guards for their future security. Such has been the patient sufferance of these colonies, and such is now the necessity which constrains them to alter their former systems of government. The history of the present king of Great Britain is a history of repeated injuries and usurpations, all having, in direct object, the establishment of an absolute tyranny over these States. To prove this, let facts be submitted to a candid world:

He has refused his assent to laws the most wholesome and necessary for the public good.

He has forbidden his Governors to pass laws of immediate and pressing importance, unless suspended in their operation till his assent should be obtained; and, when so suspended, he has utterly neglected to attend to them.

He has refused to pass other laws for the accommodation of large districts of people, unless those people would relinquish the right of representation in the legislature; a right inestimable to them, and formidable to tyrants only.

He has called together legislative bodies at places unusual, uncomfortable, and distant from the depository of their public records, for the sole purpose of fatiguing them into compliance with his measures.

He has dissolved representative houses repeatedly, for opposing, with manly firmness, his invasions on the rights of the people.

He has refused, for a long time after such dissolutions, to cause others to be elected; whereby the legislative powers, incapable of annihilation, have returned to the people at large for their exercise; the State remaining, in the mean time, exposed to all the danger of invasion from without, and convulsions within.

He has endeavored to prevent the population of these States; for that purpose, obstructing the laws for naturalization of foreigners; refusing to pass others to encourage their migration hither, and raising the conditions of new appropriations of lands.

He has obstructed the administration of justice, by refusing his assent to laws for establishing judiciary powers.

He has made judges dependent on his will alone, for the tenure of their offices, and the amount and payment of their salaries.

He has erected a multitude of new offices, and sent hither swarms of officers to harass our people, and eat out their substance.

He has kept among us, in times of peace, standing armies, without the consent of our legislature.

He has affected to render the military independent of, and superior to, the civil power.

He has combined, with others, to subject us to a jurisdiction foreign to our constitution, and unacknowledged by our laws; giving his assent to their acts of pretended legislation:

For quartering large bodies of armed troops among us:

For protecting them, by a mock trial, from punishment, for any murders which they should commit on the inhabitants of these States:

For cutting off our trade with all parts of the world:

For imposing taxes on us without our consent:

For depriving us, in many cases, of the benefits of trial by jury:

For transporting us beyond seas to be tried for pretended offences:

For abolishing the free system of English laws in a neighboring province, establishing therein an arbitrary government, and enlarging its boundaries, so as to render it at once an example and fit instrument for introducing the same absolute rule into these colonies:

For taking away our charters, abolishing our most valuable laws, and altering, fundamentally, the powers of our governments:

For suspending our own legislatures, and declaring themselves invested with power to legislate for us in all cases whatsoever.

He has abdicated government here, by declaring us out of his protection, and waging war against us.

He has plundered our seas, ravaged our coasts, burnt our towns, and destroyed the lives of our people.

He is, at this time, transporting large armies of foreign mercenaries to complete the works of death, desolation, and tyranny, already begun, with circumstances of cruelty and perfidy scarcely paralleled in the most barbarous ages, and totally unworthy the head of a civilized nation.

He has constrained our fellow citizens, taken captive on the high seas, to bear arms against their country, to become the executioners of their friends and brethren, or to fall themselves by their hands.

He has excited domestic insurrections amongst us, and has endeavored to bring on the inhabitants of our frontiers, the merciless Indian savages, whose known rule of warfare is an undistinguished destruction, of all ages, sexes, and conditions.

In every stage of these oppressions, we have petitioned for redress, in the most humble terms; our repeated petitions have been answered only by repeated injury. A prince, whose character is thus marked by every act which may define a tyrant, is unfit to be the ruler of a free people.

Nor have we been wanting in attention to our British brethren. We have warned them, from time to time, of attempts made by their legislature to extend an unwarrantable jurisdiction over us. We have reminded them of the circumstances of our emigration and settlement here. We have appealed to their native justice and magnanimity, and we have conjured them, by the ties of our common kindred, to disavow these usurpations, which would inevitably interrupt our connections and correspondence. They, too, have been deaf to the voice of justice and consanguinity. We must, therefore, acquiesce in the necessity, which denounces our separation, and hold them, as we hold the rest of mankind, enemies in war, in peace, friends.

We, therefore, the representatives of the UNITED STATES OF AMERICA, in GENERAL CONGRESS assembled, appealing to the Supreme Judge of the World for the rectitude of our intentions, do, in the name, and by the authority of the good people of these colonies, solemnly publish and declare, That these United Colonies are, and of right ought to be, **Free and Independent States**; that they are absolved from all allegiance to the British crown, and that all political connexion between them and the state of Great Britain, is, and ought to be, totally dissolved; and that, as *FREE AND INDEPENDENT STATES*, they have full power to levy war, conclude peace, contract alliances, establish commerce, and to do all other acts and things which INDEPENDENT STATES may of right do. And, for the support of this declaration, with a firm reliance on the protection of **DIVINE**

PROVIDENCE, we mutually pledge to each other, our lives, our fortunes, and our sacred honor.

The foregoing declaration was, by order of Congress, engrossed, and signed by the following members:

JOHN HANCOCK.

New Hampshire.
JOSIAH BARTLETT,
WILLIAM WHIPPLE,
MATTHEW THORNTON.

Rhode Island.
STEPHEN HOPKINS,
WILLIAM ELLERY.

Connecticut.
ROGER SHERMAN,
SAMUEL HUNTINGTON,
WILLIAM WILLIAMS,
OLIVER WOLCOTT.

New York.
WILLIAM FLOYD,
PHILIP LIVINGSTON,
FRANCIS LEWIS,
LEWIS MORRIS.

New Jersey.
RICHARD STOCKTON,
JOHN WITHERSPOON,
FRANCIS HOPKINSON,
JOHN HART,
ABRAHAM CLARK.

Pennsylvania.
ROBERT MORRIS,
BENJAMIN RUSH,
BENJAMIN FRANKLIN,
JOHN MORTON,
GEORGE CLYMER,
JAMES SMITH,
GEORGE TAYLOR,
JAMES WILSON,
GEORGE ROSS.

Massachusetts Bay.
SAMUEL ADAMS,
JOHN ADAMS,
ROBERT TREAT PAINE,
ELBRIDGE GERRY.

Delaware.
CÆSAR RODNEY,
GEORGE READ,
THOMAS M'KEAN.

Maryland.
SAMUEL CHASE,
WILLIAM PACA,
THOMAS STONE,
CHARLES CARROLL, of Carrollton

Virginia.
GEORGE WYTHE,
RICHARD HENRY LEE,
THOMAS JEFFERSON,
BENJAMIN HARRISON,
THOMAS NELSON, jun.
FRANCIS LIGHTFOOT LEE,
CARTER BRAXTON.

North Carolina.
WILLIAM HOOPER,
JOSEPH HEWES,
JOHN PENN.

South Carolina.
EDWARD RUTLEDGE,
THOMAS HEYWARD, jun.
THOMAS LYNCH, jun.
ARTHUR MIDDLETON.

Georgia.
BUTTON GWINNETT,
LYMAN HALL,
GEORGE WALTON.

Resolved, That copies of the Declaration be sent to the several assemblies, conventions, and committees, or councils of safety, and to the several commanding officers of the continental troops; that it be proclaimed in each of the United States, and at the head of the army.

CHAPTER XVI.

CONFEDERATION.

COMMITTEE ON CONFEDERATION APPOINTED BEFORE THE DECLARATION WAS ADOPTED —ITS REPORT—DEBATE ON THE PLAN OF CONFEDERATION—PROPORTION OF TAXATION—REMARKS OF MR. CHASE—JOHN ADAMS—MR. HARRISON—MR. PAYNE—DR. WITHERSPOON—DEBATE ON STATE VOTES IN CONGRESS—REMARKS OF MR. CHASE—DR. FRANKLIN—DR. WITHERSPOON—JOHN ADAMS—MR. HOPKINS—MR. WILSON—ADOPTION OF THE CONFEDERATION—ITS VALUE.

While the Declaration of Independence was still under the consideration of Congress, certain necessary measures were taken towards the forming of a plan of confederation among the colonies. On the 11th of June 1776, it was resolved that a committee should be appointed to propose and digest a form of confederation. On the following day, it was resolved that the committee should consist of a member from each colony, and it was appointed accordingly.

On the 12th of July, eight days after the adoption of the Declaration of Independence, the committee appointed to draw Articles of Confederation made their report, and the subject was from time to time debated in a committee of the whole, until the 15th of November 1777, when a copy of the original draft, with a few verbal amendments only, was by Congress ordered to be sent to the legislatures of all the United States to be by them considered, in order that if it should meet their approbation they might authorize their delegates to ratify the same in Congress. On the 17th of November a circular letter was approved and ordered to be sent to the several States, with copies of the Confederation; and on the 29th a committee was appointed to procure a translation of it into French, and to report an address to the inhabitants of Canada &c. Thus the plan of Confederation passed for the present from the hands of Congress to the States, with whom alone rested its final acceptance or rejection.

In Congress, as we learn from the valuable notes of Mr. Jefferson, the discussion turned chiefly on those articles which determined the proportion, or quota of money, which each State should furnish to the common treasury, and the manner of voting in Congress. The first of these articles was, in the original draft, expressed in these words.

"Art. XI. All charges of war, and all other expenses that shall be incurred for the common defence, or general welfare, and allowed by the United States assembled, shall be defrayed out of a common treasury, which shall be supplied by the several colonies in proportion to the number of inhabitants of every age, sex, and quality, except Indians not paying taxes, in each colony—a true amount of which, distinguishing the white inhabitants, shall be triennially taken and transmitted to the Assembly of the United States."

Mr. Chase moved that the quotas should be fixed, not by the number of the inhabitants of every condition, but by that of the "white inhabitants." He admitted that taxation should always be in proportion to property; that this was, in theory, the true rule; but that, from a variety of difficulties, it was a rule which could never be adopted in practice. The value of the property in every State could never be estimated justly and equally. Some other measures for the wealth of the state must, therefore, be devised, some standard referred to, which would be more simple. He considered the number of inhabitants a tolerably good criterion of property, and that this might always be obtained. He therefore thought it the best mode that we could adopt, with one exception only: he observed that negroes are property, and, as such, cannot be distinguished from the lands or personalities held in those States where there are few slaves; that the surplus of profit which a Northern farmer is able to lay by, he invests in cattle, horses &c., whereas a Southern farmer lays out the same surplus in slaves. There is no more reason, therefore, for taxing the Southern States on the farmer's head, and on his slave's head, than the Northern ones on their farmers' heads and the heads of their cattle; that the method proposed would, therefore, tax the Southern States on their numbers and their wealth conjunctly, while the Northern would be taxed on numbers only; that negroes, in fact, should not be considered as members of the state more than cattle, and that they have no more interest in it.

Mr. John Adams observed, that the numbers of people are taken by this article, as an index of the wealth of the State, and not as subjects of taxation; that, as to this matter, it was of no consequence by what name you called your people, whether by that of *freemen* or of *slaves*; that in some countries the laboring poor are called *freemen*, in others they were called *slaves*; but that the difference as to the state was imaginary only. What matters it whether a landlord, employing ten laborers on his farm, give them annually as much money as will buy them the necessaries of life, or give them those necessaries at short hand? The ten laborers give as much wealth to the state, increase its exports as much in the one case as the other. Certainly five hundred freemen produce no more profits, no greater surplus for the payment of taxes, than five hundred slaves. Therefore the state in which are the laborers called *freemen*, should be taxed no more than that in which are those called *slaves*. Suppose, by an extraordinary operation of nature or of law, one half of the laborers of a state could, in the course of one night, be transformed into slaves; would the state be made poorer or less able to pay taxes? That the condition of the laboring poor in most countries—that of the fishermen, particularly, of the Northern States—is as abject as that of slaves. It is the number of laborers which produces the surplus for taxation, and numbers, therefore, indiscriminately, are the fair index to wealth; that it is the use of the word "property" here in its application to some of the people of the state which produces the fallacy. How does the Southern farmer procure slaves? Either by importation, or by purchase from his neighbor. If he imports a slave, he adds one to the number of laborers in his country, and proportionally to its profits and ability to pay taxes. If he buys from his neighbor, it is only a transfer of a laborer from one farm to another, which does not change the annual produce of the state, and therefore should not change its tax; that if a Northern farmer works ten laborers on his farm, he can, it is true, invest the surplus of ten men's labor in cattle; but so may the Southern farmer working ten slaves; that a state of one hundred thousand freemen can maintain no more cattle than one of one hundred thousand slaves, therefore they have no more of that kind of property. That a slave may, indeed, from the custom of speech, be more properly called the wealth of his master, than the free laborer might be called the wealth of his employer; but as to the state, both were equally its wealth, and should therefore equally add to the quota of its tax.

Mr. Harrison proposed, as a compromise, that two slaves should be counted as one freeman. He affirmed that slaves did not do as much work as freemen, and doubted if two effected more than one; that this was proved by the price of labor—the hire of a laborer in the Southern colonies being from £8 to £12, while in the Northern it was generally £24.

Mr. Wilson said that if this amendment should take place, the Southern colonies would have all the benefit of slaves, whilst the Northern ones would bear the burden; that slaves increase the profits of a state, which the Southern States mean to take to themselves; that they also increase the burden of defence, which would, of course, fall so much heavier on the Northern; that slaves occupy the places of freemen and eat their food. Dismiss your slaves, and freemen will take their places. That other kinds of property were pretty equally distributed through all the colonies;—there were as many cattle, horses, and sheep in the North as the South, and South as the North; but not so as to slaves;—that experience has shown those colonies have been always able to pay most which have the most inhabitants, whether they be black or white; and the practice of the Southern colonies has always been to make every farmer pay poll taxes upon his laborers, whether they be black or white. He acknowledged that freemen work the most; but they consume the most also. They do not produce a greater surplus for taxation. The slave is neither fed nor clothed so expensively as a freeman. Again, white women are exempted from labor generally, but negro women are not. In this, then, the Southern States had an advantage as the Article now stands. It has sometimes been said that slavery is necessary because the commodities they raise would be too dear for market if cultivated by freemen; but now it is said that the labor of the slave is the dearest.

Mr. Payne urged the original resolutions of Congress, to proportion the quotas of the States to the number of souls.

Dr. Witherspoon was of opinion that the value of land and houses was the best estimate of the wealth of a nation, and that it was practicable to obtain such a valuation. This is the true barometer of wealth. The one now proposed was imperfect in itself, and unequal between the States. It has been objected that negroes eat the food of freemen, and therefore should be taxed ! horses also eat the food of freemen; therefore, they also should be taxed. It had been said, too, that in carrying slaves into the estimate of the taxes the State is to pay we do no more than those States themselves do, who always take slaves into the estimate of the taxes the individual is to pay. But the cases were not parallel. In the Southern colonies slaves pervade the whole colony; but they do not pervade the whole continent. That as to the original resolution of Congress to proportion the quotas according to the souls, it was temporary only, and related to the moneys heretofore omitted; whereas we are now entering into a new compact, and therefore stand on original ground.

The result of this interesting discussion was that on the 1st of August the proposed amendment was rejected, and the original Article adopted by the votes of New Hampshire, Massachusetts Rhode Island, Connecticut, New York, New Jersey, and Pennsylvania, against those of Delaware, Maryland, Virginia, and North and South Carolina. Georgia was divided. The arguments convinced none on either side, as the vote sufficiently proves. The Southern delegates, however, yielded gracefully to the desire of the majority; nor was there much further opposition offered to the Article on the part of the Southern legislators before whom the plan of confederation was afterwards laid for ratification or rejection.

The other article was in these words :—

"Art. XVII. In determining questions each colony shall have one vote."

It was debated on July 30th and 31st, and on the 1st of August.

Mr. Chase observed that this article was more likely to divide the colonies than any other proposed in the draft then under consideration. That the larger colonies had threatened they would not confederate at all if their weight in Congress should not be equal to the numbers of people they added to the Confederacy; while the smaller ones declared against a union if they did not retain an equal vote for the protection of their rights. That it was of the utmost consequence to bring the parties together; as, should we sever from each other, either no foreign power will ally with us at all, or the different States will form different alliances, and thus increase the horrors of those scenes of civil war and bloodshed which in such a state of separation and independence would render us a miserable people. That our importance, our interests, our peace, required that we should confederate, and that mutual sacrifices should be made to effect a compromise of this difficult question. He was of opinion the smaller colonies would lose their rights if they were not, in some instances, allowed an equal vote; and therefore, that a discrimination should take place among the questions which should come before Congress. That the smaller States should be secured in all questions concerning life or liberty, and the greater ones in all respecting property. He therefore proposed that in votes relating to money the voice of each colony should be proportioned to the number of its inhabitants.

Dr. Franklin thought that the votes should be so proportioned in all cases. He took notice that the Delaware counties had bound up their delegates to disagree to this article. He thought it very extraordinary language to be held by any State that they would not confederate with us unless we would let them dispose of our money. Certainly if we vote equally we ought to pay equally; but the smaller States will hardly purchase the privilege at this price. That had he lived in a State where the representation, originally equal, had become unequal by time and accident, he might have submitted rather than disturb government; but that we should be very wrong to set out in this practice when it is in our power to establish what is right. That at the time of the union between England and Scotland, the latter had made the objection which the smaller States now do; but experience had proved that no unfairness had ever been shown them; that their advocates had prognosticated that it would again happen as in times of old that the whale would swallow Jonah; but he thought the prediction reversed in event, and that *Jonah had swallowed the whale;* for the Scotch had, in part, got possession of the government, and gave laws to the English. He reprobated the original agreement of Congress to vote by colonies, and therefore was for their voting in all cases according to the number of taxables.

Dr. WITHERSPOON opposed every alteration of the Article. All men admitted that a confederacy is necessary. Should the idea get abroad that there is likely to be no union among us, it will damp the minds of the people, diminish the glory of our struggle, and lessen its importance; because it will open to our view future prospects of war and dissension among ourselves. If an equal vote be refused, the smaller States will become vassals to the larger; and all experience has shown that the vassals and subjects of free states are the most enslaved. He instanced the helots of Sparta and the provinces of Rome. He observed that foreign powers discovering this blemish, would make it a handle for disengaging the smaller States from so unequal a confederacy. That the colonies should, in fact, be considered as individuals; that as such, in all disputes, they should have an equal vote; and that they are now collected as individuals making a bargain with each other, and of course had a right to vote as individuals. That in the East India Company they voted by persons, and not by their proportions of stock. That the Belgic Confederacy voted by provinces. That in questions of war the smaller States were as much interested as the larger, and therefore should vote equally; and indeed that the larger States were more likely to bring war on the Confederacy in proportion as their frontier was more extensive. He admitted that equality of representation was an excellent principle, but then it must be of things which are coördinate; that is, of things similar and of the same nature; that nothing relating to individuals could ever come before Congress; nothing but what would respect colonies. He distinguished between an *incorporating* and a *federal union.* The union of England and Scotland was an incorporating one; yet Scotland had suffered by that union; for that its inhabitants were drawn from it by the hopes of places and employments; nor was it an instance of equality of representation, because, while Scotland was allowed nearly a *thirteenth* of representation, they were to pay only *one-fortieth* of the land tax. He expressed his views that in the present enlightened state of men's minds we might expect a lasting confederacy, if it was founded on fair principles.

Mr. John Adams advocated the voting in proportion to numbers. He said, that we stand here as the representatives of the people; that in some States the people are many, in others they are few; that therefore their vote here should be proportioned to the numbers from whom it comes. Reason, justice, and equity never had justice enough on the face of the earth to govern the councils of men. It is interest alone which does it, and it is interest alone which can be trusted; that therefore the interests within doors should be the mathematical representatives of the interests without doors.

Besides the fallacy of Mr. Adams' reasoning which assumed that members of the Continental Congress were representatives of the people at large instead of what they actually were, representatives of their respective States, he argued against the individuality of States themselves, and maintained that the object of confederation was to obliterate State lines and distinctions so as to incorporate all under one consolidated government.

He said that the individuality of the colonies is a mere sound. Does the individuality of a colony increase its wealth or numbers? If it does, pay equally. If it does not add weight in the scale of the confederacy, it cannot add to their rights nor weigh in argument. A has £50, B £500, C £1,000 in partnership. Is it just that they should equally dispose of the moneys of the partnership? It has been said we are independent individuals making a bargain together. The question is not what we are now, but what we ought to be when our bargain shall be made. The confederacy is to make us one individual only. It is to form us, like separate pieces of metal, into one common mass. We shall no longer retain our separate individuality, but become a single individual as to all matters submitted to the confederacy. Therefore all reasons, which prove the justice and expediency of equal representation in other assemblies, hold good here. It had been objected that a proportional vote would endanger the smaller States. He answered that an equal vote would endanger the larger. Virginia, Pennsylvania and Massachusetts were the three greater colonies. Consider their distance, their difference of products, of interest, and of manners, and it was apparent they can never have an interest or an inclination to combine for the oppression of the smaller; that the smaller would naturally divide on all questions with the larger; that Rhode Island, from its relation, similarity and intercourse, would generally pursue the same objects with Massachusetts; Jersey, Delaware, and Maryland, with Pennsylvania.

Mr. HOPKINS observed that there were four larger, four smaller and four middle sized colonies. That the four largest would contain more than half the inhabitants of the confederating States, and therefore would govern the others as they should please. That history affords no instance of such a thing as equal representation. The Germanic body vote by states; the Helvetic body does the same; and so does the Belgic Confederacy. That too little is known of the ancient confederations to say what was their practice.

Mr. WILSON went beyond even Mr. Adams in his advocacy of consolidation, maintaining that the colonies, by the mere sending of delegates to Congress had already sacrificed their individuality. As to those matters, he said, which are referred to Congress, we are not so many States; we are one large State. We lay aside our individuality whenever we come here.

The views of Mr. Adams and Mr. Wilson did not meet the approbation of Congress, and the article as it stood was triumphantly adopted.

The draft of the Confederate Constitution was presented, as we have before observed, on the 12th of July, 1776, and debated from time to time until the 15th of November, 1777, when it was approved in Congress and ordered to be transmitted to the States for their consideration. On the 26th of June a form of ratification was adopted and engrossed on parchment for signature by the delegates acting by authority of their respective States. On subsequent examination, however, it was found that only New Hampshire, New York, Virginia, and North Carolina accepted the Articles as they stood, with a proviso on the part of New York that the same should not be binding on it until all the other States in the Union should have ratified them also. Massachusetts,

Rhode Island, Connecticut, New Jersey, Pennsylvania, Maryland, and South Carolina proposed alterations, additions or amendments, which were all considered by Congress, and all rejected. The delegate from Georgia had received no instructions from his constituents, but had no doubt they would ratify the Articles of Confederation without amendment. Delaware and North Carolina, having no delegates present, made no formal report; but the unanimous accession of North Carolina to the confederation had been already signified by her Governor Caswell so early as the 26th of April. On the 9th of July, 1778, the ratification of the Articles of Confederation was signed on the part of their respective States by the delegates from New Hampshire, Massachusetts Bay, Rhode Island and Providence Plantations, Connecticut, New York, Pennsylvania, Virginia and South Carolina, acting under the powers vested in them. The delegates from New Jersey, Delaware, and Maryland informed Congress that they had not been empowered to ratify and sign; North Carolina and Georgia were not represented.

In this critical condition of affairs a letter was addressed to the States which had not authorized their delegates to ratify the confederation, urging them "to conclude the glorious compact which by uniting the wealth, strength, and councils of the whole, might bid defiance to external violence and internal dissensions whilst it secured the public credit at home and abroad." On the 21st of July the ratification was signed by the delegates of North Carolina; and on the 24th by those of Georgia. The delegates of New Jersey, having received their powers, affixed their signatures on the 26th of November following. On the 5th of May, 1779, Mr. Dickinson and Mr. Vandyke signed the Articles of Confederation in behalf of the State of Delaware, Mr. M'Kean having previously signed them on the 12th of February, at which time he had produced a power to that effect. Maryland had instructed her delegates not to agree to the Confederation until an equitable settlement should be made concerning Western lands; but on the 30th of January, 1781, finding that the enemies of the country took advantage of the circumstance to disseminate opinions of an ultimate dissolution of the Union, the Legislature of the State empowered their delegates to ratify and subscribe the Articles;

which was accordingly done on the 1st of March, 1781, and thus the ratification was completed. On the next day Congress assembled under the new powers committed to it by the Articles of Confederation.

Thus, at length, after nearly five years of continual debate and difficulty, was consummated the "Perpetual Union" of the States. It lasted practically two years, and nominally about eight. It did not materially add to the efficiency of government during the war with England; nor did it in any great degree strengthen the bond of union between the States. Its importance, nevertheless, is not to be lightly estimated. Had the colonies achieved their independence with no closer tie between them than the military alliance rendered necessary by a foreign invasion, there is little reason to believe that they would ever after have united. Hence they would have become in peace totally independent; and the usual animosities of petty states would have been likely to embroil them with each other in continual feuds, such as disturbed the petty states of Italy in the middle ages. Neither after nor before the war could the States be induced to renounce their separate individuality or independence; and all movements towards a union were suspected by the smaller States of tending to consolidated power. The confederation, therefore, which demonstrated the possibility of union without consolidation, and showed, however imperfectly, the capacity of the federative principle to meet the exigencies of their situation, was of immense importance to the future of the States. It was in fact a rough draft of the application of the Anglo-Saxon system to the circumstances of the colonies; admitting the necessity of union, but equally asserting separate sovereignty as the only possible or even safe foundation of the union. Its model was, in this view, of inestimable value to the framers of the later Constitution; showing them at once the fundamental principle of a federal republic, and the difficulties to be apprehended in its operation.

Articles of Confederation.

TO ALL TO WHOM THESE PRESENTS SHALL COME,

WE, the undersigned, Delegates of the States affixed to our names, send greeting:

WHEREAS the delegates of the United States of America, in Congress assembled, did, on the fifteenth day of November, in the year of our Lord one thousand seven hundred and seventy-seven, and in the second year of the Independence of America, agree to certain Articles of Confederation and Perpetual Union, between the states of New Hampshire, Massachusetts Bay, Rhode Island and Providence Plantations, Connecticut, New York, New Jersey, Pennsylvania, Delaware, Maryland, Virginia, North Carolina, South Carolina, and Georgia, in the words following, viz.:—

Articles of Confederation and Perpetual Union, between the States of New Hampshire, Massachusetts Bay, Rhode Island and Providence Plantations, Connecticut, New York, New Jersey, Pennsylvania, Delaware, Maryland, Virginia, North Carolina, South Carolina, and Georgia.

ARTICLE. 1. The style of this confederacy shall be "The United States of America."

ART. 2. Each state retains it sovereignty, freedom, and independence, and every power, jurisdiction, and right, which is not by this Confederation expressly delegated to the United States in Congress assembled.

ART. 3. The said states hereby severally enter into a firm league of friendship with each other for their common defence, the security of their liberties, and their mutual and general welfare; binding themselves to assist each other against all force offered to, or attacks made upon, them, or any of them, on account of religion, sovereignty, trade, or any other pretence whatever.

ART. 4. The better to secure and perpetuate mutual friendship and intercourse among the people of the different states in this Union, the free inhabitants of each of these states—paupers, vagabonds, and fugitives from justice, excepted—shall be entitled to all privileges and immunities of free citizens in the several states; and the people of each state shall have free ingress and regress to and from any other state, and shall enjoy therein all the privileges of trade and commerce, subject to the same duties, impositions, and restrictions, as the inhabitants thereof, respectively, provided that such restrictions shall not extend so far as to prevent the removal of property imported into any state from any other state, of which the owner is an inhabitant; provided also, that no imposition, duty, or restriction, shall be laid by any state on the property of the United States, or either of them.

If any person, guilty of, or charged with, treason, felony, or other high misdemeanor, in any state, shall flee from justice, and be found in any of the United States, he shall, upon demand of the governor or executive power of the state from which he fled, be delivered up, and removed to the state having jurisdiction of his offence.

Full faith and credit shall be given, in each of these states, to the records, acts, and judicial proceedings, of the courts and magistrates of every other state.

ART. 5. For the more convenient management of the general interests of the United States, delegates shall be annually appointed in such manner as the legislature of each state shall direct, to meet in Congress on the first Monday in November, in every year, with a power reserved to each state, to recall its delegates, or any of them, at any time within the year, and to send others in their stead for the remainder of the year.

No state shall be represented in Congress by less than two, nor by more than seven members; and no person shall be capable of being a delegate for more than three years in any term of six years; nor shall any person, being a delegate, be capable of holding any office under the United States, for which he, or another for his benefit, receives any salary, fees, or emolument of any kind.

Each state shall maintain its own delegates in a meeting of the states, and while they act as members of the committee of the States.

In determining questions in the United States in Congress assembled, each state shall have one vote.

Freedom of speech and debate in Congress shall not be impeached or questioned in any court or place out of Congress; and the members of Congress shall be protected in their persons from arrests and imprisonments, during the time of their going to and from, and attendance on, Congress, except for treason, felony or breach of the peace.

ART. 6. No state, without the consent of the United States in Congress assembled, shall send any embassy to, or receive any embassy from, or enter into any conference, agreement, alliance, or treaty, with any king, prince, or state; nor shall any person holding any office of profit or trust under the United States, or any of them, accept of any present, emolument, office, or title, of any kind whatever, from any king, prince, or foreign state; nor shall the United States in Congress assembled, or any of them, grant any title of nobility.

No two or more states shall enter into any treaty, confederation, or alliance whatever between them, without the consent of the United States in Congress assembled, specifying accurately the purposes for which the same is to be entered into, and how long it shall continue.

No state shall lay any imposts or duties, which may interfere with any stipulations in treaties entered into, by the United States in Congress assembled, with any king, prince, or state, in pursuance of any treaties already proposed by Congress to the courts of France and Spain.

No vessel of war shall be kept up in time of peace by any state, except such number only as shall be deemed necessary, by the United States in Congress assembled, for the defence of such state, or its trade; nor shall any body of forces be kept up by any state, in time of peace, except such number only as, in the judgment of the United States in Congress assembled, shall be deemed requisite to garrison the forts necessary for the defence of such state; but every state shall always keep up a well-regulated and disciplined militia, sufficiently armed and accoutred, and shall provide, and have constantly ready for use, in public stores, a due number of field-pieces and tents, and a proper quantity of arms, ammunition, and camp equipage.

No state shall engage in any war without the consent of the United States in Congress assembled, unless such state be actually invaded by enemies, or shall have received certain advice of a resolution being formed by some nation of Indians to invade such state, and the danger is so imminent as not to admit of a delay till the United States in Congress assembled can be consulted; nor shall any state grant commissions to any ships or vessels of war, nor letters of marque or reprisal, except it be after a declaration of war by the United States in Congress assembled, and then only against the kingdom or state, and the subjects thereof, against which war has been so declared, and under such regulations as shall be established by the United States in Congress assembled, unless such state be infested by pirates; in which case, vessels of war may be fitted out for that occasion, and kept so long as the danger shall continue, or until the United States in Congress assembled shall determine otherwise.

Art. 7. When land forces are raised by any state for the common defence, all officers of, or under the rank of colonel shall be appointed by the legislature of each state, respectively, by whom such forces shall be raised, or in such manner as such state shall direct; and all vacancies shall be filled up by the state which first made the appointment.

Art. 8. All charges of war, and all other expenses that shall be incurred for the common defence or general welfare, and allowed by the United States in Congress assembled, shall be defrayed out of a common treasury, which shall be supplied by the several States, in proportion to the value of all land, within each state, granted to or surveyed for any person, as such land, and the buildings and improvements thereon, shall be estimated, according to such mode as the United States in Congress assembled shall, from time to time, direct and appoint.

The taxes for paying that proportion shall be laid and levied by the authority and direction of the legislatures of the several states, within the time agreed upon by the United States in Congress assembled.

ART. 9. The United States in Congress assembled shall have the sole and exclusive right and power of determining on peace and war, except in the cases mentioned in the sixth article—of sending and receiving ambassadors—entering into treaties and alliances; provided that no treaty of commerce shall be made whereby the legislative power of the respective states shall be restrained from imposing such imposts and duties on foreigners as their own people are subjected to, or from prohibiting the exportation or importation of any species of goods or commodities whatsoever—of establishing rules for deciding, in all cases, what captures, on land or water, shall be legal, and in what manner prizes taken by land or naval forces in the service of the United States shall be divided or appropriated—of granting letters of marque and reprisal in times of peace—appointing courts for the trial of piracies and felonies committed on the high seas, and establishing courts for receiving and determining finally appeals in all cases of capture; provided that no member of Congress shall be appointed a judge of any of the said courts.

The United States in Congress assembled shall also be the last resort on appeal in all disputes and differences now subsisting or that hereafter may arise, between two or more states, concerning boundary, jurisdiction, or any other cause whatever; which authority shall always be exercised in the manner following: Whenever the legislative or executive authority, or lawful agent, of any state in controversy with another, shall present a petition to Congress, stating the matter in question, and praying for a hearing, notice thereof shall be given by order of Congress to the legislative or executive authority of the other state in controversy, and a day assigned for the appearance of the parties, by their lawful agents,—who shall then be directed to appoint, by joint consent, commissioners or judges to constitute a court for hearing and determining the matter in question; but if they cannot agree, Congress shall name three persons out of each of the United States, and from the list of such persons, each party shall alternately strike out one, the petitioners beginning, until the number shall be reduced to thirteen; and from that number not less than seven nor more than nine names, as Congress shall direct, shall, in the presence of Congress, be drawn out by lot; and the persons whose names shall be so drawn, or any five of them, shall be commissioners or judges, to hear and finally determine the controversy, so always as a major part of the judges, who shall hear the cause, shall agree in the determination; and if either party shall neglect to attend at the day appointed, without showing reasons which Congress shall judge sufficient, or being present shall refuse to strike, the Congress shall proceed to nominate three persons out of each state, and the secretary of Congress shall strike in behalf of such party absent or refusing; and the judgment and sentence of the court, to be appointed in the manner before prescribed, shall be final and conclusive; and if any of the parties shall refuse to submit to the authority of such court, or to appear or defend their claim or cause, the court shall nevertheless proceed to pronounce sentence or judgment, which shall, in like manner, be final and decisive—the judgment or sentence, and other proceedings, being in either case transmitted to Congress, and lodged among the acts of Congress for the security of the parties concerned; provided that every commissioner, before he sits in judgment, shall take an oath, to be administered by one of the judges of the supreme or superior court of the state where the cause shall be tried, "*well and truly to hear and determine the matter in question, according to the best of his judgment, without favor, affection, or hope of reward:*" provided, also, that no state shall be deprived of territory for the benefit of the United States.

All controversies concerning the private right of soil, claimed under different grants of two or more states, whose jurisdiction, as they may respect such lands, and the states which passed such grants, are adjusted, the said grants, or either of them, being at the same time claimed to have originated antecedent to such settlement of jurisdiction, shall, on the petition of either party to the Congress of the United States, be finally determined, as near as may be, in the same manner as is before prescribed for deciding disputes respecting territorial jurisdiction between different states.

The United States in Congress assembled shall also have the

sole and exclusive right and power of regulating the alloy and value of coin struck by their own authority, or by that of the respective states; fixing the standard of weights and measures throughout the United States; regulating the trade and managing all affairs with the Indians not members of any of the states, provided that the legislative right of any state within its own limits be not infringed or violated; establishing and regulating post-offices from one state to another throughout all the United States, and exacting such postage on the papers passing through the same as may be requisite to defray the expenses of the said office; appointing all officers of the land forces in the service of the United States, excepting regimental officers; appointing all the officers of the naval forces, and commissioning all officers whatever in the service of the United States; making rules for the government and regulation of the said land and naval forces, and directing their operations.

The United States in Congress assembled shall have authority to appoint a committee to sit in the recess of Congress, to be denominated "a committee of the states," and to consist of one delegate from each state; and to appoint such other committees and civil officers as may be necessary for managing the general affairs of the United States under their direction—to appoint one of their number to preside, provided that no person be allowed to serve in the office of president more than one year in any term of three years—to ascertain the necessary sums of money to be raised for the service of the United States, and to appropriate and apply the same for defraying the public expenses—to borrow money or emit bills on the credit of the United States, transmitting, every half year, to the respective states, an account of the sums of money so borrowed or emitted—to build and equip a navy—to agree upon the number of land forces, and to make requisitions from each state for its quota, in proportion to the number of white inhabitants in such state; which requisitions shall be binding; and thereupon the legislature of each state shall appoint the regimental officers, raise the men, and clothe, arm, and equip them in a soldier-like manner, at the expense of the United States; and the officers and men so clothed, armed, and equipped, shall march to the place appointed, and within the time agreed on by the United States in Congress assembled: but if the United States in Congress assembled shall, on consideration of circumstances, judge proper that any state should not raise men, or should raise a smaller number than its quota, and that any other state should raise a greater number of men than the quota thereof, such extra number shall be raised, officered, clothed, armed, and equipped, in the same manner as the quota of such state, unless the legislature of such state shall judge that such extra number cannot be safely spared out of the same; in which case they shall raise, officer, clothe, arm, and equip, as many of such extra number as they judge can be safely spared. And the officers and men so clothed, armed, and equipped, shall march to the place appointed, and within the time agreed on by the United States in Congress assembled.

The United States in Congress assembled shall never engage in a war; nor grant letters of marque and reprisal in time of peace; nor enter into any treaties or alliances; nor coin money; nor regulate the value thereof; nor ascertain the sums and expenses necessary for the defence and welfare of the United States, or any of them; nor emit bills; nor borrow money on the credit of the United States; nor appropriate money; nor agree upon the number of vessels of war to be built or purchased, or the number of land or sea forces to be raised; nor appoint a commander-in-chief of the army or navy,—unless nine states assent to the same; nor shall a question on any other point, except for adjourning from day to day, be determined, unless by the votes of a majority of the United States in Congress assembled.

The Congress of the United States shall have power to adjourn to any time within the year, and to any place within the United States, so that no period of adjournment be for a longer duration than the space of six months; and shall publish the journal of their proceedings monthly, except such parts thereof, relating to treaties, alliances, or military operations, as in their judgment require secrecy; and the yeas and nays of the delegates of each state on any question shall be entered on the journal, when it is desired by any delegate; and the delegates of a state, or any of them, at his or their request, shall be furnished with a transcript of the said journal, except such parts as are above excepted, to lay before the legislatures of the several states.

ART. 10. The committee of the states, or any nine of them, shall be authorized to execute, in the recess of Congress, such of the powers of Congress as the United States in Congress assembled, by the consent of nine states, shall, from time to time, think expedient to vest them with; provided that no power be delegated to the said committee, for the exercise of which, by the Articles of Confederation, the voice of nine states in the Congress of the United States assembled is requisite.

ART. 11. Canada, acceding to this Confederation, and joining in the measures of the United States, shall be admitted into, and entitled to, all the advantages of this union; but no other colony shall be admitted into the same unless such admission be agreed to by nine States.

ART. 12. All bills of credit emitted, moneys borrowed, and debts contracted, by or under the authority of Congress, before the assembling of the United States in pursuance of the present Confederation, shall be deemed and considered as a charge against the United States, for payment and satisfaction whereof the said United States, and the public faith, are hereby solemnly pledged.

ART. 13. Every state shall abide by the determination of the United States in Congress assembled, on all questions which, by this Confederation, are submitted to them. And the Articles of this Confederation shall be inviolably observed by every state, and the union shall be perpetual; nor shall any alteration, at any time hereafter, be made in any of them, unless such alteration be agreed to in a Congress of the United States, and be afterwards confirmed by the legislature of every state.

RATIFICATION.

And whereas it has pleased the Great Governor of the world to incline the hearts of the legislatures we respectively represent in Congress, to approve of and to authorize us to ratify the said Articles of Confederation and Perpetual Union: *Know ye*, That we, the undersigned delegates, by virtue of the power and authority to us given for that purpose, do, by these presents, in the name and in behalf of our respective constituents, fully and entirely ratify and confirm each and every of the said Articles of Confederation and Perpetual Union, and all and singular the matters and things therein contained; and we do further solemnly plight and engage the faith of our respective constituents, that they shall abide by the determinations of the United States in Congress assembled, on all questions which, by the said Confederation, are submitted to them; and that the articles thereof shall be inviolably observed by the states we respectively represent; and that the union shall be perpetual.

In witness whereof, we have hereunto set our hands in Congress. Done at Philadelphia, in the state of Pennsylvania, the ninth day of July, in the year of our Lord one thousand seven hundred and seventy eight, and in the third year of the Independence of America.

On the part and behalf of the state of New Hampshire.

Josiah Bartlett, John Wentworth, Jun., Aug. 8. 1778.

On the part and behalf of the state of Massachusetts Bay.

John Hancock, Francis Dana,
Samuel Adams, James Lovell,
Elbridge Gerry, Samuel Holten.

On the part and behalf of the State of Rhode Island and Providence Plantations.

William Ellery, John Collins.
Henry Marchant,

On the part and behalf of the state of Connecticut.

Roger Sherman, Titus Hosmer,
Samuel Huntington, Andrew Adams.
Oliver Wolcott,

On the part and behalf of the state of New York.

Jas. Duane, Wm. Duer,
Fra. Lewis, Gouv. Morris.

On the part and behalf of the state of New Jersey.

Jno. Witherspoon, Nath. Scudder, Nov. 26, 1778.

On the part and behalf of the state of Pennsylvania.

Robert Morris, William Clingan,
Daniel Roberdeau, Joseph Reed, 22d July, 1778.
Jona. Bayard Smith,

On the part and behalf of the state of Delaware.

Thos. M'Kean, Feb. 13, '79, Nicholas Van Dyke,
John Dickinson, May' 5, '79.

On the part and behalf of the state of Maryland.

John Hanson, March 1, '81, Daniel Carroll, do.

On the part and behalf of the state of Virginia.

Richard Henry Lee, Jno. Harvie,
John Banister, Francis Lightfoot Lee.
Thomas Adams,

On the part and behalf of the state of North Carolina.

John Penn, July 21, '78, Corns. Harnett.
Jno. Williams,

On the part and behalf of the state of South Carolina.

Henry Laurens, Richard Hutson,
William Henry Drayton, Thos. Heyward, Jun.
Jno. Mathews,

On the part and behalf of the state of Georgia.

Jno. Walton, July 24, '78, Edw'd Langworthy.
Edw'd Telfair,

CHAPTER XVII.

ADOPTION OF THE CONSTITUTION.

CIRCUMSTANCES UNDER WHICH IT WAS ADOPTED—CONSTITUTIONAL POSITION OF THE COLONIES AFTER THE DECLARATION—THAT OF LIMITED OR CONSTITUTIONAL GOVERNMENTS—INDEPENDENT OF EACH OTHER—YET UNITED—DISTINCTION BETWEEN A CONSOLIDATED AND A FEDERATIVE UNION—WEAKNESS OF THE CONFEDERATION—FINANCIAL DIFFICULTIES—DIFFICULTY IN MAKING TREATIES OF FOREIGN ALLIANCE—PROPOSITION IN CONGRESS—CALL OF VIRGINIA—CONVENTION AT ANNAPOLIS—ITS REPORT TO THE LEGISLATURES—CONGRESS CALLS UPON THE STATES TO SEND DELEGATES TO A CONVENTION—IMPORTANCE OF THE PHRASEOLOGY OF THE CALL—ASSEMBLING OF THE CONVENTION AT PHILADELPHIA—PARTIES IN THE CONVENTION—THE MONARCHICAL PARTY—THE LARGE STATE PARTY—THE STATE RIGHTS PARTY—PROPOSITIONS OF MR. RANDOLPH—OF MR. CHARLES PINCKNEY—OF MR. PATTERSON—OF COLONEL HAMILTON—TWENTY-THREE RESOLUTIONS OF CONVENTION WITH DATES OF THEIR ADOPTION—DEBATES ON THE THIRD AND FOURTH RESOLUTIONS FROM LUTHER MARTIN—EQUAL DIVISION OF THE CONVENTION ON THE SUBJECT OF REPRESENTATION IN CONGRESS—CONFERENCE—COMPROMISE—DRAFT OF CONSTITUTION REPORTED—OMISSION OF THE WORD *NATIONAL*—THE REASON—THE REVISED DRAFT—OMISSION OF THE NAMES OF STATES IN THE PREAMBLE—THE REASON—SECESSION OF STATES FROM THE CONFEDERATION—UNANIMOUS ADOPTION OF THE CONSTITUTION IN CONVENTION—ITS RECEPTION BY CONGRESS—RATIFICATIONS BY THE STATES—ACT FOR PUTTING IT IN OPERATION—WASHINGTON ELECTED PRESIDENT—IMPERFECTION OF THE CONSTITUTION AS ADOPTED—DECLARATIONS MADE AND AMENDMENTS OFFERED BY THE STATES—MASSACHUSETTS—NEW HAMPSHIRE—SOUTH CAROLINA—VIRGINIA—NEW YORK—RHODE ISLAND—TWELVE AMENDMENTS PROPOSED BY CONGRESS—TEN OF THEM ACCEPTED BY THE STATES—VALUE OF THE AMENDMENTS—THE ELEVENTH AMENDMENT—THE TWELFTH—CONCLUDING OBSERVATIONS.

As we are now about to enter on the history of the adoption of the Constitution, it is well that we should bear in mind the circumstances under which it was adopted.

From the date of the Declaration of Independence, when the

final separation of the colonies from the mother country was proclaimed to the world, each individual colony enjoyed complete self-government. Whatever portion of the sovereign authority in these communities may have been rightfully or wrongfully exercised by Britain, was at once transferred to the communities themselves. Yet not in such a way as to set the liberty or rights of the individual citizen at the mercy of a mere majority of his fellow citizens. The fundamental law of the colonies was still the common law of England. The rights and liberties for which the colonies had long been struggling and for usurpations against which they had declared the king of England to have forfeited his sovereignty over them, were the rights and liberties of English subjects. By the settlement of undivided sovereignty in the colonies themselves, the existing law was not repealed, but rather confirmed and vindicated from invasions by assumed authority. The rights and liberties of individuals, as guaranteed by the great documents and charters of the English Constitution, were not abrogated, but maintained and reasserted with more pressing instance. Hence the sovereignty of the colonies after the declaration of their independence was limited in its exercise by the same restrictions as the sovereign power in England; the rights of individuals were protected by the same inestimable constitutions as before; and the majority in each separate colony could lawfully pass no act contravening their provisions. It is an error, therefore, to imagine that the several colonies were ever without established laws or limitations to the exercise of sovereign power. They had from the moment of their independence *actually* what, from their first establishment, they had demanded *rightfully*, the whole English Constitution so far as it was applicable in their situation. It cannot be too frequently repeated that the State governments, whether in the hands of popular majorities or otherwise constituted, were from the first limited governments. Nor is it too much to say that if any constitutions had been subsequently adopted by majorities, or if any constitutions should ever hereafter be adopted by majorities in any of these States, setting at nought the franchise of the citizen as it then stood under the English Constitution, they would be mere usurpations, and their successful establishment would be revolution. Magna Charta and the English common law are still the fundamental law in every State within the territory originally belonging to the thirteen States. State constitutions are in fact only express applications of the principles of Magna Charta and the common law to novel circumstances. Did they abrogate the wise provisions of these fundamental laws they would be null and void, or at best revolutionary; for they would be subversive of the vested rights of individuals wrung from and conceded by our ancient sovereigns in England, and maintained here by a war of years.

The colonies, then, possessed from the moment of their independence governments of law. It is to be further observed that these were independent of each other. Between them there was no connection whatsoever. Each had been immediately connected with the mother country, from which it received its charter and the constitution of its separate provincial government, and such intercolonial connections as existed were entirely voluntary, conveying to none a right of governing or controlling another. The colonies had been separately organized; they became separately independent, enjoying separate sovereignty over separate territories; the new fact of separation from England made no change in their relations to each other; consequently they were still as independent of each other as they had been hitherto.

Yet in every step towards independence of the mother country they had been united. The first assembly of delegates "chosen and appointed by the several colonies and provinces in North America to take into consideration the actual situation of the same, and the differences subsisting between them and Great Britain," was immediately known as the congress of delegates of the *United Colonies.* The Declaration of Independence professed to emanate from "the representatives of the *United States of America;*" and it affirmed aud published to the world that "these *United Colonies* are, and of right ought to be, free and independent States." And the first article of the subsequent confederation was in these words: "Article I. The style of this confederacy shall be 'The United States of America.'" From the first coöperation of the colonies in an attempt to settle their difficulty with the British Government to the present day, their combination has been known as "*The Union.*" Originally a mere combination for mutual advice on an occasion of peculiar perplexity, it became successively a defensive alliance, a confederation of independent powers, and a federal republic; but in every instance it was called in popular speech "The Union." This is a circumstance of no small value in correcting the impression—unfortunately too common—that the notion of union necessarily includes that of consolidation. The Union of England and Scotland is a consolidated union, merging as it does two separate kingdoms into one united or consolidated kingdom. Even this union, according to Blackstone, is not indissoluble; but would be resolved into its original elements or at least greatly endangered by any act which should abrogate or disregard the original conditions under which it was constituted, without "the mutual consent of both." Whence it appears that even a consolidated union does not in any true sense destroy the individuality of the parties to it; and that the surrender of particular functions of individuality is dependent as to its perpetuity on an observance between the parties "of those points which, when they were separate and independent nations, it was mutually stipulated should be 'fundamental and essential conditions of the union.'" (BLACKSTONE, *Com.* i. 97.) But the notion of consolidation has no place in the American Union. Nothing of the sort was dreamed of when the first congress of delegates assembled to take common counsel in Carpenter's Hall, Philadelphia. At that time the colonies were still British dependencies; they had formed no bond of union with each other; they were united only by the influence of common dangers, sympathies, and resolutions; it was this influence alone that made their "Union;" but it was a true union for all that. There has never been a truer union than when the delegates of the United Colonies in Philadelphia "locked the doors, enjoining by word of honor secrecy on the members; and all the while the people from New Hampshire to Georgia waited quietly, willingly, resolutely prepared to do, not *the bidding* of that congress, but to *accept its conclusions* as the voice of thirteen nations." Nor was there any thought of consolidation in the Declaration of Independence, which affirmed that in their individual capacities as "free and independent States"—not as a free and independent *state*, or a free and independent *people*—they had "full power to levy war, conclude peace, and contract alliances." It was as individual States and at different times that they authorized this declaration to be made; and it was in right of their individual power "to contract alliances" that they coöperated in the war of independence, and adopted, while the war was being waged, the Articles of Confederation and Perpetual Union. Yet, without one thought of consolidation, was there ever a more perfect union than existed when the colonies, conscious of their mutual independence, "appealed to the Supreme Judge of the world for the rectitude of their intentions," and "for the support of their declaration, with a firm reliance on the protection of Divine Providence, mutually pledged to each other their lives, their fortunes, and their sacred honors"? It is true that an attempt was made by Mr. Adams and others, as we have already seen, to effect a consolidation of the States into one state. "It has been said," he remarked, "that we are independent individuals making a bargain with each other. The question is not what we are now, but what we ought to be when our bargain shall be made. The confederacy is to make us one individual only; it is to form us, like separate pieces of metal, into one common mass. We shall no longer retain our separate individuality, but become a single individual," &c. Mr. Adams was mistaken. The States, under the confederation, did not "become a single individual;" on the contrary, they did "retain their separate individuality;" and the very article—the most important in the draft of confederation—which he was so energetically opposing, was triumphantly upheld. The truth is, that the Union was never weaker or more in danger of dissolution than under its first formal bond of confederation. The first Congress assembled under its provisions in 1781. In 1784, one year after peace was proclaimed between England and the United States, the army of the latter was reduced to eighty men; and there was no means of providing for their support. "Each State," says Madison, "yielding to the voice of immediate interest or convenience, withdrew its support from the confederation, till the frail and tottering edifice was ready to fall upon our heads, and crush us beneath its ruins."

The chief difficulty experienced by Congress and the confederation was that they had received no powers to regulate commerce. The States had consequently retained the right to impose such duties on exports and imports as their several legislatures might think proper. From this a twofold embarrassment resulted. Congress had no means of sustaining the public credit by levying duties for the liquidation of the public debt, or defraying the public expenses. They could only apportion the quota to be paid by each State; and the States failing in their duty of replenishing the treasury, there was no way of compelling them. Coercion of States, however justifiable in the case of a repudiation of pecuniary obligations voluntarily entered into, was not within the powers of Congress. On the other hand, a serious embarrassment was felt by Congress in making commercial treaties with foreign states; for unless the States of the Union chose severally through their legislatures to ratify the acts of Congress in this regard, by adopting such commercial regulations in their ports as might be necessary, treaties made by Congress might be utterly inoperative; and in practice it was found that, with the best intention on the part of the States to carry out the recommendations of Congress, certain inconvenient irregularities, inseparable from the distinct action of thirteen different bodies, interfered with the efficiency of government and prevented its consistent action. In 1785 this important matter was under the consideration of Congress, and it was proposed that the first paragraph of the ninth of the Articles of Confederation should be altered so as to read thus:

"The United States in Congress assembled shall have the sole and exclusive right and power of determining on peace and war, except in the cases mentioned in the sixth article—of sending and receiving ambassadors—entering into treaties and alliances—of regulating the trade of the States, as well with foreign nations as each other, and of laying such imposts and duties, upon imports and exports, as may be necessary for the purpose; provided, that the citizens of the States shall, in no instance, be subjected to pay higher imposts and duties than those imposed on the subjects of foreign powers; provided, also, that the legislative power of the several States shall not be restrained from prohibiting the importation or exportation of any species of goods or commodities whatever; provided, also, that all such duties as may be imposed shall be collected under the authority and accrue to the use of the State in which the same shall be payable; and provided, lastly, that every act of Congress, for the above purpose, shall have the assent of nine States in Congress assembled—of establishing rules for deciding, in all cases, what captures on land or water shall be legal, and in what manner prizes taken by land or naval forces in the service of the United States shall be divided or appropriated—of granting letters of marque and reprisal in time of peace—appointing courts for the trial of piracies and felonies committed on the high seas, and establishing courts for receiving and determining finally appeals in all cases of capture; provided, that no member of Congress shall be appointed judge of any of the said courts."

A letter was also prepared to be sent to the States, setting forth the advantages to be expected from committing these powers to Congress. It was felt, however, that any proposition for amending the act of confederation ought to emanate from the State legislatures rather than from Congress; and so the matter dropped in Congress.

After various movements in the same direction, the State of Virginia appointed a commission to "meet such commissioners as might be appointed by the other States in the Union, at a time and place to be agreed on, to take into consideration the trade of the United States; to examine the relative situation and trade of the said States; to consider how far a uniform system in their commercial regulations may be necessary to their common interest and their permanent harmony; and to report to the several States such an act relative to this great object as, when unanimously ratified by them, will enable the United States in Congress assembled effectually to provide for the same." The commissioners were also directed to transmit to the several States copies of the resolution under which their appointment had been made, with a circular requesting their concurrence, and proposing a time and place for the meeting.

Only four States, New York, New Jersey, Pennsylvania, and Delaware, at first supported the proposal of Virginia. Commissioners from these met with the Virginia commission at Annapolis on the 11th of September, 1786, and remained in session till the 14th of the same month, when they made a joint report to their several legislatures. They set forth that they had felt it to be unadvisable to proceed with the business of their mission with so partial and defective a representation of the States as had assembled, a circumstance the more important as it appeared that commissioners had been appointed from New Hampshire, Massachusetts, Rhode Island, and North Carolina, though they had not attended at Annapolis. They nevertheless expressed an earnest and unanimous wish that speedy measures might be taken to effect a general meeting of the States in a future convention for the same and such other purposes as the situation of public affairs might be found to require. They also suggested that the commissioners to be appointed should be clothed with somewhat larger powers than had at first—except in the instance of New Jersey—been confided to them. The commissioners from New Jersey had been empowered "to consider how far a uniform system in their commercial regulations *and other important matters* might be necessary to the common interest and permanent harmony of the several States;" and the convention urged the States to issue similar commissions to their representatives. The reason of this recommendation they gave in these words: "That there are important defects in the system of the federal government is acknowledged by the acts of all those States which have convened in the present meeting; that the defects, upon a closer examination, may be found greater and more numerous than even these acts imply, is at least so far probable from the embarrassments which characterize the present state of our national affairs, foreign and domestic, as may reasonably be supposed to merit a deliberate and candid discussion in some mode which will unite the sentiments and councils of all the States. In the choice of the mode, your commissioners are of opinion that a convention of deputies from the different States, for the special and sole purpose of entering into this investigation, and digesting a plan for supplying such defects as may be discovered to exist, will be entitled to a preference, from considerations which will occur without being particularized. Your commissioners decline an enumeration of those national circumstances on which their opinion respecting the propriety of a future convention with more enlarged powers is founded; as it would be a useless intrusion of facts and observations, most of which have been subjects of public discussion, and none of which can have escaped the penetration of those to whom they would in this instance be addressed. They are, however, of a nature so serious as, in the view of your commissioners, to render the situation of the United States delicate and critical, calling for an exertion of the united virtue and wisdom of all the members of the confederacy."

On the 21st of Febuary, 1787, Congress resumed the consideration of this weighty matter, and the following preamble and resolution was adopted:

"Whereas there is provision in the Articles of Confederation and Perpetual Union, for making alterations therein, by the assent of a Congress of the United States, and of the legislatures of the several States; and whereas experience hath evinced that there are defects in the present confederation; as a mean to remedy which, several of the States, and particularly the State of New York, by express instructions to their delegates in Congress, have suggested a convention for the purpose expressed in the following resolution; and such convention appearing to be the most probable means of establishing in these States a firm national government,—

"*Resolved*, That, in the opinion of Congress, it is expedient that, on the second Monday in May next, a convention of delegates, who shall have been appointed by the several States, be held at Philadelphia, for the sole and express purpose of revising the Articles of Confederation, and reporting to Congress and the several legislatures such alterations and provisions therein as shall, when agreed to in Congress and confirmed by the States, render the Federal Constitution adequate to the exigencies of government and the preservation of the Union."

The language of the foregoing preamble and resolution is important to be observed, as showing at once what was and what was not contemplated in the proposed convention. The object was to "establish in these States a firm national government" by "revising" and making "alterations" in the existing Articles of Confederation. Clearly, it was *not* intended to change the form of government, nor the terms of union; but simply to render the Federal Constitution, then existing, "adequate to the exigencies of government and the preservation of the Union." Before the adoption of the Constitution then to be revised, the States had been united only by alliance as independent foreign states. By its adoption they had been combined into a federal union of states which, though still, except in a few trifling matters, *independent*, were no longer *foreign* to each other. Having in specified particulars a common administration of the affairs of government, they had a *quasi* nationality in common; and in treaties with foreign powers, they were in fact held to be a nation. But from the independent action of the States the Union was in danger of complete dissolution; and its character of nationality was being rapidly obliterated. Congress, therefore, wisely contemplated—not the dissolution, but—the strengthening of the existing federal bond; and the object of the convention was—not to create a nationality which already existed, but—to establish and confirm it.

Scarcely, however, had the convention assembled, as they did on the 2d Monday in May, 1787 (though from the absence of a quorum it was not organized by the election of Washington as president until the 25th of May), when it appeared that very radical changes in the whole form and structure of the Union were contemplated by different parties in the convention. From Mr. Luther Martin we learn that there were in fact "three parties among the delegates, of very different sentiments and views." There was, he says, "one party, whose object and wish it was to abolish and annihilate all State governments, and to bring forward one general government over all this extensive continent, of a monarchical nature, under certain restrictions and limitations. Those who openly avowed this sentiment were, it is true, but few; yet it is equally true that there was a considerable number who did not openly avow it, who were by myself and many others of the convention considered as being in reality favorers of that sentiment and acting upon those principles, covertly endeavoring to carry into effect what they well knew openly and avowedly could not be accomplished.

"The second party was not for the abolition of State governments, nor for the introduction of a monarchical government under any form; but they wished to establish such a system as could give their own States undue power and influence in the government, over the other States.

"A third party was what I considered truly federal and republican. This party was nearly equal in numbers with the other two, and was composed of the delegations from Connecticut, New York, New Jersey, Delaware, and in part from Maryland; also of some individuals from other representations. This party was for proceeding upon terms of *federal equality;* they were for taking our present *federal system* as the basis of their proceedings, and, as far as experience had shown us that there were defects, to remedy those defects; as far as experience had shown that other powers were necessary to the Federal government, to give them those powers. They considered this the object for which they were sent by their States, and what their States expected from them.

"But the favorers of monarchy, and those who wished the total abolition of State governments—well knowing that a government founded on truly federal principles, the bases of which were the thirteen State governments preserved in full force and energy, would be destructive of their views; and knowing they were too weak in numbers openly to bring forward their system; conscious, also, that the people of America would reject it if proposed to them—joined their interest with that party who wished a system giving particular States the power and influence over the others, procuring, in return, mutual sacrifices from them in giving the government great and undefined powers as to its legislative and executive; well knowing that by departing from a federal system they paved the way for their favorite object, the destruction of the State governments and the introduction of monarchy. And hence, I apprehend, in a great measure arose the objections of those honorable members, Mr. Mason and Mr. Gerry. In everything which tended to give the large States power over the smaller, the first of those gentlemen could not forget he belonged to the Ancient Dominion; nor could the latter forget that he represented old Massachusetts; that part of the system which tended to give those States power over the others met with their perfect approbation. But when they viewed it charged with such powers as would destroy all State governments, their own as well as the rest—when they saw a president so constituted as to differ from a monarch scarcely but in name, and having it in his power to become such when he pleased—they being republicans and federalists as far as an attachment to their own States would permit them, warmly and zealously opposed those parts of the system."

Such were the elements of which the Federal Convention was composed:—a party purely monarchical in its aims, an opposite party as purely republican, aiming at the freedom and equality not only of the individual citizens, but of the States in whose trust were placed all the rights of their respective citizens; and a party which, while it did not favor monarchy, desired an inequality of States, which should give greater power and influence to the larger than to the smaller.

As early as the 29th of May, Mr. Randolph laid before the convention a series of resolutions as to the best plan of amending the Constitution; and his second resolution showed the purpose of the larger States to insist upon a greater influence than should be conceded to the smaller. Under the confederation every State voted as a unit, and consequently there was perfect equality of States in the national council. Mr. Randolph's second resolution declared that, instead of an equal vote by States, "the right of suffrage in the national legislature ought to be proportioned to *the quotas of contribution* or to the number of free inhabitants." In order to carry this principle into complete operation, he, after proposing in the third resolution that the national legislature should consist of two branches, a house of representatives and a senate, insisted in the fifth that the members of the senate should be elected by the house; thus, in effect, giving to the larger States power to construct the senate as they chose, without consulting the wishes of the smaller. The only other important point in Mr. Randolph's resolutions was contained in the seventh, which proposed a limited term of office for an executive, who should be chosen by the national legislature. Had this resolution been adopted, the president, like the senate, would have been a mere appointee of the larger States, so that the executive and legislative powers would have been wholly under their control, and the smaller States would have been powerless in every case where the interests of the larger were alike.

On the same day, Mr. Charles Pinckney submitted a "draft of a federal government, to be agreed upon between the free and independent States of America," which was subsequently made the basis of the Constitution. It was a masterly and statesmanlike document, such as could only have emanated from a man equally jealous of the independence of his State and earnestly desirous of the perpetuity, efficiency, and glory of the Union. It clearly distinguished and limited the powers of the legislative, executive, and judicial branches of the government, and provided for a limited presidential term, but agreed with Mr. Randolph's resolutions in proposing that the senate should be elected by the house.

On the 15th of June, what are known as the New Jersey resolutions were offered by Mr. Patterson of that State. They proposed a restriction of the action of the convention to the purposes contemplated by the Congress in calling for it, and suggested an increase in the powers of Congress, the creation of a federal executixe, to consist of — persons, and the establishment of a supreme federal judiciary, to try certain specified causes. This plan was warmly supported by the smaller States.

On the 18th of June, Colonel Hamilton presented a paper "containing his ideas of a suitable plan of government for the United States." This was the great effort of the favorers of a complete consolidation of the States. In the construction of the federal legislature, it ignored the States, making the members of the senate, as well as those of the house, to be elected by the people in proportion to the population, without regard to States. The senators were to be elected for life. The president was to hold his office during good behavior, and was to be elected by electors chosen in the same way as the senators, according to population. The States were regarded as mere territorial provinces of the Union; and, the better to keep them in subjection, the governor of every State was to be appointed by the president, and to have an absolute veto on all acts of the State legislature, over which he might preside. As if this were not sufficient, it was further proposed that "no State should have any forces, land or naval; and that the militia of all the States should be under the sole and exclusive direction of the United States; the officers of which (*i. e.*, the State militias) should be appointed by them."

Colonel Hamilton's "ideas of a suitable plan of government" found no favor with the convention, and were summarily dismissed. The New Jersey resolutions also were respectfully considered, but in the end rejected, the convention feeling that a more radical change in the constitution of the government was necessary than could be honestly made to appear in the form of amendments to the act of confederation. The debates, therefore, continued on the various articles of the first two plans by Mr. Randolph and Mr. Pinckney, until the 26th of July, when the following resolutions, as they had, from time to time, been adopted, were, together with the propositions of these two gentlemen, referred to a select committee, with instructions to report a constitution.

RESOLUTIONS OF THE CONVENTION,

Referred on the Twenty-third and Twenty-sixth of July, 1787, *to a committee of detail* (Messrs. RUTLEDGE, RANDOLPH, GORHAM, ELLSWORTH, *and* WILSON), *for the purpose of reporting a Constitution.*

JUNE "I. *Resolved*, That the Government of the United States
1 ought to consist of a supreme legislative, judiciary, and executive.

2 "II. *Resolved*, That the legislature consist of two branches.

21 "III. *Resolved*, That the members of the first branch of
the legislature ought to be elected by the people of the sev-
22 eral States, for the term of two years; to be paid out of the
23 public treasury; to receive an adequate compensation for their services; to be of the age of twenty-five years at least; to be ineligible to, and incapable of holding any office under the authority of the United States (except those peculiarly belonging to the functions of the first branch), during the term of service of the first branch.

JUNE "IV. *Resolved,* That the members of the second branch
25 of the legislature of the United States ought to be chosen by the individual legislatures; to be of the age of thirty years at least; to hold their offices for six years, one third to go out biennially; to receive a compensation for the devotion of their time to the public service; to be ineligible to, and incapable of holding any office under the authority of the United States (except those peculiarly belonging to the functions of the second branch) during the term for which they are elected, and for one year thereafter.

"V. *Resolved,* That each branch ought to possess the right of originating acts.

Postponed, 27. "VI. *Resolved,* That the national legislature
JULY ought to possess the legislative rights vested in Congress by
16 the confederation; and, moreover, to legislate, in all cases,
17 for the general interests of the Union; and also in those to which the States are separately incompetent, or in which the harmony of the United States may be interrupted by the exercise of individual legislation.

"VII. *Resolved,* That the legislative acts of the United States, made by virtue and in pursuance of the articles of union, and all treaties made and ratified under the authority of the United States, shall be the supreme law of the respective States, as far as those acts or treaties shall relate to the said States, or their citizens and inhabitants; and that the judiciaries of the several States shall be bound thereby in their decisions, anything in the respective laws of the individual States to the contrary notwithstanding.

16 "VIII. *Resolved,* That in the original formation of the legislature of the United States, the first branch thereof shall consist of sixty-five members, of which number

New Hampshire	shall	send	3	Delaware	shall	send	1
Massachusetts	"	"	8	Maryland	"	"	6
Rhode Island	"	"	1	Virginia	"	"	10
Connecticut	"	"	5	North Carolina	"	"	5
New York	"	"	6	South Carolina	"	"	5
New Jersey	"	"	4	Georgia	"	"	3
Pennsylvania	"	"	8				

JULY But as the present situation of the States may probably alter in the number of their inhabitants, the legislature of the United States shall be authorized, from time to time, to apportion the number of representatives; and in case any of the States shall hereafter be divided, or enlarged by addition of territory, or any two or more States united, or any new States created within the limits of the United States, the legislature of the United States shall possess authority to regulate the number of representatives, in any of the foregoing cases, upon the principle of the number of their inhabitants, according to the provisions hereafter mentioned, namely: *Provided always*, that representatives ought to be proportioned according to direct taxation. And in order to ascertain the alteration in the direct taxation which may be required, from time to time, by the changes in the relative circumstances of the States—

"IX. *Resolved*, That a census be taken within six years from the first meeting of the legislature of the United States, and once within the term of every ten years afterwards, of all the inhabitants of the United States, in the manner and according to the ratio recommended by Congress, in their resolutions of April 18, 1783; and that the legislature of the United States shall proportion the direct taxation accordingly.

"X. *Resolved*, That all bills for raising or apportioning money, and for fixing the salaries of the officers of the Government of the United States, shall originate in the first
16 branch of the Legislature of the United States, and shall not be altered or amended by the second branch; and that no money shall be drawn from the public treasury but in pursuance of appropriations to be originated by the first branch.

"XI. *Resolved*, That, in the second branch of the legislature of the United States, each State shall have an equal vote.

26 "XII. *Resolved*, That a national executive be instituted, to consist of a single person, to be chosen by the national legislature for the term of seven years; to be ineligible a

JULY second time; with power to carry into execution the national laws; to appoint to offices in cases not otherwise provided for; to be removable on impeachment and conviction of malpractice or neglect of duty; to receive a fixed compensation for the devotion of his time to public service, to be paid out of the public treasury.

21 "XIII. *Resolved*, That the national executive shall have a right to negative any legislative act, which shall not be afterwards passed, unless by two third parts of each branch of the national legislature.

18 "XIV. *Resolved*, That a national judiciary be established,
21 to consist of one supreme tribunal, the judges of which shall
be appointed by the second branch of the national legisla-
18 ture; to hold their offices during good behavior; to receive
punctually, at stated times, a fixed compensation for their services, in which no diminution shall be made, so as to affect the persons actually in office at the time of such diminution.

"XV. *Resolved*, That the national legislature be empowered to appoint inferior tribunals.

18 "XVI. *Resolved*, That the jurisdiction of the national judiciary shall extend to cases arising under laws passed by the general legislature, and to such other questions as involve the national peace and harmony.

"XVII. *Resolved*, That provision ought to be made for the admission of new States lawfully arising within the limits of the United States, whether from a voluntary junction of government and territory, or otherwise, with the consent of a number of voices in the national legislature less than the whole.

"XVIII. *Resolved*, That a republican form of government shall be guaranteed to each State; and that each State shall be protected against foreign and domestic violence.

23 "XIX. *Resolved*, That provision ought to be made for the amendment of the articles of union, whensoever it shall seem necessary.

"XX. *Resolved*, That the legislative, executive, and judiciary powers, within the several States, and of the national

JULY government, ought to be bound, by oath, to support the articles of union.

"XXI. *Resolved*, That the amendments which shall be offered to the confederation by the convention ought, at a proper time or times after the approbation of Congress, to be submitted by an assembly or assemblies of representatives, recommended by the several legislatures, to be expressly chosen by the people, to consider and decide thereon.

"XXII. *Resolved*, That the representation in the second branch of the legislature of the United States consist of two members from each State, who shall vote *per capita*.

26 "XXIII. *Resolved* That it be an instruction to the committee, to whom were preferred the proceedings of the convention for the establishment of a national government, to receive a clause or clauses, requiring certain qualifications of property and citizenship, in the United States, for the executive, the judiciary, and the members of both branches of the legislature of the United States.

During the protracted debates which took place in the discussion of the foregoing resolutions, the most important were on the third and fourth. On the one hand, the larger States demanded that the members of both houses in the national legislature should be elected by the people according to population, so as to secure to them a preponderating influence in both. On the other hand, the smaller States, feeling that such a mode of representation would set them at the mercy of the larger, insisted on an equality of representation in each house; so that the States, large and small, might be equal in their voice and vote in the assembly of the Union. The arguments advanced on both sides are profoundly interesting, and we give the most important of them in the words of Mr. Luther Martin, a distinguished member of the convention. The italics are his.

"The advocates of unequal representation," he says, in his celebrated letter, "urged that, when the Articles of Confederation were formed, it was *only* from *necessity* and *expediency* that the States were admitted *each* to have an *equal vote;* but that our situation was now altered, and therefore those States who considered it contrary to their interest would no longer abide by it. They said no State ought to wish to have influence in government except in proportion to what it contributes to it; that if it contributes but little, it ought to have but a small vote; that taxation and representation ought always to go together; that if one State had *sixteen times as many inhabitants* as another, or was *sixteen times as wealthy*, it ought to have *sixteen times as many votes;* that an inhabitant of Pennsylvania ought to have as much weight and consequence as an inhabitant of Jersey or Delaware; that it was contrary to the feelings of the human mind—what *large States* would never submit to; that the *large States* would have *great objects* in view, in which they would never permit the *smaller States* to thwart them; that *equality of suffrage* was the rotten part of the Constitution, and that this was a happy time to get clear of it. In fine, it was the poison which contaminated our whole system, and the source of all the evils we experience.

" This is the substance of the arguments—if arguments they may be called—which were used in favor of *inequality of suffrage.* Those who advocated the *equality of suffrage* took the matter up on the original principles of government. They urged that all men, considered in a state of nature, before any government is formed, are equally free and independent, no one having any right or authority to exercise power over another, and this *without any regard to difference in personal strength, understanding, or wealth*—that, when such individuals enter into government they have *each* a *right* to an *equal voice* in its first formation, and afterwards have *each* a right to an *equal vote* in every matter which relates to their government:—that if it could be done conveniently they have a right to exercise it in person; where it cannot be done in person, but, for convenience, representatives are appointed to act for them, every person has a right to an equal vote in choosing that representative who is intrusted to do, for the whole, that which the whole, if they could assemble, might do in person, and in the transacting of which each would have an equal voice:—that if we were to admit, because a man was more wise, more strong, or more wealthy, he should be entitled to more votes than another, it would be inconsistent with the freedom and liberty of that other, and would reduce him to slavery.

"Suppose, for instance, ten individuals, in a state of nature, about to enter into government, nine of whom are equally wise, equally strong, and equally wealthy; the tenth is ten times as wise, ten times as strong, or ten times as rich: if, for this reason, he is to have ten votes for each vote of either of the others, the nine might as well have no vote at all—since the whole nine might assent to a measure, yet the vote of the tenth would countervail and set aside all their votes. If this tenth approved of what they wished to adopt, it would be well; but if he disapproved, he could prevent it; and in the same manner he could carry into execution any measure he wished, contrary to the opinions of all the others, he having ten votes, and the others altogether but nine. It is evident that, on these principles, the nine would have no will nor discretion of their own, but must be totally dependent on the will and discretion of the tenth; to him they would be as absolutely slaves as any negro is to his master. Hence it was urged, the inequality of representation, or giving to one man more votes than another, on account of his wealth, &c., was altogether inconsistent with the principles of liberty; and in the same proportion as it should be adopted, in favor of one or more, in that proportion are the others enslaved. It was urged that, although every individual should have an equal voice in the government, yet even the superior wealth, strength, or understanding, would give great and undue advantages to those who possessed them—that wealth attracts respect and attention; superior strength would cause the weaker and more feeble to be cautious how they offended, and to put up with small injuries rather than engage in an unequal contest. In like manner, superior understanding would give its possessor many opportunities of profiting at the expense of the more ignorant.

"Having thus established these principles with respect to the *rights of individuals* in a *state of nature*, and what is due to *each* on entering into government—the principles established by every writer on liberty—they proceeded to show that *states*, when *once formed*, are considered, *with respect* to *each other*, as *individuals* in a state of nature; that, like individuals, each *state* is considered *equally free* and *equally independent*, the *one* having no right to exercise authority over the *other*, though *more strong*, *more wealthy*, or *abound-*

ing with more inhabitants—that, when a number of *states* unite themselves under a *federal government*, the *same principles apply to them* as when a *number of individual men* unite themselves under a *state government*—that every argument which shows *one man* ought not to have *more votes* than *another*, because he is *wiser*, *stronger*, or *wealthier*, proves that one state ought not to have *more votes* than *another*, because it is *stronger*, *richer*, or *more populous;* and that by *giving one state* or *one or two states* more votes than the *others*, the *others* thereby are *enslaved to such state or states* having the *greater number of votes*, in the *same manner* as in the case before put of *individuals*, when *one* has *more votes than the others*—that the reason why each individual man, in forming a state government, should have an equal vote, is because each individual, before he enters into government, is *equally free* and *independent;* so *each state*, when *states enter* into a *federal government*, are entitled to an *equal vote*, because, before they entered into such federal government, *each state* was *equally free* and *equally independent*—that *adequate* representation of men, *formed into a state government*, consists in *each man* having an *equal voice;* either personally, or if by representatives, that he should have an equal voice in choosing the representatives—so adequate representation of *states* in a *federal government* consists in *each state* having an *equal voice*, either in person or by its representative, in everything which relates to the federal government—that this adequacy of representation is *more important* in a *federal* than in a *state* government, because the members of a state government, the *district* of which is *not very large*, have generally such a common interest, that laws can scarcely be made by *one* part *oppressive* to the *others* without *their suffering in common;* but the *different states* composing an *extensive federal empire*, widely distinct *one* from the *other*, may have *interests so totally distinct*, that the *one* part might be greatly *benefited* by what would be *destructive* to the *other*.

" It was said that the maxim that taxation and representation ought to go together was true so far that no person ought to be *taxed* who is not *represented;* but not in the extent insisted upon, to wit, that the *quantum of taxation* and representation ought to be the same; on the contrary, the *quantum of representation* depends upon the *quantum of freedom*, and therefore *all*, whether individual *states* or individual *men*, who are *equally free*, have a right to *equal representation*—that to those who insist that he who pays the greatest share of taxes ought to have the greatest number of votes, it is a sufficient answer to say, that *this rule* would be *destructive* of the *liberty* of the *others*, and would render them *slaves* to the *more rich* and *wealthy*—that if one man pays *more taxes* than another, it is because he has *more wealth* to be protected by government, and he receives greater benefits from the government; so, if one state pays more to the federal government, it is because, as a state, she enjoys greater blessings from it; she has more wealth protected by it, or a greater number of inhabitants, whose rights are secured, and who share its advantages.

"It was urged that, upon these principles, the Pennsylvanian, or inhabitant of a large state, was of as much consequence as the inhabitant of Jersey, Delaware, Maryland, or any other State That *his consequence* was to be decided by *his situation* in his *own state;* that, if he was *there* as *free*, if he had as great share in the forming of his own government, and in the making and executing its laws, as the inhabitants of those other states, then he was equally important and of equal consequence. Suppose a confederation of states had never been adopted, but every state had remained absolutely in its independent situation, no person could, with propriety, say that the citizen of the large state was not as important as the citizen of the smaller. The confederation of states cannot alter the case. It was said that, in all transactions between state and state, the freedom, independence, importance, and consequence, even the individuality of each citizen of the different states, might, with propriety, be said to be swallowed up or concentrated in the independence, the freedom, and the individuality of *the state* of which they are citizens; that the *thirteen states* are thirteen *distinct*, *political*, *individual existences*, as to each other; that this *federal* government is, or *ought to be*, a government over these thirteen political, individual existences, which forms the members of that government; and as the *largest state* is only a *single individual* of this government, it ought to have only *one vote;* the *smallest state*, also being one individual *member* of this government, ought also to have *one vote.* To those who urged that the states having equal suffrage was contrary to the feelings of the human heart, it was answered, that it was admitted to be contrary to the feelings of pride and ambition; but those were feelings which ought not to be gratified at the expense of freedom.

"It was urged that the position that great states would have great objects in view, in which they would suffer the less states to thwart them, was one of the strongest reasons why inequality of representation ought not to be admitted. If those great objects were not inconsistent with the interest of the less states, they would readily concur in them; but if they were inconsistent with the interest of a majority of the states composing the government, in that case two or three states ought not to have it in their power to aggrandize themselves at the expense of all the rest. To those who alleged that equality of suffrage, in our federal government, was the poisonous source from which all our misfortunes flowed, it was answered that the allegation was not founded in fact—that equality of suffrage had *never been complained of by the states*, as a defect in our federal system—that, among the eminent writers, foreigners and others, who had treated of the defects in our confederation, and proposed alterations, none had proposed an alteration in this part of the system; and members of the convention, both in and out of Congress, who advocated the equality of suffrage, called upon their opponents, both in and out of Congress, and challenged them to produce one single instance where a bad measure had been adopted, or a good measure had failed of adoption, in consequence of the states having an equal vote. On the contrary, they urged that all our evils flowed from the want of power in the federal head, and that, let the right of suffrage in the states be altered in any manner whatever, if no greater power were given to the government, the same inconveniences would continue.

"It was denied that the equality of suffrage was *originally* agreed to on principles of necessity or expediency; on the contrary, that it was adopted on the principles of the rights of men, and the rights of states, which were then well known, and which then influenced our conduct, although they now seem to be forgotten. For this the journals of Congress were appealed to. It was from them shown that when the committee of Congress reported to that body the Articles of Confederation, the very first article which became subject of discussion was that respecting equality of suffrage—that Virginia proposed divers modes of suffrage, all on the principle of inequality, which were *almost unanimously* rejected—that on the question of adopting the articles, it passed, Virginia being the only state which voted in the negative—that, after the Articles of Confederation were submitted to the states, by them to be ratified, almost every state proposed certain amendments, which they instructed their delegates to endeavor to obtain before ratification; and that, among all the amendments proposed, not one state, not even Virginia, proposed an amendment of that article securing the equality of suffrage; the most convincing proof it was agreed to, and adopted, not from necessity, but upon a full conviction that, according to the principles of free government, the states had a right to that equality of suffrage.

"But it was to no purpose that the futility of their objections was shown. When driven from the pretence that the equality of suffrage had been originally agreed to on principles of expediency and necessity, the representatives of the large states persisted in a declaration, that they would never agree to admit the smaller states to an equality of suffrage. In answer to this, they were informed, and informed in terms the most strong and energetic that could possibly be used, that *we never could agree* to a system giving them the undue influence and superiority they proposed—that we would risk every possible consequence—that from anarchy and confusion order might arise—that slavery was the worst that could ensue, and we considered the system proposed to be the most complete, most abject system of slavery that the wit of man ever devised, under the pretence of forming a government for free states—that we never would submit tamely and servilely to a present certain evil in dread of a future, which might be imaginary—that we were sensible the eyes of our country and the world were upon us—that we would not labor under the imputation of being unwilling to form a strong and energetic federal government; but we would publish the system which we *approved*, and also that which we *opposed*, and leave it to our country and the world at large to judge, between us, who best understood the rights of freemen and free states, and who best advocated them; and to the same tribunal we would submit, who ought to be answerable for all the consequences which might arise to the Union, from the convention breaking up without proposing any system to their constituents. During this debate we were threatened that, if we did not agree to the system proposed, we never should have an opportunity of meeting in convention to deliberate on another; and this was frequently urged In answer, we called upon them to show what was to prevent it, and from what quarter was our danger to proceed. Was it from a foreign enemy? Our distance from Europe, and the political situation of that country left us but little to fear. Was there any amibitious state or states, who, in violation of every sacred obligation, was preparing to enslave the other states, and raise itself to consequence on the ruin of the others? Or was there any such ambitious individual? We did not apprehend it to be the case. But suppose it to be true; it rendered it the more necessary that we should sacredly guard against a system which might enable all those ambitious views to be carried into effect, even *under the sanction of the Constitution and government.* In fine, all these threats were treated with contempt, and they were told that we apprehended but one reason to prevent the states meeting again in convention; that, when they discovered the part this convention had acted, and how much its members were abusing the trust reposed in them, the states would never trust another convention."

To this degree of warmth—almost of anger—did the debate on this important subject proceed, and on the vote being taken it was found to be equally divided, five States voting for an inequality of representation, and five against it. A conference committee was accordingly appointed from the different parties to endeavor to come to an agreement; and the result was that the opponents of an unequal representation agreed to yield their objections to it in the lower house—in reference to which the debate had taken place—provided its advocates would pledge themselves to support an equal representation in the senate. Thus, by an equitable compromise, the framers of the Constitution came to a determination on this cardinal question, in regard to which their radical differences of opinion threatened to destroy the Union, and to turn the convention into a direct means for the overthrow of the confederation they had been commissioned to amend.

The committee to which the twenty-three resolutions were committed on the 26th of July, reported their draft of a Constitution on the 7th of August. In its phraseology we discover one singular difference between it and the resolutions. In the latter we find the word *national* repeatedly used in connection with the United States. The legislature of the United States is called the *national* legislature, their executive a *national* executive, and their judiciary a *national* judiciary. In the draft of the committee this expression nowhere appears. It had been adopted, and its use strongly urged by the monarchical party, and those who favored the obliteration of States and the erection of a consolidated government, on which account it was opposed by the wiser men who did not desire to overthrow but to confirm the federal character of the bond between the States. In the debate upon the fourth resolution, which, in its original form, spoke of "the national legislature," it was moved to erase the word "national," and to substitute the words "of the United States," and the motion was carried in the affirmative. The same word, however, reappears in later resolutions, but from the time of their commitment it never afterwards occurs. The truth is, this word, from the characters and aims of those who sought to introduce it, was invested with a sinister significance. No one had denied that the confederation was a national confederation. No one now denied that the United States would form a national union under the new Constitution. But the use of this term by the monarchists and consolidationists, in order to impart the notion of such nationality to the Union, as is understood to exist in consolidated monarchies, was bitterly opposed by men who understood and intended it to be a simple bond between sovereign and independent States, delegating to a common agency only certain specified and well-defined functions of their independent sovereignties. Hence, though even in the committee some may have desired that it should be retained, it was felt that the mere use of this word in the Constitution would suffice to cause its absolute rejection by the States, and it was dropped accordingly.

The draft presented by the committee was submitted to a rigorous examination and discussion from the 7th of August till the 8th of September, when, with the various changes and amendments made to it in convention, it was again committed to a committee of revision, who were charged to revise its style, and arrange the articles agreed to by the house.

On the 12th of September the committee of revision delivered their report at the secretary's table; and if we compare it with the draft from which it was prepared, we find at once a very striking change in the preamble. In the first draft the preamble was as follows:—

"We, the people of the States of New Hampshire, Massachusetts, Rhode Island and Providence Plantations, Connecticut, New York, New Jersey, Pennsylvania, Delaware, Maryland, Virginia, North Carolina, South Carolina, and Georgia, do ordain, declare, and establish the following Constitution, for the government of ourselves and our posterity."

In the convention this preamble had been adopted without amendment. In the revised draft the enumeration of the States is entirely omitted; and the preamble, which is that of the Constitution as finally adopted, reads thus:

"We, the people of the United States, in order to form a more perfect union, establish justice, insure domestic tranquillity, provide for the common defence, promote the general welfare, and secure the blessings of liberty to ourselves and our posterity, do ordain and establish this Constitution for the United States of America."

From the omission of the names of the several States in the Constitution as adopted, and the substitution of the phrase, "We, the people of the United States," some, who have not yet abandoned the hope of converting the union of sovereign States established by our fathers into the consolidated empire they deliberately refused to make, have argued that, by the adoption of the latter phraseology, "the people of the United States," are represented as one corporation; that is to say, that the Constitution declares the Union to be a corporation of the individual citizens of all the States, and not a corporation of States. Nothing could be more absurd than such a train of reasoning. It might as well be asserted that the Constitution was not intended to create a government, nor to be of authority beyond the lives of its framers, because the clause ordaining, declaring, and establishing "the following Constitution for the government of ourselves and our posterity," which appears in the draft, does not appear in the revised draft nor in the Constitution. This latter inference will certainly not be admitted by the modern admirers of consolidated monarchies. The true reason of the change of phraseology in the preamble is very simple, though not a little curious, if we consider the events of the past three years.

The thirteen States were still members of the Union as constituted by the "Articles of Confederation and Perpetual Union," which had been adopted by the free vote of each of the thirteen States; and the thirteenth article provided that—

"Art. XIII. Every State shall abide by the determination of the United States in Congress assembled, on all questions which by this confederation are submitted to them. And the articles of this confederation *shall be inviolably observed* by every State, and the Union *shall be perpetual; nor shall any alteration, at any time hereafter, be made in any of them, unless such alteration be agreed to in a Congress of the United States, and be afterwards confirmed by the legislature of every State.*"

It was under this thirteenth article that Congress had requested the States to send delegates to the convention, "*for the sole and express purpose of revising the Articles of Confederation*, and reporting to Congress and the several legislatures such *alterations* and *provisions therein* as shall, when agreed to in Congress and confirmed by the States—i. e., *all* the States—render the Federal Constitution adequate to the exigencies of government and the preservation of the Union." But instead of carrying out the original designs of Congress, the convention, when it assembled, utterly refused to *revise* or *report alterations* in the Articles of Confederation. Mr. Patterson's resolutions declaring that this should be the limit of their action, were respectfully considered and then summarily dismissed. They had determined on a new Constitution such as could not honestly be called a mere amendment of the old; and foreseeing, from the differences of opinion which had appeared in the convention, that the speedy accession of all the States was not to be anticipated, they had resolved, in the seventh article of the Constitution, that—

"Art. VII. The ratification of the conventions of *nine* States shall be sufficient for the establishment of this Constitution between the States so ratifying the same."

Now the Articles of Confederation under which the United States were at that time bound together, declared their union under its existing conditions to be perpetual, and that no alteration of it should ever be made without the consent of every one of the thirteen States. Clearly, then, the adoption of the new Constitution by nine States would be a distinct repudiation of the bond of the confederation, and a secession from the Union constituted under it. As yet the novel notion of coercing States either to remain in a "perpetual Union," or to enter into a confederation which they disapproved, had not been discovered. It was doubtful what States might determine to secede from the confederation; but the secessionists had as little thought of compelling the confederates to follow them in their secession, as the latter had of forcing the former to remain. It would, however, have been a manifest absurdity in the nine seceding States to claim the confederate States as under their jurisdiction by inserting their names in the preamble of a Constitution which was binding only on themselves; and this was the only reason for the suppression of the names of the contracting States in the preamble of the Constitution. It was still uncertain what States would adopt it. It was hoped that all might ultimately ratify it. But because they could not know which might be the first nine States of the new Union, and claimed no authority over the non-complying States, they agreed to use the corporate style of "the United States" in the preamble, that it might include those only who adhered to it.

The revised draft was submitted to a searching examination until Saturday, the 15th of September, when, on the question being put to agree to the Constitution as amended, it was passed in the affirmative—ALL THE STATES CONCURRING; and the Constitution, now at length harmoniously adopted in convention, was engrossed, and transmitted to Congress, which body having approved the same, it was by unanimous resolution, on the 28th of September,

1787, sent for final approval to the legislatures of the several States. By these it was successively ratified from the 7th of December, 1787, when it was ratified by Delaware, to the 29th of May, 1790, when it was ratified by Rhode Island.

On the 2d of July, 1788, the ratification of New Hampshire having been received in the confederate Congress, and this being the ninth ratification received, Congress immediately passed an act for putting the new Constitution in operation. The first Wednesday in January, 1789, was appointed for the election by the States of presidential electors; the first Wednesday in February for the vote of the electors for President; and the first Wednesday in March for commencing proceedings under the new Constitution. Accordingly the elections of the States were held; on Wednesday, the 4th of March, 1789, proceedings commenced under the Constitution; and on the 30th of April of the same year, GEORGE WASHINGTON, unanimously elected by the suffrage of the electors, was inaugurated as President of the United States.

The Constitution, however, was as yet far from perfect. It conveyed to the United States no power of injuring the rights and liberties either of citizens or of the States. On the other hand, it did not definitely restrain the Federal authority from acts which might be ruinous to both. This defect of indefiniteness was keenly felt by the States; and in their ratifications of the Constitution, many of them made formal declarations of the understanding with which they approved it, and at the same time called for amendments to it which should more clearly guarantee the rights of States and citizens. Of these declarations and proposals of amendment the most important were the following:

MASSACHUSETTS. "That it be explicitly declared that all powers not expressly delegated by the aforesaid Constitution, are reserved to the several States, to be by them exercised."

NEW HAMPSHIRE. "That it be explicitly declared that all powers not expressly and particularly delegated by the aforesaid Constitution, are reserved to the several States, to be by them exercised.

"Congress shall never disarm any citizen, unless such as are or have been in actual rebellion.

"That no person shall be tried for any crime by which he may incur an infamous punishment, or loss of life, until he first be indicted by a grand jury, except in such cases as may arise in the government and regulation of the land and naval forces.

"In civil actions between the citizens of different States, every issue of fact, arising in actions at common law, shall be tried by jury, if the parties, or either of them, shall request it.

"Congress shall make no laws touching religion, or to infringe the rights of conscience."

SOUTH CAROLINA. "This convention doth also declare, that no section or paragraph of the said Constitution warrants a construction that the States do not retain every power not expressly relinquished by them, and vested in the .General Government of the Union."

VIRGINIA. "We, the delegates of the people of Virginia, &c., do, in the name and in behalf of the people of Virginia, declare and make known, that the powers granted under the Constitution, being derived from the people of the United States, may be resumed by them, whensoever the same shall be perverted to their injury or oppression, and that every power not granted thereby remains with them, and at their will; that, therefore, no right, of any denomination, can be cancelled, abridged, restrained, or modified, by the Congress, by the Senate, or House of Representatives, acting in any capacity, by the President, or any department or officer of the United States, except in those instances in which power is given by the Constitution for those purposes; and that, among other essential rights, the liberty of conscience, and of the press, cannot be cancelled, abridged, restrained, or modified, by any authority of the United States."

NEW YORK. "That the powers of government may be reassumed by the people whensoever it shall become necessary to their happiness; that every power, jurisdiction, and right, which is not by the said Constitution clearly delegated to the Congress of the United States, or the departments of the Government thereof, remains to the people of the several States, or to their respective State Governments, to whom they may have granted the same; and that those clauses in the said Constitution, which declare that Congress shall not have or exercise certain powers, do not imply that Congress is entitled to any powers not given by the said Constitution; but such clauses are to be construed either as exceptions to certain specified powers, or as inserted merely for greater caution.

"That the people have an equal, natural, and inalienable right freely and peaceably to exercise their religion, according to their dictates of conscience; and that no religious sect or society ought to be favored or established by law in preference to others.

"That the people have a right to keep and bear arms; that a well-regulated militia, including the body of the people capable of bearing arms, is the proper, natural, and safe defence of a free State.

"That standing armies, in times of peace, are dangerous to liberty, and ought not to be kept up except in cases of necessity; and that, at all times, the military should be under strict subordination to the civil power.

"That in time of peace no soldier ought to be quartered in any house without the consent of the owner; and in time of war only by the civil magistrate, in such manner as the laws may direct.

"That no person ought to be taken, imprisoned, or disseized of his freehold, or be exiled, or be deprived of his privileges, franchises, life, liberty, or property, but by due process of law.

"That no person ought to be put twice in jeopardy of life or limb for one and the same offence; nor, unless in case of impeachment, be punished more than once for the same offence.

"That excessive bail ought not to be required, nor excessive fines imposed, nor cruel and unusual punishments inflicted.

"That (except in the government of the land and naval forces, and of the militia when in actual service, and in cases of impeachment) a presentment or indictment by a grand jury ought to be observed as a necessary preliminary to the trial of all crimes cognizable by the judiciary of the United States; and such trial should be speedy, public, and by an impartial jury of the county where the crime was committed; and that no person can be found guilty but by the unanimous consent of such jury; . . . and that in all criminal prosecutions the accused ought to be informed of the cause and nature of his accusation, to be confronted with his accusers and the witnesses against him, to have the means of producing his witnesses, and the assistance of counsel for his defence; and should not be compelled to give evidence against himself.

"That the trial by jury, in the extent it obtained by the common law of England, is one of the greatest securities to the rights of a free people, and ought to remain inviolate.

"That every freeman has a right to be secure from all unreasonable searches and seizures of his person, his papers, or his property; and therefore, that all warrants to search suspected places, or seize any freeman, his papers, or property, without information, upon oath or affirmation, of sufficient cause, are grievous and oppressive; and that all general warrants (or such in which the place or person suspected are not particularly designated) are dangerous, and ought not to be granted.

"That the people have a right peaceably to assemble together to consult for their common good, or to instruct their representatives, and that every person has a right to petition or apply to the legislature for redress of grievances.

"That the freedom of the press ought not to be violated or restrained."

RHODE ISLAND. "That those clauses in the Constitution which declare that Congress shall not have or exercise certain powers, do not imply that Congress is entitled to any powers not given by the said Constitution; but such clauses are to be construed as exceptions to certain specified powers, or as inserted merely for greater caution.

"That religion, or the duty which we owe to our Creator, and the manner of discharging it, can be directed only by reason and conviction, and not by force and violence; and therefore all men have a natural, equal, and inalienable right to the exercise of religion according to the dictates of conscience; and that no particular religious sect or society ought to be favored or established by law in preference to others.

"That all power of suspending laws, or the execution of laws, by any authority without the consent of the representatives of the people in the legislature, is injurious to their rights, and ought not to be exercised.

"That, in all capital and criminal prosecutions, a man hath the right to demand the cause and nature of his accusation, to be confronted with the accusers and witnesses, to call for evidence, and be allowed counsel in his favor, and to a fair and speedy trial by an impartial jury in his vicinage, without whose unanimous consent he cannot be found guilty (except in the government of the land and naval forces), nor can he be compelled to give evidence against himself.

"That no freeman ought to be taken, imprisoned, or disseized of his freehold, liberties, privileges, or franchises, or outlawed, or exiled, or in any manner destroyed or deprived of his life, liberty, or property, but by the trial by jury, or by the law of the land.

"That every freeman restrained of his liberty is entitled to a remedy, to inquire into the lawfulness thereof, and to remove the same if unlawful, and that such remedy ought not to be denied or delayed.

"That in controversies respecting property, and in suits between man and man, the ancient trial by jury, as hath been exercised by us and our ancestors from the time whereof the memory of man runneth not to the contrary, is one of the greatest securities to the rights of the people, and ought to remain sacred and inviolable.

"That every freeman ought to obtain right and justice, freely and without sale, completely and without denial, promptly and without delay; and that all establishments or regulations contravening these rights, are oppressive and unjust.

"That exessive bail ought not to be required, nor excessive fines imposed, nor cruel and unusual punishments inflicted.

"That every person has a right to be secure from all unreasonable searches and seizures of his person, his papers, or his property; and therefore, that all warrants to search suspected places, to seize any person, his papers, or his property, without information upon oath or affirmation of sufficient cause, are grievous and oppressive; and that all general warrants (or such in which the place or person suspected are not particularly designated) are dangerous, and ought not to be granted.

"That the people have a right to freedom of speech, and of writing and publishing their sentiments. That freedom of the press is one of the greatest bulwarks of liberty, and ought not to be violated.

"That the people have a right to keep and bear arms; and that at all times, the military should be under strict subordination to the civil power."

The consequence of these earnest and firm representations of the States was that at the first session of the first Congress under the Constitution the following resolution was adopted:

"CONGRESS OF THE UNITED STATES;

"Begun and held at the City of New York, on Wednesday, the 4th of March, 1789.

"The conventions of a number of the States having, at the time of their adopting of the Constitution, expressed a desire, in order to prevent misconstruction or abuse of its powers, that further declaratory and restrictive clauses should be added; and as extending the ground of public confidence in the government will best insure the beneficent ends of its institution;—

"Resolved, by the Senate and House of Representatives of the United States of America, in Congress assembled, two thirds of both houses concurring, that the following Articles be proposed to the Legislatures of the several States, as amendments to the Constitution of the United States, all or any of which articles, when ratified by three fourths of the legislatures, to be valid, to all intents and purposes, as part of the said Constitution, namely,—

"Articles in Addition to, and Amendment of the Constitution of the United States of America, proposed by Congress, and ratified by the Legislatures of the several States, pursuant to the Fifth Article of the original Constitution."

Here follow twelve articles, of which all but the first two will be found among the amendments appended to the Constitution at the end of this chapter, where they are numbered from I. to X. included. The first two articles, which were not ratified by the legislatures of the States, were intended to restrict the number of members of the House of Representatives, and to prevent the compensation of members from being varied during the term of the members who might alter it. The importance of the amendments adopted is beyond expression. Overridden and despised as they have been by the present Adminstration, they stand still upon the record, an imperishable monument of the wisdom of the framers of the Constitution, and the perjury of those who, having sworn to support, maintain, and defend them, have presumed to trample their inestimable articles under the foot of factious tyranny. The Constitution, as originally made, formed a framework of free government. The amendments to it aimed to hinder its perversion to the purposes of arbitrary power. It is to the amendments we must look for our guarantee of the enjoyment of religious liberty; freedom of speech and of the press; the right of peaceable assembly, of petitioning the Government for the redress of grievances, of keeping and bearing arms; immunity from the quartering of soldiers in private houses in time of peace; the right of freedom from unreasonable searches and seizures, under any warrant issued otherwise than upon probable cause, supported by oath or affirmation, and particularly describing the place to be searched, and the persons or things to be seized; the right, before imprisonment or trial for crime, of open indictment by a grand jury, and of trial once only for the same offence, by due process of law; the right, in all criminal prosecutions, of trial by jury in the State and district where the crime may have been committed, with all the safeguards to innocence afforded by the common law; the right of jury trial in all civil suits where the value in controversy is more than twenty dollars, and to claim the inestimable privileges of the common law in every court of the United States; the right to the accused of freedom from excessive bail, and even to the convict of immunity from excessive fines and cruel or unusual punishments. These blessed provisions of the amendments to the Constitution are beyond price to the private citizen. The States are under no less obligation to them. For the ninth and tenth amendments look to their security, providing that the enumeration in the Constitution of certain rights shall not be construed to deny or to disparage others retained by the people; and that the powers not delegated to the United States by the Constitution, nor prohibited by it to the States, are reserved to the States respectively or to the people.

At the first session of the third Congress, assembled in 1793, what stands as the eleventh amendment of the Constitution was proposed by Congress, but from various delays on the part of the State legislatures, it was not ratified until the end of the year 1797.

At the first session of the eighth Congress, in 1803, the twelfth amendment was proposed, and became part of the Constitution in 1804.

We must here conclude our hasty and imperfect outline of the history of free government in England and of its establishment in the United States. We have traced the long and doubtful battle of the manly spirit of the Saxon race against a haughty subjugating power. We have seen it groaning under the yoke of feudal despotism. We have seen the Norman masters joining with their Saxon subjects in resisting the abominable tyrannies of regal power. We have traced the rise of a free representative assembly of the commons as an equal, in the English Parliament, with the House of Peers, and even with the crown. We have contrasted the opposite and hostile institutions of trial by jury and the king's court of Star Chamber. We have seen the folly of an idle and unwise attempt at summary and forced emancipation, in the natural extinction of Saxon slavery in England. We have witnessed the tremendous struggle of prerogative with freedom in the Stuart reigns, and the complete and permanent establishment of English liberty by the revolution which dethroned that most unhappy race. In all this survey of the steps by which the English Constitution has been brought into its present noble form, we have set up conspicuously the landmarks of our English forefathers. Magna Charta, the Petition of Right, the Bill of Rights, and Act of Settlement—those glorious monuments of the determined progress of a generous race, which are our boast no less than the glory of our brethren on the other side of the Atlantic—we have set up as beacon lights to point the way of safety or destruction. We have shown the earnestness with which their guarantees were claimed by our colonial ancestors in their controversy with the mother country, and that the denial of them by the Parliament was the sole cause of the American Revolution. We have traced the progress of the Union from the first assembling of colonial delegates in Philadelphia to the final ratification of the Constitution by the legislatures of thirteen sovereign and independent States. And here the first part of our task ends. The discussion of the principles inherent in free government in general, as well as the particular provisions of our own incomparable system, we reserve to the next portion of our work. We give no theory of the Constitution. On that subject let our fathers speak, while we in reverence listen to their words of wisdom, some of which we shall present hereafter. It affords no happy augury of the impending future of our country that so many and conflicting theories of the intention of the Constitution have been published by so many men, both wise and unwise.

It is impossible to close this outline of the features of the past without a dark foreboding of the coming future. We started with the wisdom of a thousand years to guide us. In three quarters of a century we have outlived our own free institutions. In three years we have perhaps destroyed them. It requires a stout heart to pursue the theme. What will be the future of America, or how the pen of the historian will trace the swiftly coming destinies of us and our posterity, what human wisdom can foretell? No other people ever yet surrendered liberty to power and afterwards regained it, without suffering a fearful retribution, to be expiated only by unmeasured torrents of its noblest blood. It is hoping much to dream that we alone of all the world can pass unscathed though the appalling circumstances that surround us. Perhaps before these lines shall issue from the press, the muse of history may have recorded the destruction of the liberties of a free people by its own hand.

Constitution

OF THE

UNITED STATES OF AMERICA.

WE the People of the United States, in order to form a more perfect Union, establish Justice, insure domestic Tranquillity, provide for the common defence, promote the general Welfare, and secure the Blessings of Liberty to ourselves and our Posterity, do ordain and establish this CONSTITUTION for the United States of America.

ARTICLE. I.

SECTION. 1. All legislative Powers herein granted shall be vested in a Congress of the United States, which shall consist of a Senate and House of Representatives.

SECTION. 2. [1]The House of Representatives shall be composed of Members chosen every second Year by the People of the several States, and the Electors in each State shall have the Qualifications requisite for Electors of the most numerous Branch of the State Legislature.

[2]No Person shall be a Representative who shall not have attained to the Age of twenty five Years, and been seven Years a Citizen of the United States, and who shall not, when elected, be an Inhabitant of that State in which he shall be chosen.

[3]Representatives and direct Taxes shall be apportioned among the several States which may be included within this Union, according to their respective numbers, which shall be determined by adding to the whole Number of free Persons, including those bound to Service for a Term of Years, and excluding Indians not taxed, three fifths of all other Persons. The actual Enumeration shall be made

within three Years after the first Meeting of the Congress of the United States, and within every subsequent Term of ten Years, in such Manner as they shall by Law direct. The Number of Representatives shall not exceed one for every thirty Thousand, but each State shall have at Least one Representative; and until such enumeration shall be made, the State of New Hampshire shall be entitled to chuse three, Massachusetts eight, Rhode Island and Providence Plantations one, Connecticut five, New-York six, New Jersey four, Pennsylvania eight, Delaware one, Maryland six, Verginia ten, North Carolina five, South Carolina five, and Georgia three.

4 When vacancies happen in the Representation from any state, the Executive Authority thereof shall issue Writs of Election to fill such Vacancies.

5 The House of Representatives shall chuse their Speaker and other Officers; and shall have the sole Power of Impeachment.

SECTION. 3. 1 The Senate of the United States shall be composed of two Senators from each State, chosen by the Legislature thereof, for six Years; and each Senator shall have one Vote.

2 Immediately after they shall be assembled in Consequence of the first Election, they shall be divided as equally as may be into three Classes. The Seats of the Senators of the first Class shall be vacated at the Expiration of the second Year, of the second Class at the Expiration of the fourth Year, and of the third Class at the Expiration of the sixth Year, so that one-third may be chosen every second Year; and if Vacancies happen by Resignation, or otherwise, during the Recess of the Legislature of any State, the Executive thereof may make temporary Appointments until the next Meeting of the Legislature, which shall then fill such Vacancies.

3 No Person shall be a Senator who shall not have attained to the Age of thirty Years, and been nine Years a Citizen of the United States, and who shall not, when elected, be an Inhabitant of that State for which he shall be chosen.

4 The Vice President of the United States shall be President of the Senate, but shall have no Vote, unless they be equally divided.

5 The Senate shall chuse their other Officers, and also a President pro tempore, in the Absence of the Vice President, or when he shall exercise the Office of President of the United States.

[6]The Senate shall have the sole Power to try all Impeachments. When sitting for that Purpose, they shall be on Oath or Affirmation. When the President of the United States is tried, the Chief Justice shall preside. And no Person shall be convicted without the Concurrence of two thirds of the Members present.

[7]Judgment in Cases of Impeachment shall not extend further than to removal from Office, and Disqualification to hold and enjoy any Office of honour, Trust or Profit under the United States: but the Party convicted shall nevertheless be liable and subject to Indictment, Trial, Judgment and Punishment, according to Law.

SECTION. 4. [1]The Times, Places and Manner of holding Elections for Senators and Representatives, shall be prescribed in each State by the Legislature thereof; but the Congress may at any time by Law make or alter such Regulations, except as to the places of chusing Senators.

[2]The Congress shall assemble at least once in every Year, and such Meeting shall be on the first Monday in December, unless they shall by Law appoint a different Day.

SECTION. 5. [1]Each House shall be the Judge of the Elections, Returns and Qualifications of its own Members, and a Majority of each shall constitute a Quorum to do Business; but a smaller Number may adjourn from day to day, and may be authorized to compel the Attendance of absent Members, in such Manner, and under such Penalties as each House may provide.

[2]Each House may determine the Rules of its Proceedings, punish its Members for disorderly Behaviour, and, with the Concurrence of two thirds, expel a Member.

[3]Each House shall keep a Journal of its Proceedings, and from time to time publish the same, excepting such Parts as may in their Judgment require Secrecy; and the Yeas and Nays of the Members of either House on any question shall, at the Desire of one fifth of those Present, be entered on the Journal.

[4]Neither House, during the Session of Congress, shall, without the Consent of the other, adjourn for more than three days, nor to any other Place than that in which the two Houses shall be sitting.

SECTION. 6. [1]The Senators and Representatives shall receive a Compensation for their Services, to be ascertained by Law, and paid out of the Treasury of the United States. They shall in all Cases, except Treason, Felony and Breach of the Peace, be privileged from Arrest during their Attendance at the Session of their respective Houses, and in going to and returning from the same; and for any Speech or Debate in either House, they shall not be questioned in any other Place.

[2]No Senator or Representative shall, during the Time for which he was elected, be appointed to any civil Office under the Authority of the United States, which shall have been created, or the Emoluments whereof shall have been encreased during such time; and no Person holding any Office under the United States, shall be a Member of either House during his Continuance in office.

SECTION. 7. [1]All Bills for raising Revenue shall originate in the House of Representatives; but the Senate may propose or concur with Amendments as on other Bills.

[2]Every Bill which shall have passed the House of Representatives and the Senate, shall, before it become a Law, be presented to the President of the United States; If he approve he shall sign it, but if not he shall return it, with his Objections to that House in which it shall have originated, who shall enter the Objections at large on their Journal, and proceed to reconsider it. If after such Reconsideration two thirds of that House shall agree to pass the Bill, it shall be sent, together with the Objections, to the other House, by which it shall likewise be reconsidered, and if approved by two thirds of that House, it shall become a Law. But in all such Cases the Votes of both Houses shall be determined by yeas and Nays, and the Names of the Persons voting for and against the Bill shall be entered on the Journal of each House respectively. If any Bill shall not be returned by the President within ten Days (Sundays excepted) after it shall have been presented to him, the Same shall be a law, in like Manner as if he had signed it, unless the Congress by their Adjournment prevent its Return, in which Case it shall not be a Law.

[3]Every Order, Resolution, or Vote to which the Concurrence of the Senate and House of Representatives may be necessary (except on a question of Adjournment) shall be presented to the President of the United States; and before the Same shall take

Effect, shall be approved by him, or being disapproved by him, shall be repassed by two thirds of the Senate and House of Representatives, according to the Rules and Limitations prescribed in the Case of a Bill.

SECTION. 8. The Congress shall have Power

[1]To lay and collect Taxes, Duties, Imposts and Excises, to pay the Debts and provide for the common Defence and general Welfare of the United States; but all Duties, Imposts and Excises shall be uniform throughout the United States;

[2]To borrow Money on the credit of the United States;

[3]To regulate Commerce with foreign Nations, and among the several States, and with the Indian Tribes;

[4]To establish an uniform Rule of Naturalization, and uniform Laws on the subject of Bankruptcies throughout the United States;

[5]To coin Money, regulate the Value thereof, and of foreign Coin, and fix the Standard of Weights and Measures;

[6]To provide for the Punishment of counterfeiting the Securities and current Coin of the United States;

[7]To establish Post Offices and post Roads;

[8]To promote the progress of Science and useful Arts, by securing for limited Times to Authors and Inventors the exclusive Right to their respective Writings and Discoveries;

[9]To constitute Tribunals inferior to the supreme Court;

[10]To define and punish Piracies and Felonies committed on the high Seas, and Offences against the Law of Nations;

[11]To declare War, grant Letters of Marque and Reprisal, and make Rules concerning Captures on Land and Water;

[12]To raise and support Armies, but no Appropriation of Money to that Use shall be for a longer Term than two Years;

[13]To provide and maintain a Navy;

[14]To make Rules for the Government and Regulation of the land and naval Forces;

[15]To provide for calling forth the Militia to execute the Laws of the Union, suppress Insurrections and repel Invasions;

[16]To provide for organizing, arming, and disciplining, the Militia, and for governing such Part of them as may be employed in the Service of the United States, reserving to the States respectively,

the Appointment of the Officers, and the Authority of training the Militia according to the Discipline prescribed by Congress;

[17]To exercise exclusive Legislation in all Cases whatsoever, over such District (not exceeding ten Miles square) as may, by Cession of particular States, and the Acceptance of Congress, become the Seat of the Government of the United States, and to exercise like Authority over all Places purchased by the Consent of the Legislature of the State in which the Same shall be, for the Erection of Forts, Magazines, Arsenals, Dock-Yards, and other needful Buildings;—And

[18]To make all Laws which shall be necessary and proper for carrying into Execution the foregoing Powers, and all other Powers vested by this Constitution in the Government of the United States, or in any Department or Officer thereof.

SECTION. 9. [1]The Migration or Importation of such Persons as any of the States now existing shall think proper to admit, shall not be prohibited by the Congress prior to the Year one thousand eight hundred and eight, but a Tax or Duty may be imposed on such Importation, not exceeding ten dollars for each Person.

[2]The Privilege of the Writ of Habeas Corpus shall not be suspended, unless when in Cases of Rebellion or Invasion the public Safety may require it.

[3]No Bill of Attainder or ex post facto Law shall be passed.

[4]No Capitation, or other direct, Tax shall be laid, unless in Proportion to the Census or Enumeration herein before directed to be taken.

[5]No Tax or Duty shall be laid on Articles exported from any State.

[6]No Preference shall be given by any Regulation of Commerce or Revenue to the Ports of one State over those of another: nor shall Vessels bound to, or from, one State, be obliged to enter, clear, or pay Duties in another.

[7]No Money shall be drawn from the Treasury, but in Consequence of Appropriations made by Law; and a regular Statement and Account of the Recipts and Expenditures of all public Money shall be published from time to time.

[8]No Title of Nobility shall be granted by the United States:

And no Person holding any Office of Profit or Trust under them, shall, without the Consent of the Congress, accept of any present, Emolument, Office, or Title, of any kind whatever, from any King, Prince, or foreign State.

SECTION. 10. [1]No State shall enter into any Treaty, Alliance, or Confederation; grant Letters of Marque and Reprisal; coin Money; emit Bills of Credit; make any Thing but gold and silver Coin a Tender in Payment of Debts; pass any Bill of Attainder, ex post facto Law, or Law impairing the Obligation of Contracts, or grant any Title of Nobility.

[2]No State shall, without the consent of the Congress, lay any Imposts or Duties on Imports or Exports, except what may be absolutely necessary for executing it's inspection Laws: and the net Produce of all Duties and Imposts, laid by any State on Imports or Exports, shall be for the Use of the Treasury of the United States; and all such Laws shall be subject to the Revision and Controul of the Congress.

[3]No State shall, without the Consent of Congress, lay any Duty of Tonnage, keep Troops, or Ships of War in time of Peace, enter into any Agreement or Compact with another State, or with a foreign Power, or engage in War, unless actually invaded, or in such imminent Danger as will not admit of Delay.

ARTICLE. II.

SECTION. 1. [1]The executive Power shall be vested in a President of the United States of America. He shall hold his Office during the Term of four Years, and, together with the Vice President, chosen for the same Term, be elected, as follows

[2]Each State shall appoint, in such Manner as the Legislature thereof may direct, a Number of Electors, equal to the whole Number of Senators and Representatives to which the State may be entitled in the Congress: but no Senator or Representative, or Person holding an Office of Trust or Profit under the United States, shall be appointed an Elector.

[* The Electors shall meet in their respective States, and vote by Ballot for two Persons, of whom one at least shall not be an Inhabitant of the same State

* This clause within brackets has been superseded and annulled by the 12th amendment, on page 542.

with themselves. And they shall make a List of all the Persons voted for, and of the Number of Votes for each; which List they shall sign and certify, and transmit sealed to the Seat of the Government of the United States, directed to the President of the Senate. The President of the Senate shall, in the Presence of the Senate and House of Representatives, open all the Certificates, and the Votes shall then be counted. The Person having the greatest Number of Votes shall be the President, if such Number be a Majority of the whole Number of Electors appointed; and if there be more than one who have such Majority, and have an equal Number of Votes, then the House of Representatives shall immediately chuse by Ballot one of them for President; and if no Person have a Majority, then from the five highest on the List the said House shall in like Manner chuse the President. But in chusing the President, the Votes shall be taken by States, the Representation from each State having one Vote; A Quorum for this Purpose shall consist of a Member or Members from two thirds of the States, and a Majority of all the States shall be necessary to a Choice. In every Case, after the Choice of the President, the Person having the greatest Number of Votes of the Electors shall be the Vice President. But if there should remain two or more who have equal Votes, the Senate shall chuse from them by Ballot the Vice President.]

[3]The Congress may determine the Time of chusing the Electors, and the Day on which they shall give their Votes; which Day shall be the same throughout the United States.

[4]No Person except a natural born Citizen, or a Citizen of the United States, at the time of the Adoption of this Constitution, shall be eligible to the Office of President; neither shall any Person be eligible to that Office who shall not have attained to the Age of thirty five Years, and been fourteen Years a Resident within the United States.

[5]In Case of the Removal of the President from Office, or of his Death, Resignation, or Inability to discharge the Powers and Duties of the said Office, the same shall devolve on the Vice President, and the Congress may by Law provide for the Case of Removal, Death, Resignation, or Inability, both of the President and Vice President, declaring what Officer shall then act as President, and such Officer shall act accordingly, until the Disability be removed, or a President shall be elected.

[6]The President shall, at stated Times, receive for his Services, a Compensation, which shall neither be encreased nor diminished during the Period for which he shall have been elected, and he shall

not receive within that Period any other Emolument from the United States, or any of them.

[7]Before he enter on the Execution of his Office, he shall take the following Oath or Affirmation :—

"I do solemnly swear (or affirm) that I will faithfully execute "the Office of President of the United States, and will to the best "of my Ability, preserve, protect and defend the Constitution of "the United States.

SECTION. 2. [1]The President shall be Commander in Chief of the Army and Navy of the United States, and of the Militia of the several States, when called into the actual Service of the United States; he may require the Opinion, in writing, of the principal Officer in each of the executive Departments, upon any Subject relating to the Duties of their respective Offices, and he shall have Power to grant Reprieves and Pardons for Offences against the United States, except in Cases of Impeachment.

[2]He shall have Power, by and with the Advice and Consent of the Senate, to make Treaties, provided two thirds of the Senators present concur; and he shall nominate, and by and with the Advice and Consent of the Senate, shall appoint Ambassadors, other public Ministers and Consuls, Judges of the supreme Court, and all other Officers of the United States, whose Appointments are not herein otherwise provided for, and which shall be established by Law: but the Congress may by Law vest the Appointment of such inferior Officers, as they think proper, in the President alone, in the Courts of Law, or in the Heads of Departments.

[3]The President shall have Power to fill up all Vacancies that may happen during the Recess of the Senate, by granting Commissions which shall expire at the End of their next Session.

SECTION. 3. He shall from time to time give to the Congress Information of the State of the Union, and recommend to their Consideration such Measures as he shall judge necessary and expedient; he may, on extraordinary Occasions, convene both Houses, or either of them, and in Case of Disagreement between them, with Respect to the Time of Adjournment, he may adjourn them to such Time as he shall think proper; he shall receive Ambassadors and other public Ministers; he shall take Care that the Laws be faithfully executed, and shall Commission all the officers of the United States.

SECTION. 4. The President, Vice President and all civil Officers of the United States, shall be removed from Office on Impeachment for, and Conviction of, Treason, Bribery, or other high Crimes and Misdemeanors.

ARTICLE. III.

SECTION. 1. The judicial Power of the United States, shall be vested in one supreme Court, and in such inferior Courts as the Congress may from time to time ordain and establish. The Judges, both of the supreme and inferior Courts, shall hold their Offices during good Behavior, and shall, at stated Times, receive for their Services, a Compensation, which shall not be diminished during their Continuance in Office

SECTION 2. [1]The judicial Power shall extend to all Cases, in Law and Equity, arising under this Constitution, the Laws of the United States, and Treaties made, or which shall be made, under their Authority;—to all Cases affecting Ambassadors, other public Ministers, and Consuls;—to all Cases of admiralty and maritime Jurisdiction;—to Controversies to which the United States shall be a Party;—to Controversies between two or more States;—between a State and Citizens of another State;—between Citizens of different States;—between Citizens of the same State claiming Lands under Grants of different States, and between a State, or the Citizens thereof, and foreign States, Citizens or Subjects.

[2]In all Cases affecting Ambassadors, other public Ministers and Consuls, and those in which a State shall be a Party, the supreme Court shall have original Jurisdiction. In all the other Cases before mentioned, the supreme Court shall have appellate Jurisdiction, both as to Law and Fact, with such Exceptions, and under such Regulations as the Congress shall make.

[3]The Trial of all Crimes, except in Cases of Impeachment, shall be by Jury; and such Trial shall be held in the State where the said Crimes shall have been committed; but when not committed within any State, the Trial shall be at such Place or Places as the Congress may by Law have directed.

SECTION. 3. [1]Treason against the United States, shall consist only in levying War against them, or in adhering to their Enemies, giving them Aid and Comfort. No Person shall be convicted of Treason unless on the Testimony of two Witnesses to the same overt Act, or on Confession in open Court.

[2]The Congress shall have Power to declare the Punishment of Treason, but no Attainder of Treason shall work Corruption of Blood, or Forfeiture except during the Life of the Person attainted.

ARTICLE. IV.

SECTION. 1. Full Faith and Credit shall be given in each State to the public Acts, Records, and judicial Proceedings of every other State. And the Congress may by general Laws prescribe the Manner in which such Acts, Records and Proceedings shall be proved, and the Effect thereof.

SECTION. 2. [1]The Citizens of each State shall be entitled to all Privileges and Immunities of Citizens in the several States.

[2]A Person charged in any State with Treason, Felony, or other Crime, who shall flee from Justice, and be found in another State, shall on Demand of the executive Authority of the State from which he fled, be delivered up, to be removed to the State having Jurisdiction of the Crime.

[3]No Person held to Service or Labour in one State, under the Laws thereof, escaping into another, shall, in Consequence of any Law or Regulation therein, be discharged from such Service or Labour, but shall be delivered up on Claim of the Party to whom such Service or Labour may be due.

SECTION. 3. [1]New States may be admitted by the Congress into this Union; but no new State shall be formed or erected within the Jurisdiction of any other State; nor any State be formed by the Junction of two or more States, or Parts of States, without the Consent of the Legislatures of the States concerned as well as of the Congress.

[2]The Congress shall have Power to dispose of and make all needful Rules and Regulations respecting the Territory or other Property belonging to the United States; and nothing in this Constitution shall be so construed as to Prejudice any Claims of the United States, or of any particular State.

SECTION. 4. The United States shall guarantee to every State in this Union a Republican Form of Government, and shall protect each of them against Invasion; and on Application of the Legislature, or of the Executive (when the Legislature cannot be convened) against domestic Violence.

ARTICLE. V.

The Congress, whenever two thirds of both Houses shall deem it necessary, shall propose Amendments to this Constitution, or, on the Application of the Legislatures of two thirds of the several States, shall call a Convention for proposing Amendments, which, in either Case, shall be valid to all Intents and Purposes, as Part of this Constitution, when ratified by the Legislatures of three fourths of the several States, or by Conventions in three fourths thereof, as the one or the other Mode of Ratification may be proposed by the Congress; Provided that no Amendment which may be made prior to the Year one thousand eight hundred and eight shall in any Manner affect the first and fourth Clauses in the Ninth Section of the first Article; and that no State, without its Consent, shall be deprived of its equal Suffrage in the Senate.

ARTICLE. VI.

[1]All Debts contracted and Engagements entered into, before the Adoption of this Constitution, shall be as valid against the United States under this Constitution, as under the Confederation.

[2]This Constitution, and the Laws of the United States which shall be made in Pursuance thereof; and all Treaties made, or which shall be made, under the authority of the United States, shall be the supreme Law of the Land; and the Judges in every State shall be bound thereby, any Thing in the Constitution or Laws of any State to the Contrary notwithstanding.

[3]The Senators and Representatives before mentioned, and the Members of the several State Legislatures, and all executive and judicial Officers, both of the United States and of the several States, shall be bound by Oath or Affirmation, to support this Constitution; but no religious Test shall ever be required as a Qualification to any Office or public Trust under the United States.

ARTICLE. VII.

The Ratification of the Conventions of nine States, shall be sufficient for the Establishment of this Constitution between the States so ratifying the Same.

DONE in Convention by the Unanimous Consent of the States present the Seventeenth Day of September in the Year of our Lord one thousand seven hundred and Eighty seven and of the Independance of the United States of America the Twelfth. **In Witness** whereof We have hereunto subscribed our Names,

GEO WASHINGTON—
Presdt and deputy from Virginia.

NEW HAMPSHIRE.

JOHN LANGDON, NICHOLAS GILMAN

MASSACHUSETTS.

NATHANIEL GORHAM, RUFUS KING

CONNECTICUT.

WM. SAML. JOHNSON, ROGER SHERMAN.

NEW YORK.

ALEXANDER HAMILTON.

NEW JERSEY.

WIL: LIVINGSTON, DAVID BREARLEY,
WM. PATERSON, JONA. DAYTON.

PENNSYLVANIA.

B. FRANKLIN, THOMAS MIFFLIN,
ROBT. MORRIS, GEO: CLYMER,
THO: FITSIMONS, JARED INGERSOLL,
JAMES WILSON, GOUV: MORRIS.

DELAWARE.

GEO: READ, GUNNING BEDFORD, Jun'r,
JOHN DICKINSON, RICHARD BASSETT,
JACO: BROOM.

MARYLAND.

JAMES M'HENRY, DAN: OF ST. THOS. JENIFER,
DANL. CARROLL.

VIRGINIA.

JOHN BLAIR, JAS. MADISON, JR.,

NORTH CAROLINA.

WM. BLOUNT, RICH'D DOBBS SPAIGHT,
HU. WILLIAMSON.

SOUTH CAROLINA.

J. RUTLEDGE, CHARLES COTESWORTH PINCKNEY,
CHARLES PINCKNEY, PIERCE BUTLER.

GEORGIA.

WILLIAM FEW, ABR. BALDWIN.

Attest: WILLIAM JACKSON, *Secretary.*

ARTICLES

IN ADDITION TO, AND AMENDMENT OF,

THE CONSTITUTION

OF THE

UNITED STATES OF AMERICA.

Proposed by Congress, and ratified by the Legislatures of the several States, pursuant to the fifth article of the original Constitution.

(ARTICLE I.)

Congress shall make no law respecting an establishment of religion, or prohibiting the free exercise thereof; or abridging the freedom of speech, or of the press; or the right of the people peaceably to assemble, and to petition the Government for a redress of grievances.

(ARTICLE II.)

A well regulated Militia, being necessary to the security of a free State, the right of the people to keep and bear Arms, shall not be infringed.

(ARTICLE III.)

No Soldier shall, in time of peace be quartered in any house, without the consent of the Owner, nor in time of war, but in a manner to be prescribed by Law.

(ARTICLE IV.)

The right of the people to be secure in their persons, houses, papers and effects, against unreasonable searches and seizures, shall not be violated, and no Warrants shall issue, but upon probable cause, supported by Oath or affirmation, and particularly describing the place to be searched, and the persons or things to be seized.

(ARTICLE V.)

No person shall be held to answer for a capital, or otherwise infamous crime, unless on a presentment or indictment of a Grand Jury, except in cases arising in the land or naval forces, or in the Militia, when in actual service in time of War or public danger; nor shall any person be subject for the same offence to be twice put in jeopardy of life or limb; nor shall be compelled in any Criminal Case to be a witness against himself, nor be deprived of life, liberty, or property, without due process of law; nor shall private property be taken for public use, without just compensation.

(ARTICLE VI.)

In all criminal prosecutions, the accused shall enjoy the right to a speedy and public trial, by an impartial jury of the State and district wherein the crime shall have been committed, which district shall have been previously ascertained by law, and to be informed of the nature and cause of the accusation; to be confronted with the witnesses against him; to have Compulsory process for obtaining Witnesses in his favour, and to have the Assistance of Counsel for his defence.

(ARTICLE VII.)

In Suits at common law, where the value in controversy shall exceed twenty dollars, the right of trial by jury shall be preserved, and no fact tried by a jury shall be otherwise re-examined in any Court of the United States, than according to the rules of the common law.

(ARTICLE VIII.)

Excessive bail shall not be required, nor excessive fines imposed, nor cruel and unusual punishments inflicted.

(ARTICLE IX.)

The enumeration in the Constitution, of certain rights, shall not be construed to deny or disparage others retained by the people.

(ARTICLE X.)

The powers not delegated to the United States by the Constitution, nor prohibited by it to the States, are reserved to the States respectively, or to the people.

(ARTICLE XII.)

The Judicial power of the United States shall not be construed to extend to any suit in law or equity, commenced or prosecuted against one of the United States by Citizens of another State, or by Citizens or Subjects of any Foreign State.

(ARTICLE XII.)

The Electors shall meet in their respective states, and vote by ballot for President and Vice-President, one of whom, at least, shall not be an inhabitant of the same state with themselves; they shall name in their ballots the person voted for as President, and in distinct ballots the person voted for as Vice-President, and they shall make distinct lists of all persons voted for as President, and of all persons voted for as Vice-President, and of the number of votes for each, which lists they shall sign and certify, and transmit sealed to the seat of the government of the United States, directed to the President of the Senate;—The President of the Senate shall, in presence of the Senate and House of Representatives, open all the certificates and the votes shall then be counted;—The person having the greatest number of votes for President, shall be the President, if such number be a majority of the whole number of Electors appointed; and if no person have such majority, then from the persons having the highest numbers not exceeding three on the list of those voted for as President, the House of Representatives shall choose immediately, by ballot, the President. But in choosing the President, the votes shall be taken by states, the representation from each state having one vote; a quorum for this purpose shall consist of a member or members from two-thirds of the states, and a majority of all the states shall be necessary to a choice. And if the House of Representatives shall not choose a President whenever the right of choice shall devolve upon them, before the fourth day of March next following, then the Viee-President shall act as President, as in the case of the death or other constitutional disability of the President. The person having the greatest number of votes as Vice-President, shall be the Vice-President, if such number be a majority of the whole number of Electors appointed, and if no person have a majority, then from the two highest numbers on the list, the Senate shall choose the Vice-President; a quorum for the purpose shall consist of two-thirds of the whole number of Senators, and a majority of the whole number shall be necessary to a choice. But no person constitutionally ineligible to the office of President shall be eligible to that of Vice-President of the United States.

*The following is prefixed to the first ten * of the preceding amendments.*

CONGRESS OF THE UNITED STATES,

Begun and held at the City of New York, on Wednesday, the fourth of March, one thousand seven hundred and eighty-nine.

The Conventions of a number of the States, having at the time of their adopting the Constitution, expressed a desire, in order to prevent misconstruction or abuse of its powers, that further declaratory and restrictive clauses should be added: And as extending the ground of public confidence in the Government, will best insure the beneficent end of its institution;

Resolved by the Senate and House of Representatives of the United States of America, in Congress assembled, two thirds of both Houses concurring, That the following Articles be proposed to the Legislatures of the several States, as amendments to the Constitution of the United States, all, or any of which articles, when ratified by three-fourths of the said Legislatures, to be valid to all intents and purposes, as part of the said Constitution; viz.

Articles in addition to, and Amendment of the Constitution of

---

* It may be proper here to state that 12 articles of amendment were proposed by the first Congress, of which but 10 were ratified by the States—the first and second in order not having been ratified by the requisite number of States.

These two were as follows:

Article the first....After the first enumeration required by the first Article of the Constitution, there shall be one Representative for every thirty thousand, until the number shall amount to one hundred, after which, the proportion shall be so regulated by Congress, that there shall not be less than one hundred Representatives, nor less than one Representative for every forty thousand persons, until the number of Representatives shall amount to two hundred, after which the pro. portion shall be so regulated by Congress, that there shall not be less than two hundred Representatives, nor more than one Representative for every fifty thousand persons.

Article second....No law, varying the compensation for the services of the Senators and Representatives, shall take effect, until an election of Representatives shall have intervened.

the United States of America, proposed by Congress, and ratified by the Legislatures of the several States pursuant to the fifth article of the original Constitution.

The first ten amendments of the Constitution were ratified by the States, as follows, viz.:

By New Jersey, 20th November, 1789.
By Maryland, 19th December, 1789.
By North Carolina, 22d December, 1789.
By South Carolina, 19th January, 1790.
By New Hampshire, 25th January, 1790.
By Delaware, 28th January, 1790.
By Pennsylvania, 10th March, 1790.
By New York, 27th March, 1790.
By Rhode Island, 15th June, 1790.
By Vermont, 3 November, 1791.
By Virginia, 15 December, 1791.

The following is prefixed to the eleventh of the preceding amendments:

THIRD CONGRESS OF THE UNITED STATES:

At the first session, begun and held at the city of Philadelphia, in the State of Pennsylvania, on Monday the second of December, one thousand seven hundred and ninety-three.

Resolved by the Senate and House of Representatives of the United States of America, in Congress assembled, two thirds of both Houses concurring, That the following Article be proposed to the Legislatures of the several States, as an amendment to the Constitution of the United States; which when ratified by three-fourths of the said Legislatures shall be valid as part of the said Constitution, viz.:

The following is prefixed to the twelfth of the preceding amendments:

EIGHTH CONGRESS OF THE UNITED STATES:

At the first session, begun and held at the city of Washington, in the Territory of Columbia, on Monday the seventeenth of October, one thousand eight hnndred and three:

Resolved by the Senate and House of Representatives of the United States of America, in Congress assembled, Two thirds of both Houses concurring, that in lieu of the third paragraph of the first section of the second article of the Constitution of the United States, the following be proposed as an amendment to the Constitution of the United States, which when ratified by three-fourths of the legislatures of the several states, shall be valid to all intents and purposes, as part of the said Constitution, to wit:

The ten first of the preceding amendments were proposed at the first session of the first Congress, of the United States, 25 September, 1789, and were finally ratified by the constitutional number of States, on the 15th day of December, 1791. The eleventh amendment was proposed at the first session of the third Congress, 5 March, 1794, and was declared in a message from the President of the United States to both houses of Congress, dated 8th January, 1798, to have been adopted by the constitutional number of States. The twelfth amendment was proposed at the first session of the eighth Congress, 12 December, 1803, and was adopted by the constitutional number of States in 1804, according to a public notice thereof by the Secretary of State, dated 25th September, of the same year.

ADDENDA TO PART SECOND.

[At a time when the very foundation of government is shaken, and the edifice of constitutional freedom tottering, few treatises can be read with greater profit than those of Locke "On Government;" from which, therefore, we have determined to present the following extracts. And at a time when the United States are occupying towards the Confederate States, an attitude almost identical with that assumed towards us by England in the Revolutionary War, it cannot be amiss to show how one of the wisest and noblest of English statesmen—Burke—proposed to deal with the revolted colonies. On this account we give here an abridgment of his greatest speech on American affairs.]

LOCKE ON GOVERNMENT.

OBJECTS OF GOVERNMENT—ARBITRARY POWER COMPARED WITH A GOVERNMENT OF LAWS—CONSENT AND FORCE—CONQUEST—RIGHT OF THE CONQUERED—LIMITS OF THE RIGHT WHICH CAN BE OBTAINED BY A RIGHTFUL CONQUEROR—OVER HIS OWN PEOPLE—OVER THE VANQUISHED—THE LATTER DESPOTICAL—BUT NOT UNIVERSAL IN ITS EXTENT—NOT INCLUDING THE PROPERTY OF THE VANQUISHED, WHICH IS HIS CHILDREN'S—BUT ONLY THE LIVES OF THOSE ACTUALLY ENGAGED IN WAR—THESE PROPOSITIONS LOGICALLY DISCUSSED—RIGHT OF REBELLION RESERVED TO THE CONQUERED EVEN AFTER FORCED CONSENT TO THE VICTOR'S AUTHORITY—THIS RIGHT AN INDEFEASIBLE INHERITANCE OF THEIR POSTERITY—CASE OF THE GREEK CHRISTIANS—SUMMARY—CASE OF HEZEKIAH—ARBITRARY RULERS PUT THEMSELVES INTO A STATE OF WAR WITH THE PEOPLE—THEREBY ABSOLVING THEM FROM ALLEGIANCE—THE PEOPLE NOT DISPOSED TO REVOLUTION—THE RIGHT OF REVOLUTION AND REBELLION—WHEN IT EXISTS—OBJECTIONS ANSWERED.

Though men, when they enter into society, give up the equality, liberty, and executive power they had in the state of nature, into the hands of the society, to be so far disposed of by the legislative as the good of the society shall require; yet it being only with an intention in every one the better to preserve himself, his liberty, and property (for no rational creature can be supposed to change his condition with an intention to be worse); the power of the society or legislative constituted by them, can never be supposed to extend farther than the common good; but is obliged to secure every one's property by providing against those three defects above mentioned, that made the state of nature so unsafe and uneasy. And so whoever has the legislative or supreme power of any commonwealth is bound to govern by *established standing laws*, promulgated and known to the people, and *not* by extemporary decrees; *by indifferent and upright judges*, who are to decide controversies by those laws; and to employ the force of the community at home only in the execution of such laws; or abroad to prevent or redress foreign injuries, and secure the community from inroads and invasion. And all this to be directed to no other end but the peace, safety, and public good of the people.

Absolute arbitrary power, or governing without settled standing laws, can neither of them consist with the ends of society and government, which men could not quit the freedom of the state of nature for, and tie themselves up under, were it not to preserve their lives, liberties, and fortunes, and by stated rules of right and property to secure their peace and quiet. It cannot be supposed that they should intend, had they a power so to do, to give to any one or more, an absolute arbitrary power over their persons and estates, and put a force in the magistrate's hand to execute his unlimited will arbitrarily upon them. This were to put themselves in a worse condition than the state of nature, wherein they had a liberty to defend their right against the injuries of others, and were upon equal terms of force to maintain it, whether invaded by a single man or many in combination. Whereas by supposing they have given up themselves to the absolute arbitrary power and will of a legislator, they have disarmed themselves, and armed him, to make a prey of them when he pleases; he being in a much worse condition who is exposed to the arbitrary power of one man, who has the command of one hundred thousand, than he that is exposed to the power of one hundred thousand single men; nobody being secure, that his will, who has such a command, is better than that of other men, though his force be one hundred thousand times stronger. And therefore whatever form the commonwealth is under, *the ruling power ought to govern by declared and received laws, and not by extem-*

porary dictates and undetermined resolutions ; for then mankind will be in a far worse condition than in the state of nature, if they shall have armed one or a few men with the joint power of a multitude, to force them to obey at pleasure the exorbitant and unlimited decrees of their sudden thoughts, or unrestrained, and till that moment unknown wills, without having any measures set down which may guide and justify their actions; *for all the power the government has* being only for the good of society, *as it ought not to be arbitrary and at pleasure, so it ought to be exercised by established and promulgated laws ;* that both the people may know their duty, and be safe and secure within the limits of the law; *and the rulers too kept within their bounds*, and not be tempted by the power they have in their hands to employ it to such purpose, and by such measures, as they would not have known, and own not willingly.—LOCKE, vol. v. pp. 420, 421.

Though governments can originally have no other rise than that before mentioned, nor politics be founded *on anything but the consent of the people*; yet such have been the disorders ambition has filled the world with, that in the noise of war, which makes so great a part of the history of mankind, this consent is little taken notice of; and, therefore, many have mistaken the force of arms for the consent of the people, and reckon conquest as one of the originals of governments. But conquest is so far from setting up any government, as demolishing a house is from building a new one in its place. Indeed it often makes way for a new frame of commonwealth by destroying the former; but without the consent of the people, can never erect a new one.

That the aggressor, who puts himself into the state of war with another, and unjustly invades another man's right, can, by such an unjust war, never come to have a right over the conquered, will be easily agreed by all men, who will not think that robbers and pirates have a right of empire over whomsoever they have force enough to master; or that men are bound by promises, which unlawful force extorts from them. Should a robber break into my house, and, with a dagger at my throat, make me seal deeds to convey my estate to him, would this give him any title? Just such a title by his sword has an unjust conqueror who forces me into submission. The injury and the crime are equal, whether committed by the wearer of a crown, or some petty villain. The title of the offender, and the number of his followers make no difference in the offence, unless it be to aggravate it. The only difference is, great robbers punish little ones, to keep them in their obedience; but the great ones are rewarded with laurels and triumphs; because they are too big for the weak hands of justice in this world, and have the power in their own possession, which should punish offenders. What is my remedy against a robber that so broke into my house? Appeal to the law for justice.

But the conquered, or their children, have no court, no arbitrator on earth to appeal to. Then they may appeal, as Jephthah did, to Heaven, and repeat their appeal till they have recovered the native right of their ancestors, which was to have *such a legislative over them as the majority should approve, and freely acquiesce in.*

But supposing victory favors the right side, let us consider a conqueror in a lawful war, and see what power he gets, and over whom. First, it is plain, "he gets no power by his conquest over those that conquered with him." They that fought on his side cannot suffer by the conquest, but must at least be as much freemen as they were before. And most commonly they serve upon terms, and on conditions to share with their leader, and enjoy a part of the spoil, and other advantages that attended the conquering sword; or at least have a part of the subdued country bestowed upon them. And "*the conquering people* are not, I hope, to be *slaves by conquest*," and wear their laurels only to show they are sacrifices to their leader's triumph.

Secondly, I say then the conqueror gets no power but only over those who have actually assisted, concurred, or consented to that unjust force that is used against him; for the people having given to their governors no power to do an unjust war (for they never had such a power in themselves), they ought not to be charged as guilty of the violence and injustice that is committed in an unjust war, any farther than they actually abet it; no more than they are to be thought guilty of any violence or oppression their governors should use upon the people themselves, or any part of their fellow subjects, they having impowered them no more to the one than to the other.

The conqueror's power over the lives of the conquered being only because they have used force to do or maintain an injustice, he can have that power only over those who have concurred in that force; all the rest are innocent; and he has no more title over the people of that country, who have done him no injury, and so have made no forfeiture of their lives, than he has over any other, who, without any injuries or provocations, have lived upon fair terms with him.

Thirdly, the power a conqueror gets over those he overcomes in a just war, is perfectly despotical; he has an absolute power over the lives of those, who, by putting themselves in a state of war, have forfeited them; but he has not thereby a right and title to their possessions.

Though in all war there be usually a complication of force and damage, and the aggressor seldom fails to harm the estate, when he uses force against the persons of those he makes war upon; yet it is the use of force only that puts a man into the state of war.

It is the "unjust use of force that puts a man into the state of war" with another; and thereby he that is guilty of it makes a forfeiture of his life; for quitting reason, which is the rule given between man and man, and using force, the way of beasts, he becomes liable to be destroyed by him he uses force against, as any savage ravenous beast, that is dangerous to his being.

But because the miscarriages of the father are no faults of the children, and they may be rational and peaceable, notwithstanding the brutishness and injustice of the father; the father, by his miscarriages and violences, can forfeit but his own life, but involves not his children in his guilt or destruction. His goods, which nature, that willeth the preservation of all mankind as much as is possible, hath made them to belong to the children to keep them from perishing, do still belong to his children: for supposing them not to have joined in the war, either through infancy, absence, or choice, they have done nothing to forfeit them; nor has the conqueror any right to take them away, by the bare title of having subdued him that by force attempted his destruction; though perhaps he may have some right to them, to repair the damage he has sustained by the war, and the defence of his own right; which how far it reaches to the possessions of the conquered, we shall see by and by. So that he that by conquest has a right over a man's person to destroy him if he pleases, has not thereby a right over his estate to possess and enjoy it; for it is the brutal force the aggressor has used, that gives his adversary a right to take away his life, and destroy him if he pleases as a noxious creature; but it is damage sustained that alone gives him title to another man's goods: for though I may kill a thief that sets on me in the highway, yet I may not (which seems less) take away his money and let him go: this would be robbery on my side. His force and the state of war he put himself in, made him forfeit his life, but gave me no title to his goods. The right then of conquest extends only to the lives of those who joined in the war, not to their estates, but only in order to make reparation for the damages received, and the charges of the war; and that too with the reservation of the right of the innocent wife and children.

Let the conqueror have as much justice on his side as could be supposed, he has no right to seize more than the vanquished could forfeit: his life is at the victor's mercy; and his service and goods he may appropriate, to make himself reparation; but he cannot take the goods of his wife and children: they too had a title to the goods he enjoyed, and their shares in the estate he possessed: for example, I in the state of nature (and all commonwealths are in the state of nature one with another) have injured another man, and refusing to give satisfaction, it comes to a state of war, wherein my defending by force what I had gotten unjustly makes me the aggressor. I am conquered: my life, it is true, as forfeit, is at mercy, but not my wife's and children's. They made not the war, nor assisted in it. I could not forfeit their lives; they were not mine to forfeit. My wife had a share in my estate; that neither could I forfeit. And my children also, being born of me, had a right to be maintained out of my labor or substance. Here then is the case: the conqueror has a title to reparation for damages received, and the children have a title to their father's estate for their subsistence: for as to the wife's share, whether her labor, or compact, gave her a title to it, it is plain, her husband could not forfeit what was hers. What must be done in the case? I answer the fundamental law of nature being, that all, as much as may be, should be preserved, it follows, that if there be not enough fully to satisfy both, viz., for the conqueror's losses and children's maintenance, he that hath and to spare, must remit something of his full satisfaction, and give way to the pressing and preferable title of those who are in danger to perish without it.

Over those then that joined with him in the war, and over those of the subdued country that opposed him not, and the posterity of even those that did, the conqueror even in a just war hath, by his conquest, no right of dominion: they are free from any subjection to him, and if their former government be dissolved, they are at liberty to begin and erect another to themselves.

The conqueror, it is true, usually, by the force he has over them, compels them, with a sword at their breasts, to stoop to his conditions, and submit to such a government as he pleases to afford them; but the inquiry is, what right has he to do so? If it be said, they submit by their own consent, then this allows their own consent to be necessary to give the conqueror a title to rule over them. It remains only to be considered, whether promises extorted by force, without right, can be thought consent, and how far they bind. To which I shall say, they bind not at all; because whatsoever another gets from me by force, I still retain the right of, and he is obliged presently to restore. He that forces my horse from me, ought presently to restore him, and I have still a right to retake him. By the same reason, he that forced a promise from me, ought presenty to restore it, *i. e.*, quit me of the obligation of it: or I may resume it myself, *i. e.*, choose whether I will perform it; for the law of nature laying an obligation on me only by the rules she prescribes, cannot oblige me by the violation of her rules: such is the extorting anything from me by force. Nor does it at all alter the case to say, "I gave my promise," no more than it excuses the force, and passes the right, when I put my hand in my pocket, and deliver my purse myself to a thief, who demands it with a pistol at my breast.

From all which it follows, that the government of a conqueror, imposed by force on the subdued, against whom he had no right of war, or who joined not in the war against him where he had right, has no obligation upon them.

But let us suppose that all the men of that community, being all members of the same body politic, may be taken to have joined in that unjust war, wherein they are subdued, and so their lives are at the mercy of the conqueror.

I say this concerns not their children who are in their minority: for since a father hath not, in himself, a power over the life or liberty of his child, no act of his can possibly forfeit it. So that the children, whatever may have happened to the fathers, are freemen, and the absolute power of the conqueror reaches no farther than the persons of the men that were subdued by him, and dies with them: and should he govern them as slaves subjected to his absolute arbitrary power, he has no such right or dominion over their children. He can have no power over them but by their own consent, whatever he may drive them to say or do: and he has no lawful authority, whilst force, and not choice, compels them to submission.

The inhabitants of any country, who are descended, and derive a title to their estates from those who are subdued, and had a government forced upon them against their free consents, retain a right to the possession of their ancestors, though they consent not freely to the government, whose hard conditions were by force imposed on the possessors of that country: for, the first conqueror never having had a title to the land of that country, the people who are the descendants of, or claim under those who were forced to submit to the yoke of a government by constraint, have always a right to shake it off, and free themselves from the usurpation or tyranny which the sword had brought in upon them, till their rulers put them under such a frame of government as they willingly and of choice consent to. Who doubts but the Grecian Christians, descendants of the ancient possessors of that country, may justly cast off the Turkish yoke, which they have so long groaned under, whenever they have an opportunity to do it? For no government can have a right to obedience from a people who have not freely consented to it; which they can never be supposed to do, till either they are put in a full state of liberty to choose their government and governors, or at least till they have such standing laws, to which they have by themselves or their representatives given their free consent; and also till they are allowed their due property, which is so to be proprietors of what they have, that nobody can take away any part of it without their own consent, without which men under any government are not in the state of freemen, but are direct slaves under the force of war.

The short of the case in conquest is this: the conqueror, if he have a just cause, has a despotical right over the persons of all that actually aided and concurred in the war against him, and a right to make up his damage and cost out of their labor and estates, so he injure not the right of any other. Over the rest of the people, if there were any that consented not to the war, and over the children of the captives themselves, or the possessions of either, he has no power; and so can have, by virtue of conquest, no lawful title himself to dominion over them, or derive it to his posterity; but is an aggressor, if he attempts upon their properties, and thereby puts himself in a state of war against them: and has no better a right of principality, he, nor any of his successors, than Hingar, or Hubba, the Danes, had here in England; or Spartacus, had he conquered Italy, would have had; which is to have their yoke cast off, as soon as God shall give those under their subjection courage and opportunity to do it. This, notwithstanding whatever title the kings of Assyria had over Judah, by the sword, God assisted Hezekiah to throw off the dominion of that conquering empire. "And the Lord was with Hezekiah and he prospered; wherefore he went forth, and he rebelled against the king of Assyria, and served him not." (2 Kings xviii. 7.) Whence it is plain that shaking off a power, which force and not right hath set over any one, though it hath the name of rebellion, yet is no offence before God, but is that which he allows and countenances, though even promises and covenants, when obtained by force, have intervened: for it is very probable to any one that reads the story of Ahaz and Hezekiah attentively, that the Assyrians subdued Ahaz, and deposed him, and made Hezekiah king in his father's lifetime; and that Hezekiah by agreement had done him homage, and paid him tribute all this time.

The reason why men enter into society, is *the preservation of their property*; and the end why they choose and authorize a legislative, is, that there may be laws made, and rules set, as guards and fences to the properties of all the members of the society; to limit the power and moderate the dominion of every part and member of the society; for since it can never be supposed to be the will of the society that the legislative should have a power to destroy that which every one designs to secure by entering into society, and for which the people submitted themselves to legislators of their own making; whenever the legislators endeavor to take away and destroy the property of the people, or to reduce them to slavery under arbitary power, they put themselves into a state of war with the people, who are thereupon absolved from any further obedience, and are left to the common refuge, which God hath provided for all men, against force and violence. Whensoever therefore the legislative shall transgress this fundamental rule of society, and either by ambition, fear, folly, or corruption, endeavor to grasp themselves, or put into the hands of any other, an absolute power over the lives, liberties, and estates of the people, by this breach of trust they forfeit the power the people had put into their hands for quite contrary ends, and it devolves to the people, who have a right to resume their original liberty, and, by the establishment of a new legislative (such as they shall think fit), provide for their own safety and security, which is the end for which they are in society.

To this perhaps it will be said, that the people being ignorant, and always discontented, to lay the foundation of government in the unsteady opinion and uncertain humor of the people, is to expose it to certain ruin; and no government will be able long to subsist, if the people may set up a new legislative, whenever they take offence at the old one. To this I answer, quite the contrary. People are not so easily got out of their old forms as some are apt to suggest. They are hardly to be prevailed with to amend the acknowledged faults in the frame they have been accustomed to. And if there be any original defects, or adventitious ones introduced by time, or corruption; it is not an easy thing to get them changed, even when all the world sees there is an opportunity for it. This slowness and aversion in the people to quit their old constitutions, has in the many revolutions which have been seen in this kingdom, in this and former ages, still kept us to, or, after some interval of fruitless attempts, still brought us back again to, our old legislative of king, lords, and commons; and whatever provocations have made the crown be taken from some of our princes' heads, they never carried the people so far as to place it in another line.

This doctrine of a power in the people of providing for their safety anew, by a new legislative, when their legislators have acted contrary to their trust, by invading their property, is the best fence against rebellion, and the probablest means to hinder it; for rebellion being an opposition, not to persons, but authority, which is founded only in the constitutions and laws of the government; those, whoever they be, who by force break through, and by force justify their violation of them, are truly and properly rebels; for when men, by entering into society and civil government, have excluded force, and introduced laws for the preservation of property, peace, and unity amongst themselves; those who set up force again in opposition to the laws do *rebellare*, that is, bring back again the state of war, and are properly rebels; which they who are in power (by the pretence they have to authority, the temptation of force they have in their hands, and the flattery of those about them) being likeliest to do; the properest way to prevent the evil, is to show them the danger and injustice of it, who are under the greatest temptation to run into it.

In both the forementioned cases, when either the legislative is changed, *or the legislators act contrary to the end for which they were constituted*, those who are guilty are guilty of rebellion; for if any one by force takes away the established legislative of any society, and the laws by them made pursuant to their trust, he thereby takes away the umpirage, which every one had consented to, for a peaceable decision of all their controversies, and a bar to the state of war amongst them. They, who remove, or change the legislative, take away this decisive power, which nobody can have but by the appointment and consent of the people; and so destroying the authority which the people did, and nobody else can set up, and introducing a power which the people hath not authorized, they actually introduce a state of war, which is that of force without authority; and thus, by removing the legislative established by the society (in whose decisions the people acquiesced and united, as to that of their own will), they untie the knot, and expose the people anew to the state of war. *And if those who by force take away the legislative, are rebels, the legislators themselves, as has been shown, can be no less esteemed so; when they, who were set up for the protection and preservation of the people, their liberties and properties*, shall by force invade and endeavor to take them away; and so they, putting themselves into a state of war with those who made them the protectors and guardians of their peace, are properly, and with the greatest aggravation, *rebellantes*, rebels.

But if they who say, "it lays a foundation for rebellion," mean that it may occasion civil wars, or intestine broils, to tell the people they are absolved from obedience when illegal *attempts* are made upon their liberties or properties, and may oppose the unlawful violence of those who were their magistrates, when they invade their properties contrary to the trust put in them; and that therefore this doctrine is not to be allowed, being so destructive to the peace of the world: they may as well say, upon the same ground, that honest men may not oppose robbers or pirates, because this may occasion disorder or bloodshed. If any mischief come in such cases, it is not to be charged upon him who defends his own right, but on him that invades his neighbor's. If the innocent honest man must quietly quit all he has, for peace sake, to him who will lay violent hands upon it, I desire it may be considered, what a kind of peace there will be in the world, which consists only in violence and rapine; and which is to be maintained only for the benefit of robbers and oppressors. Who would not think it an admirable peace betwixt the mighty and the mean, where the lamb without resistance yielded his throat to be torn by the imperious wolf? Polyphemus's den gives us a perfect pattern of such a peace, and such a government, wherein Ulysses and his companions had nothing to do but quietly to suffer themselves to be devoured. And no doubt Ulysses, who was a prudent man, preached up passive obedience, and exhorted them to a quiet submission, by representing to them of what concernment peace was to mankind; and by showing the inconveniences which might happen, if they should offer to resist Polyphemus, who had now the power over them.—Locke, vol. v. 414–474, *carptim*.

BURKE ON THE AMERICAN WAR.

EXORDIUM—OCCASION OF THE SPEECH—MAGNITUDE OF THE TASK OF RESTORING ORDER IN AMERICA—BURKE'S PROPOSITION IS "PEACE NOT THROUGH THE MEDIUM OF WAR"—"IT IS SIMPLY PEACE"—WITH THE VIEW OF RESTORING CONFIDENCE AND PROCURING RECONCILIATION—THE QUESTIONS AT ISSUE—OUGHT CONCESSIONS TO BE MADE?—IF SO, WHAT CONCESSIONS?—POSITION OF THE WAR PARTY—OBJECTIONS—ADVANTAGE GAINED BY FORCE TEMPORARY—AMERICA MUST BE DESTROYED IN PRESERVING IT TO ENGLAND—EXPERIENCE AGAINST THE USE OF FORCE—AMERICAN TEMPER AND CHARACTER—THE SPIRIT OF LIBERTY—WORKING OF COLONIAL GOVERNMENT—CONDUCT OF THE GOVERNMENT TOWARDS AMERICA—MEANS OF RECONCILIATION—THE CAUSES OF DISCONTENT MUST BE REMOVED—IMPOSSIBILITY OF SUBJUGATION—INFAMY OF THE ATTEMPT—UNFITNESS OF ENGLAND FOR THE TASK—THE AMERICAN CHARACTER FIXED AND UNALTERABLE—SPIRIT OF THE SOUTHERN COLONIES—SLAVES—PROPOSITION OF CRIMINAL PROSECUTIONS AGAINST REBELS—"TOO BIG A THING"—DEFINITION OF AN EMPIRE—INFERENCE—JUDICIAL POSITION OF ENGLAND—HER CONSEQUENT DUTY OF JUSTICE—WHAT HAD BEEN GAINED BY THE MEASURES OF THE GOVERNMENT?—WHAT CONCESSIONS OUGHT TO BE MADE—COMPLAINT OF THE COLONIES—TAXATION WITHOUT REPRESENTATION—DUTY OF GOVERNMENT—NECESSITY OF A UNITY OF SPIRIT—THE COLONIES MUST BE PROTECTED BY THE CONSTITUTION—EXAMPLE OF SPAIN—PRECEDENT OF IRELAND—WALES—CHESTER—DURHAM—EXCITEMENTS OF THE AMERICAN MIND TO BE CONSIDERED AND ALLOWED FOR—EFFECT OF RECONCILIATION.

I HOPE, sir, that notwithstanding the austerity of the chair, your good nature will incline you to some degree of indulgence toward human frailty. You will not think it unnatural that those who have an object depending, which strongly engages their hopes and fears, should be somewhat inclined to superstition. As I came into the house full of anxiety about the event of my motion, I found, to my infinite surprise, that the grand penal bill, by which we had passed sentence on the trade and sustenance of America, is to be returned to us from the other house. I do confess, I could not help looking on this event as a fortunate omen. I look upon it as a sort of providential favor, by which we are put once more in possession of our deliberate capacity upon a business so very questionable in its nature, so very uncertain in its issue. By the return of this bill, which seemed to have taken its flight for ever, we are at this very instant nearly as free to choose a plan for our American government, as we were on the first day of the session. If, sir, we incline to the side of conciliation, we are not at all embarrassed (unless we please to make ourselves so) by any incongruous mixture of coercion and restraint. We are, therefore, called upon, as it were, by a superior warning voice, again to attend to America—to attend to the whole of it together—and to review the subject with an unusual degree of care and calmness.

To restore order and repose to an empire so great and so distracted as ours is, merely, in the attempt, an undertaking that would ennoble the flights of the highest genius, and obtain pardon for the efforts of the meanest understanding. Struggling a good while with these thoughts, by degrees I felt myself more firm. I derived at length some confidence from what in other circumstances usually produces timidity. I grew less anxious, even from the idea of my own insignificance. For, judging of what you are by what you ought to be, I persuaded myself that you would not reject a reasonable proposition, because it had nothing but its reason to recommend it. On the other hand, being totally destitute of all shadow of influence, natural or adventitious, I was very sure that if my proposition were futile or dangerous, if it were weakly conceived, or improperly timed, there was nothing exterior to it of power or awe, to dazzle, or delude you. You will see it just as it is; and you will treat it just as it deserves.

The proposition is peace, not peace through the medium of war; not peace to be hunted through the labyrinth of intricate and endless negotiations; not peace to arise out of universal discord, fomented upon principle, in all parts of the empire; not peace to depend on the judicial determination of perplexing questions, or the precise marking of the shadowy boundaries of a complex government. It is simply peace, sought in its natural course, and in its ordinary haunts. It is peace sought in the spirit of peace; and laid in principles purely pacific. I propose, by removing the ground of the difference, and by restoring the *former unsuspecting confidence of the colonies in the mother country*, to give permanent satisfaction to your people; and (far from a scheme of ruling by discord) to reconcile them to each other in the same act, and by the bond of the very same interest, which reconciles them to British government.

My idea is nothing more. Refined policy ever has been the parent of confusion; and ever will be so as long as the world endures. Plain good intention, which is as easily discovered at the first view, as fraud is surely detected at the last, is, let me say, of no mean force in the government of mankind. Genuine simplicity of heart is a healing and cementing principle. My plan, therefore, being formed upon the most simple grounds imaginable, may disappoint some people when they hear it. It has nothing to recommend it to the pruriency of curious ears. There is nothing at all new and captivating in it.

I mean to give peace. Peace implies reconciliation; and where there has been a material dispute, reconciliation does, in a manner, always imply concession on the one part or on the other. In this state of things I make no difficulty in affirming that the proposal ought to originate from us. Great and acknowledged force is not impaired, either in effect or in opinion, by an unwillingness to exert itself. The superior power may offer peace with honor and with safety. Such an offer, from such a power, will be attributed to magnanimity. But the concessions of the weak are concessions of fear. When such a one is disarmed he is wholly at the mercy of his superior; and he loses forever that time and those chances, which, as they happen to all men, are the strength and resources of all inferior power.

The capital leading questions on which you must this day decide, are these two: First, whether you ought to concede; and second, what your concession ought to be. On the first of these questions we have gained (as I have just taken the liberty of observing to you) some ground. But I am sensible that a good deal more is still to be done. Indeed, sir, to enable us to determine both on the one and the other of these great questions with a firm and precise judgment, I think it may be necessary to consider distinctly the true nature and the peculiar circumstances of the object which we have before us. Because after all our struggle, whether we will or not, we must govern America, according to that nature, and to those circumstances; and not according to our own imaginations; not according to abstract ideas of right; but by no means according to mere general theories of government, the resort to which appears to me, in our present situation, no better than arrant trifling.

America, gentlemen say, is a noble object. It is an object well worth fighting for. Certainly it is, if fighting a people be the best way of gaining them. Gentlemen in this respect will be led to their choice of means by their complexions and their habits. Those who understand the military art, will of course have some predilection for it. Those who wield the thunder of the state, may have more confidence in the efficacy of arms. But I confess, possibly for want of this knowledge, my opinion is much more in favor of prudent management, than of force; considering force not as odious, but as a feeble instrument, for preserving a people so numerous, so active, so growing, so spirited as this, in a profitable and subordinate connection with us.

First, sir, permit me to observe that the use of force alone is but *temporary*. It may subdue for a moment; but it does not remove the necessity of subduing again: and a nation is not governed which is perpetually to be conquered.

My next objection is uncertainty. Terror is not always the effect of force; and an armament is not a victory. If you do not succeed, you are without resource; for, conciliation failing, force remains; but force failing, no hope of reconciliation is left. Power and authority are sometimes bought by kindness; but they can never be begged as alms, by an impoverished and defeated violence.

A further objection to force is, that you *impair the object* by your very endeavors to preserve it. The thing you fought for is not the thing which you recover; but depreciated, sunk, wasted, and consumed in the contest. Nothing less will content me than *whole America*. I do not choose to consume its strength along with our own; because in all parts it is the British strength that I consume. I do not choose to be caught by a foreign enemy at the end of this exhausting conflict; and still less in the midst of it. I may escape; but I can make no insurance against such an event. Let me add that I do not choose wholly to break the American spirit, because it is the spirit that has made the country.

Lastly, we have no sort of *experience* in favor of force as an instrument in the rule of our colonies. Their growth and their utility has been owing to methods altogether different. Our ancient indulgence has been said to be pursued to a fault. It may be so. But we know, if feeling is evidence, that our fault was more tolerable than our attempt to mend it; and our sin far more salutary than our penitence.

These, sir, are my reasons for not entertaining that high opinion of untried force, by which many gentlemen, for whose sentiments in other particulars I have great respect, seem to be greatly captivated. But there is still behind a third consideration concerning this object, which serves to determine my opinion on the sort of policy which ought to be pursued in the management of America, even more than its population and its commerce. I mean its *temper and character.*

In this character of the Americans, a love of freedom is the predominating feature which marks and distinguishes the whole: and as an ardent is always a jealous affection, your colonies become suspicious, restive, and untractable, whenever they see the least attempt to wrest from them by force, or shuffle from them by chicane, what they think the only advantage worth living for. This fierce spirit of liberty is stronger in the English colonies probably than in any other people of the earth; and this from a great variety of powerful causes; which, to understand the true temper of their minds, and the direction which this spirit takes, it will not be amiss to lay open somewhat more largely. . . .

I do not mean to commend either the spirit in this excess, or the moral causes which produce it. Perhaps a more smooth and accommodating spirit of freedom in them would be more acceptable to us. Perhaps ideas of liberty might be desired, more reconcilable with an arbitrary and boundless authority. Perhaps we might wish the colonists to be persuaded that their liberty is more secure, when held in trust for them by us (as their guardians during a perpetual minority), than with any part of it in their own hands. But the question is not whether the spirit deserves praise or blame; what, in the name of God shall we do with it? You have before you the object; such as it is, with all its glories, with all its imperfections on its head. You see the magnitude; the importance; the temper; the habits; the disorders. By all these considerations we are strongly urged to determine something concerning it. We are called upon to fix some rule and line for our future conduct, which may give a little stability to our politics, and prevent the return of such unhappy deliberations as the present. Every such return will bring the matter before us in a still more untractable form. For what astonishing and incredible things have we not seen already? What monsters have not been generated from this unnatural contention? Whilst every principle of authority and resistance has been pushed, npon both sides, so far as it would go, there is nothing so solid and certain, either in reasoning or in practice, that has not been shaken. . . . We thought, sir, that the utmost which the discontented colonists could do, was to disturb authority; we never dreamt they could of themselves supply it; knowing, in general, what an operose business it is to establish a government absolutely new. . . . Some provinces have tried their experiment as we have tried ours; and theirs has succeeded. They have formed a government sufficient for its purposes, without the bustle of a revolution. Evident necessity and tacit consent have done the business in an instant. So well they have done it that Lord Dunmore (the account is among the fragments on your table) tells you that the new institution is infinitely better obeyed than the ancient government ever was in its fortunate periods. Obedience is what makes government, and not the names by which it is called; not the name of governor as formerly, or committee as at present.

Pursuing the same plan of punishing by the denial of the exercise of government to still greater lengths, we wholly abrogated the ancient government of Massachusetts. We were confident that the first feeling if not the very prospect of anarchy, would instantly enforce a complete submission. The experiment was tried. A new, strange, unexpected face of things appeared. Anarchy is found tolerable. A vast province has now subsisted, and subsisted in a considerable degree of health and vigor, for near a twelvemonth, without governor, without public council, without judges, without executive magistrates. How long it will continue in this state, or what may arise out of this unheard of situation, how can the wisest of us conjecture? Our late experience has taught us that many of those fundamental principles, formerly believed infallible, are either not of the importance they were imagined to be; or that we have not at all adverted to some other far more important, and far more powerful principles, which entirely overrule those we had considered as omnipotent. I am much against any further experiments, which tend to put to the proof any more of these allowed opinions, which contribute so much to the public tranquillity. In effect, we suffer as much at home, by this loosening of all ties, and this concussion of all established opinions, as we do abroad. For in order to prove that the Americans have no right to their liberties, we are every day endeavoring to subvert the maxims which preserve the whole spirit of our own. To prove that the Americans ought not to be free, we are obliged to depreciate the value of freedom itself; and we never seem to gain a paltry advantage over them in debate, without attacking some of those principles, or deriding some of those feelings, for which our ancestors have shed their blood.

But, sir, in wishing to put an end to pernicious experiments, I do not mean to preclude the fullest inquiry. Far from it. Far from deciding on a sudden or partial view, I would patiently go round and round the subject, and survey it minutely in every possible aspect. Sir, if I were capable of engaging you to equal attention, I would state, that as far as I am capable of discerning, there are but three ways of proceeding relative to this stubborn spirit, which prevails in your colonies and disturbs your government. These are—To change that spirit, as inconvenient, by removing the causes. To prosecute it as criminal. Or, to comply with it as necessary. I would not be guilty of an imperfect enumeration; I can think of but these three. Another has indeed been started, that of giving up the colonies; but it met so slight a reception, that I do not think myself obliged to dwell a great while upon it.

The first of these plans, to change the spirit as inconvenient, by removing the causes, I think is the most like a systematic proceeding. It is radical in its principles; but it is attended with great difficulties, some of them little short, as I conceive, of impossibilities.

You cannot station garrisons in every part of these deserts. If you drive the people from one place, they will carry on their annual tillage, and remove with their flocks and herds to another. Many of the people in the back settlements are already little attached to particular situations. Already they have topped the Apalachian mountains. From thence they behold before them an immense plain, one vast, rich, level meadow; a square of five hundred miles. Over this they would wander, without a possibility of restraint; they would change their manners with the habits of their life; would soon forget a government by which they were disowned; would become hordes of English Tartars; and pouring down upon your unfortified frontiers a fierce and irresistible cavalry, become masters of your governors, and your councillors, your collectors and comptrollers, and of all the slaves that adhered to them.

To impoverish the colonies in general, and in particular to arrest the noble course of their marine enterprises, would be a more easy task, I freely confess it. We have shown a disposition to a system of this kind; a disposition even to continue the restraint after the offence; looking on ourselves as rivals to our colonies, and persuaded that of course we must gain all that they shall lose. Much mischief we may certainly do. The power inadequate to all other things is often more than sufficient for this. I do not look on the direct and immediate power of the colonies to resist our violence, as very formidable. In this, however, I may be mistaken. But when I consider that we have colonies for no other purpose but to be serviceable to us, it seems to my poor understanding a little preposterous to make them unserviceable in order to keep them obedient. It is, in truth, nothing more than the old and, as I thought, exploded problem of tyranny, which proposes to beggar its subjects into submission. But remember, when you have completed your system of impoverishment, that nature still proceeds in her ordinary course; that discontent will increase with misery; and that there are critical moments in the fortunes of all states, when they who are too weak to contribute to your prosperity may be strong enough to complete your ruin. *Spoliatis arma supersunt.*

The temper and character which prevail in our colonies are, I am afraid, unalterable by any human art. We cannot, I fear, falsify the pedigree of this fierce people, and persuade them that they are not sprung from a nation in whose veins the blood of freedom circulates. The language in which they would hear you tell them this tale would detect the imposition; your speech would betray you. An Englishman is the unfittest person on earth to argue another Englishman into slavery.

I think it is nearly as little in our power to change their republican religion as their free descent; or to substitute the Roman Catholic as a penalty, or the Church of England as an improvement. The mode of inquisition and dragooning is going out of fashion in the Old World; and I should not confide much to their efficacy in the New. The education of the Americans is also on the same unalterable bottom with their religion. You cannot persuade them to burn their books of curious science, to banish their lawyers from the courts of law, or to quench the lights of their assemblies by refusing to choose those persons who are best read in their privileges. It would be no less impracticable to think of wholly annihilating the popular assemblies in which these lawyers sit. The army by which we must govern in their place would be far more chargeable to us; not quite so effectual, and perhaps in the end full as difficult to be kept in obedience.

With regard to the high aristocratic spirit of Virginia and the Southern colonies, it has been proposed, I know, to reduce it by declaring a general enfranchisement of their slaves. This project has had its advocates and panegyrists; yet I never could argue myself into any opinion of it. Slaves are often much attached to their masters. A general wild offer of liberty would not always be accepted. History furnishes few instances of it. It is sometimes as hard to persuade slaves to be free as it is to compel freemen to be slaves; and in this auspicious scheme we should have both these pleasing tasks on our hands at once. But when we talk of enfranchisement, do we not perceive that the American master may enfranchise too, and arm servile hands in defence of freedom? A measure to which other people have had recourse more than once, and not without success, in a desperate situation of their affairs.

Slaves as these unfortunate black people are, and dull as all men are from slavery, must they not a little suspect the offer of freedom from that very nation which has sold them to their present masters?

If then, sir, it seems almost desperate to think of any alterative course, for changing the moral causes (and not quite easy to remove the natural) which produce prejudices irreconcilable to the late exercise of our authority; but that the spirit infallibly will continue, and continuing will produce such effects as now embarrass us; the second mode under consideration is, to prosecute that spirit in its overt acts, as *criminal.*

At this proposition I must pause a moment. The thing seems a great deal too big for my ideas of jurisprudence. It should seem to my way of conceiving such matters, that there is a very wide difference in reason and policy, between the mode of proceeding on the irregular conduct of scattered individuals, or even of bands of men, who disturb order within the state, and the civil dissensions which may, from time to time, on great questions, agitate the several communities which compose a great empire. It looks to me to be narrow and pedantic to apply the ordinary ideas of criminal justice to this great public contest. I do not know the method of drawing up an indictment against a whole people. I cannot insult and ridicule the feelings of millions of my fellow creatures, as Sir Edward Coke insulted one excellent individual (Sir Walter Raleigh) at the bar. I am not ripe to pass sentence on the gravest public bodies, intrusted with magistracies of great authority and dignity, and charged with the safety of their fellow citizens, upon the same title that I am. I really think, that for wise men this is not judicious; for sober men, not decent; for minds tinctured with humanity, not mild and merciful.

Perhaps, sir, I am mistaken in my idea of an empire, as distinguished from a single state or kingdom. But my idea of it is this: that an empire is the aggregate of many states, under one common head, whether this head be a monarch or a presiding republic. It does, in such constitutions, frequently happen (and nothing but the dismal, cold, dead uniformity of servitude can prevent its happening) that the subordinate parts have many local privileges and immunities. Between these privileges and the supreme common authority the line may be extremely nice. Of course disputes, often, too, very bitter disputes, and much ill blood, will arise. But though every privilege is an exemption (in the case) from the ordinary exercise of the supreme authority, it is no denial of it. The claim of a privilege seems rather *ex vi termini*, to imply a superior power. For to talk of the privileges of a state or of a person, who has no superior, is hardly any better than speaking nonsense. Now, in such unfortunate quarrels, among the component parts of a great political union of communities, I can scarcely conceive anything more completely imprudent, than for the head of the empire to insist, that, if any privilege is pleaded against his will, or his acts, that his whole authority is denied; instantly to proclaim rebellion, to beat to arms, and to put the offending provinces under the ban. Will not this, sir, very soon teach the provinces to make no distinctions on their part? Will it not teach them that the government, against which a claim of liberty is tantamount to high treason, is a government to which submission is equivalent to slavery? It may not be always convenient to impress independent communities with such an idea.

We are, indeed, in all disputes with the colonies, by the necessity of things, the judge. It is true, sir. But I confess that the character of judge in my own cause, is a thing that frightens me. Instead of filling me with pride, I am exceedingly humbled at it. I cannot proceed with a stern, assured, judicial confidence, until I find myself in something more like a judicial character. I must have these hesitations as long as I am compelled to recollect, that, in my little reading upon such contests as these, the sense of mankind has, at least, as often decided against the superior as the subordinate power. Sir, let me add, too, that the opinion of my having some abstract right in my favor would not put me much at my ease in passing sentence; unless I could be sure that there were no rights which, in their exercise under certain circumstances, were not the most odious of all wrongs, and the most vexatious of all injustice. Sir, these considerations have great weight with me, when I find things so circumstanced, that I see the same party, at once a civil litigant against me in point of right, and a culprit before me; while I sit as criminal judge, on acts of his, whose moral quality is to be decided upon the merits of that very litigation. Men are every now and then put, by the complexity of human affairs, into strange situations; but justice is the same, let the judge be in what situation he will.

There is, sir, also a circumstance which convinces me, that this mode of criminal proceeding is not (at least in the present stage of our contest) altogether expedient; which is nothing less than the conduct of those very persons who have seemed to adopt that mode, by lately declaring a rebellion in Massachusetts Bay, as they had formerly addressed to have traitors brought hither under an act of Henry the Eighth, for trial. For, though rebellion is declared, it is not proceeded against as such; nor have any steps been taken towards the apprehension and conviction of any individual offender, either on our late or our former address; but modes of public coercion have been adopted, and such as have much more resemblance to a sort of qualified hostility towards an independent power than the punishment of rebellious subjects. All this seems rather inconsistent; but it shows how difficult it is to apply these juridical ideas to our present case.

In this situation let us seriously and coolly ponder. What is it we have got by all our menaces, which have been many and ferocious? What advantage have we derived from the penal laws we have passed, and which, for the time, have been severe and numerous? What advances have we made towards our object, by the sending of a force, which, by land and sea, is of no contemptible strength? Has the disorder abated? Nothing less. When I see things in this situation, after such confident hopes, bold promises, and active exertions, I cannot, for my life, avoid a suspicion, that the plan itself is not correctly right.

If, then, the removal of the causes of this American liberty be, for the greater part, or rather entirely, impracticable; if the ideas of criminal process be inapplicable, or if applicable, are in the highest degree inexpedient, what way yet remains? No way is open, but the third and last—to comply with the American spirit as necessary; or, if you please, to submit to it as a necessary evil.

If we adopt this mode, if we mean to conciliate and concede, let us see of what nature the concession ought to be; to ascertain the nature of our concession, we must look at their complaint. The colonies complain that they have not the characteristic mark and seal of British freedom. They complain that they are taxed in a Parliament in which they are not represented. If you mean to satisfy them all, you must satisfy them in regard to this complaint. If you mean to please any people, you must give them the boon which they ask; not what you may think better for them, but of a kind totally different. Such an act may be a wise regulation, but it is no concession; whereas our present theme is the mode of giving satisfaction.

The question with me is, not whether you have a right to render your people miserable; but whether it is not your interest to make them happy. It is not, what a lawyer tells me, I *may* do; but what humanity, reason, and justice, tell me I ought to do. Is a politic act the worse for being a generous one? Is no concession proper but that which is made from your want of right to keep what you grant? Or does it lessen the grace or dignity of relaxing in the exercise of an odious claim, because you have your evidence room full of titles, and your magazines stuffed with arms to enforce them? What signify all those titles, and all those arms? Of what avail are they, when the reason of the thing tells me that the assertion of my title is the loss of my suit; and that I could do nothing but wound myself by the use of my own weapons?

Such is steadfastly my opinion of the absolute necessity of keeping up the concord of this empire by a unity of spirit, though by a diversity of operations, that if I were sure the colonists had, at their leaving this country, sealed a regular compact of servitude; that they had solemnly abjured all the rights of citizens; that they had made a vow to renounce all ideas of liberty for them and their posterity, to all generations, yet I should hold myself obliged to conform to the temper I found universally prevalent in my own day, and to govern two millions of men, impatient of servitude, on the principles of freedom. I am not determining a point of law; I am restoring tranquillity; and the general character and situation of a people must determine what sort of government is fitted for them. That point nothing else can or ought to determine.

My idea, therefore, without considering whether we yield as matter of right, or grant as matter of favor, is, to *admit the people of our colonies into an interest in the constitution;* and by recording that admission in the journals of Parliament, to give them as strong an assurance as the nature of the thing will admit, that we mean forever to adhere to that solemn declaration of systematic indulgence.

In forming a plan for this purpose, I endeavored to put myself in that frame of mind, which was the most natural, and the most reasonable; and which was certainly the most probable means of securing me from all error. I set out with a perfect distrust of my own abilities; a total renunciation of every speculation of my own; and with a profound reverence for the wisdom of our ancestors, who have left us the inheritance of so happy a constitution, and so flourishing an empire, and what is a thousand times more valuable, the treasury of the maxims and principles which formed the one, and obtained the other.

During the reigns of the kings of Spain of the Austrian family, whenever they were at a loss in the Spanish councils, it was common for their statesmen to say, that they ought to consult the genius of Philip the Second. The genius of Philip the Second might mislead them, and the issue of their affairs showed that they had not chosen the most perfect standard. But sir, I am sure that I shall not be misled, when, in a case of constitutional difficulty, I consult the genius of the English Constitution. Consulting at that oracle (it was with all due humility and piety) I found four capital examples in a similar case before me: those of Ireland, Wales, Chester, and Durham.

Ireland, before the English conquest, though never governed by a despotic power, had no parliament. How far the English Parliament itself was at that time modelled according to the present form, is disputed among antiquarians. But we have all the reason in the world to be assured, that a form of parliament, such as England then enjoyed, she instantly communicated to Ireland; and we are equally sure that almost every successive improvement in constitutional liberty, as fast as it was made here, was transmitted thither. The feudal baronage and the feudal knighthood, the roots of our primitive constitution, were equally transplanted into that soil; and grew and flourished there. Magna Charta, if it did not give us originally the House of Commons, gave us at least a House of Commons of weight and consequence. But your ancestors did not churlishly sit down alone at the feet of Magna Charta. Ireland was made immediately a partaker. This benefit of English laws and liberties, I confess, was not extended to *all* Ireland. Mark the consequence. English authority and English liberty had exactly the same boundaries. Your standard could never be advanced an inch before your privileges. Sir John Davis shows beyond a doubt, that the refusal of a general communication of these rights, was the true cause why Ireland was five hundred years in subduing; and after the vain projects of a military government attempted in the reign of Queen Elizabeth, it was soon discovered that nothing could make that country English, in civility and allegiance, but your laws and your forms of legislature. It was not English arms, but the English Constitution, that conquered Ireland. From that time, Ireland has ever had a general parliament, as she had before, a partial parliament. You changed the people, you altered the religion; but you never touched the form of the vital substance of free government in that kingdom. You deposed kings, you restored them; you altered the succession to theirs, as well as to your own crown; but you never altered their constitution; the principle of which was respected by usurpation; restored with the restoration of monarchy, and established, I trust, forever by the glorious Revolution. This has made Ireland the great and flourishing kingdom that it is; and from a disgrace and a burden, intolerable to this nation, has rendered her a principal part of our strength and ornament.

My next example is Wales. This country was said to be reduced by Henry the Third. It was said more truly to be so by Edward the First. But though then conquered, it was not looked upon as any part of the realm of England. Its old constitution, whatever that might have been, was destroyed, and no good one was substituted in its place. The care of that tract was put into the hands of lord marchers—a form of government of a very singular kind; a strange, heterogeneons monster, something between hostility and government; perhaps it has a sort of resemblance, according to the modes of those times, to that of commander-in-chief, at present, to whom all civil power is granted as secondary. The manners of the Welsh nation followed the genius of the government; the people were ferocious, restive, savage, and uncultivated; sometimes composed; never pacified. Wales within itself, was in perpetual disorder; and it kept the frontier of England in perpetual alarm. Benefits from it to the state, there were none. Wales was only known to England by incursion and invasion.

Sir, during that state of things, Parliament was not idle. They attempted to subdue the fierce spirit of the Welsh by all sorts of rigorous laws. They prohibited by statute the sending all sorts of arms into Wales, as you prohibit by proclamation (with something more of doubt on the legality) the sending arms to America. They disarmed the Welsh by statute, as you attempted (but with still more question on the legality) to disarm New England by an instruction. They made an act to drag offenders from Wales into England for trial, as you have done (but with more hardships) with regard to America. By another act, where one of the parties was an Englishman, they ordained that his trial should be always by English. They made acts to restrain trade, as you do; and they prevented the Welsh from the use of fairs and markets, as you do the Americans from fisheries and foreign ports. In short, when the statute book was not quite so much swelled as it is now, you find no less than fifteen acts of penal regulation on the subject of Wales.

Here we rub our hands—a fine body of precedents for the authority of Parliament and the use of it!—I admit it fully; and pray add likewise to these precedents, that all the while Wales rid this kingdom like an incubus; that it was an unprofitable and oppressive burden; and that an Englishman in that country could not go six yards from the high road without being murdered.

The march of the human mind is slow. Sir, it was not until after two hundred years discovered, that by an eternal law, Providence had decreed vexation to violence, and poverty to rapine. Your ancestors did however at length open their eyes to the ill husbandry of injustice. They found that the tyranny of a free people, could of all tyrannies the least be endured; and that laws made against a whole nation were not the most effectual methods for securing its obedience. Accordingly, in the 27th year of Henry VIII., the course was entirely altered. With a preamble stating the entire and perfect rights of the crown of England, it gave to the Welsh all the rights and privileges of English subjects. A political order was established; the military power gave way to the civil; the marches were turned into counties. But that a nation should have a right to English liberties, and yet no share at all in the fundamental security of these liberties, the grant of their own property, seemed a thing so incongruous, that eight years after, that is, in the thirty-fifth of that reign, a complete and not ill-proportioned representation by counties and boroughs was bestowed upon Wales, by act of Parliament. From that moment, as by a charm, the tumults subsided; obedience was restored; peace, order, and civilization followed in the train of liberty. When the day star of the English Constitution had arisen in their hearts, all was harmony within and without.

> Simul alba nautis,
> Stella refulsit;
> Defluit saxis agitatus humor;
> Concidunt venti, fugiuntque nubes,
> Et minax (quod sic voluere) ponto
> Unda recumbit.

The very same year the county palatine of Chester received the same relief from its oppressions, and the same remedy to its disorder. Before this time Chester was little less distempered than

Wales. The inhabitants, without rights themselves, were the fittest to destroy the rights of others; and from thence Richard II. drew the standing army of archers with which for a time he oppressed England.

Here is my third example. It was attended with the success of the two former. Chester, civilized as well as Wales, has demonstrated that freedom and not servitude is the cure of anarchy; as religion and not atheism, is the true remedy for superstition.

I do not know that the colonies have, in any general way, or in any cool hour, gone much beyond the demand of immunity in relation to taxes. It is not fair to judge of the temper or dispositions of any man, or any set of men, when they are composed and at rest, from their conduct, or their expressions, in a state of disturbance and irritation. It is, besides, a very great mistake to imagine that mankind follow up practically any speculative principle, either of government or of freedom, as far as it will go in argument and logical illation. We Englishmen stop very short of the principles upon which we support any given part of our constitution; or even the whole of it together. I could easily, if I had not altogether tired you, give you very striking and convincing instances of it. This is nothing but what is natural and proper. All government, indeed every human benefit and enjoyment, every virtue, and every prudent act, is founded on compromise and barter. We balance inconveniences; we give and take; we remit some rights that we may enjoy others; and we choose rather to be happy citizens than subtle disputants. As we must give away some natural liberty, to enjoy civil advantages; so we must sacrifice some civil liberties, for the advantages to be derived from the communion and fellowship of a great empire. But in all fair dealings, the thing bought must bear some proportion to the purchase paid. None will barter away the immediate jewel of his soul. Though a great house is apt to make slaves haughty, yet it is purchasing a part of the artificial importance of a great empire too dear, to pay for it all essential rights, and all the intrinsic dignity of human nature. None of us who would not risk his life, rather than fall under a government purely arbitrary. But, although there are some amongst us who think our constitution wants many improvements to make it a complete system of liberty, perhaps none who are of that opinion would think it right to aim at such improvement, by disturbing his country, and risking everything that is dear to him. In every arduous enterprise, we consider what we are to lose, as well as what we are to gain; and the more and better stake of liberty every people possess, the less they will hazard in a vain attempt to make it more. These are *the cords of man.* Man acts from adequate motives relative to his interest, and not on metaphysical speculations. Aristotle, the great master of reasoning, cautions us, and with great weight and propriety, against this species of delusive geometrical accuracy in moral arguments, as the most fallacious of all sophistry.

The Americans will have no interest contrary to the grandeur and glory of England, when they are not oppressed by the weight of it; and they will rather be inclined to respect the acts of a superintending legislature, when they see them the acts of that power, which is itself the security, not the rival of their secondary importance. In this assurance my mind most perfectly acquiesces; and I confess I feel not the least alarm from the discontents which are to arise from putting people at their ease; nor do I apprehend the destruction of this empire, from giving, by an act of free grace and indulgence, to two millions of my fellow citizens, some share of those rights upon which I have always been taught to value myself.

www.ingramcontent.com/pod-product-compliance
Lightning Source LLC
LaVergne TN
LVHW021229110826
845150LV00002B/281

* 9 7 8 1 4 2 5 5 6 3 2 3 3 *